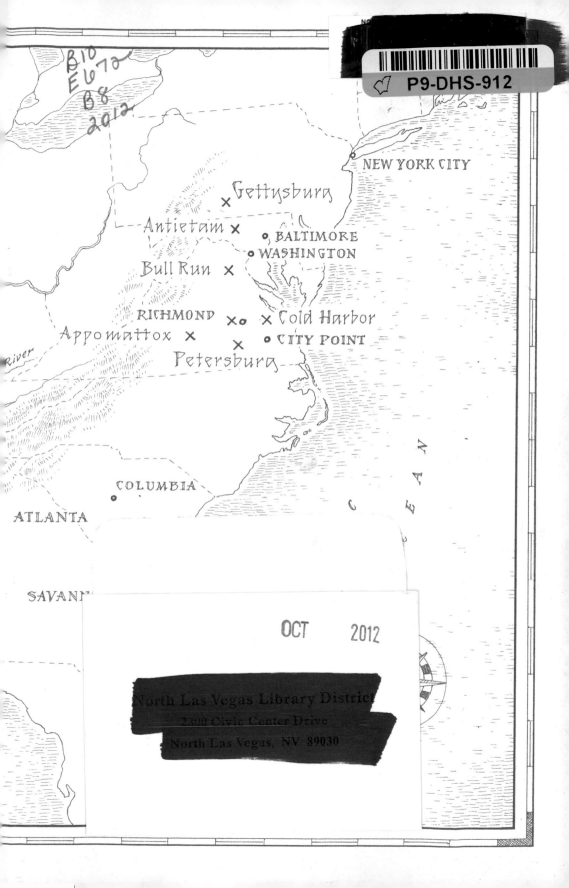

NEW YORK CITY

Gettysburg ✕

Antietam ✕

○ BALTIMORE

○ WASHINGTON

Bull Run ✕

RICHMOND ✕○ ✕ Cold Harbor

Appomattox ✕ ○ CITY POINT

Petersburg ✕

COLUMBIA ○

ATLANTA

OCEAN

SAVANN

THE MAN WHO SAVED THE UNION

Also by H. W. Brands

The Reckless Decade
T.R.
The First American
The Age of Gold
Lone Star Nation
Andrew Jackson
Traitor to His Class
American Colossus
The Murder of Jim Fisk for the Love of Josie Mansfield

Doubleday

NEW YORK   LONDON   TORONTO   SYDNEY   AUCKLAND

THE MAN
WHO SAVED THE UNION

ULYSSES GRANT IN WAR AND PEACE

⊰ ⊰ H. W. BRANDS ⊱ ⊱

www.doubleday.com

DOUBLEDAY and the portrayal of an anchor with a dolphin
are registered trademarks of Random House, Inc.

Photographs courtesy of the Library of Congress Prints and Photographs
Division and the National Archives and Records Administration.

Book design by Maria Carella
Jacket design by John Fontana
Photo courtesy of the Library of Congress
Endpaper map by John T. Burgoyne

Library of Congress Cataloging-in-Publication Data
Brands, H. W.
The man who saved the union : Ulysses Grant in war and peace /
H. W. Brands. — 1st ed.
p. cm.
Includes index.
1. Grant, Ulysses S. (Ulysses Simpson), 1822–1885. 2. Presidents—United
States—Biography. 3. Generals—United States—Biography. I. Title.
E672.B8 2012
355.0092—dc23
[B]   2011043795

ISBN 978-0-385-53241-9

MANUFACTURED IN THE UNITED STATES OF AMERICA

1   3   5   7   9   10   8   6   4   2

First Edition

CONTENTS

THE MAN WHO SAVED THE UNION

PROLOGUE

IN A CHAIR ON THE PORCH OF A COTTAGE IN THE MOUNTAINS, AN OLD man sits. The summer sun warms the air, the trees, the cottage, the porch; but the old man wears a wool cap and wraps himself in a blanket and still feels cold. Yet he pushes aside his discomfort, even as he ignores the sharp pain in his throat, to focus on his work. Paper and pencil are his instruments, a lap desk his work space. The task transports him beyond his chill, beyond his pain, across the years. He recounts his life for a public that he cannot see but that is watching him, and has been watching him for the two decades since he became the nation's hero. He hadn't intended to write his story; he was willing to let the other officers of the Civil War duel for historical reputation. His own reputation was secure: he had commanded the army that defeated the rebellion and held the Union together. Not even Lincoln ranked higher in popular esteem at the moment of victory, and Lincoln was murdered within the week of Appomattox. Other Union generals—Sherman, Sheridan, Meade—had their partisans, including the thousands of soldiers who had served under them. He didn't begrudge them their laurels, nor did he seek any for himself. The laurels came to him unsought.

He had always had a gift for conjuring images in his mind's eye; it was one of the secrets of his military success. He could visualize a battlefield and perceive where the enemy's weaknesses were and how to exploit them, where his own weaknesses were and how to remedy them. He can visualize his battlefields even now: Fort Donelson, Shiloh, Vicksburg, Chattanooga, the Wilderness, Cold Harbor, Richmond. He can hear the whistle of the artillery shells, feel their concussion as they exploded, smell the burned powder and the sweat of horses and men.

Most of all he can summon the secret blessing of war: the liberating clarity of purpose felt by those who thrive amid war's chaos. He remembers his first taste of battle, in Mexico after his graduation from West Point. He had been frightened on approaching the enemy but discovered that he never functioned better than when under fire. Others became rattled and confused; he grew calm and focused. The end of the Mexican War left him at a loss; he fumbled through the following decade disappointing himself and those who knew him. He was resigned to mediocrity when another war, the great war for the Union, rescued him.

He doesn't write so swiftly now as he did when issuing dozens of orders a day. He fell out of the physical habit of writing during his eight years as president, when secretaries took his dictation. That was almost the only advantage life in politics had over life in the military. The business of the military is war, and war is simple and straightforward. In war the objective is plain and the measure of success undeniable. Your side wins or it loses; you live or you die. War is brutal, but its brutality allows differences of opinion to be resolved definitively. In politics things are never so straightforward. In politics differences of opinion are rarely resolved and almost never definitively; in politics the best outcomes are typically compromises that leave all parties grumbling. In politics the ignorant and venal have as much right to their votes as the educated and upstanding.

Of the ignorant and venal he encountered plenty as president. But his problem with politics ran deeper than that, for even good men could differ on solutions to the troubles that vexed America in the wake of the Civil War. He often felt as though he was the last elected official who cared about the freedmen, such criticism did he receive from both parties for the strong measures he took to defend the former slaves against the Ku Klux Klan and kindred tormentors. He felt likewise lonely trying to secure belated fair treatment for the Indians. He could claim only modest and passing success in these endeavors, not because bad men defeated him but because good men, weary of the strife of sectional crisis, war and reconstruction, found other things to worry about.

Yet his efforts weren't wasted. By the time he left office the Union was secure, which was something that could not have been said during most of his sixty-three years of life. The nation was at peace, after a war that had killed six hundred thousand. Democracy survived, for all its flaws and frustrations.

His parents had named him for Homer's hero of war and wandering, and as his journey nears its end he marvels at what a strange trip it has been. "I never thought of acquiring rank in the profession I was educated for," he jots in a journal he keeps to record the final miles. "Yet it came with two grades higher prefixed to the rank of General officer for me. I certainly never had either ambition or taste for a political life; yet I was twice President of the United States."

The remaining challenge of the journey is to finish his tale. "I must try to get some soft pencils," he writes as the light fades and his scratchings grow harder to read. "I could then write plainer and more rapidly." His son is helping. "Buck has brought up the last of the first volume in print. In two weeks if they work hard they can have the second volume copied ready to go to the printer." If he can hold out that long, he will be able to rest. "I will then feel that my work is done."

PART ONE

PROUD WALLS

"Ye kings and warriors! may your vows be crowned,
And Troy's proud walls lie level with the ground."

1

THE JOURNEY BEGAN GENERATIONS BEFORE HE WAS BORN. HIS ANCES-
tor Mathew Grant crossed the Atlantic from England with the Puri-
tans in the 1630s, and subsequent Grants migrated progressively west:
to Connecticut in the seventeenth century, Pennsylvania in the eighteenth, Ohio in the nineteenth. Jesse Grant, of the sixth generation of
American Grants, for a time lived in Deerfield, Ohio, with a family
named Brown, of whom a son, John, would attempt to start a slave
revolt at Harpers Ferry, Virginia, in 1859.

Jesse Grant never got much formal education and always felt the lack;
he vowed that his sons would not suffer similarly. Jesse married Hannah
Simpson in 1821; ten months later, on April 27, 1822, Hannah bore a son
they named Hiram Ulysses on the partial inspiration of an aunt with a
penchant for the classics. The boy attended private schools, since public
education hadn't reached Georgetown, in southwestern Ohio, where he
grew up. At fourteen he was sent across the Ohio River to Maysville,
Kentucky, to boarding school, but the experience didn't take and he
returned to Georgetown. At sixteen he enrolled in an academy in Ripley,
on the Ohio bank of the Ohio River, with no greater success. He later
acknowledged that the failure was his own fault. "I was not studious in
habit," he said, "and probably did not make progress enough to compensate for the outlay for board and tuition."

Yet he was no rebel. "He was always a steady, serious sort of boy, who
took everything in earnest," his mother recalled. "Even when he played
he made a business of it." For this reason his parents paid attention when
he registered his preferences and dislikes. Jesse owned and operated a
tannery, in which Ulys, as family and friends called the boy, was expected

to work. But he detested the place and what went on there. "He would rather do anything else under the sun than work in the tannery," Jesse recounted. Jesse remembered informing Ulys a few times that he would have to grind bark (for the tannic acid it contained). "He would get right up without saying a word and start straight for the village, and get a load to haul, or passengers to carry, or something another to do, and hire a boy to come back and grind the bark." Other aspects of tanning were equally distasteful. In the "beam room" hides were defleshed by being drawn forcefully over beams; Ulys entered only under paternal duress and told his father that as soon as he could support himself he would never go near the smelly place again. Jesse excused him. "I don't want you to work at it now if you don't like it and mean to stick to it," Jesse recalled saying.

So he let the boy work outdoors. Ulys loved horses and early displayed a gift for riding and managing them. "He had the habit of riding our horses to water, standing up on their bare backs," Jesse remembered. "He began this practice at about five years old. At eight or nine he would ride them at the top of their speed, he standing upon one foot and balancing himself by the bridle reins." Ulys drove the team that transported wood and other supplies for the tannery; from the age of eleven, when he was big enough to handle a plow, he took charge of all the horse-powered tasks on the family farm.

He impressed his father with his self-sufficiency, and Jesse let the boy travel by horse and wagon around southwestern Ohio and into Kentucky. The journeys often involved some aspect of the family business: purchasing supplies, delivering messages or finished products. Ulys especially liked to buy horses and felt much older than his years when he made a good bargain.

Sometimes the bargains weren't so good. A neighbor had a colt that Ulys, then eight, fancied; the neighbor asked twenty-five dollars for it. Jesse didn't want to spend more than twenty, but Ulys pleaded and persuaded his father to let him offer more if necessary. As the story was later told, the boy approached the neighbor: "Papa says I may offer you twenty dollars for the colt, but if you won't take that, I am to offer twenty-two and a half, and if you won't take that, to give you twenty-five." The neighbor laughed and received his full price.

Grant remembered the incident sixty years later, not fondly. "This transaction caused me great heart-burning," he said. "The story got out among the boys of the village, and it was a long time before I heard the end of it. Boys enjoy the misery of their companions, at least village boys

in that day did, and in later life I have found that all adults are not free
from the peculiarity."

*I*n his eighteenth year Ulysses looked forward to leaving school,
but Jesse had other plans. An acquaintance and former friend, Thomas
Hamer, represented Georgetown's district in Congress; the friendship
had foundered in the breakup of the old Republican party of Thomas
Jefferson and the emergence of the Democratic and Whig parties. The
Democrats favored Andrew Jackson and opposed the Bank of the United
States, while the Whigs backed Henry Clay and supported the national
bank. Thomas Hamer was a Jackson man, Jesse Grant a Clay man, and
sharp political words led to a personal rupture.

Yet Jesse needed Hamer's help six years later when he learned that
a West Point cadet from the district had to withdraw from the military academy. Jesse wanted Ulysses to receive the nomination in the
young man's place. He approached Ohio senator Thomas Morris but was
informed that Hamer held the right of appointment. Jesse suspended his
hostility toward Hamer long enough to ask him to nominate Ulysses.

Hamer was willing to move beyond their differences; moreover, with
the nomination deadline swiftly approaching, he had no other nominee.
He put Ulysses forward.

Only at this point did Jesse apprise his son of what he had been doing
on his behalf. "Ulysses, I believe you are going to receive the appointment," he said. "What appointment?" Ulysses asked. "West Point," Jesse
answered.

Ulysses was less grateful than Jesse thought fitting. The young man
didn't know much about the military academy, but what he thought he
knew disposed him against it. "I had a very exalted idea of the aquire-
ments necessary to get through," he recalled later. "I did not believe I
possessed them, and could not bear the idea of failing."

One thing alone, the prospect of a journey, made the appointment
appealing. "I had always a great desire to travel," he explained. He had
ventured as far as a horse could conveniently take him from Georgetown,
and the prospect of crossing the eastern mountains was alluring. "Going
to West Point would give me the opportunity of visiting the two great
cities of the continent, Philadelphia and New York." His curiosity overcame his fear and he agreed to go.

Yet even as he imagined what he would see in the big cities, he secretly hoped fate would spare him from actually becoming a cadet. "When these places were visited," he recalled, "I would have been glad to have had a steamboat or railroad collision, or any other accident happen, by which I might have received a temporary injury sufficient to make me ineligible, for a time, to enter the Academy."

The journey was everything he hoped for, save the accident. Steamboats had arrived on the Mississippi and Ohio Rivers about the time Grant was born; by 1839 they had transformed the economy of America's central valley, permitting travelers and cargoes to move upriver almost as easily as down. Grant boarded a steamboat at Ripley and rode three days to Pittsburgh. Many travelers on the Ohio in that period remarked the difference in development between the thriving Ohio side of the river, where free farmers tilled the fields and free workers manned the wharves, and the languishing Kentucky and Virginia side, where slaves, with no stake in their labors, did the toiling. If the young Grant noticed the difference, he didn't record it.

At Pittsburgh he switched to a canal boat. Canals had served the American East since the eighteenth century; during the first third of the nineteenth century they penetrated the interior, with the Erie Canal, completed in 1825, connecting the Hudson River to the Great Lakes and launching New York City to commercial primacy. The narrow-beamed canal boats, pulled by horses or mules on canal-side towpaths, were slow but sure. "No mode of conveyance could be more pleasant, when time was not an object," Grant wrote of his own trip. His vessel was comfortable, and the artificial waterway afforded excellent views of the western Pennsylvania landscape. For Grant, the slowness of travel was a mark in the canal's favor. "I had rather a dread of reaching my destination."

At Harrisburg he encountered the revolutionary transport technology of the era. American railroads were younger than Grant, but their effect on locomotion was evident the moment he stepped aboard. "We travelled at least eighteen miles an hour, when at full speed," he remembered, "and made the whole distance averaging probably as much as twelve miles an hour. This seemed like annihilating space. . . . I thought the perfection of rapid transit had been reached."

He stepped off the train at Philadelphia, which entranced him so much that he spent five days exploring nearly every street and alley, visiting the sites associated with the landmark events of America's founding, attending the theater and generally acting the young man with pocket money and no desire to leave.

New York held him less long, in part because he feared he had spent too much money in Philadelphia. But there was also less to see in New York; its urban glory remained prospective. After three days he headed north to West Point and arrived there at the end of May 1839.

*T*he academy wasn't expecting him, at least not under his given name. Congressman Hamer knew him as Ulysses and assumed this was his first name. For some reason Hamer recorded Grant's middle initial as S, apparently from the family name, Simpson, of Grant's mother. In consequence the academy's registry listed the new cadet as "U. S. Grant."

Grant accepted Ulysses as a first name, having used it as such since he learned to talk. But he clung to Hiram, which he now adopted as a middle name.

The academy was unmoved. He had been appointed as "U. S. Grant," and so he remained in the academy's records. Grant's classmates drew the inevitable connection to "Uncle Sam" and started calling him "Sam Grant." Grant signed his papers "Ulysses H. Grant" or "U. H. Grant" until the weight of the army's authority wore him down and he became "U. S. Grant" in his own hand.

*H*is introduction to cadet life didn't diminish his ambivalence toward a military education. "I slept for two months upon one single pair of blankets," he wrote McKinstry Griffith, a cousin, at the end of the summer's encampment that served as orientation to the academy. "I tell you what, coz, it is *tremendous hard*. Suppose you try it by way of experiment for a night or two." The drilling was tedious and the discipline vexing. The more he reflected on what he had gotten himself into, the deeper his spirits sank. "When the 28th of August came—the date for breaking up camp and going into barracks—I felt as though I had been at West Point always," he later recalled, "and that if I stayed to graduation, I would have to remain always."

The autumn scarcely improved his mood. "We have tremendous long and hard lessons to get in both French and Algebra," he told his cousin in late September. Though the cadets nominally earned twenty-eight dollars per month, he had yet to see any of it. The rules of daily life could be maddening. "If we want anything from a shoestring to a coat, we must go to the commandant of the post and get an order for it." He missed the girls he knew from Ohio. "I have been here about four months and have not seen a single familiar face or *spoken* to a single lady. I wish some of the pretty girls of Bethel were here just so I might look at them."

The code of conduct was rigid and enforced by a system of black marks. "They give a man one of these black marks for almost nothing," Grant explained. "If he gets 200 a year they dismiss him." A cadet from New York had received eight black marks for not attending church one Sunday and was confined to his room besides. Grant shook his head. "We are not only obliged to go to church but must *march* there by companies. This is not exactly republican."

The uniforms struck Grant as ludicrous. "If I were to come home now with my uniform on . . . ," he wrote Griffith, "you would laugh at my appearance. . . . My pants sit as tight to my skin as the bark to a tree, and if I do not walk *military*—that is, if I bend over quickly or run—they are very apt to crack with a report as loud as a pistol. My coat must always be buttoned up tight to the chin. . . . It makes me look very singular. If you were to see me at a distance, the first question you would ask would be, 'Is that a fish or an animal?'"

Yet there were compensations. The cadets received visits from important officials. Martin Van Buren had followed Andrew Jackson in the White House, and though Van Buren lacked the war record of the hero of New Orleans, he *was* president, the only one Grant had encountered thus far.

Winfield Scott was even more impressive. Scott had covered himself with blood and glory in the War of 1812, and unlike Jackson, who had left the military for politics, he had remained in the army. By 1839 he was the ranking American general and the model, in the eyes of Grant and the other cadets, of what a soldier should be. "With his commanding figure, his quite colossal size and showy uniform, I thought him the finest specimen of manhood my eyes had ever beheld, and the most to be envied," Grant recalled.

Visits like Scott's combined with his own adjustment to the ways of the military to make Grant think the academy wasn't so bad after all. "There is much to dislike but more to like," he wrote Griffith. "On the whole I like the place very much, so much that I would not go away on any account." His teachers emphasized the usefulness of the education he was receiving, and he drew some conclusions of his own. "The fact is if a man graduates here he is safe for life, let him go where he will. I mean to study and stay if it be possible. If I cannot—very well, the world is wide."

———

*H*e did stay, although he never became a model cadet. He preferred novels to his schoolbooks, searching the academy library for works by Washington Irving, James Fenimore Cooper and others and ordering additional volumes from booksellers. Mathematics eventually came easily to him; French never did. All cadets were required to take drawing; Grant's sketches showed a steady hand and an eye for detail and nuance.

During his first year Congress debated whether to continue funding the military academy. The financial panic of 1837 had crimped the federal budget, and a certain part of the electorate had long distrusted a professional army, which brought to mind Europe and what the citizen-soldiers of the American Revolution had rebelled against. The chill of winter and the chafing of regulations revived Grant's earlier doubts about West Point, and he later recalled rooting for the opponents of the academy. "I saw in this an honorable way to obtain a discharge," he explained. But the academy survived and he remained.

He made no strong impression on his superiors or classmates, except in horsemanship. James Fry was a few years behind Grant at the academy and remembered observing a riding exercise at the end of which the riding master placed the leaping bar more than six feet high and called out for Cadet Grant. "A clean-faced, slender, blue-eyed young fellow, weighing about 120 pounds, dashed from the ranks on a powerfully built chestnut-sorrel horse, and galloped down the opposite side of the hall," Fry recorded. "As he turned at the farther end and came into the straight stretch across which the bar was placed, the horse increased his pace, and, measuring his strides for the great leap before him, bounded into the air and cleared the bar, carrying his rider as if man and beast had been welded together."

Otherwise Grant simply did what was required, and that not especially well. As the cadets advanced from class to class, their leaders became the academy's officers. Grant briefly made sergeant, but a rash of demerits knocked him back down to private.

Questionable health contributed to his failure to distinguish himself. Consumption—tuberculosis—ran in his family, killing two of his uncles and later two of his siblings. In his final year at the academy he suffered a cough that lasted six months and intimated an early end for him too. At graduation he weighed less than he had when he entered the academy, though he had gained half a foot in height.

The army registered its doubts in the assignment he was given on completing his studies. He requested the cavalry and should have gotten it on the basis of his equestrian talents. But he received the infantry instead.

He hid his disappointment behind the spanking blue uniform he ordered for his commissioning. He took his oath in July 1843 before a justice of the peace of Ohio's Clermont County, to which his family had moved while he was at West Point. He mounted a horse and rode to Cincinnati, to see the sights and show himself off. "While I was riding along a street of that city," he remembered many years afterward, "imagining that everyone was looking at me, with a feeling akin to mine when I first saw General Scott, a little urchin, bareheaded, barefooted, with dirty and ragged pants held up by a single gallows—that's what suspenders were called then—and a shirt that had not seen a wash-tub for weeks, turned to me and cried: 'Soldier! will you work? No, sir-ee; I'll sell my shirt first!!'"

The taunt stung, recalling, as he later admitted, the barbs of his boyhood mates after he paid too much for his colt. When he returned to his parents' town he caught another shaft. A drunken stableman saw him coming and donned blue pants with a strip of white down the sides, in mocking imitation of Grant's uniform pants. "The joke was a huge one in the mind of many of the people, and was much enjoyed by them," Grant wrote. "But I did not appreciate it so highly."

2

NOT EVERYONE THOUGHT THE NEW SECOND LIEUTENANT LUDICROUS.
Grant's West Point roommate Fred Dent was from St. Louis, conveniently close to Jefferson Barracks, Grant's first posting. The Dents
opened their home to Fred's friend, who visited during the winter and
spring of 1843–44. Mary Robinson, a slave in the Dent household,
remembered Grant as "an exceedingly fine looking young man." Fred's
sister Julia shared the opinion or something enough like it to encourage
the visits. Grant required little nudging. "At first sight he fell in love
with Miss Dent," Mary Robinson said. The visits grew more frequent.

The springtime of Grant and Julia's romance became a summer of
America's discontent. For decades American expansionists had eyed
Texas, initially a province of New Spain and then a state of the Mexican republic. Illegal American emigrants had crossed the Sabine River,
the boundary between Louisiana and Texas, until the Mexican government, unable to populate Texas with Mexican nationals and hoping to
build a buffer against the Comanche Indians, invading from the northwest, authorized Virginia native Stephen Austin to settle three hundred
American families on Texas soil. But this simply opened the floodgates,
and by the mid-1830s the Americans in Texas, most of whom had arrived
illegally, outnumbered the Mexicans ten to one. In 1836 they declared
independence, which they confirmed in a brief, bloody war. They then
requested annexation to the United States.

The request reopened the debate over slavery. The debate had started
at the Constitutional Convention of 1787, when the framers accepted
the anomaly of slavery in a republic in order to secure the support of
the Southern states. Most Americans, including many Southerners,

expected slavery to decline and disappear. And so it might have done if cotton hadn't emerged as a cash crop ideally suited to lands wrested from Indian tribes in the South during the early nineteenth century. As settlement spread west along the Gulf Plain, cotton and slavery spread with it, entrenching both in the minds of Southerners, who came to identify their region with the "peculiar institution."

By 1820 the culture of cotton and slavery had reached Missouri, which was admitted to the Union as part of a grand bargain that balanced free-state Maine against slave Missouri and split the rest of the Louisiana Purchase into a northern region off limits to slavery and a southern region open to the institution. The balancing was essential to the deal, for by this time the free North had outstripped the slave South in population and therefore in seats in the House of Representatives. The Senate, with its representation by states, formed the crucial redoubt of Southern influence in Washington, and the Southerners insisted that each new free state be matched with a new slave state.

Northerners insisted on the same principle, reversed, and when Texas applied for admission they were the ones who objected. The Texans practiced slavery, and Texas was so large that it seemed likely to spawn multiple slave states. Such Northerners as John Quincy Adams, returned to Congress from Massachusetts after being evicted from the White House by Andrew Jackson, decried the Texas project as a slaveholder conspiracy. Adams and the adamant antislavery bloc formed a minority in Congress, but a minority was all that was necessary to prevent the Senate from granting a Texas treaty the two-thirds support required for ratification.

Rejected by Washington, the Texans embarked on a career as an independent republic. They established diplomatic and commercial relations with Britain and France, but their finances were in shambles and they couldn't defend themselves against attack from Mexico, which refused to acknowledge the loss of its erstwhile state. Twice the Mexican army reoccupied San Antonio, deep in Texas territory.

The government of Texas, headed by Sam Houston, once more turned to the United States. Houston, a protégé of Jackson's, informed his retired mentor that if the American government continued to spurn Texas, he and the Texans would have no choice but to ally with Britain. Houston knew that the teenage Jackson had been taken prisoner during the Revolutionary War and been mistreated by his British captors; he knew that Jackson had unleashed his pent-up anger upon the British army at New Orleans in 1815; he knew that Jackson still smoldered whenever he pondered the perfidiousness of Albion. And he guessed that Jackson would move heaven and earth to prevent an alliance between Texas and Britain.

Jackson remained the dominant Democrat despite advanced age and ill health, and he responded to Houston's challenge by insisting that the contenders for the 1844 Democratic presidential nomination pledge their support for Texas annexation. When Martin Van Buren, Jackson's former vice president and then successor in the White House, waffled, Jackson singlehandedly crushed his candidacy. And when James Polk, a dark horse from Tennessee, enthusiastically endorsed annexation, Jackson ensured his nomination.

Polk's embrace of Texas revived the opposition of Adams and others; it also roiled American relations with Mexico. The Mexican government asserted that annexation would be tantamount to a declaration of war against Mexico and that, if war came, Mexico would defend itself.

John Tyler, the current occupant of the White House, hadn't been elected president, merely vice president, and when William Henry Harrison died shortly after his 1841 inauguration no one knew for certain whether Tyler became president or simply *acting* president, since the Constitution didn't specify. But he did indeed *act* like a president, on no subject more than Texas. He ordered American troops to western Louisiana to meet any Mexican challenge.

Grant's regiment, the Fourth Infantry, was part of Tyler's deployment. The unit would join others near Fort Jessup, Louisiana, a short distance from the Texas border.

Grant had commenced a leave of absence to visit his parents in Ohio when the deployment order arrived. A message chased him up the Ohio and reached him in Bethel, where they now resided. His father told him that he had gotten all the good from the army he was likely to get and that he should quit to join the family business; Ulysses's deployment, to the back of beyond, was just what he could expect of a military career. Grant didn't like the leather business any more than he had as a boy, and he rejected his father's advice. But neither did he immediately follow the army's order. Instead of traveling straight from Ohio to Louisiana, he returned to Missouri for a parting word with Julia Dent.

He later recalled approaching the Dent home. The road from Jefferson Barracks to the Dent house crossed a creek, which in most seasons a man on a horse could splash across with no difficulty whatever. But recent rains had swollen the creek to flood stage. "I looked at it a moment to consider what to do," Grant related. "One of my superstitions has always been when I started to go anywhere or to do anything, not to turn back or stop until the thing intended was accomplished. I have frequently started to go to places where I had never been and to which I did not know the way, depending upon making inquiries on the road, and if I got past the place without knowing it, instead of turning back, I would go on until a road was found turning in the right direction, take that, and come in by the other side." On this day he had both a destination and a purpose, and there was no chance he would turn back. "I struck into the stream, and in an instant the horse was swimming and I being carried down by the current." Horse and man were swept swiftly along, with both becoming thoroughly soaked and more than a little worried. But the horse proved a strong swimmer, and they eventually gained the far bank.

He arrived at the Dent home drenched but determined. He explained to Julia that the prospect of leaving for Louisiana and possibly going to war had made him realize how much he loved her. He couldn't go without asking her to marry him.

She accepted his proposal conditionally. Her parents had mixed feelings about Grant. "Old man Dent was opposed to him, when he found he was courting his daughter, and did everything he could to prevent the match," Mary Robinson remembered. "But Mrs. Dent took a great fancy to him in his venture. Mrs. Dent used to say to me: I like that young man." Julia thought she and her mother could work on her father and eventually bring him around. But until he changed his mind, the engagement must be a secret.

Grant was elated. Frederick Dent's veto centered on his judgment that army life was no fitting existence for his daughter; Grant considered this merely a temporary impediment, as he didn't intend to make a career of the army. He at once wrote to his mathematics professor at West Point asking to be appointed his assistant, in which capacity he might serve out his obligation to the army and prepare himself to be a civilian mathematics professor. He laid a plan of informal study to extend his mastery of the subject. And he congratulated himself on having won his true love, in principle at least.

———

 *M*eanwhile he had to report to Louisiana. He had never been so far south or seen anything like the swamps and bayous that constituted much of the state. "The country is low and flat and overflown"—by the Red River—"to the first limbs of the trees," he wrote Julia of his journey up that stream. "Alligators and other revolting looking things occupy the swamps in thousands; and no doubt the very few people who live there shake with the ague"—the chills of malaria—"all summer."

He was pleased to report that his regiment had found a better neighborhood for its camp. "We are on the top of a high ridge, with about the best spring of water in Louisiana running near." But they had company. The pine forest surrounding the camp was "infested to an enormous degree with ticks, red bugs, and a little creeping thing looking like a lizard that I don't know the name of." The tents couldn't keep the critters out. "This last vermin is singularly partial to society, and become so very intimate and sociable on short acquaintance as to visit our tents, crawl into our beds." Water entered as easily. "We have had a hard shower and I can tell you my tent is a poor protection. The rain runs through in streams."

Grant and the Fourth Infantry remained at Camp Salubrity, as the bivouac was hopefully named, during the summer and autumn of 1844. The name proved accurate for Grant. He spent most of his time outdoors and on horseback and rid himself of the cough that had nagged him since West Point. He gained weight and forgot about the consumption that afflicted his family.

The only fighting of the season took place in American politics, where Polk and the Democrats campaigned on a platform of aggressive expansion, against the more diffident Henry Clay and the Whigs. Polk won a narrow victory, in part because the abolitionist Liberty party bled votes from Clay in the decisive state of New York. Polk prepared to implement what he pronounced a mandate for expansion, but John Tyler got there first. The lame-duck president circumvented the Senate veto of a Texas treaty by proposing to annex the Lone Star Republic by a joint resolution, requiring mere majorities in both houses of Congress. The antislavery, anti-Texas bloc lacked the votes to forestall this maneuver, and the resolution passed. When the Texans endorsed the deal in the summer of 1845, the union was consummated.

———

"*O*ur orders are for the western borders of Texas," Grant wrote Julia that July. "But how far up the Rio Grande is hard to tell." He was glad to be going, although the deployment would put more distance between him and her. "In the course of five or six months I expect to be promoted, and there are seven chances out of eight that I will not be promoted in the Fourth, so that at the end of that time I shall hope to be back to the United States," where he *would* be closer to her. This happy result would surely transpire, "unless of course there should be active service."

He missed her terribly. He wrote her often—more often than she replied, which made him wonder if she still loved him. "I have waited so long for an answer to my three letters . . . ," he lamented, "that I began to despair of ever receiving a line from you." But then a letter or two or three together would arrive and all would be well. "I have read them over and over again and will continue to do so until another comes."

The longer they were separated the more he wished to be near her and the sooner he hoped to marry her. He wasn't sure he could wait until he left the army. "Julia, can we hope that your pa will be induced to change his opinion of an army life?" he wrote. "I think he is mistaken about the army life being such an unpleasant one. It is true the movement of the troops from Jefferson Barracks so suddenly and to so outlandish a place"—the pine forest of Louisiana—"would rather create that opinion, but then such a thing hardly occurs once a lifetime."

The deployment to Texas must have seemed still more outlandish to Frederick Dent, who continued to withhold his permission. The first stop of the Fourth was Corpus Christi, at the mouth of the Nueces River. The regiment wintered there, awaiting the arrival of other units and the outcome of developments in Washington. Grant filled his time writing to Julia and touring the region. He and several other officers rode from Corpus Christi to San Antonio, which had been the capital of Mexican Texas. "San Antonio has the appearance of being a very old town," he told Julia. "The houses are all built of stone and are beginning to crumble. The whole place has been built for defense, which by the way was a wise precaution, for until within three or four years it has been the scene of more bloodshed than almost any place of as little importance in the world. . . . The inhabitants of San Antonio are mostly Mexicans. They seem to have no occupation whatever."

From the old capital Grant and his comrades rode north to Austin, the new capital. "The whole of the country is the most beautiful that I have ever seen, and no doubt will be filled up very rapidly now that the people feel a confidence in being protected," he wrote. For the present the eighty-mile stretch was uninhabited, save for a settlement of Germans at New Braunfels who had just arrived and were living in temporary huts of the sort that soldiers threw up when they lacked tents or barracks.

From Austin back to Corpus Christi the country was similarly unoccupied, except by myriad beasts and fowl. Most of the officers in his group enjoyed hunting, and the expedition feasted nightly on venison and turkey. Grant was less the nimrod. "Benjamin and I concluded to go down to the creek, which was fringed with timber, much of it the pecan, and bring back a few turkeys," he wrote of a day near Goliad. "We had scarcely reached the edge of the timber when I heard the flutter of wings overhead, and in an instant I saw two or three turkeys flying away. These were soon followed by more, then more, and more, until a flock of twenty or thirty had left from just over my head. All this time I stood watching the turkeys to see where they flew, with my gun on my shoulder, and never once thought of leveling it at the birds. . . . I came to the conclusion that as a sportsman I was a failure."

*H*ad Texas been the sum of Polk's designs on Mexico, Grant's regiment might have remained at Corpus Christi. The government of the Texas republic had asserted ownership beyond the Nueces to the Rio Grande, and the United States had accepted the Texas claim upon annexing Texas, but neither the Texans nor the Americans had ever exercised authority in that strip. The Mexican government likewise claimed ownership of the strip, but for an even longer period it too had failed to exercise authority. A diplomatic solution to the territorial dispute might have been arranged had the will existed, not least since almost no one lived in the strip.

The Mexican government doubtless would have summoned the will if given time. Mexico still resented the loss of Texas, yet little enthusiasm existed for reopening the war now that it would mean fighting the United States. Texas had been nothing but trouble for Mexico, which had experienced chronic political turmoil since independence in 1821 and didn't need any more trouble.

Trouble, though, was just what Polk wanted. Polk's election had encouraged other expansionists to agitate for more territory; foremost among the agitators was John L. O'Sullivan, a New York editor who for years had been promoting the glories of American democracy. "Our national birth was the beginning of a new history," he wrote. "The boundless future will be the era of American greatness. In its magnificent domain of space and time, the nation of many nations is destined to manifest to mankind the excellence of divine principles." Amid the Texas controversy O'Sullivan blasted the opponents of annexation and trumpeted America's "manifest destiny to overspread the continent allotted by Providence for the free development of our yearly multiplying millions."

O'Sullivan's slogan of Manifest Destiny caught on as a précis of a dominant attitude in America in the 1840s. Americans had always been acquisitive, and as they were an agricultural people their acquisitiveness took the form of a desire for land. For at least a century the American population had doubled each generation; if the American domain didn't double too, Americans would grow poorer and poorer. Since Puritan times Americans had claimed providential approval for their undertakings; since independence they had appropriated a secular sanction as well. The spread of American sovereignty would expand the realm of liberty, allowing more of the world to participate in the glorious enterprise of self-government.

Americans had never been reluctant to assert their views; a bumptious pride had marked them since the beginning. But during the middle third of the nineteenth century American politics and diplomacy took a particularly aggressive turn. The generation that had proven itself by acquiring independence from Britain departed the scene; the younger generation felt compelled to prove *its* strength and courage. The European empires that had kept American ambition in check had withdrawn or were crumbling. France abandoned the North American field with Napoleon's sale of Louisiana to the United States in 1803. Britain stopped trying to contain the Americans after its red-coated troops lost to Jackson at New Orleans in 1815. Spain surrendered Florida to the United States and suffered embarrassment after humiliation as one country after another in Central and South America broke free in the 1810s and 1820s. And the ebb of the Europeans left the indigenous peoples of North America more at the mercy of the introduced Americans than ever. The French, British and Spanish had at various times armed and encouraged Indian tribes against American expansion; without the European help the Indians' capacity for resistance diminished drastically.

James Polk understood the new psychology and balance of power, and his interpretation of Manifest Destiny caused him to look beyond Texas to California. Mexico's northwesternmost province was even more enticing than Texas, in that it fronted on the Pacific, the greatest of all oceans, and held out the promise that American expansion might continue beyond North American shores. Polk tried to purchase California from Mexico, but the loss of Texas had made the Mexicans prohibitively sensitive to any additional loss of their national domain. Moreover, the political turbulence in Mexico prevented each of the series of governments during this period from consolidating sufficient authority to accomplish a sale of California even if it had wanted to.

Polk interpreted the turbulence in Mexico as evidence of that country's unfitness to keep California, and he sought an excuse to seize what Mexico wouldn't sell. In early 1846 he ordered General Zachary Taylor to march the Fourth Infantry and parts of other regiments, totaling some three thousand troops, from Corpus Christi to the Rio Grande, deep in the disputed zone and hard against Mexico proper.

3

"Everyone rejoices at the idea of leaving Corpus Christi," Grant wrote Julia. The months of waiting had been wearing for the soldiers, and they were eager to earn their pay. The purpose of the redeployment was plain enough. "We are to go into camp on this side of the Rio Grande just opposite to Matamoras, a town of considerable importance in Mexico, and, as we are informed, occupied by several thousand troops who it is believed by many will make us fight for our ground before we will be allowed to occupy it."

Grant noted that circumstances didn't favor the American side. The Mexicans, besides outnumbering the Americans, enjoyed the advantage of position. "If we are attacked, in the present reduced state of the troops here the consequences may be much against us." Yet death appeared less likely than inconvenience. "We may be taken prisoners, it is true, and taken to the City of Mexico and then when we will be able to get away is entirely uncertain."

Hazard apart, the redeployment complicated his plans with Julia. "In my previous letters," he told her, "I have spoken a great deal of resigning, but of course I could not think of such a thing now just at a time when it is probable that the services of every officer will be called into requisition." He wouldn't stop thinking of her, though. "I will write to you very often and look forward with a great deal of anxiety to the time when I may see you again and claim a kiss for my long absence. Do you wear the ring with the letters U. S. G. in it, Julia? I often take yours off to look at the name engraved in it."

The southward march took Grant and the others across some of the finest natural pasture in America. "The country was a rolling prairie, and from the higher ground, the vision was obstructed only by the earth's curvature," he wrote later. Countless wild horses made the region their home. "As far as the eye could reach to our right, the herd extended. To the left, it extended equally. There was no estimating the number of animals in it; I have no idea that they could all have been corralled in the State of Rhode Island, or Delaware, at one time. If they had been, they would have been so thick that the pasturage would have given out the first day."

Taylor's small army encountered Mexican forces at a minor stream some thirty miles north of the Rio Grande. "A parley took place between Gen. Taylor and their commanding officer, whose name I have forgotten," Grant explained to Julia. "The result of which was that if we attempted to cross they would fire upon us. . . . He pledged his honor that the moment we put our foot into the water to cross he would fire upon us and war would commence." Taylor responded that the Americans would cross regardless of what the Mexicans did. "Whereupon they left and were seen no more," Grant remarked. This was the more noteworthy in that the Americans were quite vulnerable amid the crossing. "When the troops were in the water up to their necks a small force on shore might have given them a great deal of trouble." Grant and the others took a lesson. "I think after making such threats and speaking so positively of what they would do, to then let so fine an opportunity to execute what they had threatened pass unimproved, shows anything but a decided disposition to drive us from the soil."

A thirsty march across a sandy desert brought the Americans to their objective, which Grant found disappointing. "No doubt you suppose the Rio Grande, from its name and appearance on the map, to be a large and magnificent stream," he wrote Julia. "But instead of that it is a small muddy stream of probably from 150 to 200 yards in width and navigable for only small sized steamers."

The Americans pitched camp opposite Matamoros. "The city from this side of the river bears a very imposing appearance and no doubt contains from four to five thousand inhabitants," Grant wrote. "Apparently there are a large force of Mexican troops preparing to attack us." On the night of the Americans' arrival the Mexican defenders threw up a wall of sandbags on which they mounted small artillery pieces aimed at the American camp. The Mexican commander published a warning to the

Americans. "It was a long, wordy, and threatening document," Grant told Julia. "He said that the citizens of Mexico were ready to expose their bare breasts to the Rifles of the Hunters of the Mississippi. . . . The Invaders of the North would have to reap their Laurels at the points of their sharpened swords. . . . The Rio Grande would be our Sepulcher."

Grant wasn't worried. "Already they have boasted and threatened so much and executed so little that it is generally believed that all they are doing is mere bombast and show, intended to intimidate our troops."

Consequently the outbreak of hostilities surprised the Americans. Taylor sent patrols in various directions from his camp; in late April one of these, composed of sixty cavalrymen, tangled with a Mexican force of two thousand. A dozen Americans were killed and the rest taken prisoner.

As news of the affair was relayed to Washington, where Polk awaited just such an incident, Taylor reconsidered his situation. His supply line ran back to Port Isabel, thirty miles north and east through territory open to Mexican troops. A swift strike by the Mexicans might cut him off, trapping his outnumbered army in hostile country. He determined to leave a small force on the Rio Grande and march the rest of his troops to Port Isabel.

"We marched nearly all night the first night, and you may depend, my dear Julia, that we were all very much fatigued," Grant wrote. "We start again at 1 o'clock today." Yet even as Taylor secured his supplies, he and the other Americans received evidence that fighting had escalated behind them. "There was about six hundred troops left in our Fort opposite Matamoros," Grant told Julia, "and the presumption is they have been attacked, for we have heard the sound of artillery from that direction ever since day light this morning."

The prospect of battle filled Grant with trepidation. "A young second-lieutenant who had never heard a hostile gun before, I felt sorry that I had enlisted," he recollected from the distance of four decades and dozens of subsequent battles. "A great many men, when they smell battle afar off, chafe to get into the fray. When they say so themselves they generally fail to convince their hearers that they are as anxious as they would like to make believe, and as they approach danger they become more subdued. This rule is not universal, for I have known a few men who were always aching for a fight when there was no enemy near, who were as good as their word when the battle did come. But the number of such men is small."

Grant's test came soon. Taylor remained at Port Isabel long enough to load a train of wagons, then countermarched toward the Rio Grande. Six miles from the now besieged garrison a stand of timber lined a former channel of the river. Palo Alto, the place was called, for the tall trees. The American column approached the stand and discovered a larger number of Mexicans arrayed for battle. "Our wagons were immediately parked, and Gen. Taylor marched us up towards them," Grant wrote Julia. "When we got in range of their artillery they let us have it right and left." The first cannonballs fired at the Americans did no damage. "They would strike the ground long before they reached our line, and ricocheted through the tall grass so slowly that the men would see them and open ranks and let them pass," Grant wrote. As the Americans drew nearer to the Mexicans, however, the firing grew more dangerous. Taylor ordered the American artillery to return fire. "Every moment we could see the charges from our pieces cut a way through their ranks making a perfect road," Grant recorded. "But they would close up the interval without showing signs of retreat."

The Mexican artillery and small arms fire eventually took a toll. "Although the balls were whizzing thick and fast about me, I did not feel a sensation of fear until nearly the close of firing," Grant wrote Julia. "A ball struck close by me, killing one man instantly. It knocked Capt. Page's under jaw entirely off and broke in the roof of his mouth, and knocked Lt. Wallen and one sergeant down besides."

Dusk brought the battle to an end, with the Mexicans falling back. The Americans counted their modest casualties—nine dead, fewer than fifty wounded—and estimated the greater losses on the Mexican side. Grant and the others congratulated themselves on surviving their first action and prepared to resume the fight the next day.

In the morning, though, they discovered that the Mexicans had abandoned the field. Grant and the others for the first time witnessed the aftermath of battle. "It was a terrible sight to go over the ground . . . ," Grant wrote Julia, "and see the amount of life that had been destroyed. The ground was literally strewed with the bodies of dead men and horses."

Taylor sent scouts to find the Mexican army. Thick chaparral blocked the way, and the scouts advanced with care. They spotted the Mexicans beyond a series of ponds at Resaca de la Palma. The Mexican army from the day before had been augmented by troops from Matamoros, and the entire force had drawn up a defensive line behind the ponds. The American scouts engaged the Mexicans from a distance and sent word back to the main force.

Taylor ordered his army forward. The captain of Grant's company had gone with the scouts, leaving Grant in command of the unit—"an honor and responsibility I thought very great," he wrote. As the army made contact with the Mexicans, Grant's company was on the American right, and he led his company through the bushes wherever an opening appeared. "At last I got pretty close up without knowing it," he explained. "The balls commenced to whistle very thick overhead, cutting the limbs of the chaparral right and left. We could not see the enemy, so I ordered my men to lie down, an order that did not have to be enforced." Gradually Grant realized that the Mexicans were firing not at his unit but at some troops behind them, and he managed to extricate his men to better ground.

Meanwhile the American left had forced the Mexicans back, and the entire Mexican line began to crumple. "Our men continued to advance and did advance in spite of their shots, to the very mouths of the cannon, and killed and took prisoner the Mexicans with them, and drove off with their own teams, taking cannon ammunition and all to our side," Grant told Julia. "In this way nine of their big guns were taken and their own ammunition turned against them."

Grant himself led a charge between two ponds and was thrilled to capture a Mexican colonel and several enlisted men, who offered little resistance. He proudly sent the prisoners, under guard, to the American rear. But as he was doing so an American private, helping a wounded American officer, emerged from a thicket ahead of Grant's position, and Grant realized that his charge had been over ground already taken by the Americans. "My exploit was equal to that of the soldier who boasted that he had cut off the leg of one of the enemy," he recalled wryly. "When asked why he did not cut off the head, he replied: 'Someone had done that before.'"

The battle became a rout as the Mexicans ran short of ammunition. "The Mexicans fought very hard for an hour and a half," Grant said, "but seeing their means of war fall from their hands in spite of all their efforts they finally commenced to retreat helter skelter. A great many retreated to the banks of the Rio Grande and without looking for means of crossing plunged into this water. . . . No doubt many of them were drowned."

The Mexican losses were even larger than the day before. "After the battle the woods was strewed with the dead," Grant wrote Julia. "Wagons have been engaged drawing the bodies to bury. How many wagon loads have already come in, and how many are still left, would be hard to guess. I saw three large wagon loads at one time myself." Grant mentally added in the prisoners taken and the weapons captured and concluded, "The victory for us has been a very great one."

And it was a satisfying victory for Grant personally. "There is no great sport in having bullets flying about one in every direction," he told Julia. "But I find they have less horror when among them than when in anticipation."

4

IN THE HALF-DAY LULL BETWEEN THE BATTLES OF PALO ALTO AND
Resaca de la Palma, while Grant was counting the carnage of his first
action at arms, James Polk convened his cabinet in Washington. The
president didn't know that one pitched battle had occurred and another
was imminent, for dispatches from the Texas frontier required a week
or more to reach the East. Polk didn't even know of the earlier incident
in which Taylor's scouting party had been overwhelmed by the much
larger Mexican force, with the loss of several American lives.

Yet Polk wanted to declare war anyway. The Mexican government
continued to refuse to relinquish California, and the more often the Mexicans refused, the more determined Polk became to have it. In his mind
and to his cabinet he escalated some minor commercial disputes into a
justification for war. The cabinet agreed. A strong majority endorsed the
president's decision to ask Congress for a war declaration.

The president sent the cabinet members home and pondered the
wording of his request. He would explain how Mexico's sins against the
business interests of American citizens had insulted American honor and
how the American government was left with no choice but to defend that
honor. He knew his case was weak, but it was the best he had and he was
prepared to press it forward.

Then, on the evening of May 9, about the time the Mexicans were
fleeing the field at Resaca de la Palma, Polk received word of the first
skirmish. The welcome news made his task much easier. The opponents
of expansion toward the southwest—John Quincy Adams and the antislavery forces—might have blocked a war for territory but wouldn't be
able to stymie a war for redress of mortal injury to American soldiers.

"After reiterated menaces," Polk wrote in his recomposed message to Congress, "Mexico has passed the boundary of the United States, has invaded our territory and shed American blood on the American soil."

Adams and his allies challenged the accuracy of Polk's assertion. They noted that the soil described was disputed between the two countries. They demanded more information about the circumstances of the skirmish and accused the president of provoking the conflict for his own aggressive purposes.

Yet they lacked the votes to stem the rush to war. The House of Representatives approved the president's war request within hours by a vote of 174 to 14. The Senate, wishing to preserve its image of deliberation, made Polk wait overnight before delivering an even stronger war vote of 40 to 2.

When Grant was nine years old a French aristocrat named Alexis de Tocqueville toured America to discover the meaning of democracy and perhaps, if democracy caught on, the direction of the world. When Grant was thirteen Tocqueville published the first volume of *Democracy in America*, which focused on the domestic institutions of the Americans; when Grant was eighteen Tocqueville released the second volume, which treated, among other subjects, the way American democracy waged war. The author contended that the Americans were a peaceful people, in part from the luck of their location. "Fortune, which has showered so many peculiar favors on the inhabitants of the United States, has placed them in the midst of a wilderness where one can almost say that they have no neighbors," Tocqueville wrote. "For them a few thousand soldiers are enough."

No less important was the pacific influence of the social equality and opportunity that characterized American life, Tocqueville said. Under aristocratic regimes the army afforded a means of advancement denied to commoners in civilian life; in democratic systems ordinary men could get ahead in other fields, and for this reason and others, the culture of the warrior weakened. "The ever-increasing number of men of property devoted to peace, the growth of personal property which war so rapidly devours, mildness of mores, gentleness of heart, that inclination to pity which equality inspires, that cold and calculating spirit which leaves little room for sensitivity to the poetic and violent emotions of wartime—all these causes act together to damp down warlike fervor." Tocqueville pro-

posed a general rule: "Among civilized nations, warlike passions become
rarer and less active as social conditions get nearer to equality." And a
corollary: "Men living in times of democracy seldom choose a soldier's
life."

Time would test Tocqueville's predictions, but his characterization
of America as a nation almost without an army was accurate enough
during the first half of the nineteenth century. Whether because of the
absence of threatening neighbors, because of the presence of preferable
career alternatives, or because of a distrust of standing armies like those
that supported despots elsewhere, Americans refused to fund more than
the skeleton of an army between wars. Grant and his fellow West Point
graduates were the backbone of that skeleton; for the muscle and flesh
the nation looked to volunteers summoned once war was declared. The
result was a predictable lag between the events that triggered a war and
the onset of sustained fighting.

In the case of the war with Mexico, the enlistment, training and
transport of volunteers filled most of the summer of 1846. Grant spent
the time encamped at Matamoros, which Taylor's force occupied shortly
after the American victory at Resaca de la Palma. Grant found the
Mexican town most curious. "Matamoros contains probably about 7,000
inhabitants, a great majority of them of the lower order," he wrote an
Ohio friend. "It is not a place of as much business importance as our
little towns of 1,000." Mexican society was no less strange. "The people
of Mexico are a very different race of people from ours. The better class
are very proud and tyrannize over the lower and much more numerous
class as much as a hard master does over his negroes, and they submit to
it quite as humbly. The great majority are either pure or more than half
blooded Indians, and show but little more signs of neatness or comfort
in their miserable dwellings than the uncivilized Indian." To Julia he
described the typical Mexican home: "Low with a flat or thatched roof,
with a dirt or brick floor, with but little furniture and in many cases the
fire in the middle of the house as if it was a wigwam."

When the summer rains arrived the Mexican houses began to look
better—at least better than the American tents. "The whole country is
low and flat," Grant wrote Julia. "It has rained almost incessantly so that
now the whole country is under water. Our tents are so bad that every
time it rains we get a complete shower-bath."

---

*M*ore than comfort was at stake. "I am afraid, Julia, that Mata-moros will be very sickly this summer," Grant wrote. The threat of sick-ness disposed Taylor to move his troops to higher ground. But James Polk weighed matters other than the health of the army. During the 1844 campaign Polk had quieted concerns about a potential dynasty of Tennessee Democrats—his supporters called him "Young Hickory"—by promising to serve but a single term if elected. As a result the 1848 race was wide open, and everyone knew that a victorious general would have an advantage over mere civilians. Winfield Scott, the ranking army gen-eral, was the obvious person to lead an invasion of Mexico in the event an invasion proved necessary. But Scott was a Whig with badly disguised political ambitions, and Polk had no desire to make him a war hero and hand the Whigs the presidency.

Zachary Taylor was the obvious alternative to Scott. Taylor was also a Whig, but he appeared content to remain a soldier. The trouble with Taylor was that he was junior to Scott; in fact he was only a colonel by permanent rank, having been brevetted a brigadier general to lead the border operation. To put Taylor over Scott would cause problems in the army and among the army's supporters in Congress.

Polk proceeded nonetheless to favor Taylor and undermine Scott. When Scott proposed a war plan based on a landing at Vera Cruz, on the central Mexican coast, followed by a thrust to Mexico City, the presi-dent countered with an assertion that the fighting should be confined to Taylor's theater in northern Mexico, the part of the country the United States desired. Scott wanted a large army of volunteers; Polk, knowing that volunteers tended to vote for their generals, maneuvered to limit the enlistments. After the American victories at Palo Alto and Resaca de la Palma, Polk arranged to have Taylor promoted to major general, equal in rank to Scott.

*G*rant observed the Washington machinations from afar and dimly. As a cadet at West Point he had considered Scott the sum of what a soldier should be, but as a second lieutenant in Mexico he found himself drawn to Taylor. "General Taylor never made any great show or parade, either of uniform or retinue," Grant remembered later. "In dress he was possibly too plain, rarely wearing anything in the field to indicate his rank, or even that he was an officer; but he was known to every soldier in his army and was respected by all." Taylor was considerate, to the point of inadvertent humor. The senior naval officer on the Rio Grande said he was coming to Taylor's camp to pay his respects; Taylor knew that the navy instructed its officers to wear all the uniform to which they were entitled, and, not wishing to make his visitor uncomfortable, he dusted off his own good uniform and put it on. The navy man, meanwhile, having heard of Taylor's distaste for show, dressed down for the meeting. The result was that both men were embarrassed and uncomfortable and spent most of the session apologizing to each other.

Grant took something else from Taylor. "General Taylor was not an officer to trouble the administration much with his demands, but was inclined to do the best he could with the means given him," Grant recalled. "If he had thought he was sent to perform an impossibility with the means given him, he would probably have informed the authorities of his opinion and left them to determine what should be done. If the judgment was against him he would have gone on and done the best he could with the means at hand without parading his grievance before the public. No soldier could face either danger or responsibility more calmly than he. These are qualities more rarely found than genius or physical courage."

Taylor's force remained at Matamoros long enough for the arriving volunteers to fill out its ranks, and then it moved a hundred miles inland to Camargo, the head of Rio Grande navigation and the gateway to Monterrey, the most important city in northern Mexico. Monterrey beckoned not simply because its capture would indicate American seriousness about the war but also because, at a higher elevation than Matamoros and Camargo, it was less prone to the diseases that constituted Taylor's principal concern for his troops.

"When we left Matamoros," Grant wrote Julia in mid-August, "it had been raining a great deal so that the roads were very bad, and as you may well guess, in the low latitude the weather was none of the coolest. The troops suffered considerably from heat and thirst." Camargo had little to recommend it. "Matamoros is a perfect paradise compared to this place." The village was small and poor, with adobe buildings with earthen floors lining its dirt streets. The water supply and sanitary facilities barely accommodated the resident population and were quickly overwhelmed by the needs of the invading force. Grant and the army regulars understood how to dig latrines and where to find clean water, but the volunteers made a horrible mess of their hydraulics and paid the price.

"About one in five is sick all the time," Grant wrote Julia. Many of the soldiers recovered, but some fifteen hundred died of their illnesses.

Grant received a new assignment for the welcome journey away from the fever zone. His obvious ability with horses caused his commanders to think he would be good with mules, and so he was named quartermaster of the regiment, with the chief task of arranging transport for the provisions required for the advance to Monterrey. He resisted the reassignment. "I respectfully protest against being assigned to a duty which removes me from sharing in the dangers and honors of service with my company at the front," he wrote his colonel. The protest was rejected.

The mules were necessary on account of the rough terrain between Camargo and Monterrey, and Mexicans were needed to help with the mules. This put Grant in the curious position of having to hire enemy citizens to support an invasion of their own country. Most who heard of Grant's offer of employment refused, but others were glad for the work and pay.

The mules reminded Grant why he liked horses better. The troops would start marching early each day, leaving Grant and his helpers to break camp. "The tents and cooking utensils had to be made into packages, so that they could be lashed to the backs of the mules," he explained later. "Sheet-iron kettles, tent-poles and mess chests were inconvenient articles to transport in that way." The loading took hours, and the delay caused the first-loaded mules to get restless. "Sometimes one would start to run, bowing his back and kicking up until he scattered his load; others would lie down and try to disarrange their loads by attempting to get on the top of them by rolling on them; others with tent-poles for part of their loads would manage to run a tent-pole on one side of a sapling while they would take the other." The experience tested Grant's patience. "I am not aware of ever having used a profane expletive in my life," he said (in a statement none who knew him then or later would have disputed). "But I would have the charity to excuse those who may have done so, if they were in charge of a train of Mexican pack mules at the time."

After two weeks the American army reached Monterrey. Grant was more impressed than by anything he had seen in Mexico till then. "Monterrey is a beautiful city enclosed on three sides by the mountains, with a pass through them to the right and to the left," he wrote Julia. "There are points around the city which command it, and these the Mexicans fortified and armed. The city is built almost entirely of stone and with very thick walls."

The Americans pitched camp north of the city at a place they called Walnut Springs, apparently mistaking pecan trees for walnut. Taylor's plan was to strike the city from three directions at once. The American general dispatched one division to the west to cut the road to Saltillo and then advance on the city from that direction. A second division would attack from the east, first reducing some gun emplacements at the edge of town and subsequently fighting toward the central plaza. A third division would close from the north, beginning with an assault on a structure called the Black Fort, which guarded the road by which the Americans had approached.

Preparations for the attack began during the night of September 20 when American soldiers established an artillery battery within range of the Black Fort. At dawn the next day the battery opened fire on the fort, whose gunners responded in kind. The sound of the barrages rolled back to the camp at Walnut Springs, where Quartermaster Grant remained with the reserves while the rest of the Fourth Infantry moved forward. "My curiosity got the better of my judgment," he explained afterward, "and I mounted a horse and rode to the front to see what was going on." He was watching the exchange of salvos when the Fourth received the order to charge. "Lacking the moral courage to return to camp, where I had been ordered to stay, I charged with the regiment."

The Americans raced forward, straight into a murderous fire from Mexican artillery and muskets. To Grant's left and right his comrades fell by the dozen. Realizing their mistake, or rather their commander's mistake, the regiment retreated to the east of the Walnut Springs road, where the terrain offered momentary shelter.

Grant was one of the few Americans on horseback, and a superior commandeered his mount. Grant looked about until he saw a subordinate on horseback and claimed that man's animal in turn. He and the others sought better cover in a canebrake northeast of the city. There he learned that the officer who had taken his horse had been killed.

The other prongs of the attack went better. American troops gained the eastern edge of the city and climbed to the roofs of some of the houses there. From this elevation they fired down into the Mexican batteries and drove the gunners out. They turned the Mexican guns against other Mexican positions and began advancing toward the plaza. West of the city the Americans severed the Saltillo road and captured fortifications nearby. By the end of the day Monterrey had been cut off from the outside world.

The Americans and Mexicans spent the next twenty-four hours consolidating their positions. For the Americans this meant resupplying forward troops and reinforcing the positions they had taken. For the Mexicans it entailed abandoning the least tenable of the buildings and streets they still held.

What the Americans hoped would be the final thrust began on the morning of the third day. Grant joined the forces fighting in from the east, against stiff resistance. The Mexicans had mounted artillery on rooftops from which they poured punishing fire upon American troops trying to advance along the streets. The Third Regiment lost nearly half its officers; Grant's Fourth fared only a little better, although Grant himself escaped injury.

The Fourth had almost reached the central plaza when the ammunition ran short. The commanding officer asked for a volunteer to return to the rear with a message for help. Grant tightened the girth on his saddle and offered to go. "I adjusted myself on the side of my horse furthest from the enemy," he explained afterward, "and with only one foot holding to the cantle of the saddle, and an arm over the neck of the horse exposed, I started at full run." He was most vulnerable at the intersections of streets, where dozens of Mexicans had clear shots at him. Yet he dashed across at such a gallop that he was behind the next row of buildings before most of the defenders even saw him. He completed his ride winded but unscathed, only to learn that his effort had been wasted. Before the needed ammunition could be sent forward his comrades had been compelled to fall back.

The Americans on the western side of the city had better luck. Their commander, General William Worth, ordered them to advance not through the streets but through the houses. The Americans would enter a house, drive out its defenders, and then with picks and axes cut holes through the wall into the adjoining house. They would hurl grenades through the holes, forcing the Mexican troops backward long enough to climb through and secure that dwelling. Slowly but inexorably they chopped and blasted their way to within a short distance of the plaza.

At the end of the third day the Mexican commander, Pedro de Ampudia, concluded that his position was hopeless. He dispatched an emissary to Taylor to negotiate a truce. Taylor, with the momentum of battle on his side, initially demanded a surrender of the city and of

Ampudia's army. Ampudia rejected the demand, pointing out that Taylor might capture the city and the army by force but only at great additional cost to the Americans. He offered to surrender the city but not his army, which would withdraw across the mountains. Taylor, not wishing to lose any more men, accepted the compromise.

The Mexicans evacuated the city the next day. Grant and the other Americans for the first time got a good look at their foes. "Many of the prisoners"—they weren't actually prisoners but seemed so to Grant— "were cavalry, armed with lances, and mounted on miserable little half-starved horses that did not look as if they could carry their riders out of town. The men looked in but little better condition. I thought of how little interest the men before me had in the results of the war, and how little knowledge they had of 'what it was all about.'"

ONE OF GRANT'S COMRADES AT MONTERREY WAS THOMAS HAMER, the Ohio congressman who had nominated him for West Point. Hamer had volunteered for service upon the outbreak of the war, and he joined Taylor's army at Camargo. He was a generation older than Grant and a major to Grant's second lieutenant, but the two Ohioans spent spare time together, as Hamer observed in a letter home. "I have found in Lieutenant Grant a most remarkable and valuable young soldier," Hamer wrote. "I anticipate for him a brilliant future, if he should have an opportunity to display his powers when they mature. Young as he is, he has been of great value and service to me. Today, after being freed from the duty of wrestling with the problem of reducing a train of refractory mules and their drivers to submissive order, we rode into the country several miles, and taking our position upon an elevated mound, he explained to me many army evolutions; and, supposing ourselves to be generals commanding opposing armies, and a battle to be in progress, he explained suppositious maneuvers of the opposing forces in a most instructive way; and when I thought his imaginary force had my army routed, he suddenly suggested a strategic move for my forces which crowned them with triumphant victory, and himself with defeat, and he ended by gracefully offering to surrender his sword! Of course, Lieutenant Grant is too young for command, but his capacity for future military usefulness is undoubted."

Hamer survived the battle of Monterrey only to fall ill afterward. He died within days, leaving Grant to console the widow. "He died as a soldier dies," Grant wrote, "without fear and without a murmur. His regret was that, if death must come, it should not come to him on the field of battle. He was mindful the last of all of those at home who would most suffer. . . . Personally, his death is a loss to me which no words can express."

Years later Grant mused on how things might have happened had Hamer lived. "Hamer was one of the ablest men Ohio ever produced," Grant wrote in his memoirs. "I have always believed that had his life been spared, he would have been President of the United States during the term filled by President Pierce. Had Hamer filled that office his partiality for me was such, there is but little doubt that I should have been appointed to one of the staff corps of the army—the Pay Department probably—and would therefore now be preparing to retire. Neither of these speculations is unreasonable, and they are mentioned to show how little men control their own destiny."

The capture of Monterrey made Taylor a national hero, causing Polk to recalculate the politics of the war. Perhaps Taylor, not Scott, was the larger threat to a Democratic succession. Polk talked himself into discounting Taylor's accomplishment—he complained that Taylor shouldn't have let Ampudia's army march away—and maligning Taylor's motives. "He is evidently a weak man and has been made giddy with the idea of the Presidency," Polk wrote in his diary. "He is a narrow minded, bigoted partisan, without resources and wholly unqualified for the command he holds." To undermine Taylor, Polk commenced to favor Scott. He endorsed Scott's plan for an invasion of central Mexico and let Scott strip Taylor of some of his victorious troops.

Grant's regiment was one of those reassigned to Scott. Grant admired Taylor and was proud of what the army had achieved under the general, but he was happy to be heading to what promised to be the decisive theater of the war. The excitement of the victory at Monterrey had been followed by the tedium of camp life. "Here we are, playing war a thousand miles from home, making show and parades but not doing enough fighting to much amuse either the enemy or ourselves, consuming rations enough to have carried us to the capital of Mexico," Grant wrote from Monterrey in December 1846. "If our mission is to occupy the enemy's territory, it is a success, for we are inertly here; but if to conquer, it seems to some of us who have no control that we might as well be performing the job with greater energy. While the authorities at Washington are at sea as to who shall lead the army, the enterprise ought and could be accomplished." In his memoirs Grant would say he had doubted the justice of America's policy toward Mexico from the moment of the annexation of Texas. "I was bitterly opposed to the measure," he wrote, "and to this day regard the war which resulted as one of the most unjust ever waged by a stronger against a weaker nation. It was an instance of a republic following the bad example of European monarchies in not considering justice in their desire to acquire additional territory." But at the end of 1846 he wasn't writing so broadly. He simply told Julia he wished the war had never started. "I begin to think like one of our captains who said that if he was the Government he would whip Mexico until they would be content to take the Sabine for their boundary and he would make them take the Texans with it."

The reassignment to Scott's army injected new life into the regiment. "As soon as Gen. Scott took command, everything was changed," Grant told Julia in early 1847. The officers cracked the men into trim, and central Mexico beckoned even as it threatened. "At Vera Cruz we will probably have a desperate fight but our little Army goes so much better prepared than it has ever done before that there is no doubt as to the result. I fear, though, that there is so much pride in the Mexican character that they will not give up even if we should take every town in the Republic."

The regiment marched from Monterrey to the mouth of the Rio Grande, where they awaited naval transport to Vera Cruz. The ships arrived after several weeks, and Grant boarded the *North Carolina* with four hundred of his fellows. The voyage was rough. "A great part of the time we have had a very heavy sea and often you would think the ship would capsize," he told Julia. Grant discovered to his relief that he wasn't prone to seasickness. Meanwhile, though, several soldiers displayed the unmistakable symptoms of smallpox, putting the rest of the army on edge and reminding everyone of the other diseases endemic to the coast. "We will have to get out of this part of Mexico soon or we will be caught by the yellow fever, which I am ten to one more afraid of than the Mexicans," Grant wrote Julia.

The American fleet consisted of sailing ships primarily, but one vessel was a steam-powered dispatch boat driven by a propeller. Most of the men had seen river steamers pushed by paddle wheels, and a smaller number had seen ocean steamers, similarly driven by paddle wheels, which made a great commotion with their noise and splashing. The propeller boat overtook the sailing ships with little noise, no splashing and barely a wake. "Why, the thing looks as if it was propelled by the force of circumstances," one of Grant's fellow officers remarked.

The landing at Vera Cruz, via surfboats ordered built by Scott for the purpose, went smoothly. The Mexicans might easily have disrupted the operation, but they contented themselves with desultory artillery fire from a fort above the beach. One shot decapitated an American major, but the others fell short.

Vera Cruz frowned formidably upon the invaders. "The city is a solid, compact place, the houses generally built of stone and two or three stories high," Grant recorded. "The whole place is enclosed by a stone wall of about fifteen feet in height and four or five feet thick."

Scott decided not to waste American lives assaulting the town. Instead he besieged it, constructing a cordon from the shore north of the town through sand hills on the west and back to the shore at the south. Scott had his engineers build artillery emplacements and then issued an ultimatum to the Mexican commander, Juan Morales, to surrender the city. When Morales refused, Scott ordered the American gunners to open fire.

For three days the Americans rained solid shot and explosive shells upon the city. On the afternoon of the third day foreign consuls in the city asked Scott to suspend the bombardment long enough for foreigners, women and children to be evacuated. Scott refused, saying they could have left upon his ultimatum to Morales. The consuls thereupon appealed to Morales to surrender the town. He agreed, on the condition that his men be paroled and the rights of civilians in the city be respected by the conquerors. Scott granted the condition and took the city.

The victory came none too soon, from the American perspective. Some of Scott's lieutenants, fearing a long siege, had urged him to order an assault. Against the larger losses an assault would entail they balanced the likelihood of an epidemic among the troops should they remain on the coast when the fever season arrived. The Americans all knew of the *vomito*—yellow fever—and they not unreasonably dreaded it. Scott guessed that the siege wouldn't last long, and he was gratified when events proved him correct.

The road inland from the coast was one of the oldest and most storied routes in the history of the Americas. It was the path Cortez had followed in the early sixteenth century on his way to defeating the Aztecs and seizing Mexico for Spain, and it had been an artery for commerce ever since. Grant was impressed. "From Vera Cruz to this place the road is one of the best, and one that probably cost more labor than any other in the world," he wrote Julia from a point a hundred miles inland. The road climbed steadily, carrying the Americans from the torrid coast to a perennially temperate region where elevation offset the strength of the tropic sun. "The climate is said to be the best in the world," Grant noted, and in April he was willing to credit the claim. "It is never so warm as to be uncomfortable nor so cold as to make a fire necessary."

The approach of the Americans compelled Mexico's ablest commander to try to cut them off. Antonio López de Santa Anna had been in and out of office more times than most of his compatriots could remember. He was living in exile in Cuba at the outbreak of fighting on the Rio Grande in 1846, but with a promise to negotiate an end to the hostilities, he persuaded the Polk administration to allow him through the American blockade of the Mexican coast. He forgot his promise on reaching Mexican soil and rallied the army and people against the invaders. He hurried north from the capital to challenge Zachary Taylor, who, refusing to be Polk's pawn and Scott's coat holder, had advanced from Monterrey toward central Mexico.

The two armies met at Buena Vista, just south of Saltillo. Santa Anna's force outnumbered Taylor's, but Taylor had the better position, with mountains guarding his flanks. In two days of bloody fighting Taylor's men inflicted heavy casualties on the Mexicans, sufficient to make Santa Anna withdraw but not so grievous as to allow Taylor to continue south. Taylor treated the outcome as a triumph and headed back to the United States to accept the Whig nomination for president.

Santa Anna returned south to fend off Scott, who, as luck would have it, was approaching Santa Anna's birthplace and hometown, Jalapa, on the road from Vera Cruz to Mexico City. Grant looked forward to the collision, albeit not as much as he might have. After tasting battle on the Rio Grande and at Monterrey, he felt confined by his quartermaster's duties. He wrote to his commanding officer requesting permission to relinquish his assignment. "I *must* and *will* accompany my regiment in battle," Grant insisted. He threatened to do so even if he was not replaced as quartermaster. He realized he would be leaving the stores in his care unguarded, but he had an answer, of sorts. "I am amenable to court-martial should any loss occur to the public property in my charge by reason of my absence while in action."

Grant's superior appreciated the sentiment but was unimpressed by the logic. "Lieutenant Grant is informed that the duty of Quartermaster and Commissary is an *assigned* duty, and not an *office* that can be resigned," he responded. "However valuable his services might be, and certainly would be, in *line*, his services in his present assigned duties cannot be dispensed with."

Consequently Grant had to watch while others got the thrilling tasks. Santa Anna selected to make his stand in a narrow pass by the village of Cerro Gordo, near a mountain of the same name just west of Jalapa. The Mexicans blocked the road upon which the Americans were approaching and placed artillery on the surrounding elevations. To attack Santa Anna head-on would have been suicidal.

So Scott sent scouts behind the ridges the Mexicans controlled. Robert E. Lee, a handsome captain of engineers from Virginia who had graduated from West Point fourteen years before Grant and many places higher in his class, and who was widely deemed the most promising officer in the army, led a reconnaissance north of Santa Anna's position. Lee ventured far into the territory held by the Mexicans and at one point found himself alone and surrounded by the enemy near a spring to which they regularly resorted. Lee ducked under a fallen log to escape detection, only to have some of the Mexicans approach and sit on the very log under which he was hiding. He held his breath, and held his spot till darkness allowed him to escape.

He returned to the American camp with word that it might be possible for an American column to slip behind the ridges, improve the route he had discovered and attack the Mexican positions from the rear. This intelligence became the basis for Scott's battle plan and for the battle itself. "Perhaps there was not a battle of the Mexican war, or of any other, where orders issued before an engagement were nearer being a correct report of what afterwards took place," Grant wrote admiringly many years and battles later. "Under the supervision of the engineers, roadways had been opened over chasms to the right where the walls were so steep that men could barely climb them. Animals could not. These had been opened under cover of night, without attracting the notice of the enemy. The engineers, who had directed the opening, led the way and the troops followed. Artillery was let down the steep slopes by hand, the men engaged attaching a strong rope to the rear axle and letting the guns down, a piece at a time, while the men at the ropes kept their ground on top, paying out gradually, while a few at the front directed the course of the piece. In like manner the guns were drawn by hand up the opposite slopes." The guns were placed behind the Mexican entrenchments, which were undefended on that side.

The American artillery opened fire on the Mexican positions. "It was war pyrotechnics of the most serious and brilliant character," Grant wrote at the time. The artillery barrage covered the advance of American infantry. "I stood there watching the brigade slowly climbing those ragged heights, each minute nearer and nearer the works of the enemy with our missiles flying over their heads, while white puffs of smoke spitefully flashed out in rapid succession along the enemy's line, and I knew that every discharge sent death into our ranks." Grant wished more than ever to be at the front. "While it was a most inspiring sight, it was a painful one to me. . . . As our men finally swept over and into the works, my heart was sad at the fate that held me from sharing in that brave and brilliant assault."

But he shared the joy of the victory. "As soon as the Mexicans saw this height taken, they knew the day was up with them," he wrote an Ohio friend. "Santa Anna vamoosed with a small part of his force leaving about 6000 to be taken prisoner with all their arms, supplies &c. Santa Anna's loss could not have been less than 8000 killed, wounded, taken prisoners and missing. The pursuit was so close upon the retreating few that Santa Anna's carriage and mules were taken and with them his wooden leg and some 20 or 30 thousand dollars in money."

These first estimates were too high; Santa Anna's losses were about half what Grant reported. But the meaning of the American victory was plain. "Between the thrashing the Mexicans have got at Buena Vista, Vera Cruz, and Cerro Gordo," he wrote his Ohio friend, "they are so completely broken up that if we only had transportation we could go to the City of Mexico and where ever else we liked without resistance."

6

IN FACT TRANSPORTATION WAS NOT ALL THAT WAS REQUIRED. MUCH of Scott's army consisted of volunteers, many of whom had enlisted for terms about to expire. Scott couldn't compel them to remain beyond their terms, and few showed much inclination to do so. Rather than start for Mexico City and lose half his army at the gates of the capital, he discharged the current crop of enlistees early, in order that they clear Vera Cruz and the coastal lowlands before the fever season began, and awaited the arrival of their replacements.

The delay gave Grant time to miss Julia more than ever. The army occupied Puebla, which brought her home to mind. "It surpasses St. Louis by far both in appearance and size," he wrote her of Puebla. "It contains from 80 to 90 thousand inhabitants. The houses are large and well built." The people were all Catholic. "At a certain ring of the church bell or when the senior Priest of the place passes, you might see them on their knees in the streets all over the city." The climate was nearly perfect. "This place from its elevation is very healthy and much more pleasant both in summer and winter, so far as climate is concerned, than Jefferson Barracks."

But St. Louis had Julia and Puebla did not. "The night after I received your last letter I dreamed that I had been ordered on the recruiting service and was near where you were," he wrote. "In my dream, I said now I have often dreamed of being near my dear Julia but this time it is no dream for here are houses I recollect well, and it is only two days travel to St. Louis. But when I woke up on the morning and found that it was but a dream after all, how disappointed I was!"

He began to wish he had never gone to war. "How much, my Dearest

Julia, I regret that I had not taken my Father's advice and resigned long ago. Now, no doubt, I would have been comfortably in business and been always near one of whom I am always thinking and whom I love better than all the world besides." He might yet resign. "In the course of a few months more I will see you again if it costs me my commission, which by the way I value very low, for I have been a very long time balancing in my mind whether I should resign or not."

*H*e didn't resign but marched to Mexico City instead. Santa Anna unexpectedly declined to challenge the Americans on their route from Puebla, and after three days Scott's advance guard crested the pass that opened upon the Valley of Mexico. Several volcanoes ringed the valley, the highest being Popocatepetl, which commanded the southern horizon. Three large lakes and some smaller ones occupied the valley floor; beyond the lakes lay Mexico City. The main road to the capital ran between two of the large lakes, which served as partial moats. Santa Anna filled the gap between the lakes with trenches and troops.

Scott accordingly left the main road and skirted to the south. Santa Anna detected the maneuver and repositioned his defenders. Scott skirted further, after additional reconnaissance by Robert E. Lee. On August 20 the Americans engaged the Mexicans at the neighboring villages of Contreras and Churubusco and inflicted demoralizing defeats on the defenders, although at considerable cost.

The American victories carried Scott's force to the very gates of the capital, but he declined to enter the city. He wanted his troops to catch their breath; equally he wanted Santa Anna to catch *his* breath. Scott feared that if Santa Anna was totally discredited, there would be no one in Mexico able to make peace. When Santa Anna suggested a truce, Scott accepted, hoping negotiations would follow.

They did but didn't lead anywhere, and in early September Scott declared the truce ended. As he prepared to renew the attack he received reports that Santa Anna was melting down the church bells of Mexico City to make new guns at a cluster of mills at Molina del Rey. American intelligence indicated that the mills were lightly defended; Scott, without giving the matter much thought, ordered the site taken.

Grant was among those assigned to the task, and he soon discovered that the intelligence was badly mistaken. Santa Anna had slipped several thousand troops into the mills and vicinity, and when the Americans charged, the Mexicans raked them with musket and artillery fire. The Americans reached the walls of the mill complex but not before losing scores of officers and men.

Grant got to the walls unscathed with the first of the American troops. "I happened to notice that there were armed Mexicans still on top of the building, only a few feet from many of our men," he recorded later. "Not seeing any stairway or ladder reaching to the top of the building, I took a few soldiers and had a cart that happened to be standing near brought up, and, placing the shafts against the wall and chocking the wheels so that the cart could not back, used the shafts as a sort of ladder extending to within three or four feet of the top. By this I climbed to the roof of the building, followed by a few men." To his surprise he learned that an American private had preceded him to the rooftop, and to his greater surprise he saw that the single soldier had somehow captured a Mexican major and several other officers, all still armed. Grant pitched in, taking the swords from the officers and ordering his own men to disable the muskets the Mexicans carried.

The Mexican forces withdrew from Molina del Rey to the fortress of Chapultepec, half a mile away. In retrospect Grant observed that an opportunity was lost by not pursuing the Mexicans at once. "No doubt Americans and Mexicans would have gone over the defenses of Chapultepec so near together that the place would have fallen into our hands without further loss," he wrote. But Scott called a halt, believing that his army had sustained sufficient casualties for one battle.

When the assault on Chapultepec *did* come, five days later, it cost the Americans heavily. An artillery barrage drove the defenders back from the walls long enough for the Americans to approach. With scaling ladders they climbed the walls and engaged the Mexicans in fierce hand-to-hand fighting. The first Americans to the top suffered grievously but provided an opening for those who followed. Within minutes they were inside the castle, where the carnage continued. Several hundred of the Mexicans were cadets, and though many were brave they were no match for the battle-tested Americans. Six of the cadets refused to surrender; five stood their ground and fought to the death, leaving the sixth to wrap himself in the Mexican flag and leap off the parapet in patriotic suicide.

Chapultepec guarded the western gates of Mexico City; Grant's part in the battle was to assault one of those gates, the San Cosme. He reconnoitered ahead of his division, discovered a way to outflank the gun defending the road to the gate, and led a company that captured the gun.

Scouting forward again, he spied a church with a belfry that overlooked the San Cosme gate. He brought up a small howitzer and ordered some men to help him transport it, and they made their way across a field and through several chest-deep irrigation ditches to the entrance to the church. "When I knocked for admission a priest came to the door, who, while extremely polite, declined to admit us," he recalled. "With the little Spanish then at my command, I explained to him that he might save the property by opening the door, and he certainly would save himself from becoming a prisoner, for a time at least; and besides, I intended to go in whether he consented or not." The priest let them pass. They carried the howitzer up the stairs to the belfry, set up the gun and began dropping shells on San Cosme and the city behind it.

Grant's gun and the confusion it wreaked among the Mexicans attracted the attention of William Worth, Grant's division commander. Worth sent one of his staff, John Pemberton, to see who was responsible. Pemberton brought Grant to Worth, who complimented him on his initiative and ordered a second howitzer sent to the same belfry. Grant was too respectfully timid to explain that the belfry was only large enough for one gun. The second howitzer was sent but not used.

Grant's regimental commander subsequently praised him for performing "most nobly" in the attack on San Cosme, which left the American force poised to enter the city. Santa Anna once again judged that discretion trumped continued resistance, and he evacuated the capital. On the morning of September 14 Grant joined the other Americans in marching victoriously into Mexico City.

"Mexico is one of the most beautiful cities in the world," he wrote Julia. "And being the capital, no wonder that the Mexicans should have fought desperately to save it." Yet they hadn't fought well. "They have fought with every advantage on their side. They doubled us in numbers, doubled us and more in artillery. They behind strong breastworks had every advantage, and then they were fighting for their homes." But still they had lost.

The American performance didn't escape Grant's critical assessment. The battles of Molina del Rey and Chapultepec had cost the Americans dearly—and for no compelling reason, he concluded. During the delay at Puebla he had pondered the best approach to Mexico City. "From my map and all the information I acquired while the army was at Puebla," he wrote on the eve of Chapultepec, "I was then, and am now more than ever, convinced that the army could have approached the city by passing around north of it, and reached the northwest side"—near San Cosme—"and avoided all the fortified positions, until we reached the gates of the city at their weakest and most indefensible, as well as most approachable, points. . . . It seems to me that the northwest side of the city could have been approached without attacking a single fort or redoubt."

Grant had communicated his view to his immediate superiors, but he never learned whether they passed it up the chain of command. At the time he acceded to the wisdom of authority. "I am willing to believe," he wrote a friend, "that the opinion of a lieutenant, where it differs from that of his commanding General, *must* be founded on *ignorance* of the situation."

Additional experience, however, confirmed his opinion of Scott's misjudgment. "The battles of Molino del Rey and Chapultepec have seemed to me to have been wholly unnecessary," he wrote many years later. Even allowing for a southern approach to the capital, Scott could have skirted Molina and Chapultepec, leaving the garrisons there to evacuate or be surrounded.

But experience taught Grant something else as well—"that things are seen plainer after the events have occurred." Scott's success was the irrefutable riposte to criticism. "He invaded a populous country, penetrating two hundred and sixty miles into the interior, with a force at no time equal to one-half of that opposed to him; he was without a base; the enemy was always intrenched, always on the defensive; yet he won every battle, he captured the capital, and conquered the government. Credit is due to the troops engaged, it is true, but the plans and the strategy were the general's."

Grant reflected on the two commanders, Scott and Taylor, he fought under in Mexico. "The contrast between the two was very marked," he wrote. Scott, besides dressing in full uniform on every occasion, insisted on the stiffest protocol. "When he inspected his lines, word would be sent to all division and brigade commanders in advance, notifying them of the hour when the commanding general might be expected. This was done so that all the army might be under arms to salute their chief as he passed. . . . His staff proper, besides all officers constructively on his staff—engineers, inspectors, quartermasters, etc., that could be spared—followed, also in uniform and in prescribed order." Scott's full staff was essential to his style of command. "Scott saw more through the eyes of his staff officers than through his own." And he treated communication as a self-conscious art form. "General Scott was quite precise in language, cultivated a style peculiarly his own; was proud of his rhetoric; not averse to speaking of himself, often in the third person." His precision extended to the orders he issued. "Orders were prepared with great care and evidently with the view that they should be a history of what followed."

Taylor, on the other hand, was the soul of simplicity. Besides almost never wearing his general's uniform, he eschewed a large staff. "He moved about the field in which he was operating, to see through his own eyes the situation. Often he would be without staff officers, and when he was accompanied by them there was no prescribed order in which they followed. He was very much given to sit his horse sideways—with both feet on one side—particularly on the battlefield." He devoted little thought to his mode of expression but much to its substance. "Taylor was not a conversationalist, but on paper he could put his meaning so plainly that there could be no mistaking it. He knew how to express what he wanted to say in the fewest well-chosen words, but would not sacrifice meaning to the construction of high-sounding sentences." He didn't pretend to anticipate every contingency and "gave orders to meet the emergency without reference to how they would read in history."

Grant saw the strengths in each general, though he had a preference. "Both were great and successful soldiers; both were true, patriotic and upright in all their dealings. Both were pleasant to serve under; Taylor was pleasant to serve with."

The occupation of Mexico City began promisingly. "Everything looks as if peace should be established soon," Grant wrote Julia. "The whole Mexican army is destroyed or dispersed; they have lost nearly all their artillery and other munitions of war; we are occupying the rich and populous valley from which the great part of their revenues are collected; and all their sea ports are cut off from them."

The fighting over, he couldn't leave Mexico soon enough. "The idea of staying longer in this country is to me insupportable. Just think of the three long years that have passed since we met. My health has always been good, but exposure to weather and a tropical sun have added ten years to my apparent age. At this rate I will soon be old." Many of his companions had died. "Out of all the officers that left Jefferson Barracks with the 4th Infantry, but three besides myself now remain."

Yet nothing about the war moved quickly. Scott was right to worry that the discrediting of Santa Anna would complicate peacemaking, for upon the Mexican general's defeat at the gates of Mexico City he turned the presidency over to a caretaker government that proved unequal to the task of signing away half the country. For months the Mexicans dithered and dodged, hoping some stroke of fortune would spare them the increasingly inevitable.

James Polk seemed intent on abetting the delay. The president wished to capture for the Democrats the fruits of victories won by Whig generals, and he feared that Nicholas Trist, the envoy he had sent to Mexico City to negotiate a treaty, was falling under the influence of soldiers who, like Grant, wanted nothing more than to get home. Polk summarily ordered Trist back to Washington. But Scott talked Trist into ignoring the order and continuing the negotiations.

The political pressure on Trist persuaded the Mexican government to get more serious, and within a few weeks he and they had the outlines of a treaty in hand. The boundary between the United States and Mexico would run west from the Gulf of Mexico along the Rio Grande to New Mexico, then west via the Gila River to the Gulf of California and overland to San Diego. The American government would assume responsibility for the claims of its citizens against Mexico and would pay the Mexican government $15 million for the territory transferred from Mexico to the United States.

The treaty was signed on February 2, 1848, at the village of Guadalupe Hidalgo, outside Mexico City. Trist shortly left for Washington to deliver the treaty and explain why he had exceeded his orders. Polk was livid but perceived no alternative to submitting the treaty to the Senate. And when antislavery Whigs in the Senate tried to prevent its ratification, on grounds that it would open new territory to slavery, the president swallowed his anger at Trist and praised the treaty as a coup. "If the treaty in its present form is ratified," he said, "there will be added to the U.S. an immense empire, the value of which twenty years hence it would be difficult to calculate." Most Americans agreed with Polk, in principle if not in specifics, and after Southern Democrats began complaining that the treaty transferred too *little* territory to the United States and calling for the negotiations to be reopened, the Whigs swung to Polk and the treaty was ratified. The Mexican senate required longer to conclude that the treaty had to be approved, but in late May 1848 it took the painful step and seconded the ratification.

———

While the diplomats and politicians wrangled, Grant and the other American soldiers diverted themselves as best they could. Grant attended a bullfight—"not wishing to leave the country without having witnessed the national sport," he explained. One visit to the arena was enough. "The sight to me was sickening. I could not see how human beings could enjoy the sufferings of beasts, and often of men, as they seemed to do on these occasions."

He tackled Popocatepetl with several comrades. "The day that we arrived at the foot of the mountain we ascended about one half of the way to the top and there encamped for the night," he wrote Julia. "We had been there but a short time when it began to blow rain, hail, and snow most terrifically, and of course we were in bad plight next morning for ascending a mountain which is difficult at best. . . . However, we started through a snow storm which had continued from the night before, and the wind blowing hard enough almost to carry a person away." They couldn't see more than a few yards ahead or to the side, and in particular they couldn't see the expansive vistas that were the purpose of the climb. "We plodded on for several hours through all these difficulties, when all found that it was perfect madness to attempt to go farther, so we turned back when about 1000 feet below the crater."

Their trials weren't over. "That night about the time we were going to lay down, first one person would complain of his eyes hurting him, then another, and by 9 o'clock everyone was suffering the most excruciating pain in the eyes. There was but little sleeping done by the party that night. Next morning nine of the officers were blind so that they were obliged to have their horses led." Fortunately the descent to lower elevation relieved the symptoms with no permanent damage. The weather cleared about this time. "Popocatepetl stood out in all its beauty, the top looking as if not a mile away, and inviting us to return." Several members of Grant's party accepted the invitation. "The remainder—I was with the remainder—concluded that we had got all the pleasure there was to be had out of mountain climbing."

They visited a large cave on the road to Acapulco. "We explored to a distance of about three miles from the entrance," Grant recorded, "and found a succession of chambers of great dimensions and of great beauty when lit up with our rockets. Stalactites and stalagmites of all sizes were discovered." One stalagmite nearly filled the cave, leaving only a narrow passage on either side. Several of Grant's companions decided some while later to return to the surface. They retraced their steps to the massive stalagmite and circled around it too far before proceeding. "When the rest of us had completed our explorations," Grant wrote, "we started out with our guides, but had not gone far before we saw the torches of an approaching party. We could not conceive who these could be, for all of us had come in together, and there were none but ourselves at the entrance when we started in. Very soon we found it was our friends. It took them some time to conceive how they had got where they were."

At length the news of the peace arrived. "I have no doubt but this will be my last letter from Mexico," Grant wrote Julia near the end of May 1848. "Already every preparation is being made to move the troops to Vera Cruz." The move was fraught, as the fever season had commenced on the coast. But with the end of the war the troops couldn't stay in Mexico.

Scott's plan was to hold the troops at Jalapa, above the *vomito* region, until the transports arrived, and then have them dash through the lowlands and onto the ships. Things didn't work out this way. Grant's regiment held its breath as it passed Vera Cruz but inexplicably lingered on the beach outside the city for a week while the fever raged within. Luckily the losses were light; only one officer of the regiment contracted yellow fever and died. In July the Fourth Infantry boarded ships and sailed away from Mexico for home.

7

"I REMEMBER ONE DAY, IN THE SPRING OF 1848, THAT TWO MEN, Americans, came into the office and inquired for the Governor," William Tecumseh Sherman recalled. Sherman was an Ohioan like Grant; he was two years older than Grant and had been three years ahead of him at West Point. He earned a reputation at the academy for being quick in class and unreliable outside it. "At the Academy I was not considered a good soldier," he acknowledged, "for at no time was I selected for any office, but remained a private throughout the whole four years. Then, as now, neatness of dress and form, with a strict conformity to the rules, were the qualifications required for office, and I suppose I was found not to excel in any of these. . . . My average demerits, per annum, were about one hundred and fifty." During the months that produced the war with Mexico, Sherman was stationed at Fort Moultrie in Charleston, South Carolina, serving under Captain Robert Anderson. After the outbreak of war his unit was sent by ship to California, a journey around South America that filled six months. The principal fighting he encountered in California was between American officers John Frémont and Stephen Kearney over who had precedence in that theater of the war; after Kearney hauled Frémont off to face a court-martial in Washington, Richard Mason took over as military governor, with Sherman as his adjutant.

Sherman was in Mason's office at Monterey the spring the war ended—but before the news of the treaty arrived—when the two Americans entered. "I asked their business," Sherman recalled, "and one answered that they had just come down from Captain Sutter on special business, and they wanted to see Governor Mason, *in person*." Sherman knew John Sutter by reputation, as a Swiss immigrant with a large ranch and trading post at the confluence of the American and Sacramento Rivers. "I took them in to the colonel, and left them together. After some time the colonel came to his door and called to me. I went in, and my attention was directed to a series of papers unfolded on his table, in which lay about half an ounce of placer-gold. Mason said to me, 'What is that?' I touched it and examined one or two of the larger pieces, and asked, 'Is it gold?'" Mason asked Sherman if he had ever seen gold in its unrefined state. He answered that he had, in Georgia, several years earlier. It didn't look much like this specimen, being considerably finer. But he said that any gold could be readily tested by acid, to see if it tarnished, and by its malleability. Mason handed him the Sutter gold. "I took a piece in my teeth," Sherman remembered, "and the metallic lustre was perfect. I then called to the clerk, Baden, to bring an axe and hatchet from the backyard. When these were brought, I took the largest piece and beat it out flat, and beyond doubt it was metal, and a pure metal. Still, we attached little importance to the fact, for gold was known to exist at San Fernando, at the south, and yet was not considered of much value."

Sutter evidently had a different opinion, for he asked Mason to grant him title to the land from which the gold was taken. Mason said this was impossible, as California still belonged to Mexico. Yet Mason and Sherman were intrigued and grew more so as further reports of gold filtered in. "Stories reached us of fabulous discoveries, and spread throughout the land," Sherman wrote. "Everybody was talking of 'Gold! Gold!!' until it assumed the character of a fever. . . . I of course could not escape the infection, and at last convinced Colonel Mason that it was our duty to go up and see with our own eyes, that we might report the truth to our Government." They rode overland to San Francisco, a small village on the bay of the same name, crossed the bay by boat and then rode to Sutter's fort and the American River. They found hundreds of men working the streambed, washing the gravel to obtain flakes and nuggets of gold. "We spent nearly a week in that region, and were quite bewildered by the fabulous tales of recent discoveries." They couldn't vouch for all the stories, but their own eyes confirmed that something remarkable was afoot.

On returning to Monterey, Sherman drafted for Mason's signature a letter relating what they had seen. "The most moderate estimate I could obtain from men acquainted with the subject was that upward of four thousand men were working in the gold district . . . ," Sherman wrote for Mason, "and that from $30,000 to $50,000 worth of gold, if not more, was daily obtained. . . . I have no hesitation now in saying that there is more gold in the country drained by the Sacramento and San Joaquin rivers than will pay the cost of the present war with Mexico a hundred times over."

Sherman and Mason entrusted this letter to an army lieutenant with orders that it be carried to Washington as quickly as possible. As additional evidence they sent along a can filled with two hundred ounces of gold dust.

The envoy reached Washington in late November, just in time for Polk's annual message. Rumors of the gold in California had been circulating in the capital, but they seemed incredible. "The accounts of the abundance of gold in that territory are of such an extraordinary character as would scarcely command belief," Polk now declared, "were they not corroborated by the authentic reports of officers in the public service who have visited the mineral district." Polk told of the mission of Mason and Sherman to the gold fields, and he explained that their observations revealed that the gold mines were very rich and already employed thousands of people. "Nearly the whole of the male population of the country have gone to the gold districts. Ships arriving on the coast are deserted by their crews and their voyages suspended for want of sailors."

Polk congratulated himself and his administration for possessing the vision to further America's westward expansion. Amid the struggle with Mexico the president had negotiated a deal with Britain fixing the boundary of the Oregon country at the Forty-ninth Parallel. "The acquisition of California and New Mexico, the settlement of the Oregon boundary, and the annexation of Texas, extending to the Rio Grande, are results which, combined, are of greater consequence and will add more to the strength and wealth of the nation than any which have preceded them since the adoption of the Constitution."

None could deny that the western territories added greatly to the wealth of the United States; whether they added to American strength was another matter. Polk's message triggered a massive migration to California during the spring and summer of 1849; eighty thousand "forty-niners" poured across the plains and mountains of the American West, over the isthmus of Panama or around Cape Horn in a headlong rush to lay hands on the riches of California. Before that summer was out they numbered enough to qualify California for admission to the Union as a state. Most of them assumed Congress would be as eager to admit them as they were eager to join, and they held a constitutional convention at Monterey to draft a state charter, which they sent to Washington in December 1849.

But Congress was not eager to admit California. The war with Mexico had intensified the slavery debate, with those Whigs and antislavery Democrats who had denounced the annexation of Texas as a slaveholder conspiracy repeating their allegations and applying them, only slightly modified, to the rest of the territory Polk intended to take from Mexico. David Wilmot, a Democratic congressman from Pennsylvania, appended to a military appropriations bill a provision asserting that slavery must not be allowed in any territory acquired in the war. The Wilmot proviso passed the House of Representatives but failed in the Senate, convincing slavery advocates that their cherished institution was under mortal assault and slavery opponents that the slave bloc would stymie any restraints on slavery's expansion. Subsequently reintroduced and reintroduced again, with the same results, the proviso became a touchstone of the growing polarization between proslavery and antislavery forces in Congress.

Among those voting for the Wilmot proviso was a first-term congressman from Illinois. Abraham Lincoln shared the distrust most of his fellow Whigs felt for James Polk and the expansionist schemes of the Democratic party, and though he missed the initial vote on the proviso, not taking his seat in the House until 1847, he voted for it subsequently. He also delivered a speech casting the darkest aspersions on Polk's explanation of the events along the Rio Grande that had triggered the war. Lincoln demanded that Polk produce irrefutable evidence that the place where the first hostilities occurred was indeed American soil. "If he cannot or will not do this . . . ," Lincoln said, "then I shall be fully convinced of what I more than suspect already, that he is deeply conscious of being in the wrong; that he feels the blood of this war, like the blood of Abel, is crying to Heaven against him; that he ordered General Taylor into the midst of a peaceful Mexican settlement, purposely to bring on a war; that originally having some strong motive—what I will not stop now to give my opinion concerning—to involve the two countries in a war, and trusting to escape scrutiny by fixing the public gaze upon the exceeding brightness of military glory—that attractive rainbow that rises in showers of blood, that serpent's eye that charms to destroy—he plunged into it, and has swept on and on."

Lincoln's statement was entirely for effect; Polk ignored this gadfly,

as Lincoln supposed he would. Yet effect was the purpose of much of
what happened in Congress by now regarding slavery. The House regularly voted against slavery, reflecting the advantage the more numerous
North enjoyed in that chamber. The Senate, in which the South balanced the North, consistently beat back the House measures.

The California constitution landed like a grenade in Congress at
the beginning of 1850. The California charter banned slavery from the
new state, endangering the Senate balance on which the South increasingly depended. Southerners refused to countenance a free California
unless they got something in return. The customary quid pro quo had
been a slave state, but no slave territory possessed sufficient population
to qualify.

For weeks the California question roiled Congress. Gradually Henry
Clay of Kentucky, the Senate's master compromiser, crafted a package
that wrapped the admission of free California inside a stiffened fugitive slave law—something the South had wanted for years—and several
slightly less provocative provisions.

Clay's compromise elicited learned comments from the cerebral
members of Congress, including South Carolina's John Calhoun; elo-
quent statements from the legislature's great orators, notably Daniel
Webster of Massachusetts; threats of violence from the most passionate
lawmakers, conspicuously Thomas Hart Benton of Missouri and Henry
Foote of Mississippi; and clever cloakroom maneuvers by the political
operators, preeminently Stephen A. Douglas of Illinois. It was Douglas who, after Clay's omnibus package stalled, disassembled the measure, arranged votes on its separate pieces and put the parts delicately
back together. Douglas graciously acknowledged the inspiration of Clay.
"No man was governed by higher or purer motives," he declared. Yet the
Compromise of 1850 marked Douglas as the new arbiter of the sectional
struggle.

Most of the Americans who fought in Mexico were volunteers; in
the wake of the peace treaty these temporary warriors returned to their
permanent vocations. Farmers left battlefields for wheat fields; mechanics put down muskets and picked up tools; shopkeepers doffed uniforms
and donned aprons. For citizen soldiers, peace was the norm and war the
anomaly.

For Grant, however, and for the other professional warriors of the regular army, the situation was reversed. War was what they trained for and what allowed them to advance in their profession. Peace promised only boredom and stagnation. For some, in fact, the outbreak of peace would produce career backsliding as officers promoted by brevet during the war reverted to their lower peacetime ranks.

Grant had other things on his mind, though. He was awarded a leave of absence when he arrived from Mexico; he traveled to St. Louis to see Julia, then to Ohio to visit his family and then back to St. Louis. Julia was as eager to wed as he was, and her father decided, amid the celebrations surrounding the American victory over Mexico, that she could do worse than marry a soldier. The ceremony came together quickly. "I had had four years in which to prepare for this event and therefore required only a week or so to make the few last arrangements," Julia recalled. The wedding was simple by the standards of St. Louis, as August was predictably hot and many persons who would have attended had left the city till fall. But the bride and groom hardly noticed their absence.

Their wedding trip took them up the Ohio River to visit his family. Julia had never been away from St. Louis nor ever on a boat. "How I marveled at this great creature, as I felt it to be, gliding so swiftly along and obeying the slightest motion of the hand in the pilothouse," she remembered. "It seemed to me almost human in its breathing, panting, and obedience to man's will." At Louisville they circumvented the Falls of the Ohio via the canal and locks there. "It was like a dream to me," she said of the river journey as a whole.

The dream soured slightly when she met some of Grant's cousins. James Hewitt had married into the Grant family and obviously done well at business. He and his wife lived a few miles from Louisville. "The approach to their beautiful residence was through broad meadows until we reached the hills covered with a fine old forest," Julia recalled. "This house was filled with everything beautiful, suited to the wealth and cultivated tastes of our host and hostess." Julia imagined herself living in such a house and shared her vision with Grant, who responded as she hoped. "My dear husband intimated very modestly that if he saw any chance for a business opening he would be happy to resign"—from the army. But neither Hewitt nor his associates showed an inclination to help. "Although these gentlemen had large business connections at New Orleans, New York, Liverpool, and, I think, Paris, not one of them offered even to introduce him to any businessman." Julia added, years later, "I always remembered this, and did not forget it when my Lieutenant was General-in-Chief nor when he was President of the United States."

Her introduction to Grant's immediate family went better. Jesse Grant welcomed her cordially. "His voice was low and pleasant," Julia remembered. Hannah Grant greeted her as a daughter. "She was the most self-sacrificing, the sweetest, kindest woman I ever met, except my own dear mother," Julia said. Grant's brothers and sisters were curious about their sister-in-law. Simpson, Grant's closest sibling at three years younger, was gone from the home, but Clara, Virginia, Orvil and Mary looked her over, and she them. Neither side of this scrutiny found much to complain of. "Altogether I was well satisfied," Julia remarked of her new family.

The newlyweds traveled to Detroit when Grant's leave of absence ended. The Fourth Regiment was now headquartered at this frontier town, and he reported for duty—only to be informed that the army needed him more at Sackets Harbor, New York. He and Julia journeyed east and endured a frosty winter on the shore of Lake Ontario. In the spring the army changed its mind and decided that Detroit, after all, was where Grant could serve his country best.

"Two years were spent with but few important incidents," Grant later wrote of his time at Detroit. Among the few was the establishment of Julia and his first real home. "A little frame house, covered with wild grapes," was how one of Grant's fellow officers remembered it. "It always looked homey and cozy to me, a comfortable place for two young people just married. . . . Most of the officers lived in the hotel, all of the unmarried ones in fact, but Grant and his wife had their own little home."

Grant's professional obligations were undemanding, leaving him time for homemaking with Julia and outdoor activities with his comrades. "The town was full of lively fellows and there were many horses whose owners considered them to be fast," Grant's officer friend recalled. "On Saturdays the whole town seemed to get out on Fort Avenue and every man who had a horse took part." Grant was a regular. "He was in the forefront of any racing that was going on. . . . Grant had that little black mare and it was a horse of tremendous speed. He was the best horseman I ever saw. He could fly on a horse, faster than a slicked bullet."

In the autumn of 1849 Julia became pregnant, and as the time of her delivery approached, the post surgeon sent her to her family's home in

St. Louis. Frederick Dent Grant was born at the end of May 1850. Grant took leave to see his wife and son before bringing them back, by way of Ohio, to Detroit.

The next summer the army sent him again to Sackets Harbor. He and Julia decided she and the baby would be more comfortable living with her family until his future became clearer, and he went east alone. He missed them terribly. "Sackets Harbor is as dull a little hole as you ever saw," he wrote her. "Take good care of little Fred, and learn him to say pa. . . . Do you think he recollects me? Has he any more teeth?"

In the spring of 1852 the army found a new mission for the Fourth Regiment: protecting America's recently acquired West Coast. The decision came suddenly, preventing Grant from traveling to Missouri to visit Julia and Fred and say farewell. Julia was pregnant again, with the delivery expected almost any day, and he hated to leave without seeing her or their new child. "It distresses me, dearest, to think that this news has to be broken to you at just this time," he wrote. "But bear it with fortitude." He would try to do the same. "Our separation will not be a long one anyway. At least let's hope so." He urged her to remember him at the birth of their child. "If it is a girl name it what you like, but if a boy name it after me. I know you will do this, Julia, of your own choice, but then I want you to know it will please me too."

Army business unexpectedly called him to Washington ahead of his New York departure. He had never seen the capital before and wasn't impressed now. "I was very much disappointed in the appearance of things about Washington," he wrote Julia. "The place seems small and scattering and the character of the buildings poor." He arrived amid mourning for Henry Clay, whose recent passing betokened an end of both the Whig party, which Clay had led for twenty years, and the spirit of compromise for which the Kentucky senator was famous. "Mr. Clay's death produced a feeling of regret that could hardly be felt for any other man," Grant wrote.

The California gold rush revolutionized travel from America's East to its Far West. The impecunious still trudged across the plains and mountains, but those with even a bit more money traveled by steamship to Panama, traversed the isthmus and caught another steamer to San Francisco.

The marine legs of the journey were swift and comparatively com-

fortable. The testing part was the fifty miles in the middle. For the officers and men of the Fourth Regiment, the challenge fell peculiarly upon
Quartermaster Grant. The regiment reached the town of Aspinwall, on
the Caribbean side of the isthmus, amid the rainy season. "The streets of
the town were eight or ten inches under water, and foot passengers passed
from place to place on raised footpaths," Grant recalled. "At intervals
the rain would pour down in streams, followed in not many minutes by
a blazing, tropical summer's sun. These alternate changes, from rain to
sunshine, were continuous in the afternoons. I wondered how any person
could live many months in Aspinwall, and wondered still more why any
one tried." The town was named for William Aspinwall, the principal
of the Pacific Mail Steamship Company, which was building a railroad
across the isthmus to take travelers to its docks at Panama City. By the
summer of 1852 the railroad had reached the Chagres River, about fifteen miles inland; there travelers boarded boats for Gorgona, near the
continental divide.

"Boats on the Chagres River were propelled by natives not incon-
veniently burdened with clothing," Grant recalled. The long, narrow
boats carried three dozen or so passengers apiece. The crew of each boat,
typically six men arrayed on planks mounted on the two sides of the
boat, propelled the craft with long poles. "The men would start from the
bow, place one end of their poles against the river bottom, brace their
shoulders against the other end, and then walk to the stern as rapidly as
they could," Grant explained. The river current was strong, but the boats
made a mile an hour against it.

At Gorgona most of the soldiers of Grant's regiment reverted to
infantry form and marched off, going over the divide and down to Panama City on the Pacific. Grant kept a company behind to help him with
the baggage and with the families who accompanied some of the soldiers
to their new posting. He hunted up the man who had won the contract
to supply the mules for the baggage and the women and children. The
man, an American, didn't have the mules on hand but promised to produce them the next day. The next day he said they would arrive the day
after that. Eventually Grant realized there would be no mules; the crush
of traffic on the isthmus and the consequent demand for transport had
prompted the man to ignore the contract he had with the army and rent
his beasts to higher bidders.

The resulting delay might have been merely annoying but for the fact
that the isthmus was one of the unhealthiest places on earth. Microbes

flourished in the warm, damp climate, and the human flood swamped the rudimentary sanitary system. Cholera claimed one after another of the men in Grant's company and an even larger portion of their family members. He sent most of the still-healthy ones off on foot to join the rest of the regiment at Panama City and scrambled to find other mules for the sick, the families and the baggage. After a week he paid a local the going rate—more than twice the contracted rate—to furnish the required transport. By then the cholera had spread, killing every third person with Grant. Nor did all those who had gone ahead escape; dozens succumbed, until more than a hundred—one-seventh of those who had set out with Grant from New York—had died.

Till now Grant had sometimes wished Julia and Fred had joined him on the journey west, but the epidemic erased such thoughts. "My dearest, you never could have crossed the isthmus," he wrote her from the safety of the ship to San Francisco. "The horrors of the road, in the rainy season, are beyond description." Realizing she might fear for his own safety, he assured her he was fine. "We are fast approaching a better climate. The *Golden Gate* takes us nearly 300 miles per day."

8

CALIFORNIA DURING THE GOLD RUSH ATTRACTED AMBITIOUS, acquisitive types from around the globe, and nearly all of them entered through San Francisco. "I consider that city the wonder of the world," Grant wrote Julia after a brief visit. "It is a place of but a few years' growth and contains a wealthy population of probably fifty thousand persons." What he learned from the locals of the city's short history supplemented what he saw himself. "It has been burned down three times and rebuilt each time better than before. The ground where the houses are built have either been filled in or else the hills dug away." The fill-ins were especially interesting. Saloons and gambling houses crowded the waterfront till they ran out of room, and then they pushed out over the water on pilings. Wooden streets serviced the new neighborhoods but not always well. "Often broken places were found in the street, large enough to let a man down into the water below," Grant recalled later, still astonished. "I have but little doubt that many of the people who went to the Pacific coast in the early days of the gold excitement, and have never been heard from since, or who were heard from for a time and then ceased to write, found watery graves beneath the houses or streets built over San Francisco Bay."

The army knew enough not to expose its soldiers to the hazards and temptations of San Francisco longer than necessary. And even if it had not known, it couldn't have afforded to keep them there. The gold from the mines fueled a ferocious inflation, sending prices to levels unimagined in other American cities. Appropriations that supported a regiment for a year in the East lasted a month in California; the exorbitant cost of living forced soldiers to moonlight to supplement their salaries.

After a few weeks at Benicia, across the bay from San Francisco, Grant's regiment steamed north to Fort Vancouver, in Oregon Territory, on the right bank of the Columbia River near its confluence with the Willamette River, several miles from the emerging town of Portland. The soldiers had little to do; the Indians of the Columbia Valley were fighting a smallpox epidemic and had no energy to battle the uniformed intruders. "During my year on the Columbia River," Grant wrote, "the small-pox exterminated one small remnant of a band of Indians entirely, and reduced others materially."

Grant nonetheless fell in love with Oregon. "Everyone speaks well of the climate and the growing prospects of the country," he wrote Julia. "It has timber and agricultural land, and the best market"—California— "in the world for all they can produce. Every article of produce can be raised here that can be in the states, and with much less labor, and finds a ready cash market at four times the value the same article would bring at home." The region around Vancouver and Portland was particularly pleasing. "This is about the best and most populous portion of Oregon. Living is expensive but money can be made. I have made on one specula- tion fifteen hundred dollars since I have been here." He explained that he had loaned a fellow officer some money to set up a store. "The business proved so profitable that I got $1500 to leave the concern." And yet he kicked himself. "I was very foolish for taking it, because my share of the profits would not have been less than three thousand per year." Even so, he couldn't complain. "I have every confidence that I shall make more than five thousand within the year."

His next speculation was already afoot. "I have been up to the Dalles of the Columbia"—rapids where the river entered a narrow gorge and where immigrants from the East rested before the final push to the Wil- lamette Valley. "I there made arrangements for the purchase of quite a number of oxen and cows." The immigrants sold the animals cheap, needing the cash, and Grant intended to sell them dear, for export to California. "I have in addition to cattle some hogs from which I expect a large increase soon, and have also bought a horse upon which I have been offered an advance of more than one hundred dollars."

Autumn rains failed to dampen Grant's speculative spirits. "About pecuniary matters, dear Julia," he wrote in early December, "I am bet- ter off than ever before, if I collect all that is due me, and there is about eighteen hundred dollars that there is but little doubt about. . . . I have got a farm of about one hundred acres, all cleared and enclosed, about one mile from here which I am going to cultivate in company with Captains Brent Wallen & McConnell. . . . We expect to raise some thirty acres of potatoes which may safely be put down at one dollar and fifty cents per bushel, and may be twice that, and the yield in this country is tremendous."

The week before Christmas brought the frigid winds that blast down the Columbia in winter. "The snow is now some ten inches in depth, and still snowing more, with a strong probability of much more falling," Grant wrote. "The thermometer has been from eighteen to twenty-two degrees for several days. Ice has formed in the river to such an extent that it is extremely doubtful whether the mail steamer can get back here to take off the mail by which I have been hoping to send this." He could scarcely leave his quarters. Yet he remained as enthusiastic as ever about the promise of the Oregon country. "So far as I have seen it, it opens the richest chances for poor persons who are willing and able to work, either in cutting wood, sawing logs, raising vegetables, poultry or stock of any kind, of any place I have ever seen. Timber stands close to the banks of the river free for all. Wood is worth five dollars a cord for steamers. The soil produces almost double it does in any place I have been before, with the finest market in the world for it after it is raised."

The cold persisted unusually, freezing the Columbia from bank to bank. "Captain Ingalls and myself were the first to cross," Grant wrote Julia on the third day of the new year. But a wind shift to the west brought warm rain that caused the ice to vanish—"so you need not feel any alarm about my falling through." Grant assured his wife he was keeping snug. "I am situated quite as comfortable as any body here, or in the Territory. The house I am living in is probably the best one in Oregon." He shared the place with two other officers, their two clerks and a civilian. A cook fed them and a hired man did the chores. "Everyone says they are the best servants in the whole Territory."

The country continued to amaze. "The climate of Oregon is evidently delightful," Grant wrote in late January. "Here we are north of 45 degrees, and though the oldest inhabitants say it has been about the most severe winter they have ever known here, yet it would surprise persons even as far south as St. Louis to be here now and witness our pleasant days. Farmers are ploughing and some sorts of vegetables have been growing all winter, and will continue to grow." His neighbors were pictures of health. "I believe the usual effect of an Oregon climate is to make a person grow stout; at least I should judge so from the appearance of every body that I see here."

He joined the general activity and shared the positive effect. "I am farming extensively and I work myself as hard as any body," he wrote in early March. "I have just finished putting in barley, and I am glad to say that I put in every grain with my own hands. By the end of the coming week myself and partners will have planted twenty acres of potatoes and an acre of onions. In a week or two more we will plant a few acres of corn." The exercise was building his muscles. "I have grown out of my clothes entirely and am still getting larger."

Oregon was ideal in all respects but one. "I have my health perfectly and could enjoy myself here as well as at any place I have ever been stationed at, if only you were here," he wrote Julia. "If you, Fred, and Ulys"—the second child had turned out to be a boy and was duly named Ulysses—"were only here, I would not care to ever go back, only to visit our friends." He pondered how he might bring them out. "I am first for promotion to a full captaincy," he explained. "Capt. Alden, it is said, intends to resign in a few months." When this happened, Grant said, he would give up his position as regimental quartermaster. "I shall then apply for orders to go to Washington to settle my accounts as disbursing officer, and when I return bring you with me."

*T*he Columbia River retarded Grant's design for family reunification. A decade hence Grant would become painfully familiar with the vagaries of large rivers; an early lesson occurred in the spring of 1853. Melting snow in the Canadian Rockies sent a torrent of water south and west. "The Columbia is now far over its banks, and has destroyed all the grain, onions, corn, and about half the potatoes upon which I had expended so much money and labor," he wrote Julia dejectedly.

Much of what the floodwaters didn't sweep away, in terms of his dreams for material success, an erstwhile partner absconded with. "Poor fellow, he could not stand prosperity," Grant said charitably, speaking of the man who owed him money from their earlier joint speculation. "He was making over $1,000.00 per month and it put him beside himself. From being generous, he grew parsimonious and finally so close that apparently he could not bear to let money go to keep up his stock of goods. He quit and went home with about $8,000.00, deceiving me as to the money he had and owing me about $800.00." This was particularly distressing, Grant acknowledged to Julia, as the sum in question was money "which if you had would educate our dear little boys."

Yet he refused to be discouraged. "I have now had a chance of looking at matters and I find that we will have a crop of several thousand potatoes," Grant wrote Julia after the flooding subsided. "According to the opinion of old settlers, they will bring from three to five dollars per bushel. This is in consequence of so many being drowned out." Certain other speculations fared well. He had traveled to San Francisco on army business. "While in California I purchased a quantity of pork, its being low there, and knowing the price here, I made in partnership with another gentleman about four hundred dollars upon it. I have still another lot to arrive, and the article having risen we will clear about six hundred." He also speculated in stock on the hoof. "I made arrangements below"—in California—"for the sale of pigs and hogs. I have out now a man buying them and I am confident of clearing, for my share, a thousand dollars in the next four weeks." Being quartermaster provided valuable opportunities, as he discovered in San Francisco. "A large business firm, from whom I have purchased flour &c., wanted me to watch the markets here (they are very changeable), and when any article was, in my opinion, a speculation, to inform them. They would furnish the capital, me make the sales, and divide the profits." Grant told Julia that he had accepted the offer, and was prepared "to do a handsome business in the commission way!"

The sudden peopling of the West on account of the gold discovery in California prompted national interest in a railroad linking the Mississippi Valley to the Pacific. The obvious western terminus for such a railroad was the San Francisco Bay, but the challenges of western geography— notably the Rocky Mountains and the Sierra Nevada—caused surveyors to look well beyond the most direct line west. Some hoped to skirt the highest peaks by swinging south, others by looping north. The army, under orders from Secretary of War Jefferson Davis, made itself useful by leading the surveys.

The survey team assigned to seek a northern route was headed by an officer of the engineer corps named George McClellan, a West Point graduate three years behind Grant. He had served with distinction in Mexico among the engineers of Winfield Scott, who happened to be

a friend of McClellan's father, a famous Philadelphia doctor. He subsequently explored and mapped the sources of the Red River and the
harbors of Texas, translated (from the original French) a manual on the
proper use of the bayonet, and earned a reputation as the most promising
of the younger generation of officers except for Robert E. Lee.

McClellan and his survey team launched into the northern Cascade
Mountains from Fort Vancouver, where Grant had the task of arranging transport. "I have purchased for them within a few days some two
hundred horses besides other property and still have more to get," he told
Julia. "The present state of the Columbia"—he wrote during the flood
that drowned his crops—"makes transportation very difficult so I have
to get Indians to pack, on their backs, all the provisions of one of these
parties over the portage at the Cascades"—a turbulent stretch of river
where the Columbia breached the Cascade Mountains—"about forty five
miles above here." Grant found the horses and hired the Indians, and
McClellan set off into the mountains, where his actions (or rather inac-
tion) embroiled him in a dispute with the governor of the newly created
Washington Territory, who detected in McClellan a penchant for promising more than he delivered.

Grant's hopes for bringing Julia and the boys to Oregon foundered
upon the army's decision to reassign him to northern California. The
death of an officer ahead of him opened a captaincy at Fort Humboldt,
a recently established post on Humboldt Bay that served the northern
gold mines—the town near the fort was called Eureka—and the growing timber industry. Getting to the post required Grant to return to San
Francisco, which had grown even wilder since his last visit. "Besides the
gambling in cards there was gambling on a larger scale in city lots," he
remembered later. "These were sold 'On Change,' much the way stocks
are now sold on Wall Street. Cash, at time of purchase, was always paid
by the broker; but the purchaser had only to put up his margin. He was
charged at the rate of two or three per cent a month on the difference,
besides commissions. The sand hills, some of them almost inaccessible
to foot-passengers, were surveyed off and mapped into fifty-vara lots—a
vara being a Spanish yard. These were sold at first at very low prices, but
were sold and resold for higher prices until they went up to many thousands of dollars. The brokers did a fine business, and so did many such

purchasers as were sharp enough to quit purchasing before the final crash came."

Grant reached Fort Humboldt in January 1854, in the dreariest season on that rainy coast. "I cannot say much in favor of the place," he wrote Julia. "Imagine a place closed in by the sea having thrown up two tongues of land, closed in a bay that can be entered only with certain winds." A more isolated post was hard to imagine, and there was little to keep the soldiers busy. "I do nothing here but set in my room and read, and occasionally take a short ride on one of the public horses." Some of the officers entertained themselves by hunting the ducks, geese, deer, elk and bears that surrounded the fort, but Grant disliked the killing. The mail came infrequently and irregularly. "I got one letter from you since I have been here," he wrote Julia in February, "but it was some three months old. . . . The only way we have of getting letters off is to give them to some Captain of a vessel to mail them after he gets down"—to San Francisco. "In the same way mails are received. This makes it very uncertain as to the time a letter may be on the way."

The isolation aggravated the disappointment he experienced at not being able to bring his family west. "You do not know how forsaken I feel here!" he wrote. "I feel again as if I had been separated from you and Fred long enough, and as to Ulys, I have never seen him. He must by this time be talking about as Fred did when I saw him last. How very much I want to see all of you. I have made up my mind what Ulys looks like, and I am anxious to see if my presentiment is correct. Does he advance rapidly? Tell me a great deal about him and Fred, and Fred's pranks with his Grandpa."

The gloomy weather darkened his mood and increased his sense of isolation. Psychologists of a subsequent era would describe a syndrome called seasonal affective disorder, a depression that afflicts some people when winter sunshine is scarce. Winter sunshine is scarcer on the northern coast of California than just about anywhere else outside the polar regions, and Grant seems to have fallen victim. "I have not been a hundred yards from my door but once in the last two weeks," he moaned in March. "I get so tired and out of patience with the loneliness of this place." When no letters arrived from Julia he couldn't tell whether they had been delayed or lost or she just hadn't written. "I have had only one letter from you in three months, and that had been a long time on the way. . . . I sometimes get so anxious to see you, and our little boys, that I am almost tempted to resign and trust to Providence, and my own exertions, for a living where I can have you and them with me." He wondered if she was forgetting him. "How do I know that you are thinking as much of me as I of you? I do not get letters to tell me so." He blamed the army and his fate for their long separation, but he didn't wholly absolve her. "I could be contented at Humboldt if it was possible to have you here, but it is not. You could not do without a servant, and a servant you could not have. This is too bad, is it not? But you never complain of being lonesome so I infer you are quite contented." A recent dream made him worry the more. "I thought you were at a party when I arrived, and before paying any attention to my arrival you said you must go; you were engaged for that dance. . . . If I should see you, it would not be as I dreamed, would it, dearest?"

Additional weeks passed with no letters, and he grew more miserable. "I do not feel as if it was possible to endure this separation much longer," he wrote. "By the time you receive this, Ulys will be nearly two years old and no doubt talking as plainly as Fred did his few words when I saw him last. Dear little boys—what a comfort it would be to see and play with them a few hours every day!"

Worry about earning a living outside the army was all that kept him from resigning. "It would only require the certainty of a moderate competency to make me take the step. Whenever I get to thinking upon the subject, however, *poverty, poverty* begins to stare me in the face, and then I think what would I do if you and our little ones should want for the necessities of life."

"There is but one thing to console," he inserted amid the laments. "Misery loves company, and there are a number in just the same fix with myself."

In their distant post on that rainy shore, a world removed from those they loved, the soldiers at Fort Humboldt did what soldiers in like circumstances have done for thousands of years: they drank their sorrows away. George Crook, a young lieutenant whose path crossed Grant's during this period, later described the drinking culture among the officers of the Fourth Infantry in California. "There was not a day passed but what these officers were drunk at least once, and mostly until the wee hours of the morning," Crook declared. One officer drank himself to death and was buried with full honors. "Major Day, whose head was as white as the driven snow, commanded the escort, and when all of us officers had assembled in the room where the corpse was lying, he said, 'Well, fellows, old Miller is dead and he can't drink, so let us all take a drink.' I was never more horrified in my life."

Grant had never drunk to such regular excess, but he sometimes drank more than his constitution could handle. "One glass would show on him," a fellow officer recalled, "and two or three would make him stupid." Army practice allowed for officers who drank, but not for those who couldn't hold their liquor. George McClellan never forgot an incident at Fort Vancouver when Grant got wobbly, and Grant's commander at Fort Humboldt, Robert Buchanan, took personal offense at his subordinate's incapacity. "One day while his company was being paid off, Captain Grant was at the pay table slightly inebriated," Henry Hodges, a lieutenant at Humboldt, remembered. "This came to the knowledge of Colonel Buchanan; he gave Grant the option of resigning or having charges preferred against him."

This likely wasn't the first time Grant's drinking interfered with his work; Buchanan was known as a stickler, but at a place like Fort Humboldt, so far from home and with so few officers, even a martinet had to allow for human weakness. Perhaps Grant was the final straw in a haystack of tipsy subordinates and Buchanan wanted to make him an example for the rest. The other officers encouraged Grant to call what they considered Buchanan's bluff. "Grant's friends at the time urged him to stand trial, and were confident of his acquittal," Rufus Ingalls, one of Grant's roommates from West Point and a close friend at Humboldt, asserted afterward.

But Grant decided not to. His loneliness already had him on the brink of resigning; if he fought the charge and won, his victory would be a sentence to more of what was making him miserable. Even if he did win, the charge against him would be a matter of record. The army didn't forget, acquittals notwithstanding.

Rufus Ingalls thought a more personal consideration mattered most. "He said he would not for the world have his wife know that he had been tried on such a charge," Ingalls said. Grant already worried that Julia was drifting away, and he wouldn't risk giving her a reason for thinking less of him.

So he abruptly made a decision he had been unable to reach uncompelled. "I very respectfully tender my resignation of my commission as an officer of the Army," he wrote to the adjutant general in Washington. He did not explain but simply asked that the resignation take effect on the last day of July, four months hence. The adjutant general, on the recommendation of Colonel Buchanan, accepted the resignation and the proposed timing.

9

When Grant helped George McClellan organize his survey of a route for a transcontinental railroad, they both acted in implicit alliance with Stephen Douglas. The Illinois Democrat headed the Senate committee on federal territories, which set the rules for administering and organizing most of the trans-Missouri West. Douglas recognized railroads as the transforming technology of the era, and he saw that railroads could make Chicago, as yet a modest town on the shore of Lake Michigan but one in which he had sizable investments, the great metropolis of the West.

Accomplishing his ambition required that Douglas arrange territorial governments for the districts through which a Pacific railroad would run. The congressional Compromise of 1850, besides admitting California as a free state, had established territorial governments for New Mexico and Utah without prejudice for or against slavery. Douglas hoped to apply the same principle to Kansas and Nebraska, the territories just west of the Missouri River. The problem was that the Missouri Compromise of 1820 promised that these territories would be free. The opponents of slavery insisted that the promise be kept, but the advocates threatened to veto the organizing of Kansas and Nebraska unless slaveholders were allowed to settle there with their slaves. David Atchison of Missouri, the leader of the proslavery forces on the Kansas issue, vowed to see the region "sink in hell" before he'd vote to ban slavery there.

Douglas understood that tampering with the Missouri Compromise was asking for trouble. "It will raise a hell of a storm," he predicted. But he thrust ahead, presenting the Senate at the beginning of 1854 with a bill that placed the future of slavery in the new territories in the hands of their settlers. In the climactic debate he told his colleagues that to vote against the bill would be to stand in the way of history. "Do you suppose that you could keep that vast country a howling wilderness in all time to come, roamed over by hostile savages, cutting off all safe communication between our Atlantic and Pacific possessions?" America would expand whether the Senate willed it or not. "You cannot fix bounds to the onward march of this great and growing country. You cannot fetter the limbs of the young giant. He will burst all your chains." The Senate must act. "You must decide upon what principles the territories shall be organized; in other words, whether the people shall be allowed to regulate their domestic institutions in their own way, according to the provisions of this bill, or whether the opposite doctrine of congressional interference is to prevail."

Most Southerners supported Douglas, but not all. Sam Houston of Texas, who had learned devotion to the Union at the knee of Andrew Jackson, judged that Douglas had fashioned a formula for secession and civil war. "I adjure you to regard the contract once made to harmonize and preserve this Union," Houston pleaded. "*Maintain the Missouri Compromise! Stir not up agitation! Give us peace!*"

The opponents of slavery screamed betrayal. A group calling itself the Independent Democrats castigated the Kansas-Nebraska bill as "a gross violation of a sacred pledge" and "a criminal betrayal of precious rights." William Fessenden of Maine called the Douglas measure "a terrible outrage." Fessenden added, "The more I look at it, the more outraged I become. It needs but little to make me an out-and-out abolitionist." Slavery opponents summoned "anti-Nebraska" meetings, which voted resolutions condemning Douglas and the Kansas-Nebraska bill. "This crime shall not be consummated," one promised. "Despite corruption, bribery, and treachery, Nebraska, the heart of our continent, shall forever continue free."

Yet Douglas had the votes. The Kansas-Nebraska bill passed the Senate easily. Approval in the House came harder; the debate in the lower chamber lasted two weeks and involved the brandishing of mortal threats and personal weapons. But Alexander Stephens of Georgia, applying what he characterized as "whip and spur," delivered the votes for the bill, and President Franklin Pierce signed it into law.

*G*rant read about the Kansas-Nebraska Act en route from San Francisco to New York, via Nicaragua. He returned east deeply uncertain about his present and his future. He didn't know how Julia would respond to his resignation from the army. He had no means of supporting her and the boys. He wondered whether she had grown to enjoy being apart from him. Her infrequent and lukewarm letters suggested that perhaps she had.

He wondered as well about his father. Jesse Grant had gotten Ulysses into the army by arranging the appointment to the military academy, and he thought the army was the place his son ought to stay. When Jesse heard of Grant's resignation, he immediately sought to reverse it. He knew of Grant's loneliness in California but not of his drinking, and, supposing Grant simply needed time with his family, Jesse wrote to his congressman requesting a leave of absence for his son. Upon being told that Grant's resignation had already been accepted and therefore that a leave of absence was impossible, Jesse wrote directly to Jefferson Davis at the War Department. "I would be much gratified if you would reconsider and withdraw the acceptance of his resignation, and grant him a six months leave, that he may come home and see his family," he said. "I never wished him to leave the service. I think after spending so much time to qualify himself for the Army, and spending so many years in the service, he will be poorly qualified for the pursuits of private life."

Whether Davis thought it odder that a father should presume to manage his grown son's life or that the father had such a dismal opinion of his son's abilities, the war secretary didn't say. Doubtless Davis had heard through the army grapevine that Grant was a drinker, and he realized there was more to the story of Grant's resignation than appeared in the official record. He was sufficiently solicitous of Grant's privacy— and the army's—not to share this realization with Jesse Grant. Davis responded, "I have to inform you that Capt. Grant tendered his resignation, but assigned no reasons why he desired to quit the service, and the motives which influenced him are not known to the Department." Grant was within his rights in resigning, and the army had followed procedure in accepting the resignation, which had been recorded and published. "The acceptance is, therefore, complete, and cannot be reconsidered."

Grant saw his father before he saw Julia. He arrived in New York short of cash and appealed to Simon Bolivar Buckner, a fellow cadet from West Point and a comrade from the Mexican War. "Grant landed in New York in 1854 poor and forlorn," Buckner recalled. "One day he came into my office and asked for help. He had been staying at the old Astor House, and his money was all gone and he had been unable to get anything to do and had no means to reach home. He asked for a loan in order to repay his bills at the hotel and reach his father in southern Ohio. I went back to the hotel with him and introduced him to the proprietor of the hotel, whom I knew. And I said Captain Grant was a man of honor and though in hard luck he would see that his bills were paid. I vouched of him, and Grant wrote to his people in Ohio and received money shortly thereafter, enough to take him home."

His mother was happy to see him, but his father frowned. Jesse didn't hide his disapproval of Grant's resignation and of what his son wasn't making of his life. "West Point spoiled one of my boys for business," he said, according to a neighbor's recollection. To which Grant replied, "I guess that's about so."

Despite the tension in his parents' home, Grant tarried before continuing west. The closer he got to Julia the more he worried that she wouldn't welcome him. Since their engagement a decade earlier they had spent but three years together, and though their separations weighed depressingly on him, she seemed to stand them quite well. Would she find his presence confining? Was she disappointed in him? Her family and friends had thought she could do better in a beau when they were courting; did she now feel she could have done better in a husband?

He finally screwed up his courage and went. He hardly recognized Fred, who had grown from an infant into a small boy. And Fred didn't recognize him at all. The boy had known his father was coming, but he mistook other men for him. "Mamma, is that ugly man my papa?" he asked Julia of an officer who visited the house. Her reply reassured him, but he continued to ask about each male who walked in the door. Grant had never seen Ulys, nor Ulys him. The strange face frightened the two-year-old, who required time to let his father get close.

It was Julia's reaction that Grant studied most carefully. "How very happy this reunion was!" she wrote later. "One great boy by his knee, one curly-headed, blue-eyed Cupid on his lap, and his happy, proud wife nestled by his side. We cared for no other happiness." Maybe she really remembered things so. But if she genuinely swelled with pride for her husband she acted more the saint than she often proved to be. She knew he had thrown over the career he had been building his whole adult life;

she knew he had no profession or trade; she knew he didn't get along with his father, who might have set him up in business.

Still, the homecoming went better than he had feared. Julia greeted him warmly—warmly enough, at any rate, that their third child, Ellen, was born a bit more than nine months later.

After a month with Julia's family, Grant reluctantly returned to his parents' home, accompanied this time by Julia and the boys, to let Jesse and Hannah see their grandsons. "There are no pleasant memories of that visit," Julia recalled. She thought her father-in-law a skinflint; he judged her a spendthrift. Jesse proposed that Grant join his brothers in a leather business Jesse had established in Galena, Illinois. "My husband was much pleased with the proposition," Julia remembered. But Jesse added a condition: that Grant go alone and live with one of the brothers to save the expense of starting another household. Julia and the boys could stay with Jesse and Hannah or they could go live with her family in Missouri.

Grant refused to be separated from Julia and the boys again, and he rejected Jesse's condition and offer. Julia emphatically supported the decision, to her husband's immense relief.

*H*e tried his hand at farming, the only occupation he knew besides soldiering. Julia's father gave her sixty acres, which Grant could cultivate. But the property included no building suitable for a home, and so they lived in a house on the Dent family farm. The house suited Julia, who didn't care that it wasn't theirs and who didn't have to travel the three miles from the house to the land where Grant spent his waking hours working. But Grant wanted a house of their own, and he soon began felling trees to build it. He also cut trees for firewood and to earn money to buy the seeds and the other items a farm required.

"I worked very hard, never losing a day because of bad weather," he recalled of the winter of 1854–55. Gradually his house—a log cabin, in fact—took shape. Julia wasn't impressed. "I cannot imagine why the Captain ever built it," she said later. She much preferred the house on the Dent farm—"a beautiful English villa," she called it, "situated in a primeval forest of magnificent oaks." She blamed her father for insisting, by his lack of financial support, that Grant build a log house, of materials at hand, rather than a frame house, which would have required paying a sawyer. "So the great trees were felled and lay stripped of their boughs," she related. "Then came the hewing which required much time and labor." The house that resulted was distinctly inferior to what she had known or expected of life. "It was so crude and so homely I did not like it at all." She tried to cover its unsightliness and her disappointment by curtains, blankets and other mementos of her better days, but she soon admitted defeat. "The little house looked so unattractive that we face-tiously decided to call it Hardscrabble."

𝒜lexander Stephens was proud of the Kansas-Nebraska Act. "I feel as if the *Mission* of my life was performed," the Georgia congressman wrote from Washington to a friend upon the measure's passage. Stephens was a Southerner but no less, he believed, an American. "My sole object here now is to serve the country." He reviewed the tumult of the last eleven years, from the time the Texas question had erupted in national politics. He faulted the antislavery elements in the North for trying to stunt the growth of the South and by doing so threatening the compact that united the two sections. He took pride in having fought off these enemies of the South and of national comity, and he looked forward to an easing of hostilities. "Are we not in a much better condition today than we were in 1843 when I took my seat on the floor of the House?"

Abraham Lincoln had met Stephens during Lincoln's one term in Congress, and he respected the Georgian's intelligence and sincerity. But he couldn't have disagreed more about the national consequences of the Kansas-Nebraska law, and he told his fellow Illinoisans as much at every opportunity. "I remember he impressed me with the feeling that the country was on the brink of a great disaster," James Miner wrote later. Miner and his father were in Winchester, Illinois, when Lincoln spoke against the measure. "About one hundred and fifty or two hundred persons gathered in the upper room of the old courthouse," Miner said. "On the west side of the old courtroom there was a dais or raised plat-form for the judge's seat and desk. Lincoln stood in front of this platform on the floor and made his speech." The leading figure in Illinois politics was Stephen Douglas, the law's author; Lincoln, who hoped to rekindle a political career that had stagnated after he left Congress, challenged Douglas by attacking the Kansas-Nebraska Act. "He began by telling how in the minds of the people the Missouri Compromise was held as something sacred, more particularly by the citizens of Illinois, as the bill had been introduced in the Senate by a senator from Illinois, Jesse B. Thomas. He spoke of the aggressiveness of the slave-holding party, their eagerness to acquire more slave territory; alluded to several arguments Douglas had made in his speeches in favor of the Kansas-Nebraska bill and replied to them." Lincoln would learn to use humor to leaven his speeches, but on this day he solicited few smiles. "He was as earnest and solemn as though he had been delivering a funeral oration." Miner remembered that his father asked a friend what he thought of Lincoln's performance. The friend replied, "I have heard this winter all the big men in Congress talk on this question, but Lincoln's is the strongest speech I ever heard on the subject."

*T*he "hell of a storm" Stephen Douglas predicted burst over Kansas in the autumn of 1854. Popular sovereignty incited competition among the advocates and opponents of slavery, as each sought to fill the new territory with friends and rid it of enemies. The advocates got there first, pouring over the border into Kansas from Missouri, where slave owners feared that a free state next door would become a hotbed of abolition and a haven for fugitive slaves. The opponents of slavery, refusing to be outdone—that is, to be outnumbered and outvoted in territorial elections and in the writing of a constitution for the state Kansas would become—mobilized in response. The New England Emigrant Aid Company sent a thousand antislavery colonists to Kansas to counterbalance the proslavery settlers. Some came armed with "Beecher's Bibles," rifles so dubbed for Henry Ward Beecher, the firebrand abolitionist minister who was reported to have said that in the struggle against slavery there was greater moral power in a single Sharp's rifle than in a hundred Bibles.

The approach of the Yankees motivated the Missourians to dispatch reinforcements. The proslavery elements swamped their opponents at the polls in elections for the territorial legislature, which set about fastening slavery upon the region. The abolitionists rejoined with reinforcements of their own, including the monomaniacal John Brown. After crossing paths with Grant's father in Ohio, Brown went east to school, then into business and farming. His farm did modestly well but his spirit required a cause, which he found in abolitionism. "I pledge myself, with God's help, that I will devote my life to increasing hostility to slavery," he told an abolitionist meeting in 1837. (A dramatically revised version of this statement was the one more widely remembered: "Here, before God, in the presence of these witnesses, I consecrate my life to the destruction of slavery.") For almost two decades he opposed slavery quietly, but when the struggle for Kansas broke out he determined to take active part. He traveled to the contested region and gathered about him a group of abolitionists. In May 1856, after slavery advocates attacked the antislavery settlement of Lawrence, the Brown group pulled five proslavery settlers from their homes along Pottawatomie Creek and hacked them to death with broadswords.

The Pottawatomie massacre inflamed the country, as Brown had intended. Additional slavery advocates entered Kansas and at Osawatomie engaged Brown's followers. Several of the latter died, among them one of Brown's adult sons. Abolitionists made a hero of John Brown— "Osawatomie Brown"—and a martyr of his son, outraging the slavery advocates the more.

"Bleeding Kansas," as Horace Greeley's *New York Tribune* called the embattled territory, summarized the calamitous direction of American politics in the mid-1850s—and then some. The story was too good for the nation's newspapers to ignore or to refrain from embellishing. Abolitionist editors like Greeley painted Kansas as the place where liberty was dying at the hands of murderers from Missouri and other agents of the slaveholder conspiracy. "Startling News from Kansas," the *Tribune* proclaimed after the attack on Lawrence. "The War Actually Begun. Triumph of the Border Ruffians. Lawrence in Ruins. Several Persons Slaughtered. Freedom Bloodily Subdued." The *New York Times* echoed, "The War in Kansas. Murders Thickening," and reprinted an appeal from the front: "Unless the North send us men and means *immediately* the Free-State men will be compelled to abandon the Territory." Southern apologists for slavery decried the atrocities committed by the abolitionists and summoned their own heroes to fly to the defense of property rights and the Southern way of life. Both sides sold record numbers of papers—and angered the majority of Kansans who were *not* involved in any massacres or sackings. One Kansas editor, rightly worried that the sensational accounts were scaring away peaceable settlers, satirized the war stories. "The late civil war in Kansas did not last but a day and a half," he wrote. "A Kansas correspondent thus sums up the result:

Killed: 0
Wounded, contusion of the nose: 2
Missing: 0

Captured: 3
Frightened: 5,718

Yet there was undeniable reality beneath the exaggerations, and the events in Kansas convinced many Americans their country was heading for a wreck. Congress itself felt the violence when Representative Preston Brooks of South Carolina assaulted Senator Charles Sumner of Massachusetts on the floor of the Senate. Sumner was notorious for the invective he spewed at opponents, but he outdid himself in a speech he called the "Crime Against Kansas," in which he singled out Senator Andrew Butler of South Carolina for having "chosen a mistress to whom he has made his vows . . . I mean the harlot, slavery." Preston Brooks was kin to Butler and full of the hair-trigger dignity of the South; he judged that Sumner didn't merit a duel and so entered the Senate with his walking stick and used it to beat Sumner about the head and neck. Sumner fell to the stone floor and lay in a pool of his blood while Brooks walked away unmolested. The North was appalled at the violation of the sanctity of the temple of democracy; the South applauded the defense of Southern honor; friends of peace shuddered at what it all portended.

"Every day I like farming better," Grant wrote his father at the end of 1856. "And I do not doubt but that money is to be made at it. So far I have been laboring under great disadvantages but now that I am on my own place, and shall not have to build next summer, I think I shall be able to do much better." Yet he was pinched for capital, and the shortfall showed. "This year if I could have bought seed I should have made out still better than I did. I wanted to plant sixty or seventy bushels of potatoes, but I had not the money to buy them." Still, the twenty bushels he had been able to plant yielded well, producing more than 350 bushels, of which he had sold 225 bushels and kept the balance for this year's planting. And he aimed to diversify. "I have in some twenty five acres of wheat that looks better, or did before the cold weather, than any in the neighborhood. My intention is to raise about twenty acres of Irish potatoes, on new ground, five acres of sweet potatoes, about the same of early corn, five or six acres cabbage, beets, cucumber pickles, and melons, and keep a wagon going to market every day." Yet here again the lack of capital constrained him. "This last year my place was not half tended because I had but one span of horses, and one hand, and we had to do all the work of the place, living at a distance too, all the hauling for my building, and take wood to the city for the support of the family. . . . This year I presume I shall be compelled to neglect my farm some to make a living in the mean time, but by next year I hope to be independent."

Grant was rarely so loquacious with his father. Jesse doubtless wondered what his son was driving at; he found his answer in the letter's concluding observation: "If I had an opportunity of getting about $500.00

for a year at 10 per cent I have no doubt but it would be of great advantage to me."

Grant evidently hoped to receive the money without having to ask for it explicitly. And 10 percent was a better rate than Jesse could expect elsewhere, so the proposition could be interpreted as a strictly business deal. Jesse, moreover, had earlier told Grant, when the younger man was visiting Covington, Kentucky, to which he and Hannah had moved, that he would help him launch the farm. But Jesse now doubted his son's prospects, or perhaps he simply didn't want to part with the money, and he let Grant's hint fall unanswered.

Grant waited six weeks, until the planting season was near, and tried again. His tone this time was plaintive, almost desperate. "Spring is now approaching, when farmers require not only to till the soil, but to have the wherewith to till it, and to seed it," he wrote Jesse. "For two years I have been compelled to farm without either of these facilities." He confessed that for all the optimism of his previous letter, he was in dire shape. "The fact is, without means it is useless for me to go on farming, and I will have to do what Mr. Dent has given me permission to do: sell the farm and invest elsewhere. For two years now I have been compelled to neglect my farm to go off and make a few dollars to buy any little necessaries—sugar, coffee, etc.—or to pay hired men." He had not been extravagant. "My expenses for my family have been nothing scarcely for the last two years. Fifty dollars, I believe, would pay all that I have laid out for their clothing." But things had been very difficult. "I have worked hard and got but little."

He no longer hinted; he had to ask directly. "I am going to make the last appeal to you. I do this because, when I was in Kentucky you voluntarily offered to give me a thousand dollars to commence with, and because there is no one else to whom I could, with the same propriety, apply. It is always usual for parents to give their children assistance in beginning life (and I am only beginning, though thirty-five years of age, nearly) and what I ask is not much." He wanted not a gift but rather a loan—of the five hundred dollars at 10 percent, for two years. "With this sum I can go on and cultivate my ground." If Jesse would lend the money, Grant wouldn't approach him again. "If I do not go on prosperously I shall ask no more from you."

Grant humbled himself to no avail. Jesse continued to withhold his money. Grant toiled more diligently than ever. Mary Robinson, Julia's slave, was astonished to see a white man labor the way Grant did. "I have seen many farmers," she remembered, "but I never saw one that worked harder than Mr. Grant."

For a time Grant's renewed efforts appeared at least moderately successful. "My hard work is now over for the season, with a fair prospect of being remunerated in everything but the wheat," he wrote his sister Mary in August 1857. "My wheat, which would have produced from four to five hundred bushels with a good winter, has yielded only seventy-five. My oats were good, and the corn, if not injured by frost this fall, will be the best I ever raised. My potato crop bids fair to yield fifteen hundred bushels or more."

But even this success proved fleeting. Julia's mother had died in January 1857, and her father, complaining of loneliness, had asked Julia and Grant and the boys to live with him. Julia was glad for the excuse to trade their log home for a real house, and Grant agreed to indulge her. As part of the bargain he managed the Dent farm as well as his—or Julia's—own.

Managing the Dent farm entailed overseeing slaves. Julia's household slaves had accompanied her into marriage with Grant, but he had little to do with them. The field slaves of Fred Dent were a different matter, and they put Grant in the awkward position small slave owners often occupied in the South, with an additional difficulty besides. In the North physical labor was a badge of virtue, the measure of one's devotion to duty and the promise of one's success. In the South physical labor was the province of chattel—and of those whites who couldn't rise above the level of slaves. The more Grant sweated and strained, the farther he fell in the estimation of his Missouri neighbors, especially the neighbors whose opinion mattered most to Julia.

The added difficulty was that Grant didn't believe in the institution of slavery. Most slave owners managed to convince themselves that slavery was part of the natural order, something accepted by the Bible and therefore ordained by God. Grant was no abolitionist, but he *was* from Ohio, where slavery was broadly deemed an affront to free labor and republican principles. He couldn't have freed his father-in-law's slaves, and he wasn't inclined to make Julia dispense with her bound servants. He eventually purchased a slave of his own because he couldn't find other help. But he never got over the queasiness he felt from the ownership of another human.

His discomfort showed in his inability to get much work out of the slaves. "He was not a hand to manage Negroes," a friend remembered. "He couldn't force them to do anything. He was just so good and good tempered, and besides, he was not a slavery man."

Partly as a result, he was not a successful man. He consistently lost money at farming. Just before Christmas 1857 he was forced to pawn his gold watch for twenty-two dollars. He gave up working Julia's property, deciding to rent it out and concentrate his efforts on the Dent tract. This lessened the time he spent going from one farm to the other—a saving he valued the more as his family continued to grow. Ellen Grant, called Nellie, had been born in 1855, and Jesse Grant arrived in early 1858. Between the needs of his growing children and the expectations of his wife, not to mention his own discouragement, he fell into dark reveries about his past, present and future. "He was like a man thinking on an abstract subject all the time," a neighbor recalled.

*W*illiam Sherman did even more thinking than Grant, along similar dismal lines. Sherman, like Grant, was a West Point graduate; like Grant he had been stationed in California after the Mexican War; like Grant he experienced the speculative frenzy that infected life all up and down the coast. Like Grant he resigned from the army, at about the same time. But Sherman remained in California, determined to make the most of the opportunities there. He became a banker, the manager of the San Francisco branch of a St. Louis firm. For a time things went well, but the pricking of one of the recurrent bubbles in mining stocks triggered a panic among San Francisco banks and he was forced to close his branch's doors. Yet his St. Louis superiors liked his work well enough to send him to New York to open an office in Wall Street.

He arrived during the summer of 1857 and got the office running in time to witness the failure that August of the heretofore well-regarded Ohio Life and Trust Company. The Ohio firm was highly leveraged, and its failure, amid allegations of fraud, spooked New York's investment community. A bank panic followed but was brought under control, and Sherman thought his new bank would survive. Then, however, a hurricane off North Carolina sank the *Central America*, a steamship of the United States Mail Company, with four hundred passengers and fifteen tons of California gold. The loss of life elicited mourning among families and friends; the loss of gold renewed the panic on Wall Street. Sherman's bank was one of the many victims. "I suppose I was the Jonah that blew up San Francisco," he wrote his wife, who tolerated the bleak humor he often favored. "And it took only two months' residence in Wall Street to bust up New York."

Sherman traveled to St. Louis to settle accounts with his backers. There he encountered Grant, and the two compared stories of bad luck since leaving the army. They spoke of other comrades who had done no better and wondered what would become of them all. "West Point and the Regular Army aren't good schools for farmers, bankers, merchants and mechanics," Sherman mused.

11

THE PANIC OF 1857, BY KNOCKING DOWN FARM PRICES, MIGHT ALONE have finished off Grant's career in agriculture, but malaria helped. Like many other Americans of the Ohio and Mississippi Valleys in the nineteenth century, Grant had suffered recurrently from the mosquito-borne illness since childhood. Neither he nor they knew what caused the disease, but it appeared to be associated with low-lying areas, precisely the sort of bottomlands best suited to farming, during summer, the farming season. Black slaves, for reasons then unknown to themselves or their masters but evidently (and later demonstrably) associated with their African heritage, usually avoided the symptoms; their comparative immunity was another argument of the apologists for slavery. Heavy work and constant worry reduced resistance to malaria, as to other diseases, and both contributed to a severe bout Grant experienced during the summer of 1858. The "fever and ague" that provided the common name of malaria alternated irregularly, with Grant sweating profusely and then shivering. Julia suggested that he would get better in St. Louis, away from the disease zone, and that in any case the older children were approaching school age and would benefit from the city's schools. He had no argument to make against her suggestion, and with Frederick Dent's permission he offered the farm for sale.

He went into business with one of Julia's cousins, a man named Harry Boggs. The business bought, sold and managed real estate. Under ordinary circumstances it might have done well, for real estate had long been the ladder to success for cash-strapped but enterprising individuals in America. The relentlessly growing American population ensured the demand that pushed up prices and commissions. But the panic of 1857 briefly deranged the market, depressing prices and deterring speculation, and the firm of Boggs & Grant struggled.

Grant spent his first months in the business living with Harry Boggs and his wife, Louisa. "We gave him an unfurnished back room and told him to fit it up as he pleased," Louisa recalled. "It contained very little during the winter he lived here. He had a bed and a bowl and pitcher on a chair and he used to sit at our fire. He used to go home Saturday night to his family. He lived this way all winter"—the winter of 1858–59. "I can see him now as he used to sit humbly by my fireside. He had no exalted opinion of himself at any time, but in those days he seemed almost in despair."

His attitude improved after he brought Julia and the children to St. Louis. "We are living now in the lower part of the city, full two miles from my office," he wrote his father in the spring of 1859. "The house is a comfortable little one just suited to my means. We have one spare room and also a spare bed in the children's room so that we can accommodate any of our friends that are likely to come see us."

Grant appreciated that his father, the businessman, would want to know about his prospects. "I can hardly tell how the new business I am engaged in is going to succeed," he explained. "But I believe it will be something more than a support." Even so, he could use help, in the form of referrals. "I will send you some of our cards, which if you will distribute among such persons as may have business to attend to in this city, such as buying or selling property, collecting either rents or other liabilities, it may prove the means of giving us additional commissions."

*I*n this letter Grant told his father that Julia would not be taking the children to see Jesse and Hannah in Kentucky that season. He had urged her to make the trip while he was arranging the move to St. Louis, but she had refused. "With four children she could not go without a servant," Grant wrote Jesse. "And she was afraid that landing so often as she would have to do in free states, she might have some trouble."

Julia was right to anticipate trouble. For decades the Mason-Dixon Line and the Ohio River had symbolized the boundary between slavery and freedom in American life, but the boundary allowed loopholes and exceptions. When wealthy Americans of the nineteenth century traveled they often took personal servants with them; in the case of Americans from the South, these personal servants were typically slaves. As long as the Southerners were simply traveling, the free-state bans on slavery didn't apply to their slaves, who remained legally bound. But when the travel stretched to sojourns of weeks or months, questions arose and sometimes wound up in the courts.

Dred Scott was a slave purchased by John Emerson, an army doctor in St. Louis. Emerson was subsequently posted to Wisconsin, a free territory to which he took Scott. After several years and further postings, Emerson returned to St. Louis, again taking Scott. Emerson died, but Scott remained in the possession of Emerson's widow, the former Eliza Irene Sanford. Scott knew enough of Missouri law to appreciate that its principle of "once free, always free"—that a Missouri slave taken to live on free soil and then returned to Missouri could claim freedom—ought to apply to him. A Missouri court ruled that it did, but the Missouri supreme court, amid the rising furor of the 1850s, reversed the judgment.

Scott's lawyers appealed to the United States Supreme Court, where the case became known as *Dred Scott* v. *Sandford* (upon the misspelling of the name of John Sanford, to whom Eliza Sanford Emerson had entrusted her affairs). The case gained significance as the sectional issue grew still more divisive, and by the time the high court delivered its decision, in March 1857, the nation hung on the outcome.

The court ruled on two aspects of the case. First, it said that Scott had no standing to bring a case in federal court because he was not a citizen of the United States. Blacks could be citizens of the separate states if those states chose to make them so, but they were not citizens of the United States. The court might have stopped there and left the Missouri verdict alone. But Chief Justice Roger B. Taney hoped the judicial branch could accomplish what the legislative and executive branches had failed to do: determine once and for all what power Congress possessed over slavery. Tackling the issue squarely, Taney, a slaveholder from Maryland, declared that Congress had *no* power over slavery. The Constitution gave Congress no authority to restrict the property rights of slave owners, and hence the Missouri Compromise, the basis for making Wisconsin a free territory, had been unconstitutional from the start. On this ground as well, Scott remained a slave.

Six other justices joined Taney in the Dred Scott decision, which angered and alarmed many Northerners. Most in the North accepted that Congress lacked jurisdiction over slavery in the states, but the assertion that the federal legislature was impotent to control slavery in the federal territories seemed absurd on its face and frightening in its implications.

The hope of moderate opponents of slavery was that the obnoxious institution could be kept from expanding and would thereby be encouraged to die a gradual death as morality and perhaps the economy evolved. This hope had been dealt a blow by the Kansas-Nebraska Act, which repealed the Missouri Compromise but left in place the principle that Congress *could* restrict slavery in the territories if it once again chose to. The Dred Scott case smashed the moderates' hope. Nothing, it seemed, stood in the way of the slave power.

The Dred Scott decision, though bad news for blacks' freedom, was good news for Abraham Lincoln's career. Lincoln had been cast adrift by the breakup of the Whig party in the aftermath of the Kansas-Nebraska Act; finding a new political home required sifting among the flotsam of the Whigs and the various successors they spawned. The American party grew out of the Know Nothing movement of the 1840s, whose members complained that the large immigration of Catholics from Ireland and Germany threatened to overwhelm the English and Protestant values on which the country had been founded. When the Democrats adopted the Irish who landed in New York and other eastern cities, the American party swung into anti-Democratic opposition. There it met the new Republican party, which originated in either Wisconsin or Michigan depending on whose story was to be believed. Two issues inspired the Republicans: resistance to slavery and support for business. The antislavery resistance ranged from moderate displeasure at the Dred Scott decision to radical abolitionism. The pro-business agenda included a protective tariff and internal improvements, starting with a railroad to the Pacific.

Lincoln found his way to the Republicans, who in Illinois were a cautious bunch, at first refusing even to call themselves Republicans for fear of being branded abolitionists by the pro-Southern elements that ran strong in parts of Illinois. At their founding convention in Bloomington in 1856, the Illinois Republicans endorsed the minimal antislavery position of the national party: opposition to an extension of slavery in the western territories. Lincoln approached the Republicans with folksy humor that made some people smile and others groan. He acknowledged that most members of the party were better known than he, and he said he felt like an ugly man who met an outspoken woman on the road. "You are the homeliest man I ever saw," the woman asserted. The man replied, "I can't help it." "I suppose not," the woman retorted. "But you might stay at home."

Yet Lincoln could be serious too. At the Bloomington convention he delivered a stirring speech on the necessity of preserving the values of American democracy against the iniquitous and unconstitutional demands of the slaveholders, some of whom threatened secession if they didn't get their way. He concluded by quoting Daniel Webster: "Liberty and Union, now and forever, one and inseparable."

He sufficiently impressed his fellow Republicans in Illinois that when the national party held its first presidential nominating convention that year at Philadelphia, the Illinois delegates arranged to have Lincoln offered for vice president. The effort failed, but it won him notice outside his state. He campaigned vigorously around Illinois for the Republican presidential nominee, John Frémont, who had survived his Mexican War court-martial to become rich on California gold, famous for his audacity and envied for his beautiful and forceful wife, Jessie Benton Frémont, the daughter of Thomas Hart Benton. Though Frémont lost to Democrat James Buchanan in the general election, Lincoln earned credit for his service on behalf of the Republicans.

He redeemed some of that credit in 1858 when the Illinois Republicans nominated him for the Senate against Stephen Douglas. Lincoln understood that he needed to capture the attention of the public, and in accepting the Senate nomination he uttered a chilling prophecy. "A house divided against itself cannot stand," he said. "I believe that this government cannot endure permanently half-slave and half-free. . . . It will become all one thing or all the other. Either the opponents of slavery will arrest the further spread of it, and place it where the public mind shall rest in the belief that it is in the course of ultimate extinction; or its advocates will push it forward till it shall become alike lawful in all the states, old as well as new, North as well as South."

Lincoln's shocking prediction brought him the notice he sought, and it compelled Douglas to accept Lincoln's challenge to a series of debates on the Kansas-Nebraska Act, the Dred Scott decision and related aspects of the sectional struggle. During the late summer and early autumn of 1858 Lincoln and Douglas toured Illinois, with Douglas defending his record of compromise over slavery and Lincoln assailing that record as capitulation to the slave tyranny. "Henry Clay once said of a class of men who would repress all tendencies to liberty and ultimate emancipation, that they must, if they would do this, go back to the era of our independence and muzzle the cannon which thunders its annual joyous return," Lincoln told an audience in Ottawa, Illinois. "They must blow out the moral lights around us. They must penetrate the human soul and eradicate there the love of liberty. And then, and not till then, could they perpetuate slavery in this country. To my thinking, Judge Douglas is, by his example and vast influence, doing that very thing."

Louisa Boggs felt sorry for Grant. "It was a hard situation for him," she remembered. "He was a northern man married to a southern, slave owning family. Colonel Dent openly despised him. All the family said 'poor Julia' when they spoke of Mrs. Grant. . . . Everybody thought Captain Grant a poor match for Miss Dent."

Louisa Boggs considered Grant a decent soul who was simply out of his element in civilian life. "We thought him a man of ability but in the wrong place. His mind was not on such things as selling real estate. He did clerical work and wrote a good clear hand, but wasn't of much use. He hadn't the push of a business man. His intentions were good, but he hadn't the faculty of keeping affairs in order. Mr. Boggs went east on business, leaving the Captain in charge, and when he returned he found everything upside down. The books were in confusion, the wrong people had been let into houses and the owners were much concerned."

Grant didn't appear to resent the low esteem in which he was held. "He didn't blame us to think poorly of him," Louisa Boggs said. "He thought poorly of himself. I don't think he had any ambition further than to educate and care for his family. His mind was always somewhere else. He said very little unless some war topic came up. If you mentioned Napoleon's battles or the Mexican war or the question of secession, he was glib enough." Grant's knowledge of his ineptitude at the business of life shaped his emotions, she believed. "He seemed to me to be much depressed. Yes, he was a sad man. I never heard him laugh out loud. He would smile, and he was not a gloomy man, but he was a sad man."

He grew sadder as he realized that the partnership with Boggs wouldn't work. He couldn't object when Boggs cut him loose; there was scarcely enough business for one partner, let alone two.

He applied for a job as county engineer. His army background, even if in infantry, gave his application a certain plausibility, but the decision rested with the county board of commissioners, who took other considerations into account. His brief residence in St. Louis told against him; he lacked the friendly connections that often facilitated public appointments. And though he kept out of partisan politics, he had voted for James Buchanan in 1856. "It was evident to my mind that the election of a Republican President in 1856 meant the secession of all the Slave States, and rebellion," he explained afterward. "Under these circumstances I preferred the success of a candidate whose election would prevent or postpone secession, to seeing the country plunged into a war the end of which no man could foretell." His preference for Buchanan was known, voting being a public act in those days, and it pleased the two Democrats on the county board, but the three Republicans—or Free-Soilers, as they were still called in Missouri—were less happy.

"Should your honorable body see proper to give me the appointment," he wrote the board as part of his application, "I pledge myself to give the office my entire attention and shall hope to give general satisfaction." He produced references, including Joseph Reynolds, a West Point classmate who currently taught mechanics and engineering at Washington University in St. Louis. "He always maintained a high standing, and graduated with great credit, especially in mathematics, mechanics, and engineering," Reynolds exaggerated of Grant. "From my personal knowledge of his capacity and acquirements as well as of his strict integrity and unremitting industry I consider him in an eminent degree qualified for the office of County Engineer."

Grant didn't get the job. "The question has at length been settled, and I am sorry to say, adversely to me," he wrote his father in September. "The two Democratic Commissioners voted for me and the Freesoilers against me. . . . The Free Soil party felt themselves bound to provide for one of their own party."

His failure left him at a loss regarding his future. "What I shall now go at I have not determined," he told his father. He had swapped the Hardscrabble farmhouse for the house in St. Louis, a lot and a $3,000 note; these gave him some hope. "If I could get the $3,000 note cashed . . . I could put up with the proceeds two houses that would pay me, at least, $40 per month rent." He and Julia had pared their expenses sufficiently that this would cover much of them. "A very modest salary will support me."

But nothing turned up. "I am still unemployed," he wrote his younger brother Simpson four weeks later. Yet he did have one prospect, in the St. Louis customhouse. "My name has been forwarded for the appointment of Superintendent, which if I do not get will not probably be filled at all. In that case there is a vacant desk which I may get that pays $1200 per annum." He landed the desk job—a clerkship—but it lasted only a month, until his patron suddenly died.

His pitiful savings dwindled. Simpson, who lived in Galena, brought him a horse to sell; Grant let a potential buyer take the horse on a trial basis. "I have seen neither man nor horse," he had to report to Simpson a week later. He and Julia moved into a cheaper house. "It is much more pleasant than where we lived when you were here," he told Simpson unconvincingly.

Grant's descent was painful to witness, not least because his family fell with him. "They were very poor in money and in clothes and furniture," Louisa Boggs recalled. "They always had enough to eat, but Mrs. Grant had to dress very plainly. I remember once someone asked her to go downtown shopping and she said, 'I can't do it. I have no shoes fit to wear on the street.'"

PART TWO

THE RAGE OF ACHILLES

"Sing, goddess, the rage of Achilles . . ."

12

JOHN BROWN LEFT KANSAS AFTER A NEW GOVERNOR, JOHN GEARY, brokered a truce between the warring parties in the territory. Increasingly Brown believed that freedom for the slaves must come by the blood of their masters; a peaceful Kansas might serve the purpose of its inhabitants but would do nothing for the larger struggle of which Kansas had been a part. When other abolitionists sent petitions to Congress and sponsored lectures and symposia, Brown couldn't contain his scorn. "Talk! talk! talk! That will never free the slaves. What is needed is action—action!"

Brown's call for action shamed certain abolitionists who realized how helpless politics and the law had become to ameliorate the condition of the slaves. Several put their money at Brown's disposal; these "secret six" included individuals eminently respectable but for a willingness to foment revolution, which was what Brown now proposed. He plotted an attack on the federal arsenal at Harpers Ferry in western Virginia, with the goal of distributing the captured weapons to slaves who would use them against their masters.

Frederick Douglass tried to talk Brown out of the endeavor. Douglass, an escaped slave whose personal journey galvanized the abolitionist movement even as it steeled the slaveholders to foil potential imitators, thought the raid on Harpers Ferry would accomplish no good and much bad, beginning with the deaths of the raiders. "You will never get out alive," he warned Brown.

Brown dismissed the warning as cowardly and defeatist. "Remember the trumpets of Jericho!" he told Douglass. "Harpers Ferry will be mine. The news of its capture will be the trumpet blast that will rally slaves to my standard from miles around. Join me, Frederick; together we will bring slavery down!"

"Not this way," Douglass said. "It is you and your men who will be surrounded. Nothing will be easier for the local militia than to cut off your escape routes. And when you are captured or killed it will be worse for those in bondage than it was before."

But Brown was beyond discouragement and almost beyond reason. He assumed a false identity and rented a farm near Harpers Ferry, where he gathered and drilled a cadre of misfits and fanatics devoted to him and his cause. On the night of October 16, 1859, they slipped into Harpers Ferry and subdued the single guard on duty. Brown dispatched several of his men to spread the word among slaves in the surrounding district that the war of their liberation had begun and arms awaited them in Harpers Ferry. Others snatched hostages as defense against the inevitable counterattack.

The slaves knew better than Brown. Those who got the word wanted nothing to do with this crazy man, who clearly valued his life less than they did theirs. As a result Brown and his band were left to face the counterattack alone. Militia units from Virginia and Maryland arrived first, laying siege to the armory and killing eight of Brown's men. Federal troops reached the town on the evening after the initial attack. Colonel Robert E. Lee led a company of marines, assisted by Lieutenant J. E. B. Stuart. Lee had superintended West Point after the Mexican War, then fought Indians in Texas before returning east to manage a family plantation across the Potomac from Washington. The news of the attack on Harpers Ferry prompted James Buchanan's secretary of war, John Flood, to summon Lee back into service. "Reached Harpers Ferry at 11 p.m.," Lee wrote in his journal. "Posted marines in the United States Armory. Waited until daylight, as a number of citizens were held as hostages, whose lives were threatened. Tuesday about sunrise, with twelve marines, under Lieutenant Green, broke in the door of the engine house, secured the insurgents, and relieved the prisoners unhurt. All the insurgents killed or mortally wounded, but four, John Brown, Stevens, Coppie, and Shields."

Brown and the other survivors were tried and convicted of treason against Virginia, a capital crime. At his sentencing Brown appealed to a higher court. "I see a book kissed, which I suppose to be the Bible, or at least the New Testament, which teaches me that all things whatsoever

I would that men should do to me, I should do to them," he said. "It teaches me further to remember them that are in bonds, as bound with them. I endeavored to act up to that instruction. I say I am yet too young to understand that God is any respecter of persons. I believe that to have interfered as I have done in behalf of His despised poor is no wrong, but right. Now, if it is deemed necessary that I should forfeit my life for the furtherance of the ends of justice, and mingle my blood with the blood of millions in this slave country whose rights are disregarded by wicked, cruel, and unjust enactments, I say let it be done."

Brown's valedictory justification was published in all the Northern papers. It sent guilty chills through those abolitionists who thought more should be done on behalf of the slaves. Church bells tolled the execution of the martyr to the cause of freedom and justice. Albany fired a hundred-gun salute in Brown's honor; Akron declared a day of mourning; public prayers were offered in Syracuse, Rochester and New York City. A meeting in Cleveland resolved: "The irrepressible conflict is upon us, and it will never end until Freedom or slavery go to the wall." William Lloyd Garrison, a heretofore nonviolent abolitionist, proclaimed to a large crowd in Boston: "Success to every slave insurrection at the South."

As Southerners read of the celebrations in the North, many abandoned hope for a future in the Union. A Baltimore paper called "preposterous" the idea "that the South can afford to live under a Government the majority of whose subjects or citizens regard John Brown as a martyr and a Christian hero rather than a murderer and robber." A North Carolinian who professed to have been a "fervid Union man" said the reaction to John Brown's raid had changed his mind. "I am willing to take the chances of every possible evil that may arise from disunion sooner than submit any longer to northern insolence and northern outrage."

By early 1860 Grant was desperate. His appeals to his father had produced disapproval, rejection and then cold silence. But at Julia's urging he appealed once more. He gathered what little cash he could and bought a train ticket to Kentucky. "I arrived here at half past 11 with a head ache and feeling bad generally," he wrote her from Covington. A wreck on the track, which had delayed his arrival, seemed ominous. His trip of hundreds of miles ended with hesitation at his father's very threshold. "As I was walking up the street home, I saw him turn down another street not more than half a square ahead of me, but I supposed he was just going down town for a few minutes and would be back home for dinner." Grant couldn't get himself to call out, even to say hello. He went into the house, where his mother explained that Jesse had just left on an out-of-town trip. "I shall have to remain until his return," he told Julia. He didn't relish the wait. "My head is nearly bursting with pain."

The pain had diminished but not the embarrassment by the time Jesse returned two days later. Once more Grant had to acknowledge his ineptitude at making an independent living. Previously he had asked for help on his own terms; now he had to accept help on his father's terms. Jesse's leather store in Galena was operated by Grant's younger brothers, Simpson and Orvil; Grant could go to work for them. He would start as a salaried employee. Following a successful probation he might hope to become a profit-sharing partner.

Julia was relieved to learn of the arrangement. She didn't like leaving Missouri, which meant, among other things, having to do without her servants—that is, her slaves. Grant had already emancipated the one slave he personally owned, upon moving from the Dent farm to St. Louis. He might have sold the man, William Jones, and certainly could have used the money, but his conscience told him not to. So instead he let Jones try to find his way in the world, as Grant himself was trying. Julia had lived with slaves her whole life and had a different kind of conscience, as did Frederick Dent. "Papa was not willing they should go with me to Galena, saying the place might not suit us," Julia remembered. "And if I took them they would, of course, be free." But anything was better than slowly starving in St. Louis, and she arranged for her four house slaves to be hired out to masters in Missouri.

She and Grant gathered their children and their modest household possessions and boarded a river steamer for Galena. The April runoff made the Mississippi flow high and fast; the journey against the current took four days. The geographical distance from St. Louis to Galena was almost three hundred miles, the nautical distance twice that and the cultural distance greater still. St. Louis was part of the South, with Southern attitudes toward labor, race, politics, women, children and most other aspects of life. Galena, at the northwestern corner of Illinois, an easy walk from Wisconsin, was part of the North, with corresponding Northern attitudes. The inhabitants of Galena had more than a little Yankee in them, valuing the ambition and diligence Jesse Grant admired and Frederick Dent scorned. Visitors who knew Latin looked immediately for the lead mines that gave the town its name; beyond the mines they discovered a brashly growing economy.

The Grant leather business partook of the growth. It thrived sufficiently to support Simpson and Orvil and their dependents in reasonable comfort. Whether it could also support Grant and his family was unclear, but nobody pressed the issue since Simpson was dying of consumption. Everyone involved understood that Jesse was giving Grant the Galena job in part because Simpson wasn't long for either the world or the business.

Grant worked around the store and traveled about the region the business served: northwestern Illinois, southwestern Wisconsin, southeastern Minnesota, northeastern Iowa. Everyone liked him, and many asked for stories about the Mexican War. He wasn't the pushing type his father had always wanted him to be, but the work matched his talents and temperament better than anything he had tried since leaving the army. "In my new employment I have become pretty conversant and am much pleased with it," he wrote a friend. "I hope to be a partner soon, and am sanguine that a competency at least can be made out of the business."

Others noticed the improvement in his disposition. Orvil's wife, Mary, remembered Grant from the Galena years. "He was a bit shorter than Orvil, more muscular, a sturdily built man," Mary recalled. He had "thrower's forearms," she said, and explained: "In a leather and saddlery business there is always the strongest one who would throw the frozen hides down the chute for them to be cleaned and distributed. The Captain could take a hide which weighed over two hundred pounds and throw it with a fling of his arm, whereas Orvil could not, nor could Simpson." Mary remembered Grant as quiet but apparently at peace with himself. "He smoked a small pipe. He was reflective. He seemed like he was meditating on some project all the time, quiet, a composed man. He didn't laugh so much aloud, but smiled with his eyes."

Julia adjusted to the new surroundings, albeit with effort. Initial attempts at cooking made her long for the servants she had left behind. Mary Grant sent over a girl to help in the kitchen; Julia asked if she knew how to prepare Southern biscuits. The girl, Jennie, confessed she did not, and Julia offered to demonstrate. The biscuits proved inedible. "I told the Captain it was because the flour was not good," Julia recalled. "And then he asked me rather severely (thinking, I presume, that the cook would have done better) if I had ever prepared any before. I really had not. I had only cut out small cakes with my thimble from the dough prepared by black Mammy." The next time Julia let Jennie handle the baking. "We had delicious bread," she related. "The Captain, turning to me, said facetiously, 'I see, Julia, you have come to a good stratum in the flour.'"

Grant's home life was more satisfactory than it had ever been. He ate his meals at his own table, except when he was traveling for the business. He played daily with the children. Jesse, two, received the most attention. "Jess would challenge his father to a wrestling match," Julia recalled. "His father would say, 'I do not feel like fighting, Jess, but I can't stand being hectored in this manner by a man of your size.' Whereupon, being struck on the knees by his opponent's little fists, he would roll on the floor with Jess in his arms and, after a few struggles, place the little fellow firmly on his breast, saying, 'It is not fair to strike when a man is down.' The Captain would take twenty or more punches from the dimpled fists, and so it went on until he thought Jess had had fun enough, when he would cry for quarter, saying, 'I give up. I give up.' Then Jess would proudly step off and help his father to arise."

13

WILLIAM SHERMAN MOVED TO LOUISIANA FOR THE SAME REASON
Grant went to Galena: to take a job. Sherman's bad experience at banking had put him off that profession. "I would as soon try the faro table
as risk the chances of banking," he told his wife. He traveled to Kansas
to become a lawyer but began to wonder about the standards of the
bar when he was admitted to practice on grounds of basic intelligence
alone. "If I turn lawyer, it will be bungle, bungle from Monday to Sunday," he wrote home. "But if it must be, so be it." He stuck with law
long enough to bungle a few cases, then quit. He tried to rejoin the
army, but the army said it didn't require his services.

Sherman was better connected than Grant; his foster father (who was
also his father-in-law) was Thomas Ewing, serially senator from Ohio,
secretary of the interior and secretary of the Treasury. Sherman's connections helped him land a job as superintendent of the state-sponsored
military academy in Alexandria, Louisiana. He liked the academy and
the cadets, but the deepening rift between the sections made his position
politically uncomfortable. His neighbors knew that his younger brother
John was an ardent Republican and a rising star in Congress; many
assumed William shared his views. In fact he didn't, and he urged John
to tamp down passions on slavery. "Avoid the subject as a dirty black one,"
he wrote. He complained that everything in politics was being reduced
to "the nigger question," and he believed this a grave mistake. "I would
not if I could abolish or modify slavery," he wrote his wife's brother. "I
don't know that I would materially change the actual political relation of
master and slave. Negroes in the great numbers that exist here must of
necessity be slaves." The South had legitimate grievances, and as a resi-

dent of the South he was willing to support his neighbors. "If they design to protect themselves against negroes, or abolitionists, I will help." But he drew a sharp line at secession. "If they propose to leave the Union on account of a supposed fact that the northern people are all abolitionists like Giddings and Brown"—Joshua Giddings, a radical Republican who advocated slave rebellion, and John Brown—"then I will stand by Ohio and the Northwest."

Among his Louisiana friends Sherman tried to be diplomatic. Governor Thomas Moore owned a plantation near Alexandria; one evening Moore invited Sherman and several members of the state legislature to dinner. "Colonel Sherman," he said, "you can readily understand that, with your brother the abolitionist candidate for speaker"—of the House of Representatives—"some of our people wonder that you should be here at the head of an important state institution. Now, you are at my table, and I assure you of my confidence. Won't you speak your mind freely on this question of slavery, that so agitates the land? You are under my roof, and, whatever you say, you have my protection."

"Governor Moore," Sherman replied, "you mistake in calling my brother, John Sherman, an abolitionist. We have been separated since childhood, I in the army and he pursuing his profession of law in northern Ohio; and it is possible we may differ in general sentiment, but I deny that he is considered at home an abolitionist; and although he prefers the free institutions under which he lives to those of slavery which prevail here, he would not of himself take from you by law or force any property whatever, even slaves."

Moore solicited Sherman's own views on slavery. Sherman said Louisianans of the current generation were not responsible for the existence of slavery in the state, having inherited the institution from their forebears. And he distinguished between two classes of slaves: domestic servants and field hands. The former were treated well, probably better than any other slaves on earth. But the condition of the field hands was different and depended on the character of their owners. "Were I a citizen of Louisiana, and a member of the legislature," Sherman said, "I would deem it wise to bring the legal condition of the slaves more near the status of human beings under all Christian and civilized governments. In the first place, in the sale of slaves made by the state, I would forbid the separation of families, letting the father, mother, and children be sold together to one person, instead of each to the highest bidder." He went on to recommend the repeal of the state law forbidding the education of slaves. He told of his experience as a bank manager in California. An army officer from Rapides Parish in Louisiana had brought a slave, Henry Sampson, to San Francisco. Sherman hired Sampson to work for his bank. "At first he could not write or read, and I could only afford to pay him one hundred dollars a month; but he was taught to read and write by Reilley, our bank-teller, when his services became worth two hundred and fifty dollars a month, which enabled him to buy his own freedom and that of his brother and family."

The governor and the others listened carefully. When Sherman finished, one of the other guests suddenly struck the table with his fist, rattling the china and silver. "By God, he is right!" the guest declared. But several present rejected Sherman's counsel, and the conversation continued for an hour, with the Louisianans doing most of the talking. "I was glad to be thus relieved," Sherman remarked later, "because at the time all men in Louisiana were dreadfully excited on questions affecting their slaves, who constituted the bulk of their wealth, and without whom they honestly believed that sugar, cotton, and rice could not possibly be cultivated."

The excitement escalated during the course of 1860. The Republicans surprised the Democrats and many of themselves by nominating Abraham Lincoln over William Seward, who was much more accomplished and better known in the country at large. Yet it was precisely Seward's reputation that worried some of the Republican strategists, for the New York senator was commonly associated with the radical wing of the party and tended to frighten voters less committed to the anti-slavery cause. Lincoln's views were vaguer. His campaign against Stephen Douglas had failed to win him a Senate seat, but the effort brought him to the attention of the national party. His supporters arranged an invitation from New York's Cooper Union to deliver a lecture in February 1860. His appearance initially disconcerted some who had thought they might like him. "When Lincoln rose to speak, I was greatly disappointed," an audience member recounted. "He was tall, tall—oh, how tall, and so angular and awkward that I had, for an instant, a feeling of pity for so ungainly a man. His clothes were black and ill-fitting, badly wrinkled, as if they had been jammed carelessly into a small trunk. His bushy head, with the stiff black hair thrown back, was balanced on a long and lean headstalk, and when he raised his hands in an opening gesture,

I noticed that they were very large. He began in a low tone of voice, as if he were used to speaking outdoors, and was afraid of speaking too loud. He said, 'Mr. *Cheerman*,' instead of 'Mr. Chairman,' and employed many other words with an old-fashioned pronunciation. I said to myself: 'Old fellow, you won't do; it's all very well for the wild West, but this will never go down in New York.'"

As Lincoln warmed to his subject, however, a change came over him. "He straightened up, made regular and graceful gestures," the audience member recalled. "His face lighted as with an inward fire; the whole man was transfigured. I forgot his clothes, his personal appearance, and his individual peculiarities. Presently, forgetting myself, I was on my feet with the rest, yelling like a wild Indian, cheering this wonderful man. In the close parts of his argument, you could hear the gentle sizzling of the gas burners. When he reached a climax, the thunders of applause were terrific. It was a great speech. When I came out of the hall, my face glowing with excitement and my frame all a-quiver, a friend, with his eyes aglow, asked me what I thought of Abe Lincoln, the rail-splitter. I said, 'He's the greatest man since St. Paul.'"

Not everyone had such a conversion that night, but Lincoln's New York debut convinced the party leaders they could elect him. They calculated the arithmetic of the electoral college and concluded that he needn't carry a single Southern state, so thoroughly did the North and its electors outnumber the South. Lincoln might scare Southern slaveholders, who hadn't forgotten the prediction of his house-divided speech, but if he held the ardent antislavery vote in the North and enticed some moderates, he would be the next president.

The campaign unfolded according to plan. The Republicans nominated Lincoln on the third ballot at their Chicago convention in May 1860. Hannibal Hamlin of Maine balanced the ticket east to west. The party platform opposed slavery in the territories but said nothing about its existence in the Southern states.

The Democrats ensured Lincoln's victory by falling apart. Stephen Douglas claimed the greatest support in the party, but the Democrats' requirement that a candidate receive two-thirds of the delegates prevented their convention, meeting at Baltimore, from putting Douglas over the top. Southern zealots rejected Douglas's popular sovereignty scheme, insisting that slavery be the law in every territory regardless of the wishes of the inhabitants. The fire-eaters stormed out of Baltimore

and reconvened in Richmond, where they nominated John C. Breckinridge of Kentucky. The Baltimore rump proceeded with Douglas.

A fourth candidate in the contest was John Bell of Tennessee,
nominated on the Constitutional Union ticket by a coalition of remnant Whigs and Union-minded Southerners. Bell's supporters sought
a middle ground between the Southern Democrats and the Northern
Republicans, contending that the former were dangerous to the Union
for threatening secession, the latter for giving the former a pretext for
their threats.

Lincoln spent the general election campaign at home in Springfield
while Republican speakers rallied Northern voters on his behalf. The
party ignored the South. Douglas took the then-unusual step of mounting a traveling campaign, but his peripatetic pleas for Democratic unity
fell on deaf Southern ears. Lincoln received fewer than four votes in ten
in the popular balloting, yet these were sufficiently concentrated—he
carried every Northern state, plus California and Oregon—to earn him a
solid majority of the electors.

"Since leaving St. Louis I have become pretty well initiated into the
leather business and like it well," Grant wrote an acquaintance amid the
campaign. "Our business here"—in Galena—"is prosperous, and I have
every reason to hope, in a few years, to be entirely above the frowns of
the world, pecuniarily." Grant followed the electioneering with interest, although he hadn't lived in Galena long enough to vote there. He
remained a Democrat and favored Douglas but recognized that the
rift among the Democrats had doomed the Douglas candidacy. Yet he
believed that a loss might not be all to the bad. "I think the Democratic
party want a little purifying and nothing will do it so effectually as a
defeat." Still, he couldn't get excited about such a result. "I don't like to
see a Republican beat the party."

Grant later professed relief at not having been able to vote in 1860.
"My pledges would have compelled me to vote for Stephen A. Douglas,
who had no possible chance of election," he said. He added, "The contest
was really between Mr. Breckinridge and Mr. Lincoln, between minority rule and rule by the majority. I wanted, as between these candidates,
to see Mr. Lincoln elected."

This may have been so, but like many others in America, and especially those who lived near the border between slavery and freedom, Grant in 1860 was deeply ambivalent about Lincoln. Grant didn't like slavery, but he had married into a family of slaveholders and consequently become a slaveholder himself. And his dislike of slavery didn't equal his dread of the disruption to the Union that Lincoln's election seemed to portend. Grant had voted for Buchanan in 1856 to forestall secession and buy time for emotions to ease, yet the emotions had only intensified. Grant would have voted for Douglas in 1860, again in hopes that the storm would pass.

The election of Lincoln unleashed the furies. South Carolina had been the center of secessionist agitation for decades, notably nullifying what South Carolinians called the "tariff of abominations" of 1828 and vowing to bolt the Union if Andrew Jackson tried to enforce it. The Palmetto State men had ultimately backed down, but in the summer and early autumn of 1860 they again took the secessionist lead, warning of grave consequences in the event Lincoln carried the election. One South Carolina politician spoke for many in his state in declaring: "Should a Black Republican President be elected it is the necessary sequence of reason that a majority of the people of the country have endorsed his principles and raised a banner on which is enscribed: death to the institutions of the South. In that event it is my solemn judgment we can no longer remain in the same confederacy." The arithmetic of the campaign became clear to South Carolinians, as to the rest of the country, weeks before the election, and by the time Lincoln secured his victory, sentiment in the state had congealed around the required response. A visitor to Charleston remarked that everyone he met favored secession over submitting to the new administration. "The young men ardently desire disunion," the visitor said. "So do old men, and wise men. The tradespeople wish it, entertaining a consciousness of its disastrous entailment upon their business. The clergy add their counsels on the same side. Reliable men are freely offering their property to maintain secession."

When the tally of electors officially confirmed Lincoln's victory, the South Carolinians moved at once. A special convention on December 20 unanimously approved an ordinance repealing the state's ratification of the Constitution. "The union now subsisting between South Carolina and other States, under the name of the 'United States of America,' is hereby dissolved," the ordinance declared.

"How do you feel on the subject of secession in St. Louis?" Grant wrote a business acquaintance in that city as the South Carolinians were deciding on disunion. "The present troubles must affect business in your trade greatly." Galena had shared in the excitement of the fall campaign, with supporters of Douglas and Lincoln filling the streets with torchlight and partisan noise, but since the election the town had fallen nervously quiet. "With us the only difference experienced as yet is the difficulty of obtaining southern exchange."

Grant didn't know what to make of the talk of secession. "It is hard to realize that a State or States should commit so suicidal an act as to secede from the Union," he remarked. "Though from all the reports I have no doubt but that at least five of them will do it. And then, with the present granny of an executive"—the lame duck Buchanan, who denied the right of secession but disavowed any authority to prevent it—"some foolish policy will doubtless be pursued which will give the seceding States the support and sympathy of the southern states that don't go out."

Grant read of troubles in Missouri, where a minority of secessionists clamored for their state to join the other Union-leavers. From the vantage of Galena it looked as though they might have their way. Grant extrapolated from Missouri to the rest of the slave South: "It does seem as if just a few men have produced all the present difficulty."

*A*braham Lincoln thought so too. Lincoln got the good news of his election amid the bad news that the South was taking it so ill. He wondered whether the former outweighed the latter. "I declare to you this morning," he told a visitor, "that for personal considerations I would rather have a full term in the Senate—a place in which I would feel more consciously able to discharge the duties, and where there is more chance to make a reputation, and less danger of losing it—than four years of the presidency."

The presidency would be his, though, and he had to make the best of it. But until it actually *was* his, until he was inaugurated in March 1861, his hands were largely tied. So was his tongue, although that was his own doing rather than the Constitution's. Friends of the Union implored him to assure the South he meant that region no harm. A Kentucky editor, alarmed that the secessionists would carry away the Bluegrass State, urged Lincoln to "take from the disunionists every excuse or pretext for treason."

"Would it do any good?" Lincoln responded dubiously. "If I were to labor a month, I could not express my conservative views and intentions more clearly and strongly than they are expressed in our platform and in my many speeches already in print and before the public. . . . For the good men of the South—and I regard the majority of them as such—I have no objection to repeat seventy and seven times. But I have *bad* men also to deal with, both North and South—men who are eager for something new upon which to base new misrepresentation." These bad men would take anything he said and turn it against him. "I intend keeping my eye upon these gentlemen, and to not unnecessarily put any weapons in their hands."

Yet as he pondered the matter and received further entreaties to clarify his aims, he consented to tip his hand a little. He wrote a passage for Lyman Trumbull, an Illinois Republican and close ally, to insert in a speech. "Each and all of the States will be left in as complete control of their own affairs respectively, and at as perfect liberty to choose, and employ, their own means of protecting property and preserving peace and order within their respective limits as they have ever been under any administration," Lincoln said through Trumbull. "Those who have voted for Mr. Lincoln have expected, and still expect, this, and they would not have voted for him had they expected otherwise."

The reaction made Lincoln think he should have kept quiet. Northern abolitionists called his indirect statement a surrender to slavery; Southern radicals condemned it as a declaration of war. "This is just as I expected," Lincoln said, "and just what would happen with any speech I could make. These political fiends are not half sick enough yet. Party malice and not public good possesses them entirely." Quoting Scripture, he declared: "They seek a sign, and no sign shall be given them."

Lincoln took modest comfort from the attitude of Alexander Stephens, who told his fellow Georgians he didn't think Lincoln would do anything to endanger the South or slavery. Besides, Stephens explained to the Georgia legislature, even if Lincoln wanted to, he lacked the ability. "The President of the United States is no emperor, no dictator. He can do nothing unless he is backed by power in Congress. The House of Representatives is largely in the majority against him. In the Senate he will also be powerless." Lincoln read of Stephens's speech and requested a copy. Stephens responded that he had none to send, but he appreciated the interest and wished Lincoln well. "The country is certainly in great peril," he said, "and no man ever had heavier or greater responsibilities resting upon him than you have in this present momentous crisis."

Lincoln extended the correspondence. "Do the people in the South really entertain fears that a Republican administration would, directly or indirectly, interfere with their slaves, or with them about their slaves?" he asked Stephens. "If they do, I wish to reassure you, as once a friend and still, I hope, not an enemy, that there is no cause for such fears. The South would be in no more danger in this respect than it was in the days of Washington." Lincoln acknowledged, however, that the issue ran deeper than politics and economics. "You think slavery is right and ought to be extended, while we think it is wrong and ought to be restricted. That, I suppose, is the rub."

It remained the rub as the crisis unfolded. "The political horizon looks dark and lowering," Lincoln observed the day after news of South Carolina's secession ordinance arrived in Springfield. Yet he promised his supporters he wouldn't budge from the Republican platform. "Let there be no compromise on the question of extending slavery," he told Lyman Trumbull. "If there be, all our labor is lost, and ere long must be done again. The dangerous ground—that into which some of our friends have a hankering to run—is popular sovereignty. Have none of it. Stand firm. The tug has to come, and better now than any time hereafter." To another ally, Republican representative Elihu Washburne of Illinois, Lincoln wrote, "Hold firm, as with a chain of steel."

Lincoln began to realize he had underestimated the secessionists. Because Southern hotheads had been threatening to secede for decades and nothing had come of their threats, Lincoln initially supposed not much would come now. "They won't give up the offices," he predicted, referring to the federal postmasterships and customs agencies across the South. "Were it believed that vacant places could be had at the North Pole, the road there would be lined with dead Virginians." But as one state after another followed South Carolina's lead, Lincoln was forced to admit that secession was more than a passion of a minority and the moment.

And so he answered a call from Thurlow Weed, a New York Republican boss whose support had been crucial to his election, for a statement. Weed had gathered Northern governors in New York to coordinate their response to the South; what could the president-elect tell them of his views regarding secession?

"My opinion," Lincoln responded, "is that no state can, in any way lawfully, get out of the Union without the consent of the others, and that it is the duty of the President, and other government functionaries, to run the machine as it is."

Lincoln cautiously elaborated this view as his inauguration neared. He left Springfield for Washington in February 1861, making a circuitous journey across much of the North. En route he learned that seven Southern states—South Carolina, Mississippi, Florida, Alabama, Georgia, Louisiana and Texas—had sent delegates to a provisional congress of the "Confederate States of America," meeting in Montgomery, Alabama. The delegates elected Jefferson Davis president and inaugurated him a few days later. Lincoln read accounts from across the South that state militias were seizing federal forts. At each of his many train stops he was asked to speak; at most of them he mumbled inconsequentialities or begged off entirely.

But at Indianapolis he asserted that the South wouldn't get away with seizing the property of the nation. Southerners were warning against coercion by the federal government or an invasion of the South by federal troops; Lincoln responded with a question that connoted a threat: "If the United States should merely hold and retake its own forts, collect duties or withhold the mails, where they were habitually violated, would any or all of these things be invasion or coercion?"

The last leg of Lincoln's journey revealed that the secession dispute could get dangerously personal. The railroad company that carried Lincoln east hired a detective named Allan Pinkerton to prevent any trouble;

Pinkerton asserted that proslavery thugs in Baltimore were planning to waylay the president-elect. Lincoln took the assertion seriously enough to revise his itinerary. He slipped through Baltimore in the dead of night, cloaked as an invalid. He reached Washington safe but slightly embarrassed, and his embarrassment grew when Southern and other critics called him a coward.

On March 4 he spoke for the first time as president. The capital was crowded and edgy; Grant's old commander, Winfield Scott, positioned federal troops conspicuously about the city. Republican "Wide Awakes"—paramilitary volunteers marked by distinctive gaudy uniforms—watched suspicious-looking persons warily. Police pounced on anyone who appeared even mildly disposed toward disruption.

Lincoln emerged from the Capitol onto the east portico. Parts of the audience began to applaud, but his grim demeanor put them off. All strained to hear as he began to speak. He professed anew his peaceful intentions toward the South: "I have no purpose, directly or indirectly, to interfere with the institution of slavery in the States where it exists. I believe I have no lawful right to do so, and I have no inclination to do so." He wished he could report comparable tolerance in the South, but sadly the opposite obtained. "A disruption of the Federal Union, heretofore only menaced, is now formidably attempted." But it would not succeed. "The Union of these States is perpetual." The arguments for secession were specious on their face. "No government proper ever had a provision in its organic law for its own termination." Secession was constitutionally impossible. "No State, upon its own mere motion, can lawfully get out of the Union. . . . The Union is unbroken." And it would remain unbroken. "To the extent of my ability I shall take care, as the Constitution itself expressly enjoins upon me, that the laws of the Union be faithfully executed in all of the States."

The secessionists had pushed the country to the brink of armed conflict, and though Lincoln didn't welcome conflict, neither would he back down from it. "In *your* hands, my dissatisfied fellow-countrymen, and not in *mine*, is the momentous issue of civil war," he said. "The Government will not assail *you*. You can have no conflict without being yourselves the aggressors. *You* have no oath registered in Heaven to destroy the Government, while I shall have the most solemn one to 'preserve, protect, and defend it.'"

Lincoln let his listeners absorb his resolve before he closed on a conciliatory note. "We are not enemies, but friends. We must not be enemies. Though passion may have strained, it must not break our bonds of affection. The mystic chords of memory, stretching from every battlefield and patriot grave to every living heart and hearthstone all over this broad land, will yet swell the chorus of the Union, when again touched, as surely they will be, by the better angels of our nature."

15

Like Lincoln, Grant at first failed to appreciate the seriousness of the secession crisis. So did most of those he spoke to in
Galena and on his business travels around the region. "It was generally believed that there would be a flurry; that some of the extreme
Southern States would go so far as to pass ordinances of secession," he
recalled. "But the common impression was that this step was so plainly
suicidal for the South that the movement would not spread over much
of the territory and would not last long."

Grant had paid little attention to political theory, but he, with the
rest of America, received a crash course in constitutionalism that winter.
And he developed a fairly sophisticated view of what America's founding
framework allowed and required. "Doubtless the founders of our government, the majority of them at least, regarded the confederation of the
colonies as an experiment," he later asserted. "Each colony considered
itself a separate government; that the confederation was for mutual protection against a foreign foe, and the prevention of strife and war among
themselves. If there had been a desire on the part of any single State to
withdraw from the compact at any time while the number of States was
limited to the original thirteen, I do not suppose there would have been
any to contest the right, no matter how much the determination might
have been regretted." But things grew more complicated after the Constitution of 1787 supplanted the Articles of Confederation and as the
number of states increased. "If the right of any one State to withdraw
continued to exist at all after the ratification of the Constitution, it certainly ceased to exist on the formation of new States, at least so far as the
new States themselves were concerned. It was never possessed at all by

Florida or the States west of the Mississippi, all of which were purchased by the treasury of the entire nation." Texas was purchased, in addition, by American blood in the war with Mexico. "It would have been ingratitude and injustice of the most flagrant sort for this State to withdraw from the Union after all that had been spent and done to introduce her."

Secessionists wrapped themselves in the Constitution, claiming that it was a revocable compact among states. Defenders of the Union cited the Constitution in asserting federal supremacy. Grant considered the arguments of both sides incomplete—and irrelevant. "The fact is, the Constitution did not apply to any such contingency as the one existing from 1861 to 1865," he said. "Its framers never dreamed of such a contingency occurring." Grant acknowledged that if they *had* foreseen the sectional crisis, they might well have sided with the South. "The probabilities are they would have sanctioned the right of a State or States to withdraw rather than that there should be war between brothers." But the framers' opinions didn't matter. "It is preposterous to suppose that the people of one generation can lay down the best and only rules of government for all who are to come after them, and under unforeseen contingencies. . . . The fathers would have been the first to declare that their prerogatives were not irrevocable."

By 1860 the Union had become, to all intents and purposes, indivisible, Grant said. "Secession was illogical as well as impracticable; it was revolution." He allowed the legitimacy of revolution under certain circumstances. "When people are oppressed by their government, it is a natural right they enjoy to relieve themselves of the oppression, if they are strong enough, either by withdrawal from it or by overthrowing it and substituting a government more acceptable." Grant didn't consider the South oppressed in 1860, but even if it had been, it still had to fight its revolution. "Any people or part of a people who resort to this remedy stake their lives, their property, and every claim for protection given by citizenship, on the issue. Victory, or the conditions imposed by the conqueror, must be the result."

The test of strength began, predictably, in South Carolina. Fort Sumter had long guarded the port of Charleston against enemy attack, but little guarded Fort Sumter from Charleston. Major Robert Anderson commanded the federal garrison there; on the day of Lincoln's inauguration Anderson informed Winfield Scott that the fort's provisions would last no more than six weeks. By the end of that time, if the fort was not resupplied, he must surrender the place.

Scott forwarded Anderson's message to Lincoln, who asked Scott's expert advice on the feasibility of resupply. Scott said it would require 25,000 soldiers and a fleet of warships and transports. Since the army lacked the men and the navy the ships, Congress would have to make a special appropriation. Outfitting the expedition would take six to eight months. In other words, Anderson was on his own.

Lincoln had no reason to doubt Scott's judgment, although some others close to the president thought the general unduly pessimistic. Montgomery Blair, a West Pointer who had left the army for the law and became Lincoln's postmaster general, suggested that a night landing might keep Anderson's garrison viable.

William Seward advocated another approach. Seward had received the State Department as his consolation prize for losing the Republican nomination to Lincoln, but he hadn't yet reconciled himself to being merely first adviser. In early April he wrote an extraordinary memorandum suggesting a special role for himself. "We are at the end of a month's administration and yet without a policy either domestic or foreign," Seward chided Lincoln. "Further delay to adopt and prosecute our policies for both domestic and foreign affairs would not only bring scandal on the Administration, but danger upon the country." Seward thought the president had foolishly allowed the secessionists to frame the debate, and he urged a new course. "We must *change the question before the Public from one upon Slavery, or about Slavery*, for a question upon *Union or Disunion*. In other words, from what would be regarded as a Party question to one of *Patriotism* or *Union*." Seward recommended evacuating Fort Sumter, which he considered indefensible, but reinforcing Fort Pickens in Florida and other positions in the South still in Union hands. This would ease the immediate crisis. It would also allow the administration to do something quite audacious: to foment war with Spain, France and perhaps Britain. A pretext could be found, as one had been found by James Polk against Mexico. The result would be similar: an outpouring of patriotism by the American people, North and South, against a foreign foe. Seward saved the best part of his recommendation—best for *him*, at any rate—for the last. "Whatever policy we adopt, there must be an energetic prosecution of it. For this purpose it must be somebody's business to pursue and direct it incessantly. Either the President must do it himself, and be all the while active in it, or devolve it on some member of his Cabinet. . . . It is not in my especial province, but I neither seek to evade nor assume responsibility."

Seward's proposal tested Lincoln's patience. The president bridled at the assertion that he lacked a policy; he dismissed as madly cynical Seward's suggestion of a deliberate foreign war; he rejected as self-serving and unconstitutional the secretary of state's recommendation of what sounded like a co-presidency. Lincoln drafted a reply summarizing these reactions—and then, in the interest of cabinet comity, refrained from sending it. But he quietly let Seward know that the country had only one president, who didn't need any further such counsel.

Other cabinet members were more circumspect. Most favored bowing to the inevitable and surrendering Fort Sumter. Yet Salmon Chase, the Treasury secretary, joined Montgomery Blair in urging an effort to resupply the fort.

Lincoln had great difficulty deciding. He was no military or naval expert, and he recognized his ignorance. He had a much firmer grasp of politics, but he couldn't tell how the politics of the situation would play out. More than a few Northerners were wishing the South good riddance, and they definitely didn't want to start a war over an indefensible fort in South Carolina. But others were tired of what they considered Southern arrogance and thought the slaveholders needed to be taught a lesson.

No less crucial than the reaction of the North was the reaction of the South—in particular of those Southern states that had not seceded. Virginia wavered; a convention had gathered to discuss secession but hadn't reached a conclusion. Lincoln attempted to shape the outcome; he met secretly with a pro-Union Virginia delegate and apparently offered to swap Fort Sumter for a promise of Virginia's loyalty. "A State for a fort is no bad business," he was later reported to have said. But the Virginians preferred to see how events developed, and the offer came to nothing.

The administration continued to drift. Though Lincoln prepared a relief expedition, his lack of administrative experience revealed itself in confusion and delay, and the ships were slow leaving New York. The supplies at Sumter dwindled, all but compelling Anderson to capitulate.

Lincoln lost hope of holding the fort yet wished to make the secessionists strike first. On April 12, shortly after the relief ships arrived off Charleston but before they could attempt a landing, the Confederate battery opposite the fort commenced a bombardment. Anderson and his garrison stood the shelling for a day and a half, then surrendered.

Lincoln told the country what the fateful events in South Carolina meant. The attack on Fort Sumter constituted rebellion, he said, which must be opposed by force. The president called on the states to raise militia troops to the number of 75,000. "I appeal to all loyal citizens to favor, facilitate and aid this effort to maintain the honor, the integrity, and the existence of our National Union and the perpetuity of popular government."

Grant had been drifting, too, albeit less anxiously than Lincoln. Secession was the president's problem, not Grant's. He read the papers but out of curiosity rather than involvement. He spent his days in the leather trade and his evenings with Julia and the children. He let the world turn itself.

The onset of war abruptly terminated his disengagement. The news of the attack on Sumter electrified Galena. A large meeting was held at the courthouse; speakers vied to best one another in their devotion to the Union. Elihu Washburne, Galena's congressman, offered several resolutions affirming the community's faith in the Constitution and the Union, concluding with: "We solemnly resolve that, having lived under the Stars and Stripes, by the blessing of God we propose to die under them!" John Rawlins, an attorney who represented the Grant family's leather business, reviewed at length the transgressions of the South and the patience of the North. For three-quarters of an hour he spoke, to increasing cheers and applause from the gathered citizenry, which erupted still further at his call to arms: "I have been a Democrat all my life, but this is no longer a question of politics. It is simply country or no country. I have favored every honorable compromise; but the day for compromise is passed. Only one course is left for us. We will stand by the flag of our country, and appeal to the God of battles!"

Grant attended the meeting and shared the mounting excitement. The event brought back memories of the most fulfilling period of his life thus far, when he had fought under the American flag. He knew he had never been good at anything but war, and now that another war had begun, he wouldn't miss it for the world. And *this* war, unlike the Mexican War, was one he could believe in. The Union was a cause to stir the heart of any patriot.

Two days later another meeting took place. The captain of the local militia summoned the meeting to order and nominated Grant to chair the session. "The sole reason, possibly, was that I had been in the army and had seen service," Grant suggested later by way of explanation. "With much embarrassment and some prompting, I made out to announce the object of the meeting"—to enlist a company of volunteers in response to Lincoln's militia call. The company was quickly raised, and Grant was offered the captaincy. To the disappointment and perhaps surprise of the group, he declined. He felt the same urgency they all did, but he remembered enough of his Mexican War experience—in particular the difference between volunteer units and the regular army—to wish to rejoin the latter. He cushioned his refusal by promising to help enlist and train the volunteers.

He shortly thereafter wrote his father-in-law. "In these exciting times we are very anxious to hear from you," he told Frederick Dent. Grant knew that Dent hated Lincoln and the Republicans, but he thought the old man might still love the Union. "Now is the time, particularly in the border slave states, for men to prove their love of country. I know it is hard for men to apparently work with the Republican party, but now all party distinctions should be lost sight of and every true patriot be for maintaining the integrity of the glorious old Stars & Stripes, the Constitution and the Union." Grant blamed the secessionists for the present crisis. "No impartial man can conceal from himself the fact that in all these troubles the South have been the aggressors and the Administration has stood purely on the defensive." The strength of the North grew more evident each day. "The North is responding to the President's call in such manner that the rebels may truly quake. I tell you there is no mistaking the feelings of the people. The Government can call into the field not only 75,000 troops but ten or twenty times 75,000 if it should be necessary."

The latest reports had brought news that Virginia had joined the seceders. Grant wasn't worried, being confident of the North's overwhelming strength. "But for the influence she will have on the other border slave states this is not much to be regretted," he told Dent. Virginia shared with the other seceding states the folly of hastening the doom of slavery, the institution they claimed to cherish. "The North do not want, nor will they want, to interfere with the institution, but they will refuse for all time to give it protection unless the South shall return soon to their allegiance. . . . Then, too, this disturbance will give such an impetus to the production of their staple, cotton, in other parts of the world that they can never recover the control of the market again for that commodity. This will reduce the value of negroes so much that they will never be worth fighting over again."

Grant wrote to his own father describing the course he intended to follow. "We are now in the midst of trying times when everyone must be for or against his country, and show his colors too, by his every act," he said. "Having been educated for such an emergency, at the expense of the Government, I feel that it has upon me superior claims, such claims as no ordinary motives of self-interest can surmount. I do not wish to act hastily or unadvisedly in the matter, and as there are more than enough to respond to the first call of the President, I have not yet offered myself." But he was doing his part nonetheless. "I have promised and am giving all the assistance I can in organizing the company whose services have been accepted from this place. I have promised further to go with them to the state capital and, if I can, be of service to the Governor in organizing his state troops to do so."

Grant owed his job in the leather business to his father, and he wanted his father's permission to leave it. "What I ask now is your approval of the course I am taking," he wrote Jesse. But whether he received permission or not, he would act. "Whatever may have been my political opinions before, I have but one sentiment now. That is, we have a Government and laws and a flag, and they must all be sustained. There are but two parties now, Traitors and Patriots, and I want hereafter to be ranked with the latter."

"On account of the cars not connecting promptly, we did not arrive here until evening yesterday," Grant wrote Julia from Springfield on April 27. He had drilled the Galena company briefly at home and then traveled with them to the capital to oversee their enrollment in one of the Illinois regiments. "Our trip here was a perfect ovation," he recounted. "At every station the whole population seemed to be out to greet the troops. There is such a feeling aroused through the country now as has not been known since the Revolution." Grant's forecast of an oversubscription to Lincoln's summons for volunteers was proving true. "Every company called for in the President's proclamation has been organized, and filled to near double the amount that can be received. In addition to that, every town of 1000 inhabitants and over has from one to four additional companies organized ready to answer the next call that will be made."

Grant delivered the Galena company to its state regiment and prepared to return home. A personal request from the governor stopped him. Grant had never met Richard Yates, although they were staying at the same hotel in Springfield and eating in the same dining room. "The evening I was to quit the capital I left the supper room before the governor and was standing at the front door when he came out," Grant remembered. "He spoke to me, calling me by my old army title 'Captain,' and said he understood that I was about leaving the city." Grant replied that that was correct. Yates asked him to stay overnight and come to the office the next morning. "I complied with his request, and was asked to go into the Adjutant-General's office and render such assistance as I could, the governor saying that my army experience would be of great service there."

Grant was pleased to be noticed, and he quickly set to the task of enrolling the volunteer regiments. He soon discovered that the paperwork was more than he had encountered in the federal army. Briefly he wondered if he was up to the job. "The only place I ever found in my life to put a paper so as to find it again was either a side coat-pocket or the hands of a clerk or secretary more careful than myself," he remarked after another two decades of wrestling with documents. Fortunately he found such a clerk in Springfield, and the enlistments proceeded smoothly.

He was impressed and gratified by the patriotic fervor of the men he mustered. "I am convinced that if the South knew the entire unanimity of the North for the Union and maintenance of law, and how freely men and money are offered to the cause, they would lay down their arms at once in humble submission," he wrote his sister Mary. "There is no disposition to compromise now. Nearly everyone is anxious to see the Government fully tested as to its strength, and see if it is not worth preserving." To his father he described the masses rallying to the flag. "Galena has several more companies organized but only one of them will be able to come in under a new call for ten regiments. Chicago has raised companies enough nearly to fill all the first call. The northern feeling is so fully aroused that they will stop at no expense of money and men to insure the success of their cause." Grant acknowledged that the North had no monopoly on fervor. "I presume the feeling is just as strong on the other side," he told Jesse. But the Southerners would be overwhelmed. "They are infinitely in the minority in resources."

He began to regret that he had not joined the Illinois volunteers. "I should have offered myself for the Colonelcy of one of the regiments," he told his father. Yet the politics of a volunteer army were beyond him. "I find all those places are wanted by politicians who are up to log-rolling." He feared that the North would win before he could find his place. "My own opinion is that this war will be but of short duration," he told Jesse in early May. "A few decisive victories in some of the southern ports will send the secession army howling, and the leaders in the rebellion will flee the country." The result would be lasting. "All the states will then be loyal for a generation to come, negroes will depreciate so rapidly in value that no body will want to own them, and their masters will be the loudest in their declamations against the institution in a political and economic view. The nigger will never disturb this country again."

Events had never moved so rapidly in Grant's life. A month earlier he had been minding the store in Galena, unknown to anyone beyond his modest circle. Now he was an important man in the state, deeply involved in preparing its army for battle. He traveled the length of Illinois, from Freeport in the north to Cairo in the south, recruiting, supervising, issuing orders, signing contracts for supplies and transport. He scarcely had time to tell Julia where he was. "Kiss the children for me," he wrote from Mattoon, in the eastern part of the state. "And accept a dozen for yourself."

*E*vents moved even faster for Robert E. Lee. With the rest of Virginia, Lee watched the secession tide spread from Charleston across the South; with the rest of the officer corps of the U.S. Army, he wondered what role the military would play in the unfolding drama. On April 17 Virginia seceded; on April 18 Lee received a visit from Francis Blair, sent by Lincoln to offer him command of the federal army. The offer came as no surprise; Lee knew of his reputation as the most gifted of the emerging generation of officers. He had decided how he ought to respond to such an invitation as Blair delivered. "After listening to his remarks," he wrote later, "I declined the offer he made me, to take command of the army that was to be brought into the field; stating, as candidly and courteously as I could, that, though opposed to secession and deprecating war, I could take part in no invasion of the Southern States."

Blair left, disappointed, and Lee went straight to the office of Winfield Scott. He told Scott of the offer made to him and of his response. Scott, a Virginian himself, merely nodded gravely. Lee then crossed the Potomac to his home in Arlington, considering the matter further. By the time he entered the house his obligation had become clear. "I concluded that I ought no longer to retain the commission I held in the United States Army." On the second morning subsequent he composed a letter to Scott tendering his resignation. "It would have been presented at once but for the struggle it has cost me to separate myself from a service to which I have devoted the best years of my life, and all the ability I possessed," he explained to Scott. "During the whole of that time—more than a quarter of a century—I have experienced nothing but kindness from my superiors and a most cordial friendship from my comrades." He hoped his career at arms had ended. "Save in the defense of my native State, I never desire again to draw my sword."

Lee's hope may have been sincere, but it was also unrealistic and short-lived. The governor of Virginia, upon learning of Lee's resignation, invited him to Richmond, where the state's secession convention was meeting. The convention requested that Lee take command of Virginia's military forces. Again he wasn't surprised, and he had remarks ready. "Deeply impressed with the solemnity of the occasion on which I appear before you, and profoundly grateful for the honor conferred upon me, I accept the position your partiality has assigned me," he said.

Lee's departure from the army of the United States coincided with Grant's first efforts to get back in. "Having served for fifteen years in the regular army, including four years at West Point, and feeling it the duty of everyone who has been educated at the Government expense to offer their services for the support of that Government, I have the honor, very respectfully, to tender my services, until the close of the war, in such capacity as may be offered," he wrote the adjutant general in Washington. He suggested a colonelcy for himself. "In view of my present age, and length of service, I feel myself competent to command a regiment if the President, in his judgment, should see fit to entrust one to me." He later admitted to diffidence in drafting his letter. "I felt some hesitation in suggesting rank as high as the colonelcy of a regiment, feeling somewhat doubtful whether I would be equal to the position," he recalled. "But I had seen nearly every colonel who had been mustered in from the State of Illinois, and some from Indiana, and felt that if they could command a regiment properly, and with credit, I could also."

The army did not agree. Yet neither did it *dis*agree. Rather it lost Grant's letter, leaving him uncertain as to where his future lay. Confusion didn't affect Grant alone; during the early months of the war confusion was often the prevailing motif as the political and legal boundaries between state and federal action shifted and blurred, along with the personal and emotional frontiers between loyalty and secession. Grant encountered the latter blurring on a visit to St. Louis amid his recruiting duties. He had gone to Bellville, Illinois, to muster a regiment, but when he got there he learned that most of the soldiers were still en route and wouldn't arrive for several days. He employed the opportunity to travel the twenty miles to St. Louis and visit his in-laws. "Your father is in the room, absorbed in his paper," he wrote Julia. "Lewis Sheets"—a family friend—"is fixing a segarita to smoke and Aunt Fanny is setting by me busy with her work. All are well." But they might not stay well. Secession was splitting the Dent family. John Dent, Julia's brother, was an open sympathizer with the South. "I believe he thinks of a colonelcy in the secession army," Grant told Julia. Frederick Dent leaned in the same direction, although less forthrightly. "Your father says he is for the Union but is opposed to having an army to sustain it. He would have a secession force march where they please uninterrupted and is really what I would call a secessionist." Dent's sister, on the other hand, sided with Grant. "Aunt Fanny is strong for the Union."

The division in the Dent household was writ larger across St. Louis. Although a convention called to consider secession for Missouri had voted against such action, the state's South-leaning governor, Claiborne Jackson, evidently hoped to use his control of the Missouri militia to seize the federal arsenal at St. Louis. But a quick-thinking Union army captain in the vicinity, Nathaniel Lyon, with critical support from Francis Blair, the district's Republican congressman, rallied Union loyalists and preempted the blow. Lyon and Blair occupied the arsenal and prepared to march against Camp Jackson, where the governor's secessionist militia had gathered. "I went down to the arsenal in the morning to see the troops start out," Grant recalled. "I had known Lyon for two years at West Point and in the old army afterwards. Blair I knew very well by sight. I had heard him speak in the canvass of 1858, possibly several times, but I had never spoken to him. As the troops marched out of the enclosure around the arsenal, Blair was on his horse outside forming them into line preparatory to their march. I introduced myself to him and had a few moments' conversation and expressed my sympathy with his purpose." Grant was pleased that Blair's swift stroke produced the intended effect. "Camp Jackson surrendered without a fight and the garrison was marched down to the arsenal as prisoners of war."

The victory transformed the mood in the city. "Up to this time the enemies of the government in St. Louis had been bold and defiant, while the Union men were quiet but determined," Grant wrote. "As soon as the news of the capture of Camp Jackson reached the city the condition of affairs was changed." The Unionists gained confidence and began standing up to the secessionists. Grant observed—and got involved in—a confrontation at a downtown building that served as headquarters of the secession party, complete with a rebel flag. "I stepped on a car standing at the corner of 4th and Pine streets, and saw a crowd of people standing quietly in front of the headquarters, who were there for the purpose of hauling down the flag." Behind the Unionists was a crowd of Southern sympathizers. "They too were quiet but filled with suppressed rage, and muttered their resentment at the insult to what they called 'their' flag." One of the latter, a young man, got into the streetcar Grant was riding. "He was in a great state of excitement and used adjectives freely to express his contempt for the Union and for those who had just perpetrated such an outrage upon the rights of a free people. . . . He turned to me saying: 'Things have come to a damned pretty pass when a free people can't choose their own flag. Where I come from, if a man dares to say a word in favor of the Union we hang him to a limb of the first tree we come to.' I replied that 'after all we were not so intolerant in St. Louis as we might be; I had not seen a single rebel hung yet, nor heard of one; there were plenty of them who ought to be, however.' The young man subsided."

The surge of support for the Union made Grant wish more than ever to be under arms. After mustering the last of his regiments at Springfield, he arranged to travel to Kentucky, ostensibly to visit his parents but really to call on George McClellan, who had been promoted to army major general with headquarters at Cincinnati. "I was in hopes that when he saw me he would offer me a position on his staff," Grant explained afterward. But McClellan, likely remembering Grant's drinking troubles in the West, was too busy. "I called on two successive days at his office but failed to see him on either occasion," Grant wrote.

Grant returned to Springfield and discovered that while McClellan and the United States might not think they needed him, Governor Yates and Illinois did. The hastily mustered state regiments included some with officers who knew nothing of military command. A colonel named Simon Goode led one regiment very badly. He had never been to war and never served in an organized army. He brandished three braces of revolvers and a large hunting knife, with which he vowed to skin Jefferson Davis alive. But he boozed as flamboyantly as he walked and talked, and he kept no semblance of military discipline, leaving the conscientious among his men at the mercy of the dissolute and damaging the reputation of the regiment, the militia and the Union cause. The complaints of his men and of the neighbors reached the ears of Yates, who asked around for a replacement. Grant wasn't his first choice, being a relative newcomer to Illinois and lacking the connections that might have rendered his appointment politically valuable. Apparently Yates too had heard the stories of Grant's drinking, which gave him additional pause. But the members of the regiment knew Grant from their mustering, and they respected his calm, straightforward demeanor. Yates offered to make Grant a colonel and give him the command.

It wasn't what Grant had wanted, but it was the best position available, and he took it with relief and comparative pleasure. "In accepting this command," he informed his new subordinates, "your Commander will require the cooperation of all the commissioned and non-commissioned officers in instructing the command and in maintaining discipline, and hopes to receive also the hearty support of every enlisted man."

The instruction began at once. "Hereafter no passes to soldiers to be out of camp after sun down will be valid unless approved by the Commanding Officer of the Regiment," he said. "All men when out of camp should reflect that they are gentlemen; in camp, soldiers. . . . The guards are required in all cases to arrest all men coming into camp after retreat unless provided with a pass countersigned by the Regimental Commander."

Certain of the soldiers resisted their lessons. "It is with regret that the commanding officer learns that a number of the men composing the guard of last night deserted their posts, and their guard," Grant said in a subsequent order. "This is an offense against all military rule and law. . . . It cannot, in time of peace, be accompanied with a punishment less than the forfeiture of $10 from the pay of the soldier, together with corporal punishment such as confinement for thirty days with ball and chain at hard labor. In time of war the punishment of this is death." Grant cut the offenders some first-time slack, choosing to interpret their failure as stemming from ignorance rather than malice. But he warned the miscreants and the entire regiment: "It will not be excused again."

His firmness paid off. "The guard house was not large enough for the first few nights and days," one of Grant's lieutenants informed his wife. "But yesterday there was but two or three in and today none. . . . So you see we have the best of order and every thing moves off pleasantly." Grant himself remarked of his regiment, in a letter to Julia: "It was in a terribly disorganized state when I took it, but a very great change has taken place. Everyone says so and to me it is very observable. I don't believe there is a more orderly set of troops now in the volunteer service. I have been very strict with them and the men seem to like it. They appreciate that it is all for their own benefit."

His timing couldn't have been better. Just as his regiment was beginning to look like an army unit, it *became* an army unit. The first Northern enlistments, in response to Lincoln's April call, had been for ninety days in state militias, with Lincoln hoping that an enthusiastic show of force would overawe the rebels. When the enlistments had no such effect, the president adopted a new approach. He issued another call, this time for three-year enlistments in the federal army. The state units already in existence would be absorbed into the army if the officers and men so chose.

Grant happily accepted the transfer, but some in his regiment initially had doubts. Two Illinois congressmen came to his camp requesting to address the men. Grant knew them only by reputation, and the reputation of one—a Democrat from the southern part of Illinois, where sympathy for the South was especially strong—gave him cause for concern. But they were members of Congress and he a mere colonel, and he didn't feel he could stop them. To his relief, patriotism informed the speeches, especially the one by the Democrat. "It breathed a loyalty and devotion to the Union which inspired my men to such a point that they would have volunteered to remain in the army as long as an enemy of the country continued to bear arms against it," he remembered. The regiment overwhelmingly followed their colonel into the federal army.

From April till early summer, Lincoln conducted the war on his own authority. But as the rebellion persisted, the president decided he needed help. In particular he required money, which necessitated summoning Congress. The legislators wouldn't have met until December; Lincoln now compelled them to brave the heat of Washington for a special summer session. He greeted them with a war message. He recapitulated the events of the winter and spring, culminating in the assault on Fort Sumter. He explained the actions he had taken to defend the Union, acknowledging that in raising an army without congressional concurrence he had stretched tradition and perhaps even the Constitution. "These measures, whether strictly legal or not, were ventured upon under what appeared to be a popular demand and a public necessity, trusting then as now that Congress would readily ratify them." He requested authority to expand the army to 400,000 men at a cost of 400 million dollars. This was a great deal of money, he admitted, but it was no more per capita than what America had spent to win its independence from Britain. And it was a necessary investment in America's future—and humanity's. "A right result, at this time, will be worth more to the world than ten times the men and ten times the money."

Lincoln expanded on the universal meaning of the current conflict, in words that foretold a more famous address. "This issue embraces more than the fate of these United States. It presents to the whole family of man the question whether a constitutional republic, or a democracy—a government of the people, by the same people—can, or cannot, maintain its territorial integrity against its own domestic foes." The struggle would answer a profound question. "Must a government, of necessity, be too *strong* for the liberties of its own people, or too *weak* to maintain its own existence?" The result would culminate eighty years of republican history. "Our popular government has often been called an experiment. Two points in it our people have already settled: the successful *establishing* and the successful *administering* of it. One still remains: its successful *maintenance* against a formidable internal attempt to overthrow it. It is now for them to demonstrate to the world that those who can fairly carry an election can also suppress a rebellion."

Congress gave Lincoln what he wanted. Secession had carried off from the legislature the Southern wing of the Democratic party; sudden death, from typhoid fever in June, deprived the party's Northern wing of its leader, Stephen Douglas. The large Republican majority that resulted assured Lincoln of support in his effort to crush the rebellion. The Republicans ratified Lincoln's past actions and approved the president's request for men and money, with a bonus of a hundred thousand men more than he asked for and an additional hundred million dollars.

*F*red Grant loved soldiering as only a young boy can. The eleven-year-old's father visited Galena to see Julia and the children and gather some personal effects; when he left he took Fred with him. The two traveled by train back to camp near Springfield. "Fred was delighted with his trip," Grant wrote Julia. The boy mingled with the troops, who adopted him as a mascot. "The soldiers and officers call him Colonel and he seems to be quite a favorite."

Grant got orders from Washington to move his regiment to Quincy, just across the Mississippi from the northern part of Missouri. That state remained loyal but precariously so, and Lincoln and Winfield Scott wanted to secure it militarily. A railroad ran from Springfield to the Mississippi, yet Grant chose to march his men. "I thought it would be good preparation for the troops," he explained. The march was much easier than traversing Mexico fifteen years earlier had been, but it posed its own challenges. An enterprising Illinoisan joined Grant's column selling liquor to slake the men's thirst; Grant, learning of the commerce, immediately interdicted it. He confiscated the seller's inventory and ordered him to get away from the line of march—"which he did in double-quick time, not even taking the trouble to pick up his coat," a local reporter noted.

A change of plans caught Grant halfway to Quincy, at the Illinois

River. The War Department now wanted him to go to Ironton, Missouri, and had dispatched a steamboat up the Illinois to fetch him and his men. The regiment boarded and began their river journey, only for the vessel to run aground on a sandbar. Awaiting a rise in the river, Grant received another set of orders. A rebel force had trapped a Union regiment in Missouri on the Hannibal & St. Joseph Railroad; Grant was to relieve the regiment and capture or disperse the rebels. The train to Quincy was the shortest and quickest route.

With battle approaching, Grant thought Fred had seen enough of army life. He put the boy on a steamboat at Quincy, heading north toward Galena. "Fred started home yesterday," Grant wrote Julia. "I did not telegraph you because I thought you would be in a perfect stew until he arrived. He did not want to go at all, and I felt loath at sending him, but now that we are in the enemy's country I thought you would be alarmed if he was with me."

Grant underestimated his wife. "Do not send him home," Julia responded. She admonished her husband with a classical precedent: "Alexander was not older when he accompanied Philip. Do keep him with you."

But the boy had been sent and couldn't well be recalled. Julia nonetheless took pride from the way Fred's journey played out. The steamboat dropped him at Dubuque, which was connected to Galena by rail. The train, however, had departed when he arrived, and rather than wait for the next one he set off on foot. "He walked the whole distance from Dubuque to Galena, seventeen miles, and carried his own knapsack," Julia remembered of her little Alexander.

The prospect of meeting the enemy made Grant anxious. Anxiety often induced headaches in him, and it did so now. "Last night we had an alarm which kept me out all night with one of those terrible headaches which you know I am so subject to," he confided to Julia. "Today I have laid up all day." Patent medicine eased the symptoms without addressing the cause. He recalled his first experiences in combat and how he had gotten past the fear he had felt then, but he realized something was quite different now. "My sensations as we approached what I supposed might be a field of battle were anything but agreeable," he wrote afterward. "I had been in all the engagements in Mexico that it was possible for one person to be in, but not in command. If some one else had been colonel and I had been lieutenant-colonel I do not think I would have felt any trepidation." Possessing the command made him responsible for the fate of the whole regiment, and the experience stressed him badly.

The feeling diminished before long, though not through his own doing. As his regiment was preparing to cross the Mississippi, the besieged Union regiment that was supposed to be the object of Grant's rescue suddenly appeared, looking embarrassed and bedraggled. "My anxiety was relieved," Grant recalled. "I am inclined to think both sides got frightened and ran away."

Grant's regiment received orders to cross into Missouri all the same. "Tomorrow I start for Monroe, where I shall fall in with Colonel Palmer and one company of horse and two pieces of artillery," he explained to his father. "One regiment and a battalion of infantry will move on to Mexico, North Missouri road, and all of us together will try to nab the notorious Tom Harris with his 1200 secessionists." Harris had been tearing up the countryside and destroying railroads. Grant was willing enough to give chase with his infantry, but he wasn't hopeful about catching Harris. "His men are mounted, and I have but little faith in getting many of them."

Grant learned that the rebels had made camp near the town of Florida. He gathered teams and drivers to transport the regiment's gear and provisions forward. He had done this in Mexico many times, and the logistics of the march came easily. The psychology of the march was another matter, and the anxiety returned. "When we got on the road and found every house deserted, I was anything but easy. In the twenty-five miles we had to march we did not see a person, old or young, male or female, except two horsemen who were on a road that crossed ours. As soon as they saw us they decamped as fast as their horses could carry them."

Grant's distress intensified as he neared Harris's camp in a creek bottom between two sets of hills. "The hills on either side of the creek extend to a considerable height, possibly more than a hundred feet," Grant wrote. "As we approached the brow of the hill from which it was expected we could see Harris' camp, and possibly find his men ready formed to meet us, my heart kept getting higher and higher until it felt to me as though it was in my throat. I would have given anything then to have been back in Illinois, but I had not the moral courage to halt and consider what to do; I kept right on." He reached the crest of the road and looked down into the valley. He saw signs of a recent large encampment but neither Harris nor his mounted men.

"My heart resumed its place," Grant wrote. And a revelation came over him. "It occurred to me at once that Harris had been as much afraid of me as I had been of him. This was a view of the question I had never taken before; but it was one I never forgot afterwards. From that event to the close of the war, I never experienced trepidation upon confronting an enemy, though I always felt more or less anxiety. I never forgot that he had as much reason to fear my forces as I had his."

WILLIAM SHERMAN SPENT MUCH OF HIS LIFE IN A BAD MOOD, AND the outbreak of the war didn't make it better. Louisiana's secession compelled his resignation from the state's military academy just when his efforts with the cadets were beginning to show real progress. He respectfully told his patron, Governor Moore, that dissolution of the Union was recklessly harebrained. "I have never been a politician," he wrote Moore, "and therefore undervalue the excited feelings of present rulers, but I do think, if this people cannot execute a form of government like the present, that a worse one will result." His brother John summoned him to Washington to reclaim his commission in the federal army; to that end John, now a senator, arranged an interview with Lincoln. "Mr. President, this is my brother, Colonel Sherman, who is just up from Louisiana," John said at the introduction. "He may give you some information you want."

Lincoln, bothered by other business, inquired distractedly: "How are they getting along down there?"

"They think they are getting along swimmingly," William Sherman responded. "They are preparing for war."

"Oh, well," Lincoln rejoined. "I guess we'll manage to keep house." He turned away, indicating an end to the interview.

Sherman couldn't believe that Lincoln had such little interest in the eyewitness account of a professional soldier just arrived from behind enemy lines. "I broke out on John, damning the politicians generally," he recalled. He told John and, by extension, the other politicians: "You have got things in a hell of a fix, and you may get out of them as you best can." He said the country was sleeping on a volcano that was about to explode, but he wanted nothing to do with it. His wife and children were in Ohio; he was going there to tend to them. John implored him to have patience, but he refused. He caught the first train west.

His wife greeted him with a letter from a St. Louis street railroad offering him the firm's presidency. Still angry at the political classes, he took the job. He arrived in St. Louis on the verge of Claiborne Jackson's coup against the federal arsenal. Frank Blair, planning his countercoup and speaking with the apparent authority of the government at Washington, offered Sherman a brigadier generalship of volunteers to help suppress the rebels. Sherman refused. He explained that he had been to Washington and been rebuffed; he had since accepted a job he couldn't relinquish without injury to his reputation and family.

Blair and other Unionists in the city interpreted Sherman's refusal amiss; some began to question his loyalty. Sherman wrote to Simon Cameron, the secretary of war, to explain his action. "I hold myself now, as always, prepared to serve my country in the capacity for which I was trained," he said. But the president until recently had asked for three-month volunteers only. "I did not and will not volunteer for *three months*, because I cannot throw my family on the cold charity of the world." The latest call, which was for longer enlistments, changed things a bit. "For the three years call made by the President, an officer can prepare his command and do good service." Sherman still wouldn't volunteer, as he was new to St. Louis. "The men are not well enough acquainted with me to elect me to my appropriate place." But the army knew where to find him. "Should my services be needed, the records of the War Department will enable you to designate the station in which I can render most service."

A week later he received a dispatch appointing him colonel of the Thirteenth Infantry Regiment of the regular army. He accepted the appointment, and his opinion of the government slightly rose. But it fell again when he discovered that the Thirteenth Infantry didn't exist. Pending its formation, he was ordered to Washington, where Winfield Scott set him to inspection duty. An early scare for the safety of the capital eased upon the arrival of large numbers of volunteers; Sherman realized, however, that the recruits were far from being soldiers. "Their uniforms were as various as the States and cities from which they came," he wrote. "Their arms were also of every pattern and caliber; and they were so loaded down with overcoats, haversacks, knapsacks, tents, and baggage that it took from twenty-five to fifty wagon to move the camp of a regiment from one place to another; and some of the camps and bakeries had cooking establishments that would have done credit to Delmonico."

The swelling presence of the troops prompted demands that they march against the enemy. Winfield Scott was skeptical, believing his army unready. Besides, he hoped to suppress the rebellion by encirclement—by a blockade at sea and a flanking action along the Mississippi—rather than a frontal offensive. Critics derided this "anaconda plan," and Lincoln concluded that though it might work in time, the Northern public lacked the requisite patience. The president sought a quicker strategy.

He turned to Irvin McDowell, who headed the Union forces in Washington. McDowell proposed to attack the rebels at Manassas Junction, twenty-five miles into Virginia on the road to Richmond, which had become the Confederate capital. A single bold stroke, McDowell explained, would defeat the rebel army, scatter the insurrectionary regime and win the war.

William Sherman liked the plan, especially after it included him. Scott and McDowell realized that Sherman was underemployed as an inspector, and he was given command of a brigade in McDowell's army. "We start forth today, camp tonight at or near Vienna," Sherman wrote his brother John on July 16. "Tomorrow early we attack." He added: "Secret absolute."

But the secret was far from absolute. Washington was filled with Southern sympathizers, who traveled freely across the Potomac to Virginia. Some of the sympathizers were remarkably well informed; Rose O'Neal Greenhow, a Maryland-born matron devoted to states' rights and the preservation of slavery, hosted high officials of the Lincoln administration, senior officers in the Union army, foreign diplomats and influential journalists. She plied her guests with wine and liquor; their loosened tongues told of operations afoot and envisioned. By her assistance, Pierre G. T. Beauregard, commanding Confederate forces near Manassas, learned of McDowell's plan almost as soon as Sherman and McDowell's other subordinates did.

Fashionable Washington got the news a short while later, and hundreds of well-wishers, ill-wishers and neutral gawkers tagged behind McDowell's army to witness the first real battle of the war. The engagement commenced promisingly for the Federals, who forded Bull Run, a small stream near Manassas, and drove the Confederates back. Newspaper reporters eager to scoop their competition dashed off stories of a great Union victory and sent them by courier back to Washington.

But the Confederates dug in as reinforcements arrived. Thomas Jackson was the most visible of the defenders; this dour professor from the Virginia Military Institute earned the nickname "Stonewall" for his stubbornness that day. The inexperience of the Federals began to show, and they fell into disorder as the Confederate fire increased.

Sherman had missed the fighting in the Mexican War, being confined to quiescent California; Bull Run was his baptism by fire. "For the first time in my life I saw cannonballs strike men and crash through the trees and saplings above and around us," he recalled. His regiments endured the bombardment for a time but lost their bearings as the fighting grew hotter. One regiment, which had left the road from the river crossing to pursue the enemy, became especially disoriented. "This regiment is uniformed in gray cloth, almost identical with that of the great bulk of the secession army," Sherman explained in his after-action report. "And when the regiment fell into confusion and retreated toward the road, there was a universal cry that they were being fired on by our own men."

Discipline broke down all along the Union front. Sherman described events on a ridge to his left: "Here, about half-past 3 p.m., began the scene of confusion and disorder that characterized the remainder of the day. Up to that time, all had kept their places, and seemed perfectly cool and used to the shell and shot that fell, comparatively harmless, all around us; but the short exposure to an intense fire of small arms, at close range, had killed many, wounded more, and had produced disorder in all of the battalions that had attempted to counter it. Men fell away from their ranks, talking and in great confusion." Sherman summoned his fellow officers to rally the troops. "We succeeded in partially reforming the regiments, but it was manifest that they would not stand." A retreat order would have been superfluous; the men were retreating uncontrollably on their own. Eventually the order came, but it did nothing to organize the retreat. "This retreat was by night and disorderly in the extreme," Sherman wrote.

The next morning Sherman's troops straggled into Fort Corcoran, their base on the Potomac. "A slow, muzzling rain had set in, and probably a more gloomy day never presented itself," Sherman related. "All organization seemed to be at an end. . . . Of course, we took it for granted that the rebels would be on our heels, and accordingly prepared to defend our posts." But the Confederates had become nearly as disorganized in victory as the Federals were in defeat, and they failed to follow up. This minor blessing didn't stop some of Sherman's soldiers from attempting to desert. Most were dissuaded when he ordered his artillery officers to level their guns at them and threatened to open fire if they made a move. Yet one captain announced his decision to depart nonetheless. "Colonel," he said to Sherman, "I am going to New York today. What can I do for you?"

"How can you go to New York?" Sherman demanded. "I don't remember to have signed a leave for you."

The captain explained that he didn't want a leave; his ninety-day term was up and he was mustering out.

Sherman considered the matter. "I noticed that a good many of the soldiers had paused about us to listen, and knew that if this officer could defy me, they also would," he wrote afterward. "So I turned on him sharp and said: 'Captain, this question of your term of service has been submitted to the rightful authority, and the decision has been published in orders. You are a soldier, and must submit to orders until you are properly discharged. If you attempt to leave without orders, it will be mutiny, and I will shoot you like a dog!'"

The captain returned to his quarters, apparently chastened. The watching men went back to their business. Sherman thought the incident ended. But later that day a carriage carrying President Lincoln and Secretary of State Seward drove by the camp. The driver looked lost, and Sherman volunteered to give directions. He got into the vehicle and told the driver where to go. Meanwhile he spoke with Lincoln, who said he had come out to encourage the troops. Sherman asked if he intended to give a speech. Lincoln said he thought he would. Sherman cautioned him against anything that might elicit cheering or other noisy demonstrations. "We had had enough of it before Bull Run to ruin any set of men," he recalled telling the president. "What we needed were cool, thoughtful, hard-fighting soldiers—no more hurrahing, no humbug."

Lincoln nodded, and when he later stood up in the carriage to address the men, he stopped their cheering with a nod to Sherman. "Don't cheer, boys," he said. "I confess I rather like it myself, but Colonel Sherman here says it is not military, and I guess we had better defer to his opinion."

Lincoln continued his inspection, with Sherman as guide. The president was about to return to Washington when the captain Sherman had reprimanded earlier approached the carriage. "Mr. President, I have a cause of grievance," the captain said. "This morning I went to speak to Colonel Sherman, and he threatened to shoot me."

"Threatened to shoot you?" Lincoln replied.

"Yes, sir. He threatened to shoot me."

Lincoln looked at Sherman, then at the captain, then back at Sherman. In a whisper loud enough for all in the vicinity to hear, he said, "Well, if I were you, and he threatened to shoot, I would not trust him, for I believe he would do it."

19

"Colonel Grant is an old army officer—thoroughly a gentleman and an officer of intelligence and discretion," John Pope wrote to John Frémont in early August. Frémont commanded Union forces in the West from headquarters in St. Louis; Pope was his lieutenant for Missouri. The mission in Missouri was confused on account of the unsettled circumstances in the state. Secession forces roamed at will but did comparatively little damage, causing the Federals to give unproductive and eventually halfhearted chase. "Fighting here looks to me like gold hunting in California—always rich leads are a little farther on or in some other locality," an exhausted assistant wrote Frémont.

Grant seemed to Pope and Frémont the man for the moment and place. His discretion and intelligence enabled him to deal with fractious troops and suspicious locals, instilling discipline and pride in the former and respect for the Union in the latter. "No wandering will be permitted, and every violation of this order will be summarily and severely punished," Grant warned his troops upon learning that some of them had annoyed and abused the neighbors. "No soldier will be allowed to go more than one mile beyond his camp except under order or by special permission, on pain of being dealt with as a deserter. No expeditions will be fitted out for the purpose of arresting suspected persons without first getting authority from these Headquarters." The troops absorbed the message and so did the locals. "When we first come, there was a terrible state of fear existing among the people," Grant informed Julia. "They thought every horror known in the whole catalogue of disasters following a state of war was going to be their portion at once. But they are now becoming much more reassured. They find that all troops are not the desperate characters they took them for." Grant was especially gratified at the change in the attitudes of the inhabitants of Macon City, on the Hannibal & St. Joseph Railroad north of Jefferson City. "People of the town, many of them, left on our approach, but finding that we behave respectfully and respected private property they returned and before we left nearly every lady and child visited camp and no doubt felt as much regret at our departure as they did at our arrival."

Yet the Missourians were a puzzling bunch. "The majority in this part of the state are secessionists, as we would term them, but deplore the present state of affairs," Grant wrote his father. "They would make almost any sacrifice to have the Union restored, but regard it as dissolved and nothing is left for them but to choose between two evils. Many, too, seem to be entirely ignorant of the object of present hostilities. You can't convince them but what the ultimate object is to extinguish, by force, slavery. Then too they feel that the Southern Confederacy will never consent to give up their State and as they, the South, are the strong party, it is prudent to favor them from the start." The rebels and sympathizers controlled the newspapers of the neighborhood, with little regard for facts. "There is never a movement of troops made that the Secession journals through the country do not give a startling account of their almost annihilation at the hands of the State's troops, whilst the facts are there are no engagements. My regiment has been reported cut to pieces once that I know of, and I don't know but oftener, whilst a gun has not been fired at us. These reports go uncontradicted here and give confirmation to the conviction already entertained that one Southron is equal to five Northerners."

Grant's good work confirmed the favorable impression he had made on Pope and Frémont, and when the rapid expansion of the Union army compelled a raft of promotions, he found himself among the beneficiaries. "I see from the papers that my name has been sent in for Brigadier General!" he wrote Jesse at the beginning of August. He was as pleased as he was surprised. "This is certainly very complimentary to me, particularly as I have never asked a friend to intercede in my behalf." After learning that Elihu Washburne and other members of the Illinois delegation in Congress had pushed his promotion, Grant told Julia, "I certainly feel very grateful to the people of Illinois for the interest they seem to have taken in me, and unasked, too. Whilst I was about Springfield I certainly never blew my own trumpet and was not aware that I attracted any attention, but it seems from what I have heard from there the people, who were perfect strangers to me up to the commencement of our present unhappy national difficulties, were very unanimous in recommending me for my present position."

He nonetheless thought the promotion was no more than he deserved. To his father he described his handling of his regiment: "I took it in a very disorganized, demoralized and insubordinate condition and have worked it up to a reputation equal to the best, and I believe with the good will of all the officers and all the men. Hearing that I was likely to be promoted, the officers, with great unanimity, have requested to be attached to my command." He cautioned, however, that he was writing for Jesse's eyes alone. "This I don't want you to read to others, for I very much dislike speaking of myself."

Grant's promotion arrived on the heels of word of the Union defeat at Bull Run, which complicated his newly enlarged task. "People here will be glad to get clear of us notwithstanding their apparent hospitality," Grant wrote Julia. "They are great fools in this section of country and will never rest until they bring upon themselves all the horrors of war in its worst form. The people are inclined to carry on a guerilla warfare that must eventuate in retaliation, and when it does commence it will be hard to control. I hope from the bottom of my heart I may be mistaken, but since the defeat of our troops at Manassas things look more gloomy here."

One of the greatest Missouri fools, Grant thought, was his former business partner. "I called to see Harry Boggs the other day as I passed through St. Louis," he told Julia. "He cursed and went on like a madman. Told me that I would never be welcome in his house, that the people of Illinois were a poor miserable set of Black Republicans, Abolition paupers that had to invade their state to get something to eat. Good joke that on something to eat. Harry is such a pitiful insignificant fellow that I could not get mad at him and told him so, where upon he set the Army of Flanders far in the shade with his profanity."

Boggs made an impression on Grant all the same. "You ask my views about the continuance of the war," he wrote his sister Mary. "Well, I have changed my mind so much that I don't know what to think. That the Rebels will be so badly whipped by April next that they cannot make a stand anywhere I don't doubt. But they are so dogged that there is no telling when they might be subdued. Send Union troops among them and respect all their rights, pay for everything you get and they become desperate and reckless because their state sovereignty is invaded. Troops of the opposite side march through and take everything they want, leaving no pay but script, and they become desperate secession partisans because they have nothing more to lose. Every change makes them more desperate."

Grant wouldn't have described Sam Clemens as dogged, had he met him. Nor would Clemens have described himself that way. Clemens was a twenty-five-year-old river pilot from Hannibal, Missouri, living in St. Louis in the early summer of 1861 when a recruiter for the secessionist Missouri state guard came through. A couple of Clemens's friends, also from Hannibal, decided to enlist, and they talked Clemens into joining them. The three headed back to Hannibal to cast their lot with secession.

But their rebel careers almost ended before they began. A Union packet boat arrived at Hannibal; Clemens and his friends watched it land a company of troops. The captain somehow learned that Clemens and the others were pilots, and he dragooned them into the Federal service. The three were transported downriver to St. Louis, where a Union officer was about to compel them to sign papers of enlistment when two young women knocked at the officer's door. He left Clemens and the others alone long enough for them to make their escape and return once more to Hannibal.

But the Union troops had occupied the town, and the trio joined some rebel irregulars mustering in the forest nearby. Clemens was chosen second lieutenant in a company they formed; his mount was an undersized yellow mule named Paint Brush. One night when Clemens was on picket duty a comrade spotted what looked like Union soldiers. The comrade fired a shotgun at the moving shadows, and Clemens and the others leaped on their steeds and raced away. Paint Brush, however, was no match for the horses of the others, and Clemens was quickly left behind. "The last we heard of him," one of the swifter fellows remembered, "he was saying, 'Damn you, you want the Yanks to capture me!'"

The horsemen got to camp ahead of Clemens and girded for battle. At the approach of hoofbeats they leveled their weapons to blast the Unionists. But it was only Clemens and Paint Brush, out of control. Mule and rider charged through the camp—Clemens cursing, Paint Brush braying. Eventually they drew to a halt and the camp settled in for the night. The next morning some of the men returned to the scene of the engagement. There was no sign that Union troops had ever been there, only some wildflowers swaying soldierlike in the breeze.

The incident became the narrative center of a story Clemens wrote about his Civil War service. The story, "The Private History of a Campaign That Failed," related the misadventures of a Missouri guardsman much like Clemens who was driven from the military by the approach of a Union regiment headed by an officer apparently destined for greater things. "In time I came to learn that the Union colonel whose coming frightened me out of the war, and crippled the southern cause to that extent, was General Grant. I came within a few hours of seeing him when he was as unknown as I was myself, at a time when anybody could have said, 'Grant—Ulysses S. Grant? I do not remember hearing the name before.'"

20

GRANT'S PROMOTION GAVE HIM GREATER AUTHORITY THAN HE HAD ever expected to wield. "My present command here numbers about 3000 and will be increased to 4000 tomorrow and probably much larger the next day," he wrote Julia. The brigade included regiments unused to the Grant style. "Many of the officers seem to have so little command over their men, and military duty seems to be done so loosely, that I feel at present our resistance"—to enemy attack—"would be in the inverse ratio of the number of troops to resist with," he told John Frémont. Yet things would change soon. "In two days I expect to have a very different state of affairs, and to improve them continuously."

Again he laid out the new dispensation. "Commanders will see that the men of their respective commands are always within the sound of the drum, and to this end there must be at least five roll calls per day," he declared. "The commanding officer from each company must be present at each roll call and see that all absentees are reported and punished. . . . The strictest discipline is expected to be maintained in this camp, and the General Commanding will hold responsible for this all officers, and the degree of responsibility will be in direct ratio with the rank of the officer." Again his efforts succeeded. "Order was soon restored," he recalled succinctly.

Yet certain developments were beyond his control. The rapid expansion of the army inevitably caused mix-ups as to who was senior to whom. Benjamin Prentiss had won appointment as brigadier general of Illinois volunteers during the spring, when Grant was still a civilian; Prentiss became a brigadier in the U.S. Army at the same time as Grant, early in August. He unsurprisingly thought he outranked Grant. But Grant knew the rules of the army, which in fact gave *him* seniority on account of his prior army service. When Prentiss refused to obey Grant's orders, a confrontation ensued. Grant had relocated to southern Missouri, where he established temporary headquarters at Cape Girardeau, and had ordered Prentiss to take a position at Jackson, a short distance away. Grant set out from his office at Cape Girardeau to meet Prentiss at Jackson. "As I turned the first corner of a street after starting, I saw a column of cavalry passing the next street in front of me," he remembered. "I turned and rode around the block the other way, so as to meet the head of the column. I found there General Prentiss himself, with a large escort. He had halted his troops at Jackson for the night, and had come on himself to Cape Girardeau, leaving orders for his command to follow him in the morning." Grant confronted Prentiss and reminded him of the order to stay at Jackson. "He was very much aggrieved." Words were exchanged, with each officer staking his claim to seniority. "I then ordered the General very peremptorily to countermarch his command and take it back to Jackson." Prentiss did so but under protest.

Frémont found in Grant's favor, prompting Prentiss to threaten to resign. Frémont told him to cool off, and he gradually did so. But the incident left him angry and Grant eventually sad. "When I came to know him better, I regretted it much," Grant reflected. "He was a brave and very earnest soldier. No man in the service was more sincere in his devotion to the cause for which we were battling."

Grant's shift to southern Missouri reflected a change in the nature of the war. As long as both sides thought the conflict would be short, the fighting was chiefly tactical; each attempted to gain local advantage or show regional strength. But after Bull Run, as the prospect of a longer struggle set in, the two sides began to think strategically, in terms of total strength or weakness. And the West, which had seemed secondary to South Carolina and Virginia, suddenly became the central theater of the war. The West comprised the valleys of the Ohio and Mississippi, the heartland of the continent. Who controlled the West bid fair to control the country and decide the war.

The cockpit of the West, for the moment at least, was the hundred-mile circle centered on Cairo, Illinois, where four states—Illinois, Missouri, Kentucky and Tennessee—and three rivers—the Ohio, Mississippi and Tennessee—came together. Grant got to Cairo in early September, on the same day that Confederate forces occupied Columbus, Kentucky, on the east bank of the Mississippi twenty miles downstream. Those forces could cause trouble if augmented, but more alarming at present was word that the Confederates were planning to seize Paducah, Kentucky, where the Tennessee entered the Ohio. "There was no time for delay," Grant recalled. "I reported by telegraph to the department commander"—Frémont—"the information I had received, and added that I was taking steps to get off that night to be in advance of the enemy in securing that important point." The war had stalled traffic on the Mississippi and Ohio, and dozens of steamers and their crews lay idle at Cairo. Grant offered work to the boats and men, and the latter quickly loaded fuel and fired up boilers. He ordered two regiments and an artillery battery aboard. He telegraphed Frémont again, not having received a reply to his earlier message, and said he would set off unless ordered otherwise.

In fact Frémont *had* replied, but to avoid tipping off Confederates or sympathizers who might be eavesdropping on the telegraph lines, his message had been translated into Hungarian before being transmitted. Until now Grant hadn't received any such coded communications, and his aides didn't know what to do with the strange message. Conveniently it told him to go ahead.

The boats left Cairo a bit before midnight and reached Paducah at dawn. The sudden appearance of the Union troops took the locals by surprise. "Found numerous secession flags flying over the city, and the citizens in anticipation of the approach of the rebel army, who was reliably reported thirty eight hundred strong sixteen miles distant," Grant informed Frémont. "I landed the troops and took possession of the city without firing a gun." The secession flags were hauled down and replaced by Union flags. Grant ordered the seizure of the town's rail depot and he confiscated rations and leather intended for the Confederate army. He took control of the telegraph office and other key points. "I distributed the troops so as best to command the city and least annoy peaceable citizens."

He published a proclamation explaining his purposes. "I have come among you not as an enemy but as your friend and fellow citizen," he declared. As their friend he would be their protector. "An enemy, in rebellion against our common Government, has taken possession of and planted its guns upon the soil of Kentucky and fired upon our flag. . . . He is moving upon your city. I am here to defend you against this enemy and to assert and maintain the authority and sovereignty of your Government and mine." Peaceful citizens of whatever political views would be unmolested. "I have nothing to do with opinions. I shall deal only with armed rebellion and its aiders and abettors." And he would stay in Paducah no longer than necessary. "Whenever it is manifest that you are able to defend yourselves, to maintain the authority of your Government and protect the rights of all its loyal citizens, I shall withdraw the forces under my command."

It was his first decisive command action, and he liked the feeling it gave him. "You have seen my move upon Paducah!" he wrote Julia. "It was of much greater importance than is probably generally known." The rebels had been on the verge of seizing the town. "Our arrival therefore put quite a damper upon their hopes." The citizens seemed willing to accept his presence and authority; at least they weren't resisting. And the capture of Paducah promised to be the start of something big. "We are likely to have lively times. . . . An attack somewhere cannot be postponed many days."

The attack failed to materialize. Grant's scouts skirmished with rebel patrols, and gunboats under his Cairo command exchanged fire with Confederate batteries near Columbus. But the rebels declined to challenge him directly, and he lacked the troops to engage them in force. "All is quiet here now," he wrote Julia disappointedly from Cairo in late September. "How long it will remain so is impossible to tell. If I had troops enough not long." A month later he was still complaining. "I am very sorry that I have not got a force to go south with, at least to Columbus," he told Julia. "But the fates seem to be against any such thing. My forces are scattered and occupy posts that must be held." A defensive posture didn't suit his personality. "What I want is to advance."

He got what he wanted not much later. John Frémont set out from St. Louis in October in search of the main body of Missouri's secessionist army, led by Sterling Price. He directed Grant to detain or divert any Confederates on the Mississippi or in southeastern Missouri. Grant gathered all the troops he could and headed from Cairo toward Columbus, Kentucky, intending merely a demonstration of force, in keeping with Frémont's order. He was not planning a serious attack. "But after we started," he recalled later, "I saw that the officers and men were elated at the prospect of at last having the opportunity of doing what they had volunteered to do: fight the enemies of their country. I did not see how I could maintain discipline or retain the confidence of my command if we should return to Cairo without an effort to do something."

Grant was as eager as any of the men at the prospect of action, and when he heard that the Confederates at Columbus were sending troops across the river, he lost no time in striking against them. With three thousand men in steam transports he dropped down the Mississippi in the dark, pausing several miles above Belmont, a Missouri village opposite Columbus, where the Confederates had established a camp. "At daylight we proceeded down the river to a point just out of range of rebel guns and debarked on the Missouri shore," he related in his after-action report. "From here the troops were marched by a flank for about one mile towards Belmont, and then drawn up in a line, one battalion having been left as a reserve near the transports." Grant ordered skirmishers to locate the enemy; within a few minutes they made contact.

Jacob Lauman, a colonel heading an Iowa regiment, was in the thick of the battle that ensued. "We fought the rebels slowly but steadily, driving them before us at every volley," he recounted later. "Our advance at this point was slow in consequence of the obstructions in our way, caused by felling timber and underbrush, but we crept under and over it, at times lying down to let the fire of the artillery and musketry pass over us, and then up and onward again until we arrived at the field to the left of the rebel camp." Here they linked up with other Union troops. "We poured volley after volley on the retiring foe across the field in front of and on the battery, which was stationed at the head of the encampment, on our right. Our fire was so hot the guns were soon abandoned, the enemy, about 800, fleeing across the field in the greatest consternation." Lauman's men seized the battery, which gave them a clear view of the rest of the camp. "The rebels kept up a sharp and galling fire upon us, but a few well directed volleys induced them to abscond from their camp immediately."

To this point in the battle, Grant was delighted with the performance of his troops. "The officers and men engaged at Belmont were then under fire for the first time," he observed. "Veterans could not have behaved better than they did." But they didn't know how to follow up. "They became demoralized from their victory and failed to reap its full reward. . . . The moment the camp was reached our men laid down their arms and commenced rummaging the tents to pick up trophies. Some of the higher officers were little better than the privates. They galloped about from one cluster of men to another, and at every halt delivered a short eulogy upon the Union cause and the achievements of the command."

The Federals' distraction became the Confederates' salvation. Upon fleeing their camp the rebels took refuge beneath the bank of the river, out of sight and shot from Grant's men. Once they discovered that they weren't about to be captured or killed, they crept north along the river until they reached a spot between the Federals and the Union transports. From the Federal rear they readied a counterattack.

"I saw at the same time two steamers coming from the Columbus side towards the western shore above us, black—or gray—with soldiers from boiler-deck to roof," Grant recalled. He shouted to those of his troops who had captured the rebel battery to turn the guns against the approaching boats. But in the noise and confusion they failed to hear or heed the message. He suddenly realized that his rapid advance had led him into what had become a trap; he must withdraw as quickly as possible. Yet he hated to fall back without accomplishing something material, and so he ordered the torching of the Confederate camp—an action that increased the danger to his men, as the Confederate guns at Columbus, heretofore quiet from belief that the rebels still held the camp, opened fire.

By this time Grant's men realized they were surrounded. Some assumed they had to surrender. "But when I announced that we had cut our way in and could cut our way out just as well, it seemed a new revelation," Grant explained. The Federals charged the Confederates again, in the reverse direction from before, and fought their way back to their boats.

Grant was the last aboard. Galloping about the battlefield, he had his horse shot from beneath him. Taking another from a subordinate, he continued to race around in front of and behind his men, urging them forward—that is, to the rear. After they reached the boats and began boarding he rode along the river's edge to determine where the Confederate troops had landed. He entered a cornfield so thick with leaves and unharvested ears as to make reconnaissance nearly impossible. "I had not gone more than a few hundred yards when I saw a body of troops marching past me, not fifty yards away," he wrote. "I looked at them for a moment and then turned my horse towards the river and started back, first in a walk and, when I thought myself concealed from the view of the enemy, as fast as my horse could carry me."

At the Union boats he came under fire from Confederates contesting the Federals' escape. The engineer of the final boat to push off saw him coming and ordered a plank thrown back to the water's edge, at the bottom of a steep pitch below the field across which Grant was racing. "My horse put his fore feet over the bank without hesitation or urging, and with his hind feet well under him slid down the bank and trotted aboard the boat, twelve or fifteen feet away, over a single gang plank."

The Confederates raked the transports with small-arms fire. Grant ascended to the captain's cabin beside the pilot house and collapsed on a sofa. But after a minute to catch his breath he leaped up to check on his men. "I had scarcely left when a musket ball entered the room, struck the head of the sofa, passed through it and lodged in the floor," he recounted.

His luck was better than that of many of his men that day. At the time and afterward Grant displayed a certain defensiveness about the battle of Belmont. His losses totaled some six hundred killed, wounded, captured or missing, against about the same number for the Confederates. He nonetheless lavished praise on the performance of his regiments. "All the troops behaved with great gallantry, much of which is to be attributed to the coolness and presence of mind of the officers, particularly the colonels," he reported right after the battle. Yet at the end of the war he filed a second report on the battle, emphasizing the orders he had been given to make a show of force. And in his memoir, written another two decades later, he asserted, "The two objects for which the battle of Belmont was fought were fully accomplished. The enemy gave up all idea of detaching troops from Columbus. . . . The National troops acquired a confidence in themselves at Belmont that did not desert them through the war."

These may indeed have been Grant's objectives. But the first was negative and the second nebulous, and the cost of achieving them was high. Doubtless Grant was speaking of himself as much as of his men when he emphasized the importance of confidence. Belmont was his first battle command. He performed with conspicuous bravery and dash. Proving himself—to himself—was no small matter. But it didn't come cheaply.

21

LINCOLN WAS WILLING TO OVERLOOK THE COST. AFTER BULL RUN the president had replaced Irvin McDowell with George McClellan, who captured the hearts of Washington with his manly good looks, his uniformed flair and his solicitude for the defense of the capital. "By some strange operation of magic I seem to have become *the* power of the land," McClellan wrote his wife. "I almost think that were I to win some small success now I could become Dictator or anything else that might please me."

The magic diminished as McClellan declined to challenge the Confederates across the Potomac in Virginia. Lincoln at first said nothing, but others in Washington grumbled till McClellan in late October 1861 felt obliged to probe beyond the river in the direction of Leesburg. The effort began well but ended devastatingly when the Union force was driven back over Ball's Bluff into the river, where many drowned. A thousand Federals were killed, captured or wounded; among the Union dead was Colonel Edward D. Baker, a senator from Oregon and a close friend of Lincoln's. McClellan conceded privately that the battle was a "serious disaster"; his critics said the same thing aloud. The most bitter alleged a secessionist conspiracy, with McClellan cast as an agent of the rebellion and Lincoln as his dupe. Congress established a joint committee on the conduct of the war to second-guess the administration.

Lincoln's military problems with McClellan were matched by his political problems with John Frémont. The frustrations of partisan warfare in Missouri drove Frémont to issue a proclamation establishing martial law and emancipating the slaves of rebel owners. The emancipation decree elicited applause from abolitionists and other Republicans who believed the nettle of slavery must be grasped if the war would be won; Frémont became their hero. But the decree immensely complicated Lincoln's task of keeping the border slave states—Missouri, Kentucky, Maryland and Delaware—loyal, and it undercut all he was saying about the war's being solely to save the Union. Lincoln told Frémont's wife, sent by the general to explain his action, that the war was for "a great national idea, the Union." He added—harshly, Jessie Benton Frémont judged— that "General Frémont should not have dragged the Negro into it."

Lincoln demanded that Frémont rescind the decree. The general grudgingly did so while continuing to believe he knew better than Lincoln how the war ought to be managed. His arrogance ultimately alienated even some of his friends, allowing Lincoln in November to remove him from his command.

The news about Grant and Belmont arrived amid the president's Frémont troubles and while the evil echoes from Ball's Bluff still roiled the capital. Northern papers, hungry for good news, presented Belmont as a signal victory. The *New York Times* praised Grant and his men: "The late battle at Belmont, Mo., is considered in a high degree creditable to all our troops concerned in it, and the credit of the brilliant movement is due to General Grant." The *Chicago Journal* declared, "General Grant was everywhere in the thickest of the fight, and performed wonderful deeds of bravery. The men never tire of lauding his gallantry."

Lincoln didn't know Grant personally, but he knew John McClernand, a Democratic congressman who had resigned his seat to command a brigade of Illinois volunteers and fought under Grant at Belmont. "All with you have done honor to yourselves and the flag and service to the country," Lincoln congratulated McClernand. "Most gratefully I do thank you and them." McClernand responded by urging the president to create a new military department for the lower Mississippi Valley. "An energetic, enterprising and judicious commander would early redeem this department from the thralldom of rebellion," McClernand said. He was thinking of himself—"If a department could be established there your promotion would be almost certain," a Washington ally assured him— but Lincoln began thinking of Grant.

The positive reaction to Belmont reinforced Grant's view of the battle. "The victory was most complete," he informed his father. "It has given me a confidence in the officers and men of this command that will enable me to lead them in any future engagement without fear of the result." He laid plans to exploit his success and telegraphed Henry W. Halleck, Frémont's successor and his own new superior, for permission to visit St. Louis and explain what he required by way of troops, arms and provisions.

Halleck brushed him off. He was old army and knew the stories of Grant's drinking. He doubtless considered the popular reaction to Belmont overblown. He had his hands full dealing with the confusion Frémont had left behind. And he didn't want Grant getting carried away. He told him to stay where he was. "You will send reports in writing."

Grant was left to train his troops, integrate new arrivals into his command, reconnoiter from Cairo and ponder what he would do if given the chance. "The true line of operations for us was up the Tennessee and Cumberland rivers," he explained afterward. "With us there, the enemy would be compelled to fall back on the east and west entirely out of the State of Kentucky." Two Confederate forts commanded the two rivers: Fort Henry on the Tennessee and Fort Donelson on the Cumberland. The forts were twins and nearly conjoined, for the rivers were but a dozen miles apart at this location and the outer defenses of the forts came to within cannon shot of each other. Grant proposed to pin Fort Henry between advancing ground forces and ironclad gunboats on the Tennessee and then, with Henry secure, do the same to Donelson.

He discussed his plan with some of his fellow officers, including Charles Smith, who was a decade his senior and a distinguished veteran of the Mexican War. Smith concurred with Grant on the importance of the Tennessee and Cumberland, prompting Grant to renew his request to visit St. Louis.

Halleck this time consented, to Grant's encouragement. "I have now a larger force than General Scott ever commanded prior to our present difficulties," he wrote his sister Mary. "I believe there is no portion of our whole army better prepared to contest a battle than there is within my district, and I am very much mistaken if I have not got the confidence of officers and men. This is all important, especially with new troops."

Halleck still didn't share Grant's hopefulness, though, and he greeted the brigadier coolly. Grant blamed both Halleck and himself for the meeting's failure. "I was received with so little cordiality that I perhaps stated the object of my visit with less clearness than I might have done," he wrote. "I had not uttered many sentences before I was cut short as if my plan was preposterous. I returned to Cairo very much crestfallen."

But not dissuaded. He again wrote Charles Smith, who reaffirmed the feasibility of the Tennessee campaign. "Two ironclad gunboats would make short work of Fort Henry," Smith told John Rawlins, the Galena orator, who had become Grant's assistant. Navy commander Andrew Foote, heading the Union squadron on the Mississippi and Ohio Rivers, telegraphed Halleck: "Fort Henry on the Tennessee can be carried with four ironclad gunboats and troops to be permanent-occupied." Foote, writing in the last week of January 1862, added, "In consultation with General Grant we have come to the conclusion that the Tennessee will soon fall as the Ohio is falling above and therefore it is desirable to make the contemplated movement the latter part of this week."

Grant approached Halleck a third time. "I would respectfully suggest the propriety of subduing Fort Henry, near the Kentucky and Tennessee line, and holding the position," he wrote Halleck on January 29. "If this is not done soon there is but little doubt but that the defenses of both the Tennessee and Cumberland rivers will be materially strengthened." Taking Fort Henry would preempt such strengthening. "It will besides have a moral effect upon our troops to advance them towards the rebel states." With what might have struck Halleck as smugness, Grant concluded: "The advantages of this move are as perceptible to the General Commanding Department"—Halleck—"as to myself. Therefore further comments are unnecessary."

Grant's arguments finally caught on, and Halleck let himself be persuaded. "Make your preparations to take and hold Fort Henry," he telegraphed Grant.

Grant had already begun. "Very little preparation is necessary for this move," he wrote Smith, who commanded the garrison at Paducah. The small need for preparation was fortunate, as secrets were impossible to maintain where Southern sympathizers abounded. "If possible, the troops and community should be kept from knowing anything of the design."

"I will leave here tomorrow night," Grant telegraphed Halleck on February 1. The next day he issued marching orders to the officers and men. "No firing, except when ordered by proper authority, will be allowed. . . . Plundering and disturbing private property is positively prohibited. . . . Regimental commanders will be held strictly accountable for the acts of their regiments."

To John McClernand he gave particular orders: "On your arrival at Paducah you will proceed immediately up the Tennessee River, debarking all your cavalry excepting one company at the first ferry above, on the side between the two rivers." The cavalry should march to a spot several miles below Fort Henry and the transports return to Paducah. Pending the arrival of additional troops McClernand should hold the ground below Henry. "For this purpose you will dispose your forces to the best advantage."

Grant himself probed the defenses of Fort Henry. "I went up on the *Essex* this morning with Captain Porter, two other ironclad boats accompanying, to ascertain the range of the rebel guns," he wrote Halleck on February 4. "From a point about one mile above the place afterwards decided on for place of debarkation, several shells were thrown, some of them taking effect inside the rebel fort. This drew the enemy's fire, all of which fell far short, except from one rifled gun which threw a ball through the cabin of the *Essex* and several near it." This ball determined the point of debarkation, just out of range of the rifled guns.

That night Grant wrote Julia from the steamer *Uncle Sam*. "All the troops will be up by noon tomorrow," he said. "And Friday morning, if we are not attacked before, the fight will commence. The enemy are well fortified and have a strong force. I do not want to boast but I have a confident feeling of success." The troops did arrive the next morning, and they were arrayed, per Grant's order, along the river. "The sight of our campfires on either side of the river is beautiful and no doubt inspires the enemy, who is in full view of them, with the idea that we have full 40,000 men," he wrote Julia that evening. The reckoning was but hours away. "Tomorrow will come the tug of war. One side or the other must tomorrow night rest in quiet possession of Fort Henry."

At eleven o'clock on the morning of February 6 the attack commenced. McClernand's infantry and cavalry approached the fort on land; Foote's gunboats closed by the river. The boats did the greater damage, as high water impeded McClernand's march. The Union boats exchanged fire with the Confederate artillery, tentatively at first but escalating after noon. "The fire on both sides was now terrific," Confederate commander Lloyd Tilghman reported afterward. One by one the guns of the fort were silenced. Meanwhile only the *Essex* of the Union gunboats suffered serious damage, when a shell hit the boiler and caused an explosion that killed or wounded nearly fifty of the crew.

Gradually Tilghman's battle plan became clear. The Confederate commander had fewer than 3,000 troops, too few to defend both Fort Henry and Fort Donelson. "Fort Donelson might possibly be held, if properly re-enforced, even though Fort Henry should fall; but the reverse of this proposition was not true," Tilghman recounted. He knew he was outnumbered, though he overestimated his deficit—as Grant intended he would. "I had no hope of being able successfully to defend the fort against such overwhelming odds," Tilghman declared. He sent his infantry, cavalry, and light artillery away from Fort Henry toward Fort Donelson. He kept no more than a hundred men to fire the guns and cover the others' escape. "My object was to save the main body by delaying matters as long as possible."

His method succeeded. After two hours he struck the flag and surrendered the fort. Grant gave cavalry chase to the Confederates fleeing toward Fort Donelson, but their lead was too great and he called his horsemen back.

"Fort Henry is ours," he wired Halleck on the evening of February 6. Yet the campaign had only begun. "I shall take and destroy Fort Donelson on the 8th."

Halleck relayed the message to Washington with a flourish. "Fort Henry is ours," he telegraphed George McClellan. "The flag of the Union is re-established on the soil of Tennessee. It will never be removed."

"Thank Grant, Foote, and their commands for me," McClellan responded.

22

"I WAS VERY IMPATIENT TO GET TO FORT DONELSON, BECAUSE I KNEW the importance of the place to the enemy and supposed he would reinforce it rapidly," Grant said later. "I felt that 15,000 men on the 8th would be more effective than 50,000 a month later." And so on the day after taking Fort Henry he rode in the direction of Donelson. He expected little resistance. "I had known General Pillow"—Gideon Pillow—"in Mexico, and judged that with any force, no matter how small, I could march up to within gunshot of any entrenchments he was given to hold." Grant was aware that John Floyd, Pillow's superior, commanded Fort Donelson. "But he was no soldier, and I judged he would yield to Pillow's pretensions." Besides, Grant said, Floyd was morally unfit for his post and knew it. "His conscience must have troubled him and made him afraid. As Secretary of War"—under James Buchanan—"he had taken a solemn oath to maintain the Constitution of the United States and to uphold the same against all its enemies. He had betrayed that trust. . . . Well may he have been afraid to fall into the hands of National troops."

Grant got a good look at Donelson. The fort topped a bluff on the left, or west, bank of the Cumberland River. A creek separated the fort from the village of Dover two miles upstream. At most times the creek presented little obstacle to travel, but winter rains this February had swollen the stream and also raised the river, which backed up into the creek. A second creek, south of the fort, similarly hindered movement. The heavy guns of the fort were trained on the river, threatening any upriver traffic from the north. Trenches for riflemen protected the west-facing rear of the fort, and recently felled trees, their sharpened trunks and branches pointing outward, protected the trenches.

Grant intended to pin Fort Donelson as he had Fort Henry. Foote's flotilla of gunboats would attack from the river while ground troops under McClernand, Smith and Lew Wallace would close in on land.

But the weather frustrated his plans. "At present we are perfectly locked in by high water," Grant reported on February 8. The banks of the Cumberland rose several feet above the fields and forests behind, so when the floodwaters went over the banks they inundated much of the surrounding area. "I contemplated taking Fort Donelson today with infantry and cavalry alone, but all my troops will be kept busily engaged saving what we now have from the rapidly rising waters."

After spending the previous weeks in rapid motion, Grant found the delay vexing. "You have no conception of the amount of labor I have to perform," he wrote his sister Mary. "An army of men all helpless looking to the commanding officer for every supply. Your plain brother has, however, as yet had no reason to feel himself unequal to the task and fully believes that he will carry on a successful campaign against our rebel enemy. I do not speak boastfully but utter a presentiment. The scare and fright of the rebels up here is beyond conception. Twenty-three miles above here some were drowned in their haste to retreat, thinking us such vandals that neither life nor property would be respected. G. J. Pillow commands at Fort Donelson. I hope to give him a tug before you receive this."

Grant summoned his division commanders to a meeting aboard one of the steamers. Lew Wallace had already formed a sense of Grant; the meeting reinforced it. "From the first his silence was remarkable," Wallace remembered. "He knew how to keep his temper. In battle, as in camp, he went about quietly, speaking in a conversational tone; yet he appeared to see everything that went on, and was always intent on business. He had a faithful assistant adjutant-general"—John Rawlins—"and appreciated him; he preferred, however, his own eyes, word, and hand. His aides were little more than messengers. In dress he was plain, even negligent; in partial amendment of that his horse was always a good one and well kept. At the council—calling it such by grace—he smoked, but never said a word."

The upshot of the meeting was that the army would move. "We start this morning for Fort Donelson in heavy force," Grant wrote Halleck on February 12. As Grant expected, Pillow put up no resistance, and the

Union troops reached sight of the Donelson defenses by midday. The next twenty-four hours were occupied investing the position, cutting it off as far as possible from resupply or escape. But the high water complicated the task, and the weather tested the troops' endurance. "Last night was very severe upon the troops," Grant wrote Halleck. "At dusk it commenced raining and in a short time turned cold and changed to snow and sleet. This morning the thermometer indicated 20 degrees below freezing."

The attack commenced nonetheless. On the afternoon of February 14 Foote's gunboats chugged up the river toward the fort. Four ironclads and two wooden gunboats began blasting away. The lead vessel got within a quarter mile of the fort's batteries, and for over an hour the flotilla delivered and received heavy fire. Foote believed he had the better of the exchange. "The enemy was running from his batteries," he reported afterward. The capture of the fort seemed imminent; Confederate commander Floyd, writing from behind the batteries, dashed off a warning to his superior, General Albert Sidney Johnston: "The fort cannot hold out twenty minutes." But then the rebel guns took disabling effect. The wheel of one Union craft and the tiller of another were torn away, rendering the boats helpless before the current, which carried them downstream. The other Federal vessels were similarly compelled to retire.

Grant watched the artillery duel from the bank of the Cumberland. "The enemy had been much demoralized by the assault," he remembered. "But they were jubilant when they saw the disabled vessels dropping down the river entirely out of the control of the men on board." The afternoon ended on this high note for the Confederates. "The gunboats have been driven back," Floyd informed Johnston. "I think the fight is over today."

The next twelve hours were extremely trying for the Federals. The weather got colder; the men were without campfires, which would have made targets for the Donelson guns, and many lacked blankets and heavy coats, which they had dropped on the rapid march from Fort Henry. Grant grew worried. "If all the gunboats that can, will immediately make their appearance before the enemy, it may secure us a victory," he wrote Foote the next morning. "Otherwise all may be defeated." When Foote informed him that the gunboats would need ten days for repair, he felt the victory had slipped through his grasp. Putting the best face on things, he informed Halleck, "Appearances now indicate that we will have a protracted siege here."

But then Floyd, or perhaps Pillow, blundered. The Confederate command impatiently determined that Pillow should try to break through the Union cordon and effect an escape. At dawn on February 15 the rebels threw themselves against the Union right, where McClernand's division held the broken ground. "Here and there the musicians were beginning to make the woods ring with reveille," Lew Wallace remembered, "and the numbed soldiers of the line were rising from their icy beds and shaking the snow from their frozen garments. . . . Suddenly the pickets fired, and with the alarm on their lips rushed back upon their comrades. The woods on the instant came alive."

The hottest fighting of the western war to date ensued. The Union brigade of W. H. L. Wallace absorbed some of the heaviest blows. "The first charge against him was repulsed," Lew Wallace recounted, "whereupon he advanced to the top of the rising ground behind which he had sheltered his troops in the night. A fresh assault followed, but, aided by a battery across the valley to his left, he repulsed the enemy a second time. His men were steadfast, and clung to the brow of the hill as if it were theirs by holy right. An hour passed, and yet another hour, without cessation of the fire. Meantime the woods rang with a monstrous clangor of musketry, as if a million men were beating empty barrels with iron hammers. . . . Men fell by the score, reddening the snow with their blood. The smoke, in pallid white clouds, clung to the underbrush and treetops as if to screen the combatants from each other. Close to the ground the flame of musketry and cannon tinted everything a lurid red."

The Federals held their positions until their ammunition ran low. At this point, facing troops who seemed to have unlimited bullets and shells, they retreated, then broke and ran. The Union right, commanded by McClernand, appeared in danger of collapse.

"Just then General Grant rode up to where General McClernand and I were in conversation," Lew Wallace remembered. "He was almost unattended. In his hand there were some papers, which looked like telegrams. Wholly unexcited, he saluted and received the salutations of his subordinates." Wallace summoned later experience to reflect on Grant at that moment. "In every great man's career there is a crisis exactly similar to that which now overtook General Grant, and it cannot be better described than as a crucial test of his nature. A mediocre person would have accepted the news as an argument for persistence in his resolution to enter upon a siege. Had General Grant done so, it is very probable his history would have been then and there concluded. His admirers and detractors alike are invited to study him at this precise juncture. It cannot be doubted that he saw with painful distinctness the effect of the disaster to his right wing. His face flushed slightly. With a sudden grip he crushed the papers in his hand. But in an instant these signs of disappointment or hesitation—as the reader pleases—cleared away. In his ordinary quiet voice he said, addressing himself to both officers, 'Gentlemen, the position on the right must be retaken.' With that he turned and galloped off."

Grant's calm resolve and the orders he issued to give it effect rescued the day. He got ammunition to McClernand, who rallied his men and regained the initiative on the right. He ordered Charles Smith, on the left, to counterattack, which Smith did with such vigor as to breach the Confederate lines. That night Smith's troops slept where the rebels had rested the night before.

To Grant's eye victory was inevitable. "There was now no doubt but that the Confederates must surrender or be captured the next day," he wrote afterward. Floyd and Pillow thought so too. Both men decided to depart, leaving the third in command, Simon Bolivar Buckner, to treat with Grant. On the morning of February 16 Buckner requested an armistice to negotiate terms.

Grant replied in words that made him famous. "No terms except an unconditional and immediate surrender can be accepted," he said. Failing that, "I propose to move immediately upon your works."

Buckner complained that Grant's ultimatum was "ungenerous and unchivalrous," but he had no alternative and gave in. He and Grant spoke a short while later. They recalled their cadet days and how Buckner had loaned Grant money on his return from California. They reflected on the battle just concluded. "He said to me that if he had been in command I would not have got up to Donelson as easily as I did," Grant recounted in his memoirs. "I told him that if he had been in command I should not have tried in the way I did."

23

"Honor to the brave!" the *New York Tribune* trumpeted of Grant. Other papers echoed the plaudits and declared that the capture of Fort Donelson laid open the heart of the Confederacy.

Lincoln was thrilled but nervous. "You have Fort Donelson safe," Lincoln wrote Halleck, "unless Grant shall be overwhelmed from outside, to prevent which latter will, I think, require all the vigilance, energy and skill of yourself and Buell"—Don Carlos Buell, commander of the Army of the Ohio—"acting in full cooperation." To this point Lincoln had let his generals run the war largely unbothered by presidential advice, but after ten months of disappointment he felt obliged to weigh in. "Our success or failure at Donelson is vastly important," he said. "I beg you to put your soul in the effort."

Halleck was willing, but at the expense of Grant. "Give me command in the West," Halleck implored George McClellan. "I ask this in return for Forts Henry and Donelson." Halleck, as a theorist of war, had long advocated concentration of force; a single command west of the Alleghenies, he now said, would allow him to crush the rebellion. "Give it to me, and I will split secession in twain in one month." When McClellan was slow to answer, Halleck entreated him again. "I must have command of the armies in the West. Hesitation and delay are losing us the golden opportunity. Lay this before the President and Secretary of War. May I assume the command? Answer quickly."

Grant learned of Halleck's assertiveness only secondhand. Halleck had taken little advance interest in the Donelson campaign. "General Halleck did not approve or disapprove of my going to Fort Donelson," Grant observed afterward. "He said nothing whatever to me on the subject." Grant was surprised not to get a letter of congratulation after the victory. Halleck's headquarters at St. Louis posted a formal notice thanking Grant and Foote and their forces for the victories at Forts Henry and Donelson. But that was all. "I received no other recognition whatever from General Halleck."

Grant did agree with Halleck on the importance of a unified command. "After the fall of Fort Donelson the way was opened to the National forces all over the Southwest without much resistance," he wrote later. "If one general who would have taken the responsibility had been in command of all the troops west of the Alleghenies, he could have marched to Chattanooga, Corinth, Memphis and Vicksburg with the troops we then had, and as volunteering was going on rapidly over the North there would soon have been force enough at all these centers to operate offensively against any body of the enemy that might be found near them."

Grant could envision himself, after Fort Donelson, as that general. "'Secesh' is now about on its last legs in Tennessee," he wrote Julia. "I want to push on as rapidly as possible to save hard fighting. These terrible battles are very good things to read about for persons who lose no friends, but I am decidedly in favor of having as little of it as possible. The way to avoid it is to push forward as vigorously as possible."

He assumed Halleck concurred. "General Halleck is clearly the same way of thinking," Grant told Julia. Halleck, moreover, recommended Grant for promotion to major general, which the president duly confirmed.

But Halleck thought Grant took excessive risks. "Don't be rash," he had cautioned Grant the day before Donelson fell. "Having the place completely invested, you can afford to have a little patience." After the victory he didn't want Grant to get too much credit. His perfunctory congratulation of Grant was pallid next to his praise for Charles Smith, Grant's subordinate. "Smith, by his coolness and bravery at Fort Donelson when the battle was against us, turned the tide and carried the enemy's outworks," he wrote McClellan. "Make him a major-general. You can't get a better one. Honor him for this victory and the whole country will applaud."

The limits of technology didn't help relations between Grant and Halleck. Grant outran his telegraph line, which connected St. Louis only to Cairo. A second line was being strung from Cairo to Paducah, but the operator at the end of the advancing line neglected to forward certain crucial messages. "This operator afterwards proved to be a rebel," Grant recalled. "He deserted his post after a short time and went south, taking his dispatches with him." The result was that Halleck thought Grant was ignoring him. "Why do you not obey my orders to report strength and positions of your command?" he wrote Grant in early March.

*H*alleck's question was accompanied by a shocking order. "You will place Major General C. F. Smith in command of expedition, and remain yourself at Fort Henry," Halleck said. There was a second part to the shock. The capture of Fort Donelson had prompted the Confederates to fall back from the Cumberland, leaving Nashville defenseless. Grant ventured to the Tennessee capital to investigate, only to receive another reprimand on his return to Fort Henry. "Your going to Nashville without authority, and when your presence with your troops was of the utmost importance, was a matter of very serious concern at Washington," Halleck wrote. "So much so that I was advised to arrest you on your return."

Grant was stunned. From being a hero he now found himself subject to arrest. His first reaction was to defend himself against Halleck's charges. "I am not aware of ever having disobeyed any order from Head Quarters, certainly never intended such a thing," he wrote Halleck. "I have reported almost daily the condition of my command and reported every position occupied. . . . My reports have nearly all been made to General Cullum, Chief of Staff, and it may be that many of them were not thought of sufficient importance to forward more than a telegraphic synopsis of."

But the longer he thought things over, the less he believed he should *have* to explain himself. "I am in a very poor humor for writing," he wrote Julia. "I was ordered to command a very important expedition up the Tennessee River, and now an order comes directing one of my juniors to take the command whilst I am left behind here with a small garrison. It may be all right, but I don't now see it."

To Halleck he grew more defensive. "I have done my very best to obey orders, and to carry out the interests of the service," he wrote. "If my course is not satisfactory, remove me at once. I do not wish to impede in any way the success of our arms. I have averaged writing more than once a day since leaving Cairo, to keep you informed of my position; and it is no fault of mine if you have not received my letters. My going to Nashville was strictly intended for the good of the service, and not to gratify any desire of my own. Believing sincerely that I must have enemies between you and myself who are trying to impair my usefulness, I respectfully ask to be relieved from further duty in the Department."

Halleck realized he had gone too far. He couldn't afford to lose the country's new hero. "You are mistaken," he wrote back. "There is no enemy between you and me." He nonetheless reiterated his earlier complaint. "There is no letter of yours stating the number and position of your command since the capture of Fort Donelson."

Grant supplied the information in great detail. Yet he too held his ground. "I renew my application to be relieved from further duty."

Halleck recognized that Grant had outmaneuvered him. The press would have his head, and Lincoln too, most likely, if Grant were let go. "You cannot be relieved from your command," he wrote Grant on March 13. "There is no good reason for it." He completed the surrender by dispatching fresh troops. "I wish you as soon as your new army is in the field to assume the immediate command and lead it on to new victories."

24

WILLIAM SHERMAN WATCHED GRANT DURING THE CAMPAIGN FOR Donelson and offered what encouragement he could from the banks of the Ohio. "I should like to hear from you, and will do everything in my power to hurry forward to you reinforcements and supplies, and if I could be of service myself would gladly come, without making any question of rank," Sherman wrote.

He was senior to Grant at this point, but he had particular cause for eschewing rank. He hadn't sought advancement to command, indeed had shunned it from the start of the war. Yet his obvious talent prompted his superiors to put him at the right hand of commanders, and when Robert Anderson, who had found his way from Fort Sumter to his native Kentucky, pleaded failing nerves as reason for resigning command of the central front of the war, Sherman reluctantly took his place.

Events and Sherman's own missteps soon reinforced his reluctance. His strategist's eye informed him that Kentucky was peculiarly vulnerable, and he said as much to Simon Cameron when the secretary of war passed through Louisville. Cameron was traveling with a sizable entourage, and Sherman hesitated to be candid in front of so many strangers. Cameron reassured him. "They are all friends, all members of my family," Cameron said. "You may speak your mind freely and without restraint." Sherman nonetheless locked the door of the meeting room before turning to the matter at hand.

"I remember taking a large map of the United States," he wrote later, "and assuming the people of the whole South to be in rebellion, and that our task was to subdue them, showed that McClellan was on the left, having a frontage of less than a hundred miles, Fremont the right, about the same; whereas I, the center, had from the Big Sandy to Paducah, over three hundred miles of frontier; that McClellan had a hundred thousand men, Fremont sixty thousand, whereas to me had only been allotted about eighteen thousand." Sherman asserted that for defense he should have sixty thousand troops immediately. For offense—for subduing the South and crushing the rebellion—two hundred thousand troops would ultimately be necessary.

Cameron was propped up on a bed, resting from the travel. Sherman's comments knocked him flat. "Great God!" he said, gradually rising again. "Where are they to come from?"

Sherman responded that there were plenty of men in the North if the government would pay to enlist and equip them. But that was the government's job, not his. "We discussed all these matters fully," Sherman remembered. "And I thought I had aroused Mr. Cameron to a realization of the great war that was before us, and was in fact upon us. I heard him tell General Thomas to make a note of our conversation, that he might attend to my requests on reaching Washington."

Cameron did attend to Sherman's requests, arranging for additional men and arms to be sent to Kentucky. But he also registered his concern that Sherman appeared agitated and too easily alarmed. In the halls of the War Department—the same halls that still echoed the tales of Grant's drunkenness—Sherman developed a reputation for instability and defeatism. He fought a losing battle against the reputation. "I know that others than yourself think I take a gloomy view of affairs without cause," he wrote his brother John. "I hope to God 'tis so. All I know is the fact that all over Kentucky the people are allied by birth, interest, and preference to the South." The arms he had requested were slow in arriving. "Troops come from Wisconsin and Minnesota without arms and receive such as we have here for the first time, and I cannot but look upon it as absolutely sacrificing them. . . . Some terrible disaster is inevitable."

Sherman was satisfied to be replaced by Don Carlos Buell, but he carried his forebodings to Missouri, where he frightened his fellow officers. Henry Halleck got unsettling reports from the field, which he relayed to Washington. "General Sherman was completely 'stampeded' and was 'stampeding' the army," Halleck wrote McClellan. He summoned Sherman to St. Louis and made a personal determination. "General Sherman's physical and mental system is so completely broken by labor and care as to render him for the present entirely unfit for duty," Halleck recorded. "Perhaps a few weeks rest may restore him. I am satisfied that

in his present condition it would be dangerous to give him a command."
Halleck sent Sherman home to Ohio for twenty days to gather his wits.

The leave started badly. A journalist Sherman had jailed in Kentucky
for snooping where he wasn't authorized wrote an article calling Sherman "insane." Sherman bitterly bemoaned his fate to Halleck. "These
newspapers have us in their power, and can destroy us as they please," he
wrote. Halleck tried to reassure him. "The newspaper attacks are certainly shameless and scandalous," Halleck said, "but I cannot agree with
you that they have us in their power 'to destroy us as they please.'"

The time off did its work, though, calming Sherman and, more
importantly, persuading him to keep his worries to himself. When he
returned to St. Louis he received a temporary assignment drilling new
enlistees; after two months of good service, he was given renewed command responsibilities. "As evidence that I have every confidence in General
Sherman," Halleck wrote, "I have placed him in command of Western Kentucky—a command only second in importance in this department. As soon as divisions and columns can be organized, I propose to
send him into the field where he can render most efficient service."

*A*lbert Sidney Johnston had his own problems with the press.
Grant's victories at Forts Henry and Donelson had compelled the Confederate commander to pull his armies south in what looked to much of
the Confederacy like an ignominious retreat. Yielding Nashville without
a fight appeared to the generals of the fourth estate an act of cowardice, perhaps treachery. Tennesseans especially complained that they were
being abandoned. The Tennessee delegation in the Confederate congress
visited Jefferson Davis to demand a change of leadership in the West.
The Confederate president knew Johnston, a distinguished officer in the
United States Army during the period when Davis had been secretary of
war, and considered him to be "one of the noblest men with whom I had
ever been associated, and one of the ablest soldiers I had ever seen in the
field." Yet the Tennesseans had grounds for their fears, and Davis heard
them out. "I paused under conflicting emotions," he remembered, "and
after a time merely answered, 'If Sidney Johnston is not a general, the
Confederacy has none to give you.'"

Shortly, though, Davis wrote to Johnston. "We have suffered great
anxiety because of recent events in Kentucky and Tennessee, and I have
been not a little disturbed by the repetition of reflections upon yourself,"

he said. "I made for you such defense as friendship prompted and many years of acquaintance justified, but I needed facts to rebut the wholesale assertions made against you to cover others and to condemn my administration. The public, as you are aware, have no correct measure for military operations, and the journals are very reckless in their statements." Davis, as a former war secretary, claimed a certain strategic expertise, and now he offered a recommendation. "The audacity which the enemy exhibits would no doubt give you the opportunity to cut some of his lines of communication, to break up his plan of campaign, and, defeating some of his columns, to drive him from the soil as well of Tennessee as of Kentucky."

Johnston was a proud man and had already been stung by the public criticism; the letter from Davis was another lash. "The test of merit in my profession, with the people, is success," he acknowledged in reply. "It is a hard rule, but I think it right." He said he was already at work on a plan that would make good use of P. G. T. Beauregard. "If I join this corps to the forces of Beauregard (I confess a hazardous experiment), then those who are now declaiming against me will be without an argument."

Johnston's hazardous experiment unfolded around a log meeting-house called Shiloh near Pittsburg Landing on the Tennessee River just above Tennessee's border with northeastern Mississippi. Grant was aiming to capture the town of Corinth, Mississippi, a junction of two critical rail lines, one tying Tennessee to the cotton states farther south and the other connecting the Atlantic seaboard to Memphis and the Mississippi. "If we obtained possession of Corinth the enemy would have no railroad for the transportation of armies or supplies until that running east from Vicksburg was reached," Grant recalled. "It was the great strategic position at the West between the Tennessee and the Mississippi rivers and between Nashville and Vicksburg."

Accordingly Grant arranged to move his forces up the Tennessee to Pittsburg Landing. Sherman led one division; Lew Wallace, John McClernand, Charles Smith, Stephen Hurlbut and Benjamin Prentiss the others. Don Carlos Buell, marching overland from Nashville, would join the strike against Corinth. As Grant's divisions reached Pittsburg Landing, he arrayed them in temporary bivouac fashion. "When all reinforcements should have arrived, I expected to take the initiative by marching on Corinth, and had no expectation of needing fortifications," he explained afterward. He discussed fortifications with his chief engineer, but the engineer pointed out the difficulty of construction, given the creek-crossed and otherwise convoluted topography, and Grant let the subject go. "The fact is, I regarded the campaign we were engaged in as an offensive one and had no idea that the enemy would leave strong entrenchments"—at Corinth—"to take the initiative when he knew he would be attacked where he was if he remained."

Grant's failure of imagination was precisely what Sidney Johnston was counting on. Rather than wait for Grant to come to Corinth, Johnston proposed to take the battle to Grant, and to get there before Buell's force augmented Grant's. Some of Johnston's lieutenants fretted at the risks; Beauregard contended that the Confederate forces could never achieve the requisite surprise. Others observed that the Federals had them seriously outnumbered. But Johnston refused to be dissuaded. "I would fight them if they were a million," he told a council of war on Saturday, April 5. Pointing to a map, he explained, "They can present no greater front between these two creeks than we can, and the more men they crowd in there, the worse we can make it for them." He closed the meeting decisively: "Gentlemen, we shall attack at daylight tomorrow."

Leander Stillwell was an eighteen-year-old enlisted man with an Illinois infantry regiment who was enjoying his first trip south. "We had just left the bleak, frozen North, where all was cold and cheerless, and we found ourselves in a clime where the air was as soft and warm as it was in Illinois in the latter part of May," Stillwell remembered. "The green grass was springing from the ground, the johnny-jump-ups were in blossom, the trees were bursting into leaf, and the woods were full of feathered songsters. There was a redbird that would come every morning about sun-up and perch himself in the tall black-oak tree in our company street, and for perhaps half an hour he would practice on his impatient querulous note that said, as plain as a bird could say, 'Boys, boys! Get up! Get up! Get up!' It became a standing remark among the boys that he was a Union redbird, and had enlisted in our regiment as a musician to sound the reveille."

April 6, Sunday, promised more of the same. "The sun was shining brightly, and there was not a cloud in the sky. It really seemed like Sunday in the country at home." But a distant sound reminded Stillwell and his comrades where they were. "Away off on the right, in the direction of Shiloh Church, came a dull, heavy 'Pum!' Then another, and still another. Every man sprang to his feet as if struck by an electric shock, and we looked inquiringly into one another's faces. What is that? said everyone, but no one answered." The pums came faster and closer, followed by a different sound: a dull, steady roar. "There was no mistaking that sound. That was not a squad of pickets emptying their guns on being relieved from duty; it was the continuous roll of thousands of muskets, and told us that a battle was on."

Stillwell's colonel summoned the regiment. "Remember your state," he said. "And do your duty today like brave men." The regiment marched across an open field and awaited the Confederate attack at the edge of the wood beyond. "The rebel army was unfolding its front, and the battle was steadily advancing in our direction," Stillwell recalled. "We could begin to see the blue rings of smoke curling upward among the trees off to the right, and the pungent smell of burning gunpowder filled the air. As the roar came travelling down the line from the right it reminded me (only it was a million times louder) of the sweep of a thunder shower in summer time over the hard ground of a stubble field."

Stillwell now wished he had never left home. "My mind's eye was fixed on a little log cabin far away to the north. . . . I could see my father sitting on the porch reading the little local newspaper. . . . There was my mother getting my little brothers ready for Sunday-school, the old dog lying asleep in the sun."

The enemy drew closer before bursting into view. "Suddenly, obliquely to our right, there was a long, wavy flash of bright light, then another, and another. It was the sunlight shining on gun barrels and bayonets—and there they were at last! A long, brown line, with muskets at right shoulder shift, in excellent order, right through the woods they came."

Stillwell's colonel gave the order to fire. "From one end of the regiment to the other leaped a sheet of red flame," Stillwell remembered. He and the others reloaded and fired again. Then, to his surprise, he heard the order to fall back. They recrossed the field to their camp, where they turned and stood their ground. They held this position for nearly an hour, exchanging vigorous fire with the enemy, until their officers once more called a retreat. "The troops on our right had given way and we were flanked," Stillwell observed, adding: "Possibly those boys on our right would give the same excuse for their leaving, and probably truly too." Whatever the case, the order to retreat came just in time. "As I rose from the comfortable log, from behind which a bunch of us had been firing, I saw men in gray and brown clothes with trailed muskets running through the camp on our right, and I saw something else, too, that sent a chill all through me. It was a kind of flag I had never seen before. It was a gaudy sort of thing, with red bars. It flashed over me in a second that that thing was a rebel flag!"

The retreat swiftly became a dash. "We observed no kind of order in leaving; the main thing was to get out of there as quick as we could. I ran down our company street and in passing the big Sibley tent of our mess I thought of my knapsack with all my traps and belongings, including that precious little packet of letters from home. I said to myself, 'I will save my knapsack, anyhow,' but one quick backward glance over my left shoulder made me change my mind, and I went on. I never saw my knapsack or any of its contents afterward."

Stillwell and the others eventually halted a half mile to the rear at the crest of a brush-covered ridge. Catching his breath, he reflected on his battle experience thus far. "I was astonished at our first retreat in the morning across the field back to our camp, but it occurred to me that maybe that was only 'strategy' and was all done on purpose. But when we had to give up our camp and actually to turn our backs and run a half a mile, it seemed to me that we were forever disgraced, and I kept thinking to myself, 'What will they say about this at home?'"

Stillwell's regiment was ordered to defend a battery some distance to the right. "We were put in position about twenty rods in the rear of the battery and ordered to lie flat on the ground. The ground sloped gently down in our direction, so that by hugging the ground close, the rebel shot and shell went over us."

At this point Grant appeared. "He was on horseback, of course, accompanied by his staff, and was evidently making a personal examination of his lines," Stillwell recalled. "He rode between us and the battery, at the head of his staff. He went by in a gallop. The battery was then hotly engaged; shot and shell were whizzing overhead and cutting off the limbs of trees, but Grant rode through the storm with perfect indifference, seemingly paying no more attention to the missiles than if they had been paper wads."

Stillwell's regiment remained by the battery till two o'clock in the afternoon, when it was sent to relieve a regiment that had been fighting desperately for hours. "I remember as we went up the slope and began firing about the first thing that met my gaze was what out west we would call a windrow, of dead men in blue, some doubled up face downward, others with their white faces upturned to the sky, brave boys who had been shot to death holding the line." Stillwell's regiment held the same line until their ammunition ran out, when they were relieved by another. They refilled their cartridge boxes and returned to their position defending the battery. "The boys laid down and talked in low tones. Many of our comrades, alive and well an hour ago, we had left dead on that bloody ridge. And still the battle raged. From right to left, everywhere, it was one never-ending, terrible roar, with no prospect of stopping."

The roar persisted till late afternoon, when the fighting diminished and then ceased. "Everything became ominously quiet," Stillwell said. A staff officer rode up and spoke to the commander of the battery and then to Stillwell's colonel. The next thing Stillwell saw was the battery horses being brought up from a ravine where they had been sheltered. The horses were hitched to the guns and the battery was hauled to the rear. The strange quiet held; the loudest noise was the creak of the caissons. Stillwell's regiment followed the battery into the woods and out upon a field. "I then saw to our right and front lines of men in blue moving in the same direction we were, and it was evident that we were falling back." The quiet held barely a moment longer. "All at once, on the right, the left and from our recent front came one tremendous roar, and the bullets fell like hail. The lines took the double-quick toward the rear. For a while the attempt was made to fall back in order, and then everything went to pieces. My heart failed me utterly. I thought the day was lost. A confused mass of men and guns, caissons, army wagons, ambulances, and all the debris of a beaten army surged and crowded along the narrow dirt road to the landing, while that pitiless storm of leaden hail came crashing on us from the rear."

The flight carried Stillwell and the others to within several hundred yards of Pittsburg Landing. They rounded a bend in the road and saw a long line of soldiers in blue, at right angles to the road and stretching on each side away into the woods. "What did that mean?" Stillwell recalled asking himself. "And where had they come from?" He asked the same questions of his sergeant, who didn't know but thought the troops were intended to cover the crossing of the river by the army in retreat. "And doubtless that was the thought of every intelligent soldier in our beaten column. And yet it goes to show how little the common soldier knew of the actual situation." In fact the line, consisting of elements of the divisions of Sherman, McClernand and Hurlbut, was not covering the retreat but holding a new position. "In other words, we still had an unbroken line confronting the enemy, made up of men who were not yet ready, by any manner of means, to give up that they were whipped."

*W*illiam Sherman had seen little amiss before the battle. "From about the 1st of April we were conscious that the rebel cavalry in our front was getting bolder and more saucy," he remembered. "And on Friday, the 4th of April, it dashed down and carried off one of our picket guards, composed of an officer and seven men, posted a couple of miles out on the Corinth road. . . . But thus far we had not positively detected the presence of infantry." The next day showed nothing new, either. "All is quiet along my lines," Sherman wrote Grant on April 5. "I do not apprehend anything like an attack on our position."

At seven on Sunday morning, April 6, Sherman rode with staff along his front, which encompassed the Shiloh meetinghouse. The Confederate pickets opened fire, killing Sherman's orderly. Sherman's men returned the fire, but nothing yet indicated a general attack.

Things changed within the hour. "About 8 a.m. I saw the glistening bayonets of heavy masses of infantry to our left front in the woods," Sherman wrote in his after-action report. For the first time he realized something serious was afoot. He galloped along his line, urging his men to hold their ground.

"The battle opened by the enemy's battery, in the woods to our front, throwing shells into our camp," he later explained. Sherman's batteries answered. "I then observed heavy battalions of infantry passing obliquely to the left, across the open field in Appler's front"—Jesse Appler headed an Ohio regiment in Sherman's command. Other Confederate columns came straight toward Sherman. He gave the order to engage. "Our infantry and artillery opened along the whole line, and the battle became general."

Sherman's men held firm, but the Confederates drove past his left flank. He clung to Shiloh as long as he could, but eventually the rebels got artillery to his rear. "Some change became absolutely necessary," he wrote. He ordered his men to fall back, while one of his batteries, led by a Captain Behr, covered their retreat. "Behr gave the order, but he was almost immediately shot from his horse, when drivers and gunners fled in disorder, carrying off the caissons and abandoning five out of six guns without firing a shot." The enemy kept driving forward, and Sherman was compelled to give more ground. "This was about 10 1/2 a.m., at which time the enemy had made a furious attack on General McClernand's whole front. He struggled most determinedly, but, finding him pressed, I moved McDowell's brigade directly against the left flank of the enemy, forced him back some distance, and then directed the men to avail themselves of every cover—trees, fallen timber, and a wooded valley to our right. We held this position for four long hours, sometimes gaining ground and at others losing ground; General McClernand and myself acting in perfect concert and struggling to maintain this line."

Grant sent word that reinforcements under Lew Wallace were coming. "General McClernand and I, on consultation, selected a new line of defense, with its right covering a bridge by which General Wallace had to approach," Sherman recounted. "We fell back as well as we could, gathering in addition to our own such scattered forces as we could find, and formed the new line." Confederate cavalry charged the new position but were driven off. McClernand's men made their own charge, driving some of the rebels into a ravine. "I had a clear field, about two hundred yards wide, in my immediate front, and contented myself with keeping the enemy's infantry at that distance during the rest of the day," Sherman said.

Grant later tried to conceal his surprise at the nature and ferocity of the Confederate attack. For several days he had been hoping for battle, though the prospect strained his mind and spirit. "I wish I could make a visit anywhere for a week or two," he wrote Julia on April 3. "It would be a great relief not to have to think for a short time. Soon I hope to be permitted to move from here, and when I do there will probably be the greatest battle fought of the war. I do not feel that there is the slightest doubt about the result and therefore, individually, feel as unconcerned about it as if nothing more than a review was to take place. Knowing, however, that a terrible sacrifice of life must take place, I feel concerned for my army and their friends at home."

On the evening of April 4 he heard firing along the front and rode out to take a look. In the dark, amid torrents of rain, he saw little but what the frequent bolts of lightning illuminated. He turned and headed toward camp, giving his horse its head in the blackness. But the horse slipped descending a hill and fell, pinning Grant's ankle beneath it. Only the softness of the saturated earth prevented a crippling fracture; as it was, Grant suffered a nasty sprain that hobbled him for days.

On April 5 he learned that the outposts of Sherman and McClernand had been attacked in probing force. He gritted his teeth against the pain in his ankle and rode out again to investigate. "Found all quiet," he reported to Halleck. The Confederates had captured a handful of prisoners, wounded several and suffered comparable losses in return. The skirmish appeared to be nothing more than that. "I have scarcely the faintest idea of an attack (general one) being made upon us, but will be prepared should such a thing take place," he told Halleck.

Yet when the general attack occurred the next morning he was *not* prepared. He had kept his headquarters at Savannah, several miles downstream from Pittsburg Landing. "I was intending to remove my headquarters to Pittsburg, but Buell was expected daily and would come in at Savannah," he explained. It was at Savannah that Grant first learned of the attack. "Heavy firing is heard up the river, indicating plainly that an attack has been made up on our most advanced positions," he hurriedly wrote Buell. "I have been looking for this but did not believe the attack could be made before Monday or Tuesday." He told Buell he couldn't wait for their meeting but must get to the scene of the fighting at once. To the commander of Buell's advance force he scribbled an appeal to hurry. "The attack on my forces has been very spirited from early this morning. The appearance of fresh troops on the field now would have a powerful effect both by inspiring our men and disheartening the enemy. If you will get upon the field leaving all your baggage on the east bank of the river, it will be a move to our advantage and possibly save the day to us."

On the dispatch boat that carried him up to Pittsburg he directed the pilot to stop at Crump's Landing, where Lew Wallace had his division. He told Wallace to make ready to move wherever he was needed and to watch for further orders. When Grant reached Pittsburg and realized that the landing there was the object of the Confederate attack, he sent word to Wallace to come on as soon as he could. Wallace, however, misunderstood the message or was misinformed as to the route he was to follow, and his division lost its way and reached the battlefield only in the late afternoon.

Grant hadn't intended to fight on the field where the battle now unfolded, but he quickly assessed the terrain and the deployment of his forces. At the center was the Shiloh meetinghouse. "It stood on the ridge which divides the waters of Snake and Lick creeks," he recounted afterward. "This was the key to our position and was held by Sherman. His division was at that time wholly raw, no part of it ever having been in an engagement; but I thought this deficiency was more than made up by the superiority of the commander." To Sherman's left was McClernand, with a division that had fought at Forts Henry and Donelson. Benjamin Prentiss was next to McClernand, with untested troops. Smith's division was to Sherman's right, in reserve, although Smith himself was sick; W. H. L. Wallace commanded in Smith's absence.

The intensity of the Confederate attack surprised Grant as much as its timing. "The Confederate assaults were made with such a disregard of losses on their own side that our line of tents soon fell into their hands," he said. The rebels tried to turn Sherman's right flank, despite the troublesome terrain and the full creeks. Sherman's men, rising to their first challenge, beat back the rebels time and again. "But the front attack was kept up so vigorously that, to prevent the success of these attempts to get on our flanks, the National troops were compelled, several times, to take positions to the rear nearer Pittsburg landing," Grant wrote. By dusk his line was a mile back from where it had been in the morning.

Grant galloped from division to division throughout the day, directing and encouraging the commanders and their men. Sherman received the least attention. "Although his troops were then under fire for the first time, their commander, by his constant presence with them, inspired a confidence in officers and men that enabled them to render services on that bloody battle-field worthy of the best of veterans," Grant observed. He added: "A casualty to Sherman that would have taken him from the field that day would have been a sad one for the troops engaged at Shiloh." Grant almost did lose Sherman, who was nicked by flying metal and had a musket ball blow off his hat, besides having three horses shot from under him.

Late in the day Grant got word that Buell had reached the east bank of the Tennessee. He rode to the river to meet him, and the two generals conferred on a dispatch boat. As they left the boat, Buell observed panic-stricken troops who had fled the fighting and now cowered under the bank of the river. Inferring the state of the rest of the command from this pitiful minority, Buell asked Grant what provisions he had made for a retreat. Grant said he had made none. "I haven't despaired of whipping them yet," he said. Buell insisted: "But if you should be whipped, how will you get your men across the river? These transports will not take ten thousand men." Buell knew that Grant had thirty thousand in the field.

Grant responded grimly, "If I have to cross the river, ten thousand will be all I shall need transport for."

Grant's losses that day were unprecedented in numbers killed, wounded and captured. The captured included most of the division of Benjamin Prentiss, who had become separated from the rest of the Federal line, allowing the Confederates to surround him. The loss of Prentiss took Grant by particular surprise. "The last time I was with him was about half past four, when his division was standing up firmly and the general was as cool as if expecting victory," Grant said. But scarcely had they parted than Prentiss was forced to surrender with more than two thousand of his men.

The losses and poor performance of the Federal troops required explanation, which Grant provided over the following decades. "There was no hour during the day when there was not heavy firing and generally hard fighting at some point on the line," Grant wrote in his memoirs. "It was a case of Southern dash against Northern pluck and endurance. Three of the five divisions engaged on Sunday were entirely raw, and many of the men had only received their arms on the way from their States to the field. Many of them had arrived but a day or two before and were hardly able to load their muskets according to the manual. Their officers were equally ignorant of their duties. Under these circumstances it is not astonishing that many of the regiments broke at the first fire."

$\mathcal{P}$. G. T. Beauregard found himself unexpectedly in command of the Confederate army by the end of Sunday's fighting. Sidney Johnston had been as active on offense as Grant had been in defense; amid one of the Confederate charges in the afternoon a Union minié ball pierced his leg and severed an artery. He continued to give orders rather than tend to the wound, and he died from the bleeding. "Staff officers were immediately dispatched to acquaint the corps commanders of this deplorable casualty, with a caution, however, against otherwise promulgating the fact," Beauregard remembered. "They were also urged to push the battle with renewed vigor and, if possible, to force a speedy close."

But the Union forces stiffened, bolstered by the arrival of the first of Buell's brigades and by the covering fire of Federal gunboats on the Tennessee. Beauregard decided to call a halt. "We had now had more than eleven hours of continuous fighting, fighting without food except that hastily snatched up in the abandoned Federal encampments," he said. "The Confederate troops were not in a condition to carry such a position as that which confronted them at that late hour."

Beauregard took satisfaction from making his new headquarters in the same tent near the Shiloh meetinghouse that Sherman had occupied in the morning. His corps and division commanders gathered to learn their latest orders. "All evinced and expressed much satisfaction with the results, while no one was heard to express or suggest that more might have been achieved had the battle been prolonged. All seemed to believe that our troops had accomplished as much as could have been hoped for."

Grant later claimed he knew he would win even before Beauregard called off the attack that Sunday evening. The Confederates had thrown everything into the battle and succeeded only in pushing the Union lines back. The lines had not broken, and Grant's army still held the west bank of the Tennessee. And with the arrival of Buell's army and the belated appearance of Wallace's lost division, the Union side was growing much stronger. "I visited each division commander in person," Grant recalled. "I directed them to throw out heavy lines of skirmishers in the morning as soon as they could see, and push them forward until they found the enemy, following with their entire divisions in supporting distance, and to engage the enemy as soon as found. To Sherman I told the story of the assault at Fort Donelson, and said that the same tactics would win at Shiloh."

Grant's confidence was infectious. "It rained hard during the night," Sherman remembered. "But our men were in good spirits, lay on their arms, being satisfied with such bread and meat as could be gathered at the neighboring camps, and determined to redeem on Monday the losses of Sunday."

Grant's own night was more troubled, his optimism notwithstanding. "Rain fell in torrents and our troops were exposed to the storm without shelter," he recollected. "I made my headquarters under a tree a few hundred yards back from the river bank. My ankle was so much swollen from the fall of my horse the Friday night preceding, and the bruise was so painful, that I could get no rest." Between the storm and the pain he decided around midnight to repair to a log house he had used for directing the battle earlier in the day. "This had been taken as a hospital, and all night wounded men were being brought in, their wounds dressed, a leg or an arm amputated as the case might require, and everything being done to save life or alleviate suffering. The sight was more unendurable than encountering the enemy's fire, and I returned to my tree in the rain."

Sherman found him beneath the tree. Sherman couldn't sleep either. "Well, Grant, we've had the devil's own day, haven't we?" he said.

"Yes," Grant replied, pulling thoughtfully on his cigar. "Lick 'em tomorrow, though."

*A*nd so they proceeded to do. Grant ordered Sherman and the other division commanders to attack at dawn on Monday, and they responded with a will. The fighting grew hot, but this time all went Grant's way. Sherman later waxed lyrical in recounting the Union progress. "I saw Willich's regiment advance upon a point of water-oaks and thicket, behind which I knew the enemy was in great strength, and enter it in beautiful style," he wrote. "Then arose the severest musketry-fire I ever heard, and lasted some twenty minutes, when this splendid regiment had to fall back." The Federals kept fighting. "A whole brigade of McCook's division advanced beautifully, deployed, and entered this dreaded wood." Sherman brought up some howitzers. "I gave personal direction to the twenty-four-pounder guns, whose well-directed fire first silenced the enemy's guns to the left, and afterward at the Shiloh meeting-house. Rousseau's brigade moved in splendid order steadily to the front, sweeping everything before it, and at 4 p.m. we stood upon the ground of our original front line, and the enemy was in full retreat."

Grant again spent much of the day galloping back and forth along the front. At one point, while walking his horse with James McPherson and another officer, to give their mounts a chance to catch their breath, he approached a clearing he thought was beyond Confederate range. Without warning, a hidden battery opened fire on them from a wood across the clearing. Shells and musket balls whistled about their heads until they could scramble to safety. As they assessed the damage, they noticed McPherson's horse panting badly; seconds later the beast dropped dead from a ball that had passed entirely through its flank. Grant's sword saved him from a severe wound; a bullet hit the metal scabbard and nearly broke it in two.

By late afternoon that Monday the Federals had driven the Confederates fully from the field. Grant was tempted to try to deliver what

Beauregard had forgone the day before: the coup de grâce against a reeling enemy. But like Beauregard he decided he couldn't ask the effort of his men. "My force was too much fatigued from two days hard fighting and exposure in the open air to a drenching rain during the intervening night to pursue immediately," he explained to Halleck.

THE BATTLE OF SHILOH, OR PITTSBURG LANDING, AT FIRST WON Grant further accolades. "More Glorious News," the *New York Times* proclaimed by way of preface to introducing Grant to readers who didn't yet know him. "He is a man of plain exterior, light hair, blue eyes, five feet nine in height, plain and retiring in his manners, firm and decisive in character, esteemed by his soldiers, never wastes a word with any one, but pays strict attention to his military duties. . . . His personal bravery and dash is undoubted. . . . He is one of the hard-fighting school of Generals." Some pundits judged that the battle had demoralized the Confederates beyond repair. "Johnston, the best of their generals, is dead," one wrote, "and if it be correct that Beauregard is also dead"—as early reports suggested—"it hardly seems likely that there will be any further show of battle in the Southwest other than detached and irregular fighting."

But Beauregard wasn't dead, and as the Union casualty count—some thirteen thousand killed, wounded or captured—became known, it dulled Grant's achievement. The troops who fled the field on Sunday included men who afterward blamed their loss of nerve on the failure of their superiors to anticipate the Confederate attack; they told lurid tales of being surprised in their tents and seeing their comrades bayoneted where they slept. Buell's officers and men naturally thought their arrival had saved the day; *their* commander, they said, rather than Grant, should be the hero of the hour. Whitelaw Reid, a young reporter with the *Cincinnati Gazette*, savaged Grant in a lengthy article that furnished grist for scores of other newspapers. Horace Greeley, mightily impressed after Fort Donelson, now declared, "There was no more preparation by Gen-

eral Grant for an attack than if he had been on a Fourth of July frolic."
Governors of states that lost men complained that Grant hadn't done
enough to protect their boys; members of Congress called for an investigation. Among the many people who had heard the tales of Grant's
drinking were more than a few now willing to blame his unpreparedness
on the bottle.

Grant was sensitive to the criticism. "I will go on and do my duty to
the very best of my ability, without praise, and do all I can to bring this
war to a speedy close," he wrote his father from Pittsburg Landing. "I
am not an aspirant for anything at the close of the war"—unlike those
officers and politicians, he implied, who criticized him and *did* aspire
for place and preference. "As to the talk about a surprise here, nothing
could be more false. If the enemy had sent us word when and where they
would attack us, we could not have been better prepared. Skirmishing
had been going on for two days between our reconnoitering parties and
the enemy's advance. I did not believe, however, that they would make
a determined attack, but simply that they were making a reconnaissance
in force." The newspapers and the politicians were stressing his absence
from the front on the morning of the attack as evidence of his unreadi-
ness; this showed how little they knew, Grant said. "Troops were constantly arriving to be assigned to brigades and divisions, all ordered to
report at Savannah, making it necessary to keep an office and someone
there. I was also looking for Buell to arrive, and it was important that
I should have every arrangement complete for his speedy transit to this
side of the river."

Grant never got over the criticism of Shiloh; in the last months of
his life he was still defending his decision not to entrench. "The troops
with me, officers and men, needed discipline and drill more than they
did experience with pick, shovel and axe," he wrote in his memoirs. Yet
he couldn't deny the cost of the victory, although he noted that the Confederates paid heavily too. "Shiloh was the severest battle fought at the
West during the war, and but few in the East equaled it for hard, determined fighting. I saw an open field, in our possession on the second day,
over which the Confederates had made repeated charges the day before,
so covered with dead that it would have been possible to walk across the
clearing, in any direction, stepping on dead bodies, without a foot touching the ground."

Shiloh showed him what he could ask of his men; it also taught him
what he *must* ask of them. "Up to the battle of Shiloh I, as well as thou-

sands of other citizens, believed that the rebellion against the Government would collapse suddenly and soon if a decisive victory could be gained over any of its armies." Forts Henry and Donelson had been such victories, but Shiloh revealed that the Confederates had more fight in them than ever. "Then, indeed, I gave up all idea of saving the Union except by complete conquest."

Alexander McClure was a friend of Lincoln and for that reason, following Shiloh, a critic of Grant. "I did not know Grant at that time; had neither partiality nor prejudice to influence my judgment, nor had I any favorite general who might be benefited by Grant's overthrow," McClure remembered. "But I shared the almost universal conviction of the President's friends that he could not sustain himself if he attempted to sustain Grant by continuing him in command." McClure was an influential Pennsylvania Republican who had supported Lincoln early and strongly for president, and now he visited the White House to press the case for Grant's removal. "I appealed to Lincoln for his own sake to remove Grant at once, and in giving my reasons for it I simply voiced the admittedly overwhelming protest from the loyal people of the land against Grant's continuance in command."

McClure spoke for several minutes, constructing what he thought was a compelling case. Lincoln listened and pondered silently for some time. "He then gathered himself up in his chair," McClure recounted, "and said in a tone of earnestness that I shall never forget: '*I can't spare this man; he fights.*'"

Henry Halleck was certain he knew more about war than Lincoln did, and he was shocked at the cost of Shiloh and sure the Union couldn't stand many more such victories. For the record he congratulated Grant and his officers and men. "The soldiers of the great West have added new laurels to those which they had already won on numerous fields," he proclaimed. But he moved at once to demote Grant in practice if not in rank. He informed the War Department that he was transferring his headquarters to Pittsburg Landing and would assume direct command of Grant's army.

Grant resented the decision deeply. He had grown accustomed to command and didn't like being preempted. He felt embarrassed by Halleck's display of want of confidence and deprived of the chance to capitalize on and thereby redeem the bloody victory at Shiloh. He suffered in silence for weeks, thinking Halleck intended to attack Corinth, the objective of the battle of Shiloh. But when no attack occurred or even appeared imminent, he couldn't contain himself. "I have felt my position as anomalous, and determined to have it corrected, in some way, so soon as the present impending crisis should be brought to a close," he wrote Halleck. "I felt that censure was implied but did not wish to call up the matter in the face of the enemy." Apparently, however, no battle was at hand, and so he must speak. "My position differs but little from that of one in arrest." This was intolerable. "I deem it due to myself to ask either full restoration to duty, according to my rank, or to be relieved entirely from further duty."

Halleck professed puzzlement. "I am very much surprised, General, that you should find any cause of complaint in the recent assignment of commands," he replied to Grant. "You have precisely the position to which your rank entitles you." Grant was wrong to take offense. "You certainly will not suspect me of any intention to injure your feelings or reputation or to do you any injustice; if so you will eventually change your mind on this subject." Far from being Grant's persecutor, he was his protector. "I have done everything in my power to ward off the attacks which were made upon you." Many in Washington wanted Grant fired; Grant should be happy to retain his post. "If you believe me your friend, you will not require explanations; if not, explanations on my part would be of little avail."

Grant couldn't have refuted Halleck's explanation even if he had been sure it was specious. Perhaps Halleck was telling the truth after all. Yet this didn't change the fact that Grant was now a general without an army. And he saw little chance of regaining an army until the cloud over his reputation lifted.

He learned that Elihu Washburne, alone in Congress, had defended him. In writing Washburne a letter of thanks, Grant detailed the untenability of his situation in the face of the continuing attacks. "I have a father, mother, wife and children who read them and are distressed. . . . Then, too, all subject to my orders read these charges, and it is calculated to weaken their confidence in me and weaken my ability to render efficient service in our present cause." He told the same sad story to Julia. "I

have been so shockingly abused that I sometimes think it is almost time
to defend myself," he said. He couldn't do so where he was. "I am thinking seriously of going home."

But he wouldn't leave with Corinth unconquered. He thought the
army should have moved on Corinth immediately after Shiloh when
the Confederates were battered and vulnerable. Every day let Beauregard regroup and consolidate the town's defenses. Yet Halleck refused to
move at more than a snail's pace, insisting that each step be thoroughly
prepared and all vulnerabilities eliminated.

Grant, already upset at being ignored, grew exasperated at Halleck's slowness. He approached Halleck in late May and suggested that
an advance by night could lay Corinth open to easy assault. Halleck
rebuffed the advice as unsound and unwanted. "I was silenced so quickly
that I felt that possibly I had suggested an unmilitary movement," Grant
remembered bitterly.

Halleck's cautious approach eventually succeeded, after a fashion.
Beauregard decided that Corinth had become indefensible and ordered
the town evacuated. "We found the enemy had gone, taking with them
all their men, arms, and most of their supplies," Grant wrote Julia on
May 31. "What they did not take was mostly burned, in flames as we
entered." The Union now controlled Corinth and the rail lines in and out
of the place. But the Confederate army there had escaped.

The result left Grant unsatisfied. He believed that victory depended
less on seizing enemy territory, however crucially placed, than on destroying the enemy's armies. "They will turn up somewhere, and have to be
whipped yet," he said of Beauregard's forces.

William Sherman was astonished to hear, just days later, that Grant
intended to go home. "I rode from my camp to General Halleck's headquarters, then in tents just outside of the town, where we sat and gossiped
for some time," Sherman recalled. "He mentioned to me casually that
General Grant was going away the next morning." Sherman asked why.
"He said that he did not know, but that Grant had applied for a thirty
days' leave, which had been given him. Of course we all knew that he was
chafing under the slights of his anomalous position, and I determined to
see him on my way back."

Sherman approached Grant's camp, which consisted of a handful of
tents in the woods, surrounded by a railing of saplings. Some of Grant's

staff were outside the tents. "Piled up near them were the usual office and camp chests, all ready for a start in the morning. I inquired for the general, and was shown to his tent, where I found him seated on a camp-stool, with papers on a rude camp-table; he seemed to be employed in assorting letters, and tying them up with red tape into convenient bun-dles. After passing the usual compliments, I inquired if it were true that he was going away."

"Yes," Grant replied.

Sherman asked why.

"Sherman, you know," Grant said. "You know that I am in the way here. I have stood it as long as I can, and can endure it no longer."

Sherman asked where he was going.

"St. Louis."

Did he have any business in St. Louis?

"Not a bit."

Sherman weighed this briefly. "I then begged him to stay, illustrating his case by my own," he recalled. "Before the battle of Shiloh, I had been cast down by a mere newspaper assertion of 'crazy,' but that single battle had given me new life, and now I was in high feather; and I argued with him that if he went away events would go right along and he would be left out; whereas if he remained, some happy accident might restore him to favor and his true place."

Grant acknowledged that things had worked out for Sherman. He thanked Sherman for the advice. He sat silently for a moment and then consented to put off his travel plans. Sherman got him to promise not to leave the army without seeing or writing him.

Sherman was ordered away from Corinth soon after this meeting. But a short while later he got a message from Grant saying he had recon-sidered and would not be leaving the army after all.

"I have just received your note, and am rejoiced at your conclusion to remain," Sherman replied. "For yourself, you could not be quiet at home for a week when armies were moving, and rest could not relieve your mind of the gnawing sensation that injustice has been done you. There is a power in our land, irresponsible, corrupt and malicious, 'the press,' which has created the intense feelings of hostility that have arrayed the two parts of our country against each other, which must be curbed and brought within the just limits of reason and law before we can have peace in America." The press was the enemy as much as the rebels were, Sher-man said. "War cannot cease as long as any flippant fool of an editor may stir up the passions of the multitude, arraign with impunity the motives of the most honorable, and howl on their gang of bloody hounds to hunt down any man who despises their order. We can deal with armies who have a visible and tangible existence, but it will require tact and skill and courage to clip the wings of this public enemy, and I hope you have sufficiently felt the force of what I say to join in their just punishment before we resign our power and pass into the humble rank of citizens."

Sherman's advice and letter cemented Grant's high opinion of him. Sherman had been promoted to major general after Shiloh, but Grant's admiration transcended professional rank. "I have never done half justice by him," he wrote Julia. "With green troops he was my standby that trying day of Sunday (there has been nothing like it on this continent, nor in history). He kept his division in place all day, and aided materially in keeping those to his right and left in place." Another letter to Julia summarized Grant's judgment: "In General Sherman the country has an able and gallant defender and your husband a true friend."

*D*uring the spring and early summer of 1862 Lincoln grew as dissatisfied with George McClellan as McClellan already was with him. McClellan thought war should be left to the generals; he answered Lincoln's letters and telegrams politely but proceeded to do as he thought best. He took aim at Richmond, believing capture of the Confederate capital would disperse the rebel government and demoralize the Southern populace. He developed his strategy with care, transporting his army down the Chesapeake and then advancing slowly up the peninsula between the James and York Rivers. He took comfort in news that Robert E. Lee had replaced Joseph Johnston in charge of Richmond's defense. "I prefer Lee to Johnston," McClellan wrote Lincoln in late April. "The former is too weak and cautious under given responsibility; personally brave and energetic to a fault, he is yet wanting in moral firmness when pressed by heavy responsibility and is likely to be timid and irresolute in action." He assured the president that all was well. "I am confident of success, not only of success but of brilliant success. I think that a defeat here substantially breaks up the rebel cause."

Lincoln wasn't convinced. Like Grant he thought battles more important than cities; McClellan might capture Richmond but until he defeated the Confederate army the rebellion would continue. Anyway, he thought McClellan moved too slowly. "Your call for Parrot guns from

Washington alarms me, chiefly because it argues indefinite procrastination," he wrote McClellan in mid-May. "Is anything to be done?"

In fact nothing was to be done. "We are quietly closing in on the enemy preparatory to the last struggle," McClellan responded. But haste risked ruining all. "Situated as I am, I feel forced to take every precaution against disaster and to secure my flank against the probably superior force in front of me." He needed more men, more arms, more time.

Lincoln stewed, mostly in silence. He recognized his lack of military experience. He occasionally nudged McClellan but declined to overrule him. He doubted the wisdom of McClellan's strategy but couldn't disprove it. He gnashed his teeth when Lee in late June proved less timid than McClellan expected and drove McClellan back down the Virginia peninsula in what came to be called the Seven Days' battles.

McClellan blamed Lincoln and the War Department. "I have lost this battle because my force was too small," he wrote Edwin Stanton, the war secretary since January. "I am not responsible for this. . . . I know that a few thousand more men would have changed this battle from a defeat to a victory. As it is, the Government must not and cannot hold me responsible for the result. . . . You have done your best to sacrifice the army. . . . You must send me very large re-enforcements, and send them at once."

Lincoln smoldered at McClellan's refusal to take responsibility. "If we had a million men we could not get them to you in time," he told the general. "We have not the men to send." The next day he added, "The idea of sending you fifty thousand or any other considerable force promptly is simply absurd." Yet he tactfully tempered his criticism with encouragement. "If you are not strong enough to face the enemy you must find a place of security and wait, rest, and repair. Maintain your ground if you can but save the Army at all events. . . . We still have strength enough in the country and will bring it out."

McClellan professed to be unfazed by his reversal. "My position is very strong and daily becoming more so," he wrote Lincoln on July 7. "If not attacked today I shall laugh at them. . . . Annoy yourself as little as possible about me, and don't lose confidence in this army." He continued to rationalize his defeat. "Prisoners all state that I had two hundred thousand enemy to fight—a good deal more than two to one and they knowing the ground."

Lincoln lacked the self-confidence as yet to fire McClellan, but he determined that a change was necessary. He kept McClellan in command of the Army of the Potomac but appointed Henry Halleck general-in-chief of the entire Union army.

Halleck got the summons at Corinth on July 11. "I will start for Washington the moment I can have a personal interview with General Grant," he replied.

26

Julia Grant followed her husband in the newspapers and the comments of her neighbors and friends, and when opportunity allowed she followed him physically. His headquarters at Cairo, Illinois, were but 150 miles from her childhood home at St. Louis, and following a visit to her Missouri family she took the children and ventured south to join him. She later recounted a dream from the beginning of the journey. "The day I started, about the middle of the afternoon, I felt nervous and unable to go on with my preparations," she wrote. "I went into my room to rest for a few moments, when I distinctly saw Ulys a few rods from me. I saw only his head and shoulders, about as high as if he were on horseback. He looked at me so earnestly and, I thought, so reproachfully, that I started up and said, 'Ulys!'" She proceeded to Cairo, en route hearing of the battle of Belmont, which had occurred on the day of her dream. Grant met the train at the Cairo station. "I told him of my seeing him on the day of the battle. He asked at what hour, and when I told him, he said: 'That is singular. Just about that time I was on horseback and in great peril, and I thought of you and the children, and what would become of you if I were lost. I was thinking of you, dear Julia, and very earnestly too.'"

Julia and the children stayed with Grant in Cairo in a commandeered house and dined with him and a few other officers and their families. After Grant's forces seized Paducah, Kentucky, she and the children rode a truce boat to that city to see what her husband and their father had wrought. The boat on the return voyage carried some Kentucky women indignant at Grant's occupation of the city but more indignant at the secession that had provoked it. "I remember one of them who most industriously, I really thought spitefully, knitted all the way," Julia related. "Her knitting needles clashed like lances." A mild observation from Julia on the sentiments of Kentuckians caused the woman to explode: "Mania! Mania! Madam! Epidemic! Madam! Why the whole South has gone *ravin'* mad!"

Julia and the children, like the families of the other officers, understandably stayed clear of the battlefields, hospitals and other grim features of war, with the result that the campaigning sometimes resembled a holiday tour. Julia recalled approaching Corinth after the Confederates evacuated that town. "As we entered the encampment, which extended from near the depot to far beyond the headquarters, the campfires were lighted, and I do not think I exaggerate when I say they numbered thousands," she wrote. "The men were singing 'John Brown.' It seemed as though a hundred or so sang the words and the whole army joined in the chorus. Oh, how grand it was!" Julia remembered Grant's house at Corinth as the most pleasing residence he and the family had ever inhabited. "The General's headquarters were in a handsome and very comfortable country house, situated in a magnificent oak grove of great extent. The house was a frame one, surrounded by wide piazzas, sheltered by some sweet odor-giving vine—Madeira vine, I think. On the grounds were plantain, mimosa and magnolia trees. A wide walk extended around the house. It was like a garden walk without sand or pebbles on it, only the mold or earth. It was kept in fine order, as it was sprinkled and raked morning and evening"—by the slaves who lived on the property. "It was the delight of Nellie and Jess to make footprints with their little rosy feet in this freshly-raked earth."

*H*er Corinth holiday ended sooner than Julia would have wished. Shortly after Grant decided he mustn't leave the army, he realized he *could* leave Corinth. He detached his headquarters from Halleck's and moved to Memphis, which had fallen to Union forces following a gunboat battle in early June 1862. The trip alerted him to some of the wrinkles of the war. "With my staff and small escort I started at an early hour, and before noon we arrived within twenty miles of Memphis," he remembered. "At this point I saw a very comfortable-looking white-haired gentleman seated at the front of his house, a little distance from the road." Grant wanted to visit with the man, but not wishing to alarm him he sent his staff and escort down the road. He walked alone to the porch and asked for a glass of water. "I found my host very congenial and communicative, and stayed longer than I had intended, until the lady of the house announced dinner and asked me to join them. The host, however, was not pressing, so that I declined the invitation and, mounting my horse, rode on."

Grant caught up with the others at a shady spot two miles ahead. They waited out the heat of the summer day before continuing to Memphis, where he discovered the source of his white-haired host's disinclination to have him stay for dinner. The man's name was De Loche and he was a Union loyalist, a rarity in that region. "He had not pressed me to tarry longer with him because in the early part of my visit a neighbor, a Dr. Smith, had called and, on being presented to me, backed off the porch as if something had hit him. Mr. De Loche knew that the rebel General Jackson"—William Jackson of Tennessee—"was in that neighborhood with a detachment of cavalry. His neighbor was as earnest in the Southern cause as was Mr. De Loche in that of the Union. The exact location of Jackson was entirely unknown to Mr. De Loche, but he was sure that his neighbor would know it and would give information of my presence, and this made my stay unpleasant to him after the call of Dr. Smith."

Memphis educated Grant to issues he and other Union commanders would confront for the rest of the war. Till then he had had no experience of responsibility for a sizable Southern population living at home. Pittsburg Landing and Corinth were small villages from which the inhabitants fled on the approach of battle, but Memphis was a real city—of some 45,000 people—and most of its residents remained during the Union occupation. Grant became the de facto governor of the city and the surrounding region, and he spent hours each day hearing grievances and petitions. A local church had been seized to house Union soldiers; a deacon of the church demanded the building back. Grant said the congregation was free to join the services conducted by the Union army chaplain. The deacon expressed shock; his fellow congregants could never listen to the radical theology espoused by the Yankee preacher. Grant said they could get used to it or stay away.

Another petitioner was a lawyer who had represented Northern businesses with dealings in Memphis. His clients were owed money by Southern firms and individuals, but the Confederate congress had confiscated Northern property and claims in the South, including debts owed Northerners. The Union government, needless to say, didn't recognize the confiscation, and upon the capture of the city the Union provost marshal had seized such evidence as he could find of the debts. The lawyer had surrendered his clients' receipts but now wanted them back. He said the Confederate government would hold him personally responsible for the debts when it regained control of Memphis. Grant shook his head in astonishment. "His impudence was so sublime that I was rather amused than indignant," he recalled. "I told him, however, that if he would remain in Memphis I did not believe the Confederate government would ever molest him."

Other matters were more consequential. "There is a great disloyalty manifested by the citizens of this place," Grant wrote Halleck. "Undoubtedly spies and members of the Southern army are constantly finding their way in and out of the city in spite of all vigilance." Sabotage was a real danger. "There is every probability that an attempt will be made to burn the city." Grant tried to mitigate the hazard by suppressing newspapers he considered inflammatory. "You will suspend the further publication of your paper," his aide William Hillyer wrote to the editor of the *Memphis Avalanche*. "The spirit with which it is conducted is regarded as both incendiary and treasonable, and its issue cannot longer be tolerated."

Additional measures were more stringent. Raids and other attacks by rebel irregulars prompted Grant to declare that he would hold mere sympathizers accountable. "Government collections shall be made of personal property from persons in the immediate neighborhood sympathizing with the rebellion, sufficient to remunerate the Government all loss and expense of collection," he announced. The irregulars, moreover, had forfeited their right to appeal to the rules of war. "Persons acting as guerrillas without organization, and without uniform to distinguish them from private citizens, are not entitled to the treatment of prisoners of war when caught, and will not receive such treatment."

Grant's harshest measure was designed to flush the rebel sympathizers out of Memphis. "The families now residing in the city of Memphis of the following persons are required to move south beyond our lines," his Special Order No. 14 declared: "First, all persons holding commissions in the so-called Confederate army. . . . Second, all persons holding office under or in the employ of the so-called Confederate government. . . . Third, all persons holding State, county, or municipal offices, who claim allegiance to said so-called Confederate government and who have abandoned their families and gone south." Special Order No. 15 appended a loophole: a loyalty oath to the United States government that would allow the otherwise sanctioned to remain in their homes.

Grant knew that his orders would strain the fabric of Memphis life. To punish the men who were actively opposing the United States government was one thing; to target their wives and children was another. The loophole intensified the strain by asking family members to disavow the actions of their loved ones.

But the orders got the attention of the rebels, as Grant intended they should. Confederate general Jeff Thompson sent a courier to Memphis with a message for Grant. "I feel it my duty to remark that you must not for a moment suppose that the thousands who will be utterly unable to leave, and the many who will thus be forced to take the hateful oath of allegiance to a despised government, are to be thus converted into loyal citizens of the United States or weaned from their affection for our glorious young Confederacy," Thompson warned. "General, I would tell you to beware of the curses and oaths of vengeance which the fifty thousand brave Tennesseans who are still in our army will register in Heaven against the persecutor of helpless old men, women, and children, and the *General who cannot guard his own lines.*"

Grant didn't meet Thompson's messenger. Before the lieutenant arrived, Grant got an order from Halleck to travel to Corinth, where Halleck told him of the summons he had received from Washington. Halleck didn't say why he was going east, as he didn't know for certain. "But if it is to make him Secretary of War or Commander in Chief, Head Quarters at Washington, a better selection could not be made," Grant wrote Elihu Washburne.

Grant was learning the game of politics. Halleck left him in charge of the Department of the Mississippi, and Grant, pleased with the promotion and new authority, decided to be gracious in watching his superior go. "He is a man of gigantic intellect and well studied in the profession of arms," Grant told Washburne. "He and I have had several little spats but I like and respect him nevertheless."

27

WASHBURNE RESPONDED WITH COMPLIMENTS FOR GRANT AND AN agenda for the administration. "I learned with great pleasure that you had been placed in command of the western army," the congressman wrote. "I think the country will hail it as the precursor of more active and vigorous operations. It is scarcely possible for you to imagine the impatience of the public at the manner in which the war is being conducted. They want to see more immediate moving upon the enemy's works. In fact they want to see *war*." Washburne explained that Grant's stern policy toward rebels and their property was playing well in Washington. "Your order in regard to the secessionists of Memphis taking the oath or leaving has been accepted as an earnest of vigorous and decided action on your part." Washburne welcomed signs that Lincoln was reaching a similar view. "The administration has come up to what the people have long demanded—a vigorous prosecution of the war by all the means known to civilized warfare."

William Sherman concurred with Grant and Washburne on the need for stern treatment of rebels and their sympathizers, but he thought the administration needed firmer nudging. "I write plainly and slowly because I know you have no time to listen to trifles," Sherman wrote Salmon Chase, the Treasury secretary. "This is no trifle; when one nation is at war with another, all the people of the one are enemies of the other; then the rules are plain and easy of understanding. Most unfortunately, the war in which we are now engaged has been complicated with the belief on the one hand that all on the other are *not* enemies. It would have been better if, at the outset, this mistake had not been made, and it is wrong longer to be misled by it." Sherman explained the situation in his part of the western theater: "There is not a garrison in Tennessee where a man can go beyond the sight of the flag-staff without being shot or captured." Talk of loyal Southerners was willful deception; the North and South were effectively two nations at war.

Sherman was writing Chase because the Treasury handled matters of Southern trade, which had become dangerously perverse, in Sherman's opinion. "These people had cotton," he said of the Southerners around Memphis, "and, whenever they apprehended our large armies would move, they destroyed the cotton in the belief that, of course, we would seize it and convert it to our use. They did not and could not dream that we would pay money for it. It had been condemned to destruction by their own acknowledged government, and was therefore lost to their people; and could have been, without injustice, taken by us and sent away, either as absolute prize of war or for future compensation." But the rules established by the administration in Washington allowed the development of a lucrative trade, and a shameful one, Sherman thought. "The commercial enterprise of the Jews"—a common shorthand for speculators that revealed both the reflexive anti-Semitism of the era and the highly visible role of certain Jewish merchants in the speculation—"soon discovered that ten cents would buy a pound of cotton behind our army; that four cents would take it to Boston, where they would receive thirty cents in gold. The bait was too tempting, and it spread like fire, when here they discovered that salt, bacon, powder, fire-arms, percussion caps, etc., etc., were worth as much as gold; and, strange to say, this traffic was not only permitted but encouraged."

The encouragement was what particularly irked Sherman. He didn't expect any better behavior from those he called Jews, but he thought the administration should have weighed its policies more carefully. Sherman appreciated that Chase and the administration were facilitating the cotton trade to keep a shortfall from driving Britain and perhaps France to recognize the Confederacy. But the trade was funding and fueling the Confederate war effort. "Before we in the interior could know it, hundreds, yea thousands of barrels of salt"—bartered for the cotton—"and millions of dollars had been disbursed; and I have no doubt that Bragg's army at Tupelo, and Van Dorn's at Vicksburg, received enough salt to make bacon, without which they could not have moved their armies in mass; and that from ten to twenty thousand fresh arms, and a due supply of cartridges, have also been got, I am equally satisfied."

Sherman explained that he had taken matters into his own hands in the sector for which he was responsible. He had declared that gold and silver were contraband of war and had ordered that they not be allowed into the interior. He realized he was contradicting administration policy, but he was certain he was doing the right thing. He told Chase—and through Chase, Lincoln—not to worry about the British. "We are not bound to furnish her cotton. She has more reason to fight the South for burning that cotton than us for not shipping it."

Sherman shared his views with Grant. "I found so many Jews and speculators here trading in cotton, and secessionists had become so open in refusing anything but gold, that I have felt myself bound to stop it," he wrote Grant. "This gold has but one use—the purchase of arms and ammunition, which can always be had for gold, at Nassau, New Providence, or Cincinnati; all the guards we may establish cannot stop it. Of course I have respected all permits by yourself or the Secretary of the Treasury, but in these new cases (swarms of Jews) I have stopped it." Sherman urged Grant to issue a similar ban for the western department as a whole. "We cannot carry on war and trade with a people at the same time."

Another item of Southern commerce posed an even greater challenge. Slaves had begun fleeing their places of bondage almost as soon as Union troops came within running range. What to do with them tested the consciences, resolve and ingenuity of Union commanders. Some, including Henry Halleck, initially took the position that since Congress had not repealed the Fugitive Slave Act, Union officers were duty bound to assist slave owners who attempted to reclaim their servants. This position accorded with the Lincoln administration's policy of reassuring slaveholders in the loyal border states that slavery was safe under the Union flag. But other officers, most notably Benjamin Butler of Massachusetts, who headed the occupation of New Orleans after its surrender in the spring of 1862, considered slaves to be contraband of war and subject to seizure and retention by Union forces. The contraband label caught on, as did a policy of letting the fugitive slaves follow the Union armies to which they fled. Congress subsequently made the policy official by forbidding the return of escaped slaves to their owners. The legislature also authorized putting the slaves to work on behalf of the Union.

Details of implementation fell to the commanders in the field, who devised rules as they went along. "Fugitive slaves may be employed in the quartermaster's department, subsistence and engineer's departments, and wherever by such employment a soldier may be saved to the ranks," Grant ordered during the summer of 1862. "They may be employed as teamsters, as company cooks (not exceeding four to a company), or as hospital attendants and nurses." Officers could engage them as private servants, but in such cases the officers, rather than the government, would be responsible for their pay.

Grant perceived the Negro question as he did everything else at that time: in the context of the war effort. "I have no hobby of my own with regard to the negro, either to effect his freedom or to continue his bondage," he wrote his father. "If Congress pass any law"—regarding slavery as an institution—"and the President approves, I am willing to execute it." But until Congress and the president took definitive action on slavery, he would leave that troublesome subject to others. "One enemy at a time is enough."

Lincoln was no more eager than Grant to tackle the slavery question, but events forced his hand. The anomalies of fighting the slave power but not slavery intensified over time; Lincoln had to work ever harder to explain himself and his policy. Horace Greeley told him he was failing dismally because the administration's policy was fatuous. "On the face of this wide earth, Mr. President," the *New York Tribune* editor wrote in an open letter to Lincoln, "there is not one disinterested, determined, intelligent champion of the Union cause who does not feel that all attempts to put down the Rebellion and at the same time uphold its inciting cause are preposterous and futile—that the Rebellion, if crushed out tomorrow, would be renewed within a year if Slavery were left in full vigor." The president must terminate this intolerable situation. "Every hour of deference to Slavery is an hour of added and deepened peril to the Union."

Lincoln responded that he loved the Union no less than Greeley did. They differed simply on the best way to preserve it. "I would save the Union," Lincoln wrote in a letter Greeley published. "I would save it the shortest way under the Constitution." Slavery was secondary and would remain so. "My paramount object in this struggle *is* to save the Union, and is *not* either to save or to destroy slavery. If I could save the Union without freeing *any* slave I would do it, and if I could save it by freeing *all* the slaves I would do it; and if I could save it by freeing some and leaving others alone, I would also do that. What I do about slavery and the colored race, I do because I believe it helps to save the Union; and what I forbear, I forbear because I do *not* believe it would help to save the Union." Lincoln said that his goal was fixed, but his tactics were flexible. "I shall do *less* whenever I shall believe what I am doing hurts the cause, and I shall do *more* whenever I shall believe doing more will help the cause. I shall try to correct errors when shown to be errors; and I shall adopt new views so fast as they shall appear to be true views." Lincoln added, lest Greeley and the country think him an agnostic on the morality of slavery: "I have here stated my purpose according to my view of *official* duty; and I intend no modification of my oft-expressed *personal* wish that all men everywhere could be free."

Lincoln had more to say on slavery and the Union, but he wouldn't say it yet. For months the president had made a habit of retreating to the War Department's telegraph office to escape the crowds and bustle of the Executive Mansion. "One morning he asked me for some paper, as he wanted to write something special," Major Thomas Eckert, who headed the telegraph office, recalled. Eckert fetched some foolscap, and Lincoln began writing. The work went slowly. "He would look out of the window a while and then put his pen to paper, but he did not write much at once," Eckert said. "He would study between times and when he had made up his mind he would put down a line or two." At the end of his first session he had not filled a single sheet. He handed the paper to Eckert. "Keep it locked up until I call for it tomorrow," he said.

Lincoln repeated the exercise most mornings for a few weeks. Some days he wrote merely a line or two; other days he revised what he had written before. Finally he finished. He informed Eckert what he had been doing. "He told me he had been writing an order giving freedom to the slaves in the South, for the purpose of hastening the end of the war."

Yet he wasn't prepared to issue the order. He summoned the cabinet in July 1862 and read what he had written. "I said to the cabinet that I had resolved upon this step and had not called them together to ask their advice, but to lay the subject-matter of a proclamation before them," Lincoln remembered two years later. He nonetheless received advice. Montgomery Blair predicted that emancipation would cost the Republicans the fall elections. Salmon Chase worried that it would roil the financial markets on which the government relied for war funding. William Seward offered the most telling counsel. "Mr. President, I approve of the proclamation," the secretary of state said. "But I question the expediency of its issue at this juncture. The depression of the public mind, consequent upon our repeated reverses, is so great that I fear the effect of so important a step. It may be viewed as the last measure of an exhausted government, a cry for help; the government stretching forth its hands to Ethiopia, instead of Ethiopia stretching forth her hands to the government."

Lincoln heeded Seward and decided to wait for a victory. But the military situation got worse before it got better. As part of the reorganization that made Halleck general-in-chief, Lincoln appointed John Pope to command the hopefully named Army of Virginia. Lincoln applauded Pope's energy as he drove south from the Potomac, and he took comfort from first reports of a battle with Lee's Army of Northern Virginia at Bull Run, near where the battle of the previous summer had been fought. As late as the third day of the battle Edwin Stanton brimmed with confidence. "He said that nothing but foul play could lose us this battle," John Hay, Lincoln's secretary, remembered of the war secretary.

But Pope did lose the battle, with ten thousand men killed or wounded. The general was wholly discredited. Alpheus Williams, a brigadier general in Pope's army, summarized his superior's disastrous accomplishment: "A splendid army almost demoralized, millions of public property given up or destroyed, thousands of lives of our best men sacrificed for no purpose." Williams went on: "More insolence, superciliousness, ignorance and pretentiousness were never combined in one man. It can in truth be said of him that he had not a friend in his command from the smallest drummer boy to the highest general officer."

Lincoln bemoaned the defeat and lamented his continuing failure to find an effective general. "The President was in deep distress," Attorney General Edward Bates recorded. "He seemed wrung by the bitterest anguish—said he felt almost ready to hang himself." Lincoln had never been religious, but now he began searching for guidance from above. "The will of God prevails," he mused privately. "In great contests each party claims to act in accordance with the will of God. Both *may* be, and one *must* be wrong. God cannot be *for* and *against* the same thing at the same time. In the present civil war it is quite possible that God's purpose is something different from the purpose of either party." The ways of the Almighty were inscrutable. "He could have either *saved* or *destroyed* the Union without a human contest. Yet the contest began. And having begun, He could give the final victory to either side any day. Yet the contest proceeds."

Robert E. Lee pushed the contest by invading Maryland. His army had scoured northern Virginia of all the supplies the region could produce; the farms and fields across the Potomac beckoned to his hungry soldiers. The North was vulnerable; its army was "much weakened and demoralized," Lee told Jefferson Davis. Maryland contained numerous Southern sympathizers; a successful invasion would rally them to the Confederate cause. An invasion might demoralize Northern voters ahead of the elections and compel the Lincoln administration to change its policies. And by demonstrating Southern strength, an invasion could well prompt—or force—British and French recognition of the Confederacy, which could do for Southern independence what French help had done for American independence in the Revolutionary War.

Lee crossed the Potomac with élan. "To the People of Maryland," he proclaimed: "Our army has come among you, and is prepared to assist you with the power of its arms in regarding the rights of which you have been despoiled." Marylanders should reclaim those rights by rallying to the Confederate side.

But the Marylanders refused. Most of those bent on fighting for the South had already gone to Virginia and enlisted with the Confederacy; Marylanders still at home looked askance at Lee's invading army—whose appearance, in any case, gave little reason to anticipate victory for the Southern cause. "When I say that they were hungry, I convey no impression of the gaunt starvation that looked from their cavernous eyes," a Maryland woman recalled. "All day they crowded to the doors of our houses, with always the same drawling complaint: 'I've been a-marchin' an' a-fightin' for six weeks stiddy, and I ain't had n-a-r-thin' to eat 'cept green apples an' green cawn, an' I wish you'd please to gimme a bit to eat.'" Far from bolstering Lee's ranks, the intrusion into Maryland bled him, as thousands of his famished men succumbed to their bellies and dropped out of the line of march. Lee could do little to prevent their leaving. "My army is ruined by straggling," he confessed to a subordinate.

Those who stayed in line were the faithful and the resolute. The knowledge that they were outnumbered by the Federals didn't bother them, for their experience had convinced them that they could beat twice their weight in Yankees. They might have been worried by one thing they did not know: that the enemy commander—George McClellan, to whom Lincoln had turned again, in desperation after Pope's debacle—

was privy to Lee's battle plan. Lee had sent coordinating directives to his principal lieutenants; one of the copies went astray and was found, wrapped around some cigars, by a Union corporal, who passed it up the chain of command. McClellan could scarcely credit his good fortune. "Here is a paper with which if I cannot defeat Bobbie Lee, I will be willing to go home," he declared privately. To Lincoln he wrote: "I have all the plans of the rebels and will catch them in their own trap if my men are equal to the emergency." Lincoln responded: "God bless you, and all with you. Destroy the rebel army, if possible."

Lee's army had spread out as it crossed the Potomac, and McClellan moved to strike before the Confederates regrouped. But Lee, sensing uncharacteristic decisiveness in McClellan, ordered his commanders to coalesce, at Sharpsburg near Antietam Creek. Confederate general John Walker got the order at Harpers Ferry. "The thought of General Lee's perilous position, with the Potomac River in his rear, confronting, with his small force, McClellan's vast army, haunted me through the long hours of the night's march," Walker remembered. "I expected to find General Lee anxious and careworn." Lee surprised him. "He was calm, dignified, and even cheerful. If he had had a well-equipped army of a hundred thousand veterans at his back, he could not have appeared more composed and confident."

Lee's confidence may have been real, but it was also for effect. The disparity in forces was daunting, at any rate to James Longstreet, another of Lee's generals. "The blue uniforms of the Federals appeared among the trees that crowned the heights on the eastern bank of the Antietam," Longstreet recalled. "The number increased, and larger and larger grew the field of blue until it seemed to stretch as far as the eye could see, and from the tops of the mountains down to the edges of the stream gathered the great army of McClellan."

That army attacked in earnest on the morning of September 17. Union general Joseph Hooker led his troops to the edge of a large cornfield. The rays of the rising sun glinted off the bayonets of Confederates otherwise concealed among the stalks. Hooker ordered his cannons loaded with canister, and the gunners opened fire. The effect was immediate and devastating. "Every stalk of corn in the northern and greater part of the field was cut as closely as could have been done with a knife," Hooker reported afterward, "and the slain lay in rows precisely as they had stood in their ranks a few moments before."

But the Confederates fought back with stubborn, savage effect, till the battlefield became a scene of unparalleled violence. "To those who have not been witnesses of a great battle like this," Confederate John Walker wrote later, "where more than a hundred thousand men, armed with all the appliances of modern science and skill, are engaged in the work of slaughtering each other, it is impossible by the power of words to convey an adequate idea of its terrible sublimity. The constant booming of cannon, the ceaseless rattle and roar of musketry, the glimpses of galloping horsemen and marching infantry, now seen, now lost in the smoke, adding weirdness to terror, all together make up a combination of sights and sounds wholly indescribable."

James Longstreet perceived the fighting as something almost beyond human control. "The line swayed forward and back like a rope exposed to rushing currents," the Confederate general recalled. "A force too heavy to be withstood would strike and drive in a weak point till we could collect a few fragments, and in turn force back the advance till our lost ground was recovered." The determination of the two sides was formidable. "The Federals fought with wonderful bravery, and the Confederates clung to their ground with heroic courage as hour after hour they were mown down like grass."

All day the fighting raged and the carnage mounted. Neither side could win but neither would admit defeat. When darkness caused the shooting to stop, neither had the heart to count the casualties. The eventual tally would show two thousand Union soldiers dead and nearly ten thousand wounded, and similar numbers on the Confederate side. A terrible night of groans and death rattles gave way to an appalling dawn of visible suffering. "No tongue can tell, no mind can conceive, no pen portray the horrible sights I witnessed," a Pennsylvania soldier recorded of that awful morning.

Lee expected the battle to resume that day. "We awaited without apprehension a renewal of the attack," he reported afterward. But McClellan's caution again set in. "I concluded that the success of an attack on the 18th was not certain," McClellan explained. Unwilling to accept anything less than certainty, he regrouped and rested his forces.

Lee thereupon canceled the Maryland operation, grateful for the opportunity to escape with his diminished army intact. "As we could not look for a material increase of strength, and the enemy's force could be largely and rapidly augmented," he explained, "it was not thought prudent to wait until he should be ready again to offer battle." On the night of September 18 Lee led his army back to Virginia.

John Walker recalled the retreat. "I was among the last to cross the Potomac," he remembered. "As I rode into the river I passed General Lee, sitting on his horse in the stream, watching the crossing of the wagons and artillery. Returning my greeting, he inquired as to what was still behind. There was nothing but wagons containing my wounded, and a battery of artillery, all of which were near at hand, and I told him so. 'Thank God!' I heard him say as I rode on."

Lincoln was sorely disappointed that McClellan hadn't destroyed Lee's army. He thought the opportunity might still exist. "The President directs that you cross the Potomac and give battle to the enemy or drive him south," Halleck told McClellan. "Your army must move now while the roads are good."

But McClellan refused, and Lincoln was compelled to take from the partial victory what he could. He gathered his cabinet and presented once more the document he had labored over at the telegraph office. "The time has come now," he said. "I wish it were a better time. I wish that we were in a better condition. The action of the army against the rebels has not been quite what I should have liked." Yet he had decided to go ahead.

On September 22, speaking as "Commander-in-chief of the Army and Navy," Lincoln proclaimed broad emancipation as of January 1, 1863. "All persons held as slaves within any state, or designated part of any state, the people whereof shall then be in rebellion against the United States shall be then, thenceforward, and forever free," the president said.

The proclamation failed to satisfy the immediate abolitionists, as it didn't touch slavery in the border states. But to everyone else, Northerners and Southerners alike, it marked a watershed in American history. Lincoln, at the stroke of his pen, transformed the nature and meaning of the war. The conflict had been about union; now it was about liberty as well. Expedience and conscience had heretofore clashed in the Northern soul; henceforth they aligned. Until this point Grant and the rest of the Union army had fought to preserve the status quo; from this point forward they fought to overturn it and create a new one.

28

THE UNION CAPTURE OF CORINTH PUT GRANT ATHWART CRUCIAL lines of Confederate communication, and the Confederates naturally sought to drive him off. In the second week of September 1862 Confederate general Sterling Price descended on Iuka, Mississippi, twenty miles east of Corinth, on the Memphis & Charleston Railroad. The outmanned Union colonel at Iuka withdrew without a fight. Grant wasn't worried about his own position; he told Julia: "I am concentrated and strong. Will give the rebels a tremendous thrashing if they come." But he *did* worry that Price and perhaps the other Confederate commander in the area, Earl Van Dorn, would drive north to join Braxton Bragg, whose Kentucky campaign was alarming Lincoln and the administration almost as much as Lee's Maryland thrust was. "Have you heard anything from Covington?" Grant asked Julia of the town where his parents lived. "They must be badly frightened."

For the most part, though, he remained optimistic. The Confederates' ambitions would betray them, he told Julia. "You will see the greatest fall in a few weeks of rebel hopes that was ever known. They have made a bold effort, and with wonderful success, but it is a spasmodic effort without anything behind to fall back on. When they do begin to fall all resources are at an end and the rebellion will soon show a rapid decline." As for his own position: "There is a large force hovering around us for the last ten days, and the grand denouement must take place soon."

The Confederates kept hovering, prompting Grant to go after them. He devised a plan to corner Price at Iuka, with Union generals Edward Ord approaching from the northwest and William Rosecrans from the southwest; the Tennessee River, behind Price, would prevent an escape east. Yet the plan required careful timing, in that if Grant pulled troops from Corinth too soon, the other Confederate general, Van Dorn, might jump him there.

Midday on September 18 Ord moved into position. He made contact with Price's advance column and in a spirited encounter drove the Confederates back. Rosecrans was supposed to be coming but sent a message saying he had been delayed. He would arrive in time the next afternoon to attack, he promised. Grant was doubtful, as the roads were bad. "Besides," he remarked later, "troops after a forced march of twenty miles are not in a good condition for fighting the moment they get through. It might do in marching to relieve a beleaguered garrison, but not to make an assault." Grant nonetheless told Ord to listen for the sounds of fighting and to strike against Price at Iuka as soon as Rosecrans did.

Rosecrans indeed required longer to reach the outskirts of Iuka than he had predicted, and when he got there his troops were roughly handled by the Confederates. The wind blew the noise of the firing away from Ord, who didn't learn of the battle until hours after it ended. Grant got the news after the fact too and directed Ord to make up for Rosecrans's failure. "You must engage the enemy as early as possible in the morning," he said.

But Price was gone by then. Recognizing Grant's trap, he had slipped away in the dark. Grant rode at once to Iuka and discovered that Rosecrans, pleading the fatigue of his men, had not even sent his cavalry in pursuit. Grant ordered a chase and joined Rosecrans for a few miles before turning back toward Corinth. Rosecrans halted soon after Grant departed and Price got clean away.

Grant didn't have time to dwell on his disappointment. With Van Dorn at large and Price again afield, Grant's position was vulnerable. The neighborhood was more dangerous than it had ever been. "We were in a country where nearly all the people, except the negroes, were hostile to us and friendly to the cause we were trying to suppress," he recollected. "It was easy, therefore, for the enemy to get early information of our every move. We, on the contrary, had to go after our information in force, and then often returned without it."

For ten days the rebels circled and feinted, leaving Grant unsure where they might strike. By the beginning of October he thought he knew. "It is now clear that Corinth is the point, and that from the west or southwest," he informed Halleck. Four Confederate commands—under Price, Van Dorn, Albert Rust and John Villepigue—had come together. Grant meanwhile had been weakened by having some of his forces transferred to Kentucky to join the pursuit of Bragg. "My position is precarious but hope to get out of it all right," he told Halleck.

As the battle neared, Grant grew eager. "The rebels are now massing on Corinth in the northwest angle of the railroad," he wrote Halleck. For weeks they had eluded him; now that they were willing to do battle he hoped to crush them. He urged his generals forward. "We should attack if they do not; do it soon," he wrote Rosecrans. "Fight!" To Stephen Hurlbut he declared, "The combined force of the enemy does not exceed thirty thousand. He must be whipped."

Yet coordination remained critical. Hurlbut was coming to reinforce Rosecrans at Corinth; unless they worked in tandem, and swiftly, the Confederates would pick them off separately. "Make all dispatch," Grant ordered Hurlbut. To Rosecrans he said, "If the enemy fall back push them with all force possible and save Hurlbut, who is now on the way to your relief." The two forces must act in close concert. "Hurlbut is not strong enough to handle the rebels without very good luck," Grant told Rosecrans. "Don't neglect this warning."

The Confederates almost preempted Grant's joining of forces. Van Dorn struck at dawn on October 4, hoping to overwhelm Rosecrans before Hurlbut arrived. The attack was spirited and sanguinary, with the Confederates inflicting and receiving many casualties. But the Federals held their own, and by the time Hurlbut's column and that of James McPherson, whom Grant had summoned from Jackson, reached the scene, the Confederates were falling back.

Hurlbut contested the Confederate retreat but Rosecrans did not. Deciding his men had fought enough for one day, he let them rest overnight. "We move at daylight in the morning," he assured Grant.

Grant put the best face on things for the administration in Washington. "The enemy are in full retreat leaving their dead and wounded on the field," he informed Halleck. "Everything looks most favorable."

But he fumed at another opportunity's being lost. "Push the enemy to the wall," he demanded of Rosecrans. The next day he ordered: "You will avail yourself of every advantage and capture and destroy the rebel army to the utmost of your power."

Rosecrans belatedly gave halfhearted and ineffectual chase. Grant, disgusted, ordered him back to Corinth—only to have Rosecrans protest the return order and call for reinforcements. Grant denied the request. "Although partial success might result from further pursuit," Grant explained to Halleck, "disaster would follow in the end."

*A*braham Lincoln heard the news from Mississippi and sighed relief. "I congratulate you and all concerned on your recent victories," the president wrote Grant. "How does it all sum up?"

Grant had wished he could report the capture of an entire army. But on reflection he judged the results still substantial. "About eight hundred rebels already buried," he replied to the president. "Their loss in killed about nine to one of ours. The ground is not yet cleared of their unburied dead. Prisoners yet arriving by every wagon road and train. . . . Our killed and wounded at Corinth will not exceed nine hundred, many of them slightly."

The more Lincoln thought about it, the more he appreciated what had been accomplished. "The victory was most triumphant as it was," he asserted in his official report on Corinth. "All praise is due officers and men for their undaunted courage and obstinate resistance against an enemy outnumbering them as three to two." Grant's part of the western theater was secure and the Confederates in the region were badly weakened. Price and Van Dorn were prevented from joining Bragg, whose invasion of Kentucky collapsed.

In late October the War Department acknowledged Grant's achievement by giving him command of the Department of the Tennessee, encompassing western Tennessee, northern Mississippi, southern Illinois and western Kentucky. Halleck offered no guidance regarding operations, so Grant, the day after he took command, made a suggestion of his own: "With small reinforcements at Memphis I think I would be able to move down the Mississippi Central road and cause the evacuation of Vicksburg."

29

THE LARGER HIS RESPONSIBILITY GREW, THE MORE WORRIED GRANT became about the vulnerabilities of his position. He shared Sherman's concern that the cotton trade was arming the rebels and Sherman's conviction that the trade must be halted if the occupation of the South was to be successful. Like Sherman he expressed his views to Salmon Chase, although in terms less confrontational than those Sherman employed. He told the Treasury secretary that he understood the administration's reasons for treating occupied territory like other parts of the Union with respect to commerce. "It is, however, a very grave question in my mind, whether this policy of 'letting trade follow the flag' is not working injuriously to the Union cause," he continued. "Practically and really I think it is benefiting almost exclusively, first, a class of greedy traders whose first and only desire is gain, and to whom it would be idle to attribute the least patriotism, and secondly our enemies south of our lines." Grant said he had tried to counter the problem, to no avail. "Our lines are so extended that it is impossible for any military surveillance to contend successfully with the cunning of the traders, aided by the local knowledge and eager interest of the residents along the border. The enemy are thus receiving supplies of most necessary and useful articles which relieves their sufferings and strengthens them for resistance to our authority; while we are sure that the benefits thus conferred tend in no degree to abate their rancorous hostility to our flag and Government." The current situation must not continue. "The evil is a great and growing one, and needs immediate attention."

Charles Dana agreed. Dana had been a journalist and would become a spy for Edwin Stanton and the War Department within Grant's camp; meanwhile he thought to try his hand at cotton trading. But he had no sooner arrived in Memphis than he discovered the destructive effect the cotton trade was having on the Union war effort. "The mania for sudden fortunes made in cotton, raging in a vast population of Jews and Yankees scattered throughout this whole country, and in this town almost exceeding the numbers of the regular residents, has to an alarming extent corrupted and demoralized the army," Dana wrote to Stanton. "Every colonel, captain, or quartermaster is in secret partnership with some operator in cotton; every soldier dreams of adding a bale of cotton to his monthly pay. I had no conception of the extent of this evil until I came and saw it for myself. Besides, the resources of the rebels are inordinately increased from this source. Plenty of cotton is brought in from beyond our lines, especially by the agency of Jewish traders, who pay for it ostensibly in Treasury notes, but really in gold." Dana recommended a draconian curtailment of the cotton trade, starting with the expulsion of all private traders.

David Porter, the commander of Union naval forces in Grant's theater, was equally indignant at the cotton speculation. Porter contended that the Treasury's program of sending aides, or agents, to license the commerce was worse than no program at all. "A greater pack of knaves never went unhung," Porter wrote. "Human nature is very weak, and the poor aides, with their small pay, could easily be bribed to allow a man to land 100 barrels of salt when he had only permit for two. And so on with everything else. The thing is done now so openly that the guerrillas come down to the bank and purchase what they want."

Bolstered by the support of others who had seen the problem firsthand, Grant decided to try something new. "Gold and silver will not be paid within this district by speculators for the products of the rebel states," he ordered. "United States Treasury notes are a legal tender in all cases, and when refused, the parties refusing them will be arrested. . . . Any speculator paying out gold and silver in violation of this order will be arrested and sent North." He proposed, without yet giving an order, extending his Memphis ban on rebel sympathizers within Union lines to the western district as a whole. "There is an evident disposition on the part of many of the citizens to join the guerrillas on their approach," he explained to Halleck. "I am decidedly in favor of turning all discontented citizens within our lines out South."

Halleck told Grant to go ahead with the removal. "It is very desirable that you should clean out West Tennessee and North Mississippi of all organized enemies," Halleck said. "If necessary, take up all active sympathizers and either hold them as prisoners or put them beyond our lines. Handle that class without gloves, and take their property for public use. . . . It is time that they should begin to feel the presence of war on our side."

But the administration vetoed Grant's attempt to curtail the cotton trade. Halleck passed along orders from Stanton: "The payment of gold should not be prohibited. . . . See that all possible facilities are afforded for getting out cotton. It is deemed important to get as much as we can into market."

Grant later described the administration's reversal of his cotton policy as an "embarrassment." He understood the political and diplomatic reasons for the reversal but believed military considerations should have been given priority. "Stations on the Mississippi River and on the railroad in our possession had to be designated where cotton would be received," he wrote in his memoirs. "This opened to the enemy not only the means of converting cotton into money which had a value all over the world and which they so much needed, but it afforded them means of obtaining accurate and intelligent information in regard to our position and strength. It was also demoralizing to our troops. Citizens obtaining permits from the Treasury department had to be protected within our lines and given facilities to get out cotton by which they realized enormous profits." Speaking for himself as much as for his troops, Grant declared, "Men who had enlisted to fight the battles of their country did not like to be engaged in protecting a traffic which went to the support of an enemy they had to fight, and the profits of which went to men who shared none of their dangers."

So he tried to work around the administration's order. He required cotton brokers and purchasers of other commodities to receive permits from their local provost marshals in addition to the licenses they were issued by Washington. Moreover, they must stay in the rear of the army. "It will be regarded as evidence of disloyalty for persons to go beyond the lines of the Army to purchase cotton or other products, and all contracts made for such articles, in advance of the Army, or for cotton in the field, are null and void. . . . All parties so offending will be expelled from the Department."

The measure had little effect. Grant's inspectors couldn't be everywhere, nor could every one of them resist the bribes the traders offered. The commerce continued much as before.

He tried to focus on the Vicksburg campaign. "My plans are all complete for weeks to come," he wrote his sister on December 15. "I hope to have them all work out just as planned." But success wouldn't come easily, and the effort was exacting a personal toll. "For a conscientious person, and I profess to be one, this is a most slavish life. I may be envied by ambitious persons, but I in turn envy the person who can transact his daily business and retire to a quiet home without a feeling of responsibility for the morrow. Taking my whole department, there are an immense number of lives staked upon my judgment and acts." He was surrounded—literally—by enemies. "I am extended now like a peninsula into an enemies' country with a large army depending for their daily bread upon keeping open a line of railroad running one hundred and ninety miles through an enemy's country, or at least through territory occupied by a people terribly embittered and hostile to us. . . . With all my other trials I have to contend against is added that of speculators whose patriotism is measured by dollars and cents. Country has no value with them compared with money."

Like Sherman, Dana and others who dealt with the speculators, Grant perceived Jews as playing a large part in the cotton trade. He had accompanied his order embargoing gold and silver with a note to Isaac Quinby, the commander of the district of the Mississippi: "Examine the baggage of all speculators coming south, and when they have specie, turn them back. If medicine and other contraband articles, arrest them and confiscate the contraband articles. Jews should receive special attention." He sent a similar order to Stephen Hurlbut: "Refuse all permits to come south of Jackson for the present. The Israelites especially should be kept out." To Joseph Webster, of his staff, he wrote: "Give orders to all the conductors on the road that no Jews are to be permitted to travel on the railroad southward from any point. They may go north and be encouraged in it; but they are such an intolerable nuisance that the department must be purged of them."

As he got further into the planning for Vicksburg, Grant formulated yet another policy against the speculators. "I have long since believed that in spite of all the vigilance that can be infused into Post Commanders that the specie regulations of the Treasury Department have been violated, and that mostly by Jews and other unprincipled traders," he explained to the War Department. "So well satisfied of this have I been that I instructed the commanding officer at Columbus to refuse all permits to Jews to come south, and frequently have had them expelled from the Department. But they come in with their carpet sacks in spite of all that can be done to prevent it. The Jews seem to be a privileged class that can travel anywhere. They will land at any wood yard or landing on the river and make their way through the country. If not permitted to buy cotton themselves they will act as agents for someone else who will be at a military post with a Treasury permit to receive cotton and pay for it in Treasury notes, which the Jew will buy up at an agreed rate, paying gold. There is but one way that I know of to reach this case. That is for Government to buy all the cotton at a fixed rate and send it to Cairo, St. Louis or some other point to be sold. Then all traders—they are a curse to the Army—might be expelled."

Grant could merely recommend that the government buy the cotton at a fixed rate, but he thought he might expel the traders, or some of them, on his own. On December 17 he issued General Order No. 11, which declared: "The Jews, as a class, violating every regulation of trade established by the Treasury Department, and also Department orders, are hereby expelled from the Department." Post commanders in the Department of the Tennessee would give passes to Jews, who would have twenty-four hours to leave. Those who remained would be arrested and forcibly removed.

Grant later claimed that the language of the order—barring Jews as a people rather than simply Jewish speculators—reflected his exasperation and overwork. "The order was issued and sent without any reflection," he said, "and without thinking of the Jews as a sect or a race to themselves, but simply as persons who had successfully (I say successfully, instead of persistently, because there were plenty of others within my lines who envied their success) violated an order, which greatly inured to the help of the rebels."

This explanation gained plausibility from the fact that Grant's every other criticism of Jews centered on their role as speculators who defied the interests of the Union and damaged the war effort. Yet Grant rarely slipped in his use of language, and he may simply have decided that the only way to rid himself of Jewish speculators was to force all Jews out of his department. Grant shared the penchant for stereotyping Jews common to the age in America, and he may well have concluded that whatever loss they suffered by being treated as a group was a burden they would have to bear. If the inconvenience of this comparatively small class was the price of winning the war, he was willing to make them pay it. He demanded far more of his soldiers every day.

Had Grant been thinking politically, he would have realized that the administration in Washington could never let his order stand. Grant knew perfectly well that there were Jews in the army and that Lincoln valued the political and financial support of Northern Jews for the war effort. The president was in the process of freeing the slaves, and Grant must have supposed that Lincoln wouldn't appreciate this illiberal slap at another unfavored group. Grant would have understood that the Democrats, energized by victories in the 1862 congressional races, would assail the administration for his egregious violation of the civil liberties of Jewish Americans.

Yet Grant refused to take politics into account. He was a soldier, and he prided himself on thinking and acting like a soldier. The officers he despised most were those who acted like politicians. Perhaps he reasoned that the administration would require some weeks to respond to his order. He expected the Vicksburg campaign to be comparatively brief; by the time his order was rescinded, it should have accomplished its goal.

A personal element may have entered into Grant's thinking. During the war his chronically difficult relationship with his father underwent a decided transformation. The more confident he grew of his abilities, the more he resented his past dependence on Jesse and the more he insisted on showing he was no longer dependent. Jesse, from worthy reasons or otherwise, had taken to promoting his son's reputation wherever he could, until it became a source of embarrassment to Grant. Jesse retailed stories as coming from the rising general, to Grant's dismay and eventual anger. "I would write you many particulars," Grant declared in a letter to Jesse from Corinth in the autumn of 1862, "but you are so imprudent that I dare not trust you with them. And while on this subject let me say a word. I have not an enemy in the world who has done me so much injury as you in your efforts in my defense. . . . I have heard this from various sources, and persons who have returned to this Army and did not know that I had parents living near Cincinnati have said that they found the best feeling existing towards me every place but there. You are constantly

denouncing other General officers, and the inference with people naturally is that you get your impressions from me. Do nothing to correct
what you have already done, but for the future keep quiet on the subject."

Jesse quieted down, and Grant discovered other things to worry
about—until he learned that his father had engaged with a Jewish firm,
Mack & Brothers of Cincinnati, to trade in Southern cotton in Grant's
department. Grant didn't know the terms of the deal, but he could easily
imagine that Jesse had hinted that his son would ensure the success of
the enterprise. Grant by now considered his father incorrigible, but if the
son couldn't strike at the father effectively, he might strike at the father's
partners.

Possibly the filial issue had nothing to do with Grant's decision; he
had sufficient other reasons for trying to restrain the speculators. Vicksburg was the prize that could determine the outcome of the war; anything that facilitated its capture was worth doing, father or no father.

*T*he administration moved faster than Grant guessed it would. After
Jewish leaders complained to Lincoln, the president agreed that the
order must be rescinded. On January 4, 1863, Halleck telegraphed Grant
tersely: "It will be immediately revoked."

The next day Halleck's adjutant elaborated on the administration's
objection to Grant's order. "It excluded a whole class, instead of certain
obnoxious individuals," John Kelton said. "Had the word 'pedlar' been
inserted after Jew, I do not suppose any exception would have been taken
to the order." Halleck himself elaborated in similar vein: "The President
has no objection to your expelling traders and Jew pedlars, which I suppose was the object of your order, but as it in terms proscribed an entire
religious class, some of whom are fighting in our ranks, the President
deemed it necessary to revoke it."

Grant quietly rescinded the order and said nothing more about it. He
probably wondered whether Washington would *really* have let him expel
Jewish speculators, given the administration's resistance to any curbs on
the cotton trade. And he remembered why he hated politics. "It is a great
annoyance to gain rank and command enough to attract public attention," he told Edward Ord. "I have found it so and would now really prefer some little command where public attention would not be attracted
toward me."

HAVING GROWN UP ALONG THE OHIO RIVER AND SPENT MUCH OF HIS adulthood on the Mississippi, Grant appreciated the fundamental importance of the great waterways of the American heartland. By the beginning of 1863 the war for the West centered on a convoluted stretch of the Mississippi from Vicksburg in the north to Port Hudson, Louisiana, in the south. The straight-line distance between the two points was somewhat more than a hundred miles, but the river distance was three times that. Union gunboats commanded the river below Port Hudson, and a separate Union fleet secured the stream above Vicksburg. The Confederates controlled the river in between and with it a vital east-west corridor through which the crops and livestock of Texas and Arkansas flowed to the Confederate armies as far away as Virginia. At the same time, the Confederates blocked the north-south corridor by which the produce of the Union West would have floated down the Mississippi to the Gulf and away to the Union East. While this state of affairs persisted, the Confederacy could live and fight; should it be disrupted—should the Confederate corridor be closed and the Mississippi opened to Union traffic—the Confederacy would be crippled.

Lincoln shared Grant's midcontinental mentality, and he agreed on the strategic importance of Vicksburg. "Vicksburg is the key," Lincoln told David Porter as the two inspected a map of the region from Vicksburg to Port Hudson. "Here is the Red River, which will supply the Confederates with cattle and corn to feed their armies. There are the Arkansas and White Rivers, which can supply cattle and hogs by the thousand. From Vicksburg these supplies can be distributed by rail all over the Confederacy. Then there is that great depot of supplies on the Yazoo. Let us get Vicksburg and all that country is ours. The war can never be brought to a close until that key is in our pocket."

Though geography dictated that Vicksburg must be taken, it didn't say *how* the feat could be accomplished. If anything, geography conspired to conceal an effective strategy. Starting north of Vicksburg the Mississippi meandered across a broad valley the locals called the Delta, which was so nearly flat that the river ran west, east and even north almost as often as it ran south. One result of this meandering was that the stream had deposited a deep black soil that supported every kind of wild or cultivated plant species, particularly cotton. Some of the richest plantations in the South—including that of Jefferson Davis—lined the banks of the river near Vicksburg. But another result was that the land was frequently impossible to traverse, as the least rise in the river inundated roads along the riverbanks.

Vicksburg itself formed an exception to the rule of minimal elevation. Starting several miles above Vicksburg, near where the Yazoo River joined the Mississippi, the latter stream rubbed against a bluff that marked the eastern boundary of the alluvial plain. Vicksburg sat atop the bluff beside a sweeping bend in the river. The bluff provided the original reason for the town's existence; traders and other inhabitants didn't have to worry about being flooded. But the bluff lent additional importance to the city during the war, for it allowed artillery placed there to bombard anything that moved along the river. In fact, so high was the bluff—more than two hundred feet in spots—that gunboats on the river couldn't raise their barrels sufficiently to reach the batteries on top.

The inefficacy of gunboats rendered a frontal assault problematic and compelled Grant to consider how to get behind Vicksburg. His initial plan, as outlined to Halleck in October 1862, was to move down the Mississippi Central Railroad and threaten the city from the east. He supposed the Confederates would be forced to evacuate Vicksburg, as the city's principal defenses faced west. If they stood and fought, the result would be even better, for besides taking the fortress he would capture the garrison. As before, Grant deemed the destruction of the enemy's army more important than the seizure of his cities; the army could survive without the cities but not the cities without the army.

His instinct to attack would alone have sufficed to get his men moving, but army politics added a spur. "At this stage of the campaign against Vicksburg I was very much disturbed by newspaper rumors that General McClernand was to have a separate and independent command within mine, to operate against Vicksburg by way of the Mississippi River," he remembered. McClernand, the Illinois Democrat, had lobbied Lincoln for the command, and the president, especially after the Democratic victories in the 1862 elections, appeared inclined to give it to him. Grant didn't like the idea one bit. "Two commanders on the same field are always one too many," he remarked.

*H*e commenced the Vicksburg campaign by pressing south down the railroad from Corinth to Holly Springs, Mississippi, which he made his depot for food and ammunition. He continued to the Tallahatchie River, where a Confederate force under John Pemberton had destroyed the railroad bridge and now defied Grant to cross the rain-swollen stream. Grant dispatched his cavalry east upstream, where it found a crossing and, approaching Pemberton's rear, forced the Confederates to withdraw. Grant's engineers repaired the broken bridge and his army marched across.

He meanwhile heard that McClernand had gotten the command he desired and that an attack on Vicksburg via the Mississippi was going to happen regardless of his—Grant's—wishes. Grant decided to preempt McClernand, who was en route from Washington, by assigning Sherman the same task. He told Sherman to gather up all the troops near Memphis. "As soon as possible, move with them down the river to the vicinity of Vicksburg, and with the cooperation of the gunboat fleet under command of Flag Officer Porter, proceed to the reduction of that place in such manner as circumstances and your own judgment may dictate."

Grant intended to assist Sherman by keeping Pemberton busy. If Pemberton retreated to Vicksburg, Grant would follow him; otherwise he would hold Pemberton north of the city. But his strategy suffered a blow in late December when Confederate cavalry under Earl Van Dorn got behind Grant's lines and captured the depot at Holly Springs. Grant blamed the colonel of the garrison. "The surrender of Holly Springs was most reprehensible and showed either the disloyalty of Colonel Murphy to the cause which he professed to serve, or gross cowardice," he said later. But he also acknowledged the inherent vulnerability of a strategy that relied on long lines of transport through enemy territory.

The severing of Grant's supply delighted the Southerners around him, but only briefly. "The women came with smiling faces to Grant's headquarters, to see how he bore the loss of Holly Springs," Adam

Badeau of Grant's staff remembered. "They asked him civilly, but exult-ingly, what he would do, now that his soldiers had nothing to eat. But their exultation and smiles were of short continuance, when the quiet general informed them that his soldiers would find plenty in their barns and storehouses. They looked aghast at this, and exclaimed: 'You would not take from noncombatants!' But a commander's first necessity is to provide for his troops; so the country was stripped bare, and the army was supplied."

Grant lived off the land at this point only long enough to reestablish his rail links to the North. He remained sufficiently wedded to tradition that once he determined that he couldn't defend the railroad clear to Vicksburg he abandoned his original plan of attack. He retreated north and prepared to put all his resources into an attack down the river. But he tucked away the lesson of self-sufficiency for future use.

Sherman would put the same lesson to even greater use than Grant the following year, but for now Grant's retreat left him dangling. Sher-man distrusted McClernand as much as Grant did, and he was as happy to preempt him as Grant was to have him do so. Following Grant's order he moved down the Mississippi to the Yazoo River, which he ascended with difficulty. He led his troops among the swamps and bayous of the Delta to a place where the Confederate defenses appeared vulnerable. On December 29 his men assaulted the bluffs above Chickasaw Bayou and came within a dozen bloody yards of dislodging the rebels from their stronghold. All the while he expected to hear Grant's guns in the enemy's rear.

What he heard instead were the whistles of trains bearing Pember-ton's Confederate troops to Vicksburg. Only later, after Grant's com-munications were restored, did Sherman learn of the Confederate raid on Holly Springs and Grant's decision to move north instead of south. In the meantime he had no choice but to retreat and regroup. He descended the Yazoo to its mouth, where he met McClernand arriving with fresh troops and seniority. Sherman relinquished his command and hoped for the best.

But he also maneuvered to outflank McClernand. Grant, after with-drawing north from Mississippi, traveled to Memphis and then down the river to reconnoiter. He met with McClernand and separately with Sherman and David Porter. The latter two urged him to take personal command of the Mississippi expedition lest McClernand, through inexperience or excessive ambition, bungle it. "I found there was not sufficient confidence felt in General McClernand as a commander, either by the Army or Navy, to insure him of success," Grant reported to Halleck.

Grant didn't cross McClernand lightly. "General McClernand was a politician of very considerable prominence in his state," he observed afterward. "He was a member of Congress when the secession war broke out; he belonged to that political party which furnished all the opposition there was to a vigorous prosecution of the war for saving the Union; there was no delay in his declaring himself for the Union at all hazards."

But Grant agreed with Sherman and Porter that McClernand wasn't up to the serious fighting ahead. "It would have been criminal to send troops under these circumstances into such danger," Grant said. He concluded that he had no choice but to follow Sherman and Porter's advice and lead the Vicksburg campaign himself.

The winter of 1862–63 gravely tested the resolve of the Union. Grant's stumble at Holly Springs and Sherman's repulse at Chickasaw Bayou followed a much larger setback for the Army of the Potomac at Fredericksburg. Lincoln had replaced George McClellan after Antietam with Ambrose Burnside, who promised the kind of bold action the president couldn't elicit from McClellan. What Burnside actually delivered was a foolhardy assault on Lee's entrenched Army of Northern Virginia, resulting in horrific losses with nothing gained. The disaster deflated Unionists all across the North; Lincoln himself lamented, "We are now on the brink of destruction. It appears to me the Almighty is against us, and I can hardly see a ray of hope."

Grant felt the discouragement from the banks of the Mississippi. As he heard Sherman describe the difficulties of the Mississippi Delta and Porter explain the formidability of Vicksburg batteries, Grant briefly considered attempting a variant of his original, railroad-based plan. It would be safer and surer. But it would also be slower, and its slowness caused him to reject it. The North was watching and many would interpret delay as additional cause for despair. The army's ability to fight would be materially weakened. "The draft would be resisted, desertions ensue, and the power to capture and punish deserters lost," Grant recalled telling Sherman and Porter. "There was nothing left to be done but to *go forward to a decisive victory*."

Going forward meant getting in back of Vicksburg somehow. Sherman's failure north of the city didn't preclude a second attempt from that direction, but it made Grant consider others. Some involved audacious hydraulic engineering—nothing less, in fact, than changing the course and flow of North America's mightiest river. The bend in the Mississippi in front of Vicksburg encompassed a neck of land of barely a mile wide. Eventually the river would slit the neck and create a new channel, as it had done many times to similar necks along its course. Grant aimed to give the river some help; if successful the operation would strand Vicksburg away from the new channel and render most of its guns useless. Union engineers in 1862 had begun digging a channel across the neck, but it was poorly placed with respect to the river's currents and the enemy's guns. "I propose running a canal through, starting far enough above the old one commenced last summer, to receive the stream where it impinges against the shore with the greatest velocity," Grant wrote Halleck in January 1863. "The old canal left the river in an eddy and in a line perpendicular to the stream and also to a crest of the hills opposite with a battery directed against the outlet. This new canal will debouch below the bluffs on the opposite side of the river and give our gunboats a fair chance against any fortifications that may be placed to oppose them."

Grant set four thousand men to digging. "Work on the canal is progressing as rapidly as possible," he informed Halleck two weeks later. But heavy rains swamped the digging and lifted the river to a threatening height. "The continuous rise in the river has kept the army busy to keep out of water, and much retarded work on the canal," Grant reported.

The slowness of this first hydro-engineering project spurred Grant to attempt others. Lake Providence filled a portion of an old river bend on the west side of the Mississippi above Vicksburg; bayous and larger streams linked it eventually to the Red River, which joined the Mississippi below Vicksburg. A canal from the Mississippi to Lake Providence would allow gunboats and transports to get past the Confederate fortress without facing its guns. "There is no question but that this route is much more practicable than the present undertaking," Grant told Halleck, comparing the Lake Providence route with the Vicksburg canal.

Grant traveled to Lake Providence to observe the work himself—and soon had his optimism dashed. The diggers hadn't completed the canal from the river to Lake Providence, but engineers had managed to drag a small steamer through. "With this we were able to explore the lake and bayou as far as cleared," Grant recorded. "I saw then that there was scarcely a chance of this ever becoming a practicable route for moving troops through an enemy's country." The waterways were too narrow and tortuous. "The enemy could throw small bodies of men to obstruct our passage and pick off our troops with their sharpshooters." Yet he kept his discouragement to himself. "I let the work go on, believing employment was better than idleness for the men." Moreover, it kept the enemy guessing.

A third plan sought to improve on Sherman's experience in the Delta. Three hundred miles above Vicksburg a levee on the Mississippi's left bank was all that kept the big river from pouring into the Yazoo Pass and eventually to the Yazoo River. Grant gave the order to blow up the levee, theoretically allowing shallow-draft boats a new route to carry troops to the high ground above Vicksburg. But trees, vines, stumps and other forms of living and dead vegetation clogged the waterway, which in any case was so narrow as to invite attacks from the shore, and after an indecisive encounter between Union gunboats and Confederates at Fort Pemberton, where the Tallahatchie joined the Yazoo, this approach was abandoned.

Similar difficulties befell David Porter, who tried to push up the Yazoo from its mouth. Porter's boats carried some of Sherman's men, and he expected support from Sherman as his flotilla plunged into the tangle of the Delta. But even as Porter found the Delta too solid for effective naval operations, Sherman found it too liquid for infantry movements. Porter called for assistance as Confederate forces closed in on him. "Hurry up, for Heaven's sake," he wrote Sherman. "I never knew how helpless an ironclad could be steaming around through the woods without an army to back her." Porter managed to extricate his boats, but the Delta remained undefeated.

Grant didn't know what to do. "I am very well but much perplexed," he wrote Julia at the end of March. "Heretofore I have had nothing to do but fight the enemy. This time I have to overcome obstacles to reach him. Foot once upon dry land on the other side of the river, I think the balance would be of but short duration." But how to reach that dry land was as puzzling as ever.

Finally he decided that the best route past the defenses of Vicksburg was the most obvious. He asked Porter if his boats could run the batteries. Porter replied that they could, but given the danger and the strength of the current, it would be a one-way trip. "When these gunboats once go below, we give up all hopes of ever getting them up again."

Grant took the gamble. He decided to risk everything on a river crossing below Vicksburg. Porter's gunboats would accompany and cover vessels carrying provisions; if the provision boats got past the Vicksburg batteries they would supply Union soldiers who had made their way down the western bank and would ferry the soldiers across the river. The crossing would afford Grant the footing he desired and open the way, he hoped, to Vicksburg.

*C*harles Dana had switched from cotton speculation to administration espionage. The slowness of the Vicksburg campaign had revived the stories of Grant's drinking, and Edwin Stanton sought to confirm or silence them. Dana's ostensible role was to investigate the finances of Grant's paymasters, but his real purpose was to investigate Grant. He had a special cipher, distinct from that of Grant and the other officers, for communicating his discoveries to the war secretary.

He caught up with Grant at Milliken's Bend on the Louisiana side of the river above Vicksburg. "The Mississippi at Milliken's Bend was a mile wide," Dana remembered, "and the sight as we came down the river by boat was most imposing. Grant's big army was stretched up and down the riverbank over the plantations, its white tents affording a new decoration to the natural magnificence of the broad plains. These plains, which stretch far back from the river, were divided into rich and old plantations by blooming hedges of rose and Osage orange, the mansions of the owners being enclosed in roses, myrtles, magnolias, oaks and every other sort of beautiful and noble trees. The negroes whose work made all this wealth and magnificence were gone, and there was nothing growing in the fields. . . . I had seen slavery in Maryland, Kentucky, Virginia, and Missouri, but it was not until I saw these great Louisiana plantations with all their apparatus for living and working that I really felt the aristocratic nature of the institution, and the infernal baseness of that aristocracy."

Dana showed Grant the letter of reference explaining his ostensible mission. Grant may have guessed that Dana's true charge was broader, but he made no attempt to hide anything. "He received me cordially," Dana recalled. "Indeed, I think Grant was always glad to have me with his army. He did not like letter writing, and my daily dispatches to Mr. Stanton relieved him from the necessity of describing every day what was going on in the army. From the first neither he nor any of his staff or corps commanders evinced any unwillingness to show me the inside of things."

Dana got to know Grant's assistants and subordinates. "Grant's staff is a curious mixture of good, bad, and indifferent," Dana wrote Stanton. "As he is neither an organizer nor a disciplinarian himself, his staff is naturally a mosaic of accidental elements and family friends. It contains four working men, two who are able to accomplish their duties without work, and several who either don't think of work or who accomplish nothing no matter what they undertake." The hardest of the workers was John Rawlins. "Lieutenant-Colonel Rawlins, Grant's assistant adjutant general, is a very industrious, conscientious man, who never loses a moment, and never gives himself any indulgence except swearing and scolding. He is a lawyer by profession, a townsman of Grant's. . . . Grant thinks Rawlins a first-class adjutant, but I think this is a mistake. He is too slow, and can't write the English language correctly without a great deal of careful consideration. Indeed, illiterateness is a general characteristic of Grant's staff."

William Sherman was the best of Grant's lieutenants. "A very brilliant man and an excellent commander of a corps," Dana wrote later. "Sherman's information was great, and he was a clever talker. He always liked to have people about who could keep up with his conversation; besides, he was genial and unaffected. I particularly admired his loyalty to Grant." To Stanton, Dana declared of Sherman: "What a splendid soldier he is!"

As for Grant himself, Dana arrived a skeptic but became a believer. He observed not a drunk but a singular commanding officer. "Grant was an uncommon fellow—the most modest, the most disinterested, and the most honest man I ever knew, with a temper that nothing could disturb, and a judgment that was judicial in its comprehensiveness and wisdom," Dana wrote. "Not a great man, except morally; not an original or brilliant man, but sincere, thoughtful, deep, and gifted with courage that never faltered; when the time came to risk all, he went in like a simple-hearted, unaffected, unpretending hero, whom no ill omens could deject and no triumph unduly exalt. A social, friendly man, too, fond of a pleasant joke and also ready with one; but liking above all a long chat of an evening, and ready to sit up with you all night, talking in the cool breeze in front of his tent. Not a man of sentimentality, not demonstrative in friendship, but always holding to his friends, and just even to the enemies he hated."

By the time Grant decided to send the boats past the Vicksburg batteries, Dana had the run of the camp. He got a look at Vicksburg from the deck of a craft that ventured to within sight of the cliffs. "It was an ugly place, with its line of bluffs commanding the channel for fully seven miles, and battery piled above battery all the way," he recalled.

He remembered the critical moment. "Just before ten o'clock on the night of April 16th the squadron cast loose its moorings," he said. "It was a strange scene. . . . A mass of black things detached itself from the shore, and we saw it float out toward the middle of the stream. There was nothing to be seen except this big black mass, which dropped slowly down the river. Soon another black mass detached itself, and another, then another. It was Admiral Porter's fleet of ironclad turtles, steamboats, and barges. They floated down the Mississippi darkly and silently, showing neither steam nor light, save occasionally a signal astern, where the enemy could not see it." The vessels spaced themselves two hundred yards apart. "First came seven ironclad turtles and one heavy armed ram; following these were two side-wheel steamers and one stern-wheel, having twelve barges in tow; these barges carried the supplies." The gunboats were rounding the sharpest part of the bend before Vicksburg, just under the bluffs, when Confederate pickets spotted them in the dark and the Confederate batteries opened fire. "There was a flash from the upper forts, and then for an hour and a half the cannonade was terrific, raging incessantly along the line of about four miles in extent. I counted five hundred and twenty-five discharges." To illuminate their targets the Confederates torched some houses at the base of the bluffs; by the infernal light the gunners improved their aim.

One of the steamers, the *Henry Clay*, caught fire and burned for nearly an hour. The crew abandoned ship but the pilot stayed aboard long enough to run the vessel aground. He leaped off and clung to a plank, which kept him afloat for four miles until he was picked up.

Grant watched the battle from a river transport that kept just out of range. "The sight was magnificent, but terrible," he said. Yet not nearly as terrible as it might have been. The flotilla made it past the Confederate guns. "My mind was much relieved when I learned that no one on the transports had been killed and but few, if any, wounded." The damage to the vessels was repairable.

Grant was most pleased. "Our experiment of running the batteries of Vicksburg I think has demonstrated the entire practicability of doing so with but little risk," he wrote Halleck. "I shall send six more steamers by the batteries as soon as they can possibly be got ready."

31

THE RUNNING OF THE BATTERIES OPENED THE RIVER BELOW VICKS-
burg to Grant's army, and he proposed to exploit the opportunity at
once. "I move my headquarters to Carthage tomorrow," he told Halleck
on April 21. From the west bank of the river he would direct operations
against the Mississippi side. "Every effort will be exerted to get speedy
possession of Grand Gulf and from that point to open the Mississippi."
Grand Gulf, at the mouth of the Big Black River, was the first railhead
below Vicksburg; control of the town would enable Grant to strike at
the rear of Vicksburg or inland toward Jackson. He fairly exuded optimism. "If I do not underestimate the enemy my force is abundant with
a foothold once obtained to do the work."

His good feeling only increased during the following week. "In company with Admiral Porter I made today a reconnaissance of Grand Gulf,"
he wrote Sherman on April 24. "My impressions are that if an attack can
be made within the next two days, the place will easily fall." Preparations
took longer than expected, but three days after his letter to Sherman he
wrote to Halleck: "I am now embarking troops for the attack on Grand
Gulf. Expect to reduce it tomorrow." To Julia he said that the capture of
Grand Gulf would constitute "virtual possession of Vicksburg and Port
Hudson and the entire Mississippi River."

Grant's plan was for Porter's gunboats to engage the Confederate
batteries at Grand Gulf, silence the rebel guns and cover the landing of
the Union troops, which would storm and carry the fort there. Porter's
crews opened fire at eight o'clock in the morning of April 29. For five
hours they blasted the Confederate positions. "From a tug out in the
stream, I witnessed the whole engagement," Grant reported after the

battle. "Many times it seemed to me the gunboats were within pistol shot of the enemy's batteries." But they failed to suppress the rebel fire. The batteries were too high above the water and too well emplaced.

Changing plans midstream, Grant decided to circumvent Grand Gulf and land his troops at Bruinsburg, ten miles down the river. A slave who had escaped to the Union lines reported that a good road linked Bruinsburg to Port Gibson, several miles behind Grand Gulf. Grant again summoned Porter into action. "The gunboats made another vigorous attack and in the din the transports safely ran the blockade," Grant subsequently explained to Halleck. The troops meanwhile moved overland to a point on the Louisiana shore below Grand Gulf; the next day they were ferried to Bruinsburg.

"When this was effected I felt a degree of relief scarcely ever equaled since," Grant recalled later. "Vicksburg was not yet taken, it is true, nor were its defenders demoralized by any of our previous moves. I was now in the enemy's country, with a vast river and the stronghold of Vicksburg between me and my base of supplies. But I was on dry ground on the same side of the river with the enemy. All the campaigns, labors, hardships and exposures from the month of December previous to this time that had been made and endured were for the accomplishment of this one object."

Relief causes some persons to relax; it prompted Grant to redouble his effort. "The march immediately commenced for Port Gibson," he told Halleck a short while later. Grant's soldiers were issued three days' rations; with these in their haversacks they set off for the Mississippi interior. They made contact with the enemy a few miles from Port Gibson in the predawn darkness of May 1, and a battle ensued. "The fighting continued all day and until dark over the most broken country I ever saw," Grant explained. "The whole country is a series of irregular ridges divided by deep and impassable ravines, grown up with heavy timber, undergrowth and cane. It was impossible to engage any considerable portion of our forces at any one time." But the Union troops drove the Confederates steadily back. "General Bowen's, the rebel commander's, defense was a very bold one and well carried out," Grant told Halleck. "My force, however, was too heavy for his and composed of well disciplined and hardy men who know no defeat and are not willing to learn what it is." Bowen evacuated Port Gibson that night.

Grant proposed to maintain the pressure against the Confederates. "The country will supply all the forage required for anything like an active campaign and the necessary fresh beef," he wrote from Grand Gulf, which the Confederates had evacuated to strengthen Vicksburg. "I shall not bring my troops into this place but immediately follow the enemy, and if all promises as favorably hereafter as it does now, not stop until Vicksburg is in our possession."

Grant's subordinates thought he was moving too fast. Even the energetic Sherman warned him to slow down. "Stop all troops till your army is partially supplied with wagons," Sherman urged. "This road will be jammed as sure as life if you attempt to supply 50,000 men by one single road."

"I do not calculate upon the possibility of supplying the army with full rations from Grand Gulf," Grant answered. "I know it will be impossible without constructing additional roads. What I do expect, however, is to get up what rations of hard bread, coffee and salt we can, and make the country furnish the balance." Initial experience had been promising. "We started from Bruinsburg with an average of about two days' rations and received no more from our own supplies for seven days," he told Sherman. "Abundance was found in the meantime. Some corn-meal, bacon and vegetables was found, and an abundance of beef and mutton."

Grant knew that Halleck, especially, wouldn't like his audacious plan, but he guessed that once he started he might be out of reach of any countermanding order from Washington. "I shall communicate with Grand Gulf no more except it becomes necessary to send a train with heavy escort," he telegraphed Halleck on May 11. "You may not hear from me again for several days."

With this parting message, Grant commenced the greatest gamble of his career. Halleck wanted him to head south and join forces with Nathaniel Banks, who was approaching Port Hudson; the combined army would move deliberately against that fortress and then Vicksburg. But Banks informed Grant he couldn't reach Port Hudson for another week and then with merely fifteen thousand troops. Grant decided he couldn't wait. "The enemy would have strengthened his position and been reinforced by more men than Banks could have brought," he related afterward. "I therefore determined to move independently of Banks, cut loose from my base, destroy the rebel force in rear of Vicksburg and invest or capture the city."

But doing so required nerve in the commander and alacrity in his subordinates. One rebel army, commanded by John Pemberton, occupied Vicksburg; another, under Joseph Johnston, was near Jackson. Either one might give Grant trouble; combined they could crush him. Yet Grant self-consciously put himself between the two commands, intending to strike one and then the other and by this means beat both.

He knew that any number of things could go wrong. His men might lose their way in the unfamiliar country. His harvest of the local crops and livestock might fail. A critical message might be intercepted. His intelligence regarding the enemy's numbers might be mistaken. (In fact it was: Grant thought Pemberton had thirty thousand men when he actually had more than fifty thousand.)

Yet Grant took the gamble. His instinct, as always, was to fight, to carry the battle to the enemy, to hit him when he was off balance and then to hit him again. "The enemy is badly beaten, greatly demoralized and exhausted of ammunition," he wrote Sherman on May 3. "The road to Vicksburg is open."

It wouldn't stay open for long. Speed was essential. "Every day's delay is worth two thousand men to the enemy," Grant declared to William Hillyer on May 5. On May 9 he told Julia: "Two days more, or Tuesday next, must bring on the fight which will settle the fate of Vicksburg."

To take Vicksburg he turned away from Vicksburg, driving instead toward Jackson. "Move your command tonight to the next cross roads three or four miles to your front, if you can find water," he told James McPherson on May 11. "And tomorrow push with all activity into Raymond. . . . We must fight the enemy before our rations fail." After McPherson engaged the Confederates at Raymond in a sharp battle that left hundreds killed or wounded, Grant related the result to John McClernand: "The enemy was driven at all points. . . . He retreated towards Clinton and no doubt to Jackson. I have determined to follow and take first the capital of the State."

Grant realized that his decision would expose his rear to an attack by Pemberton, who at the least could sever his line of communication. "So I finally decided to have none—to cut loose altogether from my base and move my whole force eastward," he recalled. "I then had no fears for my communications, and if I moved quickly enough could turn upon Pemberton before he could attack me in the rear."

He issued orders more rapidly than ever. "Move one division of your corps through this place to Clinton, charging it with the duty of destroying the railroad as far as possible to a point on the direct Raymond and

Jackson road," he instructed McClernand on May 13 from Raymond. "Move another division three or four miles beyond Mississippi Springs, and eight or nine miles beyond this place, and a third to Raymond ready to support either of the others." He ordered Sherman: "Move directly towards Jackson, starting at early dawn." Just after midnight he wrote McPherson from the outskirts of Jackson: "Send me word how you are progressing; we must get Jackson or as near as it is possible tonight."

Grant discovered that Johnston at Jackson was expecting reinforcements imminently; the discovery caused him to push even harder. Heavy rains delayed the attack on Jackson, but on the morning of May 14 McPherson and Sherman struck the outer defenses of the city. The Confederates resisted primarily to cover Johnston's withdrawal of the main body of his outnumbered force lest the whole be captured by Grant's men. Johnston got away to the north, but Grant took Jackson, sleeping that night in the house where, he was told, Johnston had slept the night before.

*B*agging the capital of the home state of Jefferson Davis won Grant praise in the North, but he himself considered it merely a step to the larger goal of reducing Vicksburg. He summoned McPherson and Sherman to the Mississippi statehouse on the afternoon of May 14 and told McPherson to head back toward Vicksburg at once, with Sherman to follow after he eliminated Jackson's capacity for supporting the Confederate war effort. "He set about his work in the morning, and utterly destroyed the railroads in every direction, north, east, south, and west, for a distance, in all, of twenty miles," Adam Badeu said of Sherman's work at Jackson. "All the bridges, factories, and arsenals were burned, and whatever could be of use to the rebels destroyed. The importance of Jackson as a railroad center and a depot of stores and military factories was annihilated."

A few other facilities were wrecked as well, without authorization. "Just as I was leaving Jackson, a very fat man came to see me, to inquire if his hotel, a large frame building near the depot, were doomed to be burned," Sherman recalled. He replied that he intended nothing of the kind; he would raze only those properties that produced war-related goods. The hotel owner expressed relief, avowing that he was a loyal Union man. "I remember to have said," Sherman continued sardonically, "that this fact was manifest from the sign of his hotel, which was the

'Confederate Hotel,' the sign 'United States' being faintly painted out, and 'Confederate' painted over it." Sherman would have left the matter there with the hotel intact. "But just as we were leaving the town, it burst out in flames and was burned to the ground. I never found out exactly who set it on fire, but was told that in one of our batteries were some officers and men who had been made prisoners at Shiloh, with Prentiss's division, and had been carried past Jackson in a railroad train; they had been permitted by the guard to go by this very hotel for supper, and had nothing to pay but greenbacks, which were refused, with insult, by this same law-abiding landlord. These men, it was said, had quietly and stealthily applied the fire underneath the hotel just as we were leaving the town."

Grant meanwhile surmised that Johnston's northward retreat would bend to the west so that Johnston's army might join up with Pemberton's, and he moved to forestall the meeting. "I am concentrating my forces at Bolton to cut them off," he told Halleck. An intercepted message from Johnston to Pemberton confirmed Grant's surmise. Stephen Hurlbut had arranged to plant a spy behind the Confederate lines, a man who received a noisy expulsion from the Union army on asserted grounds of disloyalty. This person found his way to Jackson, where he fulminated against Grant and subsequently offered to carry a message from Johnston to Pemberton through territory controlled by Grant's forces. He seemed reliable enough to Johnston that the Confederate commander let him make the hazardous run, which included a stop in McPherson's Union camp.

Grant learned that Pemberton was approaching from the west, and he hoped to smash him before he got help from Johnston. "I have just received information that the enemy has crossed Big Black with the entire Vicksburg force," Grant wrote McPherson. "You will therefore pass all trains and move forward to join McClernand with all possible dispatch." He ordered Sherman to put his men on the road toward Bolton at once. "Great celerity should be shown in carrying out this movement. The fight may be brought on at any moment; we should have every man on the field."

The clash occurred at Champion's Hill on Baker's Creek, west of Bolton. Grant admired Pemberton's choice of ground. "It is one of the highest points in that section, and commanded all the ground in range,"

he wrote afterward. "On the east side of the ridge, which is quite precipi-
tous, is a ravine running first north, then westerly, terminating at Baker's
Creek. It was grown up thickly with large trees and undergrowth, making it difficult to penetrate with troops, even when not defended."

Grant's columns converged on Pemberton's position on May 16, and
after a couple hours' skirmishing the battle proper began. It lasted four
hours and left Grant in control of Champion's Hill but not of Pemberton's
army, the far greater prize. "Had I known the ground as I did afterwards,"
he said later, "I cannot see how Pemberton could have escaped with any
organized force." Yet the Confederate losses were heavy—as were those
on the Union side—and to Grant they appeared decisive. "The enemy
were driven and are now in full retreat," he wrote just after the battle.
"I am of the opinion that the battle of Vicksburg has been fought." He
added: "We must be prepared, however, for whatever turns up."

Grant gave chase as Pemberton fled back to Vicksburg. Nightfall
found him near a house where Union surgeons and nurses tended to
wounded Confederates. "While a battle is raging, one can see his enemy
mowed down by the thousand or the ten thousand, with great composure," he reflected. "But after the battle these scenes are distressing, and
one is naturally disposed to do as much to alleviate the suffering of an
enemy as of a friend."

Before dawn Grant's men caught Pemberton a dozen miles from
Vicksburg. "The enemy were found strongly posted on both sides of the
Black River," Grant explained in his postbattle report. Bluffs backed the
stream on the west side; cultivated fields filled the flood plain on the east,
surrounded by a bayou. "Following the line of this bayou the enemy had
sunk rifle pits, leaving a stagnant ditch of water from two to three feet
in depth and from ten to twenty feet wide outside." Grant's men tested
the east-bank defenses in various places, looking for a weakness. Finding
none they readied to charge.

At just this moment Grant received a letter from Halleck that had
taken a week to find him. "If possible, the forces of you and of General
Banks should be united between Vicksburg and Port Hudson, so as to
attack these places separately with your combined forces," Halleck said.
Grant pondered the obsolete direction, then told the officer bearing the
letter that it came too late. Halleck would not have written it if he had
known the current state of affairs, he said. The officer manifested alarm,
declaring that General Halleck would insist that the order be obeyed.
The words were scarcely out of his mouth when a loud cheer erupted

on the Union right, where one of Grant's brigadiers, Michael Lawler, was leading a charge. "I immediately mounted my horse and rode in the direction of the charge, and saw no more of the officer who delivered the dispatch, I think not even to this day," Grant recalled years later.

Lawler's charge was worth the cheering. "Notwithstanding the level ground to pass over affording no cover to his troops, and the ditch in front of the enemy's works being a great obstacle, the charge was gallantly made, and in a few minutes the entire garrison, with seventeen pieces of artillery, were the trophies of this brilliant dash," Grant recorded after the battle. The Confederates west of the river, fearing a similar result, burned the bridge and headed for the comparative safety of Vicksburg.

At the cost of another seventeen hundred troops, Pemberton had bought himself time—but not as much as he hoped. Grant's engineers fabricated pontoon bridges, employing cotton bales as pontoons, and threw them across the river by the next morning. His army reached the outer defenses of Vicksburg later that day.

Grant explained to David Porter that the reduction of Vicksburg, the object for which they had been working for months, had finally begun. "My men are now investing Vicksburg," Grant said. "Sherman's forces run from the Mississippi River above the city two miles east. McPherson is to his left, and McClernand to the left of McPherson." The defenders were severely weakened by the recent battles. "The enemy have not been able to return to the city with one half of his forces." Grant hoped to shrink that number further with Porter's help. "If you can run down and throw shell in just back of the lower part of the city, it would aid us and demoralize an already badly beaten enemy," he told Porter.

Grant rode to Sherman's position north of the city. The two men climbed the highest part of the bluff that commanded the river and its banks. "Until this moment I never thought your expedition a success," Sherman told Grant. "I never could see the end clearly until now. But this is a campaign. This is a success, if we never take the town."

32

JOE JOHNSTON AGREED. THE CONFEDERATE COMMANDER UNDER-
stood he had been out-generaled, and he determined to cut his losses.
"If Haynes' Bluff is untenable," he wrote Pemberton, who had already
decided it *was* untenable, "Vicksburg is of no value, and must ultimately
surrender. Under such circumstances, instead of losing both troops and
place, we must, if possible, save the troops. If it is not too late, evacuate
Vicksburg and its dependencies, and march to the northeast."

Pemberton convened a council of war. He polled his generals as to
the feasibility of following Johnston's order. "The opinion was unanimously expressed that it was impossible to withdraw the army from this
position with such morale and material as to be of further service to
the Confederacy," he replied to Johnston. While the Confederate officers
were meeting, Grant's guns commenced a bombardment of the Vicksburg defenses. Pemberton realized that his situation was dire. But he
wouldn't give up. "I have decided to hold Vicksburg as long as possible,
with the firm hope that the Government may yet be able to assist me in
keeping this obstruction to the enemy's free navigation of the Mississippi
River," he told Johnston. "I still consider it to be the most important
point in the Confederacy."

Grant didn't want to give Confederate assistance a chance to arrive.
The momentum of the previous month, during which his men had
marched two hundred miles and won five battles, prompted him to try to
take Vicksburg by storm. "Johnston was in my rear, only fifty miles away,
with an army not much inferior to the one I had with me, and I knew he
was being reinforced," Grant explained afterward. "There was danger of
his coming to the assistance of Pemberton, and after all he might defeat

my anticipations of capturing the garrison if, indeed, he did not prevent the capture of the city." Moreover, a quick defeat of Pemberton would let him turn on Johnston's army, whose defeat or dispersal would go far toward ending the rebellion. A final argument clinched the case for an assault: "The troops believed they could carry the works in their front, and would not have worked so patiently in the trenches if they had not been allowed to try."

The attack was scheduled for the morning of May 22. Grant had his corps commanders synchronize their watches so they could launch at precisely ten o'clock. "The assault was gallant in the extreme on the part of all the troops," Grant told Halleck afterward. In places Union soldiers managed to plant their flags on the outer works of the Confederate defenses. But the geometry and geography of the city and its surroundings prevented Grant from bringing his superior numbers to bear. "Each corps had many more men than could possibly be used in the assault over such ground as intervened between them and the enemy," he said. "More men could only avail in case of breaking through the enemy's line or in repelling a sortie."

Such a breakthrough occurred in McClernand's sector—or so McClernand reported. Grant was skeptical. "I don't believe a word of it," he told Sherman. He added later: "I occupied a position from which I believed I could see as well as he what took place in his front, and I did not see the success he reported." But Sherman pointed out that McClernand had put his report in writing and that if Grant ignored it there might be political trouble. Reluctantly Grant sent reinforcements.

He soon wished he hadn't. The initial assault had been repelled with heavy losses; the second wave, prompted by McClernand's questionable report, did no better. "This last attack only served to increase our casualties without giving any benefit whatever," Grant acknowledged.

After the unsuccessful attack on May 22, the siege proper of Vicksburg began. The modernity of the Civil War—the employment of railroads and steamboats for transport, the application of industrial techniques to the production of war matériel—meant little to the millennia-old problem of reducing a hilltop fortress. If Grant had possessed sufficient siege cannon, he might have tried to batter down Vicksburg's walls. But his six thirty-two-pounders, complemented by a battery of naval guns borrowed from Porter, hardly dented the city's defenses. His

smaller guns and some makeshift mortars—hollowed logs ringed with
iron bands—harassed the inhabitants and defenders without threatening
to breach the works.

To effect a breach Grant turned to one of the oldest techniques of
siege warfare. His sappers dug tunnels toward the walls of the city. They
dodged the tunnels Pemberton's men dug against them and after weeks
of mining reached a spot beneath the Confederate defenses. Grant's
artillerists crammed the cavern with black powder and on June 25 ignited
it. The explosion hurled dirt, rocks and rebels high into the air, leaving a
gaping hole in the Confederate works and a yawning crater in the ground.
Union soldiers, who had been expecting the explosion, poured into the
gap; Confederate troops, who hadn't, nonetheless responded almost as
quickly. The fierce battle that followed was fought at close quarters with
bayonets, rifle butts, knives, fists and teeth. Grant's men won the crater
but couldn't exploit their success as the Confederates simply retreated a
short distance and retrenched.

Grant reluctantly settled for a strategy of attrition. He hammered the
fortress mercilessly, as Pemberton explained to Johnston. "The enemy
has placed several very heavy guns in position against our works," the
Confederate commander wrote on June 15. "His fire is almost continuous. Our men have no relief; are becoming much fatigued. . . . We are
living on greatly reduced rations." Within the week Pemberton reiterated: "My men have been thirty-four days and nights in trenches, without relief, and the enemy within conversation distance. We are living on
very reduced rations, and, as you know, are entirely isolated. What aid
am I to expect from you?"

After Johnston replied that he had scant aid to send and that it
couldn't get through Grant's lines, Pemberton felt more isolated than
ever. Supplies continued to dwindle. "Our stock of bacon having been
almost exhausted, the experiment of using mule meat as a substitute was
tried," he reported. "I am gratified to say it was found by both officers and
men not only nutritious but very palatable."

The bombardment from the Union guns caused the residents of
Vicksburg to seek shelter wherever they could find it. Discovering that
their houses afforded little protection, they burrowed caves into the hill-
sides of the city. These kept them comparatively safe from the balls and
shells, but living underground added to the emotional toll. "Even the very
animals seemed to share the general fear of a sudden and frightful death,"
a woman who experienced the siege recorded. "The dogs would be seen

in the midst of the noise to gallop up the street, and then to return, as if fear had maddened them. On hearing the descent of a shell, they would dart aside—then, as it exploded, sit down and howl in the most pitiful manner." Nor did the earth above the caves invariably provide protection. "Sitting in the cave one evening, I heard the most heartrending screams and moans," the Vicksburg woman recalled. "I was told that a mother had taken a child into a cave about a hundred yards from us, and having laid it on its little bed, as the poor woman believed, in safety, she took her seat near the entrance of the cave. A mortar shell came rushing through the air and fell with much force, entering the earth above the sleeping child—cutting through into the cave—oh! most horrible sight to the mother—crushing in the upper part of the little sleeping head and taking away the young innocent life."

By the beginning of July the situation was desperate. "Unless the siege of Vicksburg is raised or supplies are thrown in, it will become necessary very shortly to evacuate the place," Pemberton wrote his generals. "I see no prospect of the former, and there are many great, if not insuperable, obstacles in the way of the latter." Pemberton requested that the officers assess the ability of the troops to stand the strain of a forced evacuation. "You will, of course, use the utmost discretion while informing yourself," he added.

The gist of the officers' response was that the men were too enfeebled to break the siege and escape the besiegers. "Under these circumstances," Major General M. L. Smith wrote, in words echoed by the others, "I deem it best to propose terms of capitulation before forced to do so from want of provisions."

Pemberton had reason for putting his subordinates on record. As a native Northerner, from Philadelphia, he remained suspect in the eyes of some in the South despite the gallant service he had performed till then. If Vicksburg fell, as appeared increasingly inevitable, he didn't want its surrender to be his decision alone. "With this unanimous opinion of my officers against the practicability of a successful evacuation, and no relief from General Johnston, a surrender with or without terms was the only alternative left to me," he reported afterward.

Accordingly, on July 3 he wrote Grant requesting an armistice for the purpose of negotiating a surrender. "I make this proposition to save the further effusion of blood, which must otherwise be shed to a frightful extent, feeling myself fully able to maintain my position for a yet indefinite period."

Two decades years later Grant recalled the moment when the truce flags appeared on the Vicksburg ramparts. "It was a glorious sight to officers and soldiers on the line where these white flags were visible," Grant wrote. "The news soon spread to all parts of the command. The troops felt that their long and weary marches, hard fighting, ceaseless watching by night and day, in a hot climate, exposure to all sorts of weather, to diseases and, worst of all, to the gibes of many Northern papers that came to them saying all their suffering was in vain, that Vicksburg would never be taken, were at last at an end and the Union sure to be saved."

Grant knew John Bowen, the Confederate officer carrying Pemberton's letter. The two had been neighbors in Missouri and Grant thought him a good man. But he rejected Pemberton's request for negotiations. There was nothing to negotiate, he said. "The useless effusion of blood you propose stopping by this course can be ended at any time you choose, by an unconditional surrender of the city and garrison." Grant promised fair consideration following a surrender. "Men who have shown so much endurance and courage as those now in Vicksburg will always challenge the respect of an adversary, and I can assure you will be treated with all the respect due to prisoners of war."

Grant was less confident than he sounded. He still worried that Johnston might attack his rear; in fact he had decided that if Pemberton didn't surrender soon he would order another assault. And so he agreed to meet with Pemberton personally between the lines in front of McPherson's corps.

Pemberton arrived at three in the afternoon. Grant greeted his former comrade from the Mexican War. Pemberton asked what terms Grant might offer for a surrender. Grant repeated that he would offer no terms; the surrender must be unconditional. "The conference might as well end," Pemberton said with what Grant took for annoyance. Grant replied, "Very well," and turned to go.

But Bowen wished the conference to continue. He engaged one of Grant's officers, proposing that the Confederates be allowed to march out of Vicksburg with their small arms and artillery. Grant rejected this at once. Yet Bowen's ploy served the purpose of extending the discussion, and Grant eventually agreed to send Pemberton a letter that evening, putting in writing his requirements for a surrender.

Grant consulted his division and corps commanders and considered the matter further. The central issue was whether the Vicksburg garrison should be taken as prisoners of war and sent north, eventually to be exchanged for Union prisoners in Confederate camps, or paroled on the spot. The former mode was more satisfying in that it would demonstrate beyond question that Pemberton's army had been beaten. But the latter was more practical because prisoners would have to be fed and transported.

Grant opted for practicality. "I will march in one division as a guard and take possession at eight a.m. tomorrow," he proposed to Pemberton. "As soon as rolls can be made out, and paroles be signed by officers and men, you will be allowed to march out of our lines, the officers taking with them their side-arms and clothing, and the field, staff and cavalry officers one horse each. The rank and file will be allowed all their clothing but not other property."

Pemberton countered by proposing as a formality to march his troops out before Grant marched in, the Confederates then to be listed and paroled. He also asked Grant to guarantee the property of Vicksburg's citizens. Grant agreed to the face-saving gesture toward the troops but refused to bind himself regarding civilian property. On these terms Pemberton capitulated, with the formal surrender to take place the next day, July 4.

33

JOHN RAWLINS SIGHED RELIEF AT VICKSBURG'S FALL, FOR REASONS beyond the obvious. Grant's adjutant minded the general's mail and the issuance of orders, but he also assumed responsibility for Grant's health and welfare. Rawlins spoke to Grant more candidly than anyone else in the army. "Rawlins could argue, could expostulate, could condemn, could even upbraid, without interrupting for an hour the fraternal confidence and good will of Grant," Jacob Cox recalled. Cox was a Union officer from Ohio who knew both men during the war and after, and he understood what Grant saw in Rawlins and why he allowed Rawlins such freedom. Cox said of Rawlins: "He had won the right to this relation by an absolute devotion which dated from Grant's appointment to be brigadier-general in 1861, and which had made him the good genius of his friend in every crisis of Grant's wonderful career. This was not because of Rawlins's great intellect, for he was of only moderate mental powers. It was rather that he became a living and speaking conscience for his general, as courageous to speak in a time of need as Nathan the prophet, and as absolutely trusted as Jonathan by David."

Rawlins had heard in Galena the stories of Grant's drinking, and he subsequently observed sufficient continuing temptation in Grant to insist on a promise to abstain, which Grant gave. But amid the siege of Vicksburg, as the summer heat set in and the excitement of the previous months' fighting and maneuvering wore off, Grant apparently allowed himself a holiday from his pledge. In early June he decided to travel up the river to observe operations on the Yazoo. He invited Charles Dana to go along. The two men boarded a river steamer and headed off. By Dana's later account Grant fell ill and took to bed in the cabin. The steamer was approached by two Union gunboats whose officers said the Confederates were active upstream and Grant's vessel should turn around. "I told them Grant was sick and asleep, and that I did not want to wake him," Dana wrote. The officers insisted that Dana apprise Grant of the situation. "Finally I did so," Dana said, "but he was too sick to decide. 'I will leave it with you,' he said." Dana gave the order to turn back. He concluded the story: "The next morning Grant came out to breakfast fresh as a rose, clean shirt and all, quite himself."

Rawlins drew more from the episode than Dana recorded. He may have spoken to Dana directly or he may have heard of Grant's indisposition from others. He concluded that Grant had been drunk. And he felt compelled to write a letter to his chief that for decades remained private. "The great solicitude I feel for the safety of this army leads me to mention what I had hoped never again to do: the subject of your drinking," Rawlins said. "This may surprise you, for I may be, and trust I am, doing you an injustice by unfounded suspicion, but if in error it had better be on the side of the country's safety than in fear of offending a friend." Rawlins explained that he had been worried about Grant even before the boat ride. "I have heard that Dr. McMillan at General Sherman's a few days ago induced you, notwithstanding your pledge to me, to take a glass of wine, and today when I found a box of wine in front of your tent and proposed to move it, which I did, I was told you had forbid its being taken away, for you intended to keep it until you entered Vicksburg, that you might have it for your friends." The incident with Dana and additional evidence made Rawlins worry the more. "Tonight, when you should, because of the condition of your health, if nothing else, have been in bed, I find you where the wine bottle has just been emptied, in company with those who drink and urge you to do likewise; and the lack of your usual promptness and decision, and clearness of expressing yourself in writing, conduces to confirm my suspicion." Grant knew better, Rawlins said. "You have full control of your appetite, and can let drinking alone. Had you not pledged me the sincerity of your honor early last March, that you would drink no more during the war, and kept that pledge during your recent campaign, you would not today have stood first in the world's history as a military leader. Your only salvation depends upon your strict adherence to that pledge. You cannot succeed in any other way."

Grant didn't reply to Rawlins's letter, at least not in a form that survived. He carried the siege of Vicksburg to its successful conclusion. The incident was set aside if not forgotten.

*R*obert E. Lee's July Fourth was as dismal as Grant's was triumphant. Lee's campaign season had commenced auspiciously when Joseph Hooker, Lincoln's latest commanding general, forced a battle at Chancellorsville, west of Fredericksburg. Hooker's army outnumbered Lee's two to one and Hooker had a reputation as a fighter. But Lee outmaneuvered Hooker by daringly splitting his force and striking at Hooker's flank. The result was Lee's most brilliant victory and a stunning defeat for the North. "My God! My God!" Lincoln moaned on getting the news. "What will the country say?"

The defeat at Chancellorsville made Grant's campaign for Vicksburg more essential to Union hopes for victory in the war; it also gave Lee the encouragement he needed to mount a second invasion of the North. As in 1862, Lee hoped to ease his provisioning problems by living off the land in Maryland and Pennsylvania; to an even greater degree than before, he aimed to demoralize residents of the North and energize the peace movement for the 1864 elections. "If successful this year, next fall there will be a great change in public opinion at the North," he wrote his wife. "The Republicans will be destroyed and I think the friends of peace will become so strong that the next administration will go in on that basis."

Jefferson Davis and others in the Confederate government weren't sure a Northern invasion was the best use of Lee's army. Davis judged Vicksburg more central to the future of the Confederacy than any position in Maryland or Pennsylvania; he wanted Lee to release part of his force to fight Grant on the Mississippi. But Lee's reputation and self-confidence, especially after Chancellorsville, were such that Davis acquiesced in his desire to invade the North. Lee said that he had no realistic alternative. "Our resources in men are constantly diminishing, and the disproportion in this respect between us and our enemies, if they continue united in their efforts to subjugate us, is steadily augmenting," Lee told Davis. "Under these circumstances we should neglect no honorable means of dividing and weakening our enemies, that they may feel some of the difficulties experienced by ourselves."

In early June Lee began shifting troops to the Shenandoah Valley; by the middle of the month the advance units of his army had reached the Potomac. Joe Hooker's first thought, on learning of the Confederates' northward movement, was to attack Lee's rear. "Will it not promote the true interest of the cause for me to march to Richmond at once?" the Union commander wrote Lincoln. "I should adopt this course as being the most speedy and certain mode of giving the rebellion a mortal blow."

Lincoln responded that Hooker had his priorities wrong. "I think Lee's army and not Richmond is your sure objective point," he said. "If he comes towards the upper Potomac, follow on his flank, and on the inside track, shortening your lines, whilst he lengthens his. Fight him when the opportunity offers. If he stays where he is, fret him and fret him."

So Hooker went after Lee, who crossed into Maryland in late June and continued toward Pennsylvania. "If Harrisburg comes within your means, capture it," Lee told Richard Ewell, one of his generals. The Confederate invasion evoked alarm across the North. Lincoln feared for Baltimore and Washington; residents of Pittsburgh and Philadelphia thought *they* were the targets. Farmers and their families fled the advance of the Confederate columns, driving their livestock before them. The governor of Pennsylvania called for sixty thousand men to defend the commonwealth; the governor of New York promised to spare no effort to stop the Confederates before they reached the Empire State. Lincoln summoned one hundred thousand new volunteers.

Yet even as Lincoln feared for the safety of the North, he sensed an opening. "I really think the attitude of the enemies' army in Pennsylvania presents us the best opportunity we have had since the war began," he observed. The president hoped to pin Lee between Hooker's army in the east and the Union garrison at Harpers Ferry.

But Hooker insisted that Harpers Ferry should be abandoned and its troops attached to his main army. When Henry Halleck, speaking for Lincoln, rejected the idea, Hooker offered his resignation.

To the general's apparent surprise, Lincoln accepted the resignation, appointing George Gordon Meade in his place. Meade was a solid soldier with commendable experience but nothing that made him an obvious choice to head the Army of the Potomac. "Yesterday morning, at 3 a.m., I was aroused from my sleep by an officer from Washington entering my tent and, after waking me up, saying he had come to give me trouble," Meade wrote his wife. "At first I thought that it was either to relieve or arrest me, and promptly replied to him that my conscience was clear, void of offense toward any man; I was prepared for his bad news. He then handed me a communication to read, which I found was an order relieving Hooker from the command and assigning me to it." Having at some length recovered from his shock, Meade added: "I am moving at once against Lee. . . . A battle will decide the fate of our country and our cause."

Meade's strategy was simplicity itself: "to find and fight the enemy," he said. Finding the Confederates wasn't hard, for on the approach of Meade's army Lee concentrated his troops for battle. Lee's foragers could obtain food from the neighborhood, but his army required ammunition from Virginia. He couldn't let Meade cut him off.

When the battle began, at Gettysburg on July 1, most of the country concurred with Meade that its outcome would determine the fate of the Union. The first day's fighting favored the Confederates but not decisively; Lee and Meade brought up their whole armies to settle the issue the next day. "The sun of the 2nd of July rose brightly upon these two armies marshalling for battle," Carl Schurz remembered. Schurz was a German native who had fled his homeland after agitating unsuccessfully for democratic change during the abortive revolution of 1848. He became a Republican in the 1850s and an officer in the Union army after the outbreak of the war. He commanded a division of Meade's army at Gettysburg. "Neither of them was ready," he continued, regarding the two armies. "But as we could observe from Cemetery Hill, the Confederates were readier than we were." Cemetery Hill was the strong point of the Union defenses, and Meade arrived on the morning of July 2 to examine the position. "His long-bearded, haggard face, shaded by a black military felt hat the rim of which was turned down, looked careworn and tired, as if he had not slept that night," Schurz said. "The spectacles on his nose gave him a somewhat magisterial look. There was nothing in his appearance or his bearing—not a smile nor a sympathetic word addressed to those around him—that might have made the hearts of the soldiers warm up to him, or that called forth a cheer. . . . His mind was evidently absorbed by a hard problem." Schurz nonetheless thought Meade inspired confidence. "The officers and men, as much as was permitted, crowded around and looked up to him with curious eyes, and then turned away, not enthusiastic but clearly satisfied."

Schurz asked Meade how many men he had for the battle. "In the course of the day I expect to have about 95,000," Meade replied. "Enough, I guess, for this business." He gazed across the battlefield and said quietly, as if to himself: "We may fight it out here just as well as anywhere else."

Lee thought so too, and he hurled his 70,000 against Meade's force. His spearhead was a corps under James Longstreet, which attacked

Schurz's sector of the Union lines. "We heard a confused noise on our left," Schurz remembered, "a continuous rattle of musketry, discharges of artillery now thundering with rapid vehemence, then slackening as if batteries were silenced, then breaking out again with renewed violence, and from time to time something like an echo of a Union cheer or a rebel yell." A projection of Cemetery Ridge blocked Schurz's view from Cemetery Hill; for a time he couldn't tell whether the Union troops or the Confederates were gaining the advantage. "But looking to our rear we observed how regiment after regiment was taken from our right wing to be hurried as quickly as possible toward the left of the army as reinforcement. The fire grew more furious from minute to minute, and about half after six, the roar of the battle actually seemed to indicate that our line was yielding." At that moment one of Schurz's captains galloped up with word that the Union Third Corps had been routed and the enemy was closing in. Without help, Schurz and his division would be surrounded and forced to surrender. "It was a moment of most anxious suspense," Schurz said. "But it did not last long. Loud and repeated Union cheers on our left, which could be heard above the din of battle, told us that relief had come in time and had rolled back the hostile wave."

The day ended in a bloody draw. "We had a great fight yesterday, the enemy attacking and we completely repulsing them," Meade wrote his wife the next morning. "Both armies shattered."

But not shattered enough not to fight a third day. Lee awoke early and rode with James Longstreet to the highest point on Seminary Ridge, which overlooked most of the battlefield. George Edward Pickett had arrived with his division the day before, and he came upon Lee and Longstreet as the former was explaining his battle plan. Longstreet was loudly skeptical. "Great God!" he said. "Look, General Lee, at the insurmountable difficulties between our line and that of the Yankees: the steep hills, the tiers of artillery, the fences, the heavy skirmish line. And then we'll have to fight our infantry against their batteries. Look at the ground we'll have to charge over, nearly a mile of that open ground there under the rain of their canister and shrapnel." Lee replied calmly: "The enemy is there, General Longstreet, and I am going to strike him."

Lee's third-day attack began with an artillery barrage that lasted two hours. The Confederate guns gradually silenced the Union batteries, although Lee couldn't tell whether the cessation was voluntary on Meade's part or compelled by the pounding of the Southern bombardment. As the Union salvos started to ease, Pickett rode up to Longstreet.

"I found him like a great lion at bay," Pickett wrote his wife just moments later. "I have never seen him so grave and troubled. For several minutes after I had saluted him he looked at me without speaking. Then in an agonized voice, the reserve all gone, he said: 'Pickett, I am being crucified at the thought of the sacrifice of life which this attack will make. I have instructed Alexander'—the Confederate artillery commander—'to watch the effect of our fire upon the enemy, and when it begins to tell he must take the responsibility and give you your orders, for I can't.'"

Longstreet was still speaking when a messenger rode up with a note for Pickett from Alexander. "If you are coming at all, come at once," the note said. Pickett read it, handed it to Longstreet and asked if he should obey it. "He looked at me for a moment, then held out his hand," Pickett told his wife. "Presently, clasping his other hand over mine without speaking, he bowed his head upon his breast. I shall never forget the look in his face nor the clasp of his hand when I said: 'Then, General, I shall lead my division on.'"

Frank Haskell of the Union Second Corps observed Pickett's division from across the valley. "Every eye could see his legions, an overwhelming, resistless tide of an ocean of armed men, sweeping upon us," Haskell wrote. "Regiment after regiment, and brigade after brigade, move from the woods and rapidly take their places in the lines forming the assault. . . . More than half a mile their front extends, more than a thousand yards the dull gray masses deploy, man touching man, rank pressing rank, and line supporting line. Their red flags wave; their horsemen gallop up and down; the arms of eighteen thousand men, barrel and bayonet, gleam in the sun, a sloping forest of flashing steel. Right on they move, as with one soul, in perfect order, without impediment of ditch or wall or stream, over ridge and slope, through orchard and meadow and cornfield, magnificent, grim, irresistible."

Union skirmishers opened fire with muskets on the Confederate advance, then fell back. Union artillery cut gaping holes in the rebel ranks, but other troops stepped forward and filled the holes. "And so all across that broad open ground they have come," Haskell wrote, "nearer and nearer, nearly half the way with our guns bellowing in their faces, until now a hundred yards, no more, divide our ready left from their advancing right." As the distance diminished to almost nothing, the fighting intensified to a hellish pitch. "All along each hostile front, a thousand yards, with narrowest space between, the volleys blaze and roll, as thick the sound as when a summer hailstorm pelts the city roofs, as thick the fire as when the incessant lightning fringes a summer cloud." Haskell wondered how long the rebels, fighting in the open, could stand the fury of the Union fire, when his own line suddenly weakened. "Great Heaven! Were my senses mad? The larger portion of Webb's brigade—my God, it was true—there by the group of trees and the angles of the wall, was breaking from the cover of their works, and without orders or reason, with no hand lifted to check them, was falling back a fear-stricken flock of confusion! The fate of Gettysburg hung on a single spider's thread!"

Haskell and his fellow officers frantically attempted to rally the men. For a time their efforts appeared in vain. "Those red flags were accumulating at the wall every moment. . . . Webb's men are falling fast, and he is among them to direct and encourage; but however well they may now do, with that walled enemy in front, with more than a dozen flags to Webb's three, it soon becomes apparent that in not many minutes they will be overpowered, or that there will be none alive for the enemy to overpower."

But additional troops arrived to bolster the failing part of the Union line. The combat grew more desperate than ever. "The jostling, swaying lines on either side boil and roar and dash their flamy spray, two hostile billows of a fiery ocean. Thick flashes stream from the wall; thick volleys answer from the crest." The men fought reflexively, savagely. "Individuality is drowned in a sea of clamor, and timid men, breathing the breath of the multitude, are brave. The frequent dead and wounded lie where they stagger and fall; there is no humanity for them now, and none can be spared to care for them. The men do not cheer or shout, they growl; and over that uneasy sea, heard with the roar of musketry, sweeps the muttered thunder of a storm of growls." A Pennsylvania regiment, refusing to yield another foot of its home soil, charged toward the wall. "The line springs; the crest of the solid ground, with a great roar, heaves forward its maddened load: men, arms, smoke, fire, a fighting mass. It rolls to the wall. Flash meets flash. The wall is crossed. A moment ensues of thrusts, yells, blows, shots, and undistinguishable conflict, followed by a shout, universal, that makes the welkin ring again—and the last and bloodiest fight of the great battle of Gettysburg is ended and won."

It wasn't as simple as that, but almost. The blunting of Pickett's charge against Cemetery Ridge left the field at Gettysburg in the control of Meade and the Union. At staggering cost—some fifty thousand killed, wounded or missing, divided almost equally between the two sides—Lee and Meade had fought to a draw, but one that required Lee, the invader, to return south. "All this has been my fault," Lee acknowledged grimly. "It is I who have lost this fight."

34

As Lee withdrew, word of the Union's twin victories—at Vicksburg and Gettysburg—sparked celebrations in Washington. Revelers gathered at Lincoln's White House window; the president responded as awkwardly as he often did when speaking extemporaneously. "How long ago is it?—eighty-odd years—since on the Fourth of July for the first time in the history of the world a nation by its representatives assembled and declared as a self-evident truth that 'all men are created equal,'" he said. "And now, on this last Fourth of July just passed, when we have a gigantic rebellion, at the bottom of which is an effort to overthrow the principle that all men were created equal, we have the surrender of a most powerful position and army on that very day, and not only so, but in a succession of battles in Pennsylvania, near to us, through three days, so rapidly that they might be called one great battle on the 1st, 2nd, and 3rd of the month of July; and on the 4th the cohorts of those who opposed the declaration that all men are created equal turned tail and run." Lincoln realized he hadn't done the moment justice. "This is a glorious theme, and the occasion for a speech, but I am not prepared to make one worthy of the occasion."

Lincoln would make his worthy speech in a few months; for the present he worried that the opportunity afforded by Meade's victory was being lost. "If General Meade can complete his work, so gloriously prosecuted thus far, by the literal or substantial destruction of Lee's army, the rebellion will be over," he wrote Halleck. Heaven—or the heavens—appeared to favor this goal: summer rains had swollen the Potomac, preventing Lee from getting across. Meade merely had to pin Lee's army against the river. But Meade declined to move until it was too late.

Lincoln could scarcely contain his anger. "If I had gone up there I could have whipped them myself," he declared. He wrote a blistering letter to Meade. "I do not believe you appreciate the magnitude of the misfortune involved in Lee's escape," the president said. "He was within your easy grasp, and to have closed upon him would, in connection with our other late successes, have ended the war. As it is, the war will be prolonged indefinitely." Meade had pleaded concern for the safety of his force in not attacking Lee north of the Potomac; Lincoln now demanded: "If you could not safely attack Lee last Monday, how can you possibly do so south of the river, when you can take with you very few more than two-thirds of the force you then had in hand? . . . Your golden opportunity is gone, and I am distressed immeasurably by it."

Lincoln never sent this letter, realizing that until he had a replacement for Meade he couldn't afford to alienate the general. But the missed chance still rankled. "I was deeply mortified by the escape of Lee across the Potomac," he wrote General Oliver Howard, "because the substantial destruction of his army would have ended the war and because I believed such destruction was perfectly easy—believed that General Meade and his noble army had expended all the skill, and toil, and blood, up to the ripe harvest, and then let the crop go to waste."

As Lincoln sought Meade's replacement, his gaze turned west. Grant's capture of Vicksburg prompted the Confederate commander of Port Hudson to surrender that fortress; Lincoln lauded the regaining of the Mississippi with the words: "The Father of Waters again goes unvexed to the sea." The president knew whom to thank. "Look at his campaign since May 1," he told a visitor regarding Grant. "Where is anything in the Old World that equals it? It stamps him as the greatest general of the age, if not of the world."

Lincoln wrote to Grant directly. "I do not remember that you and I ever met personally," he said. "I write this now as a grateful acknowledgment for the almost inestimable service you have done the country." Lincoln admitted he had doubted the wisdom of Grant's strategy in approaching Vicksburg. "I thought it was a mistake." But the outcome of the campaign had revealed where wisdom truly lay. "I now wish to make the personal acknowledgment that you were right and I was wrong."

Lincoln's need for a general grew more pressing two weeks after Vicksburg and Gettysburg. The war had never been popular in New

York City, where the Democrats who controlled city politics had tried to declare neutrality in the conflict for the Union. They failed, but their efforts encouraged resentment against Republican policies. The Emancipation Proclamation, by converting the struggle to preserve the Union into a crusade to free the slaves, antagonized many New Yorkers, especially Irish immigrants who feared a flood of low-wage labor that would render their currently tenuous position even more so. The deployment of black strikebreakers against Irish dockworkers in a strike in the early summer of 1863 intensified the fear and distrust.

More immediately threatening than the Emancipation Proclamation was the Enrollment Act of March 1863. The measure aimed to induce voluntary enlistment but did so by requiring compulsory enlistment—a draft—if congressional districts didn't achieve their quotas. Loopholes allowed individuals to avoid service; of these the most noticed were the options of hiring a substitute and of paying a three-hundred-dollar commutation fee. Both evoked anger among the working class for permitting the gentry to buy their way out of serving; the latter became the more notorious for seeming to place a monetary value on the lives of conscripts.

The anger erupted in New York that summer. Papers on July 12 carried the names of potential conscripts chosen by the local draft board; the victims—for so they accounted themselves—and their friends had that day and night to consider their response. Many plotted together, as became evident the next morning. Just as the local draft administrator finished calling the names, a rock crashed through the window of his office; this proved the signal for a mob to sack the building housing the draft office and set it alight. The fire spread, as did the violence. Initial targets bore some relation to the draft: other federal facilities, the offices of the pro-war *New York Tribune*, gentlemen presumed to have purchased exemption. But the mob soon branched out, assaulting Protestant churches (most of the rioters were Irish Catholics), factories unfriendly to unions, the Colored Orphan Asylum. The police attempted to quell the rioting but lacked the tools or training to do so effectively. The police fired on the rioters, who fired back, until the streets of New York assumed the appearance of a war zone. A reporter recounted the hand-to-hand combat within one building: "On every floor were the ruffians busy at their work; and on every floor were they met and attacked; they fought desperately but were driven from rooms and hallways, from windows and roof-top; those who were not knocked senseless inside or killed themselves by jumping to the ground rushed down stairs and into the street. . . . Not one man, it is thought, escaped." As in a war zone, medics dealt with the casualties. The reporter described a makeshift treatment center: "The room had all the appearance of an army hospital after a battle—the floor covered with blood, bandages, lint, surgical instruments, pails of bloody water, with Surgeon Kennedy, his shirt-sleeves rolled up, examining, dressing, and ordering. . . . There were wounds of all descriptions—the incised, contused, lacerated, punctured, and pistol-shot."

The rioting raged for a week. Only after the War Department rushed troops from Meade's camp at Gettysburg to the city did the authorities manage to bring the violence under control. The episode shocked New York, where initial estimates placed the body count above a thousand. Even after this figure was corrected downward—to a few more than a hundred, finally—the riot made plain that the North was far from united and that if Lincoln didn't find his general soon, the effort to save the Union might implode.

35

AT THE END OF AUGUST 1863 HENRY HALLECK WROTE A CONFIDEN-
tial letter to William Sherman on a difficult question: how to reconstruct the governments of Southern states occupied by Union forces.
The question had arisen to some degree already, but the capture of
Vicksburg and the opening of the Mississippi made it suddenly more
pressing. "Not only the length of the war, but our ultimate and complete success, will depend upon its decision," Halleck told Sherman.
Reconstruction would raise vexing issues, to be sure. "But I believe it
can be successfully solved if the President will consult opinions of cool
and discreet men who are capable of looking at it in all its bearings and
effects. I think he is disposed to receive the advice of our generals who
have been in these States, and know much more of their condition than
gassy politicians in Congress." Halleck was writing Sherman because
Sherman had been forthright in expressing his views on matters of
occupation. But Halleck wanted him to sound out his fellow officers as
well. "I wish you would consult with Grant, McPherson, and others of
cool, good judgment, and write me your views fully, as I may wish to
use them with the President." Halleck added a caution he knew Sherman would appreciate: "You had better write me unofficially, and then
your letter will not be put on file, and cannot hereafter be used against
you. You have been in Washington enough to know how everything a
man writes or says is picked up by his enemies and misconstrued."

Sherman's reply was probably fuller than Halleck expected, but it was
quite as candid as the general-in-chief hoped. Lincoln had already commenced reconstruction in Louisiana with an eye toward using that state
as a model for the restoration of Southern participation in national politi-

cal life. Sherman thought the president should slow down, especially as Louisiana's reconstruction involved the lower Mississippi, which controlled so much of the rest of America. "The inhabitants of the country on the Monongahela, the Illinois, the Minnesota, the Yellowstone, and Osage are as directly concerned in the security of the lower Mississippi as are those who dwell on its very banks in Louisiana," Sherman asserted. "And now that the nation has recovered its possession, this generation of men will make a fearful mistake if they again commit its charge to a people liable to misuse their position, and assert, as was recently done, that, because they dwelt on the banks of this mighty stream, they had a right to control its navigation."

Sherman spoke with experience of the region based on his residence in Louisiana before the war, and he identified four classes of the white inhabitants of the South. First were the planters. "These are, on the whole, the ruling class. They are educated, wealthy, and easily approached. . . . None dare admit a friendship for us, though they say freely that they were at the outset opposed to war and disunion." Sherman thought the planters could be managed but only by action rather than words. "Argument is exhausted, and words have lost their usual meaning. Nothing but the logic of events touches their understanding." The recent Union victories were having an effect; a few more would clinch the case. "When these are done, then, and not until then, will the planters of Louisiana, Arkansas, and Mississippi, submit."

Sherman's second class comprised the small farmers and the merchants and laborers of the South. "They are essentially tired of the war, and would slink back home if they could," he said. But they would take their cues from the planters. "They will want the old political system of caucuses, legislatures, etc., to amuse them and make them believe they are real sovereigns; but in all things they will follow blindly the lead of the planters."

The third group were the Unionists of the South. "I have little respect for this class," Sherman said. "They allowed a clamorous set of demagogues to muzzle and drive them as a pack of curs. Afraid of shadows, they submit tamely to squads of dragoons, and permit them, without a murmur, to burn their cotton, take their horses, corn, and everything; and, when we reach them, they are full of complaints if our men take a few fence rails for fire, or corn to feed our horses." They weren't worth bothering about. "I account them as nothing in this great game of war."

Sherman's last group was "the young bloods of the South: sons of planters, lawyers about towns, good billiard players and sportsmen, men who never did work and never will." These were the most worrisome. "War suits them, and the rascals are brave, fine riders, bold to rashness, and dangerous subjects in every sense. They care not a sou for niggers, land, or anything. They hate Yankees per se, and don't bother their brains about the past, present, or future. As long as they have good horses, plenty of forage, and an open country, they are happy. . . . They are the most dangerous set of men that this war has turned loose upon the world." And they had to be dealt with, one way or the other. "These men must all be killed or employed by us before we can hope for peace. They have no property or future, and therefore cannot be influenced by anything, except personal considerations."

The nature of the Southern population caused Sherman to advocate continued military rule for the occupied South. "A civil government now, for any part of it, would be simply ridiculous," he told Halleck. The people of the region had little respect for their own civil institutions and would have still less respect for institutions imposed by the North. Considerations of force were all that guided their actions. "The only government needed or deserved by the States of Louisiana, Arkansas, and Mississippi now exists in Grant's army." Force should be applied to the utmost degree; any lessening of the war effort, any reaching out to Southerners, would be a mistake. "I would not coax them, or even meet them half-way, but make them so sick of war that generations would pass away before they would again appeal to it." The South must realize that the North would stop at nothing to achieve victory—"that we will remove and destroy every obstacle, if need be, take every life, every acre of land, every particle of property, everything that to us seems proper; that we will not cease till the end is attained."

Sherman's conception of total war would inform Union strategy before long, but meanwhile Grant had his own ideas about governing the region his army occupied. He renewed his battle with the Treasury over trade. "The people in the Mississippi Valley are now nearly subjugated," he explained to Salmon Chase. "Keep trade out for but a few months and I doubt not but that the work of subjugation will be so complete that trade can be opened freely with the states of Arkansas, Louisiana and Mississippi." To let the traders in prematurely would risk losing what had been gained. "My experience in West Tennessee has convinced me that any trade whatever with the rebellious states is weakening to us of at least thirty per cent of our force. No matter what the restrictions thrown around trade, if any whatever is allowed it will be made the means of supplying to the enemy all they want."

Grant lost this battle as he had lost previous rounds. Chase again proved a more formidable foe than Pemberton or Johnston. Southern cotton was too important to American diplomacy and, increasingly, to the economy of the North, which traded and processed the white stuff, for a mere theater commander to meddle with it.

A more complicated matter involved treatment of former slaves. The Emancipation Proclamation rode south in Grant's saddlebags; with each county his army occupied he extended the writ of freedom. But the freedmen had to be fed, and Grant was reluctant to provision them from the stores that fed his soldiers. He decided that they should support themselves whenever they could. "It is earnestly recommended that negroes who can will make contracts to labor for their former owners," Grant declared in a general order on August 1. "When such contracts cannot be made, then to hire themselves to such persons as are willing to employ their services."

Grant's earnest recommendation failed to overcome the reluctance of former slaves to return to the plantations where they had been bound and of former slaveholders to pay their servants and field hands. The dearth of cash in an economy erected on unpaid labor multiplied the difficulty of implementing his policy. So ten days later he authorized a supplementary order: "At all military posts in States within the Department, where slavery has been abolished by the Proclamation of the President of the United States, camps will be established for such freed people of color as are out of employment." The freedmen would be fed at these camps, whose superintendents would be responsible for finding them work. "All such persons supported by the Government will be employed in every practicable way, so as to avoid, as far as possible, their becoming a burthen upon the Government." They might be hired out to planters; they might be put to work building roads and bridges; they might be sent to gather crops from abandoned plantations. To encourage cash-short planters to join the program, Grant authorized sharecropping, with the freedmen to receive "not less than one-twentieth of the commercial part of their crops."

When the freedmen poured into the Union camps but the planters still failed to cooperate, Grant issued another order, this one foreshadow-

ing aspects of the "black codes" of the postwar Southern state governments. "All able-bodied negro men who are found, ten days after the
publication of this order, without a certificate of the officers or persons
employing them, will be regarded as unemployed and may be pressed
into service," Grant's order declared. "Certificates given to negroes must
show how, where, and by whom they are employed."

From employing the former slaves to arming them was a natural
step, but one fraught with difficulty for the Union government and danger for the freedmen. Negro soldiers from the North served in segregated
regiments and more capably than many whites had thought they would.
Black troops fought bravely at Port Hudson in the spring of 1863 and
with special gallantry at Fort Wagner, South Carolina, that summer.
Yet sufficient prejudice existed in the North toward blacks that the War
Department refused to accord them anything like equality in the ranks
or particularly in the officer corps.

Service in the Union army entailed hazards for the black troops
beyond those experienced by white soldiers. The mere idea of weapons
in the hands of black men conjured the longstanding nightmare of slave
insurrection in the minds of Southern soldiers, who were disinclined to
give quarter to surrendering black troops. If the black troops were Southerners—former slaves—the nightmare became a reality and the reaction
was even stronger.

Lincoln understood the danger the freedmen-soldiers faced, yet he
decided he couldn't forgo the added strength the new troops could bring
to the Union cause. "I believe it is a resource which, if vigorously applied
now, will soon close the contest," he wrote Grant in August 1863. "It
works doubly, weakening the enemy and strengthening us." Lincoln
thought the timing auspicious. "We were not fully ripe for it until the
river"—the Mississippi—"was opened. Now, I think at least a hundred
thousand can and ought to be rapidly organized along its shores, relieving all the white troops to serve elsewhere."

Grant concurred. "I have given the subject of arming the negro my
hearty support," he wrote Lincoln. "This, with the emancipation of the
negro, is the heaviest blow yet given the Confederacy. . . . By arming the
negro we have added a powerful ally. They will make good soldiers, and
taking them from the enemy weakens him in the same proportion they
strengthen us." White Southerners understood the equation. "The South
rave a great deal about it and profess to be very angry," Grant said. The
Confederates were doing their best to keep slaves out of the path of his

army and keep freedmen out of his ranks. "There has been great difficulty in getting able-bodied negroes to fill up the colored regiments in consequence of the rebel cavalry running off all that class to Georgia and Texas." A twenty-mile stretch on either side of the Mississippi had been emptied of young male slaves. But Grant told Lincoln he had dispatched two expeditions in search of black recruits. "I am also moving a brigade of cavalry from Tennessee to Vicksburg which will enable me to move troops to a greater distance into the interior and will facilitate materially the recruiting service."

The value of the black troops confirmed Grant's conversion on the issue now twinned in Northern war aims with preservation of the Union. "I never was an abolitionist, not even what could be called anti-slavery," he wrote Elihu Washburne. "But I try to judge fairly and honestly, and it became patent to my mind early in the rebellion that the North and South could never live at peace with each other except as one nation and that without slavery. As anxious as I am to see peace reestablished, I would not therefore be willing to see any settlement until this question is forever settled."

36

THE CAPTURE OF VICKSBURG GUARANTEED THAT GRANT WOULD BE given a larger command. Many in Washington wanted to bring him east to replace Meade at the head of the Army of the Potomac. But Grant resisted the idea. "My going could do no possible good," he wrote Elihu Washburne, his continuing advocate in the nation's capital. "They have there able officers who have been brought up with that army, and to import a commander to place over them certainly could produce no good." He was happy and useful where he was. "I can do more with this army than it would be possible for me to do with any other without time to make the same acquaintance with others I have with this. I know that the soldiers of the Army of the Tennessee can be relied on to the fullest extent. I believe I know the exact capacity of every general in my command to command troops, and just where to place them to get from them their best services."

Lincoln saw the wisdom in Grant's reasoning and let him stay in the West with greater responsibilities. In October Grant traveled to Indianapolis to meet with Edwin Stanton, who explained that a new command was being created for him. The Military Division of the Mississippi would stretch from the Alleghenies to the Mississippi and comprise the Departments of the Ohio, the Cumberland and the Tennessee. Ambrose Burnside would head the Ohio department and William Rosecrans the Cumberland; Sherman would take over the Tennessee.

Grant's first action in his new post was to fire William Rosecrans. He remembered the troubles Rosecrans had caused him during the summer of 1862, and he recounted them to Stanton, who related them to Halleck. "He considers it indispensible that Rosecrans should be relieved because he would not obey orders," Stanton told Halleck of Grant. Halleck accepted Grant's decision. The firing came easier since Rosecrans had just suffered a serious setback on Chickamauga Creek, near where southeastern Tennessee meets northwestern Georgia, at the hands of Confederate forces commanded by Braxton Bragg and James Longstreet. Rosecrans blundered in the battle while George Thomas, his subordinate, showed decisiveness and courage in covering the Union retreat to Chattanooga. Grant knew and respected Thomas, and he gave him Rosecrans's job.

Thomas could have wished for better timing. The Union hold on Chattanooga was uncertain at best. "By the middle of October it began to look as if we were in a helpless and precarious position," Charles Dana wrote of the Union position in eastern Tennessee. Dana had left Grant after the capture of Vicksburg and gone to spy for Stanton on Rosecrans. He rode to the battle of Chickamauga and joined the retreat to Chattanooga. "No reinforcements had yet reached us," he continued. "The enemy was growing stronger each day, and, worse still, we were threatened with starvation." Supplies for Chattanooga traveled by rail from Nashville to Bridgeport, forty miles west of Chattanooga, where the railroad crossed to the south bank of the Tennessee River. But the Confederates controlled the south bank, depriving the Union of the railroad from Bridgeport. And their batteries prevented steam transports from getting through, while sharpshooters made the road on the north bank of the river nearly impassable. As a result the Chattanooga garrison was reduced to surviving on what trickled down inferior roads through the mountains north of the river. "These were not only disturbed by the enemy, but were so bad in places that the mud was up to the horses' bellies," Dana wrote. "On October 15 the troops were on half-rations, and officers as they went about where the men were working on the fortifications frequently heard the cry of 'Crackers!' "—a plea for hardtack, even. The situation grew only worse. "On the 17th of October five hundred teams were halted between the mountain and the river without forage for the animals, and unable to move in any direction. The whole road was strewn with dead animals." Dana nearly despaired for the garrison's survival. "I never saw anything which seemed so lamentable and hopeless. Our animals were starving, the men had starvation before them, and the enemy was bound soon to make desperate efforts to dislodge us."

Chattanooga became Grant's responsibility at just this moment. He set off for the city to determine for himself its condition and prospects. He could have gone faster but for the effects of a second injury suffered when his horse again slipped and fell on him. For three weeks in September he was unable to move. "Am still confined to my bed, lying flat on my back," he wrote Halleck. "My injuries are severe but still not dangerous. My recovery is simply a matter of time. Although fatiguing I will still endeavor to perform my duties, and hope soon to recover, that I may be able to take the field."

The threat to Chattanooga left him no choice. "Hold Chattanooga at all hazards," he telegraphed Thomas upon assuming command. "I will be there as soon as possible." The journey wasn't easy. "I arrived here in the night of the 23rd, after a ride on horseback of fifty miles, from Bridgeport, over the worst roads it is possible to conceive of, and through a continuous drenching rain," he wrote Halleck. The experience made him realize that his first task was to improve the route from Nashville. "It is barely possible to supply this Army from its present base. But when winter rains set in it will be impossible." Beyond that, he wasn't sure how to proceed. "What force the enemy have to my front I have no means of judging accurately. Deserters come in every day, but their information is limited to their own brigades or divisions at furthest. The camps of the enemy are in sight, and for the last few days there seems to have been some moving of troops. But where to I cannot tell."

He conducted a reconnaissance the next day. Riding out from Chattanooga with George Thomas and William F. Smith, the chief engineer of the Cumberland army, as well as some members of his staff, Grant crossed the Tennessee to the north bank and ventured west to Brown's Ferry, a few miles downstream from Lookout Mountain, the height that commanded Chattanooga's valley. Confederate pickets occupied the south bank. "We were within easy range," Grant recalled. "They did not fire upon us nor seem to be disturbed by our presence. They must have seen that we were all commissioned officers. But, I suppose, they looked upon the garrison of Chattanooga as prisoners of war, feeding or starving themselves, and thought it would be inhuman to kill any of them except in self-defense." (His surmise was correct. "We held him at our mercy," Braxton Bragg subsequently reported to Jefferson Davis. "His destruction was only a question of time.")

The complacency of the Confederates afforded Grant an opening. Weeks earlier Halleck had detached a force under Joseph Hooker from the Army of the Potomac and sent it west to reinforce Chattanooga. It had reached Bridgeport by the time Grant came through, but it waited there lest its advance to Chattanooga simply add to the strain on the supply line. Grant ordered Hooker to advance by a route south of the Tennessee, driving away such Confederates as he encountered. Meanwhile William Smith would float a contingent down the Tennessee from Chattanooga with pontoon boats, which would glide in the dark past the Confederates on Lookout Mountain and form the basis for a bridge across the river at Brown's Ferry. A column from Chattanooga would march across and connect via Lookout Valley, west of Lookout Mountain, with Hooker's force.

The operation proceeded to Grant's entire satisfaction. The Confederates caught north of the new Union line and south of the river realized their isolation and surrendered. Their removal opened the river and the road on its north bank to Union transports and mule teams, which shortly established the "cracker line" the Chattanooga garrison had been crying for, and more. "In a week the troops were receiving full rations," Grant recalled. "It is hard for anyone not an eyewitness to realize the relief this brought. The men were soon reclothed and also well fed; an abundance of ammunition was brought up, and a cheerfulness prevailed not before enjoyed in many weeks."

Yet Chattanooga remained besieged. The Confederate positions approached so near the Union defenses that the troops of the two sides were within speaking distance. They often did speak and otherwise observed a comity at striking odds with the larger conflict. One day Grant examined the Union troops along Chattanooga Creek, south of the city. "When I came to the camp of the picket guard of our side, I heard the call, 'Turn out guard for the commanding general,'" he remembered. "I replied, 'Never mind the guard,' and they were dismissed and went back to their tents. Just back of these, and about equally distant from the creek, were the guards of the Confederate pickets. The sentinel on their post called out in like manner, 'Turn out the guard for the commanding general,' and, I believe, added, 'General Grant.' Their line in a moment front-faced to the north, facing me, and gave a salute, which I returned."

The informal ceasefire grew even stranger. A tree had fallen across the creek at one point near which soldiers from both sides drew water. Some Confederates from James Longstreet's corps, in blue uniforms nearly the same shade as those of Grant's troops, camped there. Grant, again inspecting the Union lines, saw a blue-coated soldier sitting on the log. "I rode up to him, commenced conversing with him, and asked whose corps he belonged to. He was very polite, and, touching his hat to me, said he belonged to General Longstreet's corps." Grant, hiding his surprise and perhaps embarrassment, nonchalantly continued the conversation. "I asked him a few questions—but not with a view of gaining any particular information—all of which he answered, and I rode off."

*C*hattanooga was but half of Grant's Tennessee challenge. Farther up the Tennessee River, Ambrose Burnside's army anchored eastern Tennessee for the Union, but problematically. Burnside's difficulties of provision were reported similar to those Thomas had experienced at Chattanooga, and they rendered his prospects doubtful. Yet the government in Washington considered it imperative that he hang on. The mountaineers of eastern Tennessee favored the Union, and Lincoln was loath to let them down. The valley of eastern Tennessee formed a natural corridor between Georgia and Virginia; control of the valley would tighten the screws on the Confederacy still further. Conversely the loss of the valley would endanger Nashville and possibly Kentucky and western Virginia. "If we can hold Chattanooga and East Tennessee, I think the rebellion must dwindle and die," Lincoln wrote William Rosecrans before the latter's dismissal. "I think you and Burnside can do this; and hence doing so is your main object."

After Grant secured Chattanooga from starvation and surrender, the attention of the government centered on Burnside. So did the attention of the Confederates. Bragg sent Longstreet and twenty thousand troops up the river to threaten Burnside. Grant was tempted to reinforce Burnside but realized that, until the supply problem was solved, reinforcements would only weaken Burnside's garrison. "There was no relief possible for him except by expelling the enemy from Missionary Ridge and about Chattanooga," Grant explained afterward. In the meantime he ordered Burnside to stand fast. "I do not know how to impress on you the necessity of holding on to East Tennessee, in strong enough terms," he wrote.

*T*o drive off Bragg, Grant summoned Sherman. "Drop everything east of Bear Creek and move with your entire force towards Stevenson," Grant wrote Sherman in late October, referring to a railroad town in northeastern Alabama. Sherman had marched his army from Vicksburg up the Mississippi to Memphis and from there had been working his way east along the Memphis & Charleston Railroad, rebuilding and defending the line as he went. Grant determined that the danger to eastern Tennessee required risking the railroad and other recent gains in the western part of his theater. "The enemy are evidently moving a large force towards Cleveland"—a rail town northeast of Chattanooga—"and may break through our lines and move on Nashville," he told Sherman. "With your forces here before the enemy cross the Tennessee, we could turn their position so as to force them back and save the probability of a move northward this winter."

Sherman later recollected the circumstances of his receiving Grant's message, which traveled circuitously on account of disrupted telegraph traffic. "As I sat on the porch of a house I was approached by a dirty, black-haired individual with mixed dress and strange demeanor, who inquired for me," Sherman said. "The bearer of this message was Corporal Pike, who described to me, in his peculiar way, that General Crook"—the commander at Huntsville, Alabama, the relay point for Grant's telegrams—"had sent him in a canoe; that he had pulled down the Tennessee River, over Muscle Shoals, was fired at all the way by guerrillas, but on reaching Tuscumbia he had providentially found it in possession of our troops. He had reported to General Blair, who sent him on to me." Corporal Pike apparently thrived on danger; he subsequently asked the impressed Sherman for a hazardous assignment that would make him a hero. Sherman told him about a railroad bridge behind Confederate lines that ought to be burned. "I explained to Pike that the chances were three to one that he would be caught and hanged," Sherman recalled. "But the greater the danger, the greater seemed to be his desire to attempt it." Pike disappeared into enemy territory and Sherman lost touch with him. As the bridge wasn't burned, Sherman assumed Pike had been captured and executed. But he turned up two years later in South Carolina while Sherman was marching through. "Pike gave me a graphic narrative of his adventures, which would have filled a volume; told me how he had made two attempts to burn the bridge and failed, and said that at the time of our entering Columbia he was a prisoner in the hands of the rebels, under trial for his life, but in the confusion of their retreat he made his escape and got into our lines, where he was again made a prisoner because of his looks." Sherman cleaned him up and put him back into service as a courier.

Sherman responded to Grant's call with his usual energy. He suspended rail work, gathered his available troops and hastened east. He personally reached Bridgeport on November 13, with his troops trailing by various roads. A fresh message from Grant awaited him. "Leave directions for your command and come up here yourself," Grant said. "Telegraph when you start and I will send a horse to Kelly's Ferry for you."

Grant meanwhile informed Burnside that aid was coming. "Sherman's advance has reached Bridgeport," Grant wrote. "His whole force will be ready to move from there by Tuesday"—November 17. "If you can hold Longstreet in check until he gets up, or by skirmishing and falling back can avoid serious loss to yourself and gain time, I will be able to force the enemy back from here and place a force between Longstreet and Bragg that must inevitably make the former take to the mountain passes by every available road to get back to supplies."

Grant reassured the administration in Washington that Burnside would receive help. Lincoln and the War Department were growing frantic over the danger to eastern Tennessee. Stanton's agent Dana had gone to Knoxville, and he reported that Burnside was on the verge of withdrawing his force. Halleck wrote Burnside telling him to hold his ground. "If you retreat now it will be disastrous to the campaign," Halleck said. With the next stroke of his pen he wrote Grant regarding Burnside: "I fear he will not fight, although strongly urged to do so. Unless you can give him immediate assistance he will surrender his position to the enemy. . . . Immediate aid from you is now of vital importance."

Grant redoubled his efforts. "I am pushing everything to give General Burnside early aid," he told Halleck. "I have impressed on him in the strongest terms the necessity of holding on to his position. General Sherman's troops are now at Bridgeport. They will march tomorrow and an effort will be made to get a column between Bragg and Longstreet as soon as possible."

He sent a new message to Burnside, conveying more confidence than perhaps he felt and certainly more than Halleck and Lincoln did. "So far you are doing exactly what appears to me right," he told Burnside. He added a stiffener, though: "I want the enemy's progress retarded at every foot, all it can be, only giving up each place when it becomes evident that it cannot longer be held without endangering your force to capture." And he said that help was closer than ever. "Sherman moved this morning from Bridgeport with one division. The remainder of his command moves in the morning. There will be no halt until a severe battle is fought or the railroads cut supplying the enemy."

Grant made a habit of exuding confidence. Adam Badeau recalled of this period: "Grant was always sanguine, amid the greatest difficulties and dangers." Charles Dana later observed, "There was the greatest hopefulness everywhere." Grant himself told Halleck that a bold stroke by Bragg against Burnside might lead to a setback but that it would be temporary. "I think the rebel force making such a movement would be totally annihilated," he said.

He was nervous all the same, as he later admitted to Halleck. "I felt restless beyond anything I had before experienced in this war, at my inability to either move to reinforce Burnside or to attack the enemy in his position, to make him feel the necessity of retaining at Chattanooga all his troops. I was forced to leave Burnside to contend alone against vastly superior forces until Sherman could arrive with his men and means of transportation."

When Sherman reached Chattanooga, he saw what Grant had to be nervous about. He, Grant and Thomas walked to the edge of the city to examine their position. "We had a magnificent view of the panorama," Sherman remembered. "Lookout Mountain, with its rebel flags and batteries, stood out boldly, and an occasional shot fired toward Wauhatchee or Moccasin Point gave life to the scene. . . . All along Missionary Ridge were the tents of the rebel beleaguering force; the lines of trench from Lookout up toward the Chickamauga were plainly visible; and rebel sentinels, in a continuous chain, were walking their posts in plain view." Sherman turned to his commander. "Why, General Grant, you are besieged," he said. Grant replied, "It is too true." Sherman retrospectively added: "Up to that moment I had no idea that things were so bad."

But Grant had been reckoning how to make things better. With his field glasses he could see that the Confederates were thinly placed on the north end of Missionary Ridge and near the mouth of Chickamauga Creek. This weakness afforded the opening he sought. "Every arrangement is now made to throw Sherman's force across the river just at and below the mouth of Chickamauga Creek, as soon as it arrives," he told Burnside by way of explaining what must be done before reinforcements could be sent north. "Thomas will attack on his left at the same time and together it is expected to carry Missionary Ridge and from there push a force on the railroad between Cleveland and Dalton. Hooker will at the same time attack and, if he can, carry Lookout Mountain."

Grant intended to attack on November 21, a Saturday, and promised Burnside he would do so. Burnside was more beset than ever; Longstreet's approach had driven him back and cut his telegraph lines. "If you can communicate with General Burnside, say to him that our attack on Bragg will commence in the morning," Grant wrote on that Friday to Orlando Willcox, who had the command now closest to Burnside. "If successful, such a move will be made as, I think, will relieve East Tennessee, if he can hold out."

But the bad roads and two days' downpour postponed the start. "It will be impossible to attack Bragg before Monday," Grant wrote Halleck on Saturday afternoon. The mud bogged down Sherman too; even on Monday his men weren't quite in place. Yet Grant decided to go ahead.

"It was the beginning of the most spectacular military operations I ever saw," Charles Dana remembered. "Our army lay to the south and east of the town of Chattanooga, the river being at our back. Facing us, in a great half circle, and high above us on Lookout Mountain and Missionary Ridge, were the Confederates. Our problem was to drive them from these heights." In most battles even the commanding general could see only a portion of the field, the rest being obscured by terrain, vegetation, distance or weather. The field at Chattanooga, by contrast, formed a natural amphitheater, permitting Grant and his staff to view almost every action. Dana stuck close to Grant and shared his view.

The battle opened with a ground-clearing action in Grant's immediate front. Three of Thomas's brigades moved rapidly forward against Confederates guarding two detached hills below Missionary Ridge. Their close order and precise discipline apparently lulled the enemy. "Until we opened fire, prisoners assert that they thought the whole movement was a review and general drill," Montgomery Meigs, Grant's quartermaster general, reported. "And then it was too late to send to their camps for reinforcements, and they were overwhelmed by force of numbers." The Confederates inflicted serious damage on the Federals, killing or wounding more than a thousand, but were driven back with heavy losses of their own. By Monday evening the hills had been secured.

That night Sherman struggled to get his men across the river for the assault on Missionary Ridge. The first wave of boats reached the south bank in the blackness before dawn; Sherman's men quickly overpowered the Confederate pickets and established a bridgehead. While some of the boats and a small steamer ferried more of the troops, other boats began to be formed into a bridge. Dana detached from Grant to watch the crossing. "It was marvelous with what vigor the work went on," he wrote. "Sherman told me he had never seen anything done so quietly and so well." The bridge spanned more than thirteen hundred feet of a river that flowed swiftly in the main channel, yet by early afternoon it was complete, and in a short space of time the rest of Sherman's army was marching across.

Without so much as pausing for breath they assaulted the north end of Missionary Ridge. This was the lightly defended portion of the height, and Sherman captured it with little loss. He brought up additional troops and artillery—the guns being dragged by hand—under the cover of rain and low clouds, which prevented Bragg from appreciating what Sherman was doing. When Bragg did catch on, he ordered a counterattack, but Sherman beat it back.

Hooker's actions on Grant's right complemented those of Thomas in the center and Sherman on the left. Hooker's troops captured a bridge over Lookout Creek and approached the base of Lookout Mountain. His orders were conditional—"Hooker will attack Lookout and carry it if possible," Grant explained to Halleck—but his men seemed not to give the condition a thought. They barely slowed at the base of the mountain and headed straight up. Confederate infantry manned rifle pits directly above them and Confederate guns commanded the mountaintop. But Hooker's men fought their way to, through and over the Confederate positions and gained the upper slopes. As fighting continued into the afternoon they dug themselves in; at four o'clock Hooker sent word that his position was secure. Grant nonetheless sent a fresh brigade from the city to bolster him. Clouds had blocked the view from below for much of the day, but after nightfall the sky cleared. "A full moon made the battlefield as plain to us in the valley as if it were day, the blaze of their camp fires and the flashes of their guns displaying brilliantly their position and the progress of their advance," Charles Dana recalled.

Grant made time that evening to telegraph Washington. "The fight today progressed favorably," he said. "Sherman carried the end of Missionary Ridge, and his right is now at the Tunnel"—a railroad tunnel through the ridge—"and left at Chickamauga Creek. Troops from Lookout Valley carried the point of the Mountain and now hold the eastern slope and point high up. I cannot yet tell the amount of casualties but our loss is not heavy. Hooker reports 2000 prisoners taken, besides which a small number have fallen into our hands from Missionary Ridge."

Lincoln was most pleased. "Well done," he replied. "Many thanks to all." Yet the president immediately added, "Remember Burnside." Halleck seconded both sentiments. "I congratulate you on the success thus far of your plans," he wrote Grant. "I fear that General Burnside is hard pressed and that any further delay may prove fatal. I know that you will do all in your power to relieve him."

Grant thought he *was* doing all in his power to help Burnside, by defeating Bragg. The successes of Monday and Tuesday positioned him for what he believed would prove the decisive action of Wednesday. On one part of the battlefield, however, the decision came sooner than he expected. Bragg, reckoning that he couldn't defend Lookout Mountain any longer, withdrew his troops between Tuesday nightfall and Wednesday dawn. "At daylight on the 25th, the Stars and Stripes were discerned on the peak of Lookout," Montgomery Meigs recalled. "The rebels had evacuated the mountain."

The weight of the fighting shifted to Missionary Ridge. Grant ordered Sherman to attack at dawn, driving against Bragg's right on the ridgetop. Hooker would cross over from Lookout Mountain to hit the Confederates in the left or rear. Thomas, awaiting Hooker's arrival, would move against Bragg's center. Grant and Thomas prepared to watch from Orchard Knob, one of the promontories captured on Monday.

The day broke clear and sunny. "The whole field was in full view from the top of Orchard Knob," Grant remembered. "It remained so all day. Bragg's headquarters were in full view, and officers—presumably staff officers—could be seen coming and going constantly."

Bragg, likewise, could see Grant. "The enemy kept firing shells at us," Charles Dana, with Grant on Orchard Knob, recounted. "They had got the range so well that the shells burst pretty near the top of the elevation where we were, and when we saw them coming we would duck—that is, everybody did except Generals Grant and Thomas and Gordon Granger." Granger was one of Thomas's corps commanders, and he took the Confederate shelling personally. "Granger got a cannon," Dana related. "How he got it I do not know. And he would load it with the help of one soldier and would fire it himself over at the ridge." Grant's adjutant John Rawlins didn't like this at all. "Rawlins was very much disgusted at the guerrilla operations of Granger, and induced Grant to order him to join his troops elsewhere."

The fighting in Sherman's sector was heavy all morning. Grant expected Hooker to ease the pressure on Sherman, but the Confederates, in their retreat from Lookout Mountain, had burned the one bridge over

Chattanooga Creek. Hooker spent most of the morning trying to get his troops across. Grant had intended to wait on Hooker before throwing Thomas against the Confederate center, but Sherman's condition appeared critical and so he issued the order. Nothing happened. Somehow the chain of command had broken. Grant gave the order again, this time directly to one of the division commanders who would carry it out. The embarrassed officer dashed away, and in what seemed mere moments Thomas's men charged forward shouting. His skirmishers fired at Confederates in front of rifle pits at the base of Missionary Ridge. "The rebel pickets discharged their muskets and ran into their rifle pits," Montgomery Meigs, observing with Grant from Orchard Knob, recalled. "Our skirmishers followed on their heels. The line of battle was not far behind, and we saw the gray rebels swarm out of the long line of rifle pits in numbers which surprised us, and spread over the base of the hill. A few turned and fired their pieces, but the greater number collected into the various roads which creep obliquely up its steep face, and went on to the top."

The troops' orders were to pause and regroup after taking the first line of the enemy's defense, but the passion of the moment impelled many of them forward. "Some regiments pressed on and began to swarm up the steep sides of the ridge," Meigs recounted. "Here and there a color was advanced beyond the line. The attempt appeared most dangerous, but the advance was supported, and the whole line ordered to storm the heights, upon which not less than forty pieces of artillery, and no one knew how many muskets, stood ready to slaughter the assailants. With cheers answering to cheers, the men swarmed upward. They gathered to the lines of least difficult ascent, and the line was broken. Color after color was planted on the summit, while musketry and cannon vomited their thunder upon them."

Charles Dana by this time was willing to credit Grant with gifts of military genius. But the attack on Missionary Ridge required explanation of a different sort, he said. "The storming of the ridge by our troops was one of the greatest miracles in military history. No man who climbs the ascent by any of the roads that wind along its front can believe that eighteen thousand men were moved in tolerably good order up its broken and crumbling face unless it was his fortune to witness the deed. It seemed as awful"—that is, awe-full—"as a visible interposition of God."

After the battle, Dana found Philip Sheridan, one of the corps commanders whose troops made the spontaneous assault. "Why did you go up there?" Dana asked.

"When I saw the men were going up," Sheridan replied, "I had no idea of stopping them. The rebel pits had been taken and nobody had been hurt, and after they had started I commanded them to go right on. I looked up at the head of the ridge as I was going up, and there I saw a Confederate general on horseback. I had a silver whiskey flask in my pocket, and when I saw this man on the top of the hill I took out my flask and waved my hand toward him, holding up the shining, glittering flask." Sheridan's men interpreted this as an order. "The whole corps went up."

"Glory to God!" Dana reported to Edwin Stanton that afternoon. "The day is decisively ours. Missionary Ridge has just been carried by the magnificent charge of Thomas's troops, and the rebels routed."

Grant was slightly more circumspect. "Although the battle lasted from early dawn till dark this evening, I believe I am not premature in announcing a complete victory over Bragg," he wrote Halleck that night. "Lookout Mountain top, all the rifle pits in Chattanooga Valley, Missionary Ridge entire have been carried and now held by us. I have no idea of finding Bragg here tomorrow."

Grant's announcement was not premature; Bragg withdrew what remained of his battered army to Georgia. But Grant was already looking past Chattanooga. "The next thing now will be to relieve Burnside," he wrote Sherman. Grant appreciated the hundreds of miles Sherman's army had marched already, and he initially sent Gordon Granger north to Knoxville. But when Granger moved too slowly for Grant's tastes, he called on Sherman again. "I made this change knowing Sherman's promptness and ability," he explained to Halleck. "If Burnside holds out a short time, he will be relieved." To Burnside, Grant dispatched another stiffening message: "Do not be forced into a surrender by short rations. Take all the citizens have, to enable you to hold out yet a few days longer."

Sherman sent a cavalry column up the Tennessee Valley ahead of his main army to let Burnside know help was on the way. Sherman's information indicated that if Burnside didn't receive help by the first days of December he would have to surrender. The cavalry reached Knoxville during the night of December 3, delivering moral support and word that Sherman's main army was close behind.

Sherman's arrival persuaded James Longstreet to lift the siege. As the Confederates pulled back, Sherman rode into the city. "Approaching from the south and west, we crossed the Holston on a pontoon bridge," he remembered. "And in a large pen on the Knoxville side I saw a fine lot of cattle, which did not look much like starvation. I found General Burnside and staff domiciled in a large, fine mansion, looking very comfortable." Sherman was puzzled, and more so that evening. "We all sat down to a good dinner, embracing roast turkey. There was a regular dining table, with clean tablecloth, dishes, knives, forks, spoons, etc., etc. I had seen nothing of this kind in my field experience, and could not help exclaiming that I thought 'they were starving.'" Burnside admitted that the siege of the city had never been complete and that he had been well supplied from the valley settlements throughout. He didn't explain the reports to the contrary. Sherman held his tongue at the moment, but he later reflected, with unusual understatement: "Had I known of this, I should not have hurried my men so fast."

37

THE WESTERN VICTORY. CONFIRMATION OF THE GLORIOUS NEWS.
BRAGG'S OVERWHELMING DEFEAT. HIS ARMY CRUMBLING AWAY
AND SURRENDERING BY SQUADS. THE REBEL TROOPS CANNOT BE
MADE TO RALLY. IMMENSE ADDITIONS TO OUR CAPTURES.

The multiple heads on the *New York Times* story typified the reaction in the North to Grant's victory on the Tennessee. Lincoln lauded Grant and his army in a public letter of congratulations for the securing of eastern Tennessee. "I wish to tender you, and all under your command, my more than thanks—my profoundest gratitude—for the skill, courage, and perseverance with which you and they, over so great difficulties, have effected that important object," the president wrote. "God bless you all."

When the new Congress convened in December, the first resolution of the House, approved unanimously, thanked Grant and his army and called for the striking of a gold medal in his honor; the Senate shortly added its endorsement. Elihu Washburne introduced a bill authorizing the president to revive the rank of lieutenant general, last held permanently by George Washington, and confer it on the commander "most distinguished for courage, skill, and ability." All in Congress understood that Grant was the sole candidate for nomination, but Washburne made the understanding explicit. "Look at what this man has done for his country, for humanity and civilization," the Illinois representative declared. "He has fought more battles and won more victories than any living man. He has captured more prisoners and taken more guns than any general of modern times." Some members of Congress counseled waiting until the war was over to confer the honor; Washburne asserted that to delay would be to forget what military rank was for. "I want it conferred now because it is my most solemn and earnest conviction that General Grant is the man upon whom we must depend to fight out this rebellion in the field and bring this war to a speedy and triumphant close." The nation demanded no less, he said. "The people of this country now want a fighting and a successful general to lead their armies. They want a man who is willing to risk his own life upon the field. They have seen General Grant successful in every fight from Belmont to Lookout Mountain, and they now wish to see him marshal our whole armies and strike the last, greatest and most deadly blow at the rebellion."

*I*nevitably, given American democracy's admiration for victorious generals, Grant's name surfaced in discussions of who would be the next president. The Republicans had their candidate, Lincoln, who would run on a platform of completing the task at hand. The Democrats struggled to find both a candidate and a cause. The larger wing of the party, reflecting the party's Southern antecedents, opposed the war and especially emancipation. But a minority of Democrats rejected the defeatism and surrender to slavery they considered implicit in the antiwar demands of the majority. One of the "War Democrats," Barnabas Burns of Ohio, wrote Grant in December 1863. "Your successful military career," he said, "your unfaltering devotion to your country in its darkest hours of trial, your indomitable energy in overcoming all obstacles, your consummate skill and dauntless courage on the field of battle, have all combined to call the public mind to you as the man to whom the affairs of this great nation should be committed at the close of the present incumbent's term of office." Would Grant consent to have his name presented as a candidate to a convention of the War Democrats in January?

On reading this letter Grant reflected on what remarkable turns life took. Three years earlier he had had to beg his father for a menial job in the family leather store; now he was being promoted for the most powerful job in America. "The question astonishes me," he replied to Burns.

Of course he had to decline the offer as unbecoming and wholly unsought. "I do not know of anything I have ever done or said which would indicate that I could be a candidate for any office whatever within the gift of the people," he said. "I shall continue to do my duty, to the best of my ability, so long as permitted to remain in the Army, supporting whatever Administration may be in power, in their endeavor to suppress the rebellion and maintain national unity." He wanted Burns to appreciate that this response was no stratagem. "Nothing likely to happen would pain me so much as to see my name used in connection with a political office. I am not a candidate for any office nor for favors from any party. Let us succeed in crushing the rebellion in the shortest possible time, and I will be content with whatever credit may then be given me."

Grant's admirers—including those who saw him as a vehicle for their own political hopes—needed more than a single rebuff to be dissuaded. Isaac Morris, a former Democratic congressman from Illinois, wrote Grant urging a reconsideration.

Grant amplified his rejection. "I am not a politician, never was and hope never to be," he declared. "In your letter you say that I have it in my power to be the next President! This is the last thing in the world I desire. I would regard such a consummation as being highly unfortunate for myself, if not for the country. Through Providence I have attained to more than I ever hoped, and with the position I now hold in the Regular Army, if allowed to retain it will be more than satisfied. . . . I scarcely know the inducement that could be held out to me to accept office, and unhesitatingly say that I infinitely prefer my present position to that of any civil office within the gift of the people."

Yet the solicitations kept coming. Francis Blair, the Missouri politician turned soldier, sent Grant another inquiring letter. Grant responded, "It is on a subject upon which I do not like to write, talk, or think. Everybody who knows me knows I have no political aspirations either now or for the future." He wished people would get the message. "I hope to remain a soldier as long as I live."

Grant's emergence as his country's warrior hero amazed many who had scarcely heard of him before Vicksburg and even now couldn't credit that a man so young could have accomplished so much. Forty-one years old, Grant looked, if anything, younger than he had when the war began. He affected approaching middle age; when a supporter requested that he donate a clipping from his hair to be placed in a locket and sold at a benefit for disabled soldiers, but only if the supply wasn't growing scarce, Grant responded, "I am glad to say that the stock is yet as abundant as ever, though time or other cause is beginning to intersperse here and there a reminder that winters have passed." In fact a photograph taken a short while later showed his hair as youthfully dark as ever. During the month after Chattanooga he toured eastern Tennessee, and the locals, mostly Unionists, turned out to see the vanquisher of the Confederates. Grant's entourage included his chief surgeon, a man in his fifties with graying hair; at more than one stop the crowds mistook the surgeon for the conquering general.

Grant's apparent reversal of the aging process reflected his unusual comfort with war. At the time of secession he appeared older than his chronological age; a decade of frustration and failure had worn him down. Now he was refreshed by his string of victories. The terrible responsibility of sending soldiers to their deaths didn't trouble his sleep. His conviction of the rightness of his cause afforded him proof against self-doubt, but so did something that was as much temperamental as political or moral. Other commanders—other leaders—second-guessed themselves: their plans, their preparations, their decisions. Grant, for reasons perhaps partly inborn and partly acquired, rarely revisited choices once made. He planned according to the information at hand; he prepared for all reasonable contingencies; he decided what to do as events unfolded. Then, calm in the conviction that he could have done no more, he accepted what destiny delivered.

*H*is confidence grew with each victory and as he took the measure of his opponents. During the Chattanooga campaign he and others on the Union side inferred that Bragg and Longstreet didn't trust each other and that Jefferson Davis put little faith in either. Grant respected Bragg as a man, if not especially as a soldier. "Bragg was a remarkably intelligent and well-informed man, professionally and otherwise," he later wrote. "He was also thoroughly upright. But he was possessed of an irascible temper, and was naturally disputatious. . . . As a subordinate he was always on the lookout to catch his commanding officer infringing his prerogatives; as a post commander he was equally vigorous to detect the slightest neglect, even of the most trivial order." Grant told a story that had circulated in the army before the war. Bragg was stationed at a distant post where he served simultaneously as commander of one of several companies there and as quartermaster of the whole post. In his capacity as company commander he requisitioned certain supplies; in his role as quartermaster he denied the requisition. According to the story, Bragg appealed the decision and then denied his own appeal. When the post commander discovered what was happening, he exclaimed, in uncomprehending exasperation: "My God, Mr. Bragg, you have quarreled with every officer in the army, and now you are quarreling with yourself!"

Longstreet was quite a different character, one bound to have trouble with Bragg, Grant thought. "He was brave, honest, intelligent, a very capable soldier, subordinate to his superiors, just and kind to his subordinates, but jealous of his own rights, which he had the courage to maintain. He was never on the lookout to detect a slight, but saw one as soon as anybody when intentionally given."

As for Jefferson Davis, who had traveled to Tennessee just before Grant's arrival at Chattanooga, to patch up the quarrel between Bragg and Longstreet, Grant had little but scorn. "Mr. Davis had an exalted opinion of his own military genius," he said, on the basis of his observation of Davis at the War Department before secession and of Davis's performance in the Confederate presidency. Grant was content—even pleased—for Davis to hold that opinion. "On several occasions during the war," he observed afterward, "he came to the relief of the Union army by means of his *superior military genius*."

*A*s modern as the Civil War was in certain respects, notably the application of industrial processes to organized destruction, it was almost ancient in other ways. The fighting tended to be seasonal, as fighting had been for millennia. Winter rains made roads in Tennessee and Virginia impassable; snow exposed soldiers to frostbite and hypothermia. By convention, too, as well as necessity, winter was a time for regrouping. Soldiers were furloughed to visit their families: to tend the home fires, if only briefly, and to remind themselves what they were fighting for.

Grant had less need for a furlough, with his family often at hand. Julia and the children resumed their visits to his headquarters during the months after the capture of Vicksburg. She ardently supported her husband without possessing either deep feeling or basic knowledge about the cause for which he fought. She later described discussions she had with some Confederate women in Mississippi who observed that she was accompanied by one of the Dent family's slaves. "You are Southern, are you not?" they said. "No," she said, "I am from the West. Missouri is my native state." "But Missouri is a Southern state," they rejoined. "Surely you are Southern in feeling and principle." "No, indeed," she answered. "I am the most loyal of the loyal." Her interlocutors lifted the discussion to constitutional grounds, asserting that secession was constitutional and suppressing it was not. Julia at once felt herself out of her depth. "I did not know a thing about this dreadful Constitution and told them so," she recalled. They were astonished. "Surely you have studied it?" they said. "No, I have not," she replied. "I would not know where to look for it even if I wished to read it." Decades later she confessed embarrassment at her ignorance, yet added: "But since then I have learned that even the chief justice is sometimes puzzled over the interpretation of this same Constitution."

Grant continued to keep Julia and the children away from the battle front with its dangers of violent death, but he couldn't shield them from the more insidious hazards of war—and of nineteenth-century life. Fred, who turned thirteen during the siege of Vicksburg, contracted a fever at the captured city and was sent with Julia and the other children to St. Louis, where the Dents and their doctor looked after him. The illness lingered for months and in the following winter worsened till his parents feared for his life. Grant traveled to St. Louis in January 1864 to be at the bedside. A change of doctor and medication fortunately reversed the situation, and soon Fred was his hale normal self.

William Sherman had a similar experience during this period, with sadly different results. Sherman had likewise brought his family to Vicksburg after the fall of the city, and when he arranged to return to Memphis that autumn they prepared to travel up the river with him. As the boat was about to leave, Sherman's nine-year-old son, Willie, was missing. Sherman thought he was with his mother; she thought Willie was with his father. Soldiers were dispatched to find the boy, who arrived on the dock carrying a double-barreled shotgun—"captured property," his proud father joked. On the voyage north the boy didn't appear well, and his mother put him to bed. An army surgeon was called in; the doctor diagnosed typhoid. The best chance for recovery lay in reaching Memphis and the medicines that might be found there. But low water slowed the journey, and Willie sank fast. By the time they reached Memphis he was beyond help. He died a short while later.

Sherman was devastated. "Why should I ever have taken them to that dread climate?" he asked himself. "It nearly kills me when I think of it. Why was I not killed at Vicksburg, and left Willy to grow up?" Years afterward he wrote: "Of all my children he seemed the most precious. I had watched with intense interest his development, and he seemed more than any of the children to take an interest in my special profession." One of Sherman's battalions had informally adopted Willie, and its officers and men stood at attention at a military funeral for the boy. That evening Sherman thanked its commanding officer:

My Dear Friend:

I cannot sleep tonight till I record an expression of the deep feelings of my heart to you, and to the officers and soldiers of the battalion, for their kind behavior to my poor child. I realize that you all feel for my family the attachment of kindred, and I assure you of full reciprocity.

Consistent with a sense of duty to my profession and office, I could not leave my post, and sent for the family to come to me in that fatal climate, and in that sickly period of the year, and behold the result! The child that bore my name, and in whose future I reposed with more confidence than I did in my own plan of life, now floats a mere corpse, seeking a grave in a distant land, with a weeping mother, brother, and sisters clustered about him. For myself, I ask no sympathy. On, on I must go, to meet a soldier's fate, or live to see our country rise superior to all factions. . . .

But Willie was, or thought he was, a sergeant in the Thirteenth. I have seen his eye brighten, his heart beat, as he beheld the battalion under arms, and asked me if they were not real soldiers. Child as he was, he had the enthusiasm, the pure love of truth, honor, and love of country which should animate all soldiers.

God only knows why he should die this young. He is dead, but will not be forgotten till those who knew him in life have followed him to that same mysterious end.

Please convey to the battalion my heart-felt thanks, and assure each and all that if in after-years they call on me or mine, and mention that they were with the Thirteenth Regulars when Willie was sergeant, they will have a key to the affections of my family that will open all it has; that we will share with them our last blanket, our last crust!

38

THE EXCEPTIONS TO THE WINTER RULE OF RESTING FROM COMBAT involved those parts of the war zone where winters were mild. Grant had tried to fight in Mississippi during the early months of 1863, without much luck; he sent Sherman to fight from a base at Vicksburg during early 1864 and hoped for better. The Chattanooga campaign, by pulling Union troops east, had permitted the Confederates to recommence sporadic operations in central Mississippi and to look to that region to provision rebel armies elsewhere. "I shall direct Sherman therefore to move out to Meridian with his spare force, the cavalry going to Corinth, and destroy the roads east and south of there so efficiently that the enemy will not attempt to rebuild them during the rebellion," Grant told Halleck. "The destruction which Sherman will do the roads around Meridian will be of material importance to us in preventing the enemy from drawing supplies from Mississippi and in clearing that section of all large bodies of rebel troops."

Sherman understood what was needed to accomplish his destructive goal. "The expedition is one of celerity," he told his officers and men at the start of the Meridian campaign. "All things must tend to that. Corps commanders and staff officers will see that our movements are not encumbered by wheeled vehicles improperly loaded. Not a tent, from the commander-in-chief down, will be carried. . . . Wagons must be reserved for food and ammunition. . . . The sick will be left behind."

Sherman's army swept across Mississippi, driving Confederate forces ahead of it, laying waste to arsenals and storehouses and tearing up rail lines. Sherman hoped to catch Nathan Bedford Forrest and his irregular cavalry, which roamed across Mississippi and Tennessee striking against

Union forces and positions. In this he failed, for as swiftly as Sherman moved, Forrest moved even faster. Yet the campaign succeeded in its larger purpose. It deprived the Confederacy of Mississippi and freed perhaps twenty thousand Union troops for missions elsewhere.

"The bill reviving the grade of Lieutenant General in the Army has become a law and my name has been sent to the Senate for the place," Grant wrote Sherman in early March. "I now receive orders to report at Washington, *in person*, immediately, which indicates either a confirmation or a likelihood of confirmation." He would leave the next morning for Washington, though not to remain. "I shall say very distinctly on my arrival there that I accept no appointment which will require me to make that city my headquarters."

But he was writing Sherman for another reason. "Whilst I have been eminently successful in this war, in at least gaining the confidence of the public, no one feels more than me how much of this success is due to the energy, skill, and harmonious putting forth of that energy and skill, of those who it has been my good fortune to have occupying a subordinate position under me." This applied to all the officers in his command, but to two in particular. "What I want is to express my thanks to you and McPherson as *the men* to whom, above all others, I feel indebted for whatever I have had of success. How far your advice and suggestions have been of assistance, you know. How far your execution of whatever has been given you to do entitles you to the reward I am receiving you cannot know as well as I do. I feel all the gratitude this letter would express, giving it the most flattering construction."

Sherman thanked Grant for the generous sentiments and congratulated him on the promotion. And he offered more of the candid advice he had been giving Grant since they started collaborating. "You are now Washington's legitimate successor, and occupy a position of almost dangerous elevation," Sherman said. "But if you can continue as heretofore to be yourself—simple, honest, and unpretending—you will enjoy through life the respect and love of friends, and the homage of millions of human beings who will award you a large share for securing to them and their descendants a government of law and stability."

Sherman said he valued Grant's quiet style of leadership above all. "The chief characteristic in your nature is the simple faith in success you have always manifested, which I can liken to nothing else than the faith a Christian has in his Saviour. This faith gave you victory at Shiloh and Vicksburg. Also, when you have completed your best preparations, you go into battle without hesitation, as at Chattanooga—no doubts, no reserve—and I tell you it was this that made us act with confidence. I knew wherever I was that you thought of me, and if I got in a tight place you would come, if alive." Sherman conceded that he had wondered at first whether Grant possessed the knowledge of strategy commanders typically acquired from books. "But I confess your common sense seems to have supplied all this."

Sherman urged Grant to stick with his aim of keeping clear of politics. "Do not stay in Washington," he said. Grant should let Halleck deal with the War Department and Congress. "Come out West; take to yourself the whole Mississippi Valley; let us make it dead-sure, and I tell you the Atlantic slope and Pacific shores will follow its destiny as sure as the limbs of a tree live or die with the main trunk! We have done much; still much remains to be done. Time and time's influences are all with us; we could almost afford to sit still and let these influences work. Even in the seceded States your word *now* would go further than a President's proclamation or an act of Congress." Sherman couldn't make this point strongly enough. "For God's sake and for your country's sake, come out of Washington! . . . Come out West. Here lies the seat of the coming empire; and from the West, when our task is done, we will make short work of Charleston and Richmond and the impoverished coast of the Atlantic."

*G*rant could face enemy fire without flinching, and he could send armies into battle without faltering. But the thought of speaking before a group caused him to tremble and flush. He often flatly refused. The loyal citizens of St. Louis feted him on his visit in January 1864, throwing lavish dinners in his honor. In return they asked him to say a few words. "I cannot make a speech," he responded. "It is something I have never done, and never intend to do." When they insisted, he simply repeated himself: "Making speeches is not my business. I never did it in my life, and never will."

The president was harder to deny. Grant followed orders to travel to Washington, on what he naively hoped would be a low-key journey. But word of his transit outpaced his train and at every stop large crowds gathered to cheer the man who seemed destined to save the Union. In Washington he was whisked to a White House reception, where another horde waited. All eyes followed the general as he approached the president. The two men had never met, but they of course recognized each other and shook hands without an introduction. They chatted briefly before Lincoln introduced Grant to William Seward and then Mrs. Lincoln. They walked to the East Room, where the guests abandoned decorum and rushed Grant at once. Their insistence to shake his hand drove him to climb onto a sofa lest he be buried by the onslaught.

After an exhausting hour of this, Lincoln pulled Grant aside to a drawing room. They agreed on a time the next day for the presentation of his new commission. "I shall make a very short speech to you, to which I desire for you to reply," Lincoln said. "And that you may be properly prepared to do so, I have written what I shall say, only four sentences in all, which I will read from my manuscript as an example which you may follow and also read your reply—as you are perhaps not so much accustomed to public speaking as I am."

Grant didn't know that Lincoln liked speaking extemporaneously almost as little as he did, but with this modest gesture, which put the two of them on the same footing, with both allowed to read their remarks, Lincoln won Grant to his side forever. Not that Grant didn't sweat during that night and the next morning. Lincoln gathered his cabinet, Halleck and a few others, including Grant's son Fred, and, as promised, read his remarks. "The nation's appreciation of what you have done and its reliance upon you for what remains to do in the existing great struggle are now presented with this commission, constituting you lieutenant general in the Army of the United States," the president said. "With this high honor devolves upon you also a corresponding responsibility. As the country herein trusts you, so, under God, it will sustain you. I scarcely need to add that with what I here speak for the nation goes my own hearty personal concurrence."

John Nicolay, Lincoln's private secretary, described Grant's response. "The general had hurriedly and almost illegibly written his speech on half of a sheet of note paper in lead pencil," Nicolay recalled. "His embarrassment was evident and extreme; he found his own writing very difficult to read." But his words suited the moment. "I accept the commission with gratitude for the high honor conferred," Grant said in a low voice that gradually gained strength. "With the aid of the noble armies that have fought on so many fields for our common country, it will be my earnest endeavor not to disappoint your expectations. I feel the full weight of

the responsibilities now devolving on me and know that if they are met it
will be due to those armies, and above all to the favor of that Providence
which leads both nations and men."

On the completion of this ordeal, Grant turned to matters more in
his line. His new commission gave him command of all the armies of the
Union, and though he had intended to return to the West, he decided he
needed to be closer to the seat of government. Telegraphy could accomplish only so much; regular meetings between the commanding general
and the commander in chief would facilitate the war effort in ways communication from a distance never could. Besides, Lincoln seemed more
sensible than most politicians. He didn't attempt to intrude in matters
beyond his understanding. He told Grant in their initial interview that
he had never claimed to be a military expert and would have left matters
entirely to his generals had they acted with greater energy and success.
Lincoln acknowledged that political pressure in the capital was intense
and he had felt compelled to respond to it. He said the military orders
he had issued might have been all wrong; he was certain *some* of them
were wrong. What he looked for in Grant was the ability and willingness
to act independently. He didn't expect Grant to share his military plans
with him; he didn't even *want* Grant to share his plans. If Grant would
simply take responsibility and act, he would receive all the manpower
and resources at the president's disposal.

Yet Lincoln couldn't resist offering one suggestion. He produced a
map of Virginia with the positions of the Union and Confederate forces
carefully marked. He indicated two of the rivers that flowed into the
Potomac and said the transfer of Union troops to the strip between them
would allow the landing of ammunition and provisions nearby, while the
rivers would protect the Union flanks. Grant said nothing. "I listened
respectfully but did not suggest that the same streams would protect
Lee's flanks while he was shutting us up," he recalled.

Edwin Stanton and Henry Halleck had their own reasons for thinking the president shouldn't be apprised of military plans. As they told
Grant, Lincoln was a soft touch for those who wanted to seem knowl-
edgeable, and he sometimes couldn't keep a secret. Grant nodded, further
persuaded to spare the president the details of his strategy. He simultaneously determined not to reveal more of his plans than necessary to Stanton, who seemed susceptible to the very temptations the war secretary

ascribed to Lincoln. Halleck, who became chief of staff upon Grant's promotion, learned more but by no means all.

Lincoln, for his part, proved quite happy with Grant's reticence. William Stoddard, assistant to John Nicolay, remembered asking Lincoln what he thought of Grant. "Well, I hardly know *what* to think of him," Lincoln replied. "He's the quietest little fellow you ever saw. . . . He makes the least fuss of any man you ever saw. I believe two or three times he has been in this room a minute or so before I knew he was here. It's about so all around. The only evidence that you have that he's in any place is that he makes things *git!* Wherever he is, things move!"

Stoddard asked what kind of general Lincoln thought Grant would be. Lincoln's answer surprised him. "Grant is the *first* general I've had!" the president said. "He's a *general*." As Stoddard seemed puzzled, Lincoln elaborated. "I'll tell you what I mean," he said. "You know how it's been with all the rest. As soon as I put a man in command of the army, he'd come to me with a plan of campaign and about as much as say, 'Now, I don't believe I can do it, but if you say so I'll try it on'; and so put the responsibility of success or failure on me. They all wanted me to be the general. Now it isn't so with Grant. He hasn't told me what his plans are. I don't know, and I don't want to know. I'm glad to find a man who can go ahead without me."

LINCOLN LEARNED OF GRANT'S STRATEGY FOR THE SPRING OF 1864 only as it developed. Grant conceived of the entire South as a single battlefield. Facing south from his new headquarters at Culpeper Court House, Virginia, north of the Rapidan River, he saw a battle line that stretched from the Mississippi on his right to the Atlantic on his left. The western armies of Sherman, who had been promoted to Grant's old position as commander of the Mississippi division, formed his right wing. The Army of the Potomac, nominally commanded by George Meade but under Grant's personal direction, was his center. The Army of the James, under Benjamin Butler, was his left. Opposing him were two Confederate armies, that of Joseph Johnston, who had replaced Bragg, in the West, and Lee's Army of Northern Virginia.

Grant's strategy was simple. Union forces would pursue and capture or destroy Johnston's and Lee's armies and by that means eliminate the enemy's ability to continue fighting. As before, he considered the capture of Confederate cities secondary, although he didn't dismiss the symbolic and logistical value of Richmond, Atlanta and Mobile.

Sherman would deal with Johnston, whose army now sat between Chattanooga and Atlanta. Grant ordered Sherman "to move against Johnston's army, to break it up and to get into the interior of the enemy's country as far as you can, inflicting all the damage you can against their war resources." Grant's confidence in Sherman made him comfortable providing this mere sketch. "I do not propose to lay down for you a plan of campaign but simply to lay down the work it is desirable to have done and leave you free to execute in your own way."

Grant himself, with the assistance of Meade and Butler, would handle Lee. Grant moved slowly in making the Army of the Potomac his own. He knew few of its officers and none of its men. He had met Meade during the war with Mexico but hadn't encountered him personally since. The day after receiving his commission at the White House he traveled to Meade's headquarters in Virginia. Meade acknowledged that Grant might wish to put his own lieutenant, perhaps one who had served with him in the West, at the head of the Army of the Potomac. Meade even encouraged him to do so if he thought it for the good of the army and the war effort. "This incident gave me even a more favorable opinion of Meade than did his great victory at Gettysburg the July before," Grant observed later. "It is men who wait to be selected, and not those who seek, from whom we may always expect the most efficient service."

Grant impressed Meade rather differently. "Grant is not a striking man, is very reticent, has never mixed with the world, and has but little manner, indeed is somewhat ill at ease in the presence of strangers," Meade wrote his wife. "Hence a first impression is never favorable. His early education was undoubtedly very slight; in fact, I fancy his West Point course was pretty much all the education he ever had, as since his graduation I don't believe he has studied or read any. At the same time, he has natural qualities of a high order, and is a man whom, the more you see and know him, the better you like him."

Grant aimed for the spring campaign to begin in early May. He and Sherman would move simultaneously lest Lee reinforce Johnston or vice versa. But his plans were nearly disrupted, in a most personal way, even before they commenced. Grant traveled from Culpeper to Washington regularly during April to meet with Lincoln and Stanton. One day, returning by train from the capital, he spotted a cloud of dust to the side of the road and inferred a movement of cavalry. He subsequently was informed that Confederate colonel John Mosby's horsemen were tangling with Union cavalry guarding the railroad. "I do not know that the enemy's attack on the road last Friday was with the view of ketching me," he wrote Julia a few days later. "But it was well timed." He decided to stick closer to his camp. "In the first place I do not like being seen so much about Washington. In the second it is not altogether safe. I cannot move without it being known all over the country, and to the enemy who are hovering within a few miles of the railroad all the time."

———

*L*ee had learned to respect Grant's talents from afar, and he assumed Grant would make the Army of the Potomac a more formidable force than it had been. But Lee's primary concern during the late winter and early spring of 1864 was holding his own army together. The same shortages that had driven him into Maryland in 1862 and Pennsylvania in 1863 had worsened after the retreat from Gettysburg. That August Lee complained to Jefferson Davis that he couldn't move for lack of horse power. "Nothing prevents my advancing now but the fear of killing our artillery horses," he said. Deprived of forage, the animals were starving. "The cavalry also suffer, and I fear to set them at work. Some days we get a pound of corn per horse and some days more; some none. . . . You can judge of our prospects." During the autumn the men began to suffer, too; in January 1864 Lee lamented to Davis of "our crying necessity for food." He reported that his army was down to three days' provisions of four ounces of salt meat per man per day. "I can learn of no supply of meat on the road to the army, and fear I shall be unable to obtain it in the field," he told Davis. He argued that the Confederate government should take sterner measures to ensure that civilians sacrificed on behalf of the war effort. "If it requires all the meat in the country to support the army, it should be had."

The food shortages translated into troop shortages. Lee sent soldiers home on furlough, in part to avoid having to feed them; many never returned. Conscription yielded fewer and fewer recruits as the likely ones had already been taken and the unlikely got better at eluding the draft agents. A sense of despondency fell across the Confederacy. "Today closes the gloomiest year of our struggle," the *Richmond Examiner* observed on December 31. "No sanguine hope of intervention buoys up the spirits of the Confederate public as at the end of 1861. No brilliant victory like that of Fredericksburg encourages us to look forward to a speedy and successful termination of the war, as in the last weeks of 1862." Southern finance had fallen into chaos, and for most Southerners mere existence was a grinding struggle. "Hoarders keep a more resolute grasp than ever on the necessaries of life. . . . What was once competence has become poverty, poverty has become penury, penury is lapsing into pauperism." The future was grim. "We do not know what our resources are, and no one can tell us whether we shall have a pound of beef to eat at the end of 1864."

To offset the desertions Lee appealed to his soldiers' love of their homeland. "A cruel enemy seeks to reduce our fathers and our mothers, our wives and our children, to abject slavery; to strip them of their property and drive them from their homes," he proclaimed. "Upon you these helpless ones rely to avert these terrible calamities, and to secure to them the blessings of liberty and safety."

Some soldiers responded; others did not. Desertions mounted to a point where Lee had to shelter himself from certain of their consequences. Until lately he had listened to appeals from decisions by courts martial in cases of desertion and other failures of soldierly will. He now ordered his aides to keep the supplicants away from his tent. "He said that with the great responsibilities resting on him he could not bear the pain and distress of such applications," Charles Venable of Lee's staff recalled.

As the fighting season of 1864 approached, Lee's army dwindled to fifty thousand. These were tested veterans, to be sure, and loyal to the end. And they would have the advantage of fighting on familiar ground. But they knew they were outnumbered and getting more so each day. "The reports of General Lee's scouts were scarcely necessary to our appreciation of the fact that the odds against were constantly and rapidly increasing," Confederate general John B. Gordon recalled. "From the highland which bordered the southern banks of the Rapidan one could almost estimate the numbers that were being added to Grant's ranks by the growth of the city of tents spreading out in full view below."

Gordon and the others knew the enemy commander by reputation. "Grant had come from his campaigns in the Southwest with the laurels of Fort Donelson, Shiloh, Vicksburg, and Missionary Ridge on his brow," Gordon said. Yet he and his comrades considered their own commander fully a match for Grant. "Lee stood before him with a record as military executioner unrivaled by that of any warrior of modern times. He had, at astoundingly short intervals and with unvarying regularity, decapitated or caused the official 'taking off' of the five previously selected commanders-in-chief of the great army which confronted them." Gordon and the others were confident Grant would be Lee's next victim.

Grant couldn't decide initially whether to cross the Rapidan above Lee, to the west, or below him, to the east. "Each plan presents great advantages over the other, with corresponding objections," he mused to Meade. "By crossing above, Lee is cut off from all chance of ignoring Richmond and going north on a raid. But if we take this route, all we do must be done whilst the rations we start with hold out." The roads weren't sufficient to sustain an army as large as that of the Potomac. The alternate route—below Lee—was longer but would allow access by water. "Brandy Station can be used as a base of supplies until another is secured on the York or James River." This approach, however, would tempt Lee to move north, perhaps against Washington. One thing was essential, Grant told Meade. "Lee's army will be your objective point. Wherever Lee goes there you will go also."

Benjamin Butler would worry Lee's right. Grant ordered that the Army of the James be reinforced with units drawn from the coast. "What I ask is that with them, and all you can concentrate from your own command, you seize upon City Point"—on the James River below Richmond—"and act from there looking upon Richmond as your objective point," he told Butler. He and Meade would keep Lee busy to the north of the Confederate capital, creating an opportunity for Butler. "If it should prove possible for you to reach Richmond, so as to invest all on the south side of the river, and fortify yourself there, I shall have but little fear of the result." As with Sherman, Grant furnished Butler only an outline. "I do not pretend to say how your work is to be done but simply lay down what, and trust to you and those under you for doing it well."

By late April he had made his decision about the Rapidan. He characteristically opted for directness in ordering that the Army of the Potomac cross above Lee and force him to fight or retreat toward Richmond. "I will move against Lee's army, attempting to turn him by one flank or the other," Grant told Halleck. "Should Lee fall back within his fortifications at Richmond, either before or after giving battle, I will form a junction with Butler, and the two forces will draw supplies from the James River." Until then the Army of the Potomac would be self-sufficient. "The Army will start with fifteen days' supplies. All the country affords will be gathered as we go along. This will no doubt enable us to go twenty or twenty-five days without further supplies, unless we should be forced to keep in the country between the Rapidan and Chickahominy, in which case supplies might be required by way of the York or the Rappahannock River." Halleck should see to those. "I would like to have about one million rations, and two hundred thousand forage rations, afloat to be sent wherever it may prove they will be required."

———

"This is my forty-second birthday," Grant wrote Julia on April 27. "Getting old, am I not?" Yet he remained steady and calm. "Before you receive this I will be away from Culpepper and the Army will be in motion. I know the greatest anxiety is now felt in the North for the success of this move, and that the anxiety will increase when it is once known that the Army is in motion." But he wasn't worried. "I feel well myself. Do not know that this is any criterion to judge results, because I have never felt otherwise. I believe it has never been my misfortune to be placed where I lost my presence of mind—unless indeed it has been when thrown in strange company, particularly of ladies."

Lincoln was more nervous than Grant but nonetheless supportive. "Not expecting to see you again before the spring campaign opens, I wish to express, in this way, my entire satisfaction with what you have done up to this time, so far as I understand it," the president wrote Grant on April 30. "The particulars of your plan I neither know or seek to know. You are vigilant and self-reliant; and, pleased with this, I wish not to obtrude any constraints or restraints upon you. While I am very anxious that any great disaster, or the capture of our men in great numbers, shall be avoided, I know these points are less likely to escape your attention than they would be mine. If there is anything wanting which is within my power to give, do not fail to let me know it. And now with a brave Army, and a just cause, may God sustain you."

"The confidence you express for the future, and satisfaction with the past, in my military administration is acknowledged with pride," Grant responded. "From my first entrance into the volunteer service of the country, to the present day, I have never had cause of complaint, have never expressed or implied a complaint, against the Administration or the Secretary of War for throwing any embarrassment in the way of my vigorously prosecuting what appeared to me my duty." And since his promotion to command of the armies the administration had been especially helpful. "I have been astonished at the readiness with which everything asked for has been yielded without even an explanation being asked." The burden was now on him. "It will be my earnest endeavor that you, and the country, shall not be disappointed."

"The movement of this Army will commence at 12 o'clock tomorrow night," Grant ordered on May 2. "The attempt will be made to turn the right flank of the enemy—that is, to cross the Rapidan east of or below the railroad. Ely's Ford, Germanna Ford, and Culpeper Mine Ford will be the crossing places." The early start was to surprise Lee; the three crossings would allow Grant's army to get over the Rapidan before Lee could react.

The first phase of the operation went well. Grant's cavalry seized the fords in the dark and captured or dispersed the Confederate pickets on the south bank. At dawn his engineers began building pontoon bridges, which were helpful to the infantry and indispensable to the artillery and supply trains.

Lee didn't contest the crossing, leaving Grant to wonder whether he would oppose the advance at all or retreat to Richmond. "The crossing of Rapidan effected," Grant informed Halleck in the late morning of May 4. "Forty-eight hours now will demonstrate whether the enemy intends giving battle this side of Richmond." Grant hoped for a fight, as his advantage in numbers would have greater effect in the open field than if Lee's army fought from the fortifications of the Confederate capital.

Lee might well have fallen back had the ground been different. But the Wilderness, as the region south of the Rapidan was called, was hardly an open field. "It was uneven, with woods, thickets, and ravines right and left," one of Grant's generals, Alexander Webb, explained. "Tangled thickets of pine, scrub-oak, and cedar prevented our seeing the enemy, and prevented anyone in command of a large force from determining accurately the position of the troops he was ordering to and fro." Lee knew the Wilderness better than Grant did, and he counted on its confusing nature to work to his advantage. He would hit Grant hard; if Grant recoiled, the way his predecessors had, Lee would emerge the winner. If Grant kept coming, Lee would make him pay for each mile he gained. By the time they got to Richmond the odds would be more nearly even. And even odds favored the defender.

As Grant's columns pressed south from the river to the Wilderness Tavern, a local landmark, Lee brought up his forces to attack him from the west. The Federals turned to face the Confederates and on May 5 the serious fighting began. The overall clash took the apparent form of discrete engagements as the vegetation and terrain often prevented both Grant and Lee from knowing where their own units were, let alone those of the enemy. The fighting was heavy, lethal and utterly disorienting. "My command had cut its way through the Union center," Confederate John Gordon recalled, "and at that moment it was in the remarkably strange position of being on identically the same general line with the enemy, the Confederates facing in one direction, the Federals in the other. Looking down that line from Grant's right toward his left, there would first have been seen a long stretch of blue uniforms, then a short stretch of gray, then another still longer of blue, in one continuous line. The situation was both unique and alarming." Gordon had never experienced, or read of, such a position, and he didn't know how to get out of it. "Further movement to Grant's rear was not to be considered, for his unbroken lines on each side of me would promptly close up the gap which my men had cut through his center, thus rendering the capture of my whole command inevitable." Retreat was almost as fatal. "Those same unbroken and now unopposed ranks on each side of me, as soon as such retrograde motion began, would instantly rush from both directions upon my retreating column and crush it." So Gordon improvised. He ordered half his line to file right and the other to file left, thereby arraying each half perpendicular to the flank of the corresponding segment of the Union line. He then ordered a double charge, with his twin lines surging away from each other but wreaking havoc on the Federal flanks.

The fighting continued throughout the day, with both sides taking satisfaction. "By the blessing of God, we maintained our position against every effort until night, when the contest closed," Lee reported to Jefferson Davis. Grant was equally, if paradoxically, upbeat. "We have engaged with the enemy in full force since early yesterday," he wrote Halleck on the morning of May 6. "So far there is no decisive result, but I think all things are progressing favorably."

The paradox persisted through the second day. Each general brought up reinforcements, which swelled the casualty count without materially changing the balance of battle. "The enemy advanced and created some confusion," Lee acknowledged of the morning's fighting. But the Confederates quickly regrouped. "The ground lost was recovered as soon as the fresh troops got into position, and the enemy driven back to his original line. Afterward we turned the left of his front line and drove it from the field, leaving a large number of dead and wounded. . . . Every advance on his part, thanks to a merciful God, has been repulsed. Our loss in killed is not large."

Grant again saw things differently. "Yesterday the enemy attacked our lines vigorously first at one point and then another, from right to left," he wrote on May 7. "They were repulsed at all points before reaching our lines, except once during the afternoon on Hancock's front, and just after night on Sedgwick's. . . . Our losses to this time in killed, wounded and prisoners will not probably exceed 12,000, of whom an unusually large proportion are but slightly wounded." The slightness of the wounding reflected the fact that the nature of the battlefield prevented either side from using much artillery, which normally inflicted the heaviest wounds. "I think the loss of the enemy must exceed ours," Grant continued. "But this is only a guess, based upon the fact that they attacked and were repulsed so often." Grant was willing to call the contest a draw. "At present we can claim no victory over the enemy; neither have they gained a single advantage."

He subsequently revised his estimate of the battle of the Wilderness. "More desperate fighting has not been witnessed on this continent than that of the 5th and 6th of May," he wrote after the war. "Our losses in the Wilderness were very severe." Still, he believed the results repaid the cost. "Our victory consisted in having successfully crossed a formidable stream, almost in the face of an enemy, and in getting the army together as a unit. . . . As we stood at the close, the two armies were relatively in about the same condition to meet each other as when the river divided them. But the fact of having safely crossed was a victory."

How many more such victories the Union could endure was the central question of the late spring and summer of 1864. The tragedy of that season was that the fighting, sanguinary as it was, suited both sides. Lee calculated that by bleeding Grant he could slow or stall the Union advance to Richmond, wearing out Northern patience if not Grant himself. Grant reasoned that every soldier Lee lost made one less Confederate to fight, while every soldier he himself lost could be replaced. Equal losses favored the more populous North.

Charles Dana witnessed the implications of Grant's thinking. Lincoln and Stanton weren't getting information from the front as quickly as they desired. "We are very much troubled, and have concluded to send you down there," the president told Dana, who thereupon rode off to Grant's headquarters. He discovered that the officers and men of Grant's command were just getting used to their new leader. "The previous history of the Army of the Potomac had been to advance and fight a battle, then either to retreat or lie still, and finally to go into winter quarters," Dana recounted. "Grant did not intend to proceed in that way. As soon as

he had fought a battle and had not routed Lee, he meant to move nearer
to Richmond and fight another battle." And so he informed his army
shortly after the Wilderness. Grant's order to press ahead surprised the
troops but also pleased them. "As the army began to realize that we were
really moving south, and at that moment were probably much nearer
Richmond than was our enemy, the spirits of men and officers rose to
the highest pitch of animation. On every hand I heard the cry: 'On to
Richmond!'"

But Lee was quicker than Grant's army guessed. Lee thought he
understood Grant, and he related his understanding to John Gordon.
"He discussed the dominant characteristics of his great antagonist," Gordon recalled: "his indomitable will and untiring persistency; his direct
method of waging war by delivering constant and heavy blows upon
the enemy's front rather than by seeking advantage through strategical
maneuver. General Lee also said that General Grant held so completely
and firmly the confidence of the Government that he could command to
any extent its limitless resources in men and materials, while the Confederacy was already practically exhausted in both. He, however, hoped—
perhaps I may say he was almost convinced—that if we could keep the
Confederate army between General Grant and Richmond, checking him
for a few months longer, as we had in the past two days, some crisis in
public affairs or change in public opinion at the North might induce the
authorities at Washington to let the Southern States go."

Gordon also remembered Lee's predicting what Grant would do
next. In a conversation with Lee, Gordon transmitted intelligence
reports indicating that Grant was preparing to retreat, as his predecessors had retreated in the face of stiff resistance. Lee waved the reports
aside. "General Grant is not going to retreat," he said. "He will move
his army to Spotsylvania." Gordon asked Lee if he had particular intelligence to that effect. "Not at all, not at all," Lee said. "But that is the
next point at which the armies will meet. Spotsylvania is now General
Grant's best strategic point." Gordon later accounted for Lee's foresight:
"This notable prophecy by General Lee and its fulfillment by General
Grant show that the brains of these two foemen had been working at the
same problem. The known quantities in that problem were the aims of
Grant to crush Lee and capture Richmond, to which had been added the
results of the last two days' fighting. The unknown quantity which both
were endeavoring to find was the next movement which the aggressor

would probably make. Grant stood in his own place and calculated from his own standpoint; Lee put himself in Grant's place and calculated from the same standpoint; and both found the same answer—Spotsylvania."

The second great battle of the 1864 campaign was more protracted than the Wilderness, in part because of bad weather, but at times equally brutal. The most intense fighting occurred at the "Bloody Angle," where Union troops and Confederates locked at close quarters from before dawn on May 12 till hours past sunset. Horace Porter, a Grant aide, never saw anything to equal the fighting that day. "Rank after rank was riddled by shot and shell and bayonet thrusts, and finally sank, a mass of torn and mutilated corpses; then fresh troops rushed madly forward to replace the dead, and so the murderous work went on," Porter remembered. "Guns were run up close to the parapet, and double charges of canister played their part in the bloody work. The fence rails and logs in the breastworks were shattered into splinters, and trees over a foot and a half in diameter were cut completely in two by the incessant musketry fire. A section of the trunk of a stout oak tree thus severed was afterward sent to Washington, where it is still on exhibition at the National Museum. We had not only shot down an army, but also a forest."

John Gordon took part in the contest on the Confederate side. "Firing into one another's faces, beating one another down with clubbed muskets, the front ranks fought across the embankment's crest almost within an arm's reach, the men behind passing up to them freshly loaded rifles as their own were emptied," Gordon recalled. "As those in front fell, others quickly sprang forward to take their places. On both sides the dead were piled in heaps. As Confederates fell their bodies rolled into the ditch, and upon their bleeding forms their living comrades stood, beating back Grant's furiously charging columns. The bullets seemed to fly in sheets. Before the pelting hail and withering blast the standing timber fell. The breastworks were literally drenched in blood. The coming of the darkness failed to check the raging battle. It only served to increase the awful terror of the scene."

The fighting ended only with the eventual exhaustion of both sides. Charles Dana went out the next day with John Rawlins to inspect the lines. "The ground around the salient had been trampled and cut in the struggle until it was almost impassable for one on horseback, so Rawlins and I dismounted and climbed up the bank over the outer line of the rude breastworks," Dana wrote. "Within we saw a fence over which earth evidently had been banked, but which now was bare and half down. It was here the fighting had been fiercest. We picked our way to this fence and stopped to look over the scene. The night was coming on, and after the horrible din of the day, the silence was intense; nothing broke it but distant and occasional firing or the low groans of the wounded. I remember that as I stood there I was almost startled to hear a bird twittering in a tree. All around us the underbrush and trees, which were just beginning to be green, had been riddled and burnt. The ground was thick with dead and wounded men, among whom the relief corps was at work. The earth, which was soft from the heavy rains we had been having before and during the battle, had been trampled by the fighting of the thousands until it was soft, like thin hasty pudding. Over the fence against which we leaned lay a great pool of this mud, its surface as smooth as that of a pond. As we stood there, looking silently down at it, of a sudden the leg of a man was lifted up from the pool and the mud dripped off his boot. It was so unexpected, so horrible, that for a moment we were stunned. Then we pulled ourselves together and called to some soldiers nearby to rescue the owner of the leg." The man recovered, but Dana never learned how many other soldiers lay beneath the mud, dead of their wounds or drowned.

The fighting around Spotsylvania stretched over two weeks on account of the mud and the inability of either side to win a decisive victory. Grant sent reports piecemeal to Washington, hesitant to draw premature conclusions and reluctant to record the totals of dead and wounded. "Our losses have been heavy as well as those of the enemy," he informed Stanton while the fighting continued. "I think the loss of the enemy must be greater. We have taken over five thousand prisoners in battle, while he has taken from us but few except stragglers."

Other men—starting with Grant's predecessors in command of the Army of the Potomac, but including anyone less dedicated to the cause of the Union and the calling of war—would have quailed at the toll the fighting exacted. But Grant remained undaunted. "I propose to fight it out on this line if it takes all summer," he told Stanton.

40

YET HE DIDN'T THINK IT WOULD TAKE ALL SUMMER. "I AM SATISFIED the enemy are very shaky and are only kept up to the mark by the greatest exertion on the part of their officers," Grant wrote Halleck. To Julia he declared, "The world has never seen so bloody or so protracted a battle as the one being fought, and I hope never will again. The enemy were really whipped yesterday. . . . Their situation is desperate beyond anything heretofore known. To lose this battle, they lose their cause." After several additional days of fighting, interspersed by spring downpours, Grant suggested that ultimate victory was nigh. "Lee's army is really whipped," he told Halleck. "The prisoners we now take show it, and the actions of his army show it unmistakably. A battle with them outside of entrenchments cannot be had. Our men feel that they have gained morale over the enemy and attack with confidence. I may be mistaken but I feel that our success over Lee's army is already ensured."

Charles Dana detected the same good omens. "One of the most important results of the campaign thus far was the entire change which had taken place in the feelings of the armies," Dana remembered. "The Confederates had lost all confidence, and were already morally defeated. Our army had learned to believe that it was sure of ultimate victory. Even our officers had ceased to regard Lee as an invincible military genius." Lee looked slower to attack and more tentative than Dana had known him, even when circumstances favored the Confederates. The prisoners Dana talked to seemed discouraged, almost defeated. "Rely upon it," he wrote Stanton by his special channel, "the end is near as well as sure."

Grant's confidence initially disposed him to conserve his resources. By the last week of May, Lee had retreated across the North Anna

River; Grant's forces confronted him, but the terrain strongly favored the defenders. A swamp secured Lee's right and three streams his left. His center was well entrenched. "To make a direct attack from either wing would cause a slaughter of our men that even success would not justify," Grant concluded to Halleck. Consequently and uncharacteristically, he disengaged and headed farther south.

He aimed for Cold Harbor, which was neither a harbor nor cold; the name originally indicated a crossroads tavern that didn't serve hot meals. Lee again anticipated him, and by the time Grant's army was ready for battle, Lee's had dug itself in. The forces collided on June 1. "There has been a very severe battle this afternoon," Grant informed Julia. "And as I write, now 9 o'clock at night, firing is still continued on some parts of the battle line. What the result of the day's fighting has been I will know little about before midnight and possibly not then. The rebels are making a desperate fight and I presume will continue to do so as long as they can get a respectable number of men to stand."

Grant intended to renew the attack the next day. But the unusual heat of the early summer and the weariness of his men from a month of marching and fighting caused him to postpone the second assault until June 3. Horace Porter walked among the troops on the night of the 2nd and saw something that was, in his opinion, later misinterpreted. "In passing along on foot among the troops at the extreme front that evening while transmitting some of the final orders, I observed an incident which afforded a practical illustration of the deliberate and desperate courage of the men," he recounted. "As I came near one of the regiments which was making preparations for the next morning's assault, I noticed that many of the men had taken off their coats and seemed to be engaged in sewing up rents in them. This exhibition of tailoring seemed rather peculiar at such a moment, but upon closer examination it was found that the men were calmly writing their names and home addresses on slips of paper, and pinning them on the backs of their coats, so that their dead bodies might be recognized upon the field, and their fate made known to their families at home." Some persons who later heard of this interpreted the soldiers' actions as demoralization and defeatism, but Porter judged it otherwise. "They were veterans who knew well from terrible experience the danger which awaited them. . . . Their minds were occupied not with thoughts of shirking their duty, but with preparation for the desperate work of the coming morning. Such courage is more than heroic—it is sublime."

It was desperate work indeed for the soldiers the next day. "The Second Corps assaulted the enemy's position at 4:45 this a.m., the enemy in entrenchments," Winfield Scott Hancock, the corps commander, reported. "After a desperate and bloody fight Barlow and Gibbon both penetrated the enemy's works; Brooke's brigade of Barlow's division capturing 4 guns and 1 color. The enemy, however, rapidly threw fresh troops (Bushrod Johnson's division) upon our forces and compelled them to return with terrible slaughter." Hancock's troops maintained good discipline even as they fell back. "They did not retreat in any disorder but gallantly held on and entrenched themselves by throwing up the sand with their bayonets, hands, etc., under a scathing fire of musketry." The effort was to no avail. The Confederates were too well protected and the Federals too exposed. "By 6 a.m. the battle on our front was over, and the brave old Second Corps had lost over 3,000 of its bravest and best."

The story was similar for much of the rest of Grant's army that day. "It is understood that our whole line has been repulsed, from the right to the left of our army, wherever we attacked," Hancock wrote. "If so the loss must be grievous indeed." Hancock didn't know that the total loss would come to seven thousand, but he understood the implication. "Altogether this has been one of the most disastrous days the Army of the Potomac has ever seen."

Grant at first acted as though nothing unusual had happened. "Our loss was not severe," he wrote Halleck that afternoon. Perhaps he didn't initially appreciate the extent of his losses; doubtless he indulged his habit of putting the best face on things lest the resolve of his men or of the administration weaken.

But Cold Harbor haunted him the rest of his life. "I have always regretted that the last assault at Cold Harbor was ever made," he wrote in his memoirs, referring to the bloody morning of June 3. "No advantage whatever was gained to compensate for the heavy loss we sustained." On the contrary, the advantage was all to Lee. "Before that, the Army of Northern Virginia seemed to have acquired a wholesome regard for the courage, endurance, and soldierly qualities generally of the Army of the Potomac. They no longer wanted to fight them 'one Confederate to five Yanks.' . . . They seemed to have given up any idea of gaining any advantage of their antagonist in the open field. They had come to much prefer breastworks in their front." Cold Harbor—in particular the tragic final charge—shifted the psychological balance again. "This charge seemed to revive their hopes."

*I*n April 1864 Sherman received a letter from his brother John, the Ohio senator, regarding "the very bad news from Fort Pillow, not so bad from the loss of men, but from the question of retaliation raised by the massacre of negro troops." A Confederate force under Nathan Bedford Forrest had attacked the Union garrison at Fort Pillow, Tennessee, north of Memphis, on April 12, 1864; after driving the defenders from the fort, the Confederates killed hundreds of them. Negro troops, who constituted about half the garrison, suffered especially, with reports indicating that many had been killed after surrendering. "The river was dyed with the blood of the slaughtered for 200 yards," Forrest explained unapologetically in his battle report. He noted that his own casualties were light and added: "It is hoped that these facts will demonstrate to the Northern people that negro troops cannot cope with Southerners."

Grant heard about Fort Pillow from William Sherman. "Three hundred blacks murdered after surrender," Sherman telegraphed. The incident outraged Grant but also put him and the Union government in a quandary. "We all feel that we must disband negro troops or protect them," John Sherman explained from Washington. "It is fearful to think about the measures that may be necessary, but what else can we do?" Lincoln reflected, to an audience at Baltimore: "Having determined to use the negro as a soldier, there is no way but to give him all the protection given to any other soldier. The difficulty is not in the principle, but in practically applying it."

Lincoln consulted his cabinet and received advice that ranged from executing Forrest and the others responsible for the killings, should they be caught, to executing prisoners randomly chosen from Confederates previously captured, should Jefferson Davis not disavow Forrest's action. Lincoln drafted an order that an unspecified number of Confederate officers in Union custody be held as hostages against future massacres. But the order was never sent, and amid the larger slaughter of the Wilderness campaign, the subject was pushed aside.

THE BLOODLETTING AT COLD HARBOR CAUSED GRANT TO RECON-
sider his strategy for cornering Lee and capturing Richmond. "I now
find, after more than thirty days of trial, the enemy deems it of first
importance to run no risks with the armies they now have," he wrote
Halleck. "They act purely on the defensive, behind breastworks, or fee-
bly on the offensive immediately in front of them and where, in case
of repulse, they can instantly retire behind them. Without a greater
sacrifice of human life than I am willing to make, all cannot be accomplished that I had designed outside of the city."

A change was required. Grant determined to extricate his army from
its close quarters with Lee and move south across the James River. "Once
on the south side of the James River," he told Halleck, "I can cut off all
sources of supply to the enemy except what is furnished by the canal"—
the James River Canal, to Richmond's west. He would then attack the
canal and complete Lee's encirclement.

The new strategy lifted the gloom of Cold Harbor for Grant and, he
thought, his men. "Our army is not only confident of protecting itself,
without entrenchments, but that it can beat and drive the enemy whenever and wherever he can be found without this protection," he told Halleck.

Yet for one as used to fighting as Grant, *not* fighting came as a challenge. Moreover, disengaging from the Confederate lines and marching
south through hostile territory entailed the risk that Lee would attack
him at his most vulnerable. "But the move had to be made," Grant
reflected later. "And I relied upon Lee's not seeing my danger as I saw it."

What Lee saw was his own danger. He had to keep Grant off balance and off the James River, his outlet to the sea. "We must destroy this army of Grant's before he gets to James River," Lee told Jubal Early, one of his generals. "If he gets there it will become a siege, and then it will be a mere question of time."

But Grant was too quick and clever for Lee. To cover his southward move he dispatched Phil Sheridan west to strike against the Virginia Central Railroad. "Every rail on the road destroyed should be so bent or twisted as to make it impossible to repair the road without supplying new rails," he told Sheridan. At the same time he ordered General David Hunter, currently in the Shenandoah Valley, to move against the railroad and then the James Canal. "The complete destruction of this road and of the canal is of great importance to us," Grant said. He expected his order to reach Hunter between Staunton and Lynchburg. "Immediately turn east by the most practicable road until you strike the Lynchburg branch of the Virginia Central road. From there move eastward along the line of the road, destroying it completely and thoroughly until you join General Sheridan." Hunter should then drive for the canal. "Lose no opportunity to destroy the canal."

Grant meanwhile readied to move his main army south. He shared his plans with a mere handful of officers, reasoning that broader distribution would inevitably alert Lee. As a result, when the order to march went down the line on the evening of June 12, the rank and file could only guess where they were bound. The advance guard forded the Chickahominy and dispersed the Confederate pickets there; Grant's engineers threw over pontoon bridges for the others to cross upon. Lee didn't miss Grant from the Cold Harbor front till the next morning when Grant's army was halfway to the James. That river posed a more serious obstacle, being nearly half a mile wide at Grant's point of crossing. But the engineers again came through, building a hundred-pontoon bridge in seven hours. At once the infantry, led by Winfield Hancock's corps, headed across.

Grant observed the operation as it proceeded the next morning. "His cigar had been thrown aside, his hands were clasped behind him, and he seemed lost in the contemplation of the spectacle," Horace Porter remembered. "The great bridge was the scene of a continuous movement of infantry columns, batteries of artillery, and wagon trains. The approaches to the river on both banks were covered with masses of troops moving briskly to their positions or waiting patiently their turn to cross. . . . Drums were beating the march; bands were playing stirring quicksteps. . . . The bright sun, shining through a clear sky upon the scene, cast its sheen upon the water, was reflected from the burnished gun barrels and glittering cannon, and brought out with increased brilliancy the gay colors of the waving banners."

Grant took quiet pride in the operation. "Since Sunday we have been engaged in one of the most perilous movements ever executed by a large army, that of withdrawing from the front of an enemy and moving past his flank, crossing two rivers over which the enemy has bridges and railroads whilst we have bridges to improvise," he wrote Julia on June 15. "So far it has been eminently successful and I hope will prove so to the end." To Halleck he wrote: "The enemy show no signs of yet having brought troops to the south of Richmond. I will have Petersburg secured if possible before they get there in much force."

Halleck sent Lincoln a copy of Grant's message. Grant had withheld his intentions from the president as from the rest of the administration. Lincoln now learned of the operation with appreciative pleasure. "I begin to see it," he wrote Grant. "You will succeed. God bless you all."

Grant considered Petersburg, a rail junction on the Appomattox River twenty miles south of Richmond, to be an outer work of the Confederate capital; seizing its rail lines would help him starve Richmond and Lee's army. Grant guessed that Petersburg was poorly defended, and he ordered an attack as his army approached the town. General William F. Smith drove back the defenders, who indeed were few and inexperienced, consisting primarily of old men and young boys. But then he paused, awaiting reinforcements, which through a miscommunication were slow to arrive. By the time the second assault occurred, Lee had gotten more of his own troops into place. Two days of heavy fighting left the Confederates in control of Petersburg and several thousand Union troops dead or wounded.

Grant lamented the opportunity lost. "I believed then, and still believe, that Petersburg could have been easily captured," he wrote later. There was nothing to be done now except mount a siege. "We will rest the men and use the spade for their protection until a new vein can be struck," he told Meade.

Grant judged that his move south of the James marked the beginning of his endgame with Lee. He had tried to slug it out in the Wilderness and at Cold Harbor and discovered he couldn't bear the cost. So he would settle for a siege, a more deliberate but no less certain version of the war of attrition he had commenced at the Rapidan. "Our work progresses here slowly and I feel will progress securely until Richmond finally falls," he wrote Julia from City Point, where he established his headquarters.

With Lee contained near Richmond and Sherman dogging Johnston in Georgia, victory was inevitable, Grant thought. All that was required was patience on the part of the Union's advocates. "You people up North must be of good cheer," he wrote Chicago acquaintance Russell Jones. "Recollect that we have the bulk of the Rebel Army in two grand Armies both besieged and both conscious that they cannot stand a single battle outside their fortifications with the Armies confronting them. The last man in the Confederacy is now in the Army. They are becoming discouraged, their men deserting, dying and being killed and captured every day. We lose too but can replace our losses. If the rebellion is not perfectly and thoroughly crushed it will be the fault and through the weakness of the people North. Be of good cheer and rest assured that all will come out right."

*B*ut good cheer was scarce in the North in the summer of 1864. The Virginia campaign thus far had been singular for its slow progress and sobering casualties. In killed, wounded and missing, Grant had lost some sixty thousand since crossing the Rapidan, and he was only marginally nearer Richmond than when he started. Lee looked no closer to surrendering than he had in May; if anything, the Confederate performances at Cold Harbor and Petersburg suggested that the rebel troops had more fight left in them than Grant's troops did. Northern newspapers wondered how long the army would follow Grant; even members of the Lincoln administration began to register doubts. "The immense slaughter of our brave men chills and sickens us all," Gideon Welles, the secretary of the navy, wrote in his diary. "The hospitals are crowded with the thousands of mutilated and dying heroes who have poured out their blood for the Union cause."

Lincoln shared Welles's concern, and he decided to pay Grant a visit. He traveled by river steamer down the Potomac and the Chesapeake Bay and up the James to City Point. Grant greeted him at the wharf. "I hope you are very well, Mr. President," he said.

"I am in very good health," Lincoln replied. "But I don't feel very comfortable after my trip last night on the bay. It was rough, and I was considerably shaken up."

A messmate of Grant's with unusual powers of procurement stepped forward. "Try a glass of champagne, Mr. President," he said. "That is always a certain cure for seasickness."

Lincoln demurred. "No, my friend, I have seen too many fellows seasick ashore from drinking that very stuff."

Grant offered to escort the president along the Union lines. Lincoln accepted. Horace Porter grinned at the sight of the president on horseback. "Like most men who had been brought up in the West, he had good command of a horse," Porter said. "But it must be acknowledged that in appearance he was not a very dashing rider. . . . By the time he had reached the troops he was completely covered with dust, and the black color of his clothes had changed to Confederate gray. As he had no straps, his trousers gradually worked up above his ankles, and gave him the appearance of a country farmer riding into town wearing his Sunday clothes. A citizen on horseback is always an odd sight in the midst of a uniformed army, and the picture presented by the President bordered on the grotesque."

Yet the troops appreciated his coming. They gathered around and offered cheers to "Uncle Abe." Most appreciative were the black troops who had fought at Petersburg. They saluted Lincoln as their commander but revered him as their liberator. They crowded close, some merely to touch his coat or his horse. Lincoln was obviously moved. "The President rode with bared head," Porter recalled. "The tears had started to his eyes, and his voice was so broken with emotion that he could scarcely articulate the words of thanks and congratulation which he tried to speak."

Lincoln spent the evening in front of Grant's tent on a bluff above the James. He told stories of life in Illinois and among the political classes of Washington. As the shadows lengthened he sank deeper into his camp chair till his torso all but disappeared and he seemed entirely legs and arms, with the latter waving here and there to emphasize his anecdotes. He retired to his boat on the James and returned the next day to Washington.

Brief though it was, Lincoln's visit established a new level of trust and understanding between the president and his commanding general. "They parted with unfeigned regret," Porter said. "Both felt that their acquaintance had already ripened into a genuine friendship."

42

LINCOLN NEEDED ALL THE FRIENDS HE COULD GET. THE 1864 ELECtion loomed, and voters were restive that the war continued inconclusively more than three and a half years after its start. The Republican party reconfigured itself, with the addition of pro-war Democrats, as the National Union party and nominated Lincoln for a second term. The president eased Vice President Hannibal Hamlin off the ticket in favor of Tennessee Democrat Andrew Johnson, whom he had previously appointed military governor of the Volunteer State. Johnson's background was as humble as Lincoln's, but while life broadened Lincoln it seemed to narrow Johnson, who grew stubborn and suspicious as an adult. Yet his stubbornness favored the Union, and it disposed Lincoln to overlook Johnson's rough edges.

The Democrats who maintained their party identity had difficulty deciding what to do. A few sought to nominate Grant despite his repeated denials of interest. Their efforts went nowhere. A larger group looked to another soldier, George McClellan. Grant had never figured out how to employ McClellan since assuming command of the Union armies, and the underoccupied general concluded that he should replace Lincoln as president. The delegates to the Democratic national convention, held at Chicago, nearly all thought the war had gone on too long, and they nominated McClellan on a platform demanding that "immediate efforts be made for a cessation of hostilities." McClellan put some distance between himself and the platform, but he made clear that a vote for him was a vote against the war policies of the present administration.

McClellan ran formally against Lincoln but implicitly against Grant. The two generals—McClellan didn't bother resigning his commission to run for office—competed for the favor of voters and, via the voters, for the right to determine the fate of the Union. Each battlefield success for Grant was a boon to Lincoln and a setback for McClellan; each reversal for Grant was a blow to Lincoln and a gain for McClellan.

Grant rarely commented on politics except to decry the absence of spine in certain elected officials. And he would have been outraged at any accusation that he made military decisions for political reasons. But he understood that his army existed and persisted by the will of the people of the Union. "Be of good cheer," he had said to his Chicago friend in urging that the people of the North continue to support the war. Grant understood that Lee might beat him yet if the Northern will to continue the fight flagged. And it might indeed flag if he couldn't show greater progress than he had shown since spring.

To that end he authorized another assault on Petersburg. The lines hadn't moved for over a month—the lines above ground, that is. Below the surface there was more action. Some Pennsylvania miners in Ambrose Burnside's Ninth Corps mimicked the tunneling Grant's engineers had done at Vicksburg; they dug a passage that stretched more than five hundred feet to beneath the Confederate lines. Eight thousand pounds of gunpowder were carted into the tunnel and set in place. The fuse was lit shortly after three o'clock on the morning of July 30, and the troops of the Ninth waited anxiously for the explosion. Nothing happened. Two intrepid miners crawled along the tunnel to find out what had gone wrong; they discovered that the fuse had failed at a splicing point. They relit the fuse and hurried out of the tunnel. A bit before five o'clock an enormous explosion rocked the hillside around the tunnel, blasting the Confederate position above it and hundreds of Confederates too.

But the follow-up was even more disappointing than the comparable effort before Vicksburg had been. Burnside's men were slow into the crater, and by the time they arrived in force the Confederates had recovered from their shock and repaired the breach in their defenses. They proceeded to beat back the assault, inflicting heavy damage in the process. "It was the saddest affair I have witnessed in this war," Grant told Halleck. "Such opportunity for carrying fortifications I have never seen and do not expect again to have."

The bungle of the Petersburg crater caused many in the North and some in the Lincoln administration to doubt that Grant was the man to beat Lee. "Admiral Porter has always said there was something wanting in Grant, which Sherman could always supply, and vice versa, as regards Sherman, but that the two together made a very perfect general officer and they ought never to be separated," Gideon Welles said. "Grant relies on others, but does not know men—can't discriminate." Welles feared that Grant might have been given more responsibility than he could shoulder. "God grant that I may be mistaken, for the slaughtered thousands of my countrymen who have poured out their rich blood for three months on the soil of Virginia from the Wilderness to Petersburg under his generalship can never be atoned in this world or the next if he without Sherman prove a failure. A blight and sadness comes over me like a dark shadow when I dwell on the subject, a melancholy feeling of the past, a foreboding of the future. A nation's destiny almost has been committed to this man, and if it is an improper committal, where are we?"

As before when Grant stumbled, his critics asserted he was drinking. William Smith, whom Grant had relieved after his failure of nerve at Petersburg, wrote to Senator Solomon Foot of his home state of Vermont to say that his firing had nothing to do with his performance. "I write to put you in possession of such facts in the case as I am aware of and think will throw light upon the subject," Smith said. "About the very last of June, or the first of July, Generals Grant and Butler came to my headquarters, and shortly after their arrival General Grant turned to General Butler and said: 'That drink of whiskey I took has done me good'; and then, directly afterward, asked me for a drink. My servant opened a bottle for him, and he drank of it, when the bottle was corked and put away. I was aware at this time that General Grant had within six months pledged himself to drink nothing intoxicating, but did not feel it would better matters to decline to give it upon his request in General Butler's presence. After the lapse of an hour or less, the General asked for another drink, which he took. Shortly after, his voice showed plainly that the liquor had affected him, and after a little time he left. I went to see him upon his horse, and as soon as I returned to my tent, I said to a staff officer of mine, who had witnessed his departure: 'General Grant has gone away drunk. General Butler has seen it, and will never fail to use the weapon which has been put into his hands.'" Smith proceeded to assert that Grant had wanted to relieve not him but Butler and would have done so if not for Butler's secret knowledge. "I have heard from two different sources (one being from General Grant's headquarters, and one a staff officer of a general on intimate official relations with General

Butler), that General Butler went to General Grant and threatened to expose his intoxication." Smith closed his account by saying, "I have not referred to the state of things existing at headquarters when I left, and to the fact that General Grant was then in the habit of getting liquor in a surreptitious manner, because it was not relevant to my case; but if you think at any time the matter may be of importance to the country, I will give it to you."

John Rawlins heard the part of the story about Grant's taking a drink. "The General was at the front today, and I learn from one of his staff he deviated from the only path he should ever travel by taking a glass of liquor," Rawlins wrote his wife. "It is the first time I have failed to accompany him to Petersburg, and it was with misgivings I did so. Nothing but indisposition induced me to remain behind. I shall hereafter, under no circumstances, fail to accompany him."

Ben Butler denied Smith's whole tale, which didn't become public until after Grant's death. Smith was simply trying to explain away his own firing, Butler said. "There never was any such happening as Smith relates," Butler wrote in his memoir. "I never saw General Grant drink a glass of spirituous liquor in my life." The story was ludicrous on its face, Butler asserted, especially the part about Grant getting liquor surreptitiously. "Surreptitiously? The lieutenant general could have commanded all the whiskey of the United States to his army if he thought proper, and it would have come. If he had let it be known that he would use it, his admiring friends all over the North and West would have sent him the choicest brands in the most boundless profusion."

*W*hatever the basis of Smith's story, it did nothing to boost confidence in Grant at a time when the political classes in Washington required reassuring. The impatience at the slow pace of the war transmuted into fear when the fighting accelerated dramatically and came shockingly close to home. Since the spring Grant and Lee had fought for control of the Shenandoah Valley. Grant got the upper hand first, as David Hunter rolled south seizing everything he could put to use and destroying much of the remainder. Hunter's success, which Grant valued for the damage it did to Lee's supply base, served the additional purpose of compelling the Confederate general to dispatch forces from his own army to stop Hunter. Jubal Early met Hunter at Lynchburg and drove him back north. Early reclaimed the valley for the Confederacy before crossing the Potomac into Maryland and heading for Washington.

Grant was slow to respond. He knew Early lacked the troops to do serious damage to the Union capital, and he remained as convinced as ever that Lee's army was the objective that truly mattered. Yet political Washington didn't uniformly share his priorities and his equanimity, and as Early approached the city many there took fright. "I have sometimes thought that Lee might make a sudden dash in the direction of Washington or above, and inflict great injury before our troops could interfere or Grant move a column to protect the city," Gideon Welles recorded in his diary on July 6. Two days later Welles asserted, "Profound ignorance reigns at the War Department concerning the Rebel raid in the Shenandoah Valley. . . . They know absolutely nothing of it—its numbers, where it is, its destination. . . . I think we are in no way prepared for it, and a fierce onset could not well be resisted." In another three days the enemy was at the capital's edge. "The Rebels are upon us," Welles cried.

Lincoln alarmed less easily than Welles, and he did his best to appear calm. "Let us be vigilant but keep cool," he told a resident of Baltimore who feared for his own city. "I hope neither Baltimore or Washington will be sacked." Yet the president's nervousness showed in a telegram to Grant. "General Halleck says we have absolutely no force here fit to go to the field," he said. He wanted Grant to march his army to Washington at once. "What I think is that you should provide to retain your hold where you are, certainly, and bring the rest with you personally and make a vigorous effort to destroy the enemy's force in this vicinity."

Grant believed the situation was under control or soon would be. He had already dispatched reinforcements, which should be arriving shortly. "I have sent from here a whole corps commanded by an excellent officer, besides over 3000 troops," he assured the president. And he respectfully declined the suggestion that he should head the capital's defenses himself. "It would have a bad effect for me to leave here."

Grant's measures saved the situation, although not without additional shudders in Washington. Lew Wallace, the Union commander first on the scene, suffered significant casualties but bought time for the forces behind him to dig in. Early approached to within sight of the Capitol, where he exchanged fire with Union troops holding Fort Stevens. Lincoln rode out to watch; his tall figure on the parapets became a target for Confederate sharpshooters. Gideon Welles went to the front too. "Could see the line of pickets of both armies," the navy secretary recorded. "There was continual firing. . . . Two houses in the vicinity were in flames, set on fire by our own people because they obstructed the range of our guns and gave shelter to Rebel sharpshooters." Welles still wasn't sure the defenses would hold, and he blamed Grant for leaving the city vulnerable. "The forts around Washington have been vacated and the troops sent to General Grant, who was promised reinforcements to take Richmond. But he has been in its vicinity more than a month, resting, apparently, after his bloody march, but has effected nothing since arrival on the James, nor displayed any strategy." Welles expressed the nakedness many residents of Washington felt. "We are without force for its defense."

In fact the defense was already in place. Early realized he lacked the troops to occupy the capital and, after frightening the residents a bit more, backed off. "We haven't taken Washington, but we've scared Abe Lincoln like hell," Early remarked. Gideon Welles finally exhaled as the danger passed, but he gave no credit to the men who were supposed to safeguard the government. "The Rebels have lost a remarkable opportunity," he said. "They might easily have captured Washington. Stanton, Halleck, and Grant are asleep or dumb."

*T*he fright of July segued into the angst of August. Lincoln felt and exhibited it. For weeks the cost of the war and the lack of progress had burdened his soul. Isaac Arnold, an Illinois Republican, saw the president conclude an encounter with a line of ambulances carrying the wounded to hospitals. "The sun was just sinking behind the desolate and deserted hills of Virginia," Arnold recalled. "The flags from the forts, hospitals, and camps drooped sadly. . . . The haze of evening was gathering over the landscape, and when I met the President his attitude and expression spoke the deepest sadness. He paused as we met, and pointing his hand towards the line of wounded men, he said, 'Look yonder at those poor fellows. I cannot bear it. This suffering, this loss of life is dreadful.'" Arnold responded that victory would eventually come. "Yes, victory will come," Lincoln replied. "But it comes slowly."

Its slowness drove increasing numbers of Americans to look away from Lincoln for leadership. "The people are wild for peace," Thurlow Weed observed in August. Weed, a charter member of New York's Republican party and a figure essential to Lincoln's 1860 election, had visited Lincoln to convey the opinion that the president's reelection was "an impossibility." Weed told William Seward that defeat for the president and for the party was unavoidable. "Nobody here doubts it, nor do I see anybody from other states who authorizes the slightest hope of success."

Lincoln understood the odds against him. He asked New York's Schuyler Hamilton to stump for the administration, but Hamilton replied, "No, sir. As things stand at present I don't know what in the name of God I could say, as an honest man, that would help you. Unless you clean these men away who surround you and do something with your army, you will be beaten overwhelmingly."

Lincoln responded that Hamilton's words were harsh but not unwarranted. "You think I don't know I am going to be beaten," he said. "*But I do*, and unless some great change takes place, *badly beaten.*"

Unable to foresee the requisite change, Lincoln prepared for defeat. In late August he drafted a memorandum unlike anything composed by a president before him or after. "This morning, as for some days past, it seems exceedingly probable that this Administration will not be reelected," he wrote. "Then it will be my duty to so cooperate with the President elect as to save the Union between the election and the inauguration, as he will have secured his election on such ground that he cannot possibly save it afterwards."

Lincoln folded and sealed this memo and took it to a meeting of his cabinet. He had the secretaries sign the back, without telling them what it said. He later explained that he intended, in the event of McClellan's election, to approach the general personally. "I would say, 'General, the election has demonstrated that you are stronger, have more influence with the American people than I. Now let us together, you with your influence and I with all the executive power of the Government, try to save the country. You raise as many troops as you possibly can for this final trial, and I will devote all my energies to assisting and finishing the war.'"

William Seward answered, on hearing the later explanation, that McClellan would have responded as he always did: by saying yes but doing nothing.

"At least I should have done my duty and have stood clear before my own conscience," Lincoln replied.

"IT IS ENOUGH TO MAKE THE WHOLE WORLD START AT THE AWFUL amount of death and destruction that now stalks abroad," William Sherman had written his wife, Ellen, in June 1864. "Daily for the last two months has the work progressed and I see no signs of a remission till one or both or all the armies are destroyed. . . . I begin to regard the death and mangling of a couple thousand men as a small affair, a kind of morning dash—and it may be well that we become so hardened."

Sherman was speaking of Grant's grim work in Virginia but also of his own in Georgia. At the same time that Grant crossed the Rapidan toward Richmond, Sherman moved south from Chattanooga toward Atlanta. He traveled light, leaving behind inessentials and hoping to live off the land to the extent he could. His staff had acquired the 1860 federal census tables and data derived by Georgia's prewar tax office, which showed where the best farms and most prosperous villages were located. He didn't abandon the railroad, relying on the line from Chattanooga for ammunition and other vitals that didn't spring from the ground, but his men ranged far out from the road in their search for food and forage.

"Dalton will be our first point, Kingston next, then Allatoona and then Atlanta," Sherman explained to Ellen. "Thomas is my centre and has about 45,000 men; McPherson my right, 25,000; and Schofield my left, 15,000—in all 85,000." His destination was Atlanta, but his objective was Joe Johnston's army. If Johnston would stand, they would settle the issue at once; if Johnston retreated, Sherman would follow.

Johnston chose to do a bit of both. With fewer men than Sherman, he couldn't afford to fight in the open, so he prepared defensive positions and invited attack. Sherman accepted, and a series of small battles ensued, in each of which Johnston fought awhile and then fell back. Engagements at Resaca, Dallas and Kennesaw Mountain cost Sherman two to three thousand casualties each but left the overall balance between his and Johnston's forces unchanged.

Sherman wished he could push the campaign harder but couldn't see how to do so. "I cannot leave the railroad to swing on Johnston's flank or rear without giving him the railroad, which I cannot do without having a good supply on hand," he told Ellen. Nor could he be careless with his men. "At this distance from home we cannot afford the losses of such terrible assaults as Grant has made." The landscape, besides, favored the defenders. "All of Georgia, except the cleared bottoms, is densely wooded, with few roads. And at any point an enterprising enemy can, in a few hours with axes and spades, make across our path formidable works, whilst his sharpshooters, spies, and scouts, in the guise of peaceable farmers, can hang around us and kill our wagon-men, messengers, and couriers. It is a big Indian war." Yet Sherman was satisfied so far. "I have won four strong positions, advanced a hundred miles, and am in possession of a large wheat-growing region and all the iron mines and works of Georgia."

In early July, Johnston retreated to the Chattahoochee, the last stream before Atlanta. Sherman readied what he hoped would be the final blow. "I propose to study the crossings of the Chattahoochee, and when all is ready to move quick," he wrote Halleck, for Grant's eyes. "As a beginning I keep the wagons and troops well back from the river and display to the enemy only the picket line, with a few batteries along at random." Timing would depend on the weather. "The waters are turbid and swollen by the late rains, but if the present hot weather lasts the water will run down very fast." Sherman's engineers had pontoons ready for bridges. He expected resistance at the river and even more in Atlanta if he let Johnston fight from behind his fortifications. This he intended not to do. "Instead of attacking Atlanta direct, or any of its forts, I propose to make a circuit, destroying all its railroads." Johnston would have to come out and fight or surrender the isolated city.

Johnston did neither. He fell back from the Chattahoochee, burning his bridges as he went. But before he took his next step, he was fired. Jefferson Davis concluded that endless retreat would never win the war, and he replaced Johnston with John Bell Hood. Sherman, surprised, sought information about the new man. "I immediately inquired of General Schofield, who was his classmate at West Point, about Hood, as to his general character, etc., and learned that he was bold even to rashness, and courageous in the extreme."

Sherman took this as a good sign, for it might lead to the battle that would decide the war in the western theater. In the event, Hood gave him all he wanted. He came out of the city and struck Sherman's lines furiously. The attack caught Sherman off guard and the Confederates got the better of the early fighting. But Sherman's advantage in numbers and experience eventually told and Hood had to withdraw, leaving a large part of his army on the field or in Union hands.

One Union casualty cost Sherman dearly. James McPherson had become to Sherman what Sherman was to Grant: a close friend and invaluable lieutenant. Sherman remembered the last time he saw McPherson alive. Sudden artillery fire from an unexpected direction had caused the two officers to exchange puzzled looks. "McPherson was then in his prime (about thirty-four years old), over six feet high, and a very handsome man in every way, was universally liked, and had many noble qualities," Sherman wrote. "He had on his boots outside his pantaloons, gauntlets on his hands, had on his major-general's uniform, and wore a sword-belt but no sword. He hastily gathered his papers (save one, which I now possess) into a pocket-book, put it in his breast-pocket, and jumped on his horse, saying he would hurry down his line and send me back word what these sounds meant."

A short while later one of McPherson's aides galloped breathlessly back, to report his superior either killed or taken prisoner. They had been riding behind the Union lines when McPherson entered a wood and got separated from the aide. His horse emerged shortly, wounded and without its rider.

"Poor Mac, he was killed dead instantly," Sherman told Ellen after the details became known. McPherson's death revealed the essential caprice of war. "He was not out of his place or exposing himself more than I and every General does daily. He was to the rear of his line, riding by a road he had passed twice that morning. The thing was an accident that resulted from the blind character of the country we are in. Dense woods fill all the ravines and hollows, and what little cleared ground there is is on the ridge levels, or the alluvion of creek bottoms. The hills are all chestnut ridges with quartz and granite boulders and gravel. You can't find a hundred acres of level, clear ground between here and Chattanooga, and not a day passes but what every general officer may be shot as McPherson was." Sherman understood his own reputation in the South, and he recognized that for every bullet with McPherson's name on it there were several with his. "I know the country swarms with thousands who would shoot me and thank their God they had slain a monster."

There was nothing to do except press on. "We have Atlanta close aboard, as the sailors say," he told Ellen. "But it is a hard nut to handle. These fellows fight like devils and Indians combined, and it calls for all my cunning and strength. Instead of attacking the forts, which are really unassailable, I must gradually destroy the roads which make Atlanta a place worth having. This I have partially done, two out of three are broken and we are now maneuvering for the third."

The campaign became a siege. "Atlanta is on high ground and the woods extend up to the forts which look strong and circle the whole town," Sherman observed during the first week in August. "Most of the people are gone—it is now simply a big fort." The static nature of the contest made him more irritable than usual. He fretted that some of his soldiers would leave at the expiration of their terms of service and not be replaced. "I have no faith in the people of the North. They ever lose their interest when they should act." The regular army was too good for the nation it defended. "I sometimes think our people do not deserve to succeed in war; they are so apathetic." He refought old battles, telling his father-in-law how he had resolved a conflict in Nashville regarding civilian-military priorities. Merchants were crying for space on the trains that served the city, but he forbade anything that didn't advance the war effort. "It was the Gordian knot, and I cut it. People may starve, and go without, but an army cannot and do its work. A howl was raised, but the President and Secretary of War backed me, and now all recognize the wisdom and humanity of the thing."

At length he severed Atlanta's final link to the outside world. "That night I was so restless and impatient that I could not sleep," he remembered. "About midnight there arose toward Atlanta sounds of shells exploding, and other sound like that of musketry. I walked to the house of a farmer close by my bivouac, called him out to listen to the reverberations which came from the direction of Atlanta (twenty miles to the north of us), and inquired of him if he had resided there long. He said he had, and that these sounds were just like those of a battle."

But the battle had already been fought. What Sherman and the farmer were hearing was Hood exploding the ordnance in Atlanta as he abandoned the city.

"Atlanta is ours, and fairly won," Sherman telegraphed Washington on September 3. Lincoln proclaimed the nation's thanks to Sherman and his men. "The marches, battles, sieges, and other military operations that have signalized this campaign must render it famous in the annals of war," the president said.

Grant got the news via Washington. He congratulated Sherman for a mission well accomplished and said he had arranged a practical demonstration of thanks. "In honor of your great victory I have ordered a salute to be fired with shotted guns from every battery bearing upon the enemy."

Even as he congratulated Sherman, Grant urged him to fight all the harder. "As soon as your men are properly rested and preparations can be made, it is desirable that another campaign should be commenced," he said. "We want to keep the enemy continually pressed to the end of the war. If we give him no peace whilst the war lasts, the end cannot be distant."

CAVALRY COMMANDERS WERE THE POPULAR IDOLS OF THE CIVIL
War. They were typically young, invariably dashing, necessarily brilliant on horseback, temperamentally headstrong, famously brave and
utterly irresistible to the smitten journalists who chronicled their
exploits for rapt readers. J. E. B. Stuart captured the imagination of
every Southerner and more than a few Northerners as he rode circles,
literally, around the Union army, galloping across hundreds of miles
of forest and farm, leaping and swimming creeks and rivers, seizing
enemy soldiers, horses and supplies and sowing fright and confusion far
behind Union lines. Lee called Stuart the "eyes of the army" and relied
on him for intelligence regarding the disposition and movements of
Union forces. A Stuart slip at Gettysburg, where he let the thrill of the
ride distract him from his informational mission, cost the Confederates
but didn't alienate Lee, who saw much of his younger self in Stuart and
continued to indulge the junior officer's audacity.

Stuart's exploits evoked envy and then emulation among the Union
horse soldiers. Phil Sheridan complained to George Meade after the
battle of the Wilderness that he hadn't been allowed to do his job. He
insisted—in language "highly spiced and conspicuously italicized with
expletives," Horace Porter remembered—that if he could concentrate his
forces and strike directly at Stuart, he would whip the Confederate cavalryman. Meade told Grant of the exchange. "Did Sheridan say that?"
Grant responded. "Well, he generally knows what he is talking about.
Let him start right out and do it."

Sheridan detached his cavalry from the main body of the Army of
the Potomac and skirted Lee's left en route to Richmond. Stuart raced

to cut him off. The battle Sheridan sought took place at Yellow Tavern, just north of the Confederate capital, and in a sharp clash he beat Stuart, who died of wounds suffered in the engagement. Sheridan might have entered Richmond, but, lacking the heft to hold the city, he veered off to disrupt Lee's supply lines. He destroyed many miles of railroad and telegraph, liberated a large group of Union prisoners and killed or captured hundreds of Confederates.

His achievements inspired Grant to give him greater authority in a major campaign in the Shenandoah Valley. "I want Sheridan put in command of all the troops in the field"—infantry and artillery, as well as cavalry—"with instructions to put himself south of the enemy and follow him to the death," Grant wrote Halleck in early August 1864. "Wherever the enemy goes let our troops go also."

Lincoln liked Grant's plan. "This, I think, is exactly right," the president said. But he warned Grant that others in Washington would resist it. "It will neither be done nor attempted unless you watch it every day and hour and force it."

Halleck and Stanton proved Lincoln right, asserting that Sheridan was too young—at thirty-three—for command of an entire army. But Grant insisted, and he sent Sheridan off to the Shenandoah. Sheridan's first objective was to keep Jubal Early away from Washington; his broader mission was to deny Lee the resources of the valley, including its manpower. "Carry off the crops, animals, negroes, and all men under fifty years of age capable of bearing arms," Grant ordered. "All male citizens under fifty can fairly be held as prisoners of war and not as citizen prisoners. If not already soldiers, they will be made so the moment the rebel army gets hold of them." Grant particularly wanted to neutralize the partisan forces mobilized by John Mosby. "The families of most of Mosby's men are known and can be collected," he told Sheridan. "They should be taken and kept at Fort McHenry or some secure place as hostages for good conduct of Mosby and his men. When any of them are caught with nothing to designate what they are, hang them without trial." In a subsequent dispatch Grant reiterated his basic message and described his desired outcome: "Do all the damage to railroads and crops you can. Carry off stock of all descriptions and negroes, so as to prevent further planting. If the war is to last another year we want the Shenandoah Valley to remain a barren waste."

Sheridan showed himself to be the general for the job. "I endorsed the program in all its parts," he recalled afterward, "for the stores of meat and grain that the valley provided, and the men it furnished for Lee's depleted regiments, were the strongest auxiliaries he possessed in the whole insurgent section. In war a territory like this is a factor of great importance, and whichever adversary controls it permanently reaps all the advantages of its prosperity." Sheridan articulated the philosophy of modern war that was coming to summarize much of the Union approach. "I do not hold war to mean simply that lines of men shall engage each other in battle, and material interests be ignored. This is but a duel, in which one combatant seeks the other's life; war means much more, and is far worse than this. Those who rest at home in peace and plenty see but little of the horrors attending such a duel, and even grow indifferent to them as the struggle goes on, contenting themselves with encouraging all who are able-bodied to enlist in the cause, to fill up the shattered ranks as death thins them. It is another matter, however, when deprivation and suffering are brought to their own doors. Then the case appears much graver, for the loss of property weighs heavily with the most of mankind—heavier, often, than the sacrifices made on the field of battle. Death is popularly considered the maximum of punishment in war, but it is not; reduction to poverty brings prayers for peace more surely and more quickly than does the destruction of human life."

Sheridan initially heard prayers of another sort. Grant's failure to produce a victory over Lee or prevent the Confederates from reaching the suburbs of Washington had put the Republicans in a partisan panic. Their hopes came to rest, for the moment, on Sheridan. "Mr. Stanton kept reminding me that positive success was necessary to counteract the political dissatisfaction existing in some of the Northern states," Sheridan recounted.

Sheridan first answered the Republican prayers at Winchester on September 19. After weeks of skirmishing he got Early to stand and fight, and the Union general put his greater numbers to good effect. He lost more than Early did, but he could afford to, and he forced the Confederate commander to withdraw. "I have just received the news of your great victory and ordered each of the armies here to fire a salute of one hundred guns in honor of it," Grant telegraphed. He urged Sheridan to follow up at once. "If practicable push your success and make all you can of it."

Sheridan did push and a month later delivered the decisive blow. His signal officers had broken the Confederate flagging code and they deciphered a message sent from James Longstreet to Early: "Be ready

to move as soon as my forces join you, and we will crush Sheridan."
Sheridan wasn't sure the message wasn't deliberate disinformation, but
he didn't feel he could ignore it, and consequently when Halleck summoned him to Washington for consultation he initially refused. But Halleck assured him Longstreet couldn't link up with Early imminently and
insisted that he come ahead. Sheridan went to Washington, consulted
quickly and headed back to the valley. He arrived at Winchester on his
return on the night of October 18, intending to reach his command at
Cedar Creek the next day.

At six o'clock the next morning the picket officer awoke him and
said he heard artillery fire from the direction of Cedar Creek. Sheridan asked if the fire was continuous or intermittent. The officer said it
sounded intermittent, leading Sheridan to conclude that his own artillery was simply feeling out the enemy. He lay back in bed but couldn't
sleep. A short while later the picket officer said the firing was louder
and still intermittent. Sheridan grew a bit more worried and ate a hasty
breakfast. He mounted his horse and with a cavalry escort rode through
the streets of Winchester. "I noticed that there were many women at the
windows and doors of the houses who kept shaking their skirts at us and
who were otherwise markedly insolent in their demeanor," he recalled.
"But supposing this conduct to be instigated by their well-known and
perhaps natural prejudices, I ascribed to it no unusual significance." By
the time he reached the edge of town the distant artillery rumbled a constant thunder, and he concluded that a regular battle had begun. "I now
felt confident that the women along the street had received intelligence
from the battlefield by the 'grape-vine telegraph' and were in raptures
over some good news while I as yet was utterly ignorant of the actual
situation."

Sheridan and his escort raced toward the battle sounds. Several miles
from Cedar Creek they crested a low hill. "There burst upon our view
the appalling spectacle of a panic-stricken army—hundreds of slightly
wounded men, throngs of others unhurt but utterly demoralized, and
baggage wagons by the score, all pressing to the rear in hopeless confusion, telling only too plainly that a disaster had occurred at the front."
Sheridan stopped some of the fugitives and demanded to know what
was happening. "They assured me that the army was broken up, in full
retreat, and that all was lost—all this with a manner true to that peculiar
indifference that takes possession of panic-stricken men."

Sheridan ordered part of his escort to remain behind and try to halt the headlong retreat. He took two aides and the rest of his escort and pushed toward the front. At first the going was difficult, for the rearward tide clogged the road. But as the men recognized their commander, first a few and then more stopped, reconsidered their retreat and reversed their steps, following him toward the front. Officers galloped beside the road spreading the word that Sheridan was back. More and more of the stragglers shouldered the muskets they had been trailing and turned again toward the enemy. "I already knew that even in the ordinary condition of mind enthusiasm is a potent element with soldiers," Sheridan remarked, "but what I saw that day convinced me that if it can be excited from a state of despondency its power is almost irresistible."

Among those happiest to see Sheridan was George Armstrong Custer, who had rocketed from West Point cadet at the start of the war to commander of a cavalry brigade and then a division. Custer caught Sheridan in a bear hug of relief before tearing off to lead his men against the enemy.

Sheridan's appearance at the front transformed the battle. His troops repulsed the Confederate attack and launched a counterattack. The dazed rebels surrendered by the hundreds; those who avoided surrender fled the field as quickly as they could.

Grant again congratulated Sheridan on a brilliant victory, which definitively deprived the Confederacy of the Shenandoah Valley. To Edwin Stanton he boasted of his protégé: "Turning what bid fair to be a disaster into glorious triumph stamps Sheridan what I have always thought him, one of the ablest of generals."

45

Sherman's capture of Atlanta and Sheridan's sweep of the Shenandoah Valley brought relief and joy to Lincoln and the Republicans. Where the summer's defeatism had favored the Democrats, the autumn's resurgence revived the Republicans. Lincoln's reelection suddenly seemed not merely possible but likely.

And Grant appeared poised to be his successor. The guiding genius of the Union victories, the common man become defender of democracy, Grant was the obvious heir to George Washington and Andrew Jackson in the lineage of hero-presidents. Reporters flocked to his camp to describe the great man to their readers and to solicit his views on the issues before the public. Candidates for office vied for his endorsement.

Grant disliked politics as much as ever, but more than ever he appreciated that tending to politics was the cost of defending the Union. Elihu Washburne wrote him asking for a statement that would benefit the Republicans. Washburne had sponsored Grant so well and long in Congress that Grant couldn't refuse his request, but he probably would have answered anyway, for he believed that a Republican victory over the Democrats was vital to a republican victory over the disunionists.

He chose his words carefully. "All we want now to insure an early restoration of the Union is a determined unity of sentiment North," Grant said. "The rebels have now in their ranks their last man. The little boys and old men are guarding prisoners, guarding railroad bridges and forming a good part of their garrisons for entrenched positions. A man lost by them cannot be replaced. They have robbed the cradle and the grave equally to get their present force. Besides what they lose in frequent skirmishes and battles they are now losing from desertions and other causes at least one regiment per day. With this drain upon them the end is visible if we will but be true to ourselves. Their only hope now is a divided North." Grant detected the influence of the approaching election upon Lee's strategy, which had reduced to playing for time. "The enemy are exceedingly anxious to hold out until after the Presidential election. . . . They hope the election of a peace candidate." Northern peace advocates, however sincere, were gravely mistaken that acquiescence in separation could result in an end of hostilities. "The South would demand the restoration of slaves already freed. They would demand indemnity for losses sustained, and they would demand a treaty which would make the North slave hunters for the South. . . . It would be but the beginning of war."

Grant's words were widely reproduced and disseminated. Lincoln's advisers, notably Washburne, urged the president to use various of Grant's other letters to confirm the case for returning the administration to office. Washburne asked for Grant's permission and received it. "I have no objection to the President using anything I have ever written to him as he sees fit," Grant said. Yet as a tactical matter he wondered how effective such letters or any rebuttals to the president's critics would be. "For him to attempt to answer all the charges the opposition will bring against him will be like setting a maiden to work to prove her chastity."

Grant felt obliged to weigh in, albeit confidentially, on one of the most contentious political issues facing the administration. While no subsequent single protest against the draft had matched the New York riots of 1863, the administration worried that resistance to the draft would intensify as the election approached. Some of Lincoln's advisers urged the president to suspend the draft until after the balloting and rely on voluntary enlistments, which for obvious reasons were much less unpopular. Grant understood that this was a question that properly belonged to civilian officials, but he also realized that it would influence his ability to carry on the fight against Lee. "I hope it is not the intention to postpone the draft to allow time to fill up with recruiting," he wrote Edwin Stanton in September. "The men we have been getting in that way are nearly all deserters, and out of five reported north as having enlisted, we do not get more than one effective soldier."

Another matter had philosophical/conduct implications for the future of American democracy. The administration and the Republicans wanted to ensure that soldiers voted, as they assumed that most of those who had taken up arms in the Union cause would wish to see their efforts carried to a successful conclusion. Some in the administration desired to furlough troops to let them return home to vote, especially in states where the outcome might be close. "The first, third, and fourth regiments of Delaware Volunteers are now near Petersburg, two of them numbering about one hundred each, one numbering about four hundred," Stanton informed Grant. "The vote of the State will depend on them. If it be possible, please give them leave of absence to go home for the election."

Grant acquiesced in this case and in others where the men could get home and back quickly. But he preferred a kind of absentee balloting whereby special election officials would visit the camps and collect the troops' ballots. He appreciated the objections some people might have to this mingling of the military and civilian realms. "The exercise of the right of suffrage by the officers and soldiers of armies in the field is a novel thing," he wrote Stanton. "It has, I believe, generally been considered dangerous to constitutional liberty and subversive of military discipline." But novel circumstances required novel solutions. "A very large proportion of legal voters of the United States are now either under arms in the field, or in hospitals, or otherwise engaged in the military service of the United States." The traditional concern about the militarization of politics didn't apply now. "Most of these men are not regular soldiers in the strict sense of that term; still less are they mercenaries who give their services to the Government simply for its pay, having little understanding of political questions and feeling little or no interest in them. On the contrary, they are American citizens, having still their homes and social and political ties, binding them to the States and districts from which they come and to which they expect to return." They had demonstrated their devotion to the Constitution by defending it against its enemies. "In performing this sacred duty, they should not be deprived of a most precious privilege. They have as much right to demand that their votes shall be counted, in the choice of their rulers, as those citizens who remain at home. Nay, more, for they have sacrificed more for their country."

Still another issue was essentially military but had profound political ramifications for the future. Grant had tried to keep out of matters relating to race, leaving emancipation and civil rights for African Americans to the president, Congress, the states and perhaps the courts. Yet he found himself championing black equality at least as it pertained to his soldiers. Lee and the Confederate government refused to grant prisoner-of-war status to captured Union soldiers who had been Southern slaves, but instead reenslaved them. Grant retaliated by halting prisoner exchanges. "The Government is bound to secure to all persons received into her Armies the rights due to soldiers," Grant wrote Lee. "This being denied by you in the persons of such men as have escaped from Southern masters induces me to decline making the exchanges you ask." He added a further sanction: putting Confederate prisoners to work in circumstances similar to those forced upon the captured black Union troops. "I shall always regret the necessity of retaliating for wrongs done our soldiers, but regard it my duty to protect all persons received into the Army of the United States, regardless of color."

Grant was happy when the political season ended, and even happier that it resulted in Lincoln's reelection. The Union army, with most soldiers voting by Grant's absentee method, returned heavy majorities for Lincoln. The rest of the voting country—which was to say those states still or newly in the Union (Kansas and Nevada emerged from territorial status to statehood in 1861 and 1864, respectively; Unionist West Virginia was carved from Virginia in 1863)—favored Lincoln by a smaller but still decisive margin. George McClellan carried Kentucky, Delaware and New Jersey, but Lincoln won the other twenty-two states, garnering 55 percent of the popular vote and 212 electors to McClellan's 45 percent and 21 electors.

"Congratulate the President for me," Grant wrote Stanton. Preelection rumors had raised concern that Southern sympathizers would disrupt the balloting; the event showed the rumors false. Grant took this as a vote in favor of democracy itself. "The election having passed off quietly, no bloodshed or riot throughout the land, is a victory worth more to the country than a battle won," he told Stanton.

46

SHORTLY AFTER THE FALL OF ATLANTA, JEFFERSON DAVIS HAD TRAV-
eled to Georgia to buck up the people in the rest of the state. "It would
have gladdened my heart to have met you in prosperity instead of adversity," the Confederate president said. "But friends are drawn together
in adversity." He couldn't deny that Confederate arms had been dealt a
blow, but the spirit of the South remained strong. "Our cause is not lost.
Sherman cannot keep up his long line of communication, and retreat
sooner or later he must. And when that day comes, the fate that befell
the army of the French empire on its retreat from Moscow will be reen-
acted. Our cavalry and our people will harass and destroy his army as
did the Cossacks that of Napoleon, and the Yankee general, like him,
will escape with only a body guard."

Sherman read the speech and sneered. "Davis seemed to be perfectly
upset by the fall of Atlanta, and to have lost all sense and reason," he
remarked. But he couldn't discount the possibility that a long retreat from
Atlanta, through country hostile in spirit and difficult of terrain, might
indeed exact a serious toll on his army. He weighed the alternatives. Suppose the Union navy established a foothold on the Atlantic coast south-
east of Atlanta, perhaps at Savannah. "It once in our possession, and the
river open to us," he wrote Grant on September 20, "I would not hesitate
to cross the State of Georgia with 60,000 men, hauling some stores and
depending on the country for the balance. Where a million of people
live, *my* Army won't starve, but as you know in a country like Georgia,
with few roads and innumerable streams, an inferior force could so delay
an army and harass it that it would not be a formidable object." Yet if
the Confederates realized Sherman had supplies waiting on the coast,

they would have to come out and fight or let the state be ravaged. Either result, Sherman told Grant, would hasten the end of the war. "They may stand the fall of Richmond, but not of all Georgia. . . . If you can whip Lee, and I can march to the Atlantic, I think Uncle Abe will give us a twenty days leave of absence to see the young folks."

Grant had to think this over. Sherman's suggestion entailed unusual risks, and with the election still in the balance Grant didn't want to take unnecessary chances. He told Sherman to concentrate on defending the lines to his rear. "It will be better to drive Forrest from Middle Tennessee as a first step, and do anything else that you may feel your force sufficient for," he said. "When a movement is made on any part of the sea coast I will advise you."

Sherman did as ordered. "I take it for granted that Forrest will cut our road, but think we can prevent him from making a serious lodgment," he wrote Halleck. His troops kept Forrest off long stretches of the line and his engineers, working around the clock, repaired breaches in the road as fast as the Confederates effected them. "It was by such acts of extraordinary energy that we discouraged our adversaries," Sherman reflected of the repair crews, "for the rebel soldiers felt that it was a waste of labor for them to march hurriedly, on wide circuits, day and night, to burn a bridge and tear up a mile or so of track, when they knew we could lay it back so quickly." The rebels seemed to think Sherman had duplicates of rails, bridges, culverts and everything else needed to maintain a railroad. Sherman told a story he heard of a company of Confederates expressing pleasure that they had blown up a tunnel, which would surely require months to fix. "Oh, hell," a less hopeful member of the group reflected. "Don't you know that old Sherman carries a duplicate tunnel along?"

But it was Sherman who ultimately grew discouraged. The rebels roamed through friendly territory and attacked at will. "It will be a physical impossibility to protect the roads now that Hood, Forrest and Wheeler, and the whole batch of devils, are turned loose without home or habitation," Sherman wrote Grant in October. It was time to regain the offensive. "I propose we break up the railroad from Chattanooga and strike out with wagons for Milledgeville, Millen, and Savannah. Until we can repopulate Georgia, it is useless to occupy it, but the utter destruction of its roads, houses and people will cripple their military resources. By attempting to hold the roads we will lose 1,000 men monthly, and will gain no result. I can make the march, and make Georgia howl."

Grant still wasn't convinced. Sherman had indicated he didn't worry about encountering the Confederate army of John Bell Hood, but Grant saw other dangers. "I do not believe you would meet Hood's army, but would be bushwhacked by all the old men, little boys and such railroad guards as are still left at home," he said. And he thought Sherman *should* encounter Hood. "Hood would probably strike for Nashville, thinking by going north he could inflict greater damage upon us than we could upon the enemy by going south. If there is any way of getting at Hood's army, I would prefer that." Yet Grant had faith in Sherman. "I must trust to your own judgment."

Sherman continued to press his case for a march to the sea. "We cannot now remain on the defensive," he told Grant. Hood had too many advantages. "With 25,000 infantry and the bold cavalry he has, he can constantly break my road. I would infinitely prefer to make a wreck of the road and of the country from Chattanooga to Atlanta, including the latter city, send back all my wounded and worthless, and with my effective army move through Georgia, smashing things to the sea. Hood may turn into Tennessee and Kentucky, but I believe he will be forced to follow me. Instead of being on the defensive, I would be on the offensive. Instead of my guessing at what he means to do, he will have to guess at my plans. The difference in war is full 25 per cent. I can make Savannah, Charleston, or the mouth of the Chattahoochee. Answer quick, as I know we will not have the telegraph long."

Grant was impressed by Sherman's conviction, and with the favorable outcome of the election now in sight, he let himself be persuaded. "If you are satisfied the trip to the seacoast can be made, holding the line of the Tennessee firmly," he telegraphed Sherman, "you may make it, destroying all the railroad south of Dalton or Chattanooga, as you think best."

Sherman prepared his army for the march. "I am now perfecting arrangements to put into Tennessee a force able to hold the line of the Tennessee whilst I break up the railroad in front of Dalton, including the city of Atlanta, and push into Georgia, and break up all its railroads and depots, capture its horses and negroes, make desolation everywhere, destroy the factories at Macon, Milledgeville and Augusta, and bring up with 60,000 men on the sea shore about Savannah or Charleston," he wrote Grant. "I will leave General Thomas to command all my divisions behind me, and take with me only the best fighting material." To his quartermaster in Atlanta, Sherman gave a deadline. "On the 1st of

November I want nothing but what is necessary to war," he said. "Send all trash to the rear at once and have on hand thirty days' food and but little forage. I propose to abandon Atlanta and the railroad back to Chattanooga, to sally forth to ruin Georgia."

Grant defended Sherman's plan to the Lincoln administration, which remained nervous about such an undertaking. "On mature reflection, I believe Sherman's proposition is the best that can be adopted," he wrote Stanton. "With the long line of railroad in rear of Atlanta, Sherman cannot maintain his position. If he cuts loose, destroying the road from Chattanooga forward, he leaves a wide and destitute country for the rebels to pass over before reaching territory now held by us." Grant was confident Thomas in Tennessee could handle Hood if the Confederate general went north. And if he pursued Sherman, Sherman could look out for himself. "Such an army as Sherman has (and with such a commander) is hard to corner or capture."

Grant wrote Sherman a send-off message: "Great good fortune attend you. . . . I believe you will be eminently successful."

"*O*h, God, the time of trial has come!" Dolly Sumner Lunt recorded in her diary two weeks later. Dolly Lunt had been born in Maine and was kin to Charles Sumner, the abolitionist senator. She had followed her married sister to Georgia, where she met Thomas Burge, who wooed her, won her and took her home to his plantation near Covington. They lived in such happiness as wealth and slaves could ensure until Burge died amid the sectional crisis of the late 1850s. His widow and young daughter were left to face the tribulations of the Civil War and, in the autumn of 1864, the wrath of William Sherman.

Frightful tidings of Sherman's army preceded it. "Have been uneasy all day," Dolly Lunt wrote in her diary for November 17. "At night some of the neighbors who had been to town called. They said it was a large force moving very slowly. What shall I do? Where go?" In fact there was nowhere to go and nothing to do but wait and watch. "Slept very little last night," she wrote the next day. "Went out doors several times and could see large fires like burning buildings. Am I not in the hands of a merciful God who has promised to take care of the widow and orphan?" She concealed what she could: a barrel of salt, some pieces of meat. She packed herself and her daughter as though for a trip. "I fear that we shall be homeless."

On November 19 the bluecoats arrived. "I walked to the gate. There they came filing up." She hurried back to the house to warn the servants to hide, as the Yankees would carry them off. But the invaders were too swift. "Like demons they rush in! My yards are full. To my smoke-house, my dairy, pantry, kitchen, and cellar, like famished wolves they come, breaking locks and whatever is in their way. The thousand pounds of meat in my smoke-house is gone in a twinkling, my flour, my meat, my lard, butter, eggs. . . . Wine jars and jugs are all gone. My eighteen fat turkeys, my hens, chickens, and fowls, my young pigs are shot down in my yard and hunted as if they were rebels themselves." She appealed to the officer in charge. He shrugged. "I cannot help you, Madam," he said. "It is orders."

The raiders were relentless. They drove off her horses. "There they go!" she cried. They drove off other livestock. "There go my mules, my sheep!" They drove off her servants. "My boys! Alas!" She reflected later: "Little did I think while trying to save my house from plunder and fire that they were forcing my boys from home at the point of a bayonet." One of the young slaves crawled under the floor. "A lame boy he was, but they pulled him out, placed him on a horse, and drove him off." Another was frightened nearly to death. "Jack came crying to me, the big tears coursing down his cheeks, saying they were making him go. I said, 'Stay in my room.' But a man followed him in, cursing him and threatening to shoot him if he did not go; so poor Jack had to yield." The soldiers left the slave boys' parents but took the families' meager possessions. "Their cabins are rifled of every valuable, the soldiers swearing that their Sunday clothes were the white people's, and that they never had money to get such things as they had."

An officer identified himself as Captain Webber from Illinois and said he knew Dolly Lunt's brother Orrington, an attorney in Chicago. "At that name I could not restrain my feelings, but, bursting into tears, implored him to see my brother and let him know my destitution," she remembered. "I saw nothing before me but starvation. He promised to do this, and comforted me with the assurance that my dwelling-house would not be burned, though my out-buildings might."

The author of Georgia's agony appeared and supervised additional destruction. "Sherman himself and a greater portion of his army passed my house that day," she said. "All day, as the sad moments rolled on, were they passing not only in front of my house, but from behind; they tore down my garden palings, made a road through my back-yard and lot field, driving their stock and riding through, tearing down my fences and desolating my home—wantonly doing it when there was no necessity for it. Such a day, if I live to the age of Methuselah, may God spare me from ever seeing again!"

Sherman remembered the Georgia campaign differently. Not long after capturing Atlanta he had ordered the evacuation of the city's inhabitants. The order shocked the townsfolk, who described it as inhumane and petitioned to have it revoked. Sherman refused. "My orders are not designed to meet the humanities of the case, but to prepare for the future struggles in which millions, yea hundreds of millions, of good people outside of Atlanta have a deep interest," he said. "We must have peace not only in Atlanta *but in all America.*" Sherman's petitioners had suggested he didn't appreciate the cruelty of war; they were quite wrong, he said. "You cannot qualify war in harsher terms than I will. War is cruelty, and you cannot refine it; and those who brought war on our country deserve all the curses and maledictions a people can pour out. . . . You might as well appeal against the thunderstorm as against these terrible hardships of war."

Sherman led his own tempest out of Atlanta. The first evening he camped near Lithonia. "Stone Mountain, a mass of granite, was in plain view, cut out in clear outline against the blue sky," he recounted. "The whole horizon was lurid with the bonfires of rail-ties, and groups of men all night were carrying the heated rails to the nearest trees, and bending them around the trunks. . . . I attached much importance to this destruction of the railroad, gave it my own personal attention, and made reiterated orders to others on the subject."

Sherman didn't think the destruction egregious, and he noted that not everyone feared his approach. "The negroes were simply frantic with joy," he said of his visit to Covington, where Dolly Lunt lived. "Wherever they heard my name, they clustered about my horse, shouted, and prayed in their peculiar style, which had a natural eloquence that would have moved a stone. I have witnessed hundreds, if not thousands, of such scenes, and can now see a poor girl, in the very ecstasy of the Methodist 'shout,' hugging the banner of one of the regiments and jumping up to the 'feet of Jesus.'" That night Sherman camped outside Covington. "I walked up to a plantation-house close by, where were assembled many negroes, among them an old, gray-haired man, of as fine a head as I ever saw." Sherman asked him if he knew what the war was about and how it progressed. "He said he did; that he had been looking for the 'angel of the Lord' ever since he was knee-high, and though we professed to be fighting for the Union, he supposed that slavery was the cause, and that our success was to be his freedom."

Sherman instructed his troops to be self-sufficient. "The army will forage liberally on the country during the march," he declared at the outset. The foraging Dolly Lunt experienced was part of a process Sherman's army soon perfected. Brigade commanders detailed companies of foragers who left their camps before dawn in the general direction of that day's march. They set out afoot but acquired wagons or carriages from the farms and plantations they visited. "Often I would pass these foraging parties at the roadside, waiting for their wagons to come up, and was amused at their strange collections—mules, horses, even cattle, packed with old saddles and loaded with hams, bacon, bags of corn meal, and poultry of every character and description," Sherman recalled. "Although this foraging was attended with great danger and hard work"—even widows, albeit not Dolly Lunt, sometimes defended their homes with lethal force—"there seemed to be a charm about it that attracted the soldiers, and it was a privilege to be detailed on such a party. Daily they returned mounted on all sorts of beasts, which were at once taken from them and appropriated to the general use; but the next day they would start out again on foot, only to repeat the experience of the day before." Sherman didn't deny that his foragers—known both pejoratively and affectionately as "bummers"—sometimes exceeded their orders. "No doubt many acts of pillage, robbery, and violence were committed." Civilians were handled roughly and occasionally money, jewelry and other easily concealed items never reached the commissary. "But these acts were exceptional and incidental." In any event they were part of war.

Skirmishes with Confederate forces afforded diversion from what became, for Sherman's army, almost a lark. "The weather was fine, the roads good, and everything seemed to favor us," Sherman wrote of one particularly pleasant stretch. "Never do I recall a more agreeable sensation than the sight of our camps by night, lit up by the fires of fragrant pine-knots. The trains were all in good order, and the men seemed to march their fifteen miles a day as though it were nothing."

———

Birthplace at Point Pleasant, Ohio

Earliest photograph
of Grant *(left)*, with the
army in Louisiana, 1845

Hardscrabble,
the Missouri home Grant
built for his young family

Jesse Grant, his father

Henry W. Halleck, Grant's
ambivalent superior

HARPER'S WEEKLY.

JOURNAL OF CIVILIZATION

VOL. VI.—No. 271.]   NEW YORK, SATURDAY, MARCH 8, 1862.   [SINGLE COPIES SIX CENTS.
$2 50 PER YEAR IN ADVANCE.

Entered according to Act of Congress, in the Year 1862, by Harper & Brothers, in the Clerk's Office of the District Court for the Southern District of New York.

Grant, suddenly famous though barely recognizable,
after the battle of Fort Donelson, 1862

At Chattanooga, 1863

＊＊＊

(Facing page)
At Cold Harbor, 1864

＊＊＊

The siege of Vicksburg,
1863

＊＊＊

Abraham
Lincoln promotes
Grant, 1864

＊＊＊

With John Rawlins *(left)*, his fiercely loyal adjutant

George G. Meade *(left)*, the victor at Gettysburg
and Grant's subordinate in the Virginia campaign; William T. Sherman *(right)*,
Grant's closest friend and most capable lieutenant

Consulting
his generals in
Virginia, 1864
(Grant is the one
bending over the
back of the bench
to see the map)

At City Point, Virginia, 1864

Headquarters
at City Point

Heroically rendered
for popular consumption

Lincoln, showing the strain
of the agonizing conflict

Edwin M. Stanton, the war
secretary who spied on Grant

Robert E. Lee's surrender,
reimagined

Grant for president, 1868

Young Jesse, Julia and
Nellie

❦ ❦

For reelection, 1872

❦ ❦

At Long Branch, New Jersey,
where the Grant family spent
summers, with Jesse and Julia

❦ ❦

The peace policy symbolized: Grant meets with Indian chiefs

⇥ ⇤

Grant in the Southern press *(below)*, after he used the army to safeguard civil rights in Louisiana

⇥ ⇤

MURDER of LOUISIANA SACRIFICED ON THE ALTAR OF RADICALISM

Elder statesman and world traveler

At Mount McGregor, racing death
to finish his memoirs

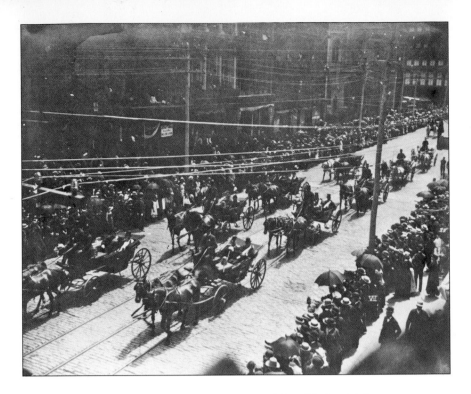

Grant's funeral procession in New York, 1885

Dedication of the tomb, New York, 1897

*F*or a month after Sherman cut loose from Atlanta, Grant heard nothing reliable of his whereabouts. Southern papers sketchily asserted that he was meeting his match or would meet it soon, that his army was surrounded and starving or nearly so. Northern papers summoned self-declared experts on Georgia geography to explain to readers what Sherman's army must be experiencing if it went this way or that. Lincoln, more confident of ultimate victory than before his reelection, nonetheless fretted that a failure by Sherman's army would lengthen the war significantly. Grant promised the president that all would be well. Sherman and his men would come out somewhere on the coast, if not necessarily at Savannah, he said. If the worst happened they could always go back north. Lincoln was calmed and paraphrased Grant to visitors: "Grant says they are safe with such a general, and that if they cannot get out where they want to, they can crawl back by the hole they went in at."

His confidence notwithstanding, Grant welcomed a report that Sherman had arrived at the coast. A copy of the *Richmond Dispatch* that reached Grant's headquarters on December 13 placed Sherman five miles from Savannah. "I congratulate you and the brave officers and men under your command on the successful termination of your brilliant campaign," Grant wrote Sherman after confirming the report and while Sherman invested Savannah. "I never had a doubt of the result. When apprehensions for your safety were expressed by the President, I assured him that with the Army you had, and you in command of it, there was no danger, but you would strike bottom on salt water some place." Grant added, "I would not feel the same security, in fact would not have entrusted the expedition to any other living commander."

Sherman prepared to assault Savannah, but at the last moment the Confederate commander evacuated the city. On December 22 Sherman sent a message that reached Washington on the 24th:

To His Excellency President Lincoln:
I beg to present you as a Christmas gift the city of Savannah, with 150 heavy guns and plenty of ammunition, and also about 25,000 bales of cotton.

GRANT SPENT THE WEEKS OF SHERMAN'S MARCH TIGHTENING THE noose about Lee and Richmond. He ordered George Thomas in Tennessee to attack Hood's Confederate army, which had gone north about the time Sherman went south. Thomas was under Sherman's command, and Grant's orders would have gone through Sherman if Sherman had been within reach by telegraph or courier. But Sherman's plunge beyond his communications compelled Grant to telegraph orders to Thomas himself. And Thomas's slowness to respond required Grant to send the same orders again and again. "If Hood is permitted to remain quietly about Nashville you will lose all the road back to Chattanooga and possibly have to abandon the line of the Tennessee," Grant wrote Thomas on December 2. "Should he attack you it is well, but if he does not you should attack him before he fortifies." Later that day he reiterated: "You will now suffer incalculable injury upon your railroads if Hood is not speedily disposed of; put forth, therefore, every possible exertion to attain this end." Thomas pleaded bad weather and said he required time to augment his forces. Grant told him to stop finding excuses. "Hood should be attacked where he is," he said. "Time strengthens him in all probability as much as it does you." The next day he put the matter more bluntly: "Attack Hood at once."

Still Thomas stalled. Grant worried that Hood would bypass Thomas and continue north to the Ohio River and perhaps beyond. At a moment when the psychological balance had tipped crucially in favor of the North, such a Confederate campaign might be disastrous. "If you delay any longer, the mortifying spectacle will be witnessed of a rebel army moving to the Ohio River," Grant wrote on December 11. "Hood cannot stand even a drawn battle so far from his supplies of ordnance stores. If he retreats and you follow, he must lose his material and much of his army. . . . Delay no longer."

When Thomas *still* refused, Grant determined to fire him. He dispatched John Logan to Nashville to relieve Thomas but told him to halt if word met him en route that Thomas had finally moved against Hood. He shortly wondered if he had done the right thing by sending a subordinate, and he traveled to Washington with the idea of continuing to Nashville himself to settle the matter directly.

At Washington he received the news he had been wanting to hear for weeks. "General Thomas with the forces under his command attacked Hood's army in front of Nashville at 9 o'clock this morning," the December 15 message from the front asserted. "The enemy were driven from the river, from his entrenchments, from the range of hills on which his left rested and forced back upon his right and center, and the center pushed back from one to three miles with the loss of 17 guns and about 1500 prisoners. . . . The whole action today was splendidly successful."

Grant suspended his plans to replace Thomas, yet he let the general know he was being watched. "I was just on my way to Nashville, but receiving a dispatch from Van Duzer"— of Thomas's staff—"detailing your splendid success of today I shall go no further," he wrote. "Push the enemy now and give him no rest until he is entirely destroyed. Your army will cheerfully suffer many privations to break up Hood's army and render it useless for future operations. . . . Much is now expected."

*T*he reduction of Fort Fisher had a similar strangling purpose. The Confederate fortress guarded the mouth of the Cape Fear River and the approach to Wilmington, North Carolina, the last important point of Atlantic access to the Confederacy. The Union naval blockade was supposed to seal the coast, but blockade runners slipped through, bringing supplies that helped keep Lee's army in the field. Grant determined to strengthen the blockade by capturing Fort Fisher. Benjamin Butler and the Army of the James were his tools of choice, but at first the tools appeared poorly suited to the task. Butler conceived a plan to assault the fort with a gunboat packed with powder that would explode and stun the defenders physically, mentally or both. Grant, recalling the failure of similar attempts at Vicksburg and Petersburg, was skeptical but didn't stop Butler from trying. Butler worked with the navy's David

Porter to fill the chosen vessel with explosive and a timer. The craft was then grounded beneath the walls of the fort. The Union side watched anxiously and the Confederate defenders wondered what was happening. A second later the boat blew up but with no more force than might have been created by a bursting boiler, which the Confederates in fact thought had caused the vessel's destruction. Butler proceeded to land troops anyway, while Porter's gunboats provided artillery cover. But Butler changed his mind upon the arrival of Confederate reinforcements, and he withdrew the troops.

Grant lamented the reversal, believing the foothold once established should not have been abandoned. "The Wilmington expedition has proven a gross and culpable failure," he wrote Lincoln from City Point on December 28. He faulted procrastination and poor security. "Delays and free talk of the object of the expedition enabled the enemy to move troops to Wilmington to defeat it. . . . Who is to blame I hope will be known."

Grant soon decided the blame was Butler's and sacked the general. Meanwhile he tried to calm the irate Porter, who had risked his own men for Butler's irresolution. "Please hold on where you are for a few days, and I will endeavor to be back again with an increased force and without the former commander," Grant wrote Porter.

He tapped Alfred Howe Terry to lead the second assault. To ensure security he didn't inform even Terry what the mission was until Terry's force had boarded transports and set off. "Here there is not the slightest suspicion where the troops are going," Grant assured Stanton. Savannah was murmured as the destination, for the benefit of ears attuned to such things.

Terry opened his orders at sea and discovered that he was to accomplish what Butler had not. The orders urged Terry to listen to Porter. "It is exceedingly desirable that the most complete understanding should exist between yourself and the Naval Commander," Grant wrote. Terry and Porter achieved the requisite meeting of minds and directed the largest amphibious operation of the war. The Confederates fought well but were outgunned and outmanned. On January 15 the commandant of Fort Fisher surrendered the place.

Lee got the word a short time later and realized that the days of his army were numbered. His men were short of everything necessary for fighting: food, clothing, shoes, ammunition, medicine. Hunger drove desertions; as Lee watched the flesh melt from the bones of his men, he saw the men melt from the ranks of his army. "Desertion is increasing in the army, notwithstanding all my efforts to stop it," he lamented. He requested broader authority from the Confederate government to shoot deserters. "A rigid execution of the law is mercy in the end. The great want in our army is firmer discipline." But he knew this wasn't true: the army's great want was food. And though he received the shooting authority he requested, the desertions continued. The fall of Fort Fisher, which severed his last link to the world beyond America, guaranteed that the desertions would accelerate.

The Confederate government responded by drafting and arming slaves. The measure revealed the rebels' desperation, given the long-standing Southern fear of armed slaves. But Lee and the army had been using slaves to dig trenches, erect parapets, repair railroads and manage mules on behalf of the Confederacy; putting guns in hands that had wielded shovels and picks was a logical if nonetheless daunting step. Lee endorsed the move as a practical necessity. "The enemy will certainly use them against us if he can get possession of them," he wrote. "And as his present numerical superiority will enable him to penetrate many parts of the country, I cannot see the wisdom of the policy of holding them to await his arrival, when we may, by timely action and judicious management, use them to arrest his progress."

The Confederate government meanwhile made Lee commander in chief. Jefferson Davis had held the post, but the Confederacy's numerous setbacks sparked calls that he relinquish the command to Lee. Davis initially resisted, as did his wife, who declared of her husband, "If I were he, I would die or be hung before I would submit to the humiliation." Eventually he realized he had no choice. Lee accepted the job with unfeigned reluctance. "Deeply impressed with the difficulties and responsibilities of the position, and humbly invoking the assistance of Almighty God," he declared, "I rely for success upon the courage and fortitude of the army, sustained by the patriotism and firmness of the people."

He then told his wife: "I think General Grant will move against us soon—within a week if nothing prevents—and no man can tell what may be the result."

Grant wasn't quite ready to move. "I could not see how it was possible for the Confederates to hold out much longer where they were," he wrote later. "There is no doubt that Richmond would have been evacuated much sooner than it was, if it had not been that it was the capital of the so-called Confederacy, and the fact of evacuating the capital would, of course, have had a very demoralizing effect upon the Confederate army."

Grant assumed that Lee would wish to save the army but that Davis might try to save the capital. He didn't know which priority would prevail. Nor had he any desire to waste more troops assaulting Richmond if that city might be abandoned imminently by the Confederates' own choice. Yet he worried that Lee might elude him. He rarely lost sleep over impending battles but he lost sleep now. "I felt that the situation of the Confederate army was such that they would try to make an escape at the earliest practicable moment, and I was afraid, every morning, that I would awake from my sleep to hear that Lee had gone, and that nothing was left but a picket line. He had his railroad by the way of Danville south, and I was afraid that he was running off his men and all stores and ordnance except such as it would be necessary to carry with him for his immediate defense. I knew he could move much more lightly and more rapidly than I, and that, if he got the start, he would leave me behind so that we would have the same army to fight again farther south—and the war might be prolonged another year."

So Grant continued to close the ring. He considered bringing Sherman north from Savannah by sea, but when sufficient transports proved hard to find, Sherman suggested simply continuing his march, across the Carolinas and into Virginia. He could cover the distance by land as surely as by water, he said, and would accomplish much good on the way. "I know this trip is necessary to the war. It must be made sooner or later, and I am on time and in the right position for it. My army is large enough, and I ask no reinforcement, but simply wish the utmost activity at all other points, so that concentration against me may not be universal." He would strike for Columbia, South Carolina, the capital of the state that had started all the trouble and a city with symbolic importance second to none. "I expect Davis will move Heaven and earth to catch me, for success to my column is fatal to his dream of empire. Richmond is not more vital to his cause than Columbia and the heart of South Carolina." Events were progressing favorably but must be exploited, Sherman said. "The poor white trash of the South are falling out of their ranks by sickness, desertion, and every available means; but there is a large class of vindictive Southerners who will fight to the last. The squabbles in Richmond, the howls in Charleston, and the disintegration elsewhere are all good omens to us, but we must not relax one iota, but on the contrary pile up our efforts." Sherman knew his business. "I will start with my Atlanta army, 60,000, supplied as before and depending on the country for all in excess of thirty days. I will have less cattle on the hoof, but I hear of hogs, cows and calves in Barnwell and the Columbia districts; even here we found some forage. Of course the enemy will carry off and destroy some forage but I will burn the houses where the people burn forage and they will get tired of that."

Grant bade Sherman good luck and turned to Phil Sheridan to bring similar pressure from the west. The winter was harsh along the Shenandoah; Sheridan wrote Grant in February that snow had covered the ground since December and was currently a foot deep on the roads. The cavalry he sent after Confederate guerrillas came back frostbitten. "It is utterly impossible to do anything here in such weather," Sheridan said. "I have never experienced a colder or worse winter." Grant acknowledged the complication of the weather but told Sheridan to come out of the valley when he could. "As soon as it is possible to travel, I think you will have no difficulty about reaching Lynchburg with a cavalry force alone. From there you could destroy the railroads and canal in every direction so as to be of no further use to the rebellion this coming spring or, I believe, during the existence of the rebellion." Sheridan should then continue as conditions warranted. "From Lynchburg, if information you might get there would justify it, you could strike south, heading the streams in Virginia to the westward of Danville, and push on and join Sherman." Sheridan and Sherman, together with smaller forces operating elsewhere, could fairly cut the ground from under the rebellion. "I would advise you to overcome great obstacles to accomplish this."

Grant's belief that the rebellion was dying gained credibility from peace feelers out of Richmond. On January 30 three civilians rode up to the Union lines at Petersburg and presented a letter for Grant. "We desire to pass your lines under safe conduct and proceed to Washington, to hold a conference with President Lincoln upon the subject of the existing war and with a view of ascertaining upon what terms it may be terminated," the letter said. It was signed by Alexander H. Stephens, John A.

Campbell, and R. M. T. Hunter—respectively the vice president of the Confederacy, the assistant secretary of war and a leading member of the Confederate senate.

Grant telegraphed the request to Lincoln, who quickly decided he didn't want the Confederate agents anywhere near Washington. Lincoln told Grant to hold them at City Point pending the administration's decision whether to talk with them. Grant had Stephens and the others shown to a passenger steamboat in the James River. He dropped by occasionally and let himself be engaged in small talk but avoided matters of substance. "I found them all very agreeable gentlemen," he recollected. He allowed them to come and go; they visited the shore and wandered about Grant's headquarters. But he refused to accord them any official status; they were simply his guests.

Like many others, Grant found Stephens curiously impressive. He had read the Georgian's speeches and thought him a reasonable man. He had also thought him a small—diminutive—man. "But when I saw him in the dusk of the evening I was very much surprised to find so large a man as he seemed to be," he recalled. The discrepancy soon came clear. "When he got down on to the boat I found that he was wearing a coarse gray woolen overcoat, a manufacture that had been introduced into the South during the rebellion. The cloth was thicker than anything of the kind I had ever seen, even in Canada. The overcoat extended nearly to his feet, and was so large that it gave him the appearance of being an average-sized man. He took this off when he reached the cabin of the boat, and I was struck with the apparent change in size, in the coat and out of it."

Lincoln was struck too. The president decided to see the Confederate commissioners and arranged for a conference at Hampton Roads. He later compared impressions with Grant, asking him if he had watched Stephens take off his coat. Grant replied that he had. "Well," Lincoln said, "didn't you think it was the biggest shuck and the littlest ear that ever you did see?"

The conference came to nothing. Lincoln's peace terms since the Emancipation Proclamation had been the preservation of the Union and the abolition of slavery. Stephens and the others accepted neither forthrightly, and Lincoln, on the verge of victory, was in no mood to let them equivocate.

Grant suspected a ploy, an effort by Davis to buy time. The envoys had wanted an armistice until the talks ended; Grant refused, with

Lincoln's approval. "The peace feeling within the rebel lines is gaining ground rapidly," he wrote Sherman. "This, however, should not relax our energies in the least, but should stimulate us to greater activity."

Sherman didn't require the encouragement. His army rolled north from Savannah, extending the swath of destruction it had wrought across Georgia. In the third week of February it approached Columbia. "General Howard will cross the Saluda and Broad Rivers as near their mouths as possible, occupy Columbia, destroy the public buildings, railroad property, manufacturing and machine shops, but will spare libraries and asylums and private dwellings," Sherman ordered. Howard and his men did cross the rivers and occupy the city; they destroyed the public buildings, railroad property and machine shops.

But the libraries, asylums and private dwellings were not wholly spared. On the night of February 17 a fire spread across much of the city. Most of those who experienced the blaze had never seen the like. "The northern and western sky was not only all aflame, but the air was filled with myriad sparks and burning brands," one eyewitness recalled. "They fell upon the wooden house-tops; they dashed against the windowpanes, lurid with reflected light; they fell in showers into the garden and among the trees; they mingled with the eddying dust which whirled along the street. It was the rain of fire, which is so sublimely expressed in music, in that grand oratorio—'Israel in Egypt.'" Residents and property owners felt the destruction personally. "Oh, that long twelve hours!" diarist Emma LeConte recorded the next day. "Never surely again will I live through such a night of horrors. The memory of it will haunt me as long as I shall live—it seemed as if the day would never come. The sun arose at last, dim and red through the thick, murky atmosphere. It set last night on a beautiful town full of women and children—it shone dully down this morning on smoky ruins and abject misery."

LeConte and other South Carolinians had heard stories of Sherman's brutal practices; the burning of their homes suggested he was indeed the monster described. "This is the way the 'cultured' Yankee nation wars upon women and children!" she wrote. "Failing with our men in the field, *this* is the way they must conquer! . . . One expects these people to lie and steal, but it does seem such an outrage even upon degraded humanity that those who practice such wanton and useless cruelty should call themselves men. It seems to us even a contamination to look at these devils. Think of the degradation of being conquered and ruled by such a people! It seems to me now as if we would choose extermination."

Sherman denied responsibility for the fire and set his men to work dousing the flames. He suggested that the retreating Confederates had ignited the cotton stored in the city, lest the Federals seize it, and that the high wind that evening had spread the flames. "If I had made up my mind to burn Columbia I would have burnt it with no more feeling than I would a common prairie dog village," he testified later. "But I did not do it."

Others blamed the chaos of the moment. Union general Oliver Howard asserted that his efforts to restore order did little good. "During the night I met Logan and Wood and other general officers, and they were taking every possible measure to stop the fire and prevent disorder. Nevertheless, some escaped prisoners, convicts from the penitentiary just broken open, army followers, and drunken soldiers ran through house after house and were doubtless guilty of all manner of villainies, and it was these men that, I presume, set new fires farther to the windward in the northern part of the city."

Grant didn't worry about culpability or weep for Columbia. "One thing is certain," he wrote long after the embers, if not the passions, had cooled. "As soon as our troops took possession, they at once proceeded to extinguish the flames to the best of their ability with the limited means at hand. In any case, the example set by the Confederates in burning the village of Chambersburg, Pennsylvania"—in July 1864—"would seem to make a defense of the act of firing the seat of government of the state most responsible for the conflict then raging, not imperative."

48

EVEN IF THE WINTER RAINS HAD NOT RENDERED THE ROADS AROUND Richmond impassable, Grant would have been reluctant to attack the fortified position Lee occupied. "Whilst the enemy holds nearly all his force for the defense of Richmond and Petersburg, the object to be gained by attacking entrenchments is not worth the risk to be run," he explained to George Meade. "In fact, for the present it is much better for us to hold the enemy where he is than to force him south." Sherman was proceeding north through the Carolinas; Sheridan was coming from the west. "To drive the enemy from Richmond now would be to endanger the success of these two columns." Patience was the virtue of the moment; when Sherman and Sheridan arrived would be the time to attack Lee.

Yet patience came hard. Sherman's operations once more took him out of reach of telegraph. "I feel no doubt of the result with him," Grant told a friend, "but cut loose as he is I necessarily feel anxious. As long as Sherman is individually safe, his army will be. But an unlucky ball to touch him would materially mar the prospects of his army. Sherman has immortalized his name and that of the army he commands. It would be too unfortunate now to have anything occur to prevent him, and those under him, enjoying their laurels." Grant didn't like to think about such an occurrence, but he couldn't help it. "My anxiety will be intense until I hear directly from Sherman."

A letter from Lee moderated Grant's anxiety somewhat. "Lieutenant General Longstreet has informed me," Lee wrote on March 2, "that in a recent conversation between himself and Major General Ord as to the possibility of arriving at a satisfactory adjustment of the present unhappy difficulties by means of a military convention, General Ord stated that if I desired to have an interview with you on the subject, you would not decline, provided I had authority to act. Sincerely desiring to leave nothing untried which may put an end to the calamities of war, I propose to meet you at such convenient time and place as you may designate." Lee added, "In such event, I am authorized to do whatever the result of the proposed interview may render necessary or advisable."

Grant read the letter as indicating Lee's desperation, and so he put him off to let the desperation deepen. "General Ord and General Long-street have probably misunderstood what I said," he replied. Grant had sent Ord to talk to Longstreet about an exchange of prisoners; he hadn't told Ord to invite broader discussions. Perhaps Ord had done so on his own; perhaps Longstreet had embellished what Ord said. Most likely, Grant surmised, Lee simply took the prisoner talks as an opportunity to suggest a more comprehensive negotiation.

In any case, Grant lacked authority to discuss any but the narrowest military questions. "General Ord could only have meant that I would not refuse an interview on any subject on which I have a right to act, which of course would be such as are purely of a military character," he told Lee.

Grant could, of course, have asked for broader authority. But now was not the time. Writing to Stanton, he said, "I can assure you that no act of the enemy will prevent me pressing all advantages gained, to the utmost of my ability."

$\mathscr{A}$ week later Grant stood uncomfortably aboard a steamboat in the James River at City Point. He had dressed more formally for the occasion than was his headquarters habit, for his companions that evening included Elihu Washburne and a number of other dignitaries visiting from Washington. Washburne carried the gold medal that had been struck by order of Congress to reward Grant for his services in Tennessee the previous year. Washburne warmly thanked and congratulated Grant, and he read a letter from Lincoln. "Please accept, for yourself and all under your command, the renewed expression of my gratitude for your and their arduous and well-performed public service," the president said.

Grant scarcely heard the words. All he could think of was that he would have to give a speech in reply. He reached in his pocket for the paper on which he had scribbled a couple of sentences, which he now mumbled in a voice so low as to be barely audible even to those standing beside him. "I accept the medal and joint resolutions of Congress which the President has commissioned you to deliver to me," he told Washburne rather than the audience. "I will do myself the honor at an early date to acknowledge the receipt of the letter of the President accompanying them, and to communicate, in orders, to the officers and soldiers who served under my command prior to the passage of the resolution, the thanks so generously tendered to them by the Congress of the United States."

He pocketed the paper and made for the door of the vessel's parlor. But his escape was interrupted when Julia, who had joined him at City Point, suggested a dance in her husband's honor. A military band was conveniently aboard, and a consensus supported the commanding general's wife. "The officers soon selected their partners from among the ladies present, and the evening's entertainment was continued to a late hour," Horace Porter recalled. Grant sat awkwardly to the side. Julia tried to get him to waltz with her, and Grant's staff lightheartedly urged him to please her. He resisted all entreaties until the band struck up a square dance reel. "He went through the cotillion," Porter observed, "not as gracefully as some of the beaux among the younger officers present, but did his part exceedingly well, barring the impossibility of his being able to keep exact time with the music."

The party broke up too late for Washburne and the others to leave for Washington. The congressman awoke early the next day—a Sunday—and readied his razor and soap brush for a shave. He looked about for a mirror, only to discover that his guest quarters lacked such amenity. He walked the short distance to Grant's office, where he found a mirror but not the general. He lathered up and raised his blade for the first stroke. Suddenly a woman burst into the room. "Save him! Oh, save him!" she cried, throwing herself at Washburne's feet. "He's my husband!"

Washburne was so startled that he nearly sliced his neck. "What's all this about your husband?" he demanded as he regained his composure.

"Oh, General! For God's sake, save my husband!" she said.

"Why, my good woman," he said, "I'm not General Grant."

"Yes you are; they told me this was your room. Oh, save him, General, they're to shoot him this very day for desertion if you don't stop them."

Washburne reiterated that he wasn't Grant, but he listened to the woman explain how her husband had taken unauthorized leave to visit her, how he had been arrested and court-martialed and how he was to be executed, all for the love of her. Washburne tried to comfort the woman, who merely cried more loudly than ever.

At this point Grant entered the room. He had heard the commotion and wondered what it meant. "The spectacle presented partook decidedly of the serio-comic," Horace Porter recalled. "The dignified member of Congress was standing in his shirt-sleeves in front of the pleading woman, his face covered with lather, except the swath which had been made down his right cheek; the razor was uplifted in his hand, and the tears were starting out of his eyes as his sympathies began to be worked upon. The woman was screaming and gesticulating frantically, and was almost hysterical with grief. I entered at the front door about the same time that the general entered from the rear, and it was hard to tell whether one ought to laugh or cry at the sight presented."

Grant took charge of the situation. He convinced the woman that he, not Washburne, was the commanding general, and he said that her husband would be pardoned. He sent the order and the man was rescued just in time.

Spring's arrival brought the war's end closer. The rains diminished and the roads began to dry out. "We are now having fine weather and I think will be able to wind up matters about Richmond soon," Grant wrote his father just before the equinox. "The rebellion has lost its vitality, and if I am not much mistaken there will be no rebel army of any great dimensions a few weeks hence."

Sherman resurfaced in North Carolina, having extended his track of destruction from Columbia. "I have never felt any uneasiness for your safety," Grant wrote Sherman with imperfect candor. "But I have felt great anxiety to know just how you were progressing. I knew, or thought I did, that with the magnificent Army with you, you would come out safely someplace." Phil Sheridan closed in from the west, and Grant directed him to sever Lee's last links to other parts of the Confederacy. "Your problem will be to destroy the South Side and Danville roads," Grant wrote. Sheridan might incidentally keep an eye out for Joe Johnston's army, which was between him and Sherman. "This, however, I care but little about, the principal thing being the destruction of the only two roads left to the enemy at Richmond."

Sheridan's thrust would shape what Grant did with the rest of the Army of the Potomac. "When this movement commences I shall move out by my left with all the force I can, holding present entrenched lines," he told Sherman. "I shall start with no distinct view further than holding Lee's forces from following Sheridan. But I shall be along myself"— rather than acting through Meade, whom he didn't quite trust to handle the endgame—"and will take advantage of anything that turns up. If Lee detaches I will attack, or if he comes out of his lines I will endeavor to repulse him and follow it up to best advantage."

Grant confessed he couldn't quite fathom Lee. "It is most difficult to understand what the rebels intend to do," he told Sherman. "So far but few troops have been detached from Lee's army. Much machinery has been sent to Lynchburg, showing a disposition to go there." Lee himself remained at Richmond.

On March 24 Grant issued detailed orders for his leftward movement, to begin on the 29th. He prescribed provisions, the route, the order of march—and the duty of those who wouldn't be making the march. "A large part of the armies operating against Richmond are left behind," he explained. "The enemy, knowing this, may, as an only chance, strip their lines to the merest skeleton in the hope of advantage not being taken of it, whilst they hurl everything upon the moving column. . . . It cannot be impressed too strongly upon commanders of troops left in the trenches not to allow this to occur without taking advantage of it. The very fact of the enemy coming out to attack, if he does so, might be regarded as almost conclusive evidence of such a weakening of his lines."

Lee did what Grant anticipated, only sooner. On March 25 Lee launched a surprise attack on Grant's right wing, against a part of the Petersburg line covered by Fort Stedman. Lee's purpose was to compel Grant to send reinforcements from his left, which was Lee's real target. He agreed with Grant that Richmond had become untenable; he wanted to break out of the city and head southwest. Grant's weakened left would be his escape route.

The attack on Fort Stedman began by stealth. Confederate troops slipped silently across the narrow gap between the lines and surprised the Union defenders. Before Grant could react, the Confederates had captured the fort and turned its guns against the Union positions nearby. But there the attack stalled. Grant's gunners returned the fire, and the Confederates in Fort Stedman found themselves bombarded from left and right. Their only hope was to press forward and get to the Union rear. This the Confederate rank and file refused to attempt. Rather than risk their lives in what appeared an ultimately hopeless task, they huddled in Fort Stedman and allowed themselves to be taken prisoner. "In the fight today we captured 2700 of the enemy and killed and wounded a great number," Grant reported matter-of-factly that afternoon.

The plans for Grant's own operation unfolded on schedule. He brought Sherman and Sheridan to City Point for a last-minute conference. The three generals met with Lincoln, who had come down from Washington. "The President was not very cheerful," Sheridan recalled. "In fact he was dejected, giving no indication of his usual means of diversion, by which (his quaint stories) I had often heard he could find relief from his cares." Lincoln had been informed of the broad outline of the move to the left, and he worried that Lee would hit once more at Grant's right, perhaps taking City Point. "I answered that I did not think it at all probable that General Lee would undertake such a desperate measure to relieve the strait he was in," Sheridan recounted. "General Grant would give Lee all he could attend to on the left."

Sherman and Sheridan possessed strong wills, which became evident in their meeting with Grant. Sherman thought Sheridan, after destroying the Confederate railroads, should bring his cavalry south to help him crush Johnston; then they would move north together and join Grant for the destruction of Lee's army. Sheridan objected strenuously and profanely. His soldiers belonged to the Army of the Potomac, he said, not to Sherman's Army of the Tennessee. The former, having fought Lee for three years, deserved the right to defeat him without the help of Sherman's westerners. And he—Sheridan—should be in at the kill.

Grant let Sherman present his case and Sheridan rebut, and he proceeded to split the difference, with some misdirection. He wrote Sheridan an order that concluded: "After having accomplished the destruction of the two railroads which are now the only avenues of supply to Lee's army, you may return to this army selecting your road further south, or you may go into North Carolina and join General Sherman." He let Sherman think that Sheridan would choose the latter course, while he told Sheridan that the suggestion of a rendezvous between him and Sherman was a ploy. "This portion of your instructions I have put in merely as a blind." He explained that he didn't want to advertise the move to the left as the final stroke of the war before it merited such a description. Even now defeatists in the North would take any misstep as an excuse to resume their peacemongering. But his true aims were bolder. "I told him that, as a matter of fact, I intended to close the war right here, with this movement, and that he should go no farther," Grant recalled. "His face at once brightened up, and slapping his hand on his leg he said, 'I am glad to hear it, and we can do it.'"

On March 29 Grant began moving. The rain had stopped and roads begun to dry. But the army was scarcely in motion when the skies opened again. "The heavy rains and horrid roads have prevented the execution of my designs, or attempting them," Grant wrote Lincoln on the 31st. To Julia he was more philosophical: "The weather is bad for us but it is consoling to know that it rains on the enemy as well."

Grant directed his men to lay corduroy roads, and the march resumed. His goal was to reach Five Forks, on Lee's extreme right. Sheridan would attack Lee there, forcing the Confederate commander to pull troops from the center of his line or risk letting Sheridan get behind him. Grant would then hit the weakened center and carry Petersburg and perhaps Richmond.

Grant's aide Horace Porter was riding with Sheridan, and he reported to Grant how the general and his men wanted a showdown and likely would carry it off. "General Sheridan will attack the enemy with everything," Porter wrote. "Our men have never fought better. All are in excellent spirits and anxious to go in. The enemy is said to be fighting badly, giving way constantly before our dismounted cavalry."

Sheridan took Five Forks and much besides. His infantry hit the Confederate flank while his cavalry charged the front. "The result of this combined movement was the complete rout of the enemy, with the loss of five pieces of artillery and caissons, a number of their wagons and ambulances, and I think at least 5,000 prisoners and several battle flags," Sheridan wrote Grant. "After the enemy broke, our cavalry pursued them for six miles down the White Oak road."

Grant immediately ordered attacks on the center of the Petersburg line. His corps commanders answered that it was getting dark and the men couldn't see to attack; Grant accepted the argument and settled for artillery barrages overnight. Yet by five o'clock on the morning of April 2 his troops were in motion, and they quickly drove the rebels back upon the inner defenses of Petersburg. Lee counterattacked and hard fighting followed. But the weight of the Federals gradually told. "We are now up and have a continuous line of troops, and in a few hours will be entrenched from the Appomattox below Petersburg to the river above," Grant reported to the War Department and Lincoln that afternoon. "The whole captures since the army started out gunning will not amount to less than 12,000 men and 50 pieces of artillery." The surrender of Richmond was a matter of time and probably not much at that. "I think the President might come out and pay us a visit tomorrow."

"I SEE NO PROSPECT OF DOING MORE THAN HOLDING OUR POSITION here till night," Lee wrote Jefferson Davis the same morning. "I am not certain that I can do that. If I can I shall withdraw tonight north of the Appomattox, and, if possible, it will be better to withdraw the whole line tonight from James River. The brigades on Hatcher's Run are cut off from us; enemy have broken through our lines and intercepted between us and them. . . . Our only chance, then, of concentrating our forces is to do so near the Danville railroad, which I shall endeavor to do at once. I advise that all preparation be made for leaving Richmond tonight."

Davis objected that the Confederate government couldn't evacuate the city on a moment's notice. "To move tonight will involve the loss of many valuables, both for want of time to pack and of transportation," he told Lee.

Lee refused to let Davis dictate the future of the Army of Northern Virginia. "It is absolutely necessary that we should abandon our position tonight or run the risk of being cut off in the morning," Lee rejoined. The army would leave whether the Confederate government did so or not. "I have given all the orders to officers on both sides of the river, and have taken every precaution I can to make the movement successful. It will be a difficult operation, but I hope not impracticable."

LaSalle Corbell Pickett was the wife of Confederate general George Pickett and a resident of Richmond. "On the morning of Sunday, April 2, in the holy calm of St. Paul's Church, we had assembled to ask the great Father of Heaven and earth to guard our loved ones and give victory to the cause so dear to us," she remembered. Jefferson Davis was there along with other Confederate leaders, and it was during the service that Davis received Lee's evacuation order. "Suddenly the glorious sunlight was dimmed by the heavy cloud of disappointment," Sallie Pickett said, "and the peace of God was broken by the deep-voiced bells tolling the death-knell of our hopes."

Clouds of more than disappointment soon covered the city. The evacuation order provoked panic. Residents recalling the recent fate of Columbia carted their furniture and other belongings through the streets, hoping to save at least these from the fires they feared were coming. The impedimenta clogged the thoroughfares, raising the fever level. Looters trailed the evacuees, perhaps consoling their consciences that they were simply taking what the owners had left behind. Soon they anticipated the flight, stealing whatever they could lay hands on. Foodstores were irresistibly tempting to a hungry populace; breaking into warehouses, they discovered that much of the shortage they suffered had been contrived. "The most revolting revelation was the amount of provisions, shoes and clothing which had been accumulated by the speculators who hovered like vultures over the scene of death and desolation," Sallie Pickett recalled. The crowds grew angry and many persons got drunk on liberated liquor. Confederate general Richard Ewell, ordered by Lee to burn the cotton and tobacco in government custody, took care to keep his authorized fires from spreading; he later asserted that the fires that destroyed the city were set by the mob. However they started, the flames quickly spread and magnified the chaos. "Throughout the night the fire raged," Sallie Pickett wrote. "The sea of darkness rolled over the town; the crowds of men, women and children went about the streets laden with what plunder they could rescue from the flames. The drunken rabble shattered the plate-glass windows of the stores and wrecked everything upon which they could seize. The populace had become a frenzied mob, and the kingdom of Satan seemed to have been transferred to the streets of Richmond."

Lee looked back on the smoking ruins the next day. "I have got my army safely out of its breastworks," he remarked from the road. He had withdrawn from the Richmond defenses and begun his flight. "In order to follow me, the enemy must abandon his lines and can derive no further benefit from his railroads on the James River."

But Grant did not intend to follow Lee; he intended to cut him off.

"The first object of the present movement will be to intercept Lee's army," Grant told Sheridan on the morning of April 3. "Make your movements according to this program." To Edward Ord, now heading the Army of the James, he wrote, "Efforts will be made to intercept the enemy, who are evidently pushing toward Danville. Push southwest with your command."

Grant finally had Lee where he wanted him: out from behind his defenses and in the open. Lee looked weaker and more vulnerable than ever. "Sheridan, who was up with him last night, reports all that is left—horse, foot, and dragoons—at 20,000, much demoralized," Grant wrote Sherman on April 5. "We hope to reduce this number fully one-half. I will push on to Burkeville, and if a stand is made at Danville will in a very few days go there." Sherman should join the hunt. "If you can possibly do so, push on from where you are and let us see if we cannot finish the job with Lee and Johnston's armies." Sherman should forget entirely about towns or other points of geography. "Rebel armies are now the only strategic points to strike at." The next day Grant reiterated: "We have Lee's army pressed hard, his men scattering and going to their homes by the thousands. He is endeavoring to reach Danville, where Davis and his cabinet have gone. I shall press the pursuit to the end. Push Johnston at the same time, and let us finish up this job all at once."

Grant knew he was on the verge of victory. He praised the swift march—twenty-eight miles in a day—of two of his divisions. "These troops were sent out to Farmville this afternoon and I am in hopes will head the enemy and enable us to totally break up the Army of Northern Virginia," he reported to City Point for relay to Washington. "The troops are all pushing now though it is after night and they have had no rest for more than one week. The finest spirit prevails among the men, and I believe that in three days Lee will not have an army of 5,000 men to take out of Virginia, and no train or supplies."

Lee felt Grant's grip tightening. He realized he couldn't win the war but thought he might prolong it. If he could feed his men he might reach Johnston's army. Together they could threaten to extend the war longer than Northern opinion could stand. Lincoln and Grant might have to negotiate yet.

Lee's army reached Amelia Court House, thirty miles southwest of Richmond, where he hoped to find supplies. But the supplies weren't there, and he was compelled to turn his men out to forage across the neighborhood. "Nearly twenty-four hours were lost in endeavoring to collect in the country subsistence for men and horses," he recounted afterward. "This delay was fatal, and could not be retrieved." The weary, hungry troops marched on. At Jetersville, on the Richmond & Danville Railroad, they encountered Sheridan's cavalry and learned that the Union infantry was close behind. "This deprived us of the use of the railroad," Lee said, "and rendered it impracticable to procure from Danville the supplies ordered to meet us at points of our march." The countryside offered nothing, having been stripped bare. Lee had no choice but to redirect his march toward Farmville, where he hoped to find provisions shipped from Lynchburg.

The march deteriorated by the mile. Sheridan's cavalry sliced across the Confederate column, disrupting its progress. Ord's infantry attacked and took many prisoners. Lee kept the men marching through the night of April 6 and reached Farmville on the morning of the 7th. But many of the troops went hungry again, as some of the supply trains had pulled out lest they be captured by the approaching Sheridan.

The march continued with greater difficulty than ever. "The roads were wretched and the progress slow," Lee recalled. Most of the men no longer thought of fighting; they simply wanted to eat. Lee had nothing to give them.

Grant offered Lee a chance to surrender. "The result of the last week must convince you of the hopelessness of further resistance," he wrote Lee on April 7. "I feel that it is so, and regard it as my duty to shift from myself the responsibility of any further effusion of blood by asking of you the surrender of that portion of the Confederate States Army known as the Army of Northern Virginia."

Lee was interested. He denied that his situation was hopeless but said he wanted to hear more. "I reciprocate your desire to avoid useless effusion of blood," he wrote Grant, "and, therefore, before considering your proposition, ask the terms you will offer."

Grant sought to make things simple. "There is but one condition I would insist upon, namely that the men and officers surrendered shall be disqualified for taking up arms again against the Government of the United States, until properly exchanged," he said. "I will meet or will designate officers to meet any officers you name for the same purpose, at any point agreeable to you, for the purpose of arranging definitely the terms upon which the surrender of the Army of Northern Virginia will be received."

Lee wasn't ready. "I did not intend to propose the surrender of the Army of Northern Virginia, but to ask the terms of your proposition," he wrote to Grant on April 8. "To be frank, I do not think the emergency has arisen to call for the surrender of this army, but as the restoration of peace should be the sole object of all, I desired to know whether your proposals would lead to that end. I cannot, therefore, meet you with a view to surrender the Army of Northern Virginia." He *could* meet for other purposes, though. "As far as your proposal may affect the Confederate States forces under my command, and tend to the restoration of peace, I should be pleased to meet you at 10 a.m. tomorrow, on the old stage road to Richmond, between the picket lines of the two armies."

That same day Sheridan's cavalry galloped toward Appomattox Station, a rail depot on the line from Lynchburg. A Union scout met them with news that four trains loaded with supplies for Lee's army were poised at the station. Sheridan pressed harder than ever. The trains meant life for Lee's army if they got through, death if they didn't. George Custer headed the Union column that reached Appomattox Station first. He sent two regiments around to the west to break the track behind the trains so they couldn't return to Lynchburg. With the rest of his force Custer rode into the depot, arriving almost simultaneously with Lee's advance guard. Custer attacked the Confederates, dealing them a sharp blow that resulted in the seizure of two dozen artillery pieces and a wagon column, besides securing the supply trains and compelling the retreat of the rebels back up the road toward Appomattox Court House, several miles away.

Sheridan ordered his skirmishers to follow the Confederates and wear them down further. He got little rest himself. "The captured trains had been taken charge of by locomotive engineers, soldiers of the command who delighted evidently to get back at their old calling," he remembered. "They amused themselves by running the trains to and fro, creating much confusion and keeping up such an unearthly screeching with the whistles that I was on the point of ordering the cars burned."

Nor did he sleep that night. His cavalry couldn't bear the weight of opposing Lee's whole army; the horse soldiers required support. "The necessity of getting Ord's column up was so obvious now that staff officer after staff officer was sent to him and to General Grant requesting that the infantry be pushed on, for if it could get to the front, all knew that the rebellion would be ended on the morrow," Sheridan said.

The night passed with nothing from Ord or Grant. Sheridan, Custer and the other officers alternately cheered the imminent end of the war and worried that Lee would arrive before Ord and frustrate them again.

Finally, just at dawn on April 9, Ord appeared. His troops had marched all night and were bone-tired. Yet they were as determined to end the war as Sheridan's men were, and they wouldn't stop till they had cornered Lee conclusively.

They arrived at the decisive moment. Lee made a final, desperate effort to break through Sheridan's cavalry line. The attack was beginning just as Ord's men reached the scene. Sheridan withdrew the cavalry to allow passage for Ord's infantry. The Confederates initially mistook the maneuver for a Federal retreat and pushed with rising hopes to the crest of a hill commanding the field. From that vantage, however, they could see Ord's columns pouring onto the battlefield, and their spirit broke. They reflexively halted and then fell back toward Appomattox Court House.

Sheridan prepared to pursue. Custer, eager as always, and Wesley Merritt, Sheridan's second in command, were about to charge when Sheridan heard that Lee had raised the white flag. Sheridan sent a courier to Ord and galloped after Custer and Merritt himself. On the way he came under fire from Confederates who hadn't got the news. He began to think that the report was wrong or Lee was engaged in deception. When one of Lee's officers, John Gordon, belatedly arrived, Sheridan said, "General, your men fired on me as I was coming over here, and undoubtedly they are treating Merritt and Custer the same way. We might as well let them fight it out." Gordon replied, "There must be some mistake." Sheridan suggested that Gordon send a staff officer to tell his men to stop firing. Gordon responded, "I have no staff officer to send."

Sheridan offered one of his own, Lieutenant Vanderbilt Allen. Gordon wrote orders to Confederate general Martin Gary, who commanded a shrunken brigade of South Carolinians opposite Merritt. Gary ignored Allen's truce flag and took the lieutenant prisoner. "I do not care for white flags," Gary said. "South Carolinians never surrender." Merritt watched from a distance and decided he'd seen enough. He launched an attack. "This in short order put an end to General Gary's last-ditch absurdity," Sheridan recalled.

Gordon told Sheridan that Gary was acting without orders. General Lee, he said, sincerely desired a truce pending talks with General Grant. Sheridan remained skeptical. He knew that Grant and Lee had been communicating but had heard nothing of talks. He told Gordon that the Confederate attempt to break through his lines that very morning belied any notion of talks. "I will entertain no terms except that General Lee shall surrender to General Grant on his arrival here," he said. "If these terms are not accepted, we will renew hostilities."

Gordon vouched for his commander. "General Lee's army is exhausted," he said. "There is no doubt of his surrender to General Grant."

Ord rode up at this point. Sheridan explained the situation. Gordon asked for time to provide proof of Lee's bona fides. Sheridan and Ord reluctantly agreed. Gordon galloped away. He returned half an hour later, accompanied by James Longstreet, who carried a note from Lee to Grant, agreeing to surrender. Sheridan and Ord extended the truce until they could locate Grant.

"On the 8th I had followed the Army of the Potomac in rear of Lee," Grant remembered. "I was suffering very severely with a sick headache, and stopped at a farmhouse on the road some distance in rear of the main body of the army." He spent a miserable night with hot water on his feet and hot mustard on his wrists and neck. A courier brought Lee's answer to his second letter, but its evasions left him unsatisfied and still suffering.

He moved out before dawn on the 9th, intending to join Sheridan beyond Appomattox Court House. But to get there he had to ride around Lee's army, and so he left the road and circled south. Sheridan's message about Lee's agreement to surrender consequently missed him. Hearing nothing, Sheridan and Ord grew nervous about the ceasefire.

Lee sent one of his own officers to look for Grant and deliver a new message. "I received your note of this morning on the picket line, whither I had come to meet you and ascertain definitely what terms were embraced in your proposal of yesterday with reference to the surrender of this army," Lee's message said. He was disappointed that Grant had not been there. But he still wanted to meet. "I now ask an interview in accordance with the offer contained in your letter of yesterday for that purpose."

Grant recalled the moment vividly two decades later. "When the officer reached me I was still suffering with the sick headache," Grant said. "But the instant I saw the contents of the note I was cured."

He halted, sat down and composed his reply. "I am at this writing about four miles west of Walker's Church and will push forward to the front for the purpose of meeting you," he wrote. "Notice sent to me on this road where you wish the interview to take place will meet me."

Lee's courier conducted Grant back through the Confederate lines to where Sheridan was impatient to attack. Sheridan still suspected a ruse and registered concern that with each hour Joe Johnston was getting closer. "Is it a trick?" he demanded of no one in particular. He gestured at Lee's army, just several hundred yards away, and snapped his open palm shut. "I've got 'em! I've got 'em like *that*!" Sheridan told Grant that if he would simply give the nod, he and Ord would settle the issue on the battlefield.

But Grant had had enough of fighting, and he chose to trust Lee. He was escorted to the house of a prosperous farmer named McLean at Appomattox Court House. Lee and a single staff officer awaited him. Several of Grant's subordinates joined their commander; all noted the contrast between the two commanding generals. "Lee was tall, large in form, fine in person, handsome in feature, grave and dignified in bearing—if anything, a little too formal," Adam Badeau recorded. "There was a suggestion of effort in his deportment, something that showed he was determined to die gracefully, a hint of Caesar muffling himself in his mantle." Lee's conqueror couldn't have been more different. "Grant as usual was simple and composed, but with none of the grand air about him," Badeau said. "No elation was visible in his manner or appearance. His voice was as calm as ever, and his eye betrayed no emotion. He spoke and acted as plainly as if he were transacting an ordinary matter of business. No one would have suspected that he was about to receive the surrender of an army, or that one of the most terrible wars of modern times had been brought to a triumphant close by the quiet man without a sword who was conversing calmly, but rather grimly, with the elaborate gentleman in grey and gold."

Grant, for his own part, tried to read Lee's emotions, without luck. "As he was a man of much dignity, with an impassible face, it was impossible to say whether he felt inwardly glad that the end had finally come, or felt sad over the result and was too manly to show it," Grant recalled.

THE RAGE OF ACHILLES

As for himself, he said: "My own feelings, which had been quite jubilant on the receipt of his letter, were sad and depressed. I felt like anything rather than rejoicing at the downfall of a foe who had fought so long and valiantly."

The two generals spoke of the old army before the war. Grant remembered Lee better than Lee remembered him, but Lee was tactful enough not to dwell on the discrepancy. Grant would have talked on if Lee hadn't reminded him what brought them together. Grant summoned his staff secretary, who produced paper, pen and ink. "In accordance with the substance of my letter to you of the 8th inst.," Grant wrote, "I propose to receive the surrender of the Army of Northern Virginia on the following terms, to wit: Rolls of all the officers and men to be made in duplicate. One copy to be given to an officer designated by me, the other to be retained by such officer or officers as you may designate. The officers to give their individual paroles not to take up arms against the Government of the United States until properly exchanged and each company or regimental commander sign a like parole for the men of their commands. The arms, artillery and public property to be parked and stacked and turned over to the officer appointed by me to receive them. This will not embrace the side arms of the officers nor their private horses or baggage. This done, each officer and man will be allowed to return to their homes not to be disturbed by United States authority so long as they observe their parole and the laws in force where they may reside."

He handed Lee the letter. The provision permitting the officers their side arms, horses and personal property was a grace note beyond the requirements of the surrender agreement. Lee acknowledged Grant's gesture, saying it would have a positive effect on his army. Lee asked whether soldiers other than officers—cavalrymen and artillerists principally—would be allowed to keep their horses, too. Grant, guessing that most were small farmers who would have difficulty planting a crop without their horses, said they would. Lee acknowledged this gesture as well.

Lee sat down and wrote a letter accepting Grant's conditions. He signed the letter, then stood once more. He said his army was hungry. He needed help feeding the men. Grant asked how many he had. Twenty-five thousand, Lee responded. Grant told him to send his commissary and quartermaster to Appomattox Station, where they would receive all they required.

The two men parted and returned to their armies. Grant's men began cheering and firing their guns on learning of the surrender. He ordered them to stop. "The Confederates were now our prisoners," he explained afterward. "We did not want to exult over their downfall."

The news was relayed to Washington at once. Edwin Stanton replied to Grant: "Thanks be to Almighty God for the great victory."

⊹ PART THREE ⊹

AND GIVE THE PEACE

"Descended from the gods, Ulysses, cease;
Offend not Jove; obey, and give the peace."

50

WHILE GRANT AND THE UNION ARMY WERE SUPPRESSING A REVOLU
tion in American politics, Lincoln and the Republicans in Congress
were making a revolution in American economics. The Republican
party had always been both antislavery and pro-business, but until 1860
it lacked the power to act on either part of its agenda. Lincoln's election and the subsequent departure of the Southern Democrats from
Congress left the party in firm control of the two lawmaking branches
of the federal government, and the Republicans soon began fashioning
their policy preferences into statutes.

The Constitution prevented a legislative assault on slavery, compelling Lincoln to employ his authority as commander in chief to justify the
Emancipation Proclamation. But the positive reaction to the proclamation inspired the president to broader reform; he called on Congress to
approve and send to the states a thirteenth, emancipating amendment to
the Constitution, which the legislature duly did.

Aiding business came more easily. Lincoln and the Republicans in
Congress raised tariffs, boosting the profits of American manufacturers. They underwrote a transcontinental railroad, immediately throwing
contracts to the hundreds of firms engaged in the construction of the
road and prospectively knitting the country into a vast single marketplace
for the purveyors of American products. They established a national currency and a national banking system, to enhance the war effort but to
facilitate commerce as well. They crafted laws to shift hundreds of millions of acres of public land and hundreds of millions of dollars in other
natural resources to the private sector. They spent previously unthink-
able amounts of money on all manner of commodities and manufactures,

for the primary purpose of defeating the rebellion but with the secondary result of accelerating the industrialization that had begun to reshape America before the war began. In dozens of other areas they made government the protector and promoter of the business interests of the country. And in providing Grant and his armies the wherewithal to defeat the Southern political revolution they ensured the extension of their economic revolution to the far corners of previously semifeudal Dixie.

The fate of the two revolutions—the failure of the South's political revolution, the success of the North's economic revolution—was stunningly apparent at the war's end. The South was devastated, its productive resources spent and shattered, its people exhausted and despondent, its legal system broken, its folkways untenable. The North was invigorated by the war, its industry surging ahead, its wealth and population growing apace, its values reigning triumphant. If characteristic Southerners were sons of planters who returned from the war to find their birthright in ruins and former slaves who, though free, had little idea how they would make a living, typical Northerners were industrialists and financiers who saw handsome opportunity in every direction, workers who manned the booming mines and mills, and farmers who were rapidly transforming agriculture into an industry of its own.

The one small cloud on the horizon of Republican dreams for more of the same was the result, ironically, of the victory so brilliantly achieved. The Republican monopoly on power wouldn't last forever; the South, upon being effectively rejoined to the Union, would send senators and representatives to Congress once again. If the old guard in the South had its way, these legislators would be Democrats likely to obstruct and subvert the Republican agenda. The Republicans in Washington, who since April 1861 had been doing everything possible to keep the South from leaving the Union, in April 1865 suddenly found reason to delay the South's return.

*J*ulia Grant grew proud as the fame of her husband increased, but she also grew worried. She had fretted since girlhood about a subtle misalignment of her eyes, which a minor operation could have corrected. "I had never had the courage to consent," she explained afterward. "But now that my husband had become so famous I really thought it behooved me to look as well as possible." She discreetly consulted a physician, who informed her that she had missed her opportunity: the surgery worked on young persons only. She went to her husband and confessed her vanity and disappointment. "What in the world put such a thought in your head?" he replied. She answered, through tears: "Why, you are getting to be such a great man, and I am such a plain little wife, I thought if my eyes were as others, I might not be so very, very plain." Years later she still remembered his response. "He drew me to him and said, 'Did I not see you and fall in love with you with these same eyes? I like them just as they are.'" She remembered as well her feeling: "My knight, my Lancelot!"

She spent the last winter of the war at City Point with him, often at his very side. Grant's associates at first wondered at her presence. During the final weeks, when Sherman arrived from Carolina for consultation, she sat in the corner of Grant's office writing personal letters. Grant asked Sherman half seriously whether Julia should move somewhere else. "I don't know," Sherman responded. "Let me see." He turned to Julia. "Mrs. Grant, can you tell me where the Tombigbee River is?" She missed by several counties. He asked if she could locate the Chattahoochee. Again far off. Sherman turned back to Grant. "I think we may trust her," he said.

She got the news of Lee's surrender from the City Point telegraph operator, who swore her to secrecy until the official word arrived. When it did she joined the celebration and urged her husband to savor his victory by returning to Richmond. "No," he replied. "I will go at once to Washington." She persisted, provoking his anger. "Hush, Julia," he said. "Do not say another word on this subject. I would not distress these people. They are feeling their defeat bitterly, and you would not add to it by witnessing their despair, would you?"

Grant went to Washington, and Julia with him. She had never been prouder of her husband. "Everyone was wild with delight," she remembered. "We received calls of congratulations all day. . . . I went with Mrs. Stanton to the War Department, where we were joined by Mr. Stanton and General Grant. Mr. Stanton was in his happiest mood, showing me many stands of arms, flags, and, among other things, a stump of a large tree perforated on all sides by bullets, taken from the field of Shiloh." A grand illumination—a fireworks display—was readied for that evening. Grant explained that Julia would ride in a carriage with the Stantons while he, at the request of the president, would ride with the Lincolns. "To this plan I protested and said I would not go at all unless he accompanied me," she wrote. Grant reacted with surprise, then said he would ride with her first and subsequently with the Lincolns. "This was all satisfactory to me," Julia concluded the story, "as it was the honor of being with him when he first viewed the illumination in honor of peace restored to the nation, in which he had so great a share—it was this I coveted."

She reveled in her husband's glory that night. The next morning she said she wanted to go to Burlington, New Jersey, where she had placed the children in school. And she wanted him to go with her, as they had seen little of their father lately. "I wish I could," he replied. "But I have promised Mr. Lincoln to go up this morning and with him see what can be done in reference to the reduction of the army." She pleaded with him to change his mind. He said he would try to finish early in order to get away that evening. Just then a messenger arrived with a note for Grant from the president, who asked to postpone their interview till afternoon so he could see his son, Robert, just back from the front. Grant sighed to Julia that this would make it even more difficult for him to get out of Washington that day, but he said he would do his best. She should see to preparing their bags.

She was doing so, hours later, when another messenger arrived. Poorly dressed, in tattered coat, trousers and hat, he asked if she was Mrs. Grant. She nodded that she was. "Mrs. Lincoln sends me, madam, with her compliments, to say she will call for you exactly at eight o'clock to go the theater," the messenger said. Julia remembered gazing at him coolly. "I replied with some feeling (not liking either the looks of the messenger or the message, thinking the former savored of discourtesy and the latter seemed like a command), 'You may return with my compliments to Mrs. Lincoln and say I regret that as General Grant and I intend leaving the city this afternoon, we will not, therefore, be here to accompany the President and Mrs. Lincoln to the theater.'" The messenger reddened. "Madam, the papers announce that General Grant will be with the President tonight at the theater." Julia was unmoved. "You may deliver my message to Mrs. Lincoln as I have given it to you. You may go now."

She was still taking pleasure in her riposte when Grant, having completed his business, arrived in time for them to catch the evening train to Philadelphia. No bridge then spanned the Delaware, and they had to wait for the train ferry to transport them across. As Grant had not eaten since morning, they visited a restaurant, where he ordered oysters. His dish was being prepared when a telegraph boy hurried in with a message from Washington. The message said that President Lincoln had been shot, perhaps fatally.

"It would be impossible for me to describe the feeling that overcame me at the news," Grant recalled. "I knew his goodness of heart, his generosity, his yielding disposition, his desire to have everybody happy, and above all his desire to see all the people of the United States enter again upon the full privileges of citizenship with equality among all." Grant realized that if Lincoln died Andrew Johnson would become president. He didn't know Johnson well, but he had heard that Johnson bore a grudge against the leaders of the South. "I feared that his course towards them would be such as to repel and make them unwilling citizens, and if they became such they would remain so for a long while. I felt that reconstruction had been set back, no telling how far."

Grant immediately summoned a special train to return him to the capital. But learning that it wouldn't arrive for a few hours, he took Julia on to Burlington, only an hour away. He retraced his path to Philadelphia and rode through the night to Washington. In the morning he learned, with the rest of the capital, of Lincoln's passing. "The joy that I had witnessed among the people in the street and in public places in Washington when I left there had been turned to grief," he recalled. "The city was in reality a city of mourning."

*I*t was also a city of fear. Lincoln's assassin, John Wilkes Booth, had organized a conspiracy that targeted Andrew Johnson and William Seward, besides Lincoln. The conspirator assigned to kill Johnson lost his nerve and didn't attack the vice president, but Seward was assaulted in his bed and was stabbed nearly to death. Who else might be in danger was anyone's guess in the hours and days that followed. And whether the attacks signaled a continuation of the war, by agents of the Confederate government or by diehard irregulars, was equally and frighteningly unclear.

Grant had to assume he was on the assassins' list. Booth had read the notices announcing his presence in the box with Lincoln at Ford's Theater; the assassin must have been surprised not to find the victorious general there. Julia later convinced herself that the plotters had been watching her. She suspected, after the fact, that the unkempt messenger at her hotel room was in league with Booth, and she concluded that some men sitting near her at lunch that day were planning her husband's murder. On the night of the shooting Charles Dana wrote Grant from the War Department warning him to be careful on the train ride back to Washington. "Permit me to suggest to you to keep a close watch on all persons who come near you in the cars or otherwise," Dana said. "Also that an engine be sent in front of the train to guard against anything being on the track." Grant directed the Union commander at Baltimore to send a company of soldiers to meet his train and join him for the rest of the trip to Washington. The next day Grant received an unsigned note indicating that the precautions had been well taken. As Julia recalled the note, it read: "General Grant, thank God, as I do, that you still live. It was your life that fell to my lot, and I followed you on the cars. Your car door was locked, and thus you escaped me, thank God!"

On arrival at the capital Grant sent orders to his generals in the field to tighten security. He told Edward Ord at Richmond to arrest the mayor, city council and any paroled Confederate officers who hadn't taken the oath of allegiance to the United States. "Extreme rigor will have to be observed whilst assassination remains the order of the day with the rebels," Grant said. When Ord replied that Lee and his staff were in the city and that to arrest them would risk reopening the rebellion, Grant rescinded the order but still urged Ord to keep close watch for assassins and saboteurs. Meanwhile he wrote Phil Sheridan to prepare to march again. Joe Johnston hadn't surrendered and Grant aimed to ensure that he not escape Sherman, who was short of cavalry. "I want you to get your cavalry in readiness to push south and make up this deficiency if it become necessary," Grant told Sheridan.

*I*t didn't become necessary; Johnston surrendered to Sherman a short while later. Grant got the news directly from Sherman. "I enclose herewith a copy of an agreement made this day between General Joseph E. Johnston and myself, which, if approved by the President of the United States, will produce peace from the Potomac to the Rio Grande," Sherman wrote proudly. Grant winced as he read these words, for Sherman had no authority to negotiate anything so sweeping. Sherman evidently had anticipated Grant's objection, for he explained: "You will observe that it is an absolute submission of the enemy to the lawful authority of the United States, and disperses his armies absolutely, and the point to which I attach most importance is that the dispersion and disbandment of these armies is done in such a manner as to prevent their breaking up into guerrilla bands." Grant couldn't dispute the importance of this accomplishment, which was the central issue at this stage of the conflict from a strictly military standpoint. His nightmare had been that the Confederate army would take to the hills and continue fighting a partisan campaign for months, even years. Yet he had to question, in light of his own experience in the Mississippi Valley, Sherman's subsequent observation: "I know that all the men of substance in the South sincerely want peace." And he wondered at Sherman's conclusion: "I have no doubt that they will in the future be perfectly subordinate to the laws of the United States."

Then he read the agreement itself, beginning with the most immediately operative clause: "The Confederate armies now in existence to be disbanded and conducted to their several State capitals, there to deposit their arms and public property in the State arsenal, and each officer and man to execute and file an agreement to cease from acts of war and to abide by the action of both State and Federal authority." Grant shook his head. Sherman appeared to be allowing the Confederates to surrender to themselves. And a promise to abide by state and federal authority begged the question of what they would do when state authority clashed with federal—which had been the central issue of the whole war.

There was more, including "the recognition by the Executive of the United States of the several State governments on their officers and legislatures taking the oaths prescribed by the Constitution of the United States." Aside from the fact that the Constitution prescribed no oaths for state officials, Grant saw this clause as the primary deal breaker. Where did Sherman think he got the authority to commit the president to recognize the governments of the Confederate states? By Sherman's interpretation, there was nothing to reconstruct; the old governments would remain in power.

And yet there was more: "a general amnesty, so far as the Executive of the United States can command, on condition of the disbandment of the Confederate armies, the distribution of the arms, and the resumption of peaceful pursuits by the officers and men hitherto composing said armies." This provision of the surrender agreement and others would take effect upon approval by the responsible authorities on both sides.

Grant appreciated that Sherman's outline for reconstruction followed the spirit of Lincoln's plan for restoring the Southern states to their places in the Union. Leniency had informed Lincoln's policy toward Louisiana and other states brought under federal control during the war. And leniency had inspired his second inaugural address, in which he summoned the spirit of charity to bind the nation's wounds.

But Grant also appreciated that Lincoln was dead, slain by a Southerner who knew nothing of charity and had no desire to bind the nation's wounds. He appreciated that the death killed the chance of an easy reconstruction. Those in the North who wanted vengeance would receive it, or at least they would fight for it. Sherman's agreement said nothing about slavery; at the very least the North would insist—rightly, Grant thought—that the South formally abjure the institution that had brought the conflict on.

He shook his head once more as he reread the letter and the agreement. He sympathized with Sherman in wanting to end the bloodletting. He understood Sherman's desire to put military considerations above politics. He himself had desired the same thing throughout war. But the war was over, to all intents and purposes. And politics again prevailed.

He forwarded Sherman's letter and agreement to Edwin Stanton. "They are of such importance that I think immediate action should be taken on them, and that it should be done by the President, in council with his whole Cabinet," Grant said.

Johnson and the cabinet convened that day and emphatically rejected Sherman's agreement. Grant was summoned to the White House and directed to travel to North Carolina to take personal charge of Sherman's army.

Grant didn't tell Sherman he was coming. Security suggested not wiring ahead lest assassins intercept the telegram and waylay the Confederacy's principal antagonist. Grant had another reason for discretion: he didn't wish to embarrass Sherman. He reached Sherman's camp at dawn; the two men repaired to Sherman's headquarters for a confidential discussion. Grant told him the president had rejected his surrender agreement with Johnston. Sherman was to resume hostilities pending Johnston's surrender on the same terms Grant had offered Lee—that is, surrender of Johnston's army, with nothing said about broader political issues.

The hostilities did not resume, however. Johnston accepted the new terms on April 26. Grant left for Washington the next day without, Sherman believed, the country's knowing that he had been in Carolina. "I thought the matter was surely at an end," Sherman recalled afterward.

*H*e discovered his mistake upon the arrival of a copy of the *New York Times*, dated April 24. The paper printed a statement by Stanton that reflected humiliatingly on Sherman. It recounted the administration's overwhelmingly negative response to Sherman's initial peace agreement with Johnston. It explained that Grant had been sent to North Carolina to take charge of Sherman's army. And it reproduced, with the specificity of a criminal indictment, Stanton's reasons why Sherman's agreement was insubordinate, wrongheaded and illegitimate: "It was an exercise of authority not vested in General Sherman. . . . It was a practical acknowledgment of the rebel government. . . . It undertook to reestablish the rebel State governments, that had been overthrown at the sacrifice of many thousand loyal lives and an immense treasure, and placed arms and munitions of war in the hands of the rebels at their respective capitals, which might be used as soon as the armies of the United States were disbanded, and used to conquer and subdue the loyal States. . . . By the restoration of the rebel authority in their respective States, they would be enabled to reestablish slavery." Adding personal insult to professional injury, Stanton asserted that Sherman was all but conspiring with Jefferson Davis in the Confederate president's efforts to escape justice. Stanton reproduced a statement from a source in Richmond regarding Davis, his fellow Confederate officials and the gold they were reported to have spirited out of the city: "They hope, it is said, to make terms with General Sherman or some other Southern commander, by which they will be permitted, with their effects, including this gold plunder, to go to Mexico or Europe. Johnston's negotiations look to this end."

Sherman was outraged at this public dressing-down. He might have acknowledged hoping for too much by way of a deal with Johnston, but as he pointed out, the agreement explicitly said it was not final until approved by the authorities in Washington. He would have accepted a quiet rejection on the order of what Grant delivered when he traveled south. But this public slap, he inferred, was raw politics, an opening round in the fight for control of reconstruction after Lincoln. And it was made at his expense.

He wrote to Grant complaining of the insult. "I have never in my life questioned or disobeyed an order," he said, "though many and many a time have I risked my life, health, and reputation in obeying orders, or even hints, to execute plans and purposes not to my liking." He reminded Grant that he had not been privy to the opinions of the politicians at Washington and therefore could not judge what they would find unacceptable. "For four years I have been in camp dealing with soldiers, and I can assure you that the conclusion at which the cabinet arrived, with such singular unanimity, differs from mine. I conferred freely with the best officers in this army as to the points involved in this controversy, and strange to say they were singularly unanimous in the other conclusion, and they will learn with pain and amazement that I am deemed insubordinate and wanting in common sense; that I, who in the complications of last year, worked day and night, summer and winter, for the cause and the Administration, and who have brought an army of 70,000 men in magnificent condition across a country deemed impassable, and placed it just where it was wanted almost on the day appointed, have brought discredit on our Government." This alone, Sherman said, should have entitled him to better consideration than he had received.

But he was happy that he would not have to endure such abuse longer, on the present subject at least. "I envy not the task of reconstruction, and am delighted that the Secretary has relieved me of it." He assumed from Grant's refusal to replace him that he still enjoyed the confidence of the general-in-chief. "I will therefore go on and execute your orders to their conclusion, and when done will with intense satisfaction leave to the civil authorities the execution of the task of which they seem to me so jealous."

HAD LINCOLN LIVED, THE WAR'S END WOULD HAVE FORCED HIM TO answer questions he had avoided amid the fighting. He would have been required to say whether emancipation implied citizenship for the freedmen; whether citizenship entailed suffrage; how far political equality, if it came to that, demanded social equality; and who would enforce the rights of African Americans against the resistance the assertion of such rights must inevitably evoke. In short, he would have been required to specify what reconstruction meant.

The task fell instead to Andrew Johnson. Little was known of the new president outside his small circle, and what *was* known wasn't promising. He had been added to Lincoln's ticket in 1864 entirely to facilitate the president's reelection; no one envisioned Johnson's becoming president himself. The Tennessee Democrat fairly represented neither the ruling party nor the war's winning section. All he brought to his new job were his personality and individual gifts, which didn't give him a great deal to work with. Oliver Temple knew Johnson from the selective world of Tennessee Unionist politics. "Johnson was a man of the coolest and most unquestioned courage," Temple granted. "When he was assailed on account of his loyalty"—to the Union—"by a mob of ruffians in Lynchburg, Virginia, on his way from Washington, in the spring of 1861, and one of them attempted to pull his nose, he drew his revolver and kept the whole pack at bay." Yet Johnson was also a man of deep character flaws. "Johnson's life was full of stormy passions," Temple said. "It had no rest, and but little sunshine in it. He was strong and self-willed; had excessive confidence in his own power; was obstinate and dogmatic, and had little respect for the opinion of others." Everything Johnson gained in life he

earned by his own effort, as he had been born poor and received no formal education. In part as a result, he despised the rich and the wellborn
even as he envied them. "He denounced aristocrats, yet imitated them,
and if not one at heart himself, he had all their worst ways," Temple said.
Johnson seemed to have but one goal in life, one interest. "Never was a
human breast fired by a more restless, inextinguishable love of power.
His ambition was boundless. To it he sacrificed everything—society,
pleasure, and ease."

Johnson's initial pronouncements as president were unexceptional and
broadly in keeping with Lincoln's sentiments. He proclaimed amnesty
and pardon for all participants in the rebellion who swore allegiance to
the laws of the United States, specifically including the laws emancipating slaves. Various persons were excluded from this amnesty offer—the
most visible of the rebels and the wealthiest—but such persons might
apply individually to the president for a case-by-case review. At the same
time, Johnson announced a protocol for reintegrating North Carolina
into the Union, a protocol that was generally interpreted as providing a
model for the reintegration of other Southern states. He appointed a provisional governor, who, with the assistance of the military commander of
the district that included North Carolina, would supervise a convention
to amend the state's constitution to make it conform with federal law.
The voters for delegates to the convention would be those citizens who
had qualified to vote under the state's laws in 1860 and who had taken
the loyalty oath.

Grant watched, at first from a distance. Some admirers in Philadelphia, hoping to entice the Union hero to take up residence in the
City of Brotherly Love, gave him a fine house. He moved the family in
and attempted to make Philadelphia his base of operations. But a brief
experiment convinced him he couldn't afford the luxury of distance from
Washington, and he accepted Henry Halleck's offer of the use of a house
in Georgetown until he and Julia could find one of their own in the
capital.

Meanwhile he did what he could to facilitate the reknitting of North
and South. He argued for the broadest possible amnesty for Confederate
officers and men. "Although it would meet with opposition in the North
to allow Lee the benefit of amnesty, I think it would have the best possible effect towards restoring good feeling and peace in the South to have

him come in," he wrote Halleck. "All the people except a few political leaders South will accept whatever he does as right and will be guided to a great extent by his example." Grant pressed to allow Confederate veterans to enlist in the Union army and urged that Confederate prisoners of war be released and transported to their home states in order to get that season's crops planted. "By going now they may still raise something for their subsistence for the coming year and prevent suffering next winter." And he worked to keep the army out of the politics of reconstruction. "Until a uniform policy is adopted for reestablishing civil government in the rebellious states, the military authorities can do nothing but keep the peace," he said.

In the fourth week of May he reviewed the victorious Union armies as they marched through Washington. "The sight was varied and grand," he recalled. "Nearly all day for two successive days, from the Capitol to the Treasury Building, could be seen a mass of orderly soldiers marching in columns of companies. The National flag was flying from almost every house and store; the windows were filled with spectators; the doorsteps and sidewalks were crowded with colored people and poor whites who did not succeed in securing better quarters from which to get a view of the grand armies." Meade's Army of the Potomac filled the first day: well equipped, carefully disciplined—the picture of martial order and strength. Sherman's westerners took up the second day. "Sherman's army was not so well dressed as the Army of the Potomac," Grant observed. "But their marching could not be excelled; they gave the appearance of men who had been thoroughly drilled to endure hardships, either by long and continuous marches or through exposure to any climate, without the ordinary shelter of a camp." Sherman's traverse of Washington recapitulated aspects of his march across the South. "In the rear of a company there would be a captured horse or mule loaded with small cooking utensils, captured chickens, and other food picked up for the use of the men. Negro families who had followed the army would sometimes come along in the rear of a company, with three or four children packed upon a single mule, and the mother leading it."

By the evidence of the applause he received, Sherman had lost nothing of popular support as a result of Stanton's rebuke. And the acclaim confirmed his ire at the secretary of war. "To say that I was merely angry . . . ," Sherman recalled, "would hardly express the state of my feelings. I was outraged beyond measure." Stanton tried to shake Sherman's hand, but Sherman glaringly refused. "He offered me his hand, but

I declined it publicly, and the fact was universally noticed," he said with satisfaction.

Grant tried to stay out of the quarrel. He respected and supported Sherman, and by his quiet but firm refusal to carry out Stanton's order to relieve Sherman he had saved his friend's job. But he had to work with Stanton, who had no desire to step aside, unless to step up to the presidency, and who was simply a difficult person. "Mr. Stanton never questioned his own authority to command," Grant wrote later. "He cared nothing for the feeling of others. In fact it seemed to be pleasanter to him to disappoint than to gratify. He felt no hesitation in assuming the functions of the executive, or in acting without advising him." In public Grant defended Stanton. A committee of Congress charged with investigating Stanton's oversight of the War Department called Grant to testify. "In what manner has Mr. Stanton, Secretary of War, performed his duties?" he was asked. "Admirably," he replied. "There has been no complaint." Grant's questioners inquired whether there had been any misunderstandings between Grant and Stanton. "Never expressed to me," Grant said.

The Stanton-Sherman contretemps receded as other matters pressed forward. The surrender of Lee and Joe Johnston hadn't quite terminated the war; Grant had to deal with the remnant Confederate armies. One headed by Richard Taylor in Mississippi surrendered in early May, ending resistance east of the Mississippi. On May 17 Grant ordered Phil Sheridan to Texas to conclude operations there.

He had a second reason for sending Sheridan to Texas. During the war the French government under Napoleon III had concocted a scheme for reviving French influence in the Americas. The centerpiece of the scheme was an underemployed Austrian prince named Maximilian, whom Napoleon's troops installed in Mexico City to the cheers of Mexican conservatives and the dismay of Mexican republicans. The American government protested this violation of the Monroe Doctrine's principle of noninterference by Europe in the affairs of the Americas, but under the duress of the war Lincoln could do little more. Grant likewise resented the French influence across the Rio Grande and upon the war's end determined that there *was* something that could be done. Sending Sheridan south was a first step. "The Rio Grande should be strongly held whether the forces in Texas surrender or not," he told Sheridan.

The Confederate forces in Texas did surrender, before Sheridan arrived. This allowed Grant to make his argument against France more explicit. "I regard the act of attempting to establish a monarchical government on this continent, in Mexico, by foreign bayonets, as an act of hostility against the Government of the United States," Grant told Andrew Johnson. "If allowed to go on until such a government is established, I see nothing before us but a long, expensive and bloody war, one in which the enemies of this country will be joined by tens of thousands of disciplined soldiers embittered against their government by the experience of the last four years." Grant amplified this last point—that the former rebels might join the French in Mexico—by noting that Maximilian's regime had allowed the Confederates free access to Mexico during the war. "It is notorious that every article held by the rebels for export was permitted to cross the Rio Grande and from there to go unmolested to all parts of the world, and they in turn to receive in pay all articles, arms, munitions of war, etc. they desired. Rebels in arms have been allowed to take refuge on Mexican soil protected by French bayonets." Grant urged Johnson to register a "solemn protest" against the French presence in Mexico. Sheridan's stationing on the Rio Grande would lend emphasis to the protest and allow additional measures if necessary.

When Johnson, under the influence of William Seward, registered a preference for quiet diplomacy, Grant made his case more strongly. "Nonintervention in Mexican affairs will lead to an expensive and bloody war hereafter, or a yielding of territory now possessed by us," he told Johnson. "To let the empire of Maximilian be established on our frontier is to permit an enemy to establish himself who will require a large standing army to watch. Military stations will be at points remote from supplies and therefore expensive to keep up. The trade of an empire will be lost to our commerce, and Americans, instead of being the most favored people of the world, throughout the length and breadth of this continent, will be scoffed and laughed at by their adjoining neighbors both north and south, the people of the British provinces and of Mexico." Grant hoped to see an ultimatum from the president. "I would have no hesitation in recommending that notice be given the French that foreign troops must be withdrawn from this continent and the people left free to govern themselves in their own way." The United States should assist the republican forces in Mexico. "I would openly sell, on credit, to the Government of Mexico all the arms, munitions and clothing they want, and aid them with officers to command troops." If the French construed such action as a provocation, the United States army would be ready.

Johnson's reluctance to pick a fight with France reflected his preoccupation with the Republicans in Congress. Johnson's first steps toward reconstruction gave the Radical Republicans—the members of the party most devoted to equal rights for the former slaves—some of what they wanted but by no means all. On paper the exclusion from amnesty of the wealthy, defined as those with taxable property worth more than $20,000, portended the destruction of the planter class; the Radicals deemed this a good thing. But the restriction of suffrage to those who had voted in 1860 transparently barred blacks from politics. Congressional Republicans were deeply divided over the question of black suffrage, but to the Radicals this exclusion was disturbing and unacceptable.

The split among the Republicans allowed Johnson's plan to proceed. Lukewarm rebels, closet Unionists and upcountry farmers dominated the constitutional conventions in the Southern states, raising the prospect that the postwar governments would be more democratic than the antebellum versions. But the constitutions the conventions wrote made no provisions for African American political participation, demonstrating that Southern democracy would stop short of the color line.

Early laws enacted by the governments elected under the new constitutions demonstrated still more: that on the race question, white resistance and reaction were rapidly setting in. In one Southern state after another the all-white legislatures approved general policies regarding the conduct of African Americans. These "black codes" addressed numerous of the issues attending the transition of blacks from slavery to freedom. They defined legal rights for the freedmen, allowing them to bring cases to court, to testify at trial, to marry, to have custody of their children. In this respect they marked an advance over slavery. But the codes also outlawed vagrancy and required blacks to find and keep employment, typically on terms dictated by white planters. Unemployed blacks could be imprisoned and hired out by the state to those same planters. As the codes took effect they revealed their central purpose: to re-create the caste system of slavery without the formal props of the peculiar institution.

The black codes convinced the Radical Republicans that Johnson couldn't be trusted with reconstruction. Thaddeus Stevens of Pennsylvania led the Radicals in the House of Representatives. Lame from birth, Stevens had long identified with the disadvantaged. He was elected to

the House as a Whig but abandoned that party in frustration at its waf-
fling on slavery. He became a founder of the Pennsylvania branch of
the Republican party and was returned to Congress in time to support
Lincoln against secession. He was chosen chairman of the House Ways
and Means Committee shortly after the war commenced and in that post
helped Lincoln raise the money to fight the rebels. But as the end of the
war approached, he increasingly differed with Lincoln over reconstruction and demanded that the South be treated not as a lapsed partner but
as a conquered province, that the planter class be broken forever, and that
African Americans be accorded their democratic rights, including full
citizenship and the vote.

Charles Sumner had an even more personal stake in reconstruction,
having given his blood, under the beating by Preston Brooks, on behalf
of African Americans. The assault crippled the Massachusetts senator,
but it silenced him only temporarily—until he regained consciousness—
and it reinforced his belief that the slave system was rooted in sin and
nurtured on violence. At the end of the war he advocated the fullest
punishment of the rebels and the fullest equality for the former slaves.

Stevens and Sumner were revolutionary idealists; their critics called
them raving zealots. But they were also practical politicians, as to an even
greater degree were their moderate Republican colleagues. The secession
of the South had been the best thing to happen to the Republican party
in its short life, giving it control of Congress and the presidency. The
return of the South, the stronghold of the Democrats, would threaten the
Republican primacy unless measures were taken to bolster the Republicans there. When the Republicans advocated giving the vote to Southern
blacks, they reasonably assumed that the freedmen would vote Republican out of gratitude toward their emancipators, hostility toward their
oppressors or simple self-defense. The last thing either the Radicals or
the moderates wanted was to let the Southern states back into the Union
without some guarantee that blacks would exercise real political power.
Because this was the result that Johnson's reconstruction plan was producing, they turned against it with a will.

Johnson provoked them further by retreating from parts of his own
initial policy. "Treason is a crime and must be made odious," he had
declared upon assuming the presidency, and his exclusion of wealthy
planters and influential Confederates from political participation had
made him look as though he meant it. But events soon proved that
though he despised the master class as a class, he couldn't resist its mem-

bers as individuals. Prominent Southerners who entreated the president for pardon discovered that he was happy to assent; the exercise apparently stroked his ego. Psychology apart, Johnson guessed that though the Republicans of the North would never embrace him, the Democrats of the South just might.

Whether or not the Southern Democrats thought they were embracing Johnson, they eagerly grasped what he offered, and when the Southern states elected federal representatives and senators, the new delegations to Congress looked suspiciously like the old, prewar delegations. Georgia's Alexander Stephens, formerly vice president of the Confederacy, was simply the most senior rebel among the many who received pardon or amnesty from Johnson in order to serve.

THE STRUGGLE BETWEEN JOHNSON AND THE REPUBLICANS REMINDED Grant why he disliked politics so. His hope for honor in politics had died with Lincoln; he distrusted Johnson and the Radicals about equally. He appreciated the praise he received wherever he went, and he understood that it rested on the perception that he was a hero who stood apart from the grubby world of politics.

But standing apart grew harder. Grant agreed with Johnson in hoping for a swift transition to peace, but he sided with the Radicals in deeming protection for the freedmen essential to ensuring the permanence of the Union victory. As general-in-chief he commanded the troops that occupied the South, and though the return of civilian government under Johnson's reconstruction program diminished the day-to-day responsibilities of the occupation force, the army might still wield considerable power across the South should Grant choose to exercise it. Yet he couldn't exercise it independently of Johnson, at least not for long.

Johnson's jealousy and ambition complicated matters further. Johnson knew that Grant was far more popular than he was, making the president reluctant to push Grant in directions Grant didn't want to go. For the same reason Johnson tried, whenever possible, to entice Grant into supporting his policies—and, Johnson hoped, improving his chances for another term as president.

At times his efforts succeeded. In the autumn of 1865, Johnson asked Grant to take a tour of the South. Grant's formal charge was to inspect federal troops and installations; the broader purpose was to assess the mind and mood of the former rebels. Grant crossed the Potomac into Virginia, then continued south through the Carolinas to Georgia before returning to Washington via Tennessee. He got back to the capital in December. "General Grant was in the council-room at the Executive Mansion today, and stated the result of his observations and conclusions during his journey south," Gideon Welles observed in his diary for December 15. "He says the people are more loyal and better disposed than he expected to find them, and that every consideration calls for the early reestablishment of the Union. His views are sensible, patriotic, and wise." Johnson agreed, and he directed Grant to summarize his assessment in writing.

"I saw much and conversed freely with the citizens of these States, as well as with officers of the army who have been stationed among them," Grant recorded. "I am satisfied that the mass of thinking men of the South accept the present situation of affairs in good faith. The questions which have heretofore divided the sentiment of the people of the two sections—slavery and states' rights, or the right of a state to secede from the Union—they regard as having been settled forever, by the highest tribunal, arms, that man can resort to." Nor was this mere acquiescence. "I was pleased to learn from the leading men whom I met that they not only accepted the decision arrived at as final but, now that the smoke of battle has cleared away and time has been given for reflection, that this decision has been a fortunate one for the whole country, they receiving like benefits from it with those who opposed them on the field and in council."

Yet the South wasn't ready for self-rule, Grant said. Four years of war had disrupted habits of yielding to civil authority. The army still had a role to play. "I did not meet anyone, either those holding place under the government or citizens of the Southern states, who think it practicable to withdraw the military force from the South at present. The white and the black mutually require the protection of the general government." Grant did not expect the troops to fight or even look particularly fearsome. "The mere presence of a military force, without regard to numbers, is sufficient to maintain order." The makeup of garrisons, however, was a matter of some delicacy. In places where there were many freedmen, the troops should be white. "The presence of black troops, lately slaves, demoralizes labor both by their advice and by furnishing in their camps a resort for the freedmen for long distances around." Moreover, black troops commanded less respect than white, most conspicuously, if somewhat surprisingly, among black civilians. "The late slave seems to be imbued with the idea that the property of his late master should by right belong to him, or at least should have no protection from the colored soldier. There is danger of collisions being brought on by such causes."

Grant elaborated on this point. Since emancipation blacks had dreamed—and been encouraged by Radical Republicans and others to dream—of being awarded the lands of their former masters. The dream hadn't been realized and by the end of 1865 looked as though it never would be. Yet it persisted among the freedmen and hindered the economic recovery of the South. "This belief is seriously interfering with the willingness of the freedmen to make contracts for the coming year," Grant wrote. Potential employers and officials of the Freedmen's Bureau tried with only mixed success to convince the former slaves that they still had to work, even if for pay. "In some instances, I am sorry to say, the freedman's mind does not seem to be disabused of the idea that a freedman has the right to live without care or provision for the future. The effect of the belief in division of lands is idleness and accumulation in camps, towns, and cities." This road would lead to disaster for the freedmen, Grant predicted. "In such cases I think it will be found that vice and disease will tend to the extermination or great reduction of the colored race." The federal government and especially the Freedmen's Bureau had the responsibility to prevent this outcome. "It cannot be expected that the opinions held by men at the South for years can be changed in a day, and therefore the freedmen require for a few years not only laws to protect them but the fostering care of those who will give them good counsel and in whom they rely."

Grant's report was as apolitically objective as he could phrase it, but it was immediately turned to politically subjective use. Johnson appended the report to a self-congratulatory message he sent to Congress formally declaring that the rebellion had been suppressed, that the United States had reclaimed control of all the insurrectionary states, that federal courts and post offices had been reopened and that federal revenues were being collected. "The aspect of affairs is more promising than, in view of all the circumstances, could well have been expected," Johnson asserted. "The people throughout the entire South evince a laudable desire to renew their allegiance to the Government and to repair the devastations of war by a prompt and cheerful return to peaceful pursuits." He acknowledged sporadic outbreaks of violence but said they weren't worrisome. "These are local in character, not frequent in occurrence, and are rapidly disappearing as the authority of civil law is extended and sustained." Race relations posed continuing challenges; this could not be otherwise given the momentous changes in Southern affairs. "But systems are gradually developing themselves under which the freedman will receive the protection to which he is justly entitled, and, by means of his labor, make himself a useful and independent member in the community in which he has a home." Johnson anticipated further rapid progress. "From all the information in my possession and from that which I have recently derived from the most reliable authority"—he cited Grant's report specifically—"I am induced to cherish the belief that sectional animosity is surely and rapidly merging itself into a spirit of nationality, and that representation, connected with a properly adjusted system of taxation, will result in a harmonious restoration of the relation of the States to the National Union."

Thaddeus Stevens didn't let Johnson's message land on his House desk before he rose to defy the president. To claim that the Southern states were full members of the Union was ludicrous, Stevens said. "They have torn their constitutional states into atoms, and built on their foundations fabrics of a totally different character." They couldn't simply resume where they had left off in 1861. "Dead men cannot raise themselves. Dead states cannot restore their own existence." Neither could the president restore them. Stevens asked his fellow legislators to consider where the Constitution reposed such restorative power. "Not in the judicial branch of Government, for it only adjudicates and does not prescribe laws. Not in the executive, for he only executes and cannot make laws. Not in the commander-in-chief of the armies, for he can only hold them under military rule until the sovereign legislative power of the conqueror shall give them law." The legislature, alone, could restore the states, Stevens said. Two provisions of the Constitution controlled the issue: "New States may be admitted by the Congress into this Union," and "The United States shall guarantee to every State in this Union a republican form of government." Who was the United States, in this context? "Not the judiciary, not the President, but the sovereign power of the people, exercised through their representatives in Congress."

Congress, moreover, should finish the egalitarian task the war had begun. The American republic, Stevens said, had been built on the principle of equality. The founders had intended for all men to exercise equal rights but were stymied by the representatives of the slave power. "For the sake of the Union they consented to wait, but never relinquished the idea of its final completion," Stevens declared. "The time to which they looked forward with anxiety has come. It is our duty to complete their work. If this Republic is not now made to stand on their great principles, it has no honest foundation, and the Father of all men will still shake it to its center."

Stevens's insistence on black equality, shared by other Radical Republicans, inspired Congress in March 1866 to pass a civil rights bill nullifying the Southern black codes, guaranteeing citizenship to the freedmen and promising equality before the law. Johnson vetoed the bill. "In all our history, in all our experience as a people living under Federal and State law, no such system as that contemplated by the details of this bill has ever before been proposed or adopted," the president declared. "They establish for the security of the colored race safeguards which go infinitely beyond any that the General Government has ever provided for the white race. In fact, the distinction of race and color is by the bill made to operate in favor of the colored and against the white race." But moderate Republicans joined the Radicals to override the veto, and the civil rights bill became law.

Yet the Radicals weren't satisfied. Stevens, Sumner and the others understood that what Congress establishes by statute the Supreme Court can disestablish by decision. The Taney court had ruled in the Dred Scott case that blacks could not be citizens, and though Taney was dead his successors on the court might follow his lead and find or conjure cause for disallowing the new civil rights act. To forestall such an outcome the Republicans proposed to write the essence of the civil rights act, the guarantee of citizenship, into the Constitution. They had revised the Constitution once already; the Thirteenth Amendment, disallowing slavery, had passed Congress in January 1865, been ratified by most of the Northern states in short order and won the approval of the Southern states as a de facto condition of their readmission under the Johnson reconstruction plan.

The Fourteenth Amendment was trickier. Johnson had endorsed the end of slavery—not that he had had much choice—but he remained stubbornly opposed to the idea of black citizenship. "This is a country for white men," he declared, "and, by God, as long as I am President, it shall be a government for white men." Nor was he alone in questioning a civil rights amendment. Several Northern states barred blacks from political participation and had no desire for a civil rights amendment to apply to *them*. Yet the status quo appeared intolerable to most Northerners. Justice to African Americans apart, the end of slavery was about to produce a side effect not many Northerners—or Southerners—had previously thought through. Abolition rendered inoperative the clause of the Constitution counting but three-fifths of slaves toward Southern representation in Congress; the black populations of the South would now be counted in full. In other words, the South, far from being punished for its crimes against the Union, would be rewarded with extra seats in the House and with the extra electoral votes for president those seats would convey. It wasn't beyond imagination that a Southerner would become president at the next election.

What to do? The Republicans couldn't fiddle the numbers back down without denying their commitment to equality and the fundamental principles of democracy. Yet they *could* insist that Southern blacks be given full rights of citizenship, including the vote, so that they might have a voice in filling those extra Southern seats. But a direct guarantee of black suffrage wouldn't sit well with the Northern states that still wanted to discriminate at the polls. The simplest solution was to count qualified voters rather than mere inhabitants in determining representation. If Southern states didn't let blacks vote, those states would gain no congressional seats. Northern states that disallowed black voting would theoretically suffer, too, but because the numbers of Northern blacks were small, in practice no Northern state was likely to lose a seat in Congress.

The Republican drafters of the civil rights amendment began by declaring that "all persons born or naturalized in the United States, and subject to the jurisdiction thereof, are citizens of the United States and of the State wherein they reside." This sentence would guarantee citizenship to African Americans (while bypassing Indians, who were not subject to federal jurisdiction). The proposed amendment went on to require that all persons in every state be accorded "the equal protection of the laws." It forbade the states to "abridge the privileges or immunities of citizens of the United States." And it guaranteed "due process of law" to all.

The "equal protection" and "due process" clauses would keep constitutional lawyers busy for the next century and a half, but the true art began in the second section of the amendment. It confirmed the end of the three-fifths rule but went on to say that when a state denied the vote to any group of adult males (excluding those barred from voting by crime or participation in the late rebellion), that state's representation in Congress would be trimmed by a proportional amount. Put otherwise, if Southern states denied the vote to blacks, they would be *worse* off than before (by roughly the three-fifths the slaves had counted). Of course, the same rule applied to Northern states that didn't allow blacks to vote, but it would have much less effect there.

As with most important works of art, what became the Fourteenth Amendment evoked strong emotions, often negative. Hardcore egalitarians complained that suffrage should have been addressed directly and that the proposed amendment left too much to chance and to the evil genius of Southern whites. Erstwhile abolitionist Wendell Phillips, still president of the Anti-Slavery Society, condemned it as a "fatal and total surrender" to the South. George W. Julian, a Radical congressman from Indiana, called it a "wanton betrayal of justice and humanity." But Thaddeus Stevens, though privately declaring the amendment a "shilly-shally bungling thing," publicly explained that nothing better could be accomplished under present circumstances. "In my youth, in my manhood, in my old age," he told the House, "I had fondly dreamed that when any fortunate chance should have broken up for a while the foundation of our institutions, and released us from obligations the most tyrannical that ever man imposed in the name of freedom, that the intelligent, pure and just men of this Republic, true to their professions and their consciences, would have so remodeled all our institutions as to have freed them from every vestige of human oppression, of inequality of rights, of the recognized degradation of the poor, and the superior caste of the rich. In short, that no distinction would be tolerated in this purified Republic but what arose from merit and conduct." This dream, however, had vanished in the crucible of the war and its turbulent aftermath. "I find that we shall be obliged to be content with patching up the worst portions of the ancient edifice, and leaving it, in many of its parts, to be swept through by the tempests, the frosts, and the storms of despotism." Stevens had reconciled himself to what was possible. "Do you inquire why, holding these views and possessing some will of my own, I accept so imperfect a proposition? I answer, because I live among men and not among angels."

53

THE REPUBLICAN LEADERSHIP DROVE THE AMENDMENT THROUGH Congress and prepared to fight the elections of 1866 under its banner. Johnson prepared to fight back, and he enlisted Grant into service with him. Even Johnson's enemies acknowledged the president's skills as a stump speaker, and he intended to put his rhetorical talents to use on a several-state "swing around the circle." He talked Grant into going by explaining that they would dedicate a memorial to Stephen Douglas in Chicago; the country would benefit from this display of bipartisan solidarity.

The crowds were tepid in the North but grew warmer as the president's group reached the border states. The turnout in St. Louis was large and enthusiastic. Johnson interpreted the positive reception as an endorsement of his reconstruction policies. "I look upon it as an indication of the popular heart moved with reference to questions now agitating the public mind," he told an afternoon rally. The audience applauded more loudly. "Believing this, I come before you with the country's flag bearing thirty-six stars, with the Constitution in one hand and the Union in the other." Johnson's reference was to his belief that all thirty-six states, North and South, were fully part of the Union, against the Radical Republican view that the eleven rebel states remained outside. "The time has come when the great masses of the people of the United States should look to a constitutional government, and an emerging from the chaotic conditions in which they were plunged, and resuming our former relations. It behooves every man who loves the law and the Constitution to see that the questions involved are properly adjusted. In leaving the stand I leave with you the Constitution your fathers purchased with their blood." More applause and rousing cheers. "I turn over to you the flag of the country, not with twenty-five but with thirty-six stars. I turn over to you the Union. It will be protected and cherished in your hands, and, so far as I am concerned, being the humble medium in the Executive Department—God being willing—they shall be protected and defended at all hazards." Louder cheers than ever.

The applause moved Johnson to greater flights that evening. He blamed violence in the South on the Radicals, who encouraged agitation against the existing Southern governments, he said. "Every drop of blood that was shed rests upon their shirts." He lampooned the Radicals who called him a Judas for betraying what they asserted was the cause of the Union. "If I have played the Judas, who has been my Christ that I have played the Judas with? Was it Thad Stevens? Was it Wendell Phillips? Was it Charles Sumner?" At each name the audience hissed and shouted. "Are these the men that set themselves up and compare themselves with the Savior of man, and everybody that differs with them in opinion, and that try to stay and arrest their diabolical and nefarious policy, to be denounced as a Judas?" Cheers and a loud "Hurrah for Andy!" from the audience. Johnson derided the motives of his opponents in Congress and their allies in the executive branch, whom he was trying to remove from office. "Don't you see, my countrymen, it is a question of power, and being in power. . . . Their object is to perpetuate themselves in power. . . . When you make an effort or struggle to take the nipple out of their mouths, how they clamor! They have stayed at home here five or six years, held the offices, grown fat, and enjoyed all the emoluments of position." He called on his listeners to rally to his side. "If you will stand by me in trying to give the people a fair chance, to have soldiers and citizens to participate in these offices, God being willing I will kick them out. I will kick them out just as fast as I can." More cheers, and shouts of "Kick 'em out!"

Grant listened and groaned. "I am getting very tired of this expedition and of hearing political speeches," he wrote Julia from Auburn, New York, when the tour had hardly begun. "I must go through, however." As Johnson's attacks on the Radicals grew more heated, Grant's tolerance diminished further. "I never have been so tired of anything before as I have been with the political stump speeches of Mr. Johnson from Washington to this place," he told Julia from St. Louis. "I look upon them as a national disgrace." He quickly added: "Of course you will not show this letter to anyone, for so long as Mr. Johnson is President I must respect him as such, and it is the country's interest that I should also have his confidence."

It complicated Grant's position that many Republicans made no secret of their preference for him. He arrived at Cincinnati ahead of Johnson and sought refuge from politics by attending the theater. But a boisterous group of Union veterans cornered him there, shouting for him to come out and address them. Grant told them to send in their commander. When the officer arrived, Grant lectured sternly: "I am no politician. The president of the United States is my commander-in-chief. I consider this demonstration in opposition to the president of the United States, Andrew Johnson. If you have any regard for me you will take your men away." A local newspaper chuckled at the denouement: "A large crowd, bent upon seeing the Union hero, joined in the clamor, but neither the seductive strains of the band nor the enthusiastic calls of the people would induce the shy little man to appear. He had in fact smelt a rat, and doubtless in consideration of the fact that the Presidential party will be here tomorrow, of which he is at this time one, he vamoosed." The crowd eventually realized that Grant had given them the slip, but they refused to be disheartened. "The boys abandoned the field with three mighty cheers for 'General Grant, the next President of the United States!'" the paper related.

Grant's unease grew into alarm as he considered the effects of Johnson's campaign upon Southerners. "I regret to say that since the unfortunate differences between the President and Congress, the former becomes more violent with the opposition he meets with until now but few people who were loyal to the Government during the rebellion seem to have any influence with him," he wrote Phil Sheridan in Texas. "None have unless they join in a crusade against Congress and declare their acts, the principal ones, illegal, and indeed I much fear that we are fast approaching the point where he will want to declare the body itself illegal, unconstitutional and revolutionary." Grant was writing Sheridan to say that the army must be on the alert. "Commanders in Southern states will have to take great care to see, if a crisis does come, that no armed headway can be made against the *Union*." Grant ordered that army weapons stored in Southern states be removed to the North, lest local militias try to seize them, and he directed Sheridan to tell the Texas governor to leave the Texas militia in their homes. The governor was citing Indian troubles as reason for summoning the citizen soldiers; Grant told Sheridan to inform the governor that the army would handle the Indians. "Texas should have no reasonable excuse for calling out the militia."

Grant's fear of Southern violence increased as the elections neared. Parts of the South had been restive for months. A riot in Memphis started after white police arrested a black man whose carriage had collided with that of a white man and some black Union veterans protested. The riot didn't end until three days had passed, nearly fifty people had been killed (all but two of them black), many more had been injured and hundreds of homes and shops had been reduced to smoldering rubble. The violent spirit spread to New Orleans, where hundreds of blacks peacefully petitioning for the vote became the victims of what Sheridan called an "absolute massacre" when angry whites, including police, assaulted the petitioners. Before Sheridan's troops were able to stop the rampage, at least thirty-four blacks (and three white sympathizers) were killed and more than a hundred persons were wounded. An eyewitness told of seeing wagons hauling away the dead and wounded, with the bodies "thrown in like sacks of corn." Contemporary accounts and subsequent investigation indicated premeditation in the attack. "We are going to shoot down all these God damned niggers," one policeman was quoted as having said.

Despite his concern at the bloodletting, Grant was reluctant to engage the army in domestic affairs unless absolutely necessary. Andrew Johnson received word from the governor of Maryland that riots could disrupt the elections in Baltimore; the president asked Grant to investigate and prepare to send in the troops. Grant inquired and concluded that though the politicking was intense, interposing the army would make things worse. "So far there seems to be merely a very bitter contest for political ascendancy in the state," he reported to Johnson. "Military interference would be interpreted as giving aid to one of the factions no matter how pure the intentions or how guarded and just the instructions. It is a contingency I hope never to see arise in this country whilst I occupy the position of General-in-Chief of the Army to have to send troops into a state *in full relations with the General Government*, on the eve of an election, to preserve the peace. If insurrection does come, the law provides the method of calling out forces to suppress it. No such condition seems to exist now."

Johnson's sources told a different story. "There is ground to apprehend danger of an insurrection in the City of Baltimore, on or about the day of the election," the attorney general, Henry Stanbery, wrote Grant,

speaking for himself and the president. "I feel great solicitude that preparations be made to meet and promptly put down such insurrection if it
should break out."

Grant went to Baltimore personally. He discovered greater cause for
concern than previously. Cyrus Comstock, a staff officer traveling with
him, wrote to George Meade: "General Grant desires me to say that
there is in Baltimore very high political feeling which may possibly result
in collision and bloodshed. It is reported that ex-soldiers called 'Boys in
Blue' exist there, and threats have been made that similar organizations
from Pennsylvania would pour into Baltimore if there should be in that
city a serious collision between the two political parties. Such an invasion would inevitably cause serious bloodshed and might lead to the most
deplorable circumstances." Grant quietly summoned troops from New
York to bolster those at Baltimore's Fort McHenry.

In public, though, he downplayed the prospect of violence. Reporters
followed him as he met with public officials and other interested parties,
calming tempers and allaying concerns. "General Grant is of the opinion
that there will be no disturbance of a serious character in Baltimore," a
correspondent with whom he had spoken informed the readers of the
New York Times.

Whether from Grant's reinforcement of the garrison, from his
soothing presence or from some other cause, the turmoil in Baltimore
didn't erupt into violence. The outcome of the elections nationwide was
a disaster for Johnson nonetheless. The Republicans won huge majorities
in both the House and Senate, claiming advantages of nearly three to one
in the lower chamber and four to one in the upper.

*T*he Republicans didn't wait for the new Congress to be sworn in to
capitalize on their triumph. On the first day of the post-election session,
in December 1866, they struck against the president. They introduced a
measure that would dissolve the Johnsonian Southern state governments
(except in Tennessee, where a rabidly anti-Johnson governor had rammed
ratification of the Fourteenth Amendment through the legislature. "Give
my respects to the dead dog of the White House," he declared). In place
of the state governments the Republican bill would reestablish military
rule, returning the South to the status of an occupied territory. Some
moderate Republicans initially balked at the measure as overly drastic,
but continuing violence in the South led to its passage in March 1867,

over Johnson's veto. The Reconstruction Act divided the South into five military districts, each under the command of an army general authorized to employ military force to ensure stability and order. It directed the occupied states to write new constitutions guaranteeing the vote to all adult males, black as well as white. And it effectively withheld congressional recognition of the new state governments until those states had ratified the Fourteenth Amendment.

In the same month the Republicans passed the Tenure of Office Act. The Republicans realized that Johnson could frustrate their legislative purposes by staffing federal positions with persons hostile to their policies. To limit Johnson's chances of doing so, the Tenure of Office Act forbade the president from removing individuals whose appointments had required Senate confirmation, without Senate endorsement of the removal. Johnson deemed the measure unconstitutional and vetoed it. The Republicans again overrode his veto.

"One of the most ridiculous veto messages that ever emanated from any president," was how Grant characterized Johnson's failed argument against the reconstruction law. Grant learned that Jeremiah Black, attorney general under James Buchanan, had drafted Johnson's message. "It is a fitting end to all our controversy . . . ," Grant wrote Elihu Washburne, "that the man who tried to prove at the beginning of our domestic difficulties that the nation had no constitutional power to save itself is now trying to prove that the nation has not now the power, after a victory, to demand security for the future." Grant cautioned Washburne that this letter was for his eyes only. "Do not show what I have said on political matters to anyone. It is not proper that a subordinate should criticize the acts of his superiors in a public manner."

Grant's efforts to keep his politics private met with diminishing success. Each week made clearer that the army was a political instrument in reconstruction and consequently that the commanding general of the army was a political figure. Grant's troops represented federal authority in the South, but with the president and Congress at loggerheads it was unclear *which* federal authority they represented. When the troops tried to protect freedmen against rioters, as Sheridan's troops did in New Orleans, they pleased the Radicals in Congress, who considered such protection necessary and appropriate. But they angered the president, who deemed the Southern states masters again of their domains. Grant appealed for guidance to his superiors, but Edwin Stanton told him one thing and Johnson another.

In his quandary Grant adopted a more advanced position politically than he had ever imagined he would. He wrote to Edward Ord at Little Rock urging him to exert what influence he could to get Arkansas to approve the Fourteenth Amendment. Ratification was inevitable eventually, he said, and Southern resistance would simply cause Congress to take harsher measures. "Delay may cause further demands, but it is scarcely in the realm of possibility that less will be accepted." He still acknowledged the wall that separated, or ought to separate, civilian affairs from those of the military. "It is not proper that officers of the Army should take part in political matters," he told Ord. But he found a door in the wall through which, in the case at hand, a conscientious officer must step. "This is hardly to be classed as a party matter. It is one of National importance. All parties agree to the fact that we ought to be united and the status of every state definitely settled. They only differ as to the manner of doing this. It ought to be seen that no way will succeed unless agreed to by Congress."

Significantly, Grant did not say "unless agreed to by the President." He recognized where political power was coming to rest, at least for the moment, and in the escalating fight between the legislature and the executive he sided increasingly with the former. Yet he resisted any overt identification with the Republicans as Republicans. "There is but little difference between the parties," he wrote Sherman.

The Republicans, however, identified with *him*. So did Johnson, when he could. Grant lamented being the object of such political fascination. "No matter how close I keep my tongue, each try to interpret from the little let drop that I am with them," he told Sherman. He said he sometimes wished he could relinquish command of the army and spend a year abroad. "But to leave now would look like throwing up a command in the face of the enemy." To Elihu Washburne he wrote, "I am not egotistical enough to suppose that my duties cannot be performed by others just as well as myself, but Congress has made it my duty to perform certain offices, and whilst there is an antagonism between the executive and legislative branches of the Government, I feel the same obligation to stand at my post that I did whilst there were rebel armies in the field to contend with."

54

THE STRUGGLE ESCALATED. AFTER JOHNSON ATTEMPTED TO SABO tage enforcement of the Reconstruction Act, the Republicans launched an impeachment effort. The House Judiciary Committee called Grant as a witness. Members asked if he had advised the president regarding reconstruction. He answered that he had. They asked what policies he had recommended for the South. "I was not in favor of anything or opposed to anything particularly," he said unhelpfully. "I was simply in favor of having a government there. That was all I wanted. I did not pretend to give my judgment as to what it should be. I was perfectly willing to leave that to the civil department." Grant was on public record as having supported speedy reconstruction; committee members inquired if he had expressed a similar opinion to the president in private? "I may have done so, and it is probable that I did," Grant said. "I do not recollect particularly. I know I conversed with the president very frequently." But there was less to the discussions than might appear, he added. "I do not suppose that there were any persons engaged in that consultation who thought of what was being done at that time as being lasting—any longer than until Congress would meet and either ratify that or establish some other form of government. I know it never crossed my mind that what was being done was anything more than temporary."

The impeachment rumblings grew louder with the spring, then diminished when Congress recessed for the summer. Johnson took the opportunity of the legislators' absence to demand Stanton's resignation. The secretary of war refused, as Johnson expected. Johnson suspended him.

Grant wished he hadn't. He warned the president against "the great danger to the welfare of the country" in defying Congress. He acknowledged that Johnson was within the letter of the law, which allowed for the suspension of officeholders while Congress was in recess. But the president's action contravened the spirit of the law. "It certainly was the intention of the legislative branch of the government to place cabinet ministers beyond the power of executive removal," Grant told Johnson. "And it is pretty well understood that, so far as cabinet ministers are affected by the Tenure of Office bill, it was intended specially to protect the Secretary of War, who the country felt great confidence in." Johnson's legal advisers sought loopholes in the law, but such an approach missed the point, Grant said. "The meaning of the law may be explained away by an astute lawyer, but common sense, and the mass of loyal people, will give to it the effect intended by its framers." Grant knew he was being forward in expressing himself so freely. But his sense of duty required nothing less. "Allow me to say as a friend, desiring peace and quiet, the welfare of the whole country, north and south, that it is in my opinion more than the loyal people of this country (I mean those who supported the government during the great rebellion) will quietly submit to, to see the very man of all others who they have expressed confidence in removed. . . . I know I am right in this matter."

His disapproval of Johnson's course didn't prevent Grant from accepting Johnson's appointment of him as acting successor to Stanton. He refused to consider becoming the actual secretary of war, believing Johnson wrong constitutionally and politically. But he believed he owed it to the army and the country to fill the post until the controversy could be resolved.

He entered his new post on good terms with his predecessor. "In notifying you of my acceptance," he told Stanton, "I cannot let the opportunity pass without expressing to you my appreciation of the zeal, patriotism, firmness and ability with which you have ever discharged the duties of Secretary of War." He initially concluded this sentence with the clause: "and also the regret I now feel at seeing you withdraw from them." But he crossed it out, apparently wanting to remain officially noncommittal as to Stanton's removal.

He thought he might have more influence with Johnson than Stanton had. The president obviously wanted some of Grant's popularity to rub off on him, and he presumably would hesitate to adopt policies Grant thought ill advised. Grant tested his influence just days after taking over the War Department. Phil Sheridan enforced the federal writ too harshly for many Texans, who appealed to the president for Sheridan's removal. Johnson told Grant to reassign Sheridan but invited him to comment on the reassignment before he sent the order out. Grant urged Johnson to think again. "It is unmistakably the expressed wish of the country that General Sheridan should not be removed from his present command," Grant said, without specifying how he had ascertained the country's will. "This is a republic where the will of the people is the law of the land. I beg that their voice may be heard." The country, especially the South, was watching. "General Sheridan has performed his civil duties faithfully and intelligently. His removal will only be regarded as an effort to defeat the laws of Congress. It will be interpreted by the unreconstructed element in the South, those who did all they could to break up this government by arms, and now wish to be the only element consulted as to the method of restoring order, as a triumph. It will embolden them to renewed opposition to the will of the loyal masses, believing they have the Executive with them."

Grant's plea failed. Johnson understood where his political support, such as it was, lay. The Republicans would never accept him; his sole hope for continuation in power was to expand his base among the Democrats, including those who called for Sheridan's removal. Besides, he believed the principle of executive independence was at stake. If he couldn't remove Stanton and reassign Sheridan, the presidency might become an impotent appendage of the legislature. He reiterated his instruction to Grant, who duly withdrew Sheridan from Texas.

The decision made Grant realize the political waters were deeper than he thought. "I feel that your relief from command of the 5th District is a heavy blow to reconstruction," he told Sheridan. "The act of removal will be interpreted as an effort to defeat the law and will encourage opposition to it. . . . I do not know what to make of present movements in this capital, but they fill me with alarm." To William Sherman, who offered sympathy at Grant's awkward position, he replied, "It is truly an unenviable one, and I wish I had never been in it. All the romance of feeling that men in high places are above personal considerations, and act only from motives of pure patriotism and for the general good of the public, has been destroyed. An inside view proves too truly very much the reverse. I am afraid to say on paper all I fear and apprehend."

When the Republicans returned to Washington in November, they were spoiling for a fight. A first attempt in the House to vote articles of impeachment failed when a majority decided that, though Johnson had made himself obnoxious, he hadn't committed the "high crimes and misdemeanors" specified by the Constitution as sole grounds for removal. If Johnson had been looking to patch over his differences with the Republicans, he could have taken this as an opportunity. But he was as determined as they were to have matters out, and he stood on his right to remove Stanton.

Grant again found himself in the crossfire. Sherman was in Washington that winter crafting a new code of army regulations. "Our place of meeting was in the room of the old War Department, second floor, next to the corner room occupied by the Secretary of War, with a door of communication," Sherman remembered. "While we were at work it was common for General Grant and, afterward, for Mr. Stanton to drop in and chat with us on the social gossip of the time." As the controversy between Johnson and the Republicans intensified, Grant told Sherman that he had only recently read the tenure of office law carefully. "It was different from what he had supposed," Sherman said. "In case the Senate did not consent to the removal of Secretary of War Stanton, and he (Grant) should hold on, he should incur a liability of ten thousand dollars and five years' imprisonment." Grant was uncomfortable heading the War Department on even an interim basis; the prospect of prison and financial ruin made continuing in the post utterly impossible. Sherman asked him if he had told this to Johnson. He said he had not but would do so soon.

What happened next became a subject of rancorous disagreement. "Learning on Saturday, the 11th instant"—that is, of January 1868—"that the Senate had taken up the subject of Mr. Stanton's suspension," Grant wrote Johnson in subsequent recapitulation, "after some conversation with Lieutenant General Sherman and some members of my staff, in which I stated that the law left me no discretion as to my action should Mr. Stanton be reinstated, and that I intended to inform the President, I went to the President for the sole purpose of making this decision known and did so make it known." Johnson at their meeting—on January 14—disputed Grant's interpretation of the tenure law, saying that he had appointed Grant under the terms of the Constitution, not of any statute, and that Grant therefore was not governed by the act. Grant demurred. "I stated that the law was binding on me, constitutional or not, until set aside by the proper tribunal. An hour or more was consumed, each reiterating his views on this subject, until getting late, the President said he would see me again." Grant was sure he had made his intentions plain. "From the 11th to the Cabinet meeting on the 14th instant, a doubt never entered my mind about the President fully understanding my position, namely that if the Senate refused to concur in the suspension of Mr. Stanton, my powers as Secretary of War ad interim would cease, and Mr. Stanton's right to resume at once the functions of his office would under the law be indisputable."

Later on January 14 Grant received official notice that the Senate had refused to support Stanton's suspension. He immediately forwarded the notice to Johnson with a letter of his own. "According to the provisions of Section 2 of 'An Act Regulating the Tenure of Certain Civil Offices,' my functions as Secretary of War, ad interim, ceased from the moment of the receipt of the within notice," he told the president.

Johnson called a meeting of the cabinet and told Grant he should come. Johnson treated Grant as though he were still war secretary. Grant reminded him that he had been removed by the Senate order. Johnson thereupon related his version of the conversations they had had. He said that Grant had agreed to remain as war secretary until removed by the courts or to resign and allow the president to name another secretary. Grant rejected Johnson's version—"though to soften the evident contradiction my statement gave, I said (alluding to our first conversation on the subject) the President might have understood me in the way he said, namely that I had promised to resign if I did not resist the reinstatement," Grant later recalled. He added, "I made no such promise."

Johnson insisted that he *had* made the promise. And in a long, angry letter to Grant that got into the papers, he said that four of the five cabinet secretaries present at the meeting attested that he had.

"I confess my surprise that the Cabinet officers referred to should so greatly misapprehend the facts in the matter," Grant replied. He refused to retreat. Referring to the letter to Johnson in which he had stated his understanding of their conversations, he said, "I here reassert the correctness of my statements in that letter, anything in yours in reply to it to the contrary notwithstanding." He said he had accepted the job of acting war secretary simply to ensure continuity in army policy in the South, not to enable Johnson to fire Stanton. And in a tone he had never imagined he would take toward a commander in chief, he concluded: "Mr. President, where my honor as a soldier and integrity as a man have been so violently assailed, pardon me for saying I can but regard this whole matter, from the beginning to the end, as an attempt to involve me in the resistance of law, for which you hesitated to assume the responsibility in orders, and thus to destroy my character before the country."

*I*f Johnson hadn't been so unpopular, Grant might have had to work harder to explain the discrepancy between what he said he had told Johnson and the cabinet and what Johnson and the four cabinet members said they had heard. But Johnson's removal of Stanton eliminated what scruples most Republicans in Congress still had about going after Johnson, and within days the big story in Washington was the first impeachment of a president in American history. The nine articles of impeachment approved by the House alleged various high crimes and misdemeanors, but the central one was Johnson's failure to fulfill his constitutional obligation to ensure that the laws of the United States—in particular the Tenure of Office Act—be faithfully executed.

Some of the Radical Republicans apparently believed that the mere threat of removal would compel Johnson to resign. Moorfield Storey, Charles Sumner's secretary, predicted privately that Johnson would growl till the last moment before retreating like a "thoroughly ill-bred dog" and submitting his resignation. Eliza Johnson, the president's wife, viewed the prospect of eviction from the White House ambivalently. "But for the humiliation and Mr. Johnson's feelings," she told a friend, "I wish they would send us back to Tennessee—if it were possible, give us our poverty and peace again, so that we might learn how to live for our children and ourselves. I have not seen a happy moment since I came to this house."

But Johnson had always been a scrapper, and he scrapped now. It helped him that the Republicans in the Senate, where the trial would be held, weren't as unified as their counterparts in the House. Though Sumner confidently declared that "never in history was there a great case more free from all just doubt," a number of his colleagues weren't so sure—about Sumner, if not about Johnson. William Fessenden of Maine, the Senate Republican leader, despised Sumner. After the first impeachment attempt had failed, Fessenden took comfort that the failure frustrated Sumner. "His bitterness beats wormwood and gall," Fessenden said. He subsequently characterized Sumner as "the most cowardly dog in the parish."

Another impediment to conviction involved the man who would

succeed Johnson. Benjamin Wade, the president pro tempore of the Senate, had almost as many enemies in the upper house as Johnson did, and these had no desire to make Wade president (on account of there being no vice president). "If impeachment fails, be sure of one fact," a Washington observer remarked. "Dislike for Mr. Wade has done it."

The trial began in early March and lasted till the middle of May. Salmon Chase, who had succeeded Roger Taney as chief justice of the Supreme Court in 1864, presided. The House sent Thaddeus Stevens and several colleagues to manage the prosecution; Johnson retained William Evarts, a distinguished member of the New York bar and a harsh critic of Johnson's reconstruction policies who nonetheless thought the president deserved capable counsel. The senators, sitting as the jury in the case, weighed matters constitutional (What precisely were "high crimes and misdemeanors"?), political (Was it smarter to remove Johnson by conviction now or by election six months hence?) and philosophical (Was this exercise of the impeachment power a vindication of democracy or its perversion?). In the end the prosecution persuaded a solid majority but not quite the necessary two-thirds. Seven Republicans crossed the line to vote with the Democrats, sparing Johnson by a single vote.

WHILE THE STRUGGLE BETWEEN JOHNSON AND THE REPUBLICANS convulsed Washington and the East, a more violent struggle of much longer duration was playing out in the West. The contest for mastery of what would become the United States, between the indigenous peoples of North America and the European settlers and their descendants, had begun with the first clashes between the Indians and the English in Virginia and New England in the early seventeenth century; it continued with King Philip's War, the French and Indian War, Pontiac's Rebellion, Tecumseh's War, the Creek War, the Seminole Wars, the Black Hawk War and the hundreds of raids, massacres and reprisals too minor to merit proper names. The battleground shifted as the frontier of white settlement pushed westward; one group of defenders gave way to another as various Indian tribes were defeated, dislocated or destroyed. By the midpoint of the nineteenth century the eastern half of the continent was essentially pacified; only the territory west of the Mississippi experienced continued resistance. And for a time that resistance was modest. The discovery of gold in California drew hundreds of thousands of adventurers to the Pacific Coast, and though they wreaked havoc on the California tribes, they provoked little conflict with the peoples of the Great Plains, the Rocky Mountains or the Great Basin. Those peoples stole cattle from unprotected wagon trains and sometimes extorted protection money from the travelers, but they typically acquiesced in the migrants' passage, recognizing them as a transient annoyance rather than an existential danger.

Things changed around 1860. The discovery of gold and silver in Nevada, Idaho, Colorado, Montana and other parts of the western interior brought permanent populations of intruders to regions previously unpeopled by whites. And the outbreak of the Civil War pulled soldiers from frontier forts where their presence had tended to keep the peace. The uncontrolled friction between settlers and Indians in southeastern Colorado in 1864 culminated in a bloody massacre of Cheyenne and Arapaho men, women and children by Colorado militia at Sand Creek. The Sand Creek massacre reverberated among the tribes of the region and touched off a general war for the Plains. The Cheyenne and Arapaho allied with the Sioux to assault white settlements and outposts across Colorado. A force of a thousand Indians swept down upon the village of Julesburg, slaughtering and scalping the residents and burning the buildings. The attackers tore out telegraph lines and severed the road to Denver, cutting off that town from supplies and reinforcements.

The Sioux took the lead in the fighting, and at the head of the Sioux was a chief of the Oglala band, Red Cloud. "The Great Spirit raised both the white man and the Indian," Red Cloud afterward told a delegation of federal officers at Fort Laramie. "I think he raised the Indian first. He raised me in this land and it belongs to me. The white man was raised over the great waters, and his land is over there. Since they crossed the sea, I have given them room. There are now white people all about me. I have but a small spot of land left. The Great Spirit told me to keep it."

Efforts by the government to open a more direct route to the gold fields of Montana prodded Red Cloud and his first lieutenant, Crazy Horse, to launch a new series of attacks. Crazy Horse ambushed parties along the Bozeman road, enticing the commander at Fort Phil Kearny to sally forth in pursuit. The commander, William Fetterman, a Civil War veteran, had boasted that with eighty men he could ride through the entire Sioux nation. With eighty-one men he rode into Crazy Horse's trap, and he and his men were annihilated.

The conflict escalated further with the approach of construction crews of the transcontinental railroad. The Indians of the region hadn't seen trains before, but they quickly realized that these trains weren't like wagon trains, here today and gone tomorrow. The railroad established a permanent white presence and consequently a more serious threat to the indigenes' way of life. When the railroad trains disgorged buffalo hunters who slaughtered the herds on which the Indians depended for food, clothing, shelter and fuel, the conflict became irrepressible. Not long after Crazy Horse crushed Fetterman, a coalition of Sioux and Cheyenne conducted raids against the Union Pacific crews in Wyoming. In one a hundred Indians attacked a special train carrying government officials and potential investors; the travelers escaped injury but quickly retreated to safer ground.

Grant inherited the Indian war when he became general-in-chief, but not until the struggle with the South ended did he pay much attention to the conflict on the Plains. In the summer of 1865 he sent Sherman to command the army forces in the West from headquarters at St. Louis; he typically worked through Sherman but occasionally received communications from the front. "I want men," Colonel Henry Carrington demanded from Fort Phil Kearny in the wake of the Fetterman debacle. "I must have reinforcements and the best of arms." Carrington related the grim details of the defeat and declared that if Grant didn't send men and weapons the country must expect more of what Fetterman and his men had suffered. "Any remissness will result in mutilation and butchery beyond precedent."

Grant was willing to reinforce the western army, but he insisted on doing so as part of a deliberate strategy. Sherman had proposed dividing the West into separate districts for whites and Indians. The Sioux would be kept north of the Platte, west of the Missouri and east of the road to Montana. "All Sioux found outside of these limits without a written pass from some military commander defining clearly their object should be dealt with summarily," Sherman wrote Grant. The Arapaho, Cheyenne and other tribes would have their own districts. "This would leave for our people exclusively the use of the wide belt, east and west, between the Platte and the Arkansas, in which lie the two great railroads and over which passes the bulk of travel to the mountain territories. As long as these Indians can hunt the buffalo and antelope within the described limits"—of the white zone—"we will have the depredations of last summer and, worse yet, the exaggerations of danger raised by our own people, often for a very base purpose."

Grant forwarded Sherman's plan to the War Department. He endorsed the recommendations, provided that they didn't conflict with existing treaty obligations. "The protection of the Pacific railroad, so that not only the portion already completed shall be entirely safe, but that the portion yet to be constructed shall in no way be delayed, either by actual or apprehended danger, is indispensable," he declared.

Grant and Sherman viewed the struggle for the Plains through their experience of the struggle for the Union. Railroads were critical; protecting the lines of communication and transport took precedence over nearly everything else. Commerce came a distant second. Grant perceived the agents licensed by the Indian Bureau of the Department of the Interior as being much like the rogue traders of the Civil War. They put personal profit before the nation's interest, to the point of selling the Indians the weapons they used against the federal soldiers. Grant judged this intolerable, and he bent every effort to bring the traders under control of the military. "The Indian Bureau should be transferred to the War Department," he told Sherman. "And Indian agencies, from among civilians, abolished. . . . No license should be given to traders among them." The army would then strictly regulate what goods might be sold to the Indians. "Keeping arms and munitions from them, trade in all other articles would weaken them more rapidly than campaigns."

Grant made the same argument more sharply and more politically to Edwin Stanton, at that time still secretary of war. Grant knew that the current regime of Indian agents had friends in Washington who would resist the changes he espoused. But he told Stanton that the government needed to make up its mind. "If the present practice is to be continued, I do not see that any course is left open to us but to withdraw our troops to the settlements, and call upon Congress to provide means and troops to carry on formidable hostilities against the Indians until all the Indians or all the whites upon the Great Plains and between the settlements on the Missouri and the Pacific slope are exterminated."

He took his case to the president and the cabinet. "War exists," he told Johnson and the secretaries. "We cannot fight them with one branch of the government and equip and food them with another, with any kind of justice to those who are called upon to expose their lives," he said. He was asked whether supplies ought to be withheld from peaceable Indians. "The military must be the judge of who are peaceable Indians," he replied.

The judgment of some military men could be harsh. The spring of 1867 brought a new round of raids by the Plains tribes upon white forts and settlements; Sherman concluded that the chances of coexistence were slim. "This conflict of authority will exist as long as the Indians exist, for their ways are different from our ways," he wrote Grant. "Either they or we must be masters on the Plains." Sherman contended that right and wrong had little to do with the matter. "I have no doubt that our people have committed grievous wrong to the Indians, and I wish I could punish them. But it is impracticable." The offenders had their political sponsors against whom a mere soldier would only break his lance. The alternatives were plain and undeniable. "Both races cannot use this country in common. . . . One or the other must withdraw."

Grant wasn't prepared to agree. When the Johnson administration refused to rein in the traders and Congress declined to increase appropriations for western defense, Grant called for a retreat from the most exposed western positions, the forts in the valley of the Powder River. "It will be well to prepare at once for the abandonment of the posts Phil Kearny, Reno, and Fetterman, and to make all the capital with the Indians that can be made out of the change," he wrote Sherman. He told Sherman to prepare the evacuation at once, lest matters on the ground force the army's hand. "I fear that, by delay, the Indians may commence hostilities and make it impossible for us to give them up." To Stanton, Grant again spoke more politically. He identified the forts he wished to evacuate and explained that the ground they occupied was more important to the Indians than to the whites. "These posts are kept up at great expense and without any benefit," he said. Prudence called for their abandonment.

Even as he urged retreat, Grant added his voice to those calling for negotiations with the Indians. He tapped Sherman to head a peace commission. Sherman had to be talked into the job, having traveled to Fort Laramie the previous autumn to meet with leaders of the Sioux, only for Red Cloud to boycott the talks. The chief sent a message that there was nothing to negotiate until the whites left the Powder River. "I did not first commence the spilling of blood," he said. "If the Great Father kept the white men out of my country, peace would last forever. But if they disturb me, there will be no peace. . . . I mean to keep this land."

Grant told Sherman to try again. "Your peace commission may accomplish a great deal of good, beside that of collecting the Indians on reservations, by attracting the attention of Indians during the season practicable for making war, and also of our white people, who never seem to be satisfied without hostilities with them." Talking was preferable to fighting. "It is much better to support a peace commission than a campaign against Indians."

Sherman consented, only to be frustrated again. Once more Red Cloud stayed away. He sent another message: "We are on the mountains looking down on the soldiers and the forts. When we see the soldiers moving away and the forts abandoned, then I will come down and talk."

Sherman left muttering at the stubbornness of the Sioux. But Red Cloud got what he wanted. In the summer of 1868, after Congress accepted Grant's calls for retrenchment, the army pulled out of the Powder River forts. Red Cloud led his warriors down from the mountains and into the forts, which he burned to the ground. He proceeded to Fort Laramie and signed a treaty Sherman had prepared. "The Government of the United States desires peace, and its honor is hereby pledged to keep it," the treaty said. "The Indians desire peace, and they now pledge their honor to maintain it."

THOUGH THE IMPEACHMENT EFFORT FAILED TO REMOVE JOHNSON from office, it confirmed congressional control of reconstruction. The president bowed to the inevitable and began to enforce the laws he had lately condemned, and the Radicals pushed ahead with the writing of Republican-friendly constitutions for the Southern states. Their haste to do justice to the former slaves was inspired by their historical sense that injustice had festered far too long in America and their political sense that if Republican-controlled Southern states could be readmitted in time for the 1868 presidential election, the electoral votes of those states would guarantee a Republican victory.

The most controversial question at the Republican convention was how severely to criticize Andrew Johnson—a question that proved not very controversial at all. "We profoundly deplore the untimely and tragic death of Abraham Lincoln," the platform declared, "and regret the accession of Andrew Johnson to the Presidency, who has acted treacherously to the people who elected him and the cause he was pledged to support; has usurped high legislative and judicial functions; has refused to execute the laws"—and so on, through a condemnation that culminated in a correct but misleading verdict: "and has been justly impeached for high crimes and misdemeanors, and properly pronounced guilty thereof by the vote of thirty-five senators."

The easy part was nominating Grant. He hadn't campaigned at all, and no one in particular had campaigned on his behalf. The delegates simply assumed that the hero of the war would make an irresistible candidate. "It would hardly seem that the Convention had met for the purpose of nominating a candidate for President, so little is that office mentioned in the canvass going on," a reporter who reached Chicago with the delegates said on Monday, May 18. "Grant's name occurs to no one save as a positively fixed result, and the only occasion when it will be prominently in the mouths of his friends is when he is nominated by acclamation, which will be done by Thursday certainly, if not sooner." The reporter added disappointedly: "This detracts in a great measure from the excitement and interest usually attending the nomination."

No other candidate challenged Grant; if one had, there might have been a riot, or perhaps a mutiny. A gathering of Union veterans took place in Chicago simultaneous with the Republican convention; the soldiers swapped battle tales and convinced themselves that none other than their old commander must now become the country's commander in chief. They passed a unanimous resolution to this effect and marched to the Republican convention to help the delegates there reach the same conclusion. At times it was hard to distinguish between the two groups. The temporary chairman of the Republican convention was Union general Carl Schurz, who introduced the permanent chairman, General Joseph Hawley. General John Logan placed Grant's name in nomination. Scores more of the delegates had been lesser Union officers. The convention hardly required the prompting from the veterans; it unanimously approved Grant's nomination on the first ballot.

Grant received word at Washington. Though he hadn't sought the nomination, he could read the newspapers and the political tea leaves as well as anyone and wasn't surprised. "The proceedings of the convention were marked with wisdom, moderation and patriotism, and, I believe, express the feelings of the great mass of those who sustained the country through its recent trials," he wrote by way of reply, complimenting the delegates and himself in a single sentence. He distanced himself from Johnson, saying, "If elected to the office of President of the United States it will be my endeavor to administer all the laws, in good faith." He avoided specifics. "In times like the present it is impossible, or at least eminently improper, to lay down a policy to be adhered to, right or wrong, through an administration of four years. New political issues, not foreseen, are constantly arising; the views of the public on old ones are constantly changing, and a purely administrative officer should always be free to execute the will of the people." He embraced tradition and essential values. "Peace, and universal prosperity, its sequence, with economy of administration, will lighten the burden of taxation, while it constantly reduces the national debt." He closed with four words that summarized

the mood of the country and made the general election almost pro forma:
"Let us have peace."

"*I* have seen in the papers the notice of your nomination and acceptance," William Sherman wrote Grant. "I feel a little strange, though
this was a foregone conclusion. If you want the office of course I want
you to have it, and now that you have accepted the nomination of course
you must succeed." But Sherman couldn't help thinking that Grant was
entering a world far removed from that in which they both had found
their calling in life. "It is a sacrifice on your part, but one which I doubt
not you feel forced to make."

"You understand my position perfectly," Grant replied. "It is one I
would not occupy for any mere personal consideration, but, from the
nature of the contest since the close of active hostilities, I have been forced
into it in spite of myself." He still disdained politics, and he entered the
political arena only to preserve the values he had served in the army. "I
could not back down without, as it seems to me, leaving the contest for
power for the next four years between mere trading politicians, the elevation of whom, no matter which party won, would lose to us, largely, the
results of the costly war which we have gone through."

*T*he Democrats gathered in New York City in early July. Their convention was a test of endurance; not till the twenty-second ballot did
Horatio Seymour, the New York governor, emerge victorious. Seymour
wasn't an inspiring candidate; the survivors of bruising conventions often
survive precisely because they inspire few strong emotions. But the convention paired him with Francis Blair of Missouri, the Union hero of the
fight for St. Louis. Blair had been a Jacksonian in youth (his father was
Old Hickory's chief propagandist), yet he grew up to be a Free-Soiler and
then a Republican. After foiling the Confederate plot against St. Louis,
he rose to the rank of major general under William Sherman. He parted
ways with the Republicans after the war and returned to his Democratic
roots, condemning the Republican reconstruction policies for trampling
the rights of the states, subordinating whites to blacks and fastening alien
regimes on Southern society. He won the vice presidential nomination
by virtue of an open letter published on the eve of the 1868 convention,
in which he called for executive nullification of the Republican recon-

struction acts—that is, for more of what had prompted the impeachment of Andrew Johnson. "The reconstruction policy of the Radicals
will be complete before the next election," Blair said. "The States so long
excluded will have been admitted; negro suffrage established, and the
carpet-baggers installed in their seats in both branches of Congress. . . .
We cannot, therefore, undo the Radical plan of reconstruction by Congressional action." So what were the Democrats to do? "There is but one
way to restore the Government and the constitution, and that is for the
President-elect to declare these acts null and void, compel the army to
undo its usurpations at the South, disperse the carpet-bag State Governments, allow the white people to reorganize their own Governments and
elect Senators and Representatives." The convention must focus entirely
on reconstruction. "This is the real and only question which we should
allow to control us: Shall we submit to the usurpations by which the
Government has been overthrown, or shall we exert ourselves for its full
and complete restoration?" Blair supplied the answer: "We must restore
the constitution. . . . We must have a President who will execute the will
of the people by trampling into dust the usurpations of Congress known
as the Reconstruction acts."

Blair's letter was strong liquor so soon after the Johnson trial. A
friendly reporter gave the vice presidential nominee an opportunity to
clarify his comments, asking him if his remarks might not alarm the
American people. "Alarm the people?" he bellowed in reply. "Why, they
are alarmed already. The country is in revolution. The liberties of one-
half of the citizens of this country have been destroyed, and those of the
other half threatened. . . . If the madness of Congress is not checked, we
will have in the South an Ireland or a Poland, and periodical insurrections will give vent to the aspirations of the people for liberty."

With Blair busy showing that the Democrats had learned nothing
from the Johnson fiasco, Grant could have been elected without saying
anything. And in fact he said very little. Presidential nominees in the
nineteenth century rarely campaigned for themselves; custom dictated
that they leave the stumping to others. For the publicly gregarious among
the nominees, the silence was a trial; for Grant it was a pleasure, besides
being tactically shrewd.

He headed west from Washington and joined Sherman and Sheridan on an inspection tour of the Great Plains. "The country to this place

is beautiful, and this is one of the most beautiful military posts in the United States," he wrote Julia from Fort Leavenworth, Kansas. "This will probably be the last chance I will ever have to visit the plains, and the rapid settlement is changing the character of them so rapidly that I thought I would avail myself of the opportunity to see them." Grant's sons Fred and Ulysses Jr., the latter called Buck, accompanied him and the other officers. "Sherman, Sheridan, Fred, Buck and myself each carry with us a Spencer carbine and hope to shoot a buffalo and elk before we return." A mix-up with luggage left the travelers stranded at Denver for two days. "I do not regret it now, however, because I shall spend the two days in the gold mines in the mountains, which probably I would never see but for this accident," Grant told Julia.

He dodged requests to speak. "I fully appreciate the compliment conveyed in the resolution which you forward, and thank the City Council and citizens for it," he told the mayor of Leavenworth, Kansas, who had delivered a formal offer to hold a reception. "But while traveling for recreation, and to inspect personally a country with which I have so much to do and have never seen, I would much prefer avoiding public demonstrations." The mayor was miffed, having hoped to bask in Grant's glory, but Grant's reticence evoked approving nods among the many voters who preferred their heroes unsullied by electioneering.

He circled back to Galena in early August. He had expected to visit only briefly. "I find it so agreeable here, however, that I have concluded to remain until about the end of September," he wrote John Rawlins, the Galenan who was still his adjutant. The people were friendly, and in the small town he could minimize his public exposure. "Whilst I remain here I shall avoid all engagements to go any place at any stated time. The turnout of people is immense when they hear of my coming. I was invited to visit Dubuque and I agreed to go over this evening but positively refused to agree to any reception." When he got to Dubuque he was nonetheless implored to speak. "My friends," he responded, reading uncomfortably from a scrap of paper: "I am very glad to see you and thank you for your kindness. Dubuque being near my old residence, I have a number of friends here whom I desire to see. I have come among you for no political purpose, and do not design to make you any speech; nor do I desire that any speeches should be made on my account. I thank you all, and wish you good evening."

The dramatic story of that summer's politics was the death of Thaddeus Stevens. The Radical leader succumbed after a long illness; tens of thousands of mourners, many of them African Americans, filed through the Capitol, where his body lay in state. Stevens delivered a final message by his burial in an integrated cemetery in Pennsylvania. "I have chosen this," he explained in his epitaph, "that I might illustrate in my death the principles which I advocated through a long life: Equality of man before his Creator."

Stevens's passing, coming after the Radicals' failure to remove Johnson and after the nomination of Grant, suggested that the center of gravity in the Republican party was shifting. The battle cry of Stevens and the Radicals was equality, which demanded continued reform. Grant's motto was peace, which implied a willingness to let things alone.

But it also implied, for Grant and his supporters, a consolidation of what had been won in the war. "If the contest was to be determined by the mere comparison of the public services of the candidates, everyone would say that General Grant ought to be elected," John Sherman, now a senator, told a gathering of Republicans in Ohio. "The highest services should be rewarded with the highest honors." But more was involved. "I do not place this election upon mere personal grounds," Sherman continued, speaking for many Republicans. "The vital importance of the election of General Grant grows out of the condition of affairs in the South. This campaign is to complete a cycle of events as important for human progress as any period of history. After a long struggle in arms with rebels and another long struggle in Congress with Andrew Johnson, we are approaching a period of rest and peace. . . . Under the prudent management of General Grant the violent spirits of the South will have no recourse but to submit to the laws. The long struggle in the South against slavery will be settled, and the right of all men to liberty will be secured."

Merits and promise aside, the arithmetic of the electoral college strongly favored Grant. Three Southern states—Virginia, Mississippi and Texas—had not been readmitted to the Union under the requirements of the Reconstruction Act; their absence handicapped the Democrats. The Southern states that *had* been readmitted leaned Republican, not least by virtue of the enfranchisement of black voters under the convoluted terms of the recently ratified Fourteenth Amendment. Grant could lose such Democratic strongholds as Seymour's New York State and still coast to electoral victory, even if the popular vote turned out to be close.

———

*T*he campaign included the usual election-season silliness. Grant was charged with being a drunkard and with having fathered a daughter by an Indian woman in the Pacific Northwest. His supporters ignored the first charge, which was old news, and they refuted the second by pointing out that Grant had been hundreds of miles away at the time the child was conceived. He was called a "nigger lover," which simply allowed his backers to link him to Lincoln.

One allegation he took personally and devoted time to answering. American Jews were a small but potentially important constituency; most remembered Grant's order expelling Jews from the military district of the Tennessee and wondered what it said about him as a man and a possible president. Jewish spokesmen inquired of the candidate; Grant replied in a letter to a supporter who had forwarded one of the inquiries, from a lawyer named Adolph Moses. He said he regretted having issued the poorly drafted order. "Give Mr. Moses assurances that I have no prejudice against sect or race but want each individual to be judged by his own merit," he wrote. "Order No. 11 does not sustain this statement, I admit, but then I do not sustain that order. It never would have been issued if it had not been telegraphed the moment penned, without one moment's reflection."

His statements allayed the concerns of at least some Jewish leaders. Simon Wolf, a prominent and well-connected Jew who shared an Ohio background with Grant, published an open letter to Jews and anyone else who happened to read the August 6 issue of the *Boston Transcript*: "I know General Grant and his motives, have corresponded with him on this very subject, and assert unhesitatingly *that he never intended to insult any honorable Jew; that he never thought of their religion*; that the order was simply directed 'against certain evil-designing persons who respected neither law nor order, and who were endangering the morale of the army.' . . . Unfortunately the order was ill-worded, but that is no reason why American citizens should be betrayed from their allegiance principles and turn to a party that advocates the reverse of what is right and true."

Little else intruded on Grant's time in Galena. "A person would not know there was a stirring canvass going on if it were not for the accounts we read in the papers," he wrote Elihu Washburne in late September. He and Julia, who had joined him, liked Galena so much he extended his stay another month, into October. "I presume military affairs get on as well without me as they would with me in Washington," he wrote

John Schofield, who had succeeded Edwin Stanton as secretary of war. In October he decided to remain another two weeks. "I want to put off the evil day, day of all work, as long as possible," he explained to Isaac Morris.

"Let us have peace," he had said, and most of the nation shared his desire. But in certain states the climax of the campaign brought anything but peace. The Ku Klux Klan had begun life in Tennessee as a fraternal gathering of Confederate veterans shortly after the war; following the Radical seizure of reconstruction it became a forum for grievances against the Republican governments in the South. Soon it was reprising the night patrols of the antebellum era, with a contemporary purpose: to intimidate blacks and Republicans and keep them from the polls. In 1868 the assaults of the Klan and kindred clubs were most violent in Louisiana and Georgia, where hundreds were killed and thousands terrorized. The Republicans of those two states, fearing for their lives, essentially surrendered the election to the Democrats before the balloting took place.

Besides Louisiana and Georgia, Grant lost Seymour's New York, neighboring New Jersey, the border states of Delaware, Maryland and Kentucky, and unpredictable Oregon. But he carried everything else, including all of New England and the Midwest and six states of the former Confederacy. He won the popular vote by 300,000 out of nearly 6 million votes cast and swamped Seymour in electors, 214 to 80.

GRANT'S ELECTION PLACED HIM IN A LINE OF AMERICAN GENERALS rewarded for their victories by elevation to the presidency. George Washington defeated the British in the Revolutionary War, Andrew Jackson the British and the Creek Indians in the War of 1812 and the Spanish in Florida thereafter, William Henry Harrison the British and Tecumseh in the War of 1812, Zachary Taylor the Mexicans in Grant's first war. Each victory expanded American territory or confirmed American rule over territory previously acquired; each allowed Americans greater freedom to extend their vision of human happiness against the competing visions of those they vanquished. Few other aspirants to office could claim to have conferred such boons on their countrymen; little wonder American voters admired and rewarded their generals.

Grant's contribution to the nation's destiny was arguably the most significant in the heroic line. Everything achieved by Washington, Jackson, Harrison and Taylor—not to mention the other presidents—was put at risk by Southern secession; the republican experiment would fail if the republic fell apart. Grant's victory was a victory for the idea that people could govern themselves; the presidency, the greatest gift the American people could confer, was hardly excessive for such a champion.

But there was a shadow across the victory and hence across the gift. The Union victory wasn't simply or even chiefly an intellectual victory; it was a military victory. Southerners were no less certain than Northerners of the legitimacy of their interpretation of the principles of self-government; the South lost from lack not of conviction but of ammunition. Grant didn't *convince* the South; he *conquered* the South.

Thus it had ever been. American ideals had always traveled armed.

The Loyalists of the American Revolution hadn't been persuaded; they had been defeated (and then, in many cases, driven away). The opponents of American expansion in the nineteenth century—the British, the Spanish, the Mexicans, the Indians—had yielded not to democracy's arguments but to democracy's might. Southerners were simply the most recent of those compelled to yield to American—in this case Northern—force majeure.

Americans disliked to admit that theirs was a nation built by war; they preferred to believe that the success of their country reflected the primacy of their values. To the extent that their democratic values fueled their military prowess, they weren't wrong. And to that extent their habit of conferring the highest democratic prize on their greatest military men made perfect sense.

It didn't make Grant's new job any easier, though. Saving the Union during the war had been difficult but straightforward; Grant and the army simply had to defeat Lee and the Confederates on the battlefield. Saving the Union after the war—preserving the gains of democracy and equality against the resistance of all those unconvinced Southerners—would doubtless be more complicated.

Grant addressed Galena the day after the election. "The choice has fallen upon me," he said. "The responsibilities of the position I feel, but I accept them without fear, if I can have the same support which has been given to me thus far. I thank you and all others who have fought together in this contest." He bade his neighbors good-bye. "I leave here tomorrow for Washington, and shall probably see but few of you again for some years to come." He added, with equal parts tact and sincerity: "It would give me great pleasure to make an annual pilgrimage to a place where I have enjoyed myself so much as I have here during the past few months."

But Washington was no place for a commanding general at odds with the president. "I am not on speaking terms with your venerable Chief," he wrote a friend in the diplomatic service who had requested Grant's intervention with Johnson. "Therefore cannot ask him to relieve you of your present duties." He traveled to New York to see his son Fred, who had enrolled at West Point. He was a guest at the Union League Club in Manhattan, where he was toasted enthusiastically. He responded as the antithesis of the politician. "You all know how unaccustomed I am to public speaking," he said. The audience smiled in appreciation. "How undesirable a talent I think it is to possess, how little good it generally does." Laughter punctuated with nods of approval. "And how desirous I am to see more of our public men follow the good example which I believe, in this particular, if in no other, I have set them." Roars of laughter, stamping of feet. "I must, however, express my acknowledgments to the Union League of this city, as well as to the Union Leagues of other cities, for the great benefits they conferred upon the government during the rebellion through which we have passed of late years." A thunderous standing ovation.

He traveled in style. "The offers of the managers of the different roads from Baltimore to Chicago to furnish a palace car to the Soldiers' Convention and return is thankfully accepted," he telegraphed Thomas Scott, the president of the Pennsylvania Railroad. If he reflected that letting the railroads do him favors might create the appearance of a conflict of interest in one who would be charged with executing government policy toward the railroads, he dismissed the concern, knowing that members of Congress rode the rails for free, courtesy of the same railroads.

Nor did he worry when a group of supporters offered him a premium price for his Washington house. "The proposition was to pay me $65,000 for the house and grounds, which I insisted was more than the property was worth or than I would take," Grant wrote Sherman. The house had cost $30,000 when Grant purchased it three years earlier. But the group making the offer refused to be rebuffed, and he let himself be persuaded. "I would sell it with the carpets, chairs, wardrobes and much of the other furniture for that price." He was telling Sherman because the buyers proposed to give the house to Sherman, whom Grant planned to promote to commanding general of the army now that he himself would be vacating the post for the presidency, and the house for the White House.

Tens of thousands of well-wishers traveled to Washington to see their hero take office. They came in good spirits, but a sleety mist cloaked the capital and, in the wake of the Johnson impeachment trial and amid the continuing fight over reconstruction, the mood of the city was somber. A reporter likened the inaugural stand to a scaffold. "People looking at it suggested, smilingly"—most smiled, at any rate—"that it was there that Andy would take his final drop and deliver his last veto." Grant showed little emotion. "Of all those present—his escort, the judges, the senators, the ladies—he appeared the least affected, and looked at the magnificent scene about him with more nonchalance than any other man who formed a part of it." And no wonder, thought the reporter, who knew Grant only by reputation. "What was this crowd to a man who had stood amid shot and shell for two whole days on Orchard Knob, and saw one hundred and twenty-five thousand men contending for Lookout Mountain and Mission Ridge? This was only the muster of the awkward squad to him." Grant gave no hint of the anxiety he always felt at giving a public speech. "General Grant betrayed on his countenance or manner neither agitation, solemnity, joy, sorrow, nervousness, pride: he remained the sphinx to the last."

Grant read his inaugural address slowly and carefully. He distanced himself from the political classes. "The office has come to me unsought," he said. "I commence its duties untrammeled." He distanced himself still further from his predecessor. He said he would speak his mind to Congress and perhaps veto bills he opposed. "But all laws will be faithfully executed, whether they meet my approval or not." The laws would be enforced consistently and rigorously. "Laws are to govern all alike— those opposed as well as those who favor them." He added, sagely but counterintuitively: "I know no method to secure the repeal of bad or obnoxious laws so effective as their stringent execution."

One issue demanded immediate attention. The Fourteenth Amendment had failed to resolve the issue of African American voting; advocates of equality urged a straightforward constitutional guarantee of the suffrage and had recently persuaded Congress to go along. Grant put the proposed Fifteenth Amendment front and center. "The question of suffrage is one which is likely to agitate the public so long as a portion of the citizens of the nation are excluded from its privileges in any state," he said. "It seems to me very desirable that this question should be settled now, and I entertain the hope and express the desire that it may be by the ratification of the fifteenth article of amendment to the Constitution."

His only additional policy prescription involved another matter left from the war. To fund the Union military effort Congress had borrowed heavily and issued paper money unbacked by gold. Grant declared a swift return to conservative financial policies essential to the nation's health and happiness. "Every dollar of government indebtedness should be paid in gold, unless otherwise expressly stipulated in the contract," he said. "Let it be understood that no repudiator of one farthing of our public debt will be trusted in a public place, and it will go far toward strengthening a credit which ought to be the best in the world."

He echoed Lincoln's second inaugural address as well as his own campaign theme in reaching out to the South as well as the North. "The country having just emerged from a great rebellion, many questions will come before it for settlement in the next four years which preceding administrations have never had to deal with. In meeting these it is desirable that they should be approached calmly, without prejudice, hate, or sectional pride, remembering that the greatest good to the greatest number is the object to be attained." Safety of persons and property and tolerance for divergent political opinions were prerequisites to national reconciliation. "All laws to secure these ends will receive my best efforts for their enforcement." Again echoing Lincoln, he closed with an appeal: "I ask patient forbearance one toward another throughout the land, and a determined effort on the part of every citizen to do his share toward cementing a happy union; and I ask the prayers of the nation to Almighty God in behalf of this consummation."

58

A reader that most of the presidents in the construction of a cabinet. New presidents mend rifts in the party by appointing persons from opposing factions; they spread the wealth among various states to broaden their base geographically. Selection of strong, respected secretaries connotes leadership and self-confidence; a stumble at this early stage augurs ill for a president's first months or years in office.

Grant hadn't studied the traditions surrounding cabinet appointments, and he appeared to ignore what little he knew of them. Determined to distinguish himself from ordinary politicians, he chose cabinet secretaries as he might have chosen officers for his military staff. Personal acquaintance and loyalty counted for much; he desired that his secretaries offer their opinions but fall in line behind decisions once made.

Grant saw little reason to consult widely in choosing his secretaries and ample reason not to. "I have come to the conclusion that there is not a man in the country who could be invited to a place in the cabinet without the friends of some other gentleman making an effort to secure the position," he told a delegation of lawmakers while the choices were pending. "Not that there would be any objection to the party named, but that there would be others whom they had set their hearts upon having in the place." From the moment of his election he had been bombarded with requests for preferment, and he didn't like the clamor. "Therefore I have come to the conclusion not to announce whom I am going to invite to seats in the cabinet until I send in their names to the Senate for confirmation."

The senior position in the cabinet—secretary of state—went to Elihu Washburne, Grant's longtime sponsor. Grant felt a personal debt to the

Illinois congressman, who had supported him at the start of the war and
stuck by him during the dark moments after Shiloh, the Wilderness and
Cold Harbor. Washburne had little talent for diplomacy and not much
ambition for it, but Grant sought to repay the many compliments Washburne had given him. Washburne's ill health made the appointment easy,
for both men understood that he would serve only briefly before yielding
to a permanent officeholder.

Alexander T. Stewart served even more briefly, as secretary of the
Treasury, but in this case the brevity was accidental rather than intended.
Grant's prewar background had given him no connections to the nation's
financial community, which typically provided Treasury secretaries. His
wartime career did nothing to remedy the lack, and after the war the
only capitalists with whom he had had much contact were the business-
men who gave him houses and other gifts. Stewart was America's most
successful merchant, with a giant emporium on Broadway in Manhattan
and other outlets elsewhere. Stewart befriended Grant and just before the
inauguration personally handed him the $65,000 check for his house.
The next day Grant announced that Stewart would be his Treasury secretary.

Grant's critics carped and some of his friends groaned at this con-
junction, but it was a federal law that spoiled the appointment. In 1789
Congress had prohibited officers of the Treasury from engaging in business that might bring them within the purview of the federal customs
bureau, which the Treasury oversaw. The customs bureau administered
the tariff, and the temptation in a customs agent to interpret the sched-
ules in favor of a superior was considered excessive. Stewart's firm paid
millions of dollars in tariffs; a close call in his direction by one of his
Treasury underlings could be worth a great deal. Grant had never heard
of the old law until after he announced the Stewart nomination, and
the Senate forgot it in approving Stewart without debate. Even when
the statute surfaced just days later, Grant thought the problem a technicality. "I would ask that he be exempted by joint resolution of the two
houses of Congress," the president wrote the legislature. John Sherman
promptly introduced an exempting measure in the Senate. But others
resisted. Charles Sumner, a self-appointed guardian of the Senate's dignity, declared, "It is a matter for profound consideration." Grant decided
not to test his luck, and Stewart resigned after a mere week on the job.

Grant's second choice for the Treasury was George Boutwell, a former governor of Massachusetts. Boutwell had been a Democrat until the

1850s, but as the party of Jefferson and Jackson fell under the sway of its Southern wing Boutwell switched to the Republicans. Lincoln made him the first commissioner of internal revenue and the voters of Massachusetts subsequently made him a congressman. He became a leader of the Radicals in the House and one of the managers of the impeachment trial of Andrew Johnson. His Radical friends touted him to Grant, citing his experience collecting taxes and his devotion to the Union. The president, eager to repair the slip with Stewart, tapped Boutwell for the Treasury. The Senate quickly confirmed.

But Boutwell's appointment created other problems. Ebenezer Rockwood Hoar was the most respected of Grant's nominees, being the least political. He had spent the decade after 1859 on the Massachusetts supreme court, where he won a reputation for honest, evenhanded dispensation of justice. Grant was pleased to nominate him for attorney general, and the Senate was pleased to approve. But when the president turned to Boutwell after the Stewart miscue, he found himself with two men from the same state in the cabinet. No law forbade this and practice on the matter was malleable. Yet Republicans from other states thought Massachusetts was receiving too much consideration, especially when one of the appointees—Boutwell—controlled the second-largest number of patronage appointments, in the customhouses.

First place in patronage rested with the postmaster general. The tens of thousands of postmasters across the country owed their jobs to the man in Washington who headed the post office. No one held much against John Creswell, who had served one term in the House and then the unexpired part of a dead man's term in the Senate before Grant made him postmaster general. He possessed a sharp legal mind, which didn't count for much at the post office, but he was from Maryland, which did. The border states had always been ticklish for the Republicans, and anything that made Marylanders feel welcome in the party was welcomed by the party in turn.

No one complained about Jacob Cox, who had won a reputation for gallantry as a general in the Army of the Ohio. Cox was elected Ohio governor after the war, and he distinguished himself for his moderation. The Radical Republicans disliked him on this account, but Grant valued him for it, and anyway Ohio, which was becoming the heartland of Republican politics, required representation in the upper echelon of the executive branch. Or so Grant decided, deeming his own Ohio connection somewhat attenuated by now. He gave Cox the Interior Department.

John Rawlins was certain to get something, having been at Grant's right hand since 1861. The War Department was the obvious choice, in part because Rawlins knew the department well and in part because he was one of the few men in the country who could handle William Sherman with anything like success. Some of those who knew Grant, and more of those who knew his reputation, judged Rawlins a good choice for the cabinet because there he could keep Grant off the bottle, as he had during the war. Grant deemed Rawlins a solid staff man and was willing to leave the matter at that.

The Navy Department went to Adolph Borie. Grant knew only a little about the navy, and with the war over and the navy largely idle he didn't feel compelled to educate himself. Borie knew even less, but he was from Pennsylvania, a keystone state for the Republicans as much as for the country, and he and Grant had become friends when Grant briefly resided in Philadelphia.

Hamilton Fish wasn't in the first round of Grant's selections, but he might as well have been. The ailing Elihu Washburne had hardly been confirmed when Grant began seeking his replacement. Fish had served in both houses of Congress, as a New York judge and as the governor of New York. But when he left the Senate in 1857 he thought his career in public office was over. He enjoyed the anonymity and comparative ease of retirement and had no urgent desire to see it end. He and Grant had become acquainted on one of Grant's visits to New York; Grant attended the wedding of Fish's daughter in the autumn of 1868. Yet Fish had no cause to think that Grant was considering him for high office, and he was surprised to receive an oddly diffident letter from the president seven days after the inauguration. "It has been my intention for some months back to offer you the position of minister etc. to England when the time came," Grant said. "Now, however, owing to my inability to secure the great services of Mr. A. T. Stewart in the Treasury Department, I will have to make another selection of Cabinet officer from New York. I have thought it might not be unpleasant for you to accept the portfolio of the State Department."

"I cannot," Fish telegraphed back. "I will write by mail this afternoon and explain why." Following lunch he continued: "Your letter reached me at a late hour this morning. I immediately sent an answer by telegraph and hope that it reached you in time for any action you may desire to take today." Fish expressed his gratitude for the honor of being considered for the secretaryship. "Nothing would give me greater pleasure than to be associated with your Administration, and to give the best of my humble abilities to aid in advancing the high objects which are the aim of your thoughts and your hopes and to which the country looks hopefully and confidently." But he had to decline. "There are pressing private and family considerations which oppose a removal to or residence in Washington. My wife's health forbids it."

But Fish had moved too slowly. "Not receiving your dispatch until about 1:50 p.m., I sent your appointment of Secretary of State to the Senate," Grant replied. "I sent to the Senate to withdraw but was too late." Grant appealed to the support Fish professed for the new administration. "Let me beg of you now, to avoid another break, to accept for the present, and should you not like the position you can withdraw after the adjournment of Congress."

Grant's unwillingness to let Fish decline was characteristic, reflecting his belief that the country had a legitimate call on the services of its talented men, in peace as in war. He himself had overcome his aversion to politics and let himself be drafted for president; Fish could certainly accept the lesser responsibilities of running the State Department. Grant's insistence also reflected his own immediate needs. As he told Fish, he didn't want another fumble like that with Stewart.

He set friends and allies to work on Fish. "You have exceptional qualifications for the position," Elihu Washburne wrote him; Fish simply must answer the president's call. Orville Babcock, a Grant aide from the war now serving as presidential secretary, explained to Fish that the country could not possibly do without his services.

Fish found himself outflanked. "I am 'in for it,' and must take the consequences," he wrote his wife.

*G*rant's cabinet choices elicited praise from Republican newspapers. "The Cabinet is a surprise to most people," the *Boston Journal* observed. "It will, however, not only stand the severest scrutiny but it makes a good impression at the outset." The *Baltimore American* declared: "The Cabinet as a whole is a strong one and we believe will secure the approval of the Republican party and the confidence of the country." The *Trenton Gazette* said, "This Cabinet will give every satisfaction not only to Republicans but to candid Democrats." The *Springfield Republican* thought Lincoln himself could have done little better in choosing advisers. "No halting or half-faced men are among them; no men of mere theories and crotchets;

and none of whom any section of the country need be ashamed," Lincoln's hometown journal declared.

Democratic papers were predictably less enthusiastic. "We hope for the best from the new Administration," the *Troy Press* of New York opined. "We believe in its honesty, but we fear that there is a strong feeling in the mind of the President that the Government can be well conducted on a sort of strategic, military plan." The *Baltimore Gazette* examined the list of secretaries and grumbled: "There is not one among them who bears an established character for disinterestedness, or who is entitled to be classed among statesmen."

John Bigelow, a well-connected New York Republican, thought the president's choices would be measured by his expectations of the secretaries. "The Cabinet is not strong, but it is respectable," Bigelow wrote a friend. "Whether it lasts or goes to pieces depends upon Grant's purpose in selecting it. If he has a policy and wanted men merely for instruments to put it into operation, it is admirably chosen. If he wants responsible ministers he has not got them."

The selection of the cabinet intensified the clamor for lesser places. Each appointment Grant made disappointed a dozen aspirants who felt equally worthy. To a man who had been told by an acquaintance that he was in line for a plum post, Grant wrote: "There was nothing in what I said to justify him coming to such a conclusion except the warmth with which I defended you against the charge of obscurity." He let the man down gently. "The object in my writing now is to state that I have often thought of you in that connection, and that there is no one in the world who would be more agreeable to me than yourself. I had, however, come to the conclusion that it would be unjust to ask you to leave your business to take a place of so much harassment in your present health." To his sister he was more candid. "I scarcely get one moment alone," he wrote Mary. "Office-seeking in this country, I regret to say, is getting to be one of the industries of the age. It gives me no peace."

The constant pounding provoked one of Grant's migraines; for three days he turned away all visitors. But in early April he had to resume work, for Congress was about to conclude its short session and adjourn till December. The legislature's single noteworthy accomplishment had been a pledge to pay the federal debt in gold, following Grant's inaugural recommendation. Grant signed the measure and urged another matter upon the lawmakers. "There is one subject which concerns so deeply the welfare of the country that I deem it my duty to bring it before you," he declared in a special message. The time had come for military reconstruction to end. Grant made no apology for the past use of force in the South. "The authority of the United States, which has been vindicated and established by its military power, must undoubtedly be asserted for the absolute protection of all its citizens in the full enjoyment of the freedom and security which is the object of a republican government." Yet military force was a wasting asset in a democracy. "Whenever the people of a rebellious State are ready to enter in good faith upon the accomplishment of this object, in entire conformity with the constitutional authority of Congress, it is certainly desirable that all causes of irritation should be removed as promptly as possible." Virginia had held a convention that wrote a new constitution for the state; Grant recommended that Congress authorize an election to ratify the constitution and allow for Virginia's full return to the federal Union. Mississippi had reached a similar stage and should receive similar treatment.

Grant's message provoked debate in Congress. Radical Republicans wanted to condition the return of Virginia and Mississippi on the ratification by those states of the Fifteenth Amendment. Moderates asserted that the Constitution was too important to be amended by such strong-arm tactics. A few Republicans noted softly that their constituents weren't crazy about letting Negroes vote outside the South.

The Radicals carried the day, and the legislature passed a new reconstruction law giving Grant the authority to call elections in Virginia and Mississippi—and Texas at the appropriate time—after those states had ratified the Fifteenth Amendment.

The departure of Congress left Grant relatively little to do. Nineteenth-century presidents took their lead from the legislature in lawmaking, and they delegated to customs agents, Treasury clerks and other employees of the executive branch the quotidian tasks of the federal government, chiefly collecting revenues and supervising spending. Absent war or national crisis, which mobilized the president's authority as commander in chief, the presidency was a seasonal job.

Grant accepted the tradition and, following the lawmakers' return to their homes, contented himself issuing a few executive orders. One that had lasting importance controlled compensation of federal workers.

Congress had mandated an eight-hour day for workers employed by the government or on its behalf, but the law lacked teeth in not preventing government agencies or private contractors from reducing pay when they reduced hours. Grant made the eight-hour mandate meaningful for workers by declaring that the shortened day must not result in diminished wages.

By early July he had accomplished all he could accomplish at the capital. "I leave here tomorrow for Long Branch and the North, to be gone all summer," he wrote Adam Badeau. Long Branch was a town on the New Jersey shore that Grant would make his recurrent summer headquarters. He told Badeau he was satisfied with his first months in office. "Public affairs look to me to be progressing very favorably. The revenues of the country are being collected as they have not been before, and expenditures are looked after more carefully. . . . The first thing, it seems to me, is to establish the credit of the country." If he could pay down the debt and balance the books, he would be happy. "This is policy enough for the present."

59

ABEL CORBIN, HAVING LOST HIS WIFE, WAS LOOKING FOR ANOTHER IN the spring of 1869. The president's sister Virginia, never having married, was looking for a husband. Their age difference—Corbin was sixty-one, Jennie Grant thirty-seven—provoked comment, as did the fact that he had evinced little interest in her before her brother's election. Corbin dabbled in finance with neither great success nor abject failure; he held his place in the small army of speculators seeking the main chance but never quite finding it. Grant didn't especially approve of the match, but he declined to spoil what looked like Jennie's last hope of marriage.

Corbin supposed that marrying Jennie would make him more popular. At least he would be mentioned in the papers as a member of the president's family. He probably didn't realize that his fame—or notoriety—would evolve so quickly. "Mr. Corbin is a very shrewd old gentleman," Jay Gould told a congressional committee just months later. Gould was one of the most powerful men on Wall Street: a principal in the Erie Railroad, which he and partner James Fisk had wrested from transport titan Cornelius Vanderbilt in a series of raids dubbed the "Erie War," and a speculator whose slightest gestures caused the markets to gyrate. "I used to meet him occasionally," Gould said of Corbin. "He owned some real estate in Jersey City, where I was building a horse-railroad through some of our own lands and also through his."

At one of these meetings Corbin diverted the discussion from real estate. "He asked me how he could make some money," Gould recalled. "I told him if we were certain we were going to have a big harvest, and if the government would facilitate it, I could see how it could be done." Gould's plan depended on the fluctuating price of gold relative to greenbacks, the Civil War currency in which domestic prices were denominated. A rising price for gold meant a falling price for the greenbacks, in turn implying more-competitive prices internationally for American farm goods, which would flow from the nation's heartland to the Atlantic coast and generate traffic for Gould's Erie Railroad. The chain of events would be good for Gould and the Erie and for the farmers, railroad workers, dockhands and many others involved in the export trade. Gould explained this to Corbin; he meanwhile suggested that profits might be garnered in the gold market itself, as part of the broader business.

"He saw at a glance the whole case, and said that he thought it was the true platform to stand on," Gould recounted of Corbin. "Whatever the government could do legitimately and fairly to facilitate the exportation of breadstuffs, and produce good prices for the products of the West, they ought to do." Corbin offered to help. "He was anxious that I should see the president and communicate to him my view of the subject." He said that Gould, as a railroad man, was just the person to make the argument. "He was anxious that I should see the president and talk with him, and he made an appointment for me to do so. I went to Mr. Corbin's and was introduced to the president."

Gould caught Grant as the president was heading for Boston to attend a peace jubilee. Gould offered transport on one of the Erie's steamboats, and Grant accepted. "He was our guest," Gould told the congressional committee, referring to the boat trip, which he and Jim Fisk joined. "We had supper about nine or ten o'clock going over. At this supper the question came up about the state of the country, the crops, prospects ahead, etc. The president was a listener; the other gentlemen were discussing." The central question was the government's role in determining the price of gold. The Treasury held sufficient gold to drive the price down should Grant and George Boutwell, the Treasury secretary, decide to sell. "Some were in favor of Boutwell's selling gold, and some were opposed to it. After they had all interchanged their views, someone asked the president what his views were."

A hush fell over the room. This was the million-dollar question on which Gould's whole scheme depended. The president spoke slowly, between puffs on his cigar. "He remarked that he thought there was a certain amount of factiousness about the prosperity of the country, and that the bubble might as well be tapped in one way as another," Gould told the committee.

Grant turned to Gould and asked what he thought of the subject. The financier made his strongest case. "I remarked that I thought if that policy"—bursting the bubble—"was carried out, it would produce great distress, and almost lead to civil war. It would produce strikes among the workmen; and the workshops, to a great extent, would have to be closed." The president could avert this outcome by doing nothing or by pitching in. "I took the ground that the government ought to let gold alone, and let it find its commercial level—that, as a matter of fact, it"—the government—"ought to facilitate an upward movement of gold."

Grant offered no encouragement. Gould judged the evening a failure. "We supposed from that conversation that the president was a contractionist," he told the committee.

Gould persisted. When Grant traveled to Newport in August to visit friends, Gould sent Jim Fisk after him. "I took a letter of introduction from Mr. Gould, in which it was written that there were three hundred sail of vessels then on the Mediterranean from the Black Sea, with grain to supply the Liverpool market," Fisk told the congressional committee. "Gold was then about 34"—134 greenback dollars bought 100 gold dollars. "If it continued at that price we had very little chance of carrying forward the crop during the fall. I know that we felt very nervous about it. I talked with General Grant on the subject and endeavored, as far as I could, to convince him that his policy was one that would only bring destruction upon us all." Grant listened; again he gave no encouragement.

But Abel Corbin continued to hope. He reflected at length on Gould's theory of gold and commerce. "I think it had become a sort of monomania with him," Gould recalled. Speaking publicly to the congressional committee, Gould credited Corbin's regard for the country in his embrace of easy money. "I think any idea of making money for himself had ceased to weigh with him." Privately Gould knew better, for he had arranged for Corbin to participate in the effort to boost gold, buying $1.5 million in gold on Corbin's behalf. If gold rose, Corbin would get rich. Corbin accordingly offered his good services again. "He was very anxious that I should come round," Gould told the committee. "I did so, and met with Mr. Corbin and the president."

Grant's views appeared to have changed. "The president said then that he was satisfied the country had a very bountiful harvest; that there was to be a large surplus; that unless we could find a market abroad for that surplus it would put down prices here. And he remarked that the government would do nothing during the fall months of the year to put down the price of gold or make money tight. On the contrary, they would do everything they could to facilitate the movement of breadstuffs. He seemed to take a very deep interest in it; it seemed to have been a matter of study with him. I was surprised at the clearness with which he seemed to comprehend the whole question."

Gould may not have been the most reliable witness on Grant's views. During September 1869 Gould's design to enhance the Erie's business by bulling gold transmuted into something larger: a scheme to corner the gold market. Contracts for gold delivery were bought and sold daily by both speculators and merchants; at any given time the gold promised often exceeded the gold available, but the market always cleared by the delivery dates. Gould aimed to purchase contracts far in excess of the existing supply, thereby "cornering" the market and compelling the gold promisers to settle on his terms. He estimated the existing supply of gold and arranged for various brokers to purchase contracts—quietly and without the brokers knowing they were working together, lest the secret get out and the plan be spoiled.

It was a delicate operation, involving various imponderables, of which the most important was the attitude of the federal government. The Treasury's gold could foil any attempted corner; at a word from the president the doors of the vaults would open, the gold would flood the market and the corner would be broken, with those holding contracts being bankrupted by the collapsing price. Grant's initial opposition to a rise in gold—his belief that the bubble ought to be burst—naturally discouraged Gould; his apparent change of mind caused Gould to press ahead.

Gould's testimony regarding Grant's reversal received corroboration from a less interested source. George Boutwell recalled Grant's endorsing views such as Gould described. "About the 4th day of September, I suppose, I think on the evening of the 4th of September, I received a letter from the president," the Treasury secretary told the congressional committee. "In that letter he expressed an opinion that it was undesirable to force down the price of gold. He spoke of the importance to the West of being able to move their crops. His idea was that if gold should fall the West would suffer and the movement of the crops would be retarded.

The impression made upon my mind by the letter was that he had rather a strong opinion to that effect. . . . I saw from the letter that it was his opinion that the sale of gold in any considerable quantity might carry down the price of it, and that if the price were to fall the West would be embarrassed."

Grant's intention to let the market find its own level persisted into mid-September. He and Julia departed for a vacation in western Pennsylvania on September 12 and left a letter for Boutwell, who was traveling to New York. "You will be met by the bulls and bears of Wall Street," Grant warned, "and probably by merchants, too, to induce you to sell gold, or pay the November interest"—on the federal debt, in gold—"in advance, on the one side, and to hold fast, on the other. The fact is, a desperate struggle is now taking place, and each party want the government to help them out. I write this letter to advise you of what I think you may expect, to put you on your guard." Grant wrote, as well, to indicate his own preference. "I think, from the lights before me, I would move on without change, until the present struggle is over."

Grant held his ground as the struggle intensified. The task wasn't easy. To bolster their argument that the government was on their side, the gold bulls circulated rumors that the president and other officeholders had a stake in the fight. "The President was reported as having a large interest, as well as every member of his cabinet, especially the secretary of the Treasury," James Hodgskin, an officer of the gold exchange, the market where gold contracts were traded, remembered. "Also a large number of the members of Congress." Hodgskin himself didn't believe the rumors. "There is no doubt but that these stories were set afloat by these men themselves in order to frighten people into buying gold." Yet the tales produced the desired effect on those who needed or wanted gold. "A great many became seriously alarmed, and began to buy back the gold they had sold. And a great many nervous people, who had no gold, and who had nothing to do with gold in a speculative way, fearing the country was going to wreck and ruin, also went and bought large amounts of gold."

Jay Gould didn't believe the rumors either, at least as they related to Grant. Whether Gould started the rumors himself or simply benefited from them, he never said. But he did declare that they were unfounded regarding Grant. Summarizing his discussions with the president, Gould told the congressional committee: "Nothing ever occurred to me in any of these interviews that did not impress me that the president was a very pure, high-minded man; that if he was satisfied what was the best thing to do, that was what he would do."

Gould went on to explain that as the battle between the bulls and bears grew hotter, Corbin became nervous that Grant might change his mind. Corbin wrote a letter to Grant, then in Pennsylvania. The gist of the letter, subsequently destroyed, was that the two sides in the gold battle would try to sway the president. Grant should stick to his decision to keep out of the fight.

Gould's partner Fisk arranged for a messenger, William Chapin of the Erie Railroad, to carry the letter to Pennsylvania. Chapin took a train to Pittsburgh and hired horses and a driver and rode through the night toward the village of Washington, Pennsylvania. "We started, lost our way once on the trip, but finally got there," Chapin told the congressional committee. "I think it was about nine o'clock in the morning." Chapin went to the house where Grant was staying. The woman of the house said that Grant had gone to another house, in the country. Chapin hired a second team of horses and drove on. "A lady came to the door," he said of the country house. "I told her I had a letter from Mr. Corbin which I was to deliver to the president in person. She showed me into the parlor. General Grant was playing croquet on the lawn, he and General Porter"—Grant's secretary, his former military aide Horace Porter. The croquet duly ended and Grant came to the house. "I told him I had a letter from Mr. Corbin, and delivered it to him," Chapin recalled. "General Grant broke his letter open, started down to the window of the parlor facing me, and read it. He seemed to be reading some of it twice."

A servant approached and said that Mrs. Grant wished to see the president. Grant went out, then returned some fifteen minutes later. "He still had the letter in his hand," Chapin testified. "I was waiting, expecting all the time he would give me some instructions, or send a message by me in return. He seemed to wait so long that, as I wanted to get back, I said to him, 'Is it all satisfactory?' or something like that. He says, 'Yes.' I asked him if there was any reply. He said, 'No, nothing,' and he wished me a good morning. I drove straight back to Pittsburgh and telegraphed to New York that the letters"—Corbin's letter and a letter of introduction of Chapin—"were delivered all right."

A committee member asked about the message to New York. "Did you mean by your telegram to say that the president answered that the contents of the letter"—Corbin's letter—"were all right?"

"No," Chapin replied. "I did not know anything about the contents of the letter. I meant to say that he had received the letters and read them; that they had been delivered all right."

The wording of Chapin's telegram became important as soon as it was delivered; in the meantime Horace Porter puzzled over the identity of the messenger. "Who is that man?" he asked Grant as Chapin drove away.

"I don't know," Grant responded. "Why?"

"I merely asked on account of the peculiarity of the letter of introduction which he brought to me. His name is not mentioned in it."

"Letter of introduction from whom?" Grant asked.

"From Mr. Corbin of New York."

"Is that messenger from New York?"

"He appears to be."

Grant frowned. Porter recalled: "He seemed quite surprised, and was silent for a few moments." He told Porter he had supposed the messenger was from the local post office, which frequently sent a courier with the mail.

Grant may or may not originally have questioned Corbin's intentions in marrying his sister, but the letter and its mode of transmission definitely made him doubt Corbin's good faith on the gold issue. He went back to Julia's room, where he found her writing a note to Jennie. He thought for a moment, then told her: "Write this: 'The General says, if you have any influence with your husband, tell him to have nothing whatever to do with Jay Gould. If he does, he will be ruined, for come what may, he (your brother) will do his duty to the country and the trusts in his keeping.'"

Jennie got the letter the next day and shared it with her husband, who shuddered at Grant's words. "I was very much excited," Corbin told the committee. "And my wife still more so. . . . Engaged in buying and selling gold—what a terrible thing! The world is about to come to an end immediately! . . . I must get out instantly—instantly!" Corbin related his and Jennie's distress to Gould. "When Mr. Gould came in that night, I at once read to him the substance of this letter. . . . I told Mr. Gould, at once, that I *must* get out of this matter; that it had created a great deal of feeling in my own family, as well as on the part of the president, and that the matter must now end."

Gould urged Corbin to reconsider. "I did not want to throw his gold on the market at that time," Gould told the committee. Corbin testified that Gould offered to indemnify him against losses. "If you remain in and take the chances of the market, I will give you my check for $100,000," Gould said, according to Corbin. "He looked at me with a look of severe distrust, as if he was afraid of treachery in the camp. He remarked, 'Mr. Corbin, I am undone if that letter gets out.'"

Grant returned to the capital the next day, Thursday, September 23. George Boutwell had been monitoring the situation from his office in the Treasury. "I became satisfied that the matter was very serious," he told the committee. "Gold was reported that day at about 145, and I was apprehensive from what I heard that it might advance to a still higher price the next day." Boutwell expressed his concerns to Grant. "I went that evening to see the president and told him what the state of the market appeared to be from the information I had received. We had a consultation about it, the result of which was that if gold advanced materially the next day, it would be our duty to sell, not for the purpose of forcing down the price of gold as a primary and specific object, but because we thought the business of the country was in danger." Boutwell remembered the panic of 1857 and feared a repetition. "I left the president without any specific understanding as to what should be done, except in a general way that if the excitement continued and gold advanced, it would be our duty to sell."

The excitement did continue. Gould's bribe kept Grant's warning to Corbin from reaching other investors; Friday, September 24, dawned with the gold bulls believing that the government still would not intervene. The price leaped upward at the opening bell; it shot past 150, then 155, then 160. The gold bears were in a frenzy, as were merchants who needed gold in their businesses and found the prices ruinous.

Boutwell at the Treasury read the telegraphed reports from Wall Street. No indication appeared of a pause in the price rise—no profit taking, no breath catching. Just after eleven he returned to the White House. "I went over to the President and told him what the state of the market was, upon the information that I had," he explained to the committee. "I went over with the idea of saying to him that I thought the time had come when we must interfere. I had a very strong conviction upon that point. I stated to him the condition of the market. . . . He expressed the opinion, almost at the beginning of the conversation, that we ought to sell $5 million. I recollect expressing the opinion that we should sell

$3 million, because that was the amount that I had in my mind when I left the office, and I thought it would be sufficient for the purpose. We had very little conversation beyond that. I returned almost immediately, without saying to him whether I would order the sale of $5 million or $3 million, or of any other sum, except that it was agreed that gold should be sold. Upon going back to my office, I came to the conclusion that I should advertise the sale of $4 million."

The order was telegraphed to New York. The effect was instantaneous. Within minutes the price fell from 160 to 135. The gold corner was broken. The gold bears and the merchants swooned with relief; the gold bulls bellowed as their dreams of instant wealth evaporated.

But damage had been done. The gold gyrations jolted the stock market, where panic afflicted many who had nothing directly to do with gold. For weeks Wall Street's affairs were in chaos. "It was each man drag out his own corpse," Jim Fisk told the committee. "Get out of it as well as you can." The troubles didn't travel much beyond the Hudson and East Rivers, sparing the nation's economy as a whole, but dark memories of "Black Friday" persisted among the investing classes.

And among those charged with their oversight. Grant's decision to burst the gold bubble didn't immediately dispel the earlier rumors that he and members of his administration had stood to gain from gold's rise. Congress convened an investigation; the various principals, from Jay Gould and Jim Fisk to Abel Corbin and George Boutwell, were called to testify. Grant was not summoned, although he agreed to speak to a representative of the Associated Press about his actions. "The President conversed with the utmost frankness on the subject," the newsman reported, "and said he had not thought proper to publicly contradict the statements concerning himself, as he had done nothing whatever to influence the money market or to afford any advantages to private parties." This reporter found Grant fully credible. "It may be repeated that the President had informed no one whomsoever of the purpose of the Administration on financial subjects," he wrote.

The congressional committee agreed. It excoriated Gould for trying to manipulate the market and Corbin for exploiting his connections to Grant. It implicated Daniel Butterfield, a Treasury official who may have served Gould as a second source of intelligence on the administration's plans. But it cleared Grant. "The committee find that the wicked and cunningly devised attempts of the conspirators to compromise the President of the United States or his family utterly failed," the committee declared in its final report. The committee excluded in-laws from this exoneration; Corbin "used all his arts to learn something from the private conversations of the President which could be made profitable to him and his co-conspirators." But he failed. "With this and all the efforts of his associates, the testimony has not elicited a word or an act of the President inconsistent with that patriotism and integrity which befit the Chief Executive of the nation."

ADOLPH BORIE THOUGHT THE PRESIDENT'S HANDLING OF THE GOLD crisis deserved comment more positive than the committee's mere exoneration. "What a wonderful shot that was of General Grant!" the navy secretary wrote Adam Badeau. "Never in all his great camps in the war did he strike a surer blow! I haven't ceased laughing about its effect ever since; that crazy wicked hole (New York) will long remember it nor cease to feel that there is a power, when ably and honestly wielded, that can thwart their evil machinations when at the worst and least expected."

In this same letter Borie conveyed sad news regarding one of Badeau's and Grant's wartime comrades. "Poor Rawlins has gone to a happier office," Borie said. "A noble fellow, truly; he was so pure, zealous, and earnest."

Mary Rawlins got the grim word from Grant. "Your beloved husband expired at twelve minutes after four o'clock this afternoon, to be mourned by a family and friends who love him for his personal worth and services to his country, and a nation which acknowledges its debt of gratitude to him," the president wrote the new widow. The death wasn't unexpected; Rawlins had been ill for months. "Yet his final taking off has produced a shock which would be felt for but few of our public men," Grant told Elihu Washburne.

Grant lamented the passing of Rawlins as any old friend and wartime comrade would have, but certain of Grant's associates felt a special concern that Rawlins would no longer be at his commander's side. James Wilson, who had served with both men, wrote Orville Babcock, Grant's secretary: "You and I know how necessary the bold, uncompromising, and honest character of our dead friend was to our living one, and how impossible it is for any stranger to exercise as good an influence over him as one who has known him from the time of his obscurity till the day he became the foremost man of the nation." Wilson recalled the drinking stories, but he interpreted Rawlins's positive influence more broadly. "He was the President's best friend and most useful counselor when engaged in denouncing rascality, which the President's unsuspicious nature has not dreamed of being near."

*H*amilton Fish had a different reaction. Fish knew Rawlins chiefly as a cabinet colleague and one whose judgments differed, quite strongly at times, from his own. When a Cuban insurgency against the Spanish colonial government triggered a brutal response from the Spanish and their Cuban loyalists, Rawlins called for American intervention on behalf of the insurgents. The insurgents' fight was democracy's fight, Rawlins said, and taking their part, at least to the degree of recognizing their belligerent status, would affirm America's position as the defender of democracy in the Western Hemisphere.

Rawlins was hardly alone in calling for a pro-insurgent policy. The Cuban cause—promoted by an energetic and imaginative political office, or *junta*, in New York—elicited substantial support among the American people and on Capitol Hill. *New York Tribune* editor Horace Greeley organized a rally at Manhattan's Cooper Union and forwarded to Grant its petition citing the Monroe Doctrine, hemispheric peace and the principles of republican self-government as grounds for American recognition of Cuban belligerency. Members of Congress lent their voices to the chorus. Some were sincere, others opportunistic. By damning Spain they could show their devotion to democracy, demonstrate their commitment to American national security and distract voters from the troublesome questions of domestic politics. They could also assert the primacy of Congress over the president in American politics. The Republicans had been glad to ride Grant's popularity to victory in the 1868 elections, but few Republican legislators wanted to relinquish even to a president of their own party the political ground they had seized from Andrew Johnson. John Sherman liked Grant and backed most of his policies, but the Ohio senator spoke for many when he argued that the president must take his cues—indeed his orders—from Congress. "The executive department of a republic like ours should be subordinate to the legislative department," Sherman declared. "The President should obey and enforce the laws, leaving to the people the duty of correcting any errors committed by their representatives in Congress."

Opposing Rawlins and the interventionists was Hamilton Fish. The secretary of state doubted the Cuban insurgents' stamina and didn't think the United States was ready for the war with Spain that recognition of the insurgents might lead to. Fish had another reason, unrelated to Cuba or Spain, for opposing recognition. He was in the middle of difficult negotiations with the British government over American claims from the Civil War, and central to his case was the contention that Britain had illegitimately aided Confederate belligerency. For the Grant administration to adopt a policy toward Cuba akin to the policy it was condemning Britain for having taken toward the South would, needless to say, weaken Fish's hand in the bargaining.

Grant initially tilted toward Rawlins. He looked on Spain in Cuba much as he had looked on France in Mexico at the close of the Civil War. He thought European soldiers anywhere near the United States posed a danger to American interests, and he believed that the sooner and more definitively they were withdrawn the better. He put great weight on the Monroe Doctrine, with its assertion of the Americas for the Americans, and he looked for opportunities to enforce it. In July 1869 he drafted a statement recognizing Cuban belligerency and declaring American neutrality between the insurgents and the government, in order to have it ready if the need arose. And he conspicuously held the possibility of recognition and neutrality over Spain's head as he volunteered America's diplomatic resources to mediate an end to the conflict. When Spain ignored his offer, announcing instead an escalation of the military effort in Cuba, Grant prepared to push forward. "I think it advisable to complete the neutrality proclamation which I signed before leaving Washington and to issue it if Gen. Sickles"—Daniel Sickles, Grant's envoy to Madrid—"has not received an entirely satisfactory reply to his proposition to mediate between Spain and the Cubans," the president told Fish in August. "In fact I am not clearly satisfied that we would not be justified in intimating to Spain that we look with some alarm upon her proposition to send 20,000 more troops to Cuba to put down, as Americans believe, the right of self-government on this Continent." Grant thought the Spanish government should be warned of the consequences of its escalation. "Such a course would arouse the sympathies of our citizens in favor of the Cubans to such a degree as to require all our vigilance to prevent them from giving material aid."

The Spanish would know what this meant. The insurgent junta, besides coordinating a publicity campaign, arranged the purchase of American weapons and the outfitting of military expeditions to Cuba. Grant had taken some pains to interdict the expeditions, which violated American statutes against launching undeclared war from American soil. By hinting that American vigilance might not suffice to stop the expeditions, Grant came close to winking at an undeclared war against Spain.

The Spanish government took the hint. Madrid tentatively accepted Grant's mediation offer. The president withheld the recognition statement but pressed harder. "The United States are willing to mediate between Spain and Cuba, on the following terms," he wrote to Sickles: "Immediate armistice; Cuba to recompense Spain for public property, etc.; all Spaniards to be protected in their persons and property if they wish to remain on the island, or to withdraw with it, at their option; the United States not to guarantee"—the Cuban payment to Spain— "except with the approval of Congress." The president added that this offer, dated August 31, would expire on September 25. He urged the Spanish not to tarry.

While Grant awaited Madrid's response, two events intruded upon his reckoning. Rawlins died, depriving the interventionists of their strongest voice in the cabinet. And Jay Gould's plot to corner the gold market climaxed, drawing the attention of the president and the country away from Cuba. The Spanish, perhaps recognizing America's distraction, let Grant's deadline pass without acceding to his demands.

Quite possibly Grant never intended more than stern words to Spain; with the wounds of the Civil War still healing, he had no desire to rush into another war. Doubtless the tumult of Black Friday made him count the costs, political as well as economic, of a foreign war more closely than he might have counted them otherwise. In any event, a carefully balanced statement in Grant's December annual message indicated a shift away from imminent intervention. "For more than a year a valuable province of Spain, and a near neighbor of ours, in whom all our people cannot but feel a deep interest, has been struggling for independence and freedom," the president said. The American people and government sympathized with Cuba, as they had sympathized with other Spanish colonies in their previous and mostly successful fights for freedom. Yet sympathy alone afforded insufficient basis for policy. "The contest has at no time assumed the conditions which amount to a war in the sense of international law or which would show the existence of a de facto political organization of the insurgents sufficient to justify a recognition of belligerency." The administration had not been idle, Grant reminded; it had offered to mediate a settlement of the conflict. Unfortunately the Spanish government had rejected the offer. But the president professed not to be discouraged. "It is hoped that the good offices of the United States may yet prove advantageous for the settlement of this unhappy strife." All the same, the Spanish should not assume infinite forbearance on America's part. "This nation is its own judge when to accord the rights of belligerency, either to a people struggling to free themselves from a government they believe to be oppressive or to independent nations at war with each other."

Grant's message didn't suit the ardent interventionists, who wanted a commitment to Cuban independence. But it calmed matters enough for Grant to focus on a Caribbean question he preferred. The sea to America's south had stirred the country's passions for decades. Prior to the Civil War those passions had been primarily Southern, as expansionists in Dixie looked on Cuba and its West Indian neighbors as suitable for the spread of slavery, to offset the continental curbs imposed by the Missouri Compromise and growing Northern antipathy. Precisely that Northern antipathy, though, prevented the Southern dreams from becoming real. The Civil War and emancipation changed the moral and political calculus, to the degree that the Cuban insurgency triggered its strongest American response among Northern liberals.

Little such sentiment existed toward the Dominican Republic, the Spanish-speaking half of Hispaniola, the second largest of the West Indies, just to Cuba's east and south. The Dominican Republic—or Santo Domingo, as it was commonly called, after its principal city—had followed a circuitous path to independence. It separated from Spain in 1821 only to be conquered by Haiti, its more populous Hispaniola neighbor; it broke loose from Haiti in 1844 but found independence fraught with such trouble that the ruling party voluntarily reattached the country to Spain in 1861. The reunion, however, didn't suit other Dominicans, who in 1863 issued a new independence declaration, which the Spanish recognized two years later. Whether independence would stick this time around—Haiti again threatened to invade the country—was the pressing question in the latter 1860s.

William Seward guessed that independence would not stick. Lincoln's and then Johnson's secretary of state was a throwback to the 1840s in his ambitions for American expansion, and he was wrapping up the purchase of Alaska from Russia when he initiated annexation talks with Santo Domingo's leaders, who all but threw themselves into his arms. Johnson, desperate for a triumph of any sort, found annexation appealing and recommended purchasing Haiti too. The Republican Congress, though, liked Johnson's Caribbean policy no better than his Southern policy and rejected the plan.

Grant entered office almost as skeptical as Congress on the subject of Santo Domingo. "I did not dream of instituting any steps for the acquisition of insular possessions," he explained later. But he was not opposed to expansion per se. Though he still considered the Mexican War to have begun illegitimately, he couldn't argue with the results; Californians and Texans had benefited by coming under American rule. The Dominicans might similarly benefit. "I believed that our institutions were broad enough to extend over the entire continent as rapidly as other peoples might desire to bring themselves under our protection," he said. Moreover, as president he had to defend the Monroe Doctrine and its assertion of American regional primacy. "We should not permit any independent government within the limits of North America to pass from a condition of independence to one of ownership or protection under a European power."

Consequently when an agent from Dominican president Buenaventura Báez arrived in Washington with hopes of restarting the annexation process, Grant allowed him an interview. Báez's man said that the Dominicans sought attachment to the United States as eagerly as ever. He expounded on the handsome resources of the country and the noble character of the people. "He stated further," Grant recalled, "that being weak in numbers and poor in purse, they were not capable of developing their great resources; that the people had no incentive to industry on account of lack of protection for their accumulations; and that if not accepted by the United States—with institutions which they loved above those of any other nation—they would be compelled to seek protection elsewhere." Grant listened but gave no response, either positive or negative.

Yet he considered the matter carefully and determined to discover more. In July 1869 he appointed a special representative to Santo Domingo. "Great and good friend," Grant wrote Báez: "Deeming it desirable to satisfy my curiosity in respect to your interesting country by obtaining information through a source upon which I rely, I have for this purpose appointed Brevet Brigadier General Orville Babcock." Grant explained that Babcock had served on his staff during the Civil War, had become one of his White House secretaries and was a man both presidents could trust. "I have entire confidence in his integrity and intelligence."

Grant later asserted that he intended Babcock to be an impartial observer. "He visited San Domingo not to secure or hasten annexation but, unprejudiced and unbiased, to learn all the facts about the government, the people, and the resources of that republic. He went certainly as well prepared to make an unfavorable report as a favorable one, if the facts warranted it." Grant probably wasn't telling the full story here, for Babcock had scarcely arrived in Santo Domingo when he became a vigorous advocate of annexation. And he didn't confine himself to reporting but negotiated a treaty of annexation—something no secretary would have done without at least tacit encouragement from the president.

Babcock's treaty caught the rest of the administration off guard. "What do you think!" an astonished Hamilton Fish said to Jacob Cox, the interior secretary. "Babcock is back, and has actually brought a treaty for the cession of San Domingo; yet I pledge you my word he had no more diplomatic authority than any other casual visitor to that island!" Fish and Cox assumed that Grant would disavow Babcock's patent overstepping. "We agreed that the proper course was to treat Babcock's action as null, and to insist upon burying the whole in oblivion as a state secret—this being the only way, apparently, to save him from the grave consequences of a usurpation of power," Cox recalled.

To their amazement just the opposite occurred at the next meeting of the cabinet. Babcock was there, obviously at Grant's request. "It had been the President's habit to call upon the members of the cabinet to bring forward the business contained in their portfolios, beginning with the secretary of state," Cox remembered. He, Fish and the other secretaries, to whom Fish had likewise spoken, expected that Fish would be recognized and would proceed to demolish Babcock's pretensions to diplomatic legitimacy. "On this occasion, however, General Grant departed from his uniform custom, and took the initiative," Cox said. "'Babcock has returned, as you see,' said he, 'and has brought a treaty of annexation. I suppose it is not formal, as he had no diplomatic powers, but we can easily cure that. We can send back the treaty, and have Perry, the consular agent, sign it; and as he is an officer of the State Department it would make it all right.'" Cox remembered the reaction around the table: "This took everybody so completely by surprise that they seemed dumbfounded. After an awkward interval, as nobody else broke the silence, I said, 'But Mr. President, has it been settled, then, that we *want* to annex San Domingo?'"

Now it was Grant's turn to appear nonplussed. "The direct question evidently embarrassed General Grant," Cox remembered. "He colored, and smoked hard at his cigar. He glanced at Mr. Fish on his right, but the face of the secretary was impassive and his eyes were fixed on the portfolio before him. He turned to Mr. Boutwell on his left, but no response met him there. As the silence became painful, the president called for another item of business, and left the question unanswered."

The embarrassment provoked a minor crisis in the administration. Hamilton Fish declared that he couldn't continue as secretary of state if the president was going to jump the chain of diplomatic command. He offered his resignation.

Grant refused to accept it. He told Fish he wouldn't go around him again. He said he needed the secretary's guidance and support. He insisted that Fish at least delay his resignation to give the matter further thought. Fish agreed, hoping Grant would reconsider the Santo Domingo scheme.

Rumors of the ruckus within the administration intensified the doubts in Congress about Santo Domingo. Annexation had gained few friends since being rebuffed under Johnson, and the Babcock demarche added an appearance of shady dealing. Critics alleged that payments to the Dominican government that the treaty specified as exchange for annexation would simply line the pockets of Báez and his friends. Báez had agreed to hold a referendum on annexation, but questions abounded regarding its fairness. Raymond Perry, the consular agent, wrote Fish that the referendum was rigged. "A list was opened in the police headquarters for citizens to register their names," Perry said. "Báez and Delmonte"— a Báez crony—"have told me several times that any man who opposed annexation, they would either shoot him or send him his passport." Ironically, Perry contended, a fair election would produce the result Báez wanted. "I am positive that a majority of San Domingo are in favor of annexation, and strongly in favor of it." Perry blamed Báez for lack of courage and said the turbulent state of Dominican politics—Báez's rivals had raised an insurgency against the government—had frightened him. "Báez seemed very timid and anxious, and often remarked that if the United States did not ratify the treaty, he and all his friends would lose their lives for taking the step he had for annexation."

The resistance to annexation puzzled Grant, who remembered how eagerly Americans had embraced the doctrine of Manifest Destiny at the time of the war with Mexico. And it made him consider carefully what annexation could mean to the United States. Grant sometimes wrote memos to himself as a way of organizing his thoughts, and he wrote one now on Santo Domingo. "It is an island of unequaled fertility," he said. The highlands were suited to coffee, the lowlands to sugar. "With the acquisition of San Domingo, the two great necessities in every family, sugar and coffee, would be cheapened by nearly one half." The country was important strategically. "San Domingo is the gate to the Caribbean Sea, and in the line of transit to the Isthmus of Darien"—Panama— "destined at no distant day to be the line of transit of half the commerce of the world." Britain's possessions in the Caribbean threatened to block American access from the Atlantic to Central America and even the Gulf of Mexico. "In case of war between England and the United States, New York and New Orleans would be as much severed as would be New York and Calais." For America to concede British predominance in the Caribbean would be imprudent and ignominious; conversely, acquiring Santo Domingo would neutralize Britain's advantage and put the world on notice of American power. "It would give us a foothold in the West Indies of inestimable value. Its acquisition is carrying out Manifest Destiny. It is a step toward clearing all European flags from this continent."

It was a step, as well, toward clearing slavery from the Americas. Cuba and Brazil were the remaining large American slaveholding countries, and the evil institution there was indirectly bankrolled by consumers in the United States. "More than 70 percent of the exports of Cuba and a large percentage of the exports of Brazil are to the United States," Grant observed. "Upon every pound"—of sugar and coffee—"we receive from them an export duty is charged to support slavery. . . . Get San Domingo and this will all be changed."

Annexation would also ease the race problem in America. "The present difficulty in bringing all parts of the United States to a happy unity and love of country grows out of the prejudice to color," Grant asserted. "The prejudice is a senseless one, but it exists. The colored man cannot be spared until his place is supplied, but with a refuge like San Domingo his worth here would soon be discovered, and he would soon receive such recognition as to induce him to stay; or if Providence designed that the two races should not live together, he would find a home in the Antilles."

61

GRANT AND CHARLES SUMNER WERE FATED TO CLASH. "WHEN WE
consider the natures and the training of the two men, it is not easy
to imagine agreeable cooperation in public affairs by Mr. Sumner
and General Grant," George Boutwell observed. "Mr. Sumner never
believed in General Grant's fitness for the office of President, and General Grant did not recognize in Mr. Sumner a wise and safe leader in
the business of government." Sumner would soon expound at length on
Grant's incompetence; Grant was pithier. Asked if he had ever heard
Sumner converse, Grant responded, "No, but I have heard him lecture."
Informed that Sumner didn't believe in the Bible, Grant said, "I suppose not. He didn't write it."

Grant wasn't alone in finding Sumner difficult. Henry Wadsworth
Longfellow, a Sumner friend, admired his devotion to equal rights for
African Americans but captured his single-mindedness in describing him
as "a colossus holding his burning heart in his hand, to light up the sea
of life." Longfellow added: "What confidence Sumner has in Sumner!"
James Russell Lowell agreed that Sumner was full of himself. Lowell
related a typical experience: "'I advise you to listen to this,' Sumner used
to say, when he was talking about himself (as he commonly was): 'This
is history.'" George Hoar, who knew Sumner from both Massachusetts
and Washington, declared, "It sometimes seemed as if Sumner thought
the Rebellion itself was put down by speeches in the Senate, and that
the war was an unfortunate and most annoying, though trifling, disturbance, as if a fire-engine had passed by." Abraham Lincoln recognized
that Sumner was irreligious but still thought him ecclesiastical. "I have
never had much to do with bishops where I live," Lincoln told a visitor,

"but do you know, Sumner is my idea of a bishop." A poor woman from Massachusetts petitioned the Senate for help; a Maine senator asked why she didn't put her request to Sumner, her own senator. "Oh, sir, I did," she replied. "But really, sir, Mr. Sumner takes no interest in claims unless they be from black people."

Sumner took great interest in Santo Domingo, not least on account of the black people there and in adjacent Haiti. After Grant sent the annexation treaty to the Senate, the president mounted a campaign on its behalf. He brought senators to the White House, where he shared his thinking on the importance of annexation. He went to the Senate to speak with members there. And he visited Charles Sumner at the senator's Washington home. The visit went well, Grant thought, with Sumner declaring, as Grant rose to leave: "Mr. President, I am an administration man, and whatever you do will always find in me the most careful and candid consideration."

Grant heard these words as a pledge of support, and when careful and candid consideration caused Sumner to oppose the treaty and persuade a majority of his colleagues on the Foreign Relations Committee to do likewise, the president judged that he had been double-crossed. Against the committee's negative recommendation, Grant stepped up his efforts to see the treaty passed. "I feel an unusual anxiety for the ratification of this treaty," he declared in a special message to the Senate. "I believe it will redound greatly to the glory of the two countries interested, to civilization, and to the extirpation of the institution of slavery." He denied any intent to impose American power upon the people of Santo Domingo; he claimed, indeed, that annexation was the Dominicans' idea. "The Government of San Domingo has voluntarily sought this annexation. It is a weak power, numbering probably less than 120,000 souls. . . . The people of San Domingo are not capable of maintaining themselves in their present condition, and must look for outside support. They yearn for the protection of our free institutions and laws, our progress and civilization. Shall we refuse them?" If the United States did not step forward, another country would. "I have information which I believe reliable that a European power stands ready now to offer $2,000,000 for the possession of Samana Bay alone. If refused by us, with what grace can we prevent a foreign power from attempting to secure the prize?"

The senators read Grant's message respectfully, for the most part, but the treaty nonetheless stalled. Opponents seized on alleged mistreatment by the Dominican government of an American named Davis Hatch, who

had traveled to Santo Domingo on behalf of an American company seeking a salt concession. He guessed wrong in the struggle for power that
resulted in the ascendance of Báez and was imprisoned. Orville Babcock
might have arranged his release, the treaty's opponents said, but instead
let him rot behind bars.

The Hatch affair put the administration on the defensive, prompting
Grant to employ yet stronger measures. He threatened to withhold federal patronage from opponents of the treaty. He removed Ebenezer Hoar
from the cabinet to placate senators the attorney general had crossed. He
offered Charles Sumner the job of minister to Britain, to get the Foreign
Relations chairman out of the country.

His efforts failed. Sumner rejected the offer and continued to
denounce the treaty. When the Senate voted in June 1870, the pact mustered but 28 approving votes, far short of the 48 required for ratification.

The silver lining in the setback was the confusion it threw upon the
matter of Cuba. Two Caribbean controversies were more than Congress
and the country could handle, especially since the advocates of intervention in Cuba typically opposed the annexation of Santo Domingo, while
the annexationists opposed intervention. The Cuban insurgents did
themselves no favor in America by committing atrocities that matched
those of the Spanish and the Cuban loyalists. One of the insurgent commanders, on a visit to Washington, casually mentioned having executed
six hundred prisoners, shocking the American public and dismaying the
interventionists.

Grant by now had lost all desire to involve America in Cuba's troubles. In the summer of 1870 he dashed the hopes of the interventionists
with his most definitive and negative statement so far. "The condition of
the insurgents has not improved," he told Congress. "The insurrection
itself, although not subdued, exhibits no signs of advance, but seems to be
confined to an irregular system of hostilities, carried on by small and illy
armed bands of men, roaming without concentration through the woods
and the sparsely populated regions of the island, attacking from ambush
convoys and small bands of troops, burning plantations and the estates
of those not sympathizing with their cause." Between the government
and the insurgents there was little to choose. "The torch of Spaniard
and of Cuban is alike busy in carrying devastation over fertile regions;
murderous and revengeful decrees are issued and executed by both par-

ties." Grant cited George Washington's parting counsel about holding aloof from other countries' quarrels and said that it continued to furnish "a safe guide to those of us now charged with the direction and control of the public safety." Nothing short of irresistible necessity should prompt American intervention. "Such necessity may yet hereafter arrive," Grant concluded, "but it has not yet arrived, nor is its probability clearly to be seen."

A cannier politician than Grant would have accepted his Dominican defeat and moved on. There were other battles to wage, of larger importance to the administration and America. But Grant had never known how to accept defeat, and the same stubbornness that had carried him to victory at Vicksburg and Richmond took hold of him again. He remarshaled his arguments for annexation after Congress recessed for the summer and autumn, and he made annexation the centerpiece of his December 1870 message. He reiterated that annexation would greatly benefit the United States and Santo Domingo both, and he again predicted that other countries would claim what the Senate wanted to throw away. "The moment it is known that the United States have entirely abandoned the project of accepting as a part of its territory the island of San Domingo a free port will be negotiated for by European nations in the Bay of Samana. A large commercial city will spring up, to which we will be tributary. . . . Then will be seen the folly of our rejecting so great a prize."

Tacitly conceding that the Senate would never ratify an annexation treaty, Grant suggested an alternative path. The Senate and House should jointly create a commission to examine the Dominican question; if the commission reported favorably, the two houses could annex Santo Domingo by joint resolution, as Texas had been annexed in 1845. Grant expressed confidence that the commission would agree with him. "So convinced am I of the advantages to flow from the acquisition of San Domingo, and of the great disadvantages—I might almost say calamities—to flow from nonacquisition, that I believe the subject has only to be investigated to be approved."

*C*harles Sumner was as stubborn as Grant. Sumner had obtained documents from the administration demonstrating that the U.S. Navy had sent warships to Santo Domingo to protect Báez against aggression from Haiti but also against his Dominican rivals; the commander of one of these vessels had raised the American flag over Dominican soil. Sumner condemned the orders and castigated the commander for not disobeying them. "Rather than carry out such instructions, he ought to have thrown his sword into the sea," Sumner declared. The ensuing occupation was an "act of war . . . war, sir, made by the executive without the consent of Congress." Andrew Johnson had acknowledged designs on Haiti as well as on Santo Domingo; Grant was simply less frank, Sumner said. "The president of the United States proceeds to menace the independence of Haiti." Grant's partner in dissimulation, Báez, was nothing but a "political jockey" with mercenary designs. "He is sustained in power by the government of the United States that he may betray his country."

The proposed joint commission was a cloak for American aggression against Santo Domingo and Haiti, Sumner continued. "The resolution before the Senate commits Congress to a dance of blood." He sneered at Grant's arguments for annexation. "We are called to consider commercial, financial, material advantages, and not one word is lisped of justice or humanity. . . . What are these, if right and humanity are sacrificed?" Sumner had long been considered a defender in Congress of America's blacks; he now appointed himself guardian of the African race generally. "The island of San Domingo, situated in tropical waters and occupied by another race, of another color, never can become a permanent possession of the United States. You may seize it by force of arms or by diplomacy, where a naval squadron does more than the minister, but the enforced jurisdiction cannot endure. Already by a higher statute is that island set apart to the colored race. It is theirs by right of possession, by their sweat and blood mingling with the soil, by tropical position, by its burning sun, and by unalterable laws of climate." Annexation was horribly wrong and must be resisted. "I protest against this resolution as another stage in a drama of blood. I protest against it in the name of justice outraged by violence, in the name of humanity insulted, in the name of the weak trodden down, in the name of peace imperiled, and in the name of the African race, whose first effort at independence is rudely assailed."

Sumner's anti-annexation speech, which he grandly titled "Naboth's Vineyard," confirmed his reputation for self-righteousness even as it accomplished his purpose of stymieing Grant. The president's allies in Congress won approval for the commission he sought, but such support for annexation as had existed outside the White House was nearly spent. The commissioners went south; on their return to Washington they reported in favor of annexation. Grant hailed the finding. "This report more than sustains all that I have heretofore said in regard to the productiveness and healthfulness of the Republic of San Domingo, of the unanimity of the people for annexation to the United States, and of their peaceable character," he said. He took comfort in the support for annexation of no less an authority on the African race than Frederick Douglass, the former slave and abolitionist. Douglass had accompanied the commission to the West Indies and he returned convinced that annexation suited the preference and interests of the Dominicans as well as of the United States. Douglass briefed Grant on his findings and told reporters he hoped Sumner would change his mind once he had pondered the commission's report. "If Mr. Sumner after that shall persevere in his present policy," Douglass said, "I shall consider his opposition fractious, and regard him as the worst foe the colored race has on this continent."

Neither the committee's endorsement nor Douglass's changed the minds of many lawmakers. Grant was compelled to conclude that he lacked the votes for annexation, and with belated pragmatism he let the subject drop.

62

IN JANUARY 1870 GRANT RECEIVED A LETTER FROM NEDOM ANGIER, the treasurer of the state of Georgia. Angier was a New Hampshire native who had moved to Atlanta before the war and become active in Republican politics afterward. He fell out with Governor Rufus Bullock, another Republican, over the disposition of state funds. Unable to get a hearing among Georgia Republicans, he traveled to Washington hoping to see the president. But Grant was busy and Angier impatient, so Angier sent Grant a letter. "Knowing your great desire and determination to have the laws fully executed," he said, "and having full confidence that you will allow no infraction of the laws where it is in your power to prevent, I most respectfully ask to be allowed to make some quotations and deductions therefrom." As Grant read Angier's painfully detailed brief on Bullock's flouting of state and federal law and his trampling of the rights of Georgians, he could imagine why the treasurer was having trouble with the governor—and probably with everyone else he encountered. But Grant couldn't deny the man's devotion to what he thought the welfare of his adopted state required. "To you we look, Most Worthy President, in the fullest confidence to curb any reckless disregard of law—to steady the restless passions and evil propensities that foment discord and mischief, and to give peace and prosperity to all portions of our beloved country."

Similar pleas about Georgia filled Grant's letter box that season, many indicting Bullock for egregiously violating the federal Reconstruction Act and the Fourteenth Amendment. "Governor Bullock has assumed the title of Provisional Governor, which is not authorized by the act of Congress, and intends to usurp authority over the legislature and people, and expects to be supported in his illegal and tyrannical course by yourself as President and the military under your command," Nelson Tift, a former congressman from Albany, Georgia, wrote Grant. "The people of Georgia are at your mercy and expect your protection."

Others besides Georgians felt themselves at Grant's mercy and hoped for his protection. Upon the seizure of control of federal reconstruction policy by the Radical Republicans, the white Democrats who had governed the South since before the war were driven from power, replaced by white and black Republicans. Some of the ousted sulked in silence, some plotted politically, some turned to violence. The Ku Klux Klan was the most visible of the groups perpetrating violence, and its victims appealed to Grant for protection. George Ashburn was a white Republican in Georgia who worked for greater rights for blacks. His activities brought him to the attention of the Klan, and in the spring of 1868 some three dozen hooded Klansmen broke into the Columbus rooming house where he was staying and shot him dead. In South Carolina a black Republican legislator named B. F. Randolph was murdered in broad daylight at a railway station in Cokesbury. In St. Helena Parish in Louisiana, Klansmen burned black churches and a schoolhouse and killed several African Americans. In the same parish Klan members dragged the coroner, a black Republican named John Kemp, from his home and shot him dead. They beat his wife and at least two of the neighbors. In Huntsville, Alabama, a Republican editor summarized the Klan violence in his vicinity: "These bands are having a great effect, in inspiring a *nameless terror* among negroes, poor whites, and even others. The mischief is taking place daily and nightly—nobody is found out, or arrested, or punished. The civil authority is seemingly powerless. The military does not act. And the thing goes on, and is getting worse daily."

The organized violence of the Klan tended to grow disorganized. The disruption of Southern society by the war, combined with the return of disillusioned young men familiar with arms but often without gainful employment, produced a general lawlessness that both contributed to the activities of the Klan and fed off it. At times it was hard to tell where political violence ended and ordinary criminality began. A visitor to Texas at the beginning of 1869 recounted events in the northeastern corner of the state. "Armed bands of banditti, thieves, cut-throats and assassins infest the country," he said. "They prowl around houses, they call men out and shoot or hang them, they attack travelers upon the road, they seem almost everywhere present, and are ever intent upon mischief.

You cannot pick up a paper without reading of murders, assassinations, and robbery. . . . And yet not the fourth part of the truth has been told; not one act in ten is reported. Go where you will, and you will hear of fresh murders and violence."

Grant had to decide whether the violence was his problem or the South's. His campaign call for peace could be interpreted in opposite ways. It might mean that he considered the sectional conflict over and the South ready to resume control of its own affairs. Or it could indicate an insistence on domestic tranquility in the South along lines specified by the newly amended Constitution, with equal rights for blacks.

Southern Republicans, governing by virtue of black votes, hoped for the latter interpretation, and from the moment Grant took office they appealed to him for protection. When their appeals were trivially political, he turned them away. A group of Georgia state legislators wired for advice on a matter of Republican politics: "Please answer quickly yes or no; should we vote for senators before repealing the black code of Georgia?" Horace Porter responded for Grant: "President has received your dispatch. He cannot advise you. Prefers that you use your own discretion."

But often the appeals invoked fundamental principles of constitutionality and political equality. In such cases Grant took a more forward stance. Describing Georgia's return to civil self-government, he told Congress: "She ratified her constitution, republican in form, elected a governor, members of Congress, a state legislature, and all other officers required. The governor was duly installed, and the legislature met and performed all the acts then required of them by the reconstruction acts of Congress." For this Georgia was to be commended. Unfortunately, however, the governor and legislature had subsequently reversed course. "They unseated the colored members of the legislature and admitted to seats some members who are disqualified by the third clause of the Fourteenth Amendment to the Constitution"—the clause barring former Confederates. Grant urged Congress to pass special legislation requiring Georgia to ensure equal treatment of blacks and adherence to the principles of republican government.

Congress complied. The legislature approved a law remanding Georgia to military rule until it obeyed the applicable federal laws and ratified the Fifteenth Amendment.

Georgia did as it was told. The bonus for Grant and the freedmen was the momentum the president's action supplied to the campaign for the Fifteenth Amendment, which by February 1870 had accumulated the necessary endorsements. "The ratification of the Fifteenth Amendment is assured!" Grant wrote Elihu Washburne, allowing himself a rare exclamation mark. His enthusiasm got the better of him as he added, prematurely: "With this question out of politics, and reconstruction completed, I hope to see such good feeling in Congress as to secure rapid legislation and an early adjournment. My peace is when Congress is not in session."

𝐵ut he couldn't send Congress off without requesting legislation to give substance to the promise of political equality. Grant appreciated the momentous nature of the latest development. "The adoption of the Fifteenth Amendment to the Constitution completes the greatest civil change and constitutes the most important event that has occurred since the nation came into life," he declared in a special message to Congress. Scarcely a decade earlier the Supreme Court had ruled that blacks were not citizens and had no rights the government and the white majority were bound to respect; now blacks were the political equals of whites. Yet he understood that paper promises often required concrete action to make them real. To this end he requested that Congress support education for the freedmen. "The framers of our Constitution firmly believed that a republican government could not endure without intelligence and education generally diffused among the people," he said. "If these recommendations were important then, with a population of but a few millions, how much more important now, with a population of forty millions?" He left the details to Congress, but he urged the legislators "to take all the means within their constitutional powers to promote and encourage popular education throughout the country" and "to see to it that all who possess and exercise political rights shall have the opportunity to acquire the knowledge which will make their share in the government a blessing and not a danger."

Congress wasn't so generous. The egalitarian zeal that had inspired the educational programs of the Freedmen's Bureau was waning; new benefits for blacks, if they cost money, were out of the question.

So Grant shifted his aim. The Fifteenth Amendment, like the Thirteenth and Fourteenth, included a clause giving Congress the authority to write enforcing legislation. At Grant's urging the legislature wielded that authority. A first enforcement act criminalized the use of "force, bribery, threats, intimidation, or other unlawful means" to keep voters from exercising their Fifteenth Amendment rights. Violations would be investigated by federal marshals and prosecuted in federal courts. Special commissioners would be appointed in the event the caseload exceeded the capacity of existing officials. The president could summon the army, navy and militia to aid in enforcement. A second enforcement act extended the federal writ to the conduct of elections, authorizing federal officials for the first time to supervise voting in the states and guard against violations of the Fifteenth Amendment.

These measures were historic in expanding the scope of federal law, which in those days rarely reached over the states to criminalize individual behavior. But Grant wanted more. "There is a deplorable state of affairs existing in some portions of the South, demanding the immediate attention of Congress," he wrote James Blaine, the Republican Speaker of the House. What was necessary, the president said, was legislation to provide "means for the protection of life and property in those sections of the country where the present civil authority fails to secure that end."

Blaine wasn't unwilling, but he wanted Grant to speak more definitively. The president seemed to have in mind something quite forceful, perhaps even revolutionary, and Blaine didn't want to accept the responsibility. The president must argue his own case.

Grant did so. "A condition of affairs now exists in some of the states of the Union rendering life and property insecure and the carrying of the mails and the collection of the revenue dangerous," he asserted in another special message to Congress. The comment about the mails and the revenues was legal cover for the audacious extension of federal authority Grant envisioned. "That the power to correct these evils is beyond the control of the state authorities I do not doubt," he continued. "That the power of the Executive of the United States, acting within the limits of existing laws, is sufficient for present emergencies is not clear." Grant insisted that Congress make it clear. "I urgently recommend such legislation as in the judgment of Congress shall effectually secure life, liberty, and property and the enforcement of law in all parts of the United States."

Grant's demand hit Congress like a mortar shell. The Democrats turned apoplectic at what they deemed Grant's power grab. "I can scarcely believe that so radical a revolution has overcome the institutions of this country," Representative Fernando Wood of New York declared as a bill embodying the president's proposal moved toward a vote. "I can scarcely believe that within the short period of ten or twelve years political sentiment on the other side has become so radical as to countenance a serious proposition in the House of Representatives to create a military despotism on the ruins of a republic." The bill was anti-American, anti-democratic, anti-republican, anti-civilized. "In no portion of our history has any such power been delegated; in no free government anywhere in the world has such power been delegated by the people," Wood said. "Nor is there any despot for the past century who would attempt to exercise it; and even the life of the present emperor of Russia, with all his great personal authority, holding in his hands not only the church but the state, not only the sword but the purse, whose subjects are vassals, would not be safe for twenty-four hours if he attempted to exercise the power now proposed to be given to the present president of the United States."

At the other end of the Capitol, Democratic senators waxed equally wroth. Francis Blair showed that he had lost none of the rhetorical verve that won him the vice presidential nomination in 1868. "He is invited to become *dictator*," the Missouri lawmaker said of the president and the power the Republican bill would give him. "It is proposed to confer this unlimited power upon a man whose history is wholly military, except for the two years of his presidency, which has been signalized by utter disregard of law." James Beck of Kentucky saw party cynicism behind the president's coup. "It is to divert the minds of the people," he said. "It is a flank movement to excite the people by the cry of murder, Ku Klux, etc." The administration's bill included a provision to let the president suspend habeas corpus in counties where the violence was unchecked; Beck warned: "An official might throw me into jail without cause and without warrant the moment I return"—from Washington—"stating that I had done something, he would not tell me what." Fear of losing control of the South was driving the desperate efforts by the Republicans to remain in charge, Beck said. "If these states of the South would only continue to be Radical, if they would only agree that they would vote for General Grant again, you would never hear anything about the Ku Klux; you would never more hear of reconstruction acts."

Even some Republicans wondered what Grant was getting them

into. "Public affairs are growing about as bad as the devil could wish if he were arranging them in his own way," Representative James Garfield of Ohio grumbled. Garfield didn't deny that the Southern violence was a problem, but the administration's solution could prove even worse. "This will virtually empower the President to abolish the state governments," he said. Garfield was no alarmist, but he feared that Grant was destroying the Republican party. "The impression is gaining ground that the election of Grant is impossible, but it is feared that his nomination is inevitable."

William Sherman didn't know where it all would lead. Sherman blamed politics for nearly everything that ailed the country, and he saw his old friend becoming ever more tainted. "Politics have again gradually but surely drawn the whole country into a situation of as much danger as before the Civil War," he wrote Edward Ord. "The Army left the South subdued, broken, and humbled. The party then in power"—the Republicans—"forgetful of the fact that sooner or later the people of the South must vote, labored hard to create voters out of Negroes and indifferent material." The results were predictable. "The Negro governments, aided by a weak force of Republican whites, have been swept aside and the Union people there are hustled, branded, and even killed." But little could be done about it, absent a thorough suspension of local rule. "Any Southern citizen may kill or abuse a Negro or Union man with as much safety as one of our frontiersmen may kill an Indian. . . . All crimes must be tried by juries on the spot, who of course protect their comrades." Sherman was more discouraged than ever about democracy. The Republicans, the party of the Union, were in disarray, and his and Ord's wartime commander faced a bleak future. "General Grant's personal popularity seems to be waning, and the opposition to his administration is such that if they can unite they will surely prevail."

But Grant persevered. He marshaled his allies in Congress and held their ranks firm when some started wavering. The result was a measure formally styled "An Act to Enforce the Provisions of the Fourteenth Amendment" but commonly called the Ku Klux Klan Act. It expanded the definition of criminal wrongdoing to include conspiracies to deprive citizens of their rights, and, most significantly, it remobilized the engines of the Civil War to deal with the Klan and the violence it practiced. Whenever "powerful and armed combinations" threatened the integrity of a state government or the enforcement of federal laws within a state, or when a state government connived at the "unlawful purposes of such powerful and armed combinations," these groups would be deemed to be in "rebellion against the government of the United States." The president was authorized to employ military force against said combinations and to suspend the writ of habeas corpus.

Grant signed the Ku Klux Klan Act in April 1871. Describing it as a measure of "extraordinary public importance," he suggested how he might put it to use. He wouldn't act precipitately. "It is my earnest wish that peace and cheerful obedience to law may prevail throughout the land and that all traces of our late unhappy civil strife may be speedily removed," he said. "These ends can be easily reached by acquiescence in the results of the conflict, now written in our Constitution, and by the due and proper enforcement of equal, just, and impartial laws in every part of our country." But the new law had not been written without cause. "The failure of local communities to furnish such means for the attainment of results so earnestly desired imposes upon the national government the duty of putting forth all its energies for the protection of its citizens of every race and color and for the restoration of peace and order throughout the entire country." He would do his part of the government's duty. "I will not hesitate to exhaust the powers thus vested in the executive."

THE SWEEPING NEW LAW GAVE HEART TO VICTIMS OF THE SOUTHERN violence; once again they appealed to Grant for help. "There is a Ku Klux organization in this county," Robert Flournoy, the editor of a paper called *Equal Rights*, wrote from Pontotoc, Mississippi. The Klansmen had closed a school for freedmen and were working to close others. "I am threatened with personal violence," Flournoy said. He appreciated the new law but said it had made matters worse in the short term, in that the Klansmen and Democrats didn't believe Grant would follow through and were trying to demonstrate as much to the locals. The president needed to act at once. "Nothing but the strong arm of the government firmly administered can prevent very serious consequences to the integrity of the Union. All the hopes of the loyal people are fixed on you; every day loyal men come to me and enquire will anything be done for them." Two weeks later Flournoy sent an update: "The Ku Klux attacked us on Friday night. We drove them off, killing one and wounding others. They threaten to return and burn the town. Can we have troops immediately to protect us?"

Allen Huggins, another Mississippi Republican, wrote Grant from the safety of Washington, having been driven from Monroe County in his home state. "The first appearance of Ku Klux in Monroe County was in the month of August 1870," Huggins informed the president. "About fifty in number at that time visited the jail at Athens seven miles from Aberdeen and forcibly took from there a colored man by the name of Saunders Flint and his two grown sons—Joseph and Moses, I think were their names—who were in jail for defending themselves against an assault made upon them by three white men. The father, Saunders Flint, escaped. The two sons were found about a week after, in the woods torn in pieces by shot." On Flint's testimony and additional evidence several of the perpetrators were arrested, but a white jury acquitted them. "From that time to this the county has been one continued scene of persecution and horror to Union men white and black," Huggins told Grant. The violence was escalating. Huggins described a gruesome series of hangings and shootings. The lucky among the victims of the terror were merely whipped and beaten. Even a white woman had been beaten simply for knowing the identity of some of the murderers.

G. T. F. Boulding of Tuscaloosa, Alabama, pleaded with Grant to act quickly against the Klansmen. "Give us poor people some guarantee of our lives," Boulding wrote. "We are hunted and shot down as if we were wild beasts. On last Saturday night, April 30, the clique known as the K. K.'s visited the house of one of our most guileless colored citizens and shot him dead, after which they robbed his house of about $200 in money and carried off his gun and pistol. This is not the only case of the kind in the last ten days but the third or fourth case. We hope as our lives, liberty, and property are in imminent peril that you will do something for us as soon as possible. We have imperiled our lives to support you, and we look to you to help us when in distress." Boulding invited Grant to publish his letter but requested that his name be omitted. "If the name was known I would not live for twenty-four hours."

From Fayette County, Alabama, arrived a petition with a similar message and a similar request for anonymity. "Armed bands styling themselves Ku Klux are committing crimes and outrages upon peaceable and law-abiding persons," the petition read. "Murders by these ruffians who have long disgraced this county are of common occurrence. *The civil authorities have been overawed and are utterly powerless to execute the laws.* . . . We do most humbly and imploringly appeal for that protection which the Constitution and laws guarantee to every citizen of the United States. . . . Please do not give publicity to our names as we are in constant danger of assassination."

Grant shared the grim news with Congress, which created a special investigative committee. Members visited several Southern states and heard testimony from hundreds of victims and witnesses. Alfred Richardson was a carpenter in Watkinsville, Georgia, who had entered politics and been elected to the state legislature. One night a band of armed white men rode to his house. "There were about twenty or twenty-five of them, I reckon," he told the committee. The whites battered down his door and chased him upstairs, where they shot him once in the arm and twice in his side. He nonetheless reached a cache of weapons he kept in his garret. "They came upstairs with their pistols in their hands, and a man behind with a light. I shot one of them as he got on the top step. They gathered him up by the legs, and then they all ran and left me." He hadn't seen them since but knew he was a marked man. In Jackson County, Florida, Emanuel Fortune had been compelled to flee Klan violence, and to the committee he described the apparent intentions of the organization. "The object of it is to kill out the leading men of the Republican party," he said. Alabamian George Moore and a neighbor were beaten in his home by Klansmen, who also raped a young girl. "The cause of this treatment, they said, was that we voted the Radical ticket," Moore related. In Chattanooga a black man named Andrew Flowers had defeated a white opponent in an election for justice of the peace. Shortly thereafter the Klan inflicted its own form of justice, whipping Flowers savagely. "When they were taking me out of the door, they said they had nothing particular against me," Flowers told the committee. "They didn't dispute I was a very good fellow, and they never heard anything wrong of me. But they did not intend any nigger to hold office in the United States."

The reports from South Carolina were the most alarming of all. "We are fast drifting into anarchy," Warren Driver wrote from Barnwell County. "I am told plainly to leave here or change my politics or they will kill me as no damned Radical will be tolerated—told so by the leading man of this section. . . . There are armed bands of ruffians roaming through the country murdering inoffensive people. There has been five murders committed in as many weeks in my vicinity. . . . No one arrested for it. . . . Mr. President, is it not time that these butcheries ceased? Is it not time that a heavy hand was laid on these demons?" Javan Bryant pleaded in like vein from Spartanburg County. "All eyes are turned to the executive of the nation," Bryant wrote Grant. "In him alone are concentrated all our hopes. We look upon the Ku Klux Klan as rebellion in its worst form." The Civil War was being waged again, and it needed to be won again. "At Appomattox Court House the great rebellion was cut off at the ground," Bryant said. "In Spartanburg County it has sprouted out from the stump, and the scions are more poisonous than the parent tree. We humbly pray, Almighty God, that he who cut it off at Appomattox Court House may declare martial law in Spartanburg County, and never stack arms until the last root has been extirpated."

The congressional investigators largely agreed with Grant's petitioners. Senator John Scott of Pennsylvania visited South Carolina and wrote Grant that in parts of the state the situation was entirely out of control. "The cruelties that have been inflicted in Spartanburg and York counties are shocking to humanity, crimes that ought not to go unpunished in any civilized country," Scott said. "The perpetrators are at large and unwhipped of justice. . . . All warnings have been disregarded and the efforts of the well-disposed citizens have proved unavailing."

Grant wanted an assessment from his own agent, and so he sent his new attorney general. Amos Akerman was an oddity in Grant's cabinet, being a Southerner and former Confederate officer. But he wasn't a full-blooded Southerner, having been born and raised in New Hampshire. Like William Sherman he went south before the war to become a teacher; unlike Sherman he stayed south, in Georgia, upon secession and eventually joined the Confederate army. Yet after Lee's surrender he abandoned the Lost Cause as utterly lost and beneficially so. "A surrender in good faith really signifies a surrender of the substance as well as of the forms of the Confederate cause," he explained in jumping ship all the way to the Republican party. He became federal district attorney for Georgia and a zealous enforcer of the civil rights of the freedmen. When Grant decided to remove Ebenezer Hoar from the cabinet, he chose Akerman to replace him. Besides being the first former Confederate to hold a cabinet position, Akerman was the first attorney general to head a federal department. The Justice Department was created in 1870 to facilitate enforcement of the Fourteenth and Fifteenth Amendments and the federal laws passed in pursuance thereof. Akerman denominated the department his civil rights army, and with Grant's approval he led his troops from the front. He traveled to South Carolina in 1871 to gather information and steel the spines of the federal marshals, attorneys and civil rights commissioners for a major campaign against the Klan.

Grant launched the campaign with troops already on the ground. "Order the troops in South Carolina to aid in making such arrests as the U.S. commissioner for South Carolina may ask, and in all cases to arrest and break up disguised night marauders," he directed William Belknap, the secretary of war. The move served symbolic notice but accomplished little constructive. The federal troops in South Carolina were few and the people unfriendly. As if to show their derision for federal authority, the Klansmen escalated the violence, and the number of murders actually increased.

Grant answered the challenge with greater sternness. He had Akerman draft language that fit the notification requirements of the Ku Klux Klan Act. "Unlawful combinations and conspiracies have long existed and do still exist in the State of South Carolina for the purpose of depriving certain portions and classes of the people of that State of the rights, privileges, immunities, and protection named in the Constitution of the United States," Grant declared on October 12, 1871. South Carolina's authorities had shown themselves unable or unwilling to secure those rights and privileges. "Therefore I, Ulysses S. Grant, President of the United States of America, do hereby command all persons composing the unlawful combinations and conspiracies aforesaid to disperse and to retire peaceably to their homes within five days."

Grant wasn't surprised that the proclamation by itself had little effect. The violence continued. Akerman reported that the Klan and its terrorist kin were most powerful in nine counties of the state. "These combinations embrace at least two-thirds of the active white men of those counties and have the sympathy and countenance of a majority of the other third," Akerman wrote Grant. "They are connected with similar combinations in other counties and states, and no doubt are part of a grand system of criminal associations pervading most of the southern states. The members are bound to obedience and secrecy by oaths which they are taught to regard as of higher obligation than the lawful oaths taken before civil magistrates. They are organized and armed. They effect their objects by personal violence often extending to murder. They terrify witnesses. They control juries in the state courts and sometimes in the courts of the United States." The president should act swiftly on the warning he had given. "Unless these combinations shall be thoroughly suppressed, no citizen who opposes their political objects will be permitted to live, and no freedman will enjoy essential liberty in the territory now subject to their sway."

Grant agreed. He augmented the federal force in South Carolina, and the moment the grace period expired he issued a second proclamation, in which he repeated his characterization of the South Carolina rebellion, noted that the perpetrators remained at large, specified the nine most troublesome counties and declared: "The public safety especially requires that the privileges of the writ of habeas corpus be suspended, to the end that such rebellion may be overthrown."

Grant's action provoked a new uproar in Congress. The Democrats' response was predictable. Francis Blair had spent the summer trying to neutralize the testimony given to the congressional investigative committee about the Klan violence. For each witness who graphically described the terror in the South, Blair brought forward another witness who asserted that all was well in Dixie. "What has been, and is now, the relation or state of feeling between the white and colored people?" Blair asked of Francis Lyon, an Alabamian who had held both federal and Confederate office. Lyon responded: "The general disposition of the white people has been, and is now, to do the blacks justice." Such trouble as occurred in the South was the fault of self-interested agitators. "If the colored people were let alone by political demagogues and unworthy office-seekers, there would be but little trouble between the races," Lyon said. "When the Loyal Leagues"—Republican organizations in the South—"were in operation, efforts were made by designing white men to control the votes of the negroes, by representing to them that their old owners would re-enslave them if they had the power, a thing which everybody ought to know is utterly false. There is no power to do any such thing, and no disposition to do it if the power existed."

Blair continued to insist that the South could handle its own affairs, and he condemned Grant's suspension of habeas corpus as tyrannically misguided. He sponsored a resolution in the Senate calling on the president to furnish proof of his allegations as to the violence in South Carolina—"giving the names of his informants, their statements when made to him in writing, and the substance of them when made verbally." Blair accused the president of making selective use of the examination of witnesses before the investigative committee. "As a member of the committee, I can give my opinion that the facts elicited by that examination did not justify the proclamation of martial law, and I suspect that I know more about the facts elicited before the committee than the President does." Blair lumped the legislature in with his attacks on the executive. "While I am not surprised that the President should have exercised the authority given to him, as his education and his genius are arbitrary and look to arbitrary measures, I am astonished, sir, at the servility of Congress in submitting the rights of all citizens of this country to his discretion, and depriving them of the guarantees of the Constitution."

If the dismay of the Democrats at Grant's bold stroke was expected, the revolt of certain Republicans was not. Carl Schurz had been a Lincoln man and a supporter of emancipation, but he thought Grant was on a power-grabbing fool's errand trying to enforce equality in the South. Southern society was in a process of "fermentation," Schurz said; the region's "inveterate habits, opinions, and ways of thinking" would change only with time. Schurz was currently a senator from Missouri; he professed familiarity with Southern Republicans, whom he considered corrupt, and African Americans, whom he deemed incapable of independent political judgment. He discounted the horror stories of Klan activity in South Carolina and elsewhere as gross mischaracterizations of actual events, and he took Grant's suspension of habeas corpus as occasion to declare his break from the president. "I stand in the Republican party as an independent man," he said. Calling himself a "liberal Republican," he characterized the creed of himself and his ideological allies: "We desire peace and good will to all men. We desire the removal of political restrictions and the maintenance of local self-government to the utmost extent compatible with the constitution as it is. We desire the questions connected with the Civil War to be disposed of forever, to make room as soon as possible for the new problems of the present and the future."

Even within his own administration Grant got little support. Amos Akerman was zealous, of course, but other members of the cabinet wished he and the president would find a more popular cause. The politically attuned secretaries feared a voter backlash; Hamilton Fish feared falling asleep. "Akerman introduces Ku Klux," Fish recorded in his diary on November 24. "He has it on the brain. He tells a number of stories, one of a fellow being castrated, with terribly minute and tedious details of each case. It has got to be a bore, to listen twice each week to this same thing."

On the scene in South Carolina federal marshals assisted by army troops rounded up many hundreds of Klansmen and associates. The habeas suspension allowed the arrests to take place far more rapidly than they would have otherwise, because the authorities didn't have to bring the persons arrested before a judge shortly and charge them with a crime. The effects of the sweep went beyond arrest numbers; many Klansmen fled their home counties ahead of the troops and marshals, some fled the state and a few even fled the country. The detainees overwhelmed the available jails and, after they were eventually indicted, clogged the dockets of the courts. Amos Akerman conceded he had bitten off more than the courts could chew. "It seems to me that it is too much for even the United States to undertake to inflict adequate penalties through the courts," he told an associate. But he defended the president's action. "Really these combinations amount to war and cannot be effectively crushed on any other theory."

To ease the backlog Akerman accepted plea bargains from scores of the arrestees and subjected to trial only those involved in what he called "deep criminality." The trials took months, spilling well over into 1872. Several hundred arrestees were ultimately convicted at trial and sentenced, but because even the most egregious Klansmen couldn't be charged under federal law with anything more serious than conspiracy to deprive individuals of their civil rights—rather than assault or murder, which remained under the exclusive jurisdiction of the states—the sentences were relatively minor. The longest prison term meted out was five years; most of the convicted served six to eighteen months. Fines ranged from ten to one hundred dollars.

Grant's critics, noting the light sentences, charged the president with laboring mightily to produce a mouse. Some noted the defection of Schurz and the "liberal Republicans" and concluded that the Klan prosecutions were a sign of the administration's weakness rather than its strength. Amos Akerman acknowledged the diminishing concern of Northerners for the problems of the South. "The feeling here is very strong that the Southern Republicans must cease to look for special support," he remarked from Washington. The Southerners would have to "stand on their own feet." Northerners had other worries. "Such atrocities as Ku Kluxery do not hold their attention. . . . The Northern mind, being full of what is called progress, runs away from the past."

But the consequences of Grant's stroke transcended the prison time served and, for the moment at least, defied the distraction of Northern liberals. Grant's campaign put the fear of federal power into the Klan and shattered its sense of impunity. Not for decades would the nightriders exercise such influence again. Albion Tourgée, a judge in North Carolina (who would go on to represent Homer Plessy in the landmark civil rights trial of the 1890s), wrote Grant explaining the effect of the president's actions on the legal system of the South. "At the Superior court of the county of Alamance, at which I had the honor to preside last week," Tourgée said, "a grand jury composed of a large majority of members of the Ku Klux organization, including one chief of a camp, presented bills of indictment of sixty-three members of the Klan for felony and eighteen for the murder of Wyatt Outlaw, who was hung as you may recollect on a tree in the Court House Square February 26th, 1870. Many of those indicted are of the most respectable families of the county. The confessions now in my hands also reveal the perpetrators of similar crimes in other counties. I do not doubt, within a month I shall hold ample evidence as to every K.K. crime in this district. Nothing, Mr. President, but the prompt and unflinching firmness of your course in relation to this vexatious question could have rendered such a thing possible." The change that had occurred was simply marvelous. "The Ku Klux was an impregnable fortress. Sixty-four times I have tried in vain to break into its walls and secure testimony sufficient to enable me to demand from juries indictment and conviction. The former had a few times been secured by a predominance of Republican jurors; the latter never. And so it would have remained until the end of time had not your wise and patriotic course so frightened the adherents of the Invisible Empire that they began to desert in squads. And this is the result: a *Ku Klux* grand jury *indicts for Ku Kluxing.*"

HAMILTON FISH'S BOREDOM WITH THE KU KLUX KLAN MIRRORED his preoccupation with Britain. For the secretary of state only one issue of international affairs really mattered. The British government had sought for decades—since American independence, in fact—to stunt or contain the growing republic on the Atlantic's western shore. Americans naturally resisted. In only one instance, in 1812, did war result, but bad feelings were chronic. During the sectional crisis the Americans seemed to be doing Britain's enervating work for it, and Southern secession promised a permanent solution to London's American problem. The loss of the South would weaken the Union irretrievably, making Britain perhaps the dominant power in the Western Hemisphere. Strategic prudence for Britain accordingly suggested aiding the South in its struggle against the North. Economics pointed in the same direction, as the South supplied the cotton essential to the textile trade on which Britain had built its industrial revolution.

Yet there were arguments against a Southern tilt. The British had abolished slavery in their empire a generation earlier and ever since spearheaded efforts to curtail the international slave trade. Their motives were as mixed as motives often are; in British antislavery policy, morality married calculations of competitiveness. Slavery was inhumane; it also gave Britain's commercial rivals an advantage if they practiced slavery while Britain didn't. During the first year of the American war, when Lincoln fought solely for the Union, the choice between North and South was ambiguous on the slave issue, but after the president issued the Emancipation Proclamation the British could have backed the South only at grave cost to conscience and credibility.

Other arguments added to London's diffidence. Since the repeal of Britain's protectionist Corn Laws in the 1840s, the British had become big purchasers of American grain; by the 1860s they relied almost as heavily on Northern wheat as on Southern cotton. British officials, charged with managing a globe-spanning empire, had troubles around the world; to meddle in America's fight would multiply their headaches. Finally, the South had to show an ability to win the war before Britain would risk alienating the North; to join a losing cause would be folly.

On balance the arguments for and against supporting the South were, from Britain's perspective, nearly equal. Consequently the British took a middle stance, recognizing Southern belligerency but not Southern independence. This passed the basic reality test: the South had created a government that was fighting for independence, but that government hadn't come close to winning. The middle way also hedged British bets. It left open the possibility of going farther, to a recognition of independence, should Southern victories on the battlefield so warrant. And it avoided provoking the North beyond the capacity of Lincoln and his administration to endure without declaring war on London.

The balanced policy also let British merchants and manufacturers do business with both sides in the American conflict. The South, in particular, coveted access to British industry, in order to acquire the weapons without which the Confederacy would quickly have collapsed. American industry clustered in the North, which supplied its own arms needs; the South looked to Britain. British arms makers and especially ship builders were pleased to accommodate. Some sleight of hand was required, as British law forbade the construction of foreign warships; the solution was for the British yards to build commercial vessels subsequently convertible to Confederate naval use. Lincoln's minister in London, Charles Francis Adams, saw past the ruse and protested, but not before two ships, which the Confederates christened the *Alabama* and the *Florida*, slipped to sea and into Confederate service. The raiders sank scores of Northern merchant vessels, costing the owners and shippers millions of dollars, requiring the Union navy to engage in a lengthy pursuit and arguably extending the war months or years.

This argument was what Grant inherited, along with the anger of the owners and shippers. They pressed the American government to file claims against Britain; eventually others added their grievances. The *Alabama* claims, as the package was called, stirred Congress, where legislators orated indignantly against British perfidy. Twisting the lion's tail had always been good politics in America, and it was never better than during the decade after the Civil War. Charles Sumner took up the task just weeks into Grant's presidency. An agreement on the *Alabama* claims concluded at the eleventh hour of Andrew Johnson's presidency required Senate approval; Sumner aimed to prevent any such approval from being given. Sumner damned Britain's actions on the *Alabama* as deliberately malign. "At a moment of profound peace between the United States and England there was a hostile expedition against the United States," he said of the construction and launch of the raider. "It was in no sense a commercial transaction but an act of war." The ship was operated by Confederate crews, but her origin was British. "Thus her depredations and burnings, making the ocean blaze, all proceeded from England." Sumner wanted to charge Britain not simply for the cost of the ships and cargoes the *Alabama* destroyed but for the cost of the lengthened war Britain's Confederate-friendly policy made inevitable. "Without British intervention the rebellion would have soon succumbed under the well-directed efforts of the national government. Not weeks or months, but years, were added in this way to our war, so full of costly sacrifice." Sumner declined to place a precise dollar figure on the losses America suffered as a result of Britain's hostile actions, but they were huge. "They stand before us mountain-high, with a base broad as the nation, and a mass stupendous as the rebellion itself." The transfer of Canada to the United States might begin to atone for the costs America had incurred as a result of Britain's crimes. But beyond repayment the British must apologize for their complicity in the rebellion and in the defense of slavery. "At a great epoch of history, not less than that of the French Revolution or that of the Reformation, when civilization was fighting a last battle with slavery, England gave her name, her influence, her material resources to the wicked cause, and flung a sword into the scale with slavery." Britain must own up and pay up. "The day of reckoning has come."

Grant had greater reason than Sumner for resenting Britain's wartime policy. The losses Grant's armies endured resulted in no small part from Britain's encouragement of the Confederacy. In private Grant's resentment sometimes surfaced. "If it were not for our debt," he told the cabinet, "I wish Congress would declare war upon Great Britain, when we would take Canada and wipe out her commerce as she has done ours, and then we would start fair. . . . Really, I am tired of all this arrogance and assumption of Great Britain."

But Grant differed from Sumner in keeping his resentment confidential. He concurred in rejecting the agreement inherited from Johnson, but he did so in language far more statesmanlike than Sumner's. "Its provisions were wholly inadequate for the settlement of the grave wrongs that had been sustained by this government, as well as by its citizens," he told Congress and the American people. He itemized the injuries: "the increased rates of insurance . . . the diminution of exports and imports . . . the decrease and transfer to Great Britain of our commercial marine . . . the prolongation of the war and the increased cost (both in treasure and in lives) of its suppression." It was not possible to make good these injuries the way one could ordinary claims, yet the Johnson agreement attempted to do so. The agreement must be abandoned, and Grant said he had so instructed Hamilton Fish. The secretary of state was eager to start a new round of negotiations; if the British were willing, talks could begin at once. "I hope that the time may soon arrive when the two governments can approach the solution of this momentous question with an appreciation of what is due to the rights, dignity, and honor of each," Grant said.

*A*lthough the British accepted Grant's offer to reopen negotiation of the *Alabama* claims, the talks moved slowly. Sumner stoked the fires of American passion on the subject by now insisting that Britain yield not merely Canada but all British possessions in the Western Hemisphere. The British rejected territorial transfer as absurd and unacceptable.

Amid the Anglo-American stalemate, France imprudently declared war on Prussia. Napoleon III had designs on German territory and had long chafed at the pretensions of Prussian king Wilhelm, and when a dispute flared over the succession to the Spanish throne, Prussian chancellor Otto von Bismarck, who was looking for an excuse to rally the other German states to Prussia's side, magnified an interchange between Wilhelm and the French ambassador into an insult to French pride. Napoleon took the bait and the war began.

Grant hadn't liked Napoleon during the Civil War, when the emperor had let the Confederacy float loans in Paris and exploited America's internal conflict to send the French troops to Mexico. Grant didn't know Bismarck, but he generally appreciated Germans, who during the war had bought Union bonds and whose German-American kinsmen had fought under the Union flag. Yet Grant kept his preferences to himself. He proclaimed American neutrality between the French and Germans and put Americans on notice that violations of neutrality would be treated severely.

The French wanted a friendlier response. After the rest of Germany linked arms with Prussia, as Bismarck anticipated, and after Napoleon's government collapsed upon the emperor's capture at Sedan in September 1870, Paris sought American help in avoiding dismemberment by the Germans. The French minister in Washington requested an American statement of support for French territorial integrity. Grant declined, saying France's troubles were none of America's business. "The President further expressed as a private opinion," Hamilton Fish recorded, "that France, having without provocation entered upon the war, with a scarcely concealed intention to dispossess Prussia of a portion of her territory, could not complain, and was not entitled to sympathy, if the result of the war deprived her of a portion of her own territory." Grant likewise declined any involvement in efforts by third parties to mediate an end to the war. Such involvement, he declared, conflicted with longstanding American policy and probably wouldn't work anyway. But to retain his options he added an element of diplomatic ambiguity: "Should the time come when the action of the United States can hasten the return of peace by a single hour, that action will be heartily taken."

The latter stages of the Franco-Prussian War produced the unification of Germany that had been Bismarck's goal; they also spawned a civil war in Paris that splashed the streets with the blood of tens of thousands of leftist Communards. Neither the bolstering of Germany nor the bleeding of France boded well for Britain, where government officials had followed the war nervously from the start and perceived the continental balance as being decisively disrupted by the new German *Reich*. The more prescient of those officials began looking toward America as a potential ally rather than an inveterate rival. To cultivate America they softened their position on the *Alabama* claims.

Other developments eased the way to a settlement. Charles Sumner's intemperance grew more pronounced, with his passion undermining his credibility. "Upon a certain class of questions," Hamilton Fish wrote in his diary, "and wherever his own importance or influence are concerned, or on anything relating to himself, or his views, past or present, or his ambition, he loses the power of logical reasoning and becomes contradictory, and violent and unreasoning. . . . This is mental derangement." To Thurlow Weed, a longtime associate, Fish declared, "Sumner is malicious. He has, I am told, declared that no settlement with Great Britain, and no determination on the foreign affairs of the country, shall be made by Grant's administration. He cannot control, and wishes to defeat." Fish told Elihu Washburne, "Sumner is bitterly vindictive and hostile. He is determined to oppose and if possible defeat everything that the President proposes or wishes or does. . . . I am convinced that he is crazy; vanity, conceit, ambition have disturbed the equilibrium of his mind. He is irrational and illogical, and raves and rants. No mad bull ever dashed more violently at a red flag than he does at anything that he thinks the President is interested in."

Sumner's self-righteousness alienated sufficient senators that when the administration's allies plotted his overthrow as chairman of the Foreign Relations Committee, the deed was readily accomplished. Grant declared that nothing beyond concern for the public interest had inspired the change. "I never asked to have any particular person put on any of the Senate standing committees," he said. "All that I have asked is that the chairman of the Committee on Foreign Relations be someone with whom the Secretary of State and myself might confer and advise. This I deemed due to the country in view of the very important questions which, of necessity, must come before it."

Coincident with Sumner's removal was the realization in the United States that Canada had no desire to join the Union. The 1867 British North America Act gave Canadians enough self-government that transfer to the United States, never popular in Canada, came to seem there more like recolonization than liberation. Americans had balked at annexing the heavily populated regions of Mexico in 1848, being unable to rationalize the takeover of a protesting people; they balked at taking over Canada now, for the same reason. This and the deposing of Sumner made it possible for Hamilton Fish, heading Grant's negotiating team, to leave Canada off the agenda without causing a stir.

Extraneous issues—fishery rights with Canada in the Atlantic Northeast, boundary claims in the Pacific Northwest—delayed a final settlement of the *Alabama* claims until the spring of 1871. But that May the pact was signed, and in June the ratifications of the American Senate and the British parliament were exchanged, resolving decades of tension between the two great English-speaking nations and paving the way, as matters turned out, for the most important and enduring alliance in modern world history.

BETWEEN THE SIGNING OF THE TREATY AND ITS RATIFICATION GRANT received a message from William Sherman. The message was contained in a letter from Sherman to his brother John, who forwarded the letter to Grant with an inquiry as to whether it should be published. James Gordon Bennett of the Democratic *New York Herald* was pushing Sherman to accept a Democratic presidential nomination for the next year; Sherman had responded to the unsought endorsement in the most forthright language he could devise. "I have never been and never will be a candidate for President," he wrote Bennett. "If nominated by either party I should peremptorily decline, and even if unanimously elected I should decline to serve."

Bennett delightedly printed Sherman's letter, which boosted circulation, as the editor intended. And he suggested that the letter shouldn't be taken at face value, since a man in Sherman's position could be expected to issue such a denial. Sherman meanwhile wrote John with the same message he had sent to Bennett. "You may say for me, and publish it, too, that in no event, and under no circumstances, will I ever be a candidate for President or any other political office, and I mean every word of it," Sherman said. John Sherman forwarded the letter to Grant.

Before Grant could respond, one of Bennett's reporters buttonholed the president at Long Branch, where he was vacationing. "General Sherman, Mr. President, is named as your successor. Would he take the nomination?" the reporter asked. Grant weighed his words carefully. "Sherman and I are warm friends, and I am not authorized to speak for him," he said. "Of one thing I feel pretty certain, however, and that is that Sherman won't stand on any platform the Democrats will make. . . .

No, sir; Sherman can have no affiliation with such men. He is no Democrat, and never was. He probably knows very well that if the Democracy
succeeded, the Southern leaders, who are still hostile to the Union of the
states, and, in that view, enemies of the republic, would gain possession
of the government and before long annul, so far as they could, the acts
of the Republican party. That will hardly be permitted, in this century,
at least."

After Grant read his remarks in the next day's *Herald*, he decided
Bennett had gotten enough mileage out of the Sherman question. He
recommended that John Sherman withhold William's letter. "Under no
circumstances would I publish it," he said. Sherman's earlier disclaimer
sufficed for his purposes, if not Bennett's; to say more would simply keep
the false boom going. Grant added, "I think his determination never to
give up his present position a wise one, for his own comfort, and the public knowing it will relieve him from the suspicion of acting and speaking with reference to the effect his acts and sayings may have upon his
chances for political preferment. If he should ever change his mind, however, no one has a better right than he has to aspire to anything within
the gift of the American people."

Sherman saw Grant in Washington a few weeks later. The general
had been traveling in the South, and he shared his sense of politics there
as it related to the presidential election. He described the conversation to
John afterward: "I told him plainly that the South would go against him
en masse, though he counts on South Carolina, Louisiana, and Arkansas. . . . The negroes were generally quiescent and could not be relied on
as voters when local questions became mixed up with political matters."
Sherman added: "I think, however, he will be renominated and reelected,
unless by personally doing small things to alienate his party adherents at
the North."

*O*thers were hardly so confident, and still others did all in their
power to undermine such confidence as existed. From its conception in
the 1850s the Republican party had comprised two philosophical factions. The conscience wing of the party focused on resisting slavery and,
after emancipation, extending equal rights to the freedmen. The capitalist wing bent its efforts to improving the fortunes of business enterprise. The two groups concurred on the need for activist government
and through the late 1860s made effective common cause. They defeated

slavery and wrote equality into the Constitution even as they fashioned a national banking system, created a flexible currency, raised tariff rates and underwrote the Pacific railroad.

But they began falling out not long after Grant's election. A separation, if not a divorce, was perhaps inevitable, on grounds of temperamental incompatibility if nothing else. The conscience Republicans were idealists; former abolitionists, many of them, they accounted politics an arena where sin battled salvation—or where sin *ought* to battle salvation—and they were never happier than when holding forth on good and evil. The capitalist Republicans, by contrast, were practical men, tracing their roots to the Whig party of Henry Clay and Daniel Webster, and though most went to church on Sunday, they went to their offices, shops and factories on Monday with greater devotion.

The falling-out likely would have commenced right after the war had Andrew Johnson not afforded the two factions an object of joint antipathy. The nomination of Grant in 1868 served as additional cement, signifying not simply appreciation for his past role in preserving the Union but hope for his future role in preserving the party. Grant sagely let both factions read what they wished into his "Let us have peace" slogan and his campaign silence on matters of policy.

Yet he was no sooner elected than the jostling for position began. Grant's refusal to consult with the party veterans in selecting his cabinet made both sides feel they were being jilted—as indeed they were, to some extent. Grant's heart aligned with the conscience Republicans; he shared their commitment to the principles of democracy and equality, including civil and political rights for African Americans. But Grant's head tilted toward the capitalist Republicans, not so much for their concern for commerce as for their practical approach to government. The conscience Republicans reminded Grant of why the Civil War had been fought, the capitalist Republicans of how the war had been won.

Grant's problem—among others—was that the two groups simply couldn't get along. Conscience Republicans like Charles Sumner disdained the capitalist Republicans for putting profits above principle and made no effort to hide their disdain. Sumner's alienation from Grant was partly personal, with their initial misunderstanding over Santo Domingo triggering a clash of stubborn temperaments, but it was mostly a protest that Grant was heeding the advice of the capitalist wing of the party. The latter made little effort to draw Sumner and the conscience men back, believing that they didn't need that self-righteous scold or his arrogant ilk so long as they had Grant on their side.

The split in the Republicans grew more evident as the 1872 election approached, and it took surprising forms. Sumner should have endorsed Grant's attack on the Ku Klux Klan if concern for the rights of African Americans had been his unerring lodestar, as he constantly claimed it was. But Sumner so loathed the capitalist types who had the president's ear that he insisted on conflating the Klan issue with the remnants of the Dominican matter. "With what face can we insist upon obedience to law and respect for the African race, while we are openly engaged in lawlessness upon the coast of St. Domingo and outrage upon the African race represented by the black republic?" he demanded, referring to Haiti. "It is difficult to see how we can condemn with proper, wholehearted reprobation our own domestic Ku Klux with its fearful outrages while the President puts himself at the head of a powerful and costly Ku Klux operating abroad in defiance of international law and the Constitution of the United States."

Carl Schurz likewise should have upheld Grant against the reactionaries of the South, but he repeatedly condemned the president as a tyrant. "The President's education was that of military life," he told the Senate. "He was unused to the operations of the checks and balances of power which constitute the rule of civil government." Schurz professed not to blame Grant for his shortcomings; he declared condescendingly: "If the habits of peremptory command on the one side and of absolute obedience on the other impressed themselves strongly on his mind, it was not his fault." Schurz continued: "If his temper is not such as to shake off the force of life-long habits with ease, if it is not supple enough to accommodate itself to a position no longer one of undivided power and responsibility, it may be called his misfortune, but let it not, by a confidence beyond reasonable bounds, become the misfortune of the American people." Schurz concluded: "I warn my Republican friends not to identify the cause of their party with one man."

Schurz thought he detected support in the resistance to Grant on Santo Domingo. "Unless I greatly mistake the signs of the times, the superstition that Grant is *the* necessary man is rapidly giving way," he wrote Jacob Cox, who had resigned from the Interior Department. "The spell is broken, and we have only to push through the breach." Schurz added, "The President, as I understand, is as *stubborn as ever*, and seems determined to risk his all upon that one card. He seems to have a genius for suicide."

Schurz announced his opposition to Grant's reelection and his intention to establish a third party. "Grant and his faction carry at present everything before them by *force majeure*," he wrote Charles Sumner. "The organization of the Republican party is almost entirely in the hands of the office-holders and ruled by selfish interest. . . . I doubt now whether we can prevent his nomination. The men who surround him stop at nothing." Schurz reiterated that he wouldn't support Grant, and he added that he couldn't support the Democrats. "But I think—in fact I firmly believe—in case of Grant's nomination we shall have a third movement on foot strong enough to beat both him and the Democrats. I have commenced already to organize it, and when the time comes I think it will be ready for action."

A positive response from New York editor Horace Greeley, former diplomat Charles Francis Adams, a variety of other Republican notables and a smattering of Republican newspapers caused Schurz to summon a public meeting of the "Liberal Republican" party for January 1872 at Jefferson City in his home state of Missouri, where a liberal wing of the state Republican party had enjoyed encouraging success in the most recent round of elections. The meeting evoked conflicting reports; the Associated Press played it as a portent of serious change in national politics, prompting the correspondent for the *New York Times* to deride the AP account as a "gross exaggeration of the importance of the whole affair." The *Times* man, writing from St. Louis, added, "The Republicans of this city feel greatly outraged at the character of the report sent out."

*G*rant observed the affair with bemusement. A friend, George Childs, and his wife were coming to Washington; Grant invited them to stay with him and Julia. He specified a particular week. "You know our house room is so limited that we have to invite friends in rotation," he explained. He added wryly: "I hope I have enough left, notwithstanding the defection of Mr. Greeley and Carl Schurz, to keep the little room we have filled during the winter." The opposition press criticized Grant for staffing the executive departments with his friends after dismissing— "decapitating," the critics luridly said—their predecessors. In a sardonic moment Grant warned one of those friends, Russell Jones, the minister to Belgium, to be on guard. "Sumner, Schurz, Dana and all your admirers think it preposterous in me to give appointments to persons who I ever knew and particularly to those who feel any personal friendship for me," he wrote. "If I am guided by this advice your decapitation is sure."

But Grant could be serious, for he thought the issue a serious one. Mischief-makers sought to sow doubt between the president and the vice president, contending that Schuyler Colfax was maneuvering to replace Grant. Colfax denied the rumors and Grant accepted the denial. He explained to the vice president how he had answered one of the rumor-mongers. "I simply replied testifying my entire confidence in the earnestness you felt in declaring to the contrary, but that if you should be the choice of the Republican party I did not know a better man to lead them, nor one that I could more earnestly work in support of. My great ambition was to save all that has been gained by so much sacrifice of blood and treasure; that I religiously believed that that could only be done through the triumph of the Republican party until their opponents get on a national, patriotic, Union platform; that the choice of the Republican party was my choice; that I held no patent right to the office, and probably had the least desire for it of anyone who ever held it or was ever prominently mentioned in connection with it."

Grant judged that whatever weakened the Republican party enhanced the possibility of a Democratic victory, which would be a disaster for the nation. "My own convictions," he told friend and business associate Charles Ford, "are that it would have been better never to have made a sacrifice of blood and treasure to save the Union than to have the Democratic party come in power now and sacrifice by the ballot what the bayonet seemed to have accomplished." After long eschewing party politics, Grant now saw his party as the necessary agent of national reconciliation. "It will be a happy day for me when I am out of public life," he told Adam Badeau. "But I do feel a deep interest in the Republican party keeping control of affairs until the results of the war are acquiesced in by all political parties. When that is accomplished we can afford to quarrel about minor matters." He didn't welcome the troubles his administration and the party were encountering, but he remained optimistic, in part because he had seen much worse. "My trials here have been considerable," he wrote Elihu Washburne. "But, I believe, so far every tempest that has been aroused has recoiled on them who got it up. . . . A great many professedly staunch Republicans acted very much as if they wanted to outdo the Democracy in breaking up the Republican party. Everything looks more favorably now, though, for the party than it did in '63, when the war was raging."

Several senior members of the party implored Grant to make peace with the defectors. "We have men among us who are not for your nomination," Senator Henry Wilson said, reiterating the obvious. "Some I fear are ready to go into any movements to defeat you, even at the sacrifice of the Republican party. I wish something could be done to unite these men with us. In your position you can make advances to them. . . . You are strong now. See to it, I pray you, that all well disposed men are invited to act with you." The president should focus on Schurz and Sumner especially, Wilson said. "I wish you could see Schurz, as he is by all odds the most influential of any of these men. I wish, too, you and Mr. Sumner would settle all your differences. This state"—Massachusetts, home to both Wilson and Sumner—"is sure for you by about the old majority, but it would be very pleasant to have unity and peace."

Grant appreciated the benefits of party unity. No more than Wilson or the other senators and representatives who urged reconciliation did he welcome a rift in the party. But he thought Sumner and Schurz were too far gone, too impressed with their own importance. In any event, he thought *they* were the ones who should take the first step back. "Whenever I have done injustice to any man," he wrote in a letter intended for Wilson, "no matter what his position, and find it out, there is no apology I am not ready to make. I have never done aught to give offense to Mr. Sumner, Mr. Schurz, the *Springfield Republican* people, the *Cincinnati Commercial* people"—two particularly vocal opposition papers—"nor Mr. Greeley. Yet they have all attacked me without mercy. . . . Before there can be peace between us, rather I should say good feeling and intimacy, the explanation *must* come from them." Grant had heard stories, apparently circulated by Sumner, that he had been drunk on the occasion of his visit to Sumner's house. Sensitive on the old subject, he considered Sumner's revival of it beyond the bounds of political difference. "Mr. Sumner has been unreasonable, cowardly, slanderous, unblushingly false," Grant said. "I should require from him an acknowledgment to this effect, from his scat in the Senate, before I would consent to meet him socially. He has not the manliness ever to admit an error. I feel a greater contempt for him than for any other man in the Senate."

Grant's differences with Schurz were less personal. "Schurz is an ungrateful man, a disorganizer by nature and one who can render much greater service to the party he does not belong to than the one he pretends to have attachment for. The sooner he allies himself with our enemies, openly, the better for us." Grant gave the critical press the back of his hand. "The *Springfield Republican* and *Cincinnati Commercial* are mere guerrilla newspapers, always finding fault with their friends, and any attempt to conciliate them would merely satisfy them of their importance." Grant proposed to do what he had always done. "I shall endeavor to perform my duty faithfully and trust to the common sense of the people to select the right man to execute their will."

Grant likely never sent this letter (the original remained in his files), but he conveyed its gist to Wilson and others. "President says he has just had a visit from Senators Morrill of Maine and Wilson, wishing to effect a reconciliation between him and Sumner," Hamilton Fish recorded in his diary. "He says he told them that whenever Sumner should retract and apologize for the slanders he has uttered against him in the Senate, in his own house, in street cars and other public conveyances, at dinners and other entertainments and elsewhere, as publicly, openly, and in the same manner in which he has uttered these slanders, he would listen to proposals for reconciliation. But even then he would have no confidence in him, or in the expectation that he would not again do just what he has done."

Grant initially underestimated the stamina of the insurgency. "It looks to me as if Mr. Schurz was not making much headway of his new departure," he wrote Charles Ford. "It will be gratifying to see such disorganizers as he is defeated." When Schurz persisted, calling a national nominating convention of the Liberal Republicans for May 1872 in Cincinnati, Grant suggested that the breakaway movement would implode with the help of the Democrats. "My prediction is that the Democratic party will attempt to hold out the idea that they will support the Cincinnati nominees in hope of permanently dividing the Republican party, that is, of committing the bolters to their ticket, and then make a straight-out nomination of their own. I believe such action will result in the withdrawal of the Cincinnati ticket just as the Fremont ticket was withdrawn in '64. We shall see what we shall see, however."

The Cincinnati group was a motley collection of former Free-Soilers from the North, Unionists from the South, frustrated office seekers from all over and a sprinkling of professional politicians who simply found themselves on the wrong side of the regular Republican organization. The moralistic tone of the gathering was set by Schurz, who, responding to a charge by Grant ally Oliver Morton that he was betraying the party, said of Morton: "He has never left his party. I have never betrayed my principles. That is the difference between him and me." The conventioneers advocated civil service reform to curb the corruption they perceived as epidemic in politics, tariff reduction to diminish the power of corporations and their lobbyists, federal withdrawal from the South to conclude the Civil War once and for all, and, especially, the removal of Grant from the White House to allow his replacement by someone of greater political refinement.

Charles Francis Adams was the early frontrunner (Schurz being disqualified by his foreign birth). The son of John Quincy Adams had his father's reformist streak, which suited the mood of the moment, and almost no record in politics, which gave his rivals little to use against him. But Grant had appointed him to the commission that was then adjudicating the *Alabama* claims in Geneva, and in his absence the delegates' eyes began to wander. Schurz, who favored Adams, might have brought them back had he applied himself in a more lively fashion. "Carl Schurz was the most industrious and the least energetic man I have ever worked with," Joseph Pulitzer, the secretary of the convention and soon the most energetic journalist in America, muttered afterward.

The convention ultimately settled on Horace Greeley. This choice was striking in that Greeley had long championed a high tariff, which most of the delegates excoriated. He did have a record as a reformer, but it was a record that roamed widely across the landscape of American politics and culture, touching socialism, vegetarianism and spiritualism, in addition to such mundane causes as abolition and temperance. He wore whiskers that would have been called a beard had they sprouted from his chin rather than his neck; observers sometimes mistook them for a mangy silver fox crawling from under his collar. Precisely how Greeley wound up as the nominee was a matter that prompted much debate. Some delegates claimed that the convention had been hijacked by the professionals, who foisted Greeley on the gathering. Others intimated that the airy reformer wasn't so clueless after all and had sold his convictions on the tariff—which he suddenly said should come down—for the nomination.

A third explanation, which overlapped the first two, was that Greeley had engaged in backroom dealings with influential Democrats who promised to deliver their party's seconding nomination. When the Democratic convention, in Baltimore, did indeed nominate Greeley—in the briefest convention in American history—this explanation gained plausibility.

*C*harles Sumner couldn't bring himself to bolt the Republican party. "I have no hesitation in declaring myself a member of the Republican party, and one of the straitest of the sect," he told his colleagues in the Senate in the wake of the Cincinnati convention, which he conspicuously avoided. "I stood by its cradle; let me not follow its hearse." Yet he would gladly send Grant to his political grave if he could. Sumner lashed the president more harshly than he ever had before. He retraced the history of the Santo Domingo affair, in which, he said, he had been basely attacked by the president's minions. "This Republican senator, engaged in a patriotic service, and anxious to save the colored people from outrage, was denounced on this floor as a traitor to the party." He had realized then, he said, that the Republican party he had learned to love was being malignantly transformed. "Too plainly it was becoming the instrument of *one man and his personal will*, no matter how much he set at defiance the Constitution and international law, or how much he insulted the colored people." Grant had transgressed the Constitution more egregiously than Andrew Johnson ever had, Schurz said; the appropriate analogy was Julius Caesar. "He has operated by a system of combinations, military, political, and even senatorial. . . . This utterly unrepublican Caesarism has mastered the Republican party and dictated the presidential will, stalking into the Senate chamber itself, while a vindictive spirit visits its good Republicans who cannot submit." But what could the country expect from a person of Grant's background? "The successful soldier is rarely changed to the successful civilian. There seems an incompatibility between the two. . . . One always a soldier cannot late in life become a statesman." Sumner recapitulated the gold conspiracy, dwelling on the role of Grant's brother-in-law Abel Corbin. He decried Grant's willingness to accept gifts from admirers who subsequently sought offices. "For a public man to take gifts is reprehensible; for a president to select cabinet councilors and other officers among those from whom he has taken gifts is an anomaly in republican annals." By the sale of offices, Sumner said, Grant had become "probably the richest president since George Washington." The Republican convention would meet shortly;

Sumner demanded that the delegates choose another nominee than the incumbent. "I protest against him as radically unfit for the presidential office, being essentially military in nature, without experience in civil life, without aptitude for civil duties, and without knowledge of Republican institutions. . . . Not without anxiety do I wait, but with the earnest hope that the convention will bring the Republican party into ancient harmony, saving it especially from the suicidal folly of an issue on the personal pretensions of one man."

The Republican regulars had written Sumner off as a crank, if not a lunatic. Many of Grant's supporters thought the senator's diatribe worked to the president's advantage. "The atrocious speech of Mr. Sumner has been deeply felt and resented by all who served under your command," John Pope wrote Grant from Fort Leavenworth, Kansas. "It is felt as a personal insult by every one of them and will secure you thousands of votes which for political reasons might have been given to another candidate."

The regulars rallied to Grant at the Republican convention, held in Philadelphia, where they renominated him unanimously. Yet they weren't insensitive to the complaints of their opponents, and they chose to replace Schuyler Colfax as Grant's running mate with Henry Wilson. Delegate Edwards Pierrepont, who would become Grant's attorney general, recounted the spirit and reasoning of the convention. "The wild enthusiasm with which your name was hailed at Philadelphia is most gratifying and is the harbinger of a November victory," Pierrepont wrote Grant. "The nomination of Wilson is well. It gives new life by awakening new hopes. . . . People like change and they must have new hopes. . . . I am glad that Colfax was not nominated, though I like him; I am glad simply because it proves to the people that all will not run in the same old ruts. New life, new hopes this people need. . . . If they were in Paradise, they would demand something that looked like progress and novelty."

Grant had no reason to dispute the judgment of the convention. "How do you like the substitution of Wilson for Colfax?" a correspondent who had followed him to Long Branch inquired. Grant replied tactfully: "The idea seems to have been to have the two candidates"—Wilson and himself—"from different sections of the country. Otherwise there is no preference between the two men"—Wilson and Colfax. "Personally

I have a great affection for both Wilson and Colfax. Mr. Colfax, so far through our term, has been a firm friend, and we have always entertained the most affectionate relations toward one another."

Greeley and Grant's other critics, elaborating on Sumner's charges of Caesarism, suggested that Grant sought to be president for life; Grant responded in his formal acceptance of the Republican nomination. He thanked the convention for the renewed vote of confidence and expressed hope that a second term would benefit from the lessons of the first. "Experience may guide me in avoiding mistakes inevitable with novices in all professions and all occupations," he said. He continued: "When relieved from the responsibilities of my present trust, by the election of a successor, whether it be at the end of this term or next, I hope to leave to him as executive a country at peace within its own borders, at peace with outside nations, with a credit at home and abroad, and without embarrassing questions to threaten its future prosperity."

This wasn't the unequivocal no-third-term promise his opponents sought, but it quieted most concerns on that point. Grant kept out of the campaign almost as much as he had four years earlier. He allowed himself a modest rejoinder to Sumner in an interview with a correspondent from the Associated Press. As the correspondent reported: "The conversation turning on the remark of Senator Sumner to the effect that Greeley is a better friend to the black man than President Grant, the President replied that he never pretended to be, as he had repeatedly said, an original abolitionist; but he favored emancipation as a war measure. When this was secured, he thought the ballot should be conferred to make the gift complete and to place those who had been liberated in full possession of the rights of freemen. . . . While he had no unkind words to utter concerning Senator Sumner, he was perfectly willing to place his acts against Senator Sumner's words."

Another reporter caught Grant at a public reception in upstate New York, where he and Julia had taken the younger children for a holiday. He reflected on the past and future. "I was not anxious to be president a second term, but I consented to receive the nomination simply because I thought that was the best way of discovering whether my countrymen, or the majority of them, really believed all that was alleged against my administration and against myself personally," he told the reporter. "The asperities of an election campaign will give my political opponents and my personal enemies an opportunity and an excuse to say all that can be said against me. That opportunity I do not grudge them, and I depend on the people to rebuke or to endorse me, as they see fit." Of course, in making their decision on him, the people would render a larger verdict. "I am anxious to ascertain whether the Republican party, whose choice I again happen to be, is to have its policy sustained or not."

Privately Grant exuded confidence. The Liberal Republicans were trying to lure the regulars away; Grant thought they would fail. Referring to a wavering Pennsylvania Republican, the president wrote Elihu Washburne: "The Greeleyites will be as liberal in their offers to him as Satan was to our Savior, and with as little ability to pay." He still guessed that the Greeley campaign would self-destruct. "I do not often indulge in predictions," he told Washburne, "but I have had a feeling that Greeley might not even be in the field in November." Greeley's supporters were growing desperate. "The opposition in this canvass seems to have no capital but slander, abuse and falsehood." Some of the slanderers were having their malicious words turn back on themselves, as reporters discovered dark corners of their careers. "They have learned that people who live in glass houses should never throw stones." Grant wished the lesson would rise to the top of the Liberal ranks but supposed it wouldn't. "The saintly Trumbull and Schurz ought to see the same thing, but their hides are thick and their impudence is sublime." In this confidential letter Grant didn't try to conceal his satisfaction that Sumner was being ignored by all three parties. "Poor old Sumner is sick from neglect and the consciousness that he is not all of the Republican party. I very much doubt whether he will ever get to Washington again. If he is not crazy his mind is at least so affected as to disqualify him for the proper discharge of his duties as senator."

The outlook only improved as the election neared. "There has been no time from the Baltimore convention to this when I have had the least anxiety," Grant remarked in September. "The soreheads and thieves who have deserted the Republican party have strengthened it by their departure." Grant forecast a big victory even if Greeley stayed in the race. "I do not think he will carry a single Northern state," he told Washburne. "In the South I give him Tennessee and Texas, with Virginia, West Virginia, Maryland, Kentucky, Georgia, Florida, and Arkansas doubtful, with the chances in our favor in all of them except Maryland. Missouri might also be added to the doubtful states."

Grant predicted well. Greeley carried Tennessee, Texas, Kentucky,

Georgia, Maryland and Missouri; Grant carried everything else and smashed his challenger in the popular vote by 56 percent to 44 percent. Grant received 286 electoral votes to what would have been 66 for Greeley if Greeley hadn't suddenly died three weeks after the election. His electoral votes were scattered among surviving adherents of his various causes.

AMID THE CAMPAIGN GRANT MET WITH SEVERAL DELEGATIONS OF Indians. Representatives of the indigenous peoples had been meeting with American presidents for decades, but in Grant they had greater hope for a sympathetic hearing than they had had in any of his predecessors. Grant remained convinced that the Indian Bureau was the principal cause of the Indian wars, but the bureau had friends on Capitol Hill and he hadn't been able to remove it from the Interior Department. He did, however, partially circumvent the bureau by creating a new Indian commission, staffed by prominent philanthropists and others of a generous persuasion regarding the Indians. At Grant's summons the commission met in Washington, and it denounced previous policy in the most scathing terms. "The history of the government connections with the Indians is a shameful record of broken treaties and unfulfilled promises," the commissioners declared. "The history of the border white man's connection with the Indians is a sickening record of murder, outrage, robbery, and wrongs committed by the former as a rule, and occasional savage outbreaks and unspeakably barbarous deeds of retaliation by the latter as the exception. . . . In our Indian wars, almost without exception, the first aggressions have been made by the white man." Cynicism fueled aggression in the most pernicious way, the commissioners asserted. "In addition to the class of robbers and outlaws who find impunity in their nefarious pursuits upon the frontiers, there is a large class of professedly reputable men who use every means in their power to bring on Indian wars, for the sake of the profit to be realized from the presence of troops and the expenditure of government funds in their midst. They proclaim death to the Indians at all times, in words and publications, making no distinction between the innocent and the guilty. They incite the lowest class of men to the perpetration of the darkest deeds against their victims, and, as judges and jurymen, shield them from the justice due to their crimes. Every crime committed by a white man against an Indian is concealed or palliated; every offense committed by one Indian against a white man is borne on the wings of the post or the telegraph to the remotest corner of the land, clothed with all the horrors which the reality or the imagination can throw around it."

The commission proposed and Grant accepted a new approach to staffing the Indian agencies in the West. Because the Society of Friends, or Quakers, had historically pursued humane policies toward Indians in Pennsylvania, and because as a group they appeared more honest and diligent than the typical Indian agents, Grant's commission gave the Quakers charge of Indian relations in about half the western agencies. In most of the rest the president replaced the Interior Department's agents with army officers, believing, as before, that men who would have to fight the Indian wars were less likely to start them.

Grant's "peace policy" had other facets. It followed the recommendation of William Sherman—and others—to separate the Indians from whites on the frontier, with the former being allotted reservations for their exclusive and presumably perpetual use. On these reservations the Indians would govern themselves, albeit with advice and instruction in the ways of white civilization from the Quakers and others of an educational and eleemosynary bent.

The peace policy bore fruit. Violence on the Indian frontier diminished, and leading men of the Sioux and other Plains tribes accepted the reservations apportioned to their peoples. Such leaders were the ones who visited Grant in 1872. "I come without an invitation," the Sioux chief Red Cloud told Grant accurately (through an interpreter). "I have come of my own will." Red Cloud had been impressed by the good faith of Grant's new agents, and he was willing to give the reservation allotted to his people a try. He explained that he had traveled to Washington to seek a better location for the Indian agency—the headquarters of the Indian agent—assigned to the Sioux reservation. "I have decided a place for my agency," Red Cloud told Grant. "I want it on the White River, and all the people that are with me want it there. We have found a good creek, and this man"—he nodded to Jared Daniels, the Indian agent who had accompanied him—"went with me to select that place, and we came down to let you know of it. That is the only place that is suitable for our agency. I don't want any other."

Grant wanted to give Red Cloud what he asked. The Sioux chief exemplified what the peace policy was trying to accomplish: a reconciliation between the Indians and modern ways of life. The old habits—of roaming, hunting and raiding widely and at will—were doomed, Grant believed, and Indians who insisted on clinging to the old habits were likely doomed too. Grant reiterated this point even as he explained that he couldn't give Red Cloud the location he wanted. "The place you mention is within the limits of Nebraska," Grant said. "And if you were to go there it would, probably, not be a great many years before the white people would be encroaching upon you, and then there would have to be another change." Grant nonetheless invited Red Cloud to speak with the secretary of the interior and the commissioner of Indian affairs. "What they say I will agree to." He added that he welcomed Red Cloud's visit and was happy that a large number of Indian braves were accompanying the chief on his tour of the East. "They will find that the whites are in number as the blades of grass upon the hill side, and their number increases every day. They come from other countries in greater numbers, every year, than the whole number of Indians in America." Red Cloud and his men should share this knowledge with those of their people who still thought war a solution to their problems.

Grant sketched the only future he thought provided a chance for the Indians' survival. "We want to do for you and your people all we can to advance and help them, and to enable them to become self-supporting," he told Red Cloud. "The time must come when, with the great growth of population here, the game will be gone, and your people will then have to resort to other means of support. While there is time we would like to teach you new modes of living that will secure you in the future and be a safe means of livelihood. I want to see the Indians get upon land where they can look forward to permanent homes for themselves and their children." Grant raised the possibility of a voluntary relocation to a gentler region. "If at any time you feel like moving to what is known as Cherokee country"—Oklahoma—"which is a large territory with an admirable climate, where you would never suffer from the cold and where you could have lands set apart to remain exclusively your own, we would set apart a large tract of land that would belong to you and your children. We would at first build houses for your chiefs and principal men, and send men among your people to instruct them so they could have houses for shelter. We would send you large herds of cattle and sheep to live upon, and to enable you to raise stock." Grant offered to supply instruction in the modern ways. "We would send, if you so desire, Indians who have been accustomed to live with white men, who would instruct you in growing and raising stock until you know how to do so yourselves. We would establish schools, so that your children would learn to read and to write, and to speak the English language, the same as white people, and in this way you and your people would be prepared, before the game is gone, to live comfortably and securely."

He didn't intend to force anything upon the Indians. "I say this only for you to think about and talk about to your people," he told Red Cloud. "Whenever you are ready to avail yourself of this offer, then you can talk to us and we will do what I say. All the treaty obligations we have entered into we shall keep with you unless it is with your own consent that the change is made, or so long as you keep those obligations yourself."

Grant made the same point to another Indian delegation. A Sioux chief known as The Grass told Grant that while his people were working hard on their reservation, they remained poor. "The President inquired as to the nature of the land on which the tribe is located, and inquired if anything had been said to them about moving into the Indian country," a reporter present at the meeting recounted afterward. Benjamin Cowen, the assistant secretary of the interior, replied that it had. "The President then, addressing the Indians, said he would like to see them on fertile lands, where it would be easy for them to make a living, and when they should be willing to go on such lands the government would send them and teach them to build houses. Their young especially should be instructed. It was for them to think about it, and unless they wanted to go he did not want to make them. They could go back to their homes now, and talk the matter over this year to their people. If they would not agree to go he would not compel them."

A third delegation was headed by the Sioux chief Spotted Tail, who wore a silver medal given him by Andrew Johnson, bearing the former president's likeness. Spotted Tail's band of Sioux had been asked to relocate their agency; he came to negotiate terms. Grant said that no one would force Spotted Tail to move but that, if he did, he and his people would receive the benefit in supplies and livestock of the $60,000 per year the government would save in transportation costs. Spotted Tail answered that he would take the offer back to his council and then give his reply. Before leaving the White House, he said he had something more to tell the president. "I hear that in a few months there will be an election for a new president," Spotted Tail said. "I hope you may be successful. This would please me very much, for you have been very kind to my people." Grant thanked him and responded, "However the election may result, I hope there will be no change in the Indian policy."

Or if there was a change in policy, he hoped it would be in the direction of greater sympathy toward the Indians. "If the present policy toward the Indian can be improved in any way, I will always be ready to receive suggestions on the subject," Grant told George Stuart, a member of the Indian commission. "But if any change is made, it must be on the side of the civilization and Christianization of the Indian. I do not believe our Creator ever placed different races of men on this earth with the view of having the stronger exert all its energies in exterminating the weaker. If any change takes place in the Indian policy of the government while I hold my present office, it will be on the humanitarian side of the question."

67

SPOTTED TAIL GOT HIS WISH IN GRANT'S REELECTION. AND GRANT raised the Indian question in his annual message a month later. "The policy which was adopted at the beginning of this Administration with regard to the management of the Indians has been as successful as its most ardent friends anticipated within so short a time," Grant declared. "It has reduced the expense of their management; decreased their forays upon the white settlements; tended to give the largest opportunity for the extension of the great railways through the public domain and the pushing of settlements into more remote districts of the country, and at the same time improved the condition of the Indians."

Annual messages have always been occasions for presidential boasting, but Grant had greater reason to boast than many of his predecessors, having been returned to office by the largest popular majority to that date in American history (a margin that would not be surpassed until the twentieth century). He reflected on the reasons for the voters' good feeling. A fire had recently scourged Boston, after the previous year's devastating fire in Chicago; he acknowledged these tragedies and commiserated with their victims even as he noted their exceptional character. "Otherwise we have been free from pestilence, war, and calamities, which often overtake nations; and, as far as human judgment can penetrate the future, no cause seems to exist to threaten our present peace." He was gratified to report that the tribunal established under the Treaty of Washington had awarded the United States $15.5 million to settle American claims against Britain. That settlement, Grant said, "leaves these two Governments without a shadow upon the friendly relations which it is my sincere hope may forever remain equally unclouded." Grant reported that the government continued to pay down the federal debt incurred during the Civil War. In the nearly four years of his administration the debt had been reduced by almost $400 million, from $2.6 billion at the beginning of his term, as a result of more efficient collection of revenues but mostly from a reduction of spending. "The preservation of our national credit is of the highest importance," Grant said; the administration was on a course to render it rock solid.

Grant's reflections took a more philosophical turn in his second inaugural address, delivered in early March 1873. "Under Providence I have been called a second time to act as executive over this great nation," he said. The responsibility was a heavy one. "It is my firm conviction that the civilized world is tending toward republicanism, or government by the people through their chosen representatives, and that our own great republic is destined to be the guiding star to all others." The principal goal of his first administration had been accomplished. "The states lately at war with the general government are now happily rehabilitated, and no executive control is exercised in any one of them that would not be exercised in any other state under like circumstances." The army had been reduced to a level below that of every substantial European power, and military expenditures had declined accordingly. Yet the nation remained secure. "Now that the telegraph is made available for communicating thought, together with rapid transit by steam, all parts of a continent are made contiguous for all purposes of government, and communication between the extreme limits of the country made easier than it was throughout the old thirteen states at the beginning of our national existence." Grant, the warrior, looked to the day when continued progress would render war obsolete. "I do not share in the apprehension held by many as to the danger of governments becoming weakened and destroyed by reason of their extension of territory. Commerce, education, and rapid transit of thought and matter by telegraph and steam have changed all this. Rather do I believe that our Great Maker is preparing the world, in His own good time, to become one nation, speaking one language, and when armies and navies will be no longer required."

In Americans' time, however, as opposed to God's time, work remained. "The effects of the late civil strife have been to free the slave and make him a citizen," Grant said. Americans could take pride in this. Yet the freedman had not achieved equality. "He is not possessed of the civil rights which citizenship should carry with it. This is wrong, and should be corrected. To this correction I stand committed, so far as executive influence can avail."

The Indians likewise deserved America's continued humane attention. The policies begun during the first term, designed "to bring the aborigines of the country under the benign influences of education and civilization," must be continued and extended. "It is either this or war of extermination. Wars of extermination, engaged in by people pursuing commerce and all industrial pursuits, are expensive even against the weakest people, and are demoralizing and wicked. Our superiority of strength and advantages of civilization should make us lenient toward the Indian. The wrong inflicted upon him should be taken into account and the balance placed to his credit. The moral view of the question should be considered and the question asked, Can not the Indian be made a useful and productive member of society by proper teaching and treatment? If the effort is made in good faith, we will stand better before the civilized nations of the earth and in our own consciences for having made it."

"These things are not to be accomplished by one individual," Grant concluded. "But they will receive my support and such recommendations to Congress as will in my judgment best serve to carry them into effect. I beg your support and encouragement."

Returning to the White House from the inauguration ceremony, Grant penned a note to Schuyler Colfax. "Will you do me the favor to come over and dine?" he asked the now former vice president. "We will have no company except our own family and some of our friends who came on to the inauguration. The dinner is early and will give you time to meet an early train for Baltimore." Grant added, in passing: "Allow me to say that I sympathize with you in the recent Congressional investigations, that I have watched them closely, and that I am as satisfied now as I have ever been of your integrity."

The investigations Grant referred to had begun the previous December, prompted by reports of a scandal in the spending of funds for the construction of the Pacific railroad. Investigations had been a staple of congressional life since the beginning of the Civil War. Congress investigated Lincoln's conduct of the war; it investigated reconstruction policy; it investigated the gold conspiracy; it investigated the Ku Klux Klan. Nor

were scandals involving the disbursement of funds anything new. Beginning in 1871 the New York press and subsequently New York state officials revealed enormous overspending by the New York City Democratic
ring of William Tweed, with millions in public money being diverted to
Tweed and his Tammany Hall cronies. Tweed was arrested; he would be
tried and convicted.

The Tweed scandal soured much of the public on politics and government, but the good news, from the standpoint of Grant and the
Republicans, was that it was a Democratic scandal. Not so the Pacific
railroad scandal, which surfaced in the autumn of 1872 under breathless headlines in the *New York Sun*: "The King of Frauds . . . Colossal
Bribery . . . Congressmen Who Have Robbed the People . . . How Some
Men Get Fortunes . . . Princely Gifts by the Chairmen of Committees in
Congress." The Pacific railroad had been a Republican project, initiated
by a Republican Congress and a Republican president and nurtured by
Republican appointed officials. As the story unfolded, the malfeasances
fell into two broad categories: misappropriation of public funds and bribery of federal officials. The dodgy money was routed through a company
called Crédit Mobilier, to which the Union Pacific board subcontracted
the construction of its portion of the Pacific road. The scandal was that
Union Pacific, underwritten by federal funds, paid too much to Crédit
Mobilier, with the latter's directors and owners siphoning the excess into
their pockets, and that to cover their tracks, the Crédit Mobilier conspirators sold shares of the company to members of Congress who benefited
from the bilking.

The conspiracy held together past the completion of the construction of the Pacific road, but after the *Sun* story appeared, with names of
legislators said to be in on the deal, Congress was obliged to investigate.
Schuyler Colfax was one of the names on the *Sun*'s list; other prominent
figures included James Garfield and Henry Wilson, Grant's new vice
president. The investigation became the highlight of the political season
in Washington, with reporters and visitors crowding into the investigation rooms and then rushing out to share what they had heard. The star
witness was Oakes Ames, a retired congressman from Massachusetts
who had been instrumental in persuading the legislature to underwrite
the railroad. Ames produced a memorandum book that listed the members of Congress who had purchased shares of Crédit Mobilier.

Most of those on the list claimed to have done nothing wrong.
Members of Congress had various business interests and some of those

interests were affected by federal legislation; this connection didn't make them crooks, they said. Neither could anyone demonstrate that Crédit Mobilier or Union Pacific had received anything substantial in exchange for spreading the wealth. Nearly every member shown to have purchased shares was a committed supporter of the Pacific railroad; the appropriations bill and other gestures of federal backing had their votes already. If bribery consisted in changing congressional minds—or congressional votes—it was unclear that any such wrongdoing had occurred.

Yet something shifty had happened. Several of those on the list at first denied involvement, only to have their involvement demonstrated beyond deniability. The eventual verdict of the committee was that bribes had been offered but no one had taken them. Oakes Ames, conveniently no longer a member of Congress, was saddled with the guilt. Ames had committed despicable offenses, the committee said, but the other members were either unaware of his designs or had simply purchased Crédit Mobilier stock as a profitable investment.

The judgment strained credulity. "Good government has received a deadly stab in the shameful result," the *New York Herald* declared. The *New York Times* lamented the "pitiful and shameful condition" of congressional ethics and asserted: "To refuse to censure the holders of that stock is to say that the Congressional standard of morals is not high enough to condemn it."

None of this had anything to do with Grant, who had been far from the scene and far from the minds of Oakes Ames and his collaborators, if any. But like the Tweed affair, from which Grant had been even farther, it strengthened a suspicion in many Americans that government had become a racket.

AGAINST ANY PREVIOUS EXPECTATION, GRANT FOUND HIMSELF DUR-
ing the summer of 1873 conducting a detailed correspondence with
a member of the British gentry and parliament. The communication
was unrelated to the settlement of the *Alabama* claims, though that
result made writing Edward John Sartoris easier for the president
than it would have been had the Civil War troubles still roiled Anglo-
American diplomacy. The correspondence, rather, involved Grant's
daughter, Ellen, who had taken a cruise to Europe with family friends
and met Sartoris's son, Algernon. "Much to my astonishment an
attachment seems to have sprung up between the two young people,"
Grant wrote the elder Sartoris. "To my astonishment because I had only
looked upon my daughter as a child, with a good home which I did
not think of her wishing to quit for years yet. She is my only daughter
and I therefore feel a double interest in her welfare." Nellie had just
turned eighteen; this was her first experience of love. "You must excuse
therefore the solicitude I entertain in her behalf, and also the enquiries
I make as to the habits, character and prospects of the one upon whom
she seems to have bestowed her affections."

Patriotism joined paternalism in causing Grant to raise a sensitive
issue with Algernon's father. "It would be with the greatest regret that
I would see Nellie quit the United States as a permanent home. It is a
country of great extent of territory, of fertility, and of great future promise. Its people have lavished upon me and mine great honors. Its institutions and people I love. During my life my desire is to see my children,
and my children's children, remain honored and respected citizens of it.
May I ask you therefore in all candor, and strictly confidentially, to state

to me whether your son expects to become a citizen of the United States? And what have been his habits? And what are his business qualifications?"

Grant conceded the delicacy of these questions. But he said he would eagerly provide answers were the situation reversed. He offered certain answers unprompted. "I must state with equal candor that my circumstances are not such as to enable me to do much for my children beyond educating them, having but little income beyond the salary of an office necessarily limited to but a few years' duration."

Grant didn't want Nellie to know he was writing. "May I ask you to keep this letter strictly confidential, and to attribute any apparent bluntness to a father's anxiety for the welfare and happiness of an only and much loved daughter?"

Sartoris's reply didn't survive to enter the historical record. But Grant's efforts to get Algernon to relocate to America had an effect. The young man purchased property in Michigan and took steps toward acquiring American citizenship.

But then his older brother died and he fell heir to the family's large estate in the south of England. This altered Grant's thinking, for he had to admit that if Nellie loved Algernon, as she evidently did, there was no sense in her rejecting such material security as he could now provide. And with Nellie saying she would go to the ends of the earth to be with him, Grant decided he couldn't and shouldn't stop her from going to England.

Julia had her own recollection of the engagement. "When Nellie came back to me," she wrote in her memoir, referring to the trip on which Nellie had met Algernon, "she was no longer a nestling, but a young woman equipped and ready—ah, too ready—for the battle of life." Nellie's decision to follow Algernon to England came as a shock. "This nearly broke my heart," Julia recalled, "and I ventured to remonstrate by saying to her: 'Nellie, is it possible you are willing to leave your father and me, who have loved and cherished you all of your life, and go with this stranger for *always*?' She looked up sweetly and, smiling, said: 'Why, yes, mamma. I am sure that is just what you did when you married papa and left grandpa.'"

*J*ulia's protest was largely for effect. That her daughter was engaged to an English aristocrat tickled the vanity she had indulged since her husband's rise to fame. She loved being the First Lady of the land, the center of social life in the capital. "The President's levees always seemed brilliant to me," she recalled. "The senators and representatives with their families, the diplomatic corps and their families, always in full dress, officers of the army and navy in full uniform, all of the society people of Washington in full dress, made a gay and brilliant gathering." From the distance of decades and the perspective of foreign travel, she judged, "I have visited many courts and, I am proud to say, I saw none that excelled in brilliancy the receptions of President Grant."

Daily life in the White House was more mundane. Julia was accustomed to servants, but until recently hers had been slaves, with no choice about where they worked or what they did. On the other hand, hired servants were cheaper to replace than slaves. "The servants I had in my home were thoroughly demoralized," she said of the staff she brought to the president's house. The Johnsons had not been good caretakers of the Executive Mansion, which Julia pronounced to be in a condition of "utter confusion." The servants were overwhelmed. "Perhaps they thought they were incapable of doing the work in the White House. I was forced to let most of them go."

She likewise let go of certain traditions linked to her new home. "I was somewhat annoyed by the fact that the grounds back of the Mansion were open to the public," she related. "Nellie and Jess, the latter just learning to ride on a velocipede, had no place to play, and I no place to walk save on the streets. Whenever we entered these grounds, we were followed by a crowd of idle, curious loungers, which was anything but pleasant." She asked Grant if the grounds were public property. He said that they were not, at least in the sense of being necessarily open to the public. She asked if he might order the gates closed and the public kept out. He said he would, and he did. "Of course a ripple of comment followed: 'The Grants are getting a little too exclusive,'" she recalled. "But the children and I had that beautiful lawn for eight years, and I assure you we enjoyed it."

In truth the children were only occasional residents of the White House. Julia's aging father joined her and Grant in the mansion, but the children spent academic years at boarding schools and much of their summers at the cottage Grant purchased for the family in Long Branch. The older children became adults during their father's presidency, with Nellie being merely the third out of the nest. Fred graduated from West Point and was assigned to accompany William Sherman when the general made a tour of Europe. Sherman's purpose was to show the American flag and register America's interest in the affairs of the continent; Fred's purpose was to see the world. "The papers make the most of Prince Fred," Sherman wrote his wife. "He is a good fellow but cares for little. He went to see his aunt at Copenhagen and joined me at Berlin, but asked to stay a few days more, and at the time he was to join me, he wrote that he would go to Paris to see Nellie and would rejoin me at Geneva or Paris. . . . I go on my course utterly regardless of him, and don't want anyone to find fault with General Grant for sending him with me, as I know Mrs. Grant did it, and of course she did it as a mother, thinking herself very smart to catch the chance." Sherman was somewhat more tactful in his letters to Grant. "I hope Fred has kept you advised of matters most interesting to himself, though I fear he has not," he wrote from Sevastopol. "He is perfectly well, and will profit much by his experience and observations on this trip." From St. Petersburg Sherman wrote of the journey's value and its cost. "We certainly have had a most interesting and instructive trip, seeing much and hearing much, but the greatest advantage will be that hereafter we can understand history, and events as they transpire. Expenses in Russia are heavy, and this cause may force us to hurry, for in spite of disclaimers I am treated as a commanding general and Fred as a sort of prince. Hotel charges and railway charges are made to correspond."

Ulysses Jr.—Buck—entered Harvard with the class of 1874. He saw his parents on college vacations but, like Fred and Nellie, made use of family connections to travel to Europe and other enticing spots. Jesse spent the most time of the children with his mother and father, and as the youngest he brought the frankness and insouciance of youth to their lives. When Grant learned that Edwin Stanton had fallen gravely ill, he paid the former war secretary a visit and took Jesse along. "Oh, mamma!" the boy exclaimed on returning to the White House. "Mr. Stanton looked so badly when we went in—just like a dead man!" When his father tried to insist that Jesse come to breakfast on time, saying that as a boy he himself had had to feed several horses and chop wood each morning before breakfast, Jesse replied: "Oh, yes, but you did not have such a papa as I have."

Grant's own father remained a complicated topic with him. In the summer of 1873, just as he learned he might be losing Nellie to marriage, Grant lost his father to death. The end came as no surprise, since the older man had been declining. "He expressed himself to friends, for several weeks before his death, as entirely resigned, and did not hope for, or wish, strength to hold out longer, saying that he had reached a ripe old age without pain or sickness," Grant wrote a friend after attending the funeral. "He had been so long gradually failing that my mother and sister, who were with him, had discounted his death in advance so that they did not grieve as they would have done for one who had suddenly sickened and died or for one who was not entirely resigned to his fate."

Grant wrote little more about his feelings upon his father's death. He must have reflected on the many difficulties in their relationship and on how, after four decades of disappointing his father, he had finally earned the old man's respect. For whatever it revealed of his thoughts and feelings about his father, his hand slipped while drafting the letter just quoted. Before corrections, the last line initially asserted of his mother and sister that "they did not grieve as they would have done for me who had suddenly sickened and died or for me who was not entirely resigned to his fate."

*D*eath elicits notice of time's fleeting nature, and it reminded Grant that he wouldn't be president forever. His first-term salary of $25,000—the same as George Washington would have received had he not refused pay—was increased to $50,000 in 1873, placing him in the top few percent of earners in the country. But the moment he left the White House he would be off the government's payroll and required to fend for himself. He had never possessed his father's knack for commerce; farming was the only enterprise he contemplated with anything like pleasure. During his first term he purchased a farm outside St. Louis and hired a manager, William Elrod, to direct operations in his absence. The appointment proved less than ideal. "You spoke of mixing lime with manure before putting it upon the ground!" Grant remonstrated to Elrod in the summer of 1871. "That will not do. Lime and manure should not be used at the same time. The lime would release the ammonia, the most valuable ingredient, from the manure." Elrod kept sloppy accounts and wrote Grant less often than Grant thought he should. "Let me hear all the news from the farm: how many cows, calves, colts, etc.," Grant insisted. "I like to hear particulars."

Grant aimed to make the farm as self-sufficient as possible. "I send you $600 to pay for a lime kiln," he wrote Elrod. "Build a good-sized one, and where another can be joined to it if it is desirable hereafter." He explained how the kiln should be fueled: "I do not want any land cleared to get wood to burn lime with. My idea was that all the dead and down timber on the place might be cut up, and the woods thinned out all over the place so as to leave the timber about the right thickness to grow. After that is gone, wood might be purchased or the kiln changed to use coal."

Grant sent instructions on cattle breeding. "I engaged a thorough-bred Alderney bull calf in the East which will be sent out to you this fall," he told Elrod in October 1871. "He will do for service in the spring. You may then sell or kill the bull you now have. . . . Alderney bulls are so vicious when they get old that it is best to dispose of them as soon as they are three."

Horses had been Grant's fancy since youth, and so they remained "You had better purchase a pair of large strong mares," he wrote Elrod in the spring of 1872. "They could be put to the horse and still do full work this year. If all should breed then next year more would have to be bought, but it is not likely that all will." Grant bred trotters for the racetrack and for his personal use. "If you think proper, take out a license and stand young Hambletonian on the farm this spring. I would not have him go to exceed fifteen or twenty mares, besides mine, and would set the price at $30 the season for this year, pasturage extra." Fred Grant visited the farm in early 1873 and sent welcome news. "Fred tells me that the two oldest colts of Topsey will make good matches, and that both promise to be fast!" Grant wrote Elrod. "If so I will probably have them, with Jennie's colt, brought east in the spring."

Grant's hopes for the farm grew despite Elrod's dubious perfor-mance. Charles Ford oversaw Grant's affairs in Missouri and consulted regarding the farm. "I telegraphed you to draw on me for money to set-tle up everything," Grant wrote Ford. "I want the program you laid out executed: that is, I want the twenty outside box stalls, the additional box stalls inside, windows in front of the stalls, cracks battened, and everything put in first rate order about the barn. I want every debt and encumbrance on the place lifted, and want the training track made. . . . I want my stallions driven, and also the colts as they become old enough. I would like also to have the stallions prepared for the fair, together with a suckling, a yearling, and a two-year-old colt of Hambletonian. If Elrod is scarce of horsepower to run the farm I think it will be well to purchase for him two large mares and let him breed them. They could do full work this year, and by next spring I expect to send twelve or fifteen mares from the East."

Grant invested heavily—for him—in upgrading the farm. An inventory taken in 1873 put the value of his horses at nearly $25,000, with equipment and other livestock amounting to $11,000. Yet the returns were disappointing. Bad luck didn't help matters. "I see by the morning papers that Elrod has been burned out, and no doubt without insurance," Grant wrote Charles Ford in February 1873. Elrod wasn't injured, and the fire didn't disrupt the operations of the farm. "No building has been burned which will have to be replaced," Grant said. But the incident seemed an evil portent. The profitability of the farm grew more distant, till Grant felt obliged to let Elrod go. "The receipts have steadily decreased," Grant's accountant explained, "and under Mr. Elrod's management it has yielded less and less the longer he stayed." Grant stopped paying Elrod that October but told him he could remain on the farm until he found a new position.

69

THE TIMING COULDN'T HAVE BEEN UNLUCKIER FOR ELROD, FOR AT almost the moment Grant gave his manager notice, new positions grew hard to find. In September 1873, four years to the week after the gold crisis of 1869, another panic seized the financial markets. This one centered on the firm of Jay Cooke, the man who had sold the bonds that kept the Union solvent during the Civil War. Cooke had diversified from government bonds to railroad securities, underwriting the Northern Pacific Railroad and other roads. He contracted to sell $100 million in Northern Pacific construction bonds, and he pitched the securities with the same enthusiasm he had applied to the war bonds, albeit relying less on patriotism than on self-interest and imagination. He painted the route of the Northern Pacific, from Lake Superior to Puget Sound, as the Eden of the continent, with fertile fields, towering forests and scenic vistas in equal profusion. He might have completed the sale had the Crédit Mobilier scandal and new raids on the Erie Railroad not spoiled the market for railroad issues. As it was, he found himself with tens of millions of bonds he couldn't dispose of, and on September 18 he closed the doors of the Cooke & Company headquarters in Philadelphia.

The Cooke default triggered a series of failures. Financial houses long on railroad issues succumbed, followed by several national banks. Oliver Morton, Grant's Senate ally, who happened to be in New York, telegraphed the president in alarm. "Results of today indicate imminent danger of general national bank panic," Morton said. The Indiana Republican urged Grant to take emergency action. "Government funds now in hands of national banks should not be drawn upon but should be increased." In other words, the government should risk its own solvency to save the banks. "Without such action it is impossible to move western produce and we cannot hope to avoid universal panic throughout the country. Immediate action necessary. This dispatch is the result of consultation with the most prominent commercial men here who are not in stock. It is hard to see how the course suggested could do harm under any circumstances and it may avert a disaster too great to be comprehended." Thomas Murphy, the customs collector at New York, added his own dire forecast. "Relief must come immediately or hundreds if not thousands of our best men will be ruined," he wired Grant.

Grant responded cautiously. He directed William Richardson, who had replaced George Boutwell as Treasury secretary at the beginning of Grant's second term, to purchase $10 million in bonds, thereby injecting that much cash into the system. But he declined to go further. He told Morton he lacked the legal authority to make large purchases and in any case wasn't inclined to save the bankers from their own folly. "All assistance of the government seems to go to people who do not need it but who avail themselves of the present depressed state of the stock market to buy dividend paying securities, thus absorbing all assistance without meeting the real wants of the country at large," he said. The speculators and bankers would have to look to themselves. "This will necessarily go on until balances are settled in all former stock gambling operations either by settlements or the breaking of operators. Money will then begin to resume channels of legitimate trade."

Though he disappointed the bankers, Grant agreed to travel to New York to register his concern and be available if things got worse. He arrived on the afternoon of Saturday, September 20, and took a suite at the Fifth Avenue Hotel, the headquarters of the effort to halt the panic. "The presence of President Grant, Secretary Richardson, and Reverdy Johnson"—formerly U.S. minister to Britain and currently thought to know the mind of London's financial community—"in this city was regarded as full of good omen," the New York Times reported, adding a plea that suggested a certain lack of faith in the efficacy of the omen: "If only through them some means might be devised for averting the almost universal ruin expected today." The paper on Monday morning described the Sunday efforts of the financial sector to stem the bleeding: "While the city was at prayer its financiers were striving to save its credit. The stairways, portico, and side halls of the hotel were crowded by men whose careworn faces told of anxious, sleepless nights. The clerks inside the desks were besieged by merchants, bankers, and brokers, inquiring whether the President could be seen or was in communication with any of the leading financiers. Nearly everybody wanted to see him and personally give him the benefit of their views." A committee of bankers arrived. "On hearing that these gentlemen were in conference with the President, the dense crowd of persons on the floor of the hotel grew restive and impatient, and eagerly devoured every rumor, no matter how ridiculous, that was circulated." Jay Gould, the gold conspirator and railroad man, came to the hotel. "It was whispered through the corridors that he was going to meet the President and discuss the crisis with him. Preposterous as this was declared to be, yet it was credited by many."

Grant told the bankers that he would neither bend the law to provide them aid nor ask Congress for extraordinary rescue powers. "The Government is desirous of doing all in its power to relieve the present unsettled condition of business affairs, which is holding back the immense resources of the country now awaiting transportation to the seaboard and a market," he explained in a letter that was immediately and widely published. "Confidence on the part of the people is the first thing needed to relieve this condition of affairs and to avert the threatened destruction of business with its accompanying disasters to all classes of people. To re-establish this feeling the Government is willing to take all legal measures at its command." But the bankers would have to do the heavy work. "It is evident that no Government efforts will avail without the active cooperation of the banks and moneyed corporations of the country." The liquidity the government had already provided ought to be sufficient. "The banks are now strong enough to adopt a liberal policy on their part, and by a generous system of discounts to sustain the business interests of the country."

After two weeks the panic showed signs of being contained. Grant gave an interview to the Associated Press. He registered the puzzlement many felt at this particular panic, considering its context. "Panics generally occur when the country lacks prosperity, such as from the failure of crops, over-purchases from abroad, and such causes," he said. "In this instance the panic has occurred in the midst of the greatest general prosperity." Exports were up; the balance of payments was in America's favor. "Everything we produce is in great abundance, and the demand for it abroad is beyond the supply we have to spare. Our manufactories are prosperous, and many articles which have been imported are, to a large extent, not only being produced at home, but we are actually competing in the supply of foreign markets." The panic was primarily a psychological phenomenon, Grant said. "The fact is, the money corporations have become stampeded, and in turn startled and stampeded the whole country." The administration's response reflected this perception. The modest extra liquidity the Treasury provided was "not so much real as moral," he said. This was as it should be, for some good might come out of these harsh developments. Grant chose his words with care, not wishing to seem callous. "The effect is going to be beneficial in many ways to the country at large, though the cost to some individuals, deserving of a better fate, may be severe." The country was still paying for the Civil War, not simply in its bonded debt but in the excess money represented by the greenbacks. Until the nation resumed support of all its currency in specie—gold or silver—the money system would be unstable; the present crisis, with its sudden demand for money of any kind, brought resumption closer by lifting the greenbacks nearly to par with specie. "Return to a specie basis can never be effected except by a shrinkage of values," Grant said. "This always works hard to a large class of people who keep all they are worth in margins. This shrinkage has now taken place."

Grant's view reflected conventional wisdom. "Pure fright more than any real danger to our industry produced the panic from whose effects we are rapidly recovering," the *New York Times* editorialized in October. The paper cited statistics demonstrating that the productive part of the economy, as distinct from the financial part, had been thriving at the time of the panic. The crisis was a bankers' crisis. The paper likewise applauded Grant's measured response. The bankers should work things out among themselves. "It is well that Government should not be mixed up with the matter."

*U*nfortunately for all concerned, though the panic proper subsided, the effects of the currency contraction spread throughout the country. The overextended railroad sector took the most damaging blows, with dozens of lines folding and spreading attendant misery to their employees, vendors and customers. The bankers' panic, the first since the full onset of the industrial revolution, became the nation's first industrial depression. The transition from agriculture to industry leveraged worker productivity in good times, but the leverage reversed wickedly in bad times. Industrial workers lacked the garden plots and farmhouses that had long sheltered farmers from the worst effects of financial panics.

Industrial workers lived in a cash economy, having to buy food and rent homes. When demand fell for their products and they lost their jobs, they soon went hungry and homeless. Industrial failures fed on themselves; the suppliers to a failed company often failed too, as did the bakeries, butcher shops, clothing stores, transit lines and myriad other businesses that had furnished goods and services to now jobless workers.

No one knew it in the autumn of 1873, but the depression would last the rest of the decade. Tens of thousands of businesses would close their doors; millions of workers would lose their jobs. The homeless and hungry would haunt the land; workers would strike for higher wages and riot when their wages fell. Angry and fearful voters would punish incumbent politicians. The last crisis of the slavery era—the crisis of the Civil War and Reconstruction—would end amid the first crisis of America's industrial age.

70

UNDER THE CIRCUMSTANCES GRANT ALMOST WELCOMED A WAR scare. The *Virginius* was a British-built blockade runner employed by the Confederates until its capture by the Union navy in 1865. Subsequently auctioned, it was put into service on behalf of the Cuban insurgency against Spanish rule and was captured again, in October 1873, by the Spanish navy. The Spanish government, declaring the ship a pirate, ordered it taken to Santiago de Cuba, where Spanish officials summarily executed more than fifty of its crew and passengers, including several Americans.

The news reached the United States in early November and immediately sparked an uproar. Individuals and groups already inclined toward intervention in the Cuban conflict shouted that the American government must defend America's citizens. Protest meetings were held in several cities; even Wall Street, craving distraction from its troubles, grew patriotically vehement. Governor Horace Austin of Minnesota was one of many who prayed for war. "Minnesota will furnish you as many regiments of troops as she may be permitted to raise," Austin promised Grant. "They will respond on short notice and many of them will be veterans."

More poignant were the plaints of those personally touched by the affair. "I appeal to you, in behalf of my daughter, the betrothed of General W. A. C. Ryan, who so bravely met his death at the horrible massacre at Santiago de Cuba, in the *noble cause of Liberty*," a distraught Mrs. J. G. Gebhard wrote Grant. "Mr. President, I have confidence in you that our *martyred dead* are *not to be forgotten*. . . . The days are long, and the nights sleepless, until *every satisfaction* that *remains is given*." Most moving were words from beyond the grave written by the American captain of the *Virginius* before his execution. Joseph Fry's call for a nationalistic response was complicated by the fact that upon Southern secession he had abandoned the U.S. Navy for that of the Confederacy. But with death impending he wrote to Grant as a fellow officer. "The United States are weak," he chided the president, "when a vessel can be captured on the high seas, with perfectly regular papers, and her captain, crew, and passengers shot without appeal to the protection of the United States."

In fact the vessel's papers were *not* perfectly regular. Doubts surrounded the ownership and registry of the *Virginius*, which proved, upon examination, to be the property not of the professed owner, an American, but of Cubans linked to the New York junta. Consequently the American papers the ship carried were invalid.

Grant didn't mind the war talk, but he had no more desire for actual war with Spain than previously, and less reason. Roughly coincident with Grant's reinauguration, Spain's monarchy had given way to a republic. The new government was well meaning but weak, and it lost control of the Spanish regime in Cuba. The Cuban Spaniards were the ones behind the *Virginius* executions, but Grant could deal with them only indirectly, through Madrid.

He moved to tamp down the war talk. He sent a message to the Spanish government registering America's concern. "The summary infliction of the death penalty upon the prisoners taken from the *Virginius* will necessarily attract much attention, and will be regarded as an inhuman act, not in accordance with the spirit of the civilization of the nineteenth century," he said. Then, having made his point, he let the Spanish know that diplomacy, not force, was his preference. He directed Hamilton Fish to explain that if Madrid disavowed the actions of the responsible officials in Cuba, released the *Virginius* and the surviving crew and passengers and apologized to the United States by ordering a salute to the American flag, the matter could be resolved. Grant gave the Spanish two weeks to comply.

The time limit was intended to focus the Spanish mind but also to conclude the matter before Congress returned to Washington. The last thing Grant wanted was for the legislature to take up the Cuban question again. He conspicuously prepared for war in case Spain resisted reason and justice. He sent American naval vessels to Florida and had the War Department plan an invasion of Cuba.

The theatrics worked. The Spanish government accepted his terms. Madrid quibbled only about the flag salute, pointing out that it would reserve this gesture until the questions about the ship's registry were resolved. "This seemed to be reasonable and just," Grant explained to Congress a few weeks later in a message in which he declared the case closed and the nation's honor satisfied.

Salmon Chase had thought he would make a better president than Abraham Lincoln, and he repeatedly threatened to resign his position as Lincoln's Treasury secretary to show his displeasure at Lincoln's handling of the war. Lincoln repeatedly rebuffed the threats, not wishing to give Chase the opportunity to challenge him for the 1864 nomination. But once Lincoln secured the nomination for himself, he surprised Chase by accepting his next resignation offer, and then he surprised the country by nominating Chase for chief justice. Chase didn't abandon his presidential hopes after donning the robe, but he couldn't resist the tide in Grant's favor in 1868. He often found himself in the minority on his own Supreme Court, not least in the so-called Slaughterhouse Cases of 1873, when the majority ruled that the "privileges and immunities" clause of the Fourteenth Amendment applied only to federal civil rights and not to state civil rights. The consequence was a rapid erosion of African American rights in the South.

The decision angered Chase and doubtless raised his blood pressure, but whether it contributed to the stroke that killed him weeks later, in May 1873, was impossible to determine. "His family and the nation have my condolence in mourning the loss of a distinguished and faithful public officer," Grant declared on hearing the news.

The death presented Grant with the opportunity and the burden of selecting a successor. He took his time, not least since the Senate wouldn't return to Washington till December. He could appoint an interim replacement, but the Senate could turn that person out. "A chief justice should never be subjected to the mortification of a rejection," Grant observed in explaining his delay. During the next several months he received much advice and not a few applications before deciding on Roscoe Conkling of New York. "My dear Senator," he wrote Conkling in November: "When the chief justiceship became vacant I necessarily looked with anxiety to someone whose appointment would be recognized

as entirely fitting and acceptable to the country at large. My own preference went to you at once." He said that he had withheld the appointment
on account of not wanting to risk rejection, before adding inconsistently,
"The possibility of your rejection of course was not dreamed of."

It wasn't dreamed of because Conkling, as a leader of the Republican majority in the Senate, would certainly be confirmed without a
struggle. In those days neither presidents nor the Senate much scrutinized the judicial philosophies of nominees to the Supreme Court; as a
solid Republican, Conkling suited the Republican Senate. Grant didn't
want a fight over the appointment, and Conkling was a sure bet not to
provoke one.

But Conkling declined the offer. "My transfer now from the Senate
to the bench involves considerations not only beyond my own interest and
wishes, but I think beyond those before you," Conkling replied vaguely.
"After much thought I am convinced that in view of the whole case,
you would agree with me that another appointment should be made. I
will not detain you with reasons, nor with expressions of the profound
sense of obligation to you which will abide with me always, but instead
I ask you to let your choice fall on another who, however else qualified,
believes as man and lawyer, as I believe, in the measures you have upheld
in war and in peace."

Grant was disappointed but not so disappointed as his wife. "When
the President, Roscoe Conkling, and I drove to the Capitol to attend the
funeral services of our lamented Chief Justice, Salmon P. Chase," Julia
wrote later, "the Senate chamber was filled with the distinguished men
of the country. When the officiating minister alluded to the mantle of
the Chief Justice and invoked divine instruction as upon whose shoulders
it should fall, I looked around and my choice, without hesitation, was
Roscoe Conkling. He was so talented and so honorable, and I must say
that woman-like I thought the flowing black robes would be becoming
to Mr. Conkling."

Had Grant possessed a grander vision of the presidency he might
have taken the opportunity of Conkling's declining to reconsider his
opportunity to reshape the court. At the least he might have pondered
the politics of an appointment more carefully, taking pains to test the
waters for a nominee before putting a name forward. But Conkling's
refusal to adopt Grant's own view of office—that when the nation
called a man, he should accept or provide compelling reason why he

couldn't—irritated him, and in his irritation he reverted to his anti-political mode.

He nominated George Williams, who had succeeded Amos Akerman as attorney general. Williams was happy to receive the honor, but members of the Senate were not happy to bestow it. Grant's critics threw hurdles in the path of the nomination. "The Judiciary Committee is sitting listening to every idle story, every lie told by political opponents, who arrive every day to feed the fight," Grant's secretary Horace Porter wrote Benjamin Bristow, the solicitor general. "They will end by confirming him, but in the meantime they are scoring him till he will be scarcely fit for the race. He is quiet and dignified through it all, but it looks more like the political fight of ward politicians than a contest over the confirmation of a Chief Justice of the United States. . . . No one has touched upon the question of his ability. It is simply a slanderous rough-and-tumble political fight."

The fight turned rougher than Porter predicted. Unable to find anything damning against Williams, the ward heelers dragged his wife into the fray. She was said to have extravagant tastes that led her to insist on a fancy carriage with elaborately attired footmen. Williams's income as attorney general appeared too meager to support such style; he was alleged to have charged the carriage to the government. Williams denied any wrongdoing, and Grant was tempted to try to force the nomination through. But when Hamilton Fish and others in the cabinet conveyed word from the Senate that Williams lacked the votes for confirmation, Grant reluctantly asked him to step aside. He remained as attorney general.

Grant's third choice was Caleb Cushing, who had been attorney general under Franklin Pierce and more recently counsel at the Geneva tribunal that awarded the United States its diplomatic victory in the *Alabama* claims. Grant assumed that Cushing's part in the triumph would make his confirmation straightforward and swift.

But by now Grant's foes were primed to resist any nomination, and when they began investigating Cushing's past they discovered a letter of recommendation he had written in March 1861 to Jefferson Davis on behalf of a former clerk in his office. Cushing doubtless was simply trying to do the young man a favor, but the letter to the Confederate president cast doubt on Cushing's common sense if not his loyalty to the Union. Grant had to drop him from consideration.

His fourth try was Morrison Waite, an Ohio lawyer and charter Republican from Ohio who had served with Cushing in Geneva and who shared the glow surrounding that success. Little else distinguished his career, leading Grant to hope the bloodhounds of the Senate would wander back to their kennels, bored. They did, and Waite was confirmed.

GRANT'S FRONTAL ASSAULT ON THE KU KLUX KLAN IN SOUTH CARO-
lina raised hopes among Republicans elsewhere in the South that he
would come to their aid against their political rivals. Edmund J. Davis
was a Texas Unionist who had fled his home state after secession and
raised a cavalry regiment of Texans for the Union army. He ran for
Texas governor as a Republican in 1869 and was elected to a four-year
term. But his testy nature soon antagonized even many of his fellow
Republicans, and when he tried for reelection in December 1873 he lost
very badly to Democrat Richard Coke. Thereupon Davis, citing "great
wrongs and frauds perpetrated by our opponents who controlled the
registry and the ballot boxes in much the most of the counties," complained to Grant that the result had been rigged. The Texas supreme
court stirred the dispute by invalidating recent elections to the state
legislature, which had authority over the gubernatorial election. "This
may cause here a conflict of authority," Davis told Grant. Violence
hadn't occurred, he said, but it wasn't out of the question. "A display
of U.S. troops will be most likely to keep the peace till the trouble is
settled. I therefore request that assistance."

At the time of his intervention in South Carolina, Grant had realized that such a blunt instrument could be used only rarely. The Constitution allowed the federal government to suppress insurrections in the
states, but insurrections were rare. Mundane violence was something for
the states to deal with themselves, and the Texas case didn't rise even
to that level. The Constitution did *not* authorize the federal government to act as registrar or election judge in the states, and though the
recent enforcement acts asserted such authority in cases where civil rights

were being systematically violated, they didn't extend to instances where Republicans had simply grown unpopular and were voted out of office. Grant had shrugged off the charges of tyranny and military despotism in using the army in South Carolina, knowing that South Carolina was singular. He couldn't have shrugged off the charges had he made a habit of intervention.

He told Davis to accept the judgment of Texas voters. "The act of the legislature of Texas providing for the recent election having received your approval," he wrote the governor, "and both political parties having made nominations and having conducted a political campaign under its provisions, would it not be prudent as well as right to yield to the verdict of the people as expressed by their ballots?"

He took a similar stance when a faction of Republicans in South Carolina sent a delegation to Washington with an appeal for help. The irresponsible elements of the electorate were wreaking havoc on the state, they asserted. The administration must act to restore order. "Gentlemen," Grant replied, according to a news account soon published, "after listening to what has been said, I do not see that there is anything that can be done, either by the executive or by the legislative branch of the national government, to better the condition of things which you have described. South Carolina has now a complete existence as a sovereign state, and must make her own laws." If those laws were bad laws, South Carolina was fully capable of changing them. Grant thought it ironic that his visitors had come from a convention where at least one speaker had railed against the administration in Washington in the most vitriolic terms. "I have never seen a speech equal to it in malignity, vileness, falsity, and slander," he told his visitors. He inquired whether any among them had refuted the slander. They said they had chosen to treat the speech with "silent contempt." Grant puffed on his cigar, eyed them skeptically and sent them away.

*W*hether to intervene in the economy was a harder question. As the depression intensified, debtors pleaded with Washington for relief. Falling prices made their debt burden heavier; they embraced any policies that promised to lift prices and ease their burden. The experience of the war seemed to show that printing money raised prices, and so they petitioned Congress to crank up the presses again. "The importance of doing something in regard to the currency is becoming more apparent every day," Oliver Morton wrote Grant in late March 1874. "The stagnation of business is increasing." The Indiana Republican contended that a widespread belief that there wasn't sufficient money in the economy to sustain a recovery was the culprit. "This conviction stands in the way of enterprise everywhere, especially in the West." Morton recounted the arguments against expanding the currency, in order to dismiss them. He knew that the president and much of the country distrusted anything that could be construed as inflation. What was being proposed was no such thing, Morton said. "An increase of the currency which simply keeps pace with the increase of population and wealth is no inflation. The currency is the instrument with which the business of the country is carried on, and the volume of it should be increased with the volume of business. To me it seems absurd that the volume of currency can be fixed at a particular point unless you can also fix the volume of business." The president had advocated a return to specie payments—in effect, to the gold standard. Morton shared this desire, but he suggested that the surest way back to gold was not necessarily the straightest way. "The first step, in my opinion, to the return to specie payments is the restoration of good times and the creation of a surplus revenue." Expanding the currency would accomplish both.

Other correspondents similarly endorsed expansion. A Philadelphia banker distanced himself from his profession to call for easier money. The interior of the nation was suffering badly, he wrote Grant. "I know from information received from all parts of the country west of the Alleghenies that the people are starving for money, for currency! There is absolutely no money *among the masses* in the far west. A gentleman in this bank today from Wisconsin told me that currency was hardly ever seen at all in his section; and he was coming to the East to get into business as he would starve there." Albert Redstone, the president of the National Labor Council, warned Grant to resist the banker groups demanding a veto of any bill that expanded the currency. "Who are these men?" Redstone asked. "How do they come?" He answered his own question: "They come representing three hundred and fifty millions of money." Their interest was the interest of wealth, not the interest of America. They were agitating for a return to gold, but what would they do once the return was effected? "They would present all the notes they obtain, take the specie to Europe, buy goods, bring them here, induce the people to buy them instead of buying goods of American manufacture, thereby depriving the American laborer of the employment requisite to the production of the goods bought with the gold, and thus continuing the process of depleting the country of gold which these same men have practiced for years."

Grant heard from the opponents of expansion as well. "In my intercourse with scholars and business men for several months past I have not met a single man who had an opinion at all who did not in the strongest terms deprecate the measures likely to be adopted by Congress," a banker wrote from Rochester, New York, at a moment when the legislature was leaning toward an inflation bill. "We believe that those who urge these measures on are either ignorant of the laws of finance or are willing to sacrifice the honor of the government and the financial future of the country to a few months of unhealthy activity of business to be followed by a depression more disastrous than any which we have suffered in the past." After Congress did approve an expansionary bill, a Manhattan banker begged the president to veto it. "This bill is a violation of the faith of the United States," he declared. "It is the first step in a fatal downward course that can but end in disgrace and repudiation." The writer challenged the notion that the ordinary people of the country were debtors and therefore would benefit from expansion. "The creditors are in an immense majority, in proof of which I need only state that the depositors in the savings banks of this state alone number more than 800,000. . . . You surely cannot sanction the defrauding these poor people out of a part of their hard earnings!" Twenty-five hundred New York bankers and merchants petitioned Grant for a veto lest the money bill "inflict a stain on the honor of the Republic and impair confidence in every future pledge and promise given in its name."

Grant found the opposing arguments almost equally compelling. He had supported the first issue of greenbacks as a war measure, but ever since the war he had spoken in favor of a return to specie. He acknowledged that expansion would encourage business activity, but he feared that the government, once started on an expansive path, would find it impossible to turn back. He inclined to the view that presidents should normally defer to the lawmaking prerogatives of Congress, but he understood that presidents sometimes had to check the impulses that pushed the legislature to approve measures that were politically expedient but fiscally imprudent.

He tried to talk himself into accepting the bill. He drafted a statement saying why the expansion bill should become law. Presidents almost never issued such statements, typically commenting only when they vetoed measures. "I deem this course due to myself and to the public also," Grant explained. "Due to me because no opponent of the measure has been more unreserved in expressing views against the expansion of irredeemable currency than I have, or advocated more earnestly than me the duty and obligation of Congress to legislate in such manner as best to carry out their repeated pledges to return to a specie basis at the earliest practicable day. Due to the public because there seems to be a general feeling that if the measure under consideration becomes law it is a triumph of industry over capital; if it fails, a triumph of capital." Grant thought this dichotomy mistaken; the bill could be a victory for labor and property together. He noted that no one in the debate over the measure had said it was unconstitutional. "Under these circumstances an executive should feel very sure of his ground before defeating the will of the majority by his veto." Grant praised ancillary parts of the measure, which reformed banking laws to prevent the resources of the country banks of the West being siphoned irresistibly to the city banks of the East. These provisions, he said, would facilitate the resumption of specie payments when the current crisis eased. Finally and perhaps most importantly, he asserted, the nation had been waiting anxiously on the outcome of the congressional deliberations. Crucial business decisions had been withheld until Congress acted. Now Congress *had* acted, and though the result wasn't perfect, it was the best achievable. "If this measure should be returned without approval"—that is, vetoed—"nothing more favorable could be expected. . . . Trade and commerce would remain paralyzed."

But his heart wasn't in it. Reading the message over, he found himself unpersuaded. He summoned the cabinet and explained his thinking on the expansion bill. "He had given it most careful consideration with an earnest desire to give it his approval," Hamilton Fish recorded of the president's remarks. "He had written a message assigning the best arguments he had heard or could think of in that direction, but the more he wrote, the more he thought, the more he was convinced that the bill should not become a law, and having written the draft of a message in that direction he felt that it was fallacious and untenable, and had come to the conclusion to return it without his signature."

Several of the cabinet secretaries protested, chiefly on political grounds. Columbus Delano, the interior secretary and an Ohioan alert to the sensitivities of the heartland, warned of the unpopularity of a veto,

especially one based on considerations of policy rather than of constitutionality. William Belknap predicted that a veto would turn the entire
West against the administration. George Williams shared the concern,
as did George Robeson, the navy secretary.

Grant conceded that they were right in the short term. "The President thought that the first effect would be one of denunciation of him,"
Hamilton Fish recorded. But Grant believed a veto was necessary, and
he guessed that the American people would agree once the initial shouting ceased. "He had confidence that the judgment of the country would
approve," Fish wrote.

So, against the opposition of a majority of his cabinet, Grant vetoed
the inflation bill. "I must express my regret at not being able to give my
assent to a measure which has received the sanction of a majority of the
legislators chosen by the people," he explained in his veto message. He
said he had tried to find sufficient arguments to sustain assent but had
failed. He quoted from his first annual message to Congress: "It is a duty,
and one of the highest duties, of Government to secure to the citizen a
medium of exchange of fixed, unvarying value. This implies a return to a
specie basis, and no substitute for it can be devised." The present bill took
the country in the opposite direction, he said. It signified "a departure
from true principles of finance, national interest, national obligations to
creditors, Congressional promises, party pledges (on the part of both
political parties), and of personal views and promises made by me in
every annual message sent to Congress and in each inaugural address."
Grant conceded that the bill's banking provisions would facilitate the
flow of money around the country, but he suggested that the existing
geographic imbalances were less dire than the bill's advocates asserted,
and he thought other methods could be employed to alleviate them. He
reminded the lawmakers that Congress in 1869 had passed a resolution
to return the currency to a specie basis as soon as feasible. "This act still
remains as a continuing pledge of the faith of the United States." The
expansion bill contradicted the pledge and must be vetoed.

The veto made Grant a hero with the hard-money crowd. "God
Almighty bless you," Edwards Pierrepont telegraphed from New York.
"The bravest battle and the greatest victory of your life." From Cincinnati a supporter wrote: "It is Vicksburg over again. The veto is as glorious and as vital to the honor and safety of the country as was the capture

of Vicksburg. It stirs my blood, like the bugles sounding a charge." A Boston correspondent echoed the military analogy, declaring, "I do not forget either Vicksburg or Richmond but think this one of the best things you have ever done. It gives us courage." The president of Princeton College, James McCosh, said, "You have done *your* duty nobly in vetoing the inflation bill, and it is now *our* duty to support you. We have little direct political influence in colleges, but we have some moral weight to throw in, and this we mean to give." Philadelphia banker Anthony Drexel praised the president's "noble stand" and said, "I have just received letters by the last mail from London and Paris and they are most just and complimentary in regard to yourself in relation to the financial question, and I may say they express the views of the ablest and best men." Drexel's American correspondents, and not only those in the East, took the same view. "I have yet to hear an adverse opinion from a really sound or solvent man from *any* section."

Yet Drexel's friends hardly constituted the country. The criticism of Grant's veto was as angry as the president had guessed it would be. "The president is mistaken if he thinks the mouth of the Mississippi can be dammed with a straw," Oliver Morton growled. William Crutchfield, a Republican congressman from Tennessee, called the veto "cold-blooded murder." Hundreds of papers in the Midwest and West denounced the veto; a new split among the Republicans, this time along regional lines, appeared entirely possible. The Democrats, for the most part, didn't bother to pile on, satisfied to let the Republicans beat themselves up. Representative James Beck of Kentucky, however, predicted, "That gives us Democrats the president next term."

AND IT MIGHT GIVE THEM CONGRESS IN THE ELECTIONS JUST SIX months away. Republican leaders in the Capitol scurried to limit the damage the depression was inflicting on the party. Some approached the president to probe his thinking more deeply on the currency question. If he wouldn't accept the inflation bill, what *would* he accept?

Grant answered in a memorandum he let some congressional allies show around. "I believe it to be the duty of the government to return to a specie basis at the earliest practicable day, not only to carry out legislative and party pledges but also as a necessary step to secure permanent national prosperity," he said. "I believe further that the time has come when this can be accomplished with less embarrassment to every branch of industry, the *country over*, than at any future time if patchwork is resorted to to stimulate apparent prosperity and speculation on other basis than that of coin, the recognized medium of exchange the world over." The principle was the essential thing; details were less important. "The method to accomplish this return to a specie basis of exchange is not so important as that a plan shall be devised, the day fixed when currency shall be convertible into coin, at par, and the plan adopted adhered to." Grant proposed a timetable. The legal tender clauses of existing statutes should be modified so that all contracts written after July 1, 1875, would specify their sums in gold dollars only. The effect would be to accustom Americans to think in terms of gold. "Instead of calling the paper dollar a dollar and quoting gold at so much premium, we would see the paper at so much discount. This alone would aid materially in bringing the two currencies near to a par with each other." The next step would be for Congress to declare that on July 1, 1876, paper dollars would be redeemable in coin on presentation at any regional office of the federal Treasury. The paper dollars so redeemed would be destroyed and thus eliminated from circulation forever. To fund the redemption Congress should issue gold bonds. Such an arrangement as he proposed, Grant said, "would secure a return to sound financial principles in two years and would not, in my judgment, work as much injustice to the debtor class as they are likely to be subjected to by a delay of the day of final settlement." Glancing back to the Civil War origin of America's legal tender, he added, "It may be recollected too that this class has had its day, in a larger degree, on the adoption of our present financial system."

Grant simultaneously recommended that paper currency in denominations of less than ten dollars be gradually withdrawn from circulation. "The benefit of this would be to strengthen the country in time of depression, whether caused by war, failure of crops or any other cause, by retaining in the hands of the people a large amount of the precious metals. All smaller transactions would be conducted in coin." At present too much coin accumulated in bank vaults and not enough stayed with ordinary people, who of necessity circulated whatever form of money they received for their labors and produce. Grant suggested that had this measure been in effect in recent years, much of the current distress could have been avoided. "Indeed I very much question whether it would have been necessary to depart far from a specie basis during the trying times which begat the legal tender act if the country had adopted the theory of no-small-bills as early as 1850."

Grant's memorandum circulated on Capitol Hill before finding its way into the press. The advocates of hard money applauded, but the Republican leaders in Congress, looking to the elections, put the president off. The speaker of the House, James Blaine, visited Hamilton Fish. "He speaks of the President's memorandum on finance, exhibiting considerable feeling, saying that if carried out it would be ruinous to the Republican party and the country," Fish recorded. "He said he should be inclined to adopt the words of Mr. Webster and say 'that when his leader turned a sharp corner into a dark lane and changed the light which he had been accustomed to follow, that it could not be expected that they would keep company longer.'"

Fish defended Grant to Blaine. He said the president had identified the national interest accurately. "I told him that without adopting all the details of the President's plan, I believed the principles underlying it were the only safeguards of the country."

The Republican majority agreed to a compromise bill that redistributed and lubricated but didn't explicitly expand the money supply. The measure afforded cover for the elections, the Republican leaders hoped, and it suited the president, who signed the bill into law.

A wedding at the White House is a very rare occurrence in the annals of that mansion, not more than one or two having been celebrated there before the wedding of Miss Grant today," the social correspondent for the *New York Times* reported on May 21, 1874. In fact there had been three White House weddings, but none in more than thirty years. And this one only partly counted, in that Grant, Julia and Nellie had decided that it would be conducted as a private affair, with guests limited to personal friends.

Reporters were allowed into the White House ahead of the wedding ceremony to satisfy the curiosity of the public. "The East Room was decorated and prepared especially for the occasion," the *Times* man recounted. "A profusion of beautiful flowers and tropical plants were disposed in suitable positions. Beneath the large middle window on the eastern side of the room a low platform was raised and carpeted. The two fluted columns on either side of the window were twined with roses."

Sources described the ceremony and reception, which the reporter reconstructed. "At 11 o'clock the guests, to the number of nearly 200, had assembled in the East Room. Mr. Sartoris was the first of the bridal party to arrive, accompanied by Lieut. Fred Grant." While the marine band played the wedding march, the eight bridesmaids entered. "Following the bridesmaids were the President and the bride, and after them came the mother of the bride and other members of the family." The vows were exchanged and the wedding party and guests sat down to lunch. The bride and groom departed after an hour; as they left, two young girls tossed slippers at them, in keeping with tradition. "The omen of good luck was made complete by the directness with which they were aimed, one striking the bride and the other her husband." The president and Mrs. Grant had announced that the newlyweds would be leaving shortly for Europe and would take up residence in Britain. "Mr. Sartoris is the only son of Mr. Edward Sartoris, of England, and is heir to a considerable estate," the *Times* explained to readers who hadn't already heard.

73

Try though he might, Grant couldn't keep clear of the politics of the South. Two Republicans, Elisha Baxter and Joseph Brooks, battled for the governorship of Arkansas. Brooks claimed to have won the popular vote in the most recent election, but the legislature, ruling on numerous irregularities in the balloting, awarded the office to Baxter. Both sides summoned supporters, who came armed and organized themselves into militias. A standoff paralyzed Little Rock, interspersed with bloody scrimmages. Baxter and Brooks each appealed to Grant for assistance.

Grant told the parties to work things out themselves. "I heartily approve any adjustment peaceably of the pending difficulties in Arkansas by means of the legislative assembly, the courts, or otherwise," he wrote Baxter. "I will give all the assistance and protection I can under the Constitution and laws of the United States to such modes of adjustment. I hope that the military on both sides will now be disbanded."

Meanwhile he had George Williams examine the merits of the competing claims. The attorney general concluded that the counting may have been crooked but that there wasn't any remedy Washington could provide that wouldn't create more problems than it solved. "Frauds may have been committed to the prejudice of Brooks," Williams told Grant, "but, unhappily, there are few elections, where partisan zeal runs high, in which the victorious party with more or less of truth is not charged with acts of fraud. There must, however, be an end to controversy upon the subject. Somebody must be trusted to count votes and declare elections." The Arkansas constitution placed that trust in the state assembly, which had decided in favor of Baxter. The president could hardly do otherwise than to encourage all Arkansans to accept the decision.

Grant did just that. He wrote to Baxter and Brooks individually, with each message tailored to its recipient but with each carrying the same core message: disband your militias and get back to ordinary politics. To the people of Arkansas the president issued a proclamation affirming the election of Baxter and commanding "all turbulent and disorderly persons to disperse and retire peaceably to their respective abodes." Lest they not think him serious, Grant reminded the Arkansans that the federal Constitution authorized him to employ military force when necessary. They had ten days to go home.

The stern words sufficed. Brooks acquiesced to the president's decision and sent his followers away. Baxter pondered treason charges against the Brooks camp but decided not to test his luck.

Louisiana took a lesson but not the one Grant intended. Republicans controlled the politics of Louisiana, but they were feeling lonely and threatened. This was striking, Governor William Kellogg explained to Grant from New Orleans, because the Republicans constituted a majority of the legal voters in the state. "Even our opponents now admit it," Kellogg said. As a result the Democrats were shifting tactics. "They have abandoned the policy of fraud upon which they relied in 1872, and have returned to the policy of murder, violence, and intimidation which they pursued in 1868." The spring of 1873 had produced a siege of Colfax, the seat of Grant Parish, where black Republicans resisted a forcible takeover by white Democrats. The whites, heavily armed with rifles and a Civil War cannon, eventually overwhelmed the blacks, massacring several dozen, including many after they had surrendered. Emboldened by the inability of the state police and the small number of federal troops in Louisiana to stop them, the insurgents in the spring of 1874 formed a "White League" dedicated to the recapture of the state by white Democrats. Governor Kellogg, watching these developments with alarm, told Grant that the president's recent actions toward Arkansas, while perhaps justified by the situation in that state, had created a dangerous impression in Louisiana. Democrats loudly declared that Grant had become a man of words rather than of actions. He had refused to protect Republicans in Arkansas, and he would refuse to protect them in Louisiana. Kellogg contended that the Louisiana Republicans were as brave as Republicans elsewhere. "But it is necessary that every Republican voter should know that he will be protected if violently interfered with in the exercise of the rights conferred upon him by Congress and the Constitution, and should feel that he is not beyond the reach of the national arm."

Grant heard from Louisiana's Democrats as well. "We assure your excellency most positively that Gov. Kellogg is in error," S. J. Ward, the president of the board of trade of Shreveport, telegraphed. Describing a riot in Caddo Parish in which he said blacks took the principal part, Ward asserted, "The action of the negroes was prompted by their white leaders with a view of bringing about such a condition of affairs as would induce your excellency to send troops to the state, which troops it was hoped and believed by the wily instigators of the trouble would over-awe and intimidate the white people and prevent them from prosecuting the present political contest against the radical party." That party—the Republicans—was wholly corrupt, Ward said, and deserving of defeat rather than outside support. "We assure your excellency that the white people of Louisiana, owning upwards of three hundred and fifty millions of property and largely interested in commerce and agriculture, desire only to elect and establish a government of competent and honest offi-cials under which all legitimate interests of all persons irrespective of race, color, or previous condition of servitude will be protected."

The unrest intensified as the 1874 election approached. On the last day of August Governor Kellogg reported a seizure by the White League of several elected officials at Coushatta in Red River Parish, who were then transported in the direction of Shreveport. "En route they were all shot in cold blood," Kellogg said. Several blacks with the misfortune of witnessing the crime were killed as well. The incident was characteris-tic of the situation in northwestern Louisiana, Kellogg said. "Predatory bands of armed men are scouring several of the Republican parishes in that portion of the state, driving out Republicans and intimidating col-ored men. Registration commenced today, and an openly avowed policy of exterminating Republicans."

The insurrection moved to New Orleans, where a small army of White Leaguers challenged city police and state militia. On September 14 the United States marshal in New Orleans reported a battle in which fifteen police were killed and thirty wounded. "The purpose of the riot is the overthrow of the state government," the marshal declared. The few federal troops in the area were having no effect on the violence. "The military force is inadequate to protect the public property and keep the peace besides." That same day Kellogg made a formal plea for federal assistance. "Under Article 4, section 4, of the Constitution of the United States, I have the honor to inform you that this state is now subject to domestic violence of a character that the state forces under existing circumstances are unable to suppress," he wired Grant. "I respectfully make requisition upon you to take measures to put down the domestic violence and insurrection now prevailing."

Grant decided that Louisiana looked less like the Arkansas of the previous spring than like the South Carolina of three years earlier. He prepared to take strong action. "Turbulent and disorderly persons have combined together with force and arms to overthrow the state government of Louisiana and to resist the laws and constituted authorities," he proclaimed. Citing his responsibility to preserve the states against domestic violence and to ensure enforcement of the laws, he gave "said turbulent and disorderly persons" five days to disperse and return to their homes. After that they would face federal troops. To emphasize his resolve he ordered infantry units from outside Louisiana to converge on the state and dispatched three warships from the Gulf of Mexico to New Orleans.

The brandishing of force sufficed. The insurgents dispersed, and Kellogg and the other officials regained control of the state, at least long enough to conduct the 1874 elections.

The Republicans expected to suffer losses in that autumn's countrywide balloting. The party had controlled the national government for fourteen years, and voters typically tire of incumbents long before then. Grant remained popular among Americans generally, but he wasn't on the ballot and, anyway, midterm elections usually hinge on perceptions of Congress rather than of the president. The depression, deeper than ever that autumn, seemingly sealed the Republicans' dismal fate.

Yet the tsunami that swept Republicans away caught the party by surprise. Many simply had grown so accustomed to office that they couldn't imagine America without them in charge. James Blaine was less prone to self-delusion than most of his colleagues, but even he failed to detect the signs of the approaching catastrophe. Blaine's home state always voted early to spare voters the rigors of Maine Novembers; Blaine reported to Grant in September: "The result of our election today is in all respects satisfactory. We have carried every Congressional district; have a majority I think in every county in the state."

But Maine proved the rare bright spot. When the rest of the country voted, the Republicans were trounced. They lost ninety-six seats in the House, where their swaggering majority became a quivering minority. The shift was less dramatic in the Senate, as such shifts typically are, with but a third of the seats in play in any election. But there too the Republicans suffered badly, with their majority sharply diminished and the survivors deeply sobered.

The outcome meant little to Grant personally. He had always shunned the role of politician, and though he had learned to play the political game on matters touching the essence of republicanism—ratification of the Fifteenth Amendment, suppression of the Ku Klux Klan—he still considered Congress hostile territory. Responding in the autumn of 1873 to a dinner invitation from Simon Cameron, the former secretary of war and then a senator from Pennsylvania, Grant had written: "Not before the meeting of Congress. After that unhappy event I would be willing to run away any Saturday from my natural enemy." The landslide winner of the 1872 presidential election had little difficulty convincing himself that the congressional Republicans' losses in 1874 were *their* losses, not his.

74

GRANT RARELY ABANDONED MISSIONS HE CONSIDERED ESSENTIAL, but that autumn he sounded retreat on a matter he been pushing forward for years. From the first weeks of his first term, when the clamor for office had induced one of his migraines, he had cajoled Congress to reform the federal civil service. "There is no duty which so much embarrasses the executive and heads of departments as that of appointments, nor is there any such arduous and thankless labor imposed on senators and representatives as that of finding places for constituents," he declared. "The present system does not secure the best men, and often not even fit men, for public place. The elevation and purification of the civil service of the government will be hailed with approval by the whole people of the United States."

Congress responded slowly and without enthusiasm. In 1871 the legislature authorized the president to recommend measures to ensure that federal positions be filled on the basis of competence rather than party affiliation and personal connections. Grant appointed a civil service commission, which prescribed competitive examinations and other techniques for putting an end to the spoils system or at least reducing its scope. Grant approved the recommendations, and in the spring of 1872 the first examinations under the new system were administered.

To Grant's mind the civil service reforms promised to be both a boon to the nation and a blessing to himself. The nation would benefit from the greater expertise and disinterestedness the new system would produce; he would benefit from not having to deal with the hordes of applicants and their noisy sponsors. Grant discovered what Lincoln and other presidents had learned: that the patronage system alienated more people than it satisfied. Successful applicants thought they deserved the jobs; the unsuccessful, who greatly outnumbered the successful ones, felt they had been deprived. Grant was happy to hand the thankless task of job-filling to the commission.

Many in Congress held a different view. Senators and representatives were the usual conduits for applications for federal jobs, and the delivery of the jobs to supporters acted as binder that held the parties together. This function of the patronage explained much of the fierceness of fights over the presidency. Having a Republican in the White House permitted Republican legislators to shower jobs on their friends and constituents; the arrival of a Democrat snatched that power away.

Grant had shamed Congress into accepting the principle of civil service reform, but the legislature stubbornly refused to fund the new system. He cajoled and expostulated for money year after year, to no effect. Finally he gave the lawmakers an ultimatum. "The rules adopted to improve the civil service of the Government have been adhered to as closely as has been practicable with the opposition with which they meet," he said in his December 1874 annual message. "But it is imprac-ticable to maintain them without direct and positive support of Con-gress. . . . If Congress adjourns without positive legislation on the subject of civil service reform I will regard such action as a disapproval of the system, and will abandon it." This would be a disservice to the country and a waste of the effort invested thus far. But there was no alternative. "It is impossible to carry this system to a successful issue without general approval and assistance and positive law to support it."

Congress remained unmoved. The lame-duck Republicans, who might have judged civil service reform a means to preserve the jobs of their protégés, were too stunned by the Democratic landslide to act coherently. The Democrats salivated at the thought of doling out thou-sands of positions when they reclaimed the White House in two years. The practice of reform withered; even the idea nearly expired.

Grant's failure on civil service reform augured ill for his seventh and eighth years in office, which threatened to be difficult enough anyway. The depression still shadowed the land, and the congressional Demo-crats made no secret of their intention to obstruct whatever the president proposed.

Grant might have helped himself, if only slightly, by holding open the possibility of a third term. His popularity persisted, and he could have forced the Democrats to guard their flanks against his potential presence on the ballot in 1876. The ambiguous disavowal of a third term he had made during the 1872 campaign left room for reinterpretation and hadn't been repeated. Even if he ultimately decided not to run, by keeping his antagonists in suspense he could throw them off balance.

This was what his advisers wanted him to do; it was what political common sense dictated. But it didn't suit him. He had silently resented the allegations of Caesarism, and he decided that the most potent refutation was a definitive disavowal of a political future. "I never sought the office for a second, nor even for a first, nomination," he reminded Harry White, the president of the Pennsylvania Republican convention, in a letter intended for the press. "To the first I was called from a life position"—as general of the army—"one created by Congress expressly for me for supposed services rendered to the Republic. The position vacated I liked. It would have been most agreeable to me to have retained it. . . . But I was made to believe that the public good called me to make the sacrifice." The vote of the people had corroborated this belief. His second nomination and second election had reinforced it. Grant didn't deny that he took personal pleasure at the result of the voting, especially the second round. "Such a fire of personal abuse and slander had been kept up for four years, notwithstanding my conscientious performance of my duties, to the best of my understanding—though I admit, in the light of subsequent events, many times subject to fair criticism—that an endorsement from the people, who alone govern republics, was a gratification that it is only human to have appreciated and enjoyed."

But enough was enough. The tradition of stepping down after two terms was a sound one, established by the first president and observed without exception since. Grant allowed that national emergency might someday require setting the tradition aside, but until such calamity occurred, the tradition should be maintained. "I am not, nor have I been, a candidate for a renomination," he wrote White and the country. "I would not accept a nomination if it were tendered unless it should come under such circumstances as to make it an imperative duty, circumstances not likely to arise."

If Grant had been half as good a politician as he was a soldier, he never would have written or sent this letter. The intelligence it contained was as valuable to Grant's political enemies as his battle plans before Vicksburg or Richmond would have been to Pemberton or Lee. It limited his flexibility, discouraged his troops and let the Democrats know they could simply outwait him.

If he had been merely as good a politician as his wife, he would have kept his thoughts to himself. "I followed the President into his office one Sunday afternoon, when one after another the cabinet officers arrived," Julia wrote afterward. The gathering seemed odd, as cabinet meetings weren't held on Sundays. She tried to draw the secretaries out, but they didn't know the purpose of the meeting. Grant knew, of course, but he wasn't saying. "I left the room feeling sure there was something of importance to be considered," she recounted. "I was restless and anxious." Half an hour later a messenger left the office and the White House. She could contain herself no longer. "I want to know what is happening," she told her husband. "I feel sure there is something and I must know." Grant said he would explain very soon; he just wanted to step out into the hall and light his cigar. After a few minutes he reentered the room. "What is it? Tell me!" she demanded. He said he had read the cabinet a letter he had written taking himself out of the running for 1876. She was dumbfounded. "Did all of these men approve?" she asked. Grant said he hadn't requested their approval; he had simply read them the letter. "Why did you not read it to me?" she asked. He answered, "I know you too well. It never would have gone if I had read it." She insisted, "Bring it and read it to me now." He smiled and said, "It is already posted. That is why I lingered in the hall." She wailed: "Oh, Ulys! Was that kind to me? Was it just?" He told her there was no use fretting; what was done was done. She gradually calmed herself. "But I did feel deeply injured," she remembered.

𝓗aving placed himself indisputably above politics, Grant proceeded to speak from the moral high ground. He knew his time in office was running out, and he feared that the chance for justice for the freedmen wouldn't survive him. In a message to Congress he recounted the violence and terror that had been directed against black voters and their white allies during the previous months and years; he defended his actions against the Ku Klux Klan, the White League and others who had violated the Constitution and federal laws; and he suggested that such remedies could not be applied forever. "The whole subject of executive interference with the affairs of a state is repugnant to public opinion, to the feelings of those who, from their official capacity, must be used in such interposition, and to him or those who must direct," he said. Without the law to support it, such interference was criminal, but even with the law, it was very unpopular. "I desire, therefore, that all necessity for executive direction in local affairs may become unnecessary and obsolete."

Grant appealed not simply to Congress but to the American people to consider the causes and consequences of the domestic violence. "Is there not a disposition on one side to magnify wrongs and outrages, and on the other side to belittle them or justify them?" A calmer, fairer mindset couldn't avoid improving policy toward the South. "A better state of feeling would be inculcated, and the sooner we would have that peace which would leave the states free indeed to regulate their own domestic affairs." Grant credited the majority of Southerners with a desire for justice and the rule of law. "But do they do right in ignoring the existence of violence and bloodshed in resistance to constituted authority?" He sympathized with the frustration white Southerners had experienced since the war, as important decisions had been made for them by Washington. "But can they proclaim themselves entirely irresponsible for this condition? They can not. Violence has been rampant in some localities, and has either been justified or denied by those who could have prevented it."

Grant knew that many people, and not in the South alone, rejected the idea that the federal government possessed continuing authority to interfere in Southern states to ensure the rights of Southern citizens. "This is a great mistake," he said of the rejection. "While I remain executive all the laws of Congress and the provisions of the Constitution, including the recent amendments added thereto, will be enforced with rigor, but with regret that they should have added one jot or tittle to executive duties or powers." This regret—that the president was having to do what the states should have done themselves—was what caused him to appeal again to the South's better nature. "Let there be fairness in the discussion of Southern questions, the advocates of both or all political parties giving honest, truthful reports of occurrences, condemning the wrong and upholding the right, and soon all will be well. Under existing conditions the negro votes the Republican ticket because he knows his friends are of that party. Many a good citizen votes the opposite, not because he agrees with the great principles of state which separate parties, but because, generally, he is opposed to negro rule. This is a most delusive cry. Treat the negro as a citizen and a voter, as he is and must remain, and soon parties will be divided, not on the color line, but on principle. Then we shall have no complaint of sectional interference."

75

L OUISIANA AGAIN WASN'T LISTENING. THE 1874 ELECTIONS THERE produced a contested result in the state legislature, with the Democrats and Republicans both claiming victory and both alleging theft. New Orleans boiled over once more, prompting Grant to direct Phil Sheridan to take command of the federal forces in the city and state. The assignment outraged much of the white South; for what purpose was the president sending the despoiler of Shenandoah if not to intimidate the citizenry? Sheridan seemed to confirm the critics' fears when the Democrats attempted a forcible seizure of the statehouse and Sheridan dispatched troops to prevent it. The federal soldiers entered the legislative chamber and physically removed the trespassers, who naturally asserted that they were not trespassers at all but the rightful occupants of the seats from which they were being evicted.

Sheridan ignored the complaints and requested greater authority. "I think the terrorism now existing in Louisiana, Mississippi, and Arkansas could be entirely removed and confidence and fair dealing established by the arrest and trial of the ringleaders of the armed White Leagues," he wrote to Washington. "If Congress would pass a bill declaring them banditti, they could be tried by a military commission. These banditti, who murdered men here on the 14th of last September, also more recently at Vicksburg, Miss."—the scene of additional lethal violence—"should, in justice to law and order and the peace and prosperity of this southern part of the country, be punished." If Congress wouldn't act, the president should. "It is possible that if the President would issue a proclamation declaring them banditti, no further action need be taken except that which would devolve upon me."

Sheridan's statement evoked a louder protest from the Democratic leaders of New Orleans, who characterized his words as malicious and misinformed and his actions as illegal and despotic. "Coming among us an almost entire stranger, General Sheridan has limited his inquiries as to the condition of affairs here to those whose interest it is not only to falsify facts but to promote that spirit of lawlessness with which we are falsely charged," a statement from the Cotton Exchange, a focus of Democratic influence in Louisiana, asserted. Democrats around the country echoed the cry; the Democratic state committee of Illinois declared, "The Administration, through the most facile of its military instruments, has dispersed the legislative assembly of a sovereign state and forced the representatives of the people from the halls of legislation at the point of the bayonet, and has given Louisiana over to her spoilers and plunderers. . . . This action imports terrorism of the whole South and its unholy subjugation to party ends."

Sheridan waved aside the protesters. "They seem to be trying to make martyrs of themselves," he telegraphed to Washington. "It cannot be done at this late day; there have been too many bleeding negroes and ostracized white citizens for their statements to be believed by fair-minded people." Sheridan said he would send a list he had compiled of the number of murders in Louisiana in the last few years, the perpetrators of which remained unpunished. "I think that the number will startle you; it will be up in the thousands." He added, "The city is perfectly quiet. No trouble is apprehended." Sheridan had received death threats; he similarly discounted them. "I am not afraid, and will not be stopped from informing the Government that there are localities in this department where the very air has been impregnated with assassination for several years."

Sheridan's assertiveness split Grant's cabinet. War Secretary William Belknap congratulated Sheridan, saying, "The President and all of us have full confidence and thoroughly approve your course." Hamilton Fish condemned Sheridan's action and hotly resented Belknap's implication that he endorsed it. Most other members sided with Fish, either on the principle of noninterference in state politics or from fear of the political repercussions to the Republican party.

Grant upheld Sheridan. The president wasn't thrilled that Sheridan had given so little weight to political sensibilities, but neither was he surprised. And he certainly didn't intend to disavow Sheridan's actions after the fact. He remembered how Lincoln had stood by him during moments of trial; so he would stand by Sheridan.

And he soon came to share the opprobrium aimed at Sheridan. Protest meetings were held in every section of the country; death threats poured into the White House. "You had better mend your course toward the southern states," a Virginian who signed himself only as "Conservative" wrote Grant. "If you do not, you will not be a living man two months from today." From New Orleans "Deadshot" warned, "If you cannot well back out of your now contemptible position you had better PREPARE FOR THE NEXT WORLD!!!" A man calling himself "Charles Howard"—not his real name, he said—claimed personal knowledge of a shadowy Southern paramilitary organization that intended to provoke a war with the Indians on the Plains, which would require the president to withdraw the federal troops from the South. "There will also be attempts made to assassinate you and all the leading members of the radical party. They have even now got their spies in Washington City."

Grant paid the threats no attention and summoned Congress to stand beside him on behalf of civil rights in Louisiana. "To say that lawlessness, turbulence, and bloodshed have characterized the political affairs of that state since its reorganization under the reconstruction acts is only to repeat what has become well known as a part of its unhappy history," he wrote the Senate. He summarized the fraud, violence and intimidation of the recent years and the actions he had taken to combat them. He acknowledged that the theory on which his actions rested— that the federal government could reach over the state governments to protect the rights of individual citizens—was new and to some people startling. "But it results as clearly from the fifteenth amendment to the Constitution and the acts that have been passed to enforce that amendment as the abrogation of state laws upholding slavery results from the thirteenth amendment."

Referring specifically to the Colfax massacre, Grant said he didn't hold the people of Louisiana at large to blame for the slaughter. "But it is a lamentable fact that insuperable obstructions were thrown in the way of punishing these murderers; and the so-called conservative papers of the state not only justified the massacre, but denounced as federal tyranny and despotism the attempt of the United States officers to bring them to justice." Democrats elsewhere were no help. "Fierce denunciations ring through the country about office holding and election matters in Louisiana, while every one of the Colfax miscreants goes unwhipped of justice, and no way can be found in this boasted land of civilization and Christianity to punish the perpetrators of this bloody and monstrous crime."

A similar failure had followed the Coushatta murders. "No one has been punished, and the conservative press of the state denounced all efforts to that end and boldly justified the crime." Again Grant was reluctant to generalize but unable not to. "To say that the murder of a negro or a white Republican is not considered a crime in Louisiana would probably be unjust to a great part of the people, but it is true that a great number of such murders have been committed and no one has been punished therefor; and manifestly, as to them, the spirit of hatred and violence is stronger than law."

Grant again disclaimed eagerness to involve the federal government in the affairs of Louisiana or any other state. "I have always refused except where it seemed to be my imperative duty to act in such a manner under the constitution and laws of the United States," he said. Without apologizing for Sheridan's actions, he made plain that those actions were exceptional and would not be repeated. "I am well aware that any military interference by the officers or troops of the United States with the organization of the state legislature or any of its proceedings, or with any civil department of the government, is repugnant to our ideas of government. I can conceive of no case, not involving rebellion or insurrection, where such interference by authority of the general government ought to be permitted or can be justified."

All the same, he wouldn't turn his back on the South. "To the extent that Congress has conferred power upon me to prevent it, neither Ku Klux Klans, White Leagues, nor any other association using arms and violence to execute their unlawful purposes can be permitted in that way to govern any part of this country; nor can I see with indifference Union men or Republicans ostracized, persecuted, and murdered on account of their opinions, as they now are in some localities." But to continue his defense of equal rights and to have a prayer of success, he needed a show of support from the legislative branch. "I now earnestly ask that such action be taken by Congress as to leave my duties perfectly clear."

Grant's appeal produced results, although not exactly the kind he sought. Charles Sumner had long advocated a civil rights law barring racial discrimination in most aspects of public life. The concept made little headway while he lived, but following his 1874 death the Senate had paid him homage by approving a bill incorporating his basic ideas. The House adjourned without voting on the bill, but the following year a similar bill—mandating equality in hotels and restaurants open to the public, in transportation facilities, in theaters and other public amusements and in the selection of juries—passed both chambers. The measure reached the White House about the time the two sides in Louisiana cobbled a compromise that allowed Grant to withdraw Sheridan and most of the federal troops. On March 1, 1875, the president signed the Civil Rights Act, the most ambitious affirmation of racial equality in American history until then (a distinction it would retain until the 1960s).

To affirm equality, however, was one thing; to enforce it another. The 1875 law lacked the teeth of the 1871 Ku Klux Klan Act; it required persons who believed their rights to have been violated to file suit in court, where the penalties were modest. Moreover, because the law intruded farther into the private sphere than any previous federal law touching race relations—or just about any other subject—it raised constitutional doubts even among many who supported the principle of equality.

Grant recognized the law's shortcomings. He understood that it might be declared unconstitutional (as indeed it was in 1883, when the Supreme Court ruled that the Fourteenth Amendment's equal protection clause applied to actions by state governments but not by individuals). But no law was perfect, and at this late date, on this vexed subject, it was the best he could hope for.

A SECOND PROMISE OF THAT SESSION OF CONGRESS PROVED MORE plausible. In January 1875 the legislature approved the Resumption Act, which embodied Grant's recommendation to put the federal government on track to wring the paper from America's currency. As of January 1, 1879, the Treasury would redeem greenbacks in gold. The date was more distant than Grant had wished, but the certain knowledge that paper dollars would eventually be worth their face value in gold would drive them toward parity even ahead of the redemption date. The country would still not be on a gold standard, as silver coins remained lawful currency and in fact would gain prevalence in response to a second provision of the new law, one enacting Grant's recommendation to replace small notes with silver coins.

Many economists of later generations would consider resumption to have been precisely the wrong prescription for curing the depression of the 1870s. Their arguments were anticipated during Grant's day by populists and debtor advocates who contended that a smaller currency would drive already falling prices further down and thereby increase the burden of debtors. Grant acknowledged the price-lowering effect of resumption, but he believed the confidence-building effect to be more important. In a statement upon his signing of the bill, he praised the "currency of a fixed known value" that resumption would produce. Grant considered the expectations of investors to be critical to recovery. When investors knew they would be paid back in dollars of value equal to those they invested, the economy would find its footing. Speaking of the measure before him, Grant explained, "By the enactment of such a law, business and industries would revive and the beginning of prosperity on a firm basis would be reached." He congratulated Congress and the American people on having the fortitude and courage to make the restoration of a sound currency a priority, and he gladly gave the measure his approval.

*B*y one common interpretation, the moral fiber of American public officials had been weakening since independence. The founders—Washington, Jefferson, Madison and the others—were selfless demigods, immune from temptation and devoted solely to the public weal in winning independence and establishing the principles of American republicanism. The second generation—Jackson, Clay, Webster, Calhoun—were towering figures but flawed; in their battles over the meaning of democracy they sometimes permitted party and section to cloud their judgment of what the nation's welfare required. The third generation included Lincoln, an undeniably great soul—undenied, at any rate, since his martyrdom—but also the jobbers and opportunists who battened on the country's distress during the Civil War and after. By this interpretation the Tweed Ring, the gold conspiracy and Crédit Mobilier were a matter of moral failure: the work of bad men doing what anyone would expect of their ilk.

Persuasive evidence supported this interpretation; the persons hauled before Congress and the courts to answer for diverting public funds were hardly a distinguished cohort ethically. But another interpretation looked less to the character of the miscreants than to the context in which they operated. George Washington Plunkitt, a Tammany successor to the Tweed Ring, distinguished between "honest graft" and "dishonest graft." The latter consisted of extortion, vice and other clear breaches of the Judeo-Christian code; such sins Plunkitt condemned. But "honest graft" was something different. It consisted chiefly of using inside information to capture profits generated by the rapid growth of the American economy. Plunkitt boasted of buying strategically placed property ahead of the announcement of new public works whose proximity caused the property to rise in value. His point was that *someone* would profit from the announcement; why not Plunkitt and friends? "I seen my opportunities and I took 'em," Plunkitt explained.

Opportunities were rife in the decade after the Civil War. The industrialization of the private sector was accompanied by the expansion of the public sector, and few laws effectively governed behavior in the interstices between the two realms. The gold conspirators and

Crédit Mobilier operated in this no-man's-land, with the former betting (wrongly) on whether the public Treasury would intrude unusually into the private gold market and the latter channeling public construction funds into private pockets.

New scandals surfaced during Grant's final eighteen months in office and fell into a similar category. The largest had been long brewing, or rather distilling: it centered on the failure of whiskey makers to pay the full tax owed on the spirits they produced. Underpayment of the whiskey tax continued a tradition of American tax dodges that dated to the eighteenth century, when resistance to rum taxes, stamp taxes and tea taxes had triggered the American Revolution and subsequently the Whiskey Rebellion of the 1790s.

The surprise of the whiskey scandal wasn't that the underpayment occurred but that it suddenly was prosecuted. And it might not have been prosecuted if Benjamin Bristow hadn't hoped to succeed Grant as president. Bristow's father had been elected to Congress from Kentucky; the son served with distinction in the Union army, being severely wounded at Shiloh and returning to defend his home state against the raids of John Hunt Morgan, whom he helped capture. Kentuckians elected him to state office and Andrew Johnson appointed him a federal district attorney. His vigorous prosecutions under the new civil rights laws displeased Johnson but won him the favorable attention of Grant, who made him the first solicitor general in the new Justice Department. Bristow's performance in that post led Grant to select him to succeed George Williams as attorney general, but the promotion fell through when Williams's nomination to the Supreme Court stalled. Bristow got another chance at the cabinet when Treasury Secretary William Richardson was forced out after being discovered to have shared fees from a tax collector he had hired. Grant sought a clean, hard-driving man at the Treasury, and Bristow seemed just the one.

Consequently it was to Bristow that the editor of the *St. Louis Democrat* wrote in 1875 saying he had information about a conspiracy among whiskey distillers in the Midwest and the Treasury agents who were supposed to be collecting whiskey taxes. Bristow followed the evidence to John McDonald, the chief tax collector at St. Louis. McDonald didn't deny wrongdoing but demanded leniency in exchange for testimony against his fellow conspirators and their sponsors in Washington. Bristow refused the request and pressed forward with the investigation.

Grant urged him on. "Let no guilty man escape if it can be avoided," he wrote Bristow. "Be specially vigilant—or instruct those engaged in the prosecutions of fraud to be—against all who insinuate that they have high influence to protect, or to protect them. No personal consideration should stand in the way of performing a public duty." Bristow, with Grant's approval, gave the press a copy of the president's instructions, and the phrase "let no man escape" became the administration's watchword.

Living up to the watchword caused great discomfort. Bristow's investigation eventually reached into the president's own office, with a trail of telegrams implicating Orville Babcock, Grant's private secretary. The telegrams were ambiguous, even mystifying, suggesting some kind of code. "Poor Ford is dead," one to Babcock stated. "McDonald is with his body. Let the President act cautiously in his successorship." The telegram that gained the greatest notoriety declared, "We have official information that the enemy weakens. Push things." It was signed "Sylph." No one knew who Sylph was, but the feminine sound of the name suggested a sexual element that lent salacious appeal to the whiskey story.

"To General Bristow and myself this looked like a very serious matter," Edwards Pierrepont, the successor to George Williams as attorney general, later testified. "We brought the telegrams to the President." Grant immediately summoned Babcock and asked what the messages meant. Babcock appeared flustered and talked around the subject for a few moments before Pierrepont and Bristow stopped him. "The Secretary of the Treasury and I then both insisted that this was a matter so serious that if he could give an explanation which, as he said, was complete and perfect, and if he was perfectly innocent, as he said he was, he should go out there and make an explanation. And we pressed it as a thing he ought to do on the spot." Grant concurred. Babcock proceeded to draft a telegram to send to the press. "It was somewhat long and somewhat, toward the end, argumentative, and I took the pen and dashed through it," Pierrepont recalled. "I said, 'You don't want to send your argument; send the fact, and go there and make your explanation.'"

Babcock had no explanation, at least none that exonerated him, and he was shortly indicted for tax fraud. Grant grew upset to think that one in whom he had reposed such trust might have betrayed him. He kept the cabinet secretaries after a regular meeting to discuss the case. "The President manifested a great deal of excitement," Hamilton Fish recorded in his diary. Grant resisted believing that Babcock was guilty. "He was as confident as he lived of Babcock's innocence," Fish wrote. "He knew he was not guilty; that were he guilty it would be an instance of the greatest ingratitude and treachery that ever was." Grant said he would testify on Babcock's behalf. "The President expressed his determination to go to St. Louis, to start either this evening or tomorrow morning, and said he should like at least two members of the Cabinet to go with him."

Pierrepont asked Grant to reconsider. The attorney general said he was the obvious one to accompany the president on such a mission and that he could rearrange his schedule to go, but he wondered about the attention Grant's appearance would attract and the precedent it would set. For a president to weigh in on the side of the defense might be interpreted as an attempt to intimidate the jury, and in an election year interpretations mattered. Bristow concurred, as did Fish, who suggested that if the president had been subpoenaed the situation would be different. The secretary of state asked Pierrepont if a president *could* be subpoenaed. "He of course replied in the negative," Fish recorded, having concluded the same thing himself. According to Fish, the cabinet was unanimous in its opposition to Grant's appearing in court.

Grant settled for giving a deposition. Pierrepont and Bristow accompanied the president; Chief Justice Morrison Waite served as notary. William Cook, counsel for the defendant, commenced the questioning. "How long have you known General Babcock, and how intimately?" Cook asked.

"I have known him since 1863, having first met him during the Vicksburg campaign that year," Grant replied. "Since March 1864 I have known him intimately." The president explained that Babcock had served as aide-de-camp on his military staff during and after the war and as his private secretary since his inauguration.

"As your private secretary, please state what were his general duties."

"He received my mails, opened my letters, and referred them to the appropriate departments, submitting to me all such as required any instructions or answer from myself."

"His relations with you were confidential?"

"Very."

"Do you know whether, during the time General Babcock has been your private secretary, he has had frequent applications from persons throughout the country to lay their special matters before you or before the various departments?"

"That was of very frequent occurrence. Indeed it happened almost daily."

In what manner had Babcock fulfilled his assignments?

"I have always regarded him as a most efficient and most faithful officer."

Cook turned to the topic of the indictment. "Did General Babcock, so far as you know, ever seek in any way to influence your action in reference to any investigation of the alleged whiskey frauds in St. Louis or elsewhere?"

"He did not," Grant replied. "I do not remember but one instance where he talked with me on the subject of these investigations, excepting since his indictment. It was then simply to say to me that he had asked Mr. Douglass"—John Douglass, the internal revenue commissioner—"why it was his department treated all their officials as though they were dishonest persons who required to be watched by spies, and why he could not make inspections similar to those which prevailed in the army, selecting for the purpose men of character who could enter the distilleries, examine the books, and make reports which could be relied upon as correct. General Babcock simply told me that he had said this to Mr. Douglass."

Cook inquired about Babcock's connection to John McDonald. "Was anything whatever said by him to you with reference to the investigation of alleged frauds in his"—McDonald's—"district?"

"I have no recollection of any word or words on any matter touching his official position or business," Grant said.

Cook asked about a particular moment when McDonald had visited Washington with reference to the whiskey investigations. "Did General Babcock at or about that time say anything to you with reference to such investigations, and to your knowledge did he in any way undertake to prevent them?"

"I have no recollection of his saying anything about that. Certainly he did not intercede with me to prevent them."

Cook mentioned an executive order transferring various of the tax agents to other districts. The order had been explained as standard practice, but the administration's critics contended that it was intended to frustrate the whiskey investigation. "Did General Babcock ever in any way directly or indirectly seek to influence your action in reference to that order?"

"I do not remember his ever speaking to me about or exhibiting any interest in the matter."

Returning to the broad question, Cook asked, "Have you ever seen anything in the conduct of General Babcock or has he ever said anything to you which indicated to your mind that he was in any way interested in or connected with the whiskey ring at St. Louis or elsewhere?"

"Never."

Grant's testimony helped Babcock defeat the allegations against him. Two weeks after Grant's deposition the St. Louis jury delivered a verdict of not guilty. Babcock treated the acquittal as vindication and prepared to resume his work at the White House. Grant briefly considered letting him do so. But when a separate investigation linked Babcock to the gold conspiracy, Grant finally realized—or admitted—that Babcock may have fooled him. "The President then, for the first time, comprehended in all its significance the fact that he had been betrayed by Babcock," Bluford Wilson of the Treasury Department, who informed Grant of the gold link, recalled. "If he (Babcock) had betrayed him in the Black Friday transactions, he was quite capable of betraying him in connection with the whiskey frauds."

𝐵abcock wasn't the only betrayer. Even as Grant's private secretary was being shown the door, his war secretary was leaving of his own volition, albeit one step ahead of impeachment. William Belknap's second wife had decided she couldn't live on her husband's eight-thousand-dollar salary; discovering that Belknap controlled the concessions of trade at army posts in the West, she arranged to share in the profits of the trade. A schedule of kickbacks was negotiated, and she received regular remittances. Belknap may or may not have known about the arrangement at first, but upon her death the payments continued, to him. He took up with his deceased's sister, a formidable beauty with a modest fortune and a determination to keep it. Upon their engagement she handed him a prenuptial agreement and asked that he sign it. "Belknap felt very much hurt at this request," Julia Grant recalled, based on her own knowledge and on hearsay. But he was smitten, and he did as his darling wished. "For two years she enjoyed to the fullest extent possible her position, her beauty and youth, and the entire control of her little fortune," Julia said.

Beauty, youth and fortune evoke envy, and after the Democrats gained control of the House in 1875 they launched an investigation into the Belknaps' affairs. The kickback scheme was discovered, and the House began moving toward impeaching Belknap.

Grant, still struggling with Babcock's betrayal, took the news of Belknap's corruption hard. "The President spoke of Belknap's defection saying that yesterday he had really, in the first part of the day, been unable to comprehend its magnitude and importance, the surprise was so great," Hamilton Fish recorded. "It was really not until evening that he could realize the crime and its gravity. He spoke of his long continued acquaintance with Belknap in the army, of his having known his father as one of the finest officers in the Old Army, when he himself was a young lieutenant."

Grant's affection for the father and the evident distress of the son, who confessed his crimes in a tearful meeting in Grant's office, disposed the president, without fully considering the consequences, to let Belknap resign. The resignation confused the congressional effort to remove the war secretary. The House adopted impeachment articles and the Senate trial went forward but amid constitutional doubt as to whether the Senate could remove from office someone who no longer held the office. Several senators decided it could not, and on this technicality Belknap was acquitted.

*T*he scandals metastasized. With the 1876 elections approaching, the Democrats broadened their investigations; hardly an executive department or office escaped scrutiny. Grant's minister to England, Robert Schenck, was found to have employed his position to promote investments in which he had a personal stake. No charges were brought, but Schenck was forced to resign. The secretary of the navy, George Robeson, seemed to be living beyond the means of his salary; when, under pressure, he released a statement of his bank account to the congressional investigators it revealed hundreds of thousands of dollars he couldn't explain. The natural presumption was that the money had come from navy contractors. But the paper trail was so confused that the investigators did nothing beyond chastising Robeson rhetorically. The secretary of the interior, Columbus Delano, resigned under the fire of an investigation into a scheme by his son to profit illegitimately from Delano's position. The investigation hit close to Grant when the president's younger brother Orvil was found to have been paid for surveying services in Wyoming Territory he failed to render. "Did you ever know Orvil Grant to do any surveying in that territory?" a congressional investigator asked the chief clerk in the Cheyenne office of the federal survey. "No, sir," the chief clerk replied. "I do not think he was ever *in* the territory."

77

WILLIAM SHERMAN THOUGHT SUFFICIENTLY LITTLE OF THE POLITI-cal classes that none of their corruption surprised him. He knew and liked William Belknap from the Georgia and Carolina campaigns and was consequently disposed to put responsibility for his part in the scandals elsewhere. "I feel sorry for Belknap," he wrote his brother John. "I don't think him naturally dishonest, but how could he live on $8000 a year in the style that you all beheld?" Sherman blamed those who set the rules for the army concessionaires. "The fault lies with Congress, which by special legislation has almost invited this very system. . . . I pity Belknap, and regard him as the 'effect' and not the 'cause.'" The president played a part, Sherman allowed. "Grant is not blameless," he told John. "He could have given an impetus in the right direction in 1869—meant to, but saw or thought he saw the danger, and made up his mind to let things *run*. The result was inevitable." Yet Belknap's demise wasn't all to the bad, Sherman suggested. The war secretary had been impossible to work under. "He acted towards me without frankness and meanly, gradually usurping all the power which had been exercised by General Grant, leaving me almost the subject of ridicule." Belknap's departure, especially under a cloud, would yield an improvement. "The whirlwind that is now let loose in Washington will do good."

The whirlwind did blow some power back toward Sherman and away from the civilians of the War Department, but it did little to strengthen the military in the West, the area of Sherman's greatest professional concern. Grant's Indian policy had always required a delicate balancing. The president had to convince Red Cloud and the other Indian leaders that the government in Washington had their welfare at heart despite recurrent unwillingness in Congress to fund the Indian agencies adequately, and he had to convince Congress that the Indians were fundamentally peaceful despite outbreaks of violence by the bands unreconciled to life on reservations. The western settlers were a wild card in his considerations. They could readily provoke attacks, and when they did they could count on a sympathetic hearing among a substantial portion of the American public.

The settlers constantly tried to seize land the president sought to reserve for the Indians. During the early 1870s rumors circulated of gold in the Dakota Black Hills, the heart of the Sioux reservation. Grant received letters and petitions from westerners demanding that the region be opened to settlement. A group of Nebraskans wrote that the Black Hills held the key to the future of the West and perhaps the nation as a whole. "Being thoroughly of the opinion that the opening of the same to occupancy by all who may desire is but simple justice and would promote the general welfare of the country," the Nebraskans said, "we would therefore humbly pray your Excellency to inaugurate such steps as will at the earliest possible moment render the said Black Hills occupiable by the white people with safety."

Western papers and western congressmen echoed the cry, as did Phil Sheridan, the general responsible for the security of the West. Sheridan didn't trust Grant's peace policy; he believed that the struggle for the West would end only with the destruction of the Indians. Sheridan was famous in the West and notorious in other parts of the country for having said that the only good Indian was a dead Indian, and he judged that the sooner the final struggle began, the better. In May 1874 he wrote Sherman from his headquarters in Chicago, "I would like to start Colonel Custer with a column of cavalry out, about the 15th of June, to examine the Black Hills country. . . . This country is entirely unknown, and a knowledge of it might be of great value in case of Indian troubles." Sheridan understood that an expedition to the Black Hills might trigger the very troubles he warned of, but he considered this an argument in favor of sending Custer out.

Bishop William Hare, one of the clerics charged with implementing the peace policy, took the opposite view. Hare wrote Grant from Dakota to say that the frontier was teeming with news of an expedition and with adventurers aiming to be first to gather the Black Hills gold. "Such an expedition would, almost beyond a doubt, provoke an Indian war," Hare told Grant. He explained that the Black Hills were sacred to the Sioux, who would defend them to the death. "An invasion of the Black Hills means, I fear, or at least will surely result in, *War*, and war to the knife." Interior Secretary Columbus Delano agreed. "A general war with the Sioux would be deplorable," Delano wrote Grant. "It would undo the good already accomplished by our efforts for peaceable relations."

Grant held the line as long as he could. But amid the continuing debate over the nation's money supply, as the president defended the gold dollar against the expansionary demands of the greenbackers, refusing even to explore a promising mineral region became politically impossible. He authorized Sheridan to dispatch Custer to the Black Hills.

The expedition didn't start a war, at least not at once, but it did confirm the gold rumors, thereby intensifying the pressure on the peace policy. "We have had great difficulty in keeping white people from going to the Black Hills in search of gold," Grant explained to Red Cloud and Spotted Tail in the spring of 1875. He had summoned the Sioux chiefs to Washington to try to get them to relinquish title to the gold region. He professed continued friendship for the Indians and said he would not force them into anything. "I do not propose to ask you to leave the homes where you were born and raised, without your consent." But he said he couldn't hold back the gold seekers forever. "Every year this same difficulty will be increased unless the right of the white people to go to that country is granted by you; and it may in the end lead to hostilities between the Indians and the white people without any special fault on either side."

Red Cloud thought Grant should try harder. "I do not believe that the Great Father has not troops enough to keep white men away from the Black Hills," he said. Yet the Sioux leader was realistic enough to see that the whites were probably going to get what they wanted sooner or later, and he reluctantly entered into negotiations.

Other Sioux chiefs were more adamant. As the stream of miners into the Black Hills grew to a flood, Sitting Bull and Crazy Horse defied the reservation regime, gathering warriors and commencing an armed resistance.

In doing so they forced Grant's hand. He couldn't fail to defend whites under assault from Indians, even if he thought—and though he continued to say—that the whites had put themselves in danger by going where the government had forbidden. The Democrats who were assailing him on every front would surely allege dereliction if he didn't suppress the Sioux uprising. His generals were agitating to have it out with the militants. "We might just as well settle the Sioux matter now," Sheridan wrote Sherman. "It will be better for all concerned."

Grant accommodated his generals partway. Judging that a defeat of Sitting Bull and Crazy Horse would strengthen Red Cloud's hand among the Sioux and facilitate a peaceful transfer of the Black Hills, the president in the spring of 1876 directed Sherman and Sheridan to send the Seventh Cavalry into the Yellowstone Valley, the stronghold of the militants.

*Y*et he didn't want Custer to lead the expedition. "The President has just sent me instructions through the Secretary of War to send someone else than General Custer in command," Sherman telegraphed Sheridan. Grant thought Custer a reckless prima donna whose disdain for authority had been revealed on a recent visit to Washington when he hadn't deigned to report to his commanders. "Please intercept him at Chicago or St. Paul and order him to halt and await further orders," Sherman wired Sheridan on Grant's behalf. "Meantime let the expedition from Fort Lincoln proceed without him."

But Custer was a difficult man to stop. The theatrically handsome cavalry officer riveted the attention of the country; reporters followed him west, detailing his every nod, look and act of horsemanship for readers back home. Custer's admirers talked of him as a presidential candidate; for Grant to hold him out of battle would be interpreted as blatantly political. Grant grudgingly let him proceed, although he insisted that General Alfred Howe Terry have formal command of the expedition.

Two months later he wished he had stood his ground. "The recent reports touching the disaster which befell a part of the 7th Regular Cavalry led by General Custer in person are believed to be true," Sherman wrote Grant on July 8. "For some reason as yet unexplained, General Custer, who commanded the 7th Cavalry and had been detached by his commander General Terry at the mouth of the Rosebud to make a wide detour up the Rosebud, a tributary of the Yellowstone, across to the Little Big Horn, and down it to the mouth of the Big Horn, the place agreed on for meeting, attacked en route a large Indian village with only a part of his force, having himself detached the rest with a view to intercept the expected retreat of the savages, and experienced an utter annihilation of his immediate command."

Grant concluded that hubris had killed Custer and his men. "I regard

Custer's massacre as a sacrifice of troops, brought on by Custer himself, that was wholly unnecessary, wholly unnecessary," he told a reporter. "He was not to have made the attack before effecting the junction with Terry and Gibbon. He was notified to meet them on the 26th, but instead of marching slowly, as his orders required in order to effect the junction on the 26th, he entered upon a forced march of eighty-three miles in twenty-four hours, and thus had to meet the Indians alone on the 25th." The result was the death of 260 good men and an irreparable stain on the army.

Whatever the cause, the consequence of Custer's defeat was another blow to Grant's peace policy. Civil War veterans from North and South volunteered their services to crush the savages who had massacred Custer; young men who had never seen battle clamored to enlist. Grant was confident Terry had sufficient men to handle Sitting Bull and Crazy Horse, but as a political matter he concluded that he couldn't take any chances. Congress was about to recess for the summer; before he let the lawmakers go he requested authority to reinforce Terry. They readily approved.

Amid the gloom of that summer Grant pondered his escape from Washington. His pledge not to seek another term seemed now almost superfluous, as the scandals that swirled around the White House caused many Republicans to want to distance themselves from the administration. Benjamin Bristow turned the scandals to his own advantage by presenting himself to the party—and to the Republican convention, meeting in Cincinnati—as the sweeper of the Augean stables. James Blaine played the role of party regular, the candidate who would defend what the Republicans had accomplished during the previous decade and a half.

Rutherford Hayes blindsided them both. The Ohio governor had fought gallantly in the Shenandoah Valley during the war, suffering multiple wounds while having several horses shot from under him. His unpretentiously pristine record as governor appealed to those convention delegates who thought Blaine *too* regular to be elected over a reformist Democrat. Hayes fended off Bristow, whittled away Blaine's early lead and captured the nomination on the seventh ballot.

Grant praised the "excellent ticket," which included William Wheeler of New York for vice president, and told a visiting group of African American leaders that it "should receive the cordial support of all races in all sections." He continued: "I know Governor Hayes personally, and I can surrender with unfeigned pleasure my present position to him, as I believe I shall do on the 5th of March next year, with a guaranteed security for your rights and liberties under the laws of the land."

———

*E*lecting Hayes took more than Grant's endorsement. The candidate carried the baggage of sixteen years of Republican rule, a dozen years of Reconstruction, half a decade of Democratic experience suppressing the Republican vote in the South, three years of depression and many months of scandals. And he wasn't the hero of the Civil War.

Yet neither was his opponent. Samuel Tilden owed his reputation to his diligence and success in busting the Tweed Ring of Tammany Hall. New York voters demonstrated their appreciation by electing him governor, in which office he extended his anticorruption campaign to statewide boodling. He lacked a Civil War record and the common touch, but the Democrats guessed that the war was losing its grip on voters and that Tilden's standoffishness, not to mention his substantial private wealth, would augment the impression that he was above any possibility of corruption.

Grant hadn't campaigned for himself, and he didn't campaign for Hayes. But he made clear that he thought Hayes far preferable to Tilden. Hayes drew notice in his acceptance statement by promising not to seek a second term if elected. Editors eager for a story portrayed this as a slap at Grant. The president assured the governor he took no offense. "I am not aware of any feeling personal to myself," he wrote Hayes regarding the pledge. Speaking from his own experience as a lame duck, he added, "Whether it was wise to allude to the subject in a letter of acceptance is a question about which people might differ. But in this you have largely the advantage of your competitor"—Tilden had called for a constitutional amendment barring consecutive terms yet did not disavow anything for himself. "You say distinctly what course you will take, without condemning what the people have done on seven distinct occasions: reelect the incumbent." Grant reiterated his endorsement of Hayes as a candidate: "I hope, and fully believe, the result in November will designate you as my successor."

*G*rant's larger contribution to the Hayes campaign was yet another effort to protect Republican voters in the South. The violence that season centered in South Carolina and Mississippi. In July Grant got a letter from South Carolina governor Daniel Chamberlain deploring the killing at Hamburg of several black men enrolled in a local militia company. A crowd of whites had surrounded the black company and demanded that they relinquish their arms. "It seems impossible to find a rational or adequate cause for such a demand except in the fact that the militia company were composed of negroes or in the additional fact that they were, besides being negroes, members of the Republican party," Chamberlain told Grant. "Those who made the demand were, on the other hand, white men and members of the Democratic party." The governor continued: "The *effect* of this massacre is more important than the motives which caused it. Upon this point I can speak with more confidence. It is not to be doubted that the effect of this massacre has been to cause widespread terror and apprehension among the colored race and the Republicans of this state. . . . It has, as a matter of fact, caused a firm belief on the part of most Republicans that this affair at Hamburg is only the beginning of a series of similar race and party collisions in our state, the deliberate aim of which is believed to be the political subjugation and control of this state. They see, therefore, in this event what foreshadows a campaign of violence and blood—such a campaign as is popularly described as a campaign conducted on the 'Mississippi plan.'"

From Mississippi came reports of that plan's local application. "The lives of white and colored Republicans are taken here with impunity," William Simonton wrote the president from Shannon, Mississippi. Simonton introduced himself: "I am a southron by birth, education, etc. I have lived where I now live twenty-five years, and here I expect to be buried. I was the presidential elector of the 1st congressional district in this state in 1872. I have never been a Rebel voluntarily nor involuntarily." But he might be forced to become a de facto Democrat. "We can have a sort of peace and protection here by voting with the Democrats and accepting a moral and political serfdom. In a short time Republicans will be curiosities here, if this Democratic guerrilla warfare is permitted to go on."

Scores of similar letters reached Grant from other parts of South Carolina and Mississippi and elsewhere in the South. The gist of their message was that without another assertion of federal power the Republican party would become operationally extinct in the South. The rights of African Americans would expire with it.

Grant understood that any action he took would be interpreted politically. To employ the army in the South on the eve of the election would raise howls that he was corrupting the democratic process. So he responded at first with words. "The scene at Hamburg, as cruel, bloodthirsty, wanton, unprovoked, and uncalled for as it was, is only a repetition of the course that has been pursued in other southern states within the last few years," he wrote Governor Chamberlain for publication. "Mississippi is governed today by officials chosen through fraud and violence such as would scarcely be credited to savages, much less to a civilized and Christian people." Southern Democrats charged that their states were being treated differently from the rest of the country; Grant denied the charge categorically. "Nothing is claimed for one state that is not freely accorded to all the others." The South, in fact, was the region demanding special dispensation, he said. "The right to kill negroes and Republicans without fear of punishment and without loss of caste or reputation—this has seemed to be a privilege claimed by a few states." Grant urged Chamberlain to perform his duties conscientiously and other Southerners to exercise their rights. "I will give every aid for which I can find law or constitutional power. Government that cannot give protection to the life, property, and all guaranteed civil rights (in this country the greatest is an untrammeled ballot) to the citizen is, in so far, a failure, and every energy of the oppressed should be exerted (always within the law and by constitutional means) to regain lost privileges or protection. Too long denial of guaranteed rights is sure to lead to revolution, bloody revolution."

Words, however, counted for little at this point, and in South Carolina especially the violence escalated into the autumn. Hundreds of members of "rifle clubs" brandished and employed their weapons against Republicans. "Our people are being shot down like dogs," a correspondent from Aiken wrote Grant in late September. "The Democratic whites are going about bushwhacking the people of color for our political opinion and throwing their threats around saying that they will kill the last one of us before the day of the election." A Republican who feared to sign his name wrote from Charleston: "Guns and pistols are continually heard throughout the upper wards. I have reason to believe that myself and at least 50 Republicans are marked for the dagger or to be mobbed. . . . I consider every man's life in danger who does not belong to the Democratic party."

Governor Chamberlain appealed officially for help. "Insurrection and domestic violence exist in various portions of this state," he wrote Grant on October 11. "I am unable with any means at my command to suppress the same."

Grant decided to brave the political storm and escalate from words to force. He published a proclamation ordering the rifle clubs and other fomenters of violence to disperse. The insurgents had three days to go home. He simultaneously directed William Sherman to gather all available troops of the Atlantic region and dispatch them to South Carolina at once.

THE TROOPS QUELLED THE VIOLENCE AND ALLOWED AN ELECTION IN South Carolina that was almost orderly. The Republicans felt sufficiently secure to deliver a slim majority to Hayes. Such, at any rate, was what the Republicans asserted. The Democrats alleged a miscount. They also alleged miscounts in the two other Southern states still controlled by Republicans, Florida and Louisiana, where the Hayes side similarly claimed majorities. The counting became crucial when the country as a whole returned a popular victory for Tilden and the tally of electors from the uncontested states tipped narrowly in Tilden's favor. If Tilden could overturn the result in any of the three contested states, he would become Grant's successor; Hayes needed all three to win the White House.

Grant sought to ensure a fair review of the ballots. Following reports of potential intimidation of review boards in Florida and Louisiana, he ordered Sherman to strengthen the army's presence there. "See that the proper and legal boards of canvassers are unmolested in the performance of their duties," he said. "Should there be any grounds of suspicion of fraudulent counting on either side, it should be reported and denounced at once. No man worthy of the office of President would be willing to hold it if 'counted in' or placed there by any fraud. Either party can afford to be disappointed in the result, but the country cannot afford to have the result tainted by the suspicion of illegal or false returns." The next day he decided to send Phil Sheridan back to New Orleans. "There is such apprehension of violence in New Orleans during the canvassing of the vote of the state that I think you should go in person," the president told Sheridan. He nonetheless warned against any overt intrusion into politics like that which Sheridan had directed on his last visit to the city. "The military have nothing to do with the counting of the vote. Its province is to keep the peace and to protect the legal canvassing board in the performance of its duties."

Grant's move evoked the kinds of passionate responses he had come to expect. An Indiana Democrat and Union veteran vowed that all the loyal men of his state would support Grant as they had supported Lincoln. "All they ask in this the second crisis of our country is, should it turn out that Governor Tilden has been legally elected President of the United States that he gets his seat as such. But on the other hand, should it be that Governor Hayes is the man, we will stand by you until *Hell freezes over.*" A pension agent from New Jersey applauded Grant's bold stroke against election fraud. "We have a government and mean to defend it. We are not Mexico nor South America, but Anglo Saxon Yankees, and (God willing) we don't mean the republic to perish yet awhile." Southerners and Democrats sent threats of new violence, some directed against Grant personally. John Mosby, the former Confederate cavalryman, crossed over from Virginia to warn the president against assassination plots. Mosby's sources were talking of a new insurrection and saying: "The President must be the first man to be gotten out of the way." A letter signed "Baltimore Secret Government" put a date on Grant's demise: "The course you have pursued does not meet the approbation of our members, and you are hereby ordered to resign the office of President by the 1st of January or you will be assassinated."

*A*mid the recounting and the threats, Grant reflected on his time in office. His eighth annual message took a different tone from the previous versions, admitting failures as often as claiming success. His Indian policy, he said, had ended armed conflict in most of the West but not in the region around the Black Hills. "Hostilities there have grown out of the avarice of the white man, who has violated our treaty stipulations in his search for gold. The question might be asked why the government has not enforced obedience to the terms of the treaty prohibiting the occupation of the Black Hills region by whites. The answer is simple: The first immigrants to the Black Hills were removed by troops, but rumors of rich discoveries of gold took into that region increased numbers. Gold has actually been found in paying quantity, and an effort to remove the miners would only result in the desertion of the bulk of the troops that might be sent there to remove them." The government had been forced to defend the miners, with results visible in Custer's defeat and the continuing effort to find and capture Crazy Horse and his warriors.

The Santo Domingo question still rankled Grant, and his perception of a lost opportunity elicited his regret. He pondered what annexation might have meant for American politics and civil rights. "The emancipated race of the South would have found there a congenial home, where their civil rights would not be disputed and where their labor would be so much sought after that the poorest among them could have found the means to go. Thus in cases of great oppression and cruelty, such as has been practiced upon them in many places within the last eleven years, whole communities would have sought refuge in Santo Domingo. I do not suppose the whole race would have gone, nor is it desirable that they should go. Their labor is desirable—indispensable almost—where they now are. But the possession of this territory would have left the negro 'master of the situation,' by enabling him to demand his rights at home on pain of finding them elsewhere." He added, at once wistfully and defensively, "I do not present these views now as a recommendation for a renewal of the subject of annexation, but I do refer to it to vindicate my previous action in regard to it."

Some of his failures, he owned, came from inexperience. "It was my fortune, or misfortune, to be called to the office of Chief Executive without any previous political training. From the age of seventeen I had never even witnessed the excitement attending a Presidential campaign but twice antecedent to my own candidacy, and at but one of them was I eligible as a voter. Under such circumstances it is but reasonable to suppose that errors of judgment must have occurred." He grew more specific in acknowledging and trying to explain the scandals of his administration. "Mistakes have been made, as all can see and I admit, but it seems to me oftener in the selections made of the assistants appointed to aid in carrying out the various duties of administering the Government—in nearly every case selected without a personal acquaintance with the appointee, but upon recommendations of the representatives chosen directly by the people. It is impossible, where so many trusts are to be allotted, that the right parties should be chosen in every instance. History shows that no Administration from the time of Washington to the present has been free from these mistakes." Yet he didn't absolve himself. "I leave comparisons to history, claiming only that I have acted in every instance from a conscientious desire to do what was right, constitutional, within the law, and for the very best interests of the whole people. Failures have been errors of judgment, not of intent."

And they had been the result of the tremendous challenges the country faced at the time of his inauguration. "Less than four years before, the country had emerged from a conflict such as no other nation had ever survived," Grant said. "Nearly one-half of the states had revolted against the government." The conflict had ended with the assassination of President Lincoln, who had carried the country through the war and hoped to lead it into peace. "The intervening time to my first inauguration was filled up with wranglings between Congress and the new executive as to the best mode of reconstruction, or, to speak plainly, as to whether the control of the government should be thrown immediately into the hands of those who had so recently and persistently tried to destroy it, or whether the victors should continue to have an equal voice with them in this control." This was the essence of Reconstruction: Should the South abide by the statutes and constitutional provisions that bound the rest of the country or should it be allowed to ignore the ones it disliked?

He had tried to apply a single rule of law to the whole country. He had succeeded in some instances, failed in others. Soon another man would take up the task. "With the present term of Congress my official life terminates. It is not probable that public affairs will ever again receive attention from me further than as a citizen of the republic, always taking a deep interest in the honor, integrity, and prosperity of the whole land."

The return of Phil Sheridan inspired Louisiana Republicans to hope for a further extension of their time in power. Members of Congress had descended on Louisiana to observe the recounting for president there; even as they did so, Governor Kellogg wrote Grant warning that the contest to determine the next governor and state legislature was getting ugly. If the Democrats who were claiming victory were inaugurated, violence might ensue, he said, whereas the installation of the Republicans would preserve the peace. But the Republicans couldn't be installed without federal troops.

Grant read Kellogg's request with mounting exasperation. It was "again the Louisiana trouble," he told Hamilton Fish. "They are always in trouble there and always wanting the United States to send troops. They want me to inaugurate their governor and legislature." The president told Kellogg that the Louisianans must look to themselves; he would send no troops to break the deadlock in the politics of the state. "To do so would be to recognize one of two rival governments for the state executive and legislative at the very time when a committee of each house of Congress is in the state capital of Louisiana investigating all the facts connected with the late election." The president allowed that if violence did indeed break out and a request for assistance came from a duly inaugurated governor, he would reconsider. Until then he would "leave constitutional authority and means to settle which is the rightful governor and which the legal legislature."

A request of another sort came from Congress. The Democrats who controlled the House wanted to see the orders the president and his subordinates had issued to the military commanders in the Southern states before and during the elections. Grant complied by sending hundreds of pages of orders and supporting documents, along with a statement describing what he had done and why. "These different kinds and sources of evidence have left no doubt whatever in my mind that intimidation has been used, and actual violence, to an extent requiring the aid of the United States government, where it was practicable to furnish such aid, in South Carolina, in Florida, and in Louisiana, as well as in Mississippi, in Alabama, and in Georgia," the president said. He explained what the soldiers had done and what they had not done. "The troops of the United States have been but sparingly used, and in no case so as to interfere with the free exercise of the right of suffrage. . . . No troops were stationed at voting places. In Florida and in Louisiana, respectively, the small number of soldiers already in the said states were stationed at such points in each state as were most threatened with violence, where they might be available as a posse for the officer whose duty it was to preserve the peace and prevent intimidation of voters." Grant pointed out that the small size of the postwar army and the other demands on the troops, especially in the West, had limited the force he could bring to bear. He volunteered that if he had had more troops he would have sent them south; their lack had contributed to the effective nullification of the Fifteenth Amendment in several states. As it was, his use of the army had been politically circumspect and entirely legal. "I have not employed troops on slight occasions nor in any case where it has not been necessary to the enforcement of the laws of the United States."

In January 1877 the two parties in Congress crafted a bill creating a special commission to oversee the counting of the electoral votes and thereby determine the next president. The commission consisted of five Republican members of Congress, five Democrats and five Supreme Court justices. Grant gave the measure his seal of approval. "The bill may not be perfect, and its provisions may not be such as would be best applicable to all future occasions, but it is calculated to meet the present condition of the question and of the country," he said. "The country is agitated. It needs and it desires peace and quiet and harmony between all parties and all sections. . . . It wants to be assured that the result of the election will be accepted without resistance from the supporters of the disappointed candidate, and that its highest officer shall not hold his place with a questioned title of right."

The peace and quiet Grant called for didn't emerge at once. In fact, as inauguration day approached, tensions mounted. Zealots on the Democratic side muttered about a coup against the government in the event Tilden was denied the presidency. "In my daily intercourse with men, which brings me largely with the rank and file," a correspondent wrote Grant from Brooklyn, "I hear threats of an uprising in the great cities of New York and Brooklyn. I not only hear it in New York state but in New Jersey, and it is not confined to the lower classes alone but to the influential and men in good social standing." A writer from New Jersey declared, "There is 200,000 men in Jersey who are ready to sustain Tilden in his claim to the presidency of the United States."

Grant doubted the authenticity of the threats but didn't want to be unprepared. He directed William Sherman to write to Phil Sheridan, who had returned from Louisiana to his headquarters in Chicago. "Wherever you can, collect your troops into as large garrisons as possible, convenient for moving," Sherman told Sheridan. The president wished to have troops ready to bring to Washington. "He might want as many as 4000 men here, and that is impossible without drawing from you."

While the electoral commission labored, Grant weighed the meaning of the alternative outcomes. "While he most earnestly desired the declaration of Governor Hayes as president," Hamilton Fish recorded of a conversation with Grant, "he thought that should he come into power with his administration embarrassed with the question of the votes of two or three states he would be much crippled in power. On the other hand, if Tilden were elected he would be unable to satisfy the expectations of the South, and with the commitment of his party against the use of the military for any purpose of the government, he would be unable to collect the internal revenue in the South. . . . He thinks that Tilden will be unable to reduce the debt, probably not to pay the running expenses of the government without an increase of taxation, and that four years of his administration will satisfy the country with the Democrats and make a better chance for the Republicans coming into power." But more than anything Grant wanted the issue resolved without resort to force. "He expressed the greatest anxiety for a peaceful solution of the question."

As the time ran down, Grant came to believe Hayes would win. "Three weeks remain until I close my official career," Grant wrote Edwards Pierrepont in February. "Although so short a time, it appears to me interminable, my anxiety to be free from care is so great. As yet the question of who is to succeed me is not definitely settled, but the chances seem to be much in favor of the Republican candidate. But he must gain every point to succeed, while his opponent requires but one." He no longer feared violence but he didn't rule out obstruction. "I believe quiet will be preserved in any event, though it seems possible now that the Democrats in the House may prevent any count unless they get their candidate declared elected."

The Democrats did obstruct for a while. The electoral commission, on which three Republican justices tipped the overall balance in favor of the Republicans, decided in a series of eight-to-seven votes that Hayes had won the disputed states. By the commission's count Hayes carried the electoral college and the election 185 to 184. Congress still had to consider the commission's verdict, and though the Republican Senate endorsed it at once, the Democratic House delayed, hoping for something in exchange. Sources close to Hayes suggested that the governor would terminate Grant's policy of using federal troops to safeguard elections in the South and otherwise enforce federal law there, and Hayes didn't deny the suggestions. This tacit bargain broke the embargo and let Hayes have the presidency.

THE COMPROMISE OF 1877, AS THE DEAL WAS CALLED, RANG DOWN the curtain on Grant's public service and on the extended crisis of American democracy. Almost since his graduation from West Point in 1843, the fate of the Union had hung in the balance. The North and the South had battled over the annexation of Texas, which gave rise to the war with Mexico, which spawned the Compromise of 1850, which polarized American politics and led to guerrilla war in Kansas, mayhem in the Senate and an attempt to start a slave rebellion in western Virginia. The 1860 election of Lincoln provoked the South to secede; secession triggered the bloodiest war in American history. After six hundred thousand deaths and the destruction of wide swaths of the South, the overt phase of the fighting ended at Appomattox, but the Union remained at risk until the terms of re-union were agreed upon. The South continued to resist federal authority, with the Ku Klux Klan and other paramilitary groups being the most visible agents of the resistance. Not until troops of the Union army had again taken the field in the South was the resistance finally suppressed.

Ulysses Grant turned fifty-five the month after he and Julia relinquished the White House to Rutherford and Lucy Hayes. He could reflect that his adult life had coincided with the Union's long crisis, and though he was not a boastful man, he took pride in his role—first as general, then as president—in bringing the Union through its crisis intact. He would have been the first to admit that the task of reconstruction was incomplete. He could scatter the Klan but he couldn't change the minds of all those who tolerated political terror. He could defend Southern blacks but he couldn't know that they would remain safe after he left office.

Yet the great public question of his lifetime had been answered. The Union was secure. Secession was a dead letter, mentioned only in the past tense. Slavery, the root of the sectional crisis, was a memory. American democracy required continual work, but the Union, democracy's receptacle, would hold.

"*After* an unusually stormy passage for any season of the year, and continuous seasickness generally among the passengers after the second day out, we reached Liverpool," Grant wrote in June 1877. "Jesse and I proved to be among the few good sailors. Neither of us felt a moment of quamishness during the voyage."

What he felt instead was relief. During his last months in office, amid the fight over the Hayes-Tilden election, the continuing demands by Southern Republicans for troops and the incessant assaults by Democrats, he had maintained his composure and sustained his spirits by thoughts of a foreign journey that would carry him far from the roils of American politics. He had lived longer in the White House than he had lived anywhere since childhood, and although a home base could be reassuring, it could also be confining. He remembered the freedom of the military campaign, the joy of life in tent and on horseback; and while he couldn't reproduce his wartime existence, he could recapitulate something of its peripatetic nature. "I have no plans laid either as to where we will go or how long remain absent," he said of his journey. "We will not return, however, until the party"—himself, Julia and Jesse— "becomes homesick, which may be in six months and may not be for two years." The trip would be funded by a rare—for Grant—good investment: mining stocks of Nevada's Comstock Lode, which were producing handsome dividends. And it would keep him clear of American politics, which weren't likely to get any kinder or less complicated.

From Washington he and Julia had traveled to New York to stay with Hamilton Fish and his wife. Grant dodged questions about Hayes's first appointments and early performance; he denied reports that he was writing a book about his life and career. "There are books enough already," he told a reporter. "Anybody can write a book. I could myself, for that matter, perhaps. But I assure you I haven't had the least thought about such a thing." On departing the Fish home he thanked his host for the hospitality but mostly for the service he had provided during eight years as secretary of state. Vexing questions that might have led to war had confronted the country, he said. "Through your statesmanship more than through any individual, these questions have been peaceably settled and in a manner highly creditable to the nation and without wounding the sensibilities of other nations." Grant appreciated no less the secretary's personal friendship and loyalty. "Our relations have at all times been so pleasant that I shall carry the remembrance of them through life."

Fish joined William Sherman and other notables in bidding Grant bon voyage at the Philadelphia waterfront. Grant was praised and thanked for his service in war and peace. He was visibly moved. "I feel overcome at the sentiments to which I have listened, and to which I feel altogether inadequate to respond," he said. "I don't think that the compliments ought all be paid to me or any one man in either of the positions which I was called upon to fill. That which I accomplished—which I was able to accomplish—I owe to the assistance of able lieutenants. . . . I believe some of these lieutenants could have filled my place, maybe better than I did." From the large crowd came shouts of "No!" Grant turned to Sherman. "I believe that my friend Sherman could have taken my place as a soldier." Cheers from the crowd for Sherman and Grant both. "And I believe, finally, that if our country ever comes into trial again, young men will spring up equal to the occasion, and if one fails, there will be another to take his place." Tremendous cheers and much waving of handkerchiefs.

$\mathcal{H}$e thought the departure from America would liberate him from making speeches, which had grown easier over time yet never comfortable. But he discovered that his words were in greater demand in Europe than they had been at home. His very person was in greater demand. "What was my surprise to find nearly all shipping in port decorated to the last flag," he wrote of his landing at Liverpool. "And from the mainmast of each ship the flag of the Union was most conspicuous. The docks were lined with as many of the population as could find standing room, and the streets to the hotel where it was understood my party would stop were packed." Liverpool hosted a lavish lunch for the American hero; the mayors of other English cities insisted he write them into his schedule. A special train with the finest Pullman cars was placed at his disposal.

It carried him first to London, where a round of receptions and dinners dizzied him and delighted Julia. They were guests of the current duke of Wellington, the heir of the Iron Duke of Waterloo. William Gladstone, the former (and future) prime minister, paid call at a soiree hosted by the American minister (and former attorney general), Edwards Pierrepont. "I doubt whether London has ever seen a private house so elaborately or so tastefully decorated," Grant said of the minister's residence. Grant thanked the hosts and guests and briefly asserted the necessity and virtue of Anglo-American friendship.

The Grants met Queen Victoria and Prince Albert at Windsor Castle. British royals had never encountered a former president—no former president had ever taken such a tour—and no one knew the protocol. Pierrepont suggested as model a previous visit by Louis Napoleon, the erstwhile emperor of France. Louis, like Grant, had been elected. The keeper of the queen's dignity was skeptical. "Once an emperor, always an emperor," he said. Pierrepont rejoined, "Once a president, always a president." The protocol chief pondered, then yielded. Grant was introduced as "President Grant."

The cheering rarely stopped. "He has been the recipient here of popular ovations like those which you witnessed at the close of the war," Adam Badeau, now consul in London, wrote Elihu Washburne, who had survived his illness to become American minister in Paris. "In Liverpool and Manchester the demonstrations were most enthusiastic and en route to London the train was stopped again for mayors to present addresses etc. When he enters a theater the play stops, and the people rise and cheer. Here in London he takes precedence in society of ambassadors and dukes; the ministers all called on him first, and the Prince of Wales came into his box at the Oaks to make his acquaintance."

Grant himself was struck by the magnitude and what he took to be the meaning of the enthusiasm. "My reception has been remarkable in two respects," he wrote Hamilton Fish. "First, by invitations from all authorities connected with the government from the Queen down to the mayors and city councils of almost every city in the United Kingdom; and second, by the hearty responses of the citizens of all the cities I have visited, or at which trains upon which I have been traveling have stopped even for a few minutes. It has been very much as it was in the United States in '65, directly after the war. I take this as indicative of a present very good feeling towards the United States." In some cases the good feeling seemed to cloak a guilty conscience. "Many persons say to me quietly that they personally were our good friends in the day of our country's trial, but they witness now many who were the reverse then that outdo their neighbors in respect and kindness of feeling for us now."

At every event Grant was called upon to speak. He tried to hide behind his reputation as the American sphinx, the man of deeds rather than words. His success varied. "Yesterday and the day before I received no less than six addresses from corporations, merchant exchange, working men etc., to all of which I had to reply, without the slightest idea beforehand what I was to hear or what I should say," he wrote his son Buck. "It being very well understood that I am no speaker makes the task much easier than it otherwise would be, but even as it is I would rather be kicked—in a friendly way—than to make these replies."

He mixed philosophy with politics in his remarks, which were always heartfelt. "My reception has been far beyond anything that I could have expected to have been accorded to me," he told a throng in Liverpool. "A soldier must die, and when a president's term of office expires he is but a dead soldier. But I have received an attention and a reception that would have done honor to any living person." Acknowledging the cooperative spirit that had informed the Treaty of Washington, he declared that Americans and Britons shared a great deal. "We are of one kindred, one blood, one language, and one civilization." Americans were the younger people, Britons the older and more experienced, but each could learn from the other.

A league of workingmen saluted him for the victory he had won for free labor. "There is no reception that I have met which I am prouder of than this one," he responded. "Whatever there is of greatness in the United States, or indeed in any other country, is due to the labor performed, and to the laborer who is the author of all greatness and wealth." He diverged from Republican party orthodoxy in embracing the free-trade principles of his hosts. "There is one subject that has been referred to here that I don't know that I should refer to," he told a Birmingham audience, "and that is the great advantage that would accrue to the United States if free trade could only be established." He remarked that the British had protected their manufactures in the early stages of the industrialization process but had dropped the protection when their industries matured. The United States had come later to industrialization than Britain but had now reached the stage where if it similarly dropped protection it would emerge as "one of the greatest free trading nations on the face of the earth." What this would mean for Anglo-American trade

competition Grant didn't say; he contented himself with a joint prediction: "When we both get to be free traders I think it is probable all other
nations had better stand aside and not contend with us at all."

*H*is party crossed the English Channel. A tour of the European
continent had the singular merit of releasing him from the obligation
to speak. He and the crowds that greeted him didn't share a language;
they were content for him to nod his thanks at their coming out. Julia
liked Paris more than he did. "We have now been in Paris for nearly
four weeks," he wrote Adolph Borie in November. "Mrs. Grant is quite
well acquainted with the places we hear most of: Worth's, Bon Marché,
Louvre"—three fashionable clothing stores. "It is a beautiful city, but
I am quite ready to leave." Autumn rains dampened the travel but not
Grant's outlook. "The weather in Paris was most atrocious," he declared
after the party had moved on. "But I got to see most of the people. My
opinion of their capacity for self-government has materially changed
since seeing for myself. Before coming here I did not believe the French
people capable of self-government. Now I believe them perfectly capable,
and they will be satisfied with nothing less."

They headed south and east across Italy and the Mediterranean to
the Middle East. The khedive of Egypt put them up in a palace in Alexandria. Grant was appreciative but not impressed. "All the romance given
to Oriental splendor in novels and guide books is dissipated by witnessing
the real thing," he wrote Buck. "Innate ugliness, slovenliness, filth and
indolence witnessed here is only equaled, in my experience, by seeing the
lowest class of Digger Indians found on the Pacific Coast." Yet Egypt's
history, in contrast to its present, was most alluring. "I have seen more
in Egypt to interest me than in all my other travels," he wrote Fred from
a steamer in the Nile above Thebes. The temples along the river were
magnificent, built by an unusual but remarkable society. "The ancient
Egyptian was a cultivated man, but governed soul and body by a ruler.
Without a thorough command of all the strength, muscle and mind of
the inhabitants such structures could never have been built. Without talent, learning and training the inscriptions could not have been made.
And without mechanical teaching the large blocks of granite and sand-
stone could never have been taken from the quarries to their present resting place nor dressed as they are."

Winter beat them to the Holy Land. "Our visit to Jerusalem was a very unpleasant one," he wrote Adam Badeau. "The roads are bad and it rained, blew and snowed all the time. We left snow six inches deep in Jerusalem." They reached Constantinople at a bad time for the Ottomans, who were at war with the Russians. "The Russian army was but eight miles outside and the road entirely open from the city to the Russian camp." Grant wanted to observe the czar's military. "But having received the hospitalities of the Turkish officials, I doubted the propriety of such a visit and therefore abstained." The Turkish sultan showed him the royal stables; Grant admired the purebred Arabians. The sultan made him a gift of one. "These horses, I am told, have their pedigrees kept for one or two hundred years back, and are of the purest blood," Grant wrote a friend. "It may be of some value to breeders in the United States to get some of this blood." He arranged for his new horse to be transported to America ahead of his own return.

The Greeks were on the right track. "They seem to me to be a very energetic and advancing people," he wrote from Athens. The Greek capital was a showplace of energy and good government. "The houses are substantial and present a fine architectural appearance; the people, high and low, are well and comfortably clad and everything indicates prosperity. I am inclined to think that if they could regain their former territory, or a good part of it, with the addition of the Greek population this would give them they would become a very respectable nation."

But they would be working against the grain of the region. "My impression of peoples are that in the East they have a form of government and a civilization that will always repress progress and development. Syria and Asia Minor are as rich of soil as the great northwest in our own country, and are blessed with a climate far more suitable to production. The people would be industrious if they had encouragement, but they are treated as slaves, and all they produce is taken from them for the benefit of the governing classes and to maintain them in a luxurious and licentious life. Women are degraded even beneath a slave. They have no more rights than a brute. In fact, the donkey is their superior in privileges."

Looping back west and then north, the travelers toured Italy before crossing the Alps to Germany. The *New York Herald* had sent John Russell Young to report on Grant's journey; he accompanied Grant to a Berlin interview with Otto von Bismarck at the chancellor's residence. "The General saunters in a kind of nonchalant way into the courtyard," Young related. "The sentinels eye him for just an instant, perhaps curiously, and then quickly present arms. Somehow or other these grim soldiers recognize at once, as the salute is returned, that it comes from a man who is himself a soldier. His visit had been expected, it is true, but it was supposed that an Ex-President of the United States would have come thundering in a coach and six accompanied by outriders, and not quietly on foot. The General throws away a half-smoked cigar, then brings up his hand to his hat, acknowledging the military courtesy, and advances in the most quiet way to the door."

Bismarck met him at the head of a marble hall. He extended his hand. "Glad to welcome General Grant to Germany," he said in slow but precise English. Grant answered that he had looked forward to this meeting. Bismarck expressed surprise that Grant seemed so young, but comparing ages they discovered that only eleven years separated them. "That shows the value of a military life," Bismarck said. "You have the frame of a young man, while I feel like an old one."

They took seats in the library of the chancellor's palace. Bismarck inquired about General Sheridan, whom he had encountered when Sheridan traveled to Europe to observe the Franco-Prussian War. "Sheridan seemed to be a man of great ability," Bismarck observed. Grant nodded. "Yes," he said, "I regard Sheridan as not only one of the great soldiers of our war, but one of the great soldiers of the world—as a man who is fit for the highest commands. No better general ever lived than Sheridan."

Bismarck apologized for the absence of Emperor Wilhelm, who was nursing wounds from an attempted assassination just weeks earlier. Grant conveyed his good wishes for the emperor's recovery. Wilhelm thanked him and said, "It is so strange, so strange and so sad. Here is an old man, one of the kindest old gentlemen in the world, and yet they must try and shoot him! . . . I should have supposed that the Emperor could have walked alone all over the empire without harm, and yet they must try and shoot him."

Grant agreed that it was a terrible turn of events. The same thing had happened to Lincoln, he said. A man of the kindest and gentlest nature had been killed by a vengeful assassin.

Bismarck said the emperor had spoken of taking Grant to see the Prussian army; his wounds prevented his doing so. The crown prince would stand in. Grant accepted the invitation but with a modest smile said that his military days were over. And he hoped his country's military days were over, too.

"You are so happily placed in America that you need fear no wars," Bismarck replied. "What always seemed so sad to me about your last great war was that you were fighting your own people. That is always so terrible in wars, so very hard."

"But it had to be done," Grant said.

"Yes, you had to save the Union just as we had to save Germany."

"Not only save the Union but destroy slavery."

"I suppose, however, the Union was the real sentiment, the dominant sentiment."

"In the beginning, yes. But as soon as slavery fired upon the flag it was felt, we all felt, even those who did not object to slaves, that slavery must be destroyed. We felt that it was a stain to the Union that men should be bought and sold like cattle."

"I suppose if you had had a large army at the beginning of the war it would have ended in a much shorter time."

"We might have had no war at all. But we cannot tell. Our war had many strange features; there were many things which seemed odd enough at the time but which now seem providential. If we had had a large regular army, as it was then constituted, it might have gone with the South. In fact, the Southern feeling in the army among high officers was so strong that when the war broke out the army dissolved. We had no army; then we had to organize one. A great commander like Sherman or Sheridan even then might have organized and put down the rebellion in six months or a year, or at the farthest two years. But that would have saved slavery, perhaps, and slavery meant the germs of a new rebellion. There had to be an end to slavery."

"It was a long war, and a great work well done. I suppose it means a long peace."

"I believe so."

Grant had left America in part to give Hayes the opportunity to establish his own presidency. "I propose to stay away till after the exciting scenes that will surround the test of Mr. Hayes's policy, for the reason that if I were at home I would be charged with having a hand in every kind of political maneuvering," he told William Copeland, a colleague of

John Young's at the *New York Herald*. But he couldn't avoid all comment on American affairs, even from a distance. The death of John Motley, a protégé of Charles Sumner's, revived talk of the dispute between Grant and Sumner, with certain of Sumner's surviving friends suggesting that Grant's removal of Motley from the post of minister to Britain somehow contributed to his death these several years later. Copeland invited Grant to defend himself. He did so, saying more about Sumner than he had said while in office or perhaps than he now intended. The *Herald* of course printed Grant's remarks, prompting the Sumnerites in America to recount their champion's side of the old story in greater detail than ever. The transatlantic rehashing did little credit to Grant, Sumner or anyone else, but it did sell papers, which had been the *Herald*'s point all along.

Other Grant comments bore on contemporary topics. The summer of 1877 saw the greatest labor strike in American history when rail workers responded to wage cuts by walking off the job and paralyzing transport from coast to coast. Violence followed the walkout, with workers battling private security forces and freelance arsonists piling in. Grant supported Hayes's decision to use federal troops to suppress the violence. "The United States should always be prepared to put down such demonstrations promptly and with severe consequences to the guilty," he wrote a friend. But he thought it ironic that many of the American papers that now praised the use of force to protect the property of the railroads had been quick to condemn his earlier use of force to protect the rights of Southern blacks and Republicans. "It does seem the rule should work both ways," he said.

Months later Congress passed a bill to expand the currency by minting new silver coins. Hayes vetoed the bill but Congress overrode, and the Bland-Allison Act became law. Grant thoroughly disapproved. "The country, and the country's credit, has not received so severe a blow since the attempt of the Southern states to secede," he wrote William Sherman. "We stand more or less disgraced." To banker Anthony Drexel he said of the law: "It shows a willingness on the part of a majority to repudiate a percentage of their indebtedness, and people who will do that are capable of repudiating the whole. The man who would steal a lamb would not be safe to trust with a sheep."

At times he felt gloomy about the direction of American politics. The Democrats were gaining, and as they did they corroded the meaning of the Union victory in the war. "It looks to me that unless the North rallies by 1880 the government will be in the hands of those who tried so hard fourteen—seventeen—years ago to destroy it," he wrote his sister's husband. Grant suspected that when he eventually returned to America he would be called upon by his old supporters to rescue the republic, and the Republicans, once more. "They have designs for me which I do not contemplate for myself," he told Adam Badeau.

He found himself refighting the war in other ways. Badeau was completing what would be published as the *Military History of Ulysses S. Grant*; he regularly wrote Grant for his recollections of this battle or that campaign. Sherman had published his own memoir, and his descriptions of some of his superiors provoked spirited rejoinders. Grant was informed he was among those Sherman criticized. "I cannot tell you how much I was shocked," he told a reporter. "I could not believe it in Sherman, the man whom I had always found so true and knightly, more anxious to honor others than win honor for himself." He sent for a copy of the book and prepared to write a rebuttal. "I do not think I ever ventured upon a more painful duty." But as he read, his mind was put at ease. "When I finished the book I found that I approved every word—that it was a true book, an honorable book—creditable to Sherman, just to his companions, to myself particularly so—just such a book as I expected Sherman to write. . . . You cannot imagine how pleased I was. . . . Sherman is not only a great soldier but a great man. He is one of the very great men in our country's history. . . . As a writer he is among the first. As a general I know of no man I would put above him. . . . There is not a false line in Sherman's character."

Sherman's memoir aside, Grant thought the South was getting the better of the war writing. "Everything that our armies did was wrong, could have been done so much better," he paraphrased the commentary on the war. "Everything that our opponents did was perfect. Lee was a demigod, Jackson was a demigod, while our generals were brutal butchers. . . . The Southern generals were models of chivalry and valor; our generals were venal, incompetent, coarse. . . . If we won a battle like Shiloh, for instance—one of the most useful victories of the war, one of the most important in its results—our own papers set to work to belittle the victory and give the enemy as much advantage as possible." Accounts of other battles were similar. "I do not recite these things to complain especially," Grant said. "I have nothing to complain about. . . . Having conquered, it is not for us to say anything unkind or in disparagement of our enemies. That is not my purpose. I merely mention these points in a general way, as points which our historians overlook."

He was happy not to be at home. More than happy, in fact: "It is bliss to be out of the United States just at a time when every bad element in the country are seemingly carrying every thing before them," he wrote Elihu Washburne. But the ill wind couldn't blow forever. "It is to be hoped, and I think confidently to be relied upon, that all the isms will have run their course before '80."

*H*e might stay away till then. By the autumn of 1878 he and Julia had completed their tour of Europe and the Mediterranean. "We have seen the capitals and most of the principal towns, and the people, of every country," he observed. "I have not yet seen any to be jealous of. The fact is we are the most progressive, freest, and richest people on earth but don't know it or appreciate it. Foreigners see this much plainer than we do."

The travelers headed east again, embarking from Marseilles in January 1879. "Anchored outside the harbor of Alexandria last night," Grant wrote at the end of the month in a journal he had just started keeping. They proceeded toward the Suez Canal. "Weather charming, fields green and flourishing. Party much pleased with the picturesque dress and manners of the people." A sunken ship delayed their passage of the canal, but eventually they made the Red Sea. "Heat increasing. . . . Light clothing coming into requisition." They reached Aden at the end of the first week of February. "All the land seems to be of volcanic origin and entirely barren. The natives are of a low order of savages; hair dyed—or colored from some process—red, curled into small corkscrew tufts. It is fortunate that enlightened nations"—Britain in this case—"take possession of such people and make them, and their soil, produce something for the advancement of civilization of the human race."

A smooth steam across the Arabian Sea carried them to Bombay, a cosmopolitan marvel. "Description could not convey an accurate idea of either the city or the people," Grant wrote. "Every nationality of the East is represented here." After a few days they traveled to Agra to see the Taj Mahal. "The splendor of this monument surpasses all the descriptions given of it." At Delhi Grant toured the site of the 1857 siege of British colonial rulers by Hindu nationalists. "It was fully explained by an intelligent officer, Colonel Harris, who was present at the siege and badly wounded." Beyond the city, on the North Indian plain, he observed the Indian method of irrigated farming. One man drew water from a well and poured it into a narrow raised ditch running along the edges of separate small fields. The owners of the fields diverted water onto their plots by breaching the ditch with their hands. The process was repeated throughout the dry season. "It is a matter of mystery—to the American traveler particularly—how a country less in area than that part of the United States east of the Mississippi River, with vast portions of this totally barren and uncultivated, can feed 230,000,000 people. But it does, and has large exports besides."

The travelers reached Benares at night. "Benares is regarded by the Hindoo as a sacred city and is believed by them to have existed from the beginning of time. It is well and solidly built, many of the houses going up three or four stories high. The streets are very narrow and many of them do not admit even a pack animal. The sight of the natives worshipping, which seems to be their principal occupation, is a curious one. There can be no doubt about their sincerity. It is a grave question whether they should be disturbed in their faith. It teaches no cruelty to beast or man, and sets up a good system of morals for the guidance of its followers."

Journeying again by ship, they landed at Rangoon in March. Burma's culture was close enough to India's to afford a comparison and different enough to draw contrasts. "The contrast is all in favor of the Burmese. In India they are divided into castes. . . . Females have no rights and must not remain single. They may be betrothed at any time from conception to the age of puberty. By the latter time they are disgraced if not married. . . . Many become widows before they are five years of age"—on account of the deaths of their much older fiancés—"and can never after marry. Through widowhood—life—they are disgraced and despised." In Burma, on the other hand, women were honored. "Marriage is a matter of choice between the contracting parties. The man must ask and the girl give consent." Nor was there a caste system in Burma. "All can compete to better their condition." The culture was broadminded. "The Burmese are not bigoted and do not object to the intermarriage of their race or religion with people of any other race or religion." They were more prosperous than the Indians. "Labor here commands about three to four times the amount it does in India, and servants receive twice as much."

Still farther eastward the party traveled. In Siam—Thailand— Grant met many dignitaries, including King Chulalongkorn. "The latter is a young man, 25 years of age, quite impressive in appearance and intelligent, speaks English fairly well and understands perfectly. He is evidently a progressive but is restrained by the older men in council." Hong Kong was stunning. "This colony is on an island reaching 1700 feet above the sea. The city is well built—mostly of granite—and the harbor is a magnificent one both in scenery and security." Canton was differently impressive. "The population is very dense and must far exceed one million of people." The Chinese people were as frugal and hard-working as any Grant had ever seen—but they got no respect from others for their industry. "The Chinese are badly treated at home by Europe-ans as well as when they emigrate. . . . I should not blame them if they were to drive out all Europeans—Americans included—and make new treaties in which they would claim equal rights." Grant supposed the Chinese would, in time, do just that. "My impression is that the day is not very far distant when they will make the most rapid strides towards modern civilization and become dangerous rivals to all powers interested in the trade of the East."

*H*e spoke with Li Hung-chang, the Chinese viceroy. Americans, especially in the West, were agitating to limit Chinese immigration; in an era of otherwise open American doors, this was accurately seen as a slap at China. Grant found himself an interpreter of American attitudes and policy. "I am ready to admit that the Chinese have been of great ser-vice to our country," he told Li. "I do not know what the Pacific Coast would be without them. They came to our aid at the time when their aid was invaluable." But there were problems. "The trouble about your coun-trymen coming to America is that they come under circumstances which make them slaves. . . . Their labor is not their own, but the property of capitalists." Grant was referring to the "coolie" system of contract labor. "We had slavery some years since, and we only freed ourselves from slav-ery at the cost of a dreadful war, in which hundreds of thousands of lives were lost and thousands of millions of dollars spent. Having made those sacrifices to suppress slavery in one form, we do not feel like encouraging it in another, in the insidious form of coolie emigration. . . . If you can stop the slavery feature, then emigration from China is like emigration from other countries." Grant suggested a temporary halt in emigration— "three or five years"—to let the labor market sort itself out. Li explained that the Chinese government officially discouraged emigration. Grant replied that the government, then, would not object to a moratorium.

He spoke with Prince Kung, the emperor's son and the ruling fam-ily's managing partner. Like Li, the prince wanted to modernize China, to improve the lot of the Chinese people and to unify and strengthen

China against foreign powers. Grant was the living symbol of American unity and strength; the prince probed him for advice, particularly about the nation-building role of railroads. Grant acknowledged the enormous value of the railroad industry to American development. "To it we owe a great deal of our material prosperity," he said. "It is difficult to say where we would be now in the rank of nations but for our railway system." The prince invited Grant to elaborate. Grant continued: "The value of railroads is to disseminate a nation's wealth and to enable her to concentrate and use her strength. We have a country as large as China. . . . We can cross it in seven days by special trains, or in an emergency in much less time. We can throw the strength of the nation upon any required point in a short time. That makes us as strong in one place as another. It leaves us no vulnerable points. We cannot be sieged, broken up and destroyed in detail, as has happened to other large nations. That, however, is not the greatest advantage. The wealth and industry of the country are utilized. A man's industry in interior states becomes valuable because it can reach a market. Otherwise his industry would be confined necessarily to his means of subsistence. . . . This adds to the revenue of the country."

The prince was well briefed on Grant's biography and itinerary; he knew that Grant had been feted in many of the great capitals of the world and was headed for Japan, with which China was in dispute over the Loochoo—Ryukyu—Islands of the East China Sea. "We all know how vast your influence must be, not only upon your people at home but upon all nations who know what you have done, and who know that whatever question you considered would be considered with patience and wisdom and a desire for justice and peace. You are going to Japan as the guest of the people and the emperor, and will have opportunities of presenting our views to the emperor of Japan and of showing him that we have no policy but justice." The prince explained that the Ryukyus had long been ruled by an independent monarchy, one with which China had had friendly relations. The Japanese had recently deposed the monarch and were asserting their own sovereignty. China could only take offense and alarm; war was not out of the question.

Grant hoped matters wouldn't come to that. "Any course short of national humiliation or national destruction is better than war," he said. "War in itself is so great a calamity that it should only be invoked when there is no way of saving a nation from a greater. War, especially in the East, and between two countries like Japan and China, would be a misfortune, a great misfortune."

"A great misfortune to the outside and neutral powers as well," Prince Kung said. "War in the East would be a heavy blow to the trade upon which other nations so much depend. That is one reason why China asks your good offices." The prince hoped Grant would convey to the Japanese government China's seriousness and resolve on the Ryukyu issue and would stress to the Japanese the justice of China's case.

Grant reminded the prince that he held no official position. He was a tourist and had no business to conduct with the Japanese.

"We have a proverb in Chinese," the prince rejoined, "that 'no business is business'—in other words that real affairs, great affairs, are more frequently transacted informally, when persons meet, as we are meeting now, over a table of entertainment for social and friendly conversation, than in solemn business sessions."

A cholera epidemic in Japan kept the travelers from seeing all they wanted. "Nagasaki we found a most beautiful city located on the slope of green hills at the head of a narrow bay some nine miles in from the Yellow Sea," Grant wrote. He received the rare honor of meeting with the Meiji emperor, who had put Japan on a westernizing path. Grant offered encouragement. "Japan is striving to become both liberal and enlightened," he said. "She deserves success, for her efforts are honest and in the interest of the whole people." But the efforts weren't uniformly appreciated. After the fact Grant learned that Japanese reactionaries had plotted to assassinate him for profaning the emperor's divinity by his western presence.

The Japanese government understood that Grant had been speaking to the Chinese about the Ryukyus, and it presented Japan's view of the case. "What I have learned in Japan is far different from what I was told in China," Grant replied to the Meiji emperor. "I can see how her case has features that cannot be answered. A nation having gone as far as Japan, and having acted as she believed in her unquestioned sovereignty, must consider what is due to her people." All the same, Grant continued: "There is an aspect to the Loochoo affair which, seen from the Chinese point of view, is worthy of attention. . . . China feels that she has not received from Japan the consideration due to her as a sovereign power, as a friendly nation, as a nation which had for a long time enjoyed a certain relation to Loochoo." Grant didn't propose to tell the Japanese emperor what to do. Yet he made a suggestion. "It seems to me that this feeling in the minds of Chinese statesmen should be well considered by Japan, and that Japan in a spirit of magnanimity and justice should make concessions to China. The importance of peace between China and Japan is so great that each country should make concessions to the other.

"I would say one word more on this question," Grant went on. "In your discussions with China on Loochoo, and on all matters at issue, do not invite or permit, so far as you can avoid it, the intervention of a foreign power. European powers have no interests in Asia, so far as I can judge from their diplomacy, that do not involve the humiliation and subjugation of the Asiatic people. Their diplomacy is always selfish, and a quarrel between China and Japan would be regarded by them as a quarrel that might ensue to their own advantage."

NOT SINCE ANDREW JACKSON HAD AMERICA POSSESSED A POPULAR hero of Grant's stature, and the country had missed him. The bells of San Francisco began ringing as the *City of Tokio*, the ship carrying Grant's party, approached the Golden Gate in September 1879. Steam whistles in the city's factories and canneries took up the chorus, joined by the cannons of Fort Point and other batteries around the bay. The spriest residents of the city ran to the heights of the Presidio and Telegraph Hill to catch a glimpse of the great man's vessel; others crowded the wharves north and east of the commercial center. City officials and a reception committee boarded a tugboat that met the ship in the bay; several thousand other persons, equally unable to wait for the Union's savior to touch shore, pushed aboard the Pacific Mail sidewheeler *China* and scores of lesser craft to greet the *City of Tokio*. The rest of the residents seemed to have dropped whatever they were doing to join the celebration; every street with a view of the bay was clogged with men, women and children craning their necks to view the ship bringing Grant home.

As the vessel reached its anchorage the crush intensified; everyone wished to be first to see the general. Police pushed the crowds back, making room for the carriages that would convey the hero and his party. A ferry pulled alongside the *City of Tokio*; Grant and his group went aboard. As the ferry approached its slip at the foot of Market Street, the crowd began cheering, and when Grant appeared at the head of the gangway, the cheering became a roar. A band played "Home Again" and the mayor declared, "Some time has passed since you departed from the Atlantic shore to seek the relief which a long period in your country's service had made necessary, but during this absence the people of the United States have not forgotten you." As if to confirm the mayor's words, which few of them could hear, the crowd burst into louder applause than ever. The mayor explained that San Francisco had changed since Grant had last been there a quarter century before. "The young city is now the rival of cities which were old when its history began." But some of the men who had known Grant in the early days were still in the city. "Many of them are here today waiting anxiously to take you by the hand once more."

The mayor's statement perhaps gave Grant pause, for some of those old-timers might remember the cloud under which he had left California in 1854. Yet he had been far from the hardest drinker in the gold rush days, and, looking at himself and what he could see of the thriving city before him, he had to say that things hadn't turned out badly for either of them. He responded succinctly to the mayor's remarks. He said he was honored by the reception and eager to see all that the San Franciscans had wrought. "It will afford me great pleasure to observe, after the lapse of a quarter of a century, the marvelous growth of your city." He and Julia entered the carriage reserved for them, and in line with many other vehicles they paraded up Market Street, to the sustained applause and shouts of the hordes that lined both sides of the avenue.

The San Francisco welcome caught the eye of America's political classes, who had been monitoring Grant's journey across Europe and Asia. Republicans realized they had no one who could inspire voters the way Grant did, and with the unexciting Hayes having taken himself out of the running for 1880, many of them hoped to put Grant atop the ticket again. Others in the party looked to a Grant candidacy not with hope but with fear—of a return of the spoilsmen who had plagued his second term. Democrats didn't want to run against Grant, fairly certain they would lose; they hoped for a squabble among the Republicans that would neutralize that party's continuing advantage in national politics and allow the Democracy to elect one of its own as president for the first time since 1856.

Grant kept quiet. His supporters contended that his decision not to run in 1876 had rested on a George Washington–like forswearing of protracted incumbent advantage rather than a rejection per se of more than eight years in office. His opponents contended that a third term was a third term, whether consecutive or not, and that Grant's earlier decision still applied—or should still apply. Grant declined to say what *he* thought.

The questions grew only more pressing as the excitement persisted and spread. "I cannot venture in the streets except in a carriage for the mob of goodnatured and enthusiastic friends, old and young," he wrote Adolph Borie after a week in San Francisco. He and Julia climbed the Sierra Nevada to Yosemite, which hadn't been discovered by whites at the time of his previous stay in California. They went back to San Francisco for a voyage north to Oregon. "It seems like returning home again," he told a tickled audience at Astoria. In Portland he addressed a Grand Army of the Republic convention. "It is gratifying to me to meet my old comrades again," he said. Noting the presence of some Confederate veterans in the audience, he added: "And it is particularly gratifying now in the time of perfect peace to take by the hand those who fought against us." After returning to California, they headed east on the Central Pacific Railroad. "No honors that I received abroad were such a real pleasure to me," he told a crowd at Virginia City, "nor were any so deeply felt, as are those bestowed upon me by my own people in their reception of me on my coming home." He spoke to audiences large and small across Utah, Nebraska, Iowa and Illinois during late October and early November.

A reporter traveling with Grant, recalling the general's aversion to public speaking, expressed surprise at the frequency of his remarks now. Grant said he couldn't help it. "When I was in Europe I had to speak, and, having done so, it seemed to me it would be very uncivil to refuse the folks at home. It is very embarrassing. I think I am improving, for my knees don't knock together like they did at first, but I don't like it, and I am sorry I yielded." Yet he still valued and practiced brevity. He teased himself before an Illinois audience: "I am very glad to get back to Illinois again, and very glad to see you all. But I have a great deal of sympathy with these press-men who are along with us and who take down every word. I am a man of economy. I believe in economy. They telegraph every word, and I want to save them expenses."

Galena greeted its adopted son ecstatically and urged him to stay. Gratitude to Grant aside, the town needed every resident it could claim, for the construction of the western railroads had deprived the river city of most of its business and much of its raison d'être. Grant expressed appreciation for the slow pace. "I always like to come here, because I can take my quiet and ease here better than anywhere else," he told a reporter.

But he wouldn't settle in Galena, at least not yet. Rutherford Hayes invited him to visit the White House and remain awhile; he declined, saying he and Julia were seeking winter quarters in warmer climes.

What he didn't say was that he preferred not to provide the endorsement a sojourn at the Executive Mansion would imply. But his search for
warmth was sincere, as was his desire to resume his travels. "We think
now of going to Havana and Mexico," he wrote Nellie. He had never
been to Cuba, where the insurgency against Spain had finally died out,
and he wanted to revisit the Mexican scenes of the war that introduced
him to the soldier's art.

"The first time I ever saw General Grant was in the fall or winter of
1866 at one of the receptions at Washington, when he was general of the
army," Samuel Clemens recalled. "I merely saw and shook hands with
him along with the crowd but had no conversation." Their next encounter occurred during Grant's first term as president. Clemens's friend and
Nevada's senator William Stewart took the author along on a visit to the
White House. Clemens by this period had acquired a certain reputation
as Mark Twain for his short stories and journalism, but Grant hadn't
heard of him. "I shook hands and then there was a pause and silence,"
Clemens wrote. "I couldn't think of anything to say. So I merely looked
into the General's grim, immovable countenance a moment or two in
silence and then I said: 'Mr. President, I am embarrassed. Are you?' He
smiled a smile which would have done no discredit to a cast-iron image
and I got away under the smoke of my volley."

Ten years passed before the third meeting. Grant had returned from
his world tour and in November 1879 traveled to Chicago for a reunion
of the Army of the Tennessee. Clemens was now famous as the author
of several bestselling books, and the two were to share the rostrum with
several other speakers. Carter Harrison, the mayor of Chicago, offered to
introduce Clemens to Grant. Clemens, assuming Grant didn't remember
him, gladly accepted the offer. The introduction was made. A pause followed, then Grant said, "I am not embarrassed. Are you?"

The Chicago reunion was an extravagant affair with eighty thousand
veterans attending. A formal dinner honored Grant; more than a dozen
speakers offered toasts to various segments of the American population
and to what the general's great victories meant for them. Clemens was
astonished by Grant's ability to remain calm amid the tempest of adula-
tion. "He never moved a muscle of his body for a single instant, during thirty minutes!" Clemens wrote. "You could have played him on a
stranger for an effigy. Perhaps he never *would* have moved, but at last

a speaker made such a particularly ripping and blood-stirring remark about him that the audience rose and roared and yelled and stamped an entire minute. . . . General Sherman stepped to him, laid his hand affectionately on his shoulder, bent respectfully down and whispered in his ear. Then Grant got up and bowed, and the storm of applause swelled into a hurricane."

Clemens had the final toast that evening, and he essayed to spike the earnestness of the affair with his characteristic irreverence. The penultimate speaker had offered a toast "to Woman"; Clemens raised his glass "to Babies." He explained: "We have not all had the good fortune to be ladies. We have not all been generals, or poets, or statesmen, but when the toast works down to the babies, we stand on common ground." The liquored crowd laughed when Clemens recounted how even a general had to bow before the infant in his home. "You could face the death-storm at Donelson and Vicksburg, and give back blow for blow, but when he clawed your whiskers and pulled your hair and twisted your nose, you had to take it." Clemens pushed his concept to a ludicrous extreme, explaining that the baby Grant had learned strategy "trying to find some way to get his big toe into his mouth." At this point the audience fell silent, and Clemens wondered if he had gone too far. He let the silence persist and the awkwardness mount. "And if the child is but a prophecy of the man," he concluded, "there are mighty few who will doubt that he *succeeded*." The silence held a half beat longer and then "the house came down with a crash," Clemens wrote his wife. The audience roared itself breathless. "And do you know, General Grant sat through fourteen speeches like a graven image, but I fetched him! I broke him up, utterly! He told me he laughed till the tears came and every bone in his body ached."

82

GRANT WAS FETED ACROSS THE EASTERN HALF OF THE COUNTRY TO Philadelphia, which threw a giant parade in his honor. He passed quietly through Washington en route to Savannah, where he and Julia boarded ship for Florida and Cuba.

In Havana in February 1880 he received a letter from Elihu Washburne, who had returned from France to resume domestic Republican politics. Washburne liked Grant as much as ever and thought the country did too. He said that James Blaine, John Sherman and others in the party were maneuvering for the presidential nomination; he hoped Grant would make himself available.

"All I want is that the government rule should remain in the hands of those who saved the Union until all the questions growing out of the war are forever settled," Grant replied. "I would much rather any one of many I could mention should be president than that I should have it." He had served his time in the White House and had no desire for more. Yet a public statement would be pretentious and counterproductive. "I shall not gratify my enemies by declining what has not been offered." To be clear, without being too explicit: "I am not a candidate for anything, and if the Chicago convention nominates a candidate that can be elected it will gratify me, and the gratification will be greater if it should be someone other than myself." Grant assumed Washburne would relay this sentiment to those who needed to know. He had a bit more for Washburne alone: "In confidence I will tell you I should feel sorry if it should be John Sherman." Grant thought Sherman misguided on the money question. "Blaine I would like to see elected, but I fear the party could not elect him. He would create enthusiasm, but he would have opposition in his own party that might lose him some northern states that the Republicans should carry."

Grant's statement triggered a full fight for the Republican nomination. While he and Julia toured Cuba, Washburne and other Grant partisans gathered forces in preparation for a show at Chicago. Grant didn't have to say a word as he returned to Galena via Vicksburg; his presence at the site of his momentous victory reminded Americans, at least those of the North, why they loved him. And the North would mean everything in the 1880 election. Hayes's withdrawal of the federal army from the affairs of the South allowed the completion of what white Southerners called "redemption" and others deemed simply the return to power of the Democrats, who sufficiently intimidated, cheated and otherwise discouraged Republicans, including most of the freedmen, that they counted for little in Southern politics. With any Democratic presidential nominee guaranteed the South, any Republican had to perform overwhelmingly in the North. Blaine's problem was that he couldn't; Grant's strength was that he could.

The Grant forces led going into the convention. Roscoe Conkling, the veteran senator from New York, directed the Grant men with skill and theatrical aplomb. After John Logan, Grant's lieutenant from the Vicksburg campaign and subsequently commander of the Army of the Tennessee, put Grant's name in nomination, Conkling leaped on a table to give a seconding speech. A military hero was the man for the hour, he said. "The election before us is the Austerlitz of American politics. It will decide for many years whether the country shall be Republican or Cossack." Grant had unified America during the war; he would unify America again. Erstwhile critics could no longer touch him. "Calumny's ammunition has all been burned once. Its force is spent. And the name of Grant will glitter a bright and imperishable star in the diadem of the republic when those who have tried to tarnish it have moldered in forgotten graves, and when their memories and their epitaphs have vanished utterly." Ohio and Illinois claimed Grant as a favorite son, but the nation as a whole owned him. Turning poetic, Conkling proclaimed: "When asked what state he hails from / Our sole reply shall be, / He hails from Appomattox / And its famous apple tree."

Grant garnered the most votes on the first ballot, leading Blaine but falling short of a majority. John Sherman came third, far behind. A second ballot showed little change. Likewise a third and a fourth. Hours passed, then days, and in Chicago's June heat the delegates grew weary and cross. Gradually it became clear that neither Grant nor Blaine could win and that Sherman had even less chance. The liberals in the party still resented Grant for Santo Domingo, the conservatives for South Carolina. Blaine's men couldn't silence questions about their candidate's connections to certain shady operators. Sherman seemed a lightweight next to Grant and Blaine.

In their exhaustion the delegates did what delegates often do in such circumstances: they turned to a compromise candidate. No one held much against James Garfield, the competent but uncharismatic congressman from Ohio, and so on the thirty-sixth ballot the convention tapped him to head the ticket. Chester Arthur of New York was nominated for vice president.

"Individually, I am much relieved at the result, having grown weary of constant abuse," Grant wrote Roscoe Conkling, whom he thanked for his "magnificent and generous support" during the convention. "I have no presentiment as to what is likely to be the result of the labors of the convention or the result of the election which is to follow, but I hope for the best to the country."

Julia was more disappointed than her husband at the outcome of the convention. She had greatly enjoyed her eight years as the president's wife and had surrendered the White House most reluctantly. "Oh, Ulys," she had cried, "I feel like a waif, like a waif on the world's wide common." (Gallantly he answered: "I, too, am a waif. So you are not alone.") The excitement surrounding their return from abroad had caused her to look forward to a third term as First Lady. She urged Grant, amid the deadlock, to take the unprecedented step of appearing before the convention in person to plead his case. He replied that he would cut off his right arm before he would do any such thing. "Do you not desire success?" she asked. "Yes, of course," he said. "Since my name is up, I would rather be nominated, but I will do nothing to further that end." "Oh, Ulys," she said, "how unwise—what mistaken chivalry. . . . Go, go tonight, I beseech you." He looked at her. "Julia, I am amazed at you," he said.

He didn't expect to participate in the campaign, and for a time after the Democrats, trying to steal a military march on the Republicans, nominated Winfield Scott Hancock for president, he resisted getting involved. "I have nothing to say against General Hancock," he told a reporter testing a story that he did have something to say. "I have known him for forty years. His personal, official, and military record is good." But he *was* a Democrat. "The record of the party which has put him in nomination is bad."

Grant's diffidence eroded as he pondered the prospect of a Democratic capture of the White House. He didn't believe that the Democrats, as heavily dependent on the South as they were, had fully accepted the outcome of the war and Reconstruction. In Congress the Democrats could be contained, but if they took the presidency they could roll back much of what Grant had spent the best years of his life working to secure. "I feel a very deep interest in the success of the Republican ticket," he told James Garfield in August, "and have never failed to say a good word in favor of the party and its candidates when I felt I could do any good. I shall not fail in the future."

He was better than his word, taking to the stump on behalf of Garfield as he had never done for himself. He presented himself as the antithesis of the politician. "I have never made a Republican speech in my life, or any kind of a political speech," he told an audience in Galena. "I am sure it would require some time and much preparation to make one of any length. . . . I never voted a Republican presidential ticket in my life, and but one Democratic ticket, and that was many years ago when I was quite a young man." But he was certainly going to vote this time. "Although I shall be some distance from you in November next, I shall return to Galena to cast a Republican vote for president of the United States. And I hope that the city of Galena will cast a Republican vote such as it never cast before."

He caught a touch more of the campaign fever as the weeks passed. "I am a Republican, as the two great political parties are now divided, because the Republican party is a national party seeking the greatest good for the greatest number of citizens," he told a rally in Ohio. "There is not a precinct in this vast nation where a Democrat cannot cast his ballot and have it counted as cast. No matter what the prominence of the opposite party, he can proclaim his political opinions, even if he is only one among a thousand, without fear and without proscription on account of his opinions." Sadly, such tolerance was not bipartisan. "There are fourteen states and localities in some other states where Republicans have not this privilege." He was a Republican for other reasons as well. "The Republican party is a party of progress and of liberality toward its opponents. It encourages the poor to strive to better their condition, the ignorant to educate their children, to enable them to compete successfully with their more fortunate associates, and, in fine, it secures an entire equality before the law of every citizen, no matter what his race, nationality, or previous condition. It tolerates no privileged class. Everyone has the opportunity to make himself all he is capable of."

In public he hewed to his decision to say nothing against Hancock. In private, reportedly, he asserted that the Democratic nominee lacked the character to be an effective president. "He is vain, selfish, weak, and easily flattered," he told two Methodist ministers who visited him in Galena, according to the instantly published recollection of one of them. "He is crazy to be president. The South will easily control him."

Grant denied using the language attributed to him. He allowed himself to be quoted as saying, "Hancock is a man who likes to hear himself praised," but against this he balanced a commendation of Hancock's courage and forthright character. Yet he never backed down from his assertion that the election of a Democrat would be a heavy blow to democracy and equality in America.

He spoke in the Midwest, the mid-Atlantic and New England. In New Jersey he praised the carpetbagger, the Reconstruction-era Yankee gone South who was the bête noire of Southern Democrats, as the quintessential American. Americans had long picked up and followed opportunity, he said. The West, the most dynamic region of the country, was filled with carpetbaggers. "Out there they are all carpetbaggers." He himself was a carpetbagger, having moved to Illinois in search of economic opportunity. "All we ask is that our carpetbag fellow citizens, and our fellow citizens of African descent, and of every other class who may choose to be Republicans, shall have the privilege to go to the polls, even though they are in the minority, and put in their ballot without being burned out of their homes and without being threatened or intimidated."

He concluded his campaign at the end of October in New York with another call for everyone's vote to be counted and a prediction as to what the counting would reveal. "Every Northern state, with the possible exception of two—California and Nevada—will give a Republican majority." The South would be solid for the Democrats. "I want you all to remember my prediction on next Tuesday," he told his audience with a smile. "If it appears that I am right, talk about it as much as you please. If you find that I am wrong, then treat the prediction as private and confidential."

They soon talked about it a lot. Grant erred only on New Jersey, which Hancock carried by a whisker. The Democratic ticket won the former slave states plus California and Nevada—and New Jersey—while Garfield and the Republicans swept the North minus those three. The totals gave the victory to Garfield by an electoral vote of 214 to 155.

"I heartily congratulate you and especially the country," Grant wrote the president-elect. "I feel as sure that the nation has escaped a calamity as one can feel about untried things." Rumors were alleging that Grant sought a cabinet post in exchange for his support of the ticket. "I want to put your mind entirely at ease on this subject," he told Garfield. "As an American citizen I felt as much interest in the result of the election as you or anyone else could." It was for this reason that he had worked hard for the victory. But he wanted nothing in return save the satisfaction of keeping the Democrats at bay another four years. "There is no position within the gift of the President which I would accept There is no public position which I want. If I can serve the country at any time I will do so freely and without reward."

83

At one of his campaign stops, in Hartford, Grant was introduced by Samuel Clemens. "By years of colossal labor and colossal achievement you at last beat down a gigantic rebellion and saved your country from destruction," Clemens said. "Then the country commanded you to take the helm of state. You preferred your great office of general of the army and the rest and comfort which it afforded, but you loyally obeyed and relinquished permanently the ample and well earned salary of the generalship and resigned your accumulating years to the chance mercies of a precarious existence." Clemens noted, with characteristic wryness, that other countries treated their heroes better. "When Wellington won Waterloo, a battle on a level with some dozen of your victories, sordid England tried to pay him for that service with wealth and grandeur. She made him a duke and gave him four million dollars. If you had done and suffered for any other country what you have done and suffered for your own, you would have been affronted in the same sordid way. But, thank God, this vast and rich and mighty republic is imbued to the core with a delicacy which will forever preserve her from so degrading a deserving son. . . . Your country stands ready from this day forth to testify her measureless love and pride and gratitude toward you in every conceivable inexpensive way."

Grant laughed with the rest of Clemens's audience, but the money question—*his* money question—was a serious one. Julia's distress at her husband's refusal to pursue the nomination revealed not only her desire to experience again the distinction of being First Lady but also her appreciation that the presidency had afforded them the only financial security they had ever enjoyed. Grant's mining stocks had provided the income for their world tour, but mining was a risky business and shares worth hundreds today might be worth tens tomorrow. As Grant cast about for business opportunities during the summer and autumn of 1880 he considered investing in Mexican railroads and taking the presidency of a Colorado mining company. "One thing is certain," he wrote Adam Badeau: "I must do something to supplement my income or continue to live in Galena or on a farm. I have not got the means to live in a city." Another thing was certain: though Grant might have settled for the rural life, Julia would not. She thrived on being at the center of American life; she would have withered in the country and made Grant's life miserable in the process.

At least he didn't have to worry about the children. Nellie was financially secure with Algernon Sartoris in England. Fred had married the daughter of a successful Chicago developer. Buck had just married the daughter of one of Colorado's charter senators, Jerome Chaffee. "You know Buck is married!" Grant wrote Nellie. "Everyone speaks most highly of the young lady." Jesse married into a prominent San Francisco family. "I do not know whether anyone has described Jesse's wife," Grant wrote Nellie. "She is quite small with beautiful large eyes, a very small face but prominent nose, light auburn hair, and by some thought quite pretty. I do not think her as pretty as either Ida"—Fred's wife—"or Buck's wife. But she is very pleasant and not a bit spoiled. The same may be said of all your sisters-in-law." The boys were prospering. "Buck and Jesse are both doing well in their business and are entirely independent." Fred was in the army and hence the poorest of the three. "But he has something outside of his pay"—something from Ida's family—"which I had not at his age."

Grant explained to Nellie that he and Julia planned to make their permanent home in New York. "We are boarding at the Fifth Avenue Hotel for the present, and will continue to do so until I know I am fixed to be entirely independent. I will then purchase or lease a house." Grant's friends determined to him. Illinois senator John Logan introduced a bill to restore Grant to the army's retired list with the full pay of a general. A similar bill was introduced in the House. Grant disapproved of the special treatment. "Under no circumstances will I accept the place if the bill passes," he wrote Logan. His moral veto helped kill the bill. Other admirers stepped privately into the breach. Anthony Drexel, George Childs and J. P. Morgan headed a group of bankers, merchants and industrialists who proposed a fund to assist the Grants financially. "In any other great nation such a fund would not be necessary," Drexel explained to Edwards Pierrepont, observing that most countries pensioned their heroes. Drexel and the others recommended that twenty persons each subscribe $5,000 toward a "presidential retiring fund."

The idea caught on. The list of contributors expanded beyond the twenty and the contribution total passed $200,000. The original plan had been to invest the money and let the Grants live off the dividends; in the event, Drexel and the others decided to apply part of it toward the purchase of a home in New York. "I am sure I turned deathly pale," Julia recalled of the moment when Drexel and Childs told her the news. The proprietor of the Fifth Avenue Hotel had cut the Grants a deal, but the rent still strained their budget. "I was so startled that I did not respond until Mr. Childs asked, 'Is not that nice?'" She replied, "Oh, yes, yes indeed, but talk with the General first. See if he approves." "Oh, no," Childs said. "We have decided it is to be yours. The General has nothing to do with it. It is yours, and what is yours is the General's." Julia's relief and joy were still palpable years later. "So I was to have a beautiful home, all my own," she wrote.

Though Garfield was president, Grant remained the most formidable figure in the Republican party. At fifty-eight he enjoyed solid health, and while Republican politicos had divergent opinions about him, the rank and file of the party adored him. Any slip by Garfield—whose popular margin over Hancock had been less than 2,000 votes out of 900,000 cast—might cause the party to turn once again to the hero of Appomattox.

Grant avoided such talk but watched Garfield carefully. "I hope with you that Garfield will give us an administration that will break up the solid South and not pander to the Republican soreheads and bolters," he wrote a political ally. "He certainly will know that a thousand friends are more deserving of favors at his hands—I should say recognitions—than one 'holier than thou art' Republican who votes our ticket only when some objectionable person, hard for the party to carry, is nominated."

As Garfield formed a cabinet, he solicited Grant's advice. "Harmony in the Republican party," Grant responded, "and at least the support of the whole party of your administration is certainly to be desired." He had heard that James Blaine was being considered for secretary of state as a fence-mending measure. Grant confessed that he was torn. "I do not like the man, have no confidence in his friendship nor in his reliability. But he is—has been—a leading member of the party and has many followers." Then again, he had many enemies and might prove a disruptive figure in the cabinet. Garfield would have to decide for himself, Grant said. He tendered his best wishes. "There is no member of your own family more desirous of seeing your administration a success than me. The good of the whole country requires harmonious Republican government until all the results of the war are secured."

Meanwhile Grant gave visibility to issues he feared Garfield would be tempted to ignore. Rutherford Hayes had bought peace with the South by abandoning African Americans there; Grant strove to recommit the Republican party to their defense. He spoke conspicuously at a benefit concert for the Colored Citizens' Association of New York and Brooklyn. "I sincerely hope with you that the time is not far distant when all the privileges that citizenship carries with it will be accorded you throughout the land without any opposition," he said. Some Republicans and very many Democrats contended that blacks couldn't be trusted to vote responsibly; Grant rejected this claim. "I have no fear that the franchise will not be exercised as carefully and judiciously by our fellow citizens of African descent as by any others. Perhaps more care will be used because it is a boon so recently given to your race and therefore prized more highly." Many blacks were taking exemplary advantage of such opportunities as they found. "I am glad to see in my travels the progress in education all over the country made by the colored people, even in the South, where the prejudice is the strongest. It is rare to see a colored child lose an opportunity to get a common-school education. Education is the first great step toward the capacity to exercise the new privileges accorded to you wisely and properly. I hope the field may be open to you, regardless of any prejudice which may have heretofore existed."

84

In January 1881 Samuel Clemens suggested that Grant write a book about his life and career. Grant responded skeptically. "Your kind letter of the 8th came to hand in due time," he said on the 14th. "I had delayed answering it until this time not because of any doubt as to how to answer it but because of the principal reason I have for not doing what you suggest, namely laziness. The same suggestion you make has been frequently made by others, but never entertained for a moment. In the first place I have always distrusted my ability to write anything that would satisfy myself, and the public would be much more difficult to please. In the second place I am not possessed of the kind of industry necessary to undertake such a work." Grant noted that Adam Badeau had been working on a book about his—Grant's—wartime experiences. John Russell Young, the *Herald* reporter who had followed him around the world, was compiling a book on that journey. "It would be unfair to them for me to do anything now that would in any way interfere with the sale of their work," he told Clemens. "Then too they have done it much better than I could if I was to try."

But he didn't want to disappoint Clemens completely. "If I ever settle down in a house of my own I may make notes which some one of my children may use after I am gone." Nothing before then, however. He closed cordially: "I am very much obliged to you for your kind suggestions and for the friendship which inspires them and will always appreciate both. If you want to see me about this, or any other matter at any time, I beg that you will feel no hesitation in calling. I will always be glad to see you and hear you no matter whether your views and mine agree or not."

   Still, he had to make a living. Grant joined a group of investors who aimed to do for Mexico what the Central Pacific and Union Pacific Railroads had done for the United States. At a dinner at Delmonico's in New York he called on his own experiences in Mexico and in the American West to expound to Jay Gould, Collis Huntington and other railroad men the opportunities Mexico afforded to them, to the United States and to Mexicans themselves. Mexico had gotten past the political turbulence of its first half century of independence and was on a promising path. "They have thirteen years really of growth," Grant said. "And I am perfectly satisfied that with the building of railroads and of telegraphs there need be no more apprehension for the safety of capital invested in Mexico than in our own country. The building of railroads will give employment to labor and will give rapid transit from one part of the country to another. . . . I look for a bright and prosperous and rapid future for Mexico, and it must result in a very large commerce with some part of the world. If we take advantage of the time, it will accrue to the benefit of the United States more than to that of any other country except Mexico, and Mexico will be necessarily more benefited than any other country."

   Grant was sufficiently persuasive that Gould immediately proposed the creation of a committee to effect Grant's vision. Gould and Huntington were members; Grant was chairman. The Mexican Southern Railroad Company was chartered in New York in early 1881 and Grant was named company president. He initially accepted neither salary nor ownership; if things worked out he would take compensation later. That spring he traveled to Mexico on the company's behalf. "I have long been of the opinion that the United States and Mexico should be the warmest of friends and enjoy the closest commercial relations," he told a Mexico City audience. The economies of the two countries were complementary, he said, with the United States producing fruits, vegetables and grains of the temperate zone while Mexico cultivated plants of the tropics. By trading with each other, the two countries would keep their gold and silver from flowing out of the hemisphere. Grant understood that some Mexicans perceived American investment as a threat to Mexican sovereignty; where American dollars went, they said, the American flag would follow. To refute this claim Grant cited one of his failures as president.

He briefly recounted his efforts to annex Santo Domingo and explained that although the interests of the two countries recommended annexation and the Dominican people desired it, the Senate had rejected it. There was a lesson for Mexico: "I am sure that even if it could be shown that all the people of Mexico were in favor of the annexation of a portion of their territory to the United States, it would still be rejected. We want no more land. We do want to improve what we have, and we want to see our neighbors improve and grow so strong that the designs of any other country could not endanger them."

Grant's visit led to a contract between the Mexican government and the Mexican Southern company, which the Mexican congress approved in May 1881. Some of the principals in Grant's firm wanted subsidies from the Mexican government like those the Union Pacific and Central Pacific had received from the American government, and the Mexican government appeared willing to supply them. But Grant, recalling the Crédit Mobilier scandal, rejected the subsidies. Investment monies for the railroad would be better spent, he said, if they came from private sources.

Grant's hopes for harmony among the Republicans foundered in a fight between the James Blaine and Roscoe Conkling factions of the party. Garfield sided with Blaine, whom he made secretary of state over Grant's objection. Conkling took offense and resigned from the Senate, hoping to be reelected with a mandate that would reveal his continuing strength. Grant backed Conkling, mostly from gratitude for the support Conkling had shown him at the 1880 convention, and his backing at times took the negative form of criticism of Garfield. At first he muttered under his breath. "I am completely disgusted with Garfield's course," he wrote Adam Badeau confidentially. He said he would never again support a dark-horse candidate, a man who slipped to the nomination by stealth and intrigue. Such an approach characterized Garfield's style of leadership. "Garfield has shown that he is not possessed of the backbone of an angleworm," Grant told Badeau.

Eventually he aired his complaints to the press. "Garfield is a man without backbone," he told a reporter from Pittsburgh. "A man of fine ability but lacking stamina. He wants to please everybody and is afraid of the enmity of all the men around him." Yet Grant refused to join the fray. He and the reporter were riding a train from Chicago to New York; the reporter asked if he was going to meet Conkling or otherwise engage directly in the contest with Garfield. "Oh, no," Grant replied. "I am out of politics except as a citizen who exercises his right to vote and think as he pleases."

Grant might subsequently have said more against Garfield had Charles Guiteau, a disappointed office seeker, not shot the president in Washington in July 1881. Grant decried the "dastardly attempt" on Garfield's life as a "terrible crime." The injury was not immediately fatal, and doctors predicted that the president would make a full recovery. Grant had doubts. "Of course my hopes are all for a favorable result," he told a reporter. "After the president rallied from the shock I really believed he might recover. But later news yesterday gave me great anxiety. I have known a great many cases of men shot very much in the same way where the ball was lodged where it could not be found. The men would rally after the shock and then suddenly change for the worse, contrary to the expectations of the patient and physicians and then die in a few hours."

Grant reflected in this interview on the crime and the criminal. "It was simply the act of a lunatic who was disappointed because he couldn't get what he wanted. I have seen this fellow Guiteau several times. When I was at the Fifth Avenue Hotel last winter he sent his card up to my room one day as I coming from Chicago. My son"—Fred—"who was then on General Sheridan's staff, happened to be in my room, and I asked him if he knew this Guiteau. 'Yes,' he said. 'He is a sort of lawyer and deadbeat in Chicago. Don't let him come up. If you do he will bore you to death.'" Grant sent word that he would not see Guiteau. But Guiteau persisted, following a waiter up to Grant's room and thrusting his way in. He said he wanted the job of minister to Austria and needed Grant's endorsement. Grant refused and finally got him to go away. "The fellow was sharp and a ready talker, and appeared as though he had some education," Grant observed. "But he was evidently an adventurer, a man I would not trust with anything."

Grant thought Garfield's doctors were doing the wrong thing treating the president in Washington at the Executive Mansion. "During the months of August and September the White House is one of the most unhealthy places in the world," he observed in September. "He should have been taken from there long ago." Ultimately the doctors agreed and transported the president to the seaside at Long Branch. But the effort was too late, or perhaps it was deficient in other respects, for Garfield took a sudden turn for the worse. In the evening of September 19 he died.

Grant had gone to bed by the time the report reached New York. A *Times* reporter roused him for a statement. "You will please excuse me from a consideration of this sad news at this time," Grant replied. "It comes with terrible force, and is unexpected. What can I say? There is nothing—absolutely nothing—to be said under circumstances such as these." In filing his story, the reporter added, "General Grant was weeping bitterly." Grant's eldest son, who happened to be visiting, confirmed his father's dismay. "Colonel Fred Grant said to the *Times*'s reporter that though he had seen his father under many trying circumstances he had never before known him to be so terribly affected."

The country was affected too. Losing Lincoln to an assassin could be accounted a cost of the Civil War; losing Garfield seemed an indictment of democracy. Had politics sunk so low that the disappointed resorted to lethal force? It was a sobering thought.

One consequence of Garfield's death was the passage of the kind of civil service reform Grant had hectored Congress about before finally giving up. The 1883 Pendleton Act established a permanent Civil Service Commission, similar in spirit and function to the commission Grant had convened, and it made possible the transfer of tens of thousands of federal patronage jobs to a nonpolitical system based on merit.

A second consequence was additional damage to the Republican party. The charitable view of Chester Arthur was that he wasn't the worst of the spoilsmen, but no one had considered him presidential material at the time of his nomination for vice president, and the fact that he now *was* president changed few minds. "I can hardly say I expect much from this administration," Grant wrote Adam Badeau. At voters' first chance to register opinions on the new leadership in Washington, in the congressional elections of 1882, they delivered a damning verdict. The Democrats gained seventy seats in the House, giving them an overwhelming majority there. "The defeat was expected, but the magnitude of the defeat was a surprise," Grant remarked. "It was deserved, and it is to be hoped the lesson will be appreciated." But he wasn't counting on it.

𝓕itz John Porter had graduated from West Point two years behind Grant and served alongside him in the war with Mexico. He remained in the army during the 1850s and won command of a division and then a corps of the Army of the Potomac. At the second battle of Bull Run he refused an attack order from John Pope on grounds that the recent arrival of James Longstreet's Confederate force rendered an attack suicidal and counterproductive. Pope, embarrassed by the Union defeat in the battle, blamed Porter, who was arrested, court-martialed and convicted.

Grant had observed the proceedings from the banks of the Mississippi. By the time he took command of the army the case was forgotten, except by Porter, who spent the decade after the war struggling to have his reputation restored. Grant reviewed the matter while general-in-chief and again as president but saw no reason to reopen the case or overturn the verdict.

Yet Porter persisted, and after Grant returned from his world tour Porter sent him the evidence he had amassed in his favor. Grant examined the material and concluded that Porter indeed had been unjustly convicted. "The reading of the whole of this record has thoroughly convinced me that for these nineteen years I have been doing a gallant and efficient soldier a very great injustice in thought and sometimes in speech," he wrote President Arthur. "I feel it incumbent upon me now to do whatever lies in my power to remove from him and from his family the stain upon his good name." He published a detailed article on the Porter case in the *North American Review*. The article carried the title "An Undeserved Stigma" and included the arguments of the prosecution, which Grant proceeded to dismantle. "A literal obedience to the order of the 27th of August"—the crucial directive—"was a physical impossibility," Grant declared. Porter was a good soldier who had been "grossly wronged."

Grant's reversal won him the gratitude of Porter and the respect of many who knew the case only by reputation. "The undersigned, once soldiers under your command, desire to express their hearty and grateful thanks for your recent paper in vindication of General Fitz John Porter," a group of Boston veterans wrote Grant. "They feel that no act, whether of valor or of policy, which has marked your great career should bring you more honor than the moral courage and the spirit of fairness and justice exhibited in this defense of a gallant Union soldier condemned on insufficient or mistaken evidence." Though Arthur's attorney general determined that the verdict of the Porter court-martial could not be overturned so long past the fact, the president commuted the remaining part of his sentence, his disability from holding public office.

James Longstreet wrote Grant as well. After the war he and Grant had resumed the acquaintance secession had suspended, and they exchanged notes on various battles and aspects of the war. Longstreet read Grant's Porter article and sent a letter saying that Porter and, belatedly, Grant were right. "As you state, it was not possible for Porter to attack under the 4:30 order, the failure to do which was alleged to be his high crime," Longstreet told Grant. Had Porter tried to attack, he would have played directly into Confederate hands. "He would have given us the opportunity that we were so earnestly seeking all of that day, and in the disjointed condition of their army"—the Union army—"on that day, the result might have been more serious than that of the next day"— when the Confederates won in a rout. Longstreet explained that in making that next-day attack, he had exceeded his own orders, reinterpreting them to suit changed circumstances, much as Porter had reinterpreted *his* orders. But because the Confederate side won, he was accounted self-confident rather than insubordinate. "Soon after this campaign I was promoted and assigned as Senior Lieutenant General of the Confederate Army," Longstreet said. Such were the fortunes of war.

At 8:15 on the morning of June 29, 1882, the commuter express train of the New Jersey Central pulled out of Long Branch for its seventy-minute run to Jersey City, where the bankers, brokers and merchants aboard would transfer to the Hudson ferry to Manhattan. The business crowd regularly pressed the railroad and its crew to make better time, that they might get to their offices earlier. The train was traveling forty miles per hour as the locomotive approached a newly installed switch at the southern end of a trestle over Parker's Creek, a tidewater arm of the Shrewsbury River. Witnesses later said that the locomotive and the first six cars of the train got safely past the switch but the final car jumped the track, lurched to the side and dragged several of the cars ahead of it into the creek.

Grant was sitting in the smoker car, third from the locomotive. About forty passengers, all men, were enjoying their cigars and the morning papers. The other cars contained some 150 passengers. Grant's car and the others came to rest on their sides in the water of the creek, which somewhat cushioned the blow of the crash. Yet water rushed in through the shattered windows of the cars, and the passengers had to clamber out as best they could. Three didn't make it and drowned in the brackish water. Grant received a cut on his leg but climbed through the window on what was now the skyward side of the smoking car. "He had lost his hat but still had his morning's cigar between his teeth," a reporter swift to the scene related. Authorities and the railroad determined that the cause of the accident was improper installation of the new switch; participants and observers agreed that, considering the velocity of the train and the number of passengers, the casualty count—seventy injured beyond the three fatalities—was thankfully light.

THE NATION KNEW OF GRANT'S COMMUTES AND OTHER MOVEMENTS
not least because the papers regularly published articles under the head-
line "General Grant's Movements." Americans learned that President
Arthur hosted Grant and Julia for a state dinner at the White House
in January 1883. They read weeks later that he had testified before
the Senate on behalf of a treaty reducing tariffs between the United
States and Mexico. They followed him on a summer trip to the Pacific
Northwest when the Northern Pacific completed the third transcontinental line—after the Union Pacific–Central Pacific and the Southern
Pacific—and Grant joined a group of notables for a test of the new
road. They winced during the Christmas holidays when he slipped on
an icy curb in front of his house on New York's East Sixty-sixth Street
and badly bruised the leg he had injured during the war.

Though he denied interest in a return to public life—"I have washed
my hands of politics," he told an interviewer—a national poll placed him
among the frontrunners for the 1884 nomination. He showed especially
well among Southern Republicans, who still influenced their party's
nomination process despite having scant luck in elections. Republicans of
both races in Dixie recalled how he had come to their aid when the rest
of the party was willing to give them up for politically dead. "There is no
man on either side who fills the public eye as Grant did in 1868, 1872,
and 1880," a poll respondent wrote from Raleigh. The chief concern of
this man and others was whether their hero wanted the nomination. "If
Grant was known to be a candidate, there would be but one opinion in
this state," the North Carolina man wrote of his fellow Republicans.

*O*f Grant's three sons Buck seemed to have the most promising financial future. He had taken work with a New York law firm with close ties to Wall Street. Professionally he preferred Ulysses Jr. to Buck, and his famous name attracted the attention of potential business associates, among whom Ferdinand Ward cut the most striking figure. Ward was about Buck's age and as charming as a young man could be. Older men wished to be his father, young women to be his wife. The wishes of one of each came to pass when he married the daughter of an officer of the Marine National Bank. The union seemed a splendid match and gave Ward entrée to the highest echelons of Wall Street influence. Buck Grant had begun to handle some of his father's finances, as well as money held in trust for other clients; Ward invited him to invest in ventures he knew to be sure winners on the basis of information not widely shared. Buck did so, the ventures paid handsomely and Ward seemed a genius. When Ward proposed that the two open a firm together, Buck considered himself very lucky. Grant & Ward leased offices at 2 Wall Street and commenced an active business. Bradstreet, the rating agency, bestowed its "gilt-edged" seal of approval on the firm; James Fish, the president of Marine Bank, extended an open line of credit.

Buck's father was proud of the boy, concluding that while the Grant family's talent for business might have skipped over him, it had landed squarely on Buck. Grant was pleased to become a nonmanaging partner in Grant & Ward, investing his entire liquid capital of $100,000. He refused to countenance dealing in government contracts, as that would seem to be trading on his position as former president, but he otherwise let Ward use his name in developing the business. "I am willing that Mr. Ward should derive what profit he can for the firm that the use of my name and influence may bring," Grant wrote James Fish, who had become a partner as well.

The firm's business boomed. The economy as a whole was rebounding from the depression of the 1870s and Grant & Ward benefited from the bounce. Its ledger books showed profits of double and triple digits, which Ward as directing partner put back into the business. His private life seemed a model of moral and ethical regularity; he had no vices and his only excess, if such it could be called, was a driving ambition to emulate the giants of Wall Street. "It is my plan to build up a great firm that shall live after Grant and Ward, its founders, have passed away," he said.

Grant reveled in the good fortune that had finally blessed his economic endeavors. "We are much better off than ever we were before," he wrote Nellie. "The family are enjoying as much prosperity as we ought to expect." His balance with Grant & Ward grew larger each month; he withdrew modest amounts for living expenses but reinvested the remainder, and the compounding interest swelled his balance the more. By the spring of 1884 he silently congratulated himself on being almost a millionaire.

The first sign that anything was amiss came on a Sunday afternoon in May. Ward paid a visit to the Grant household, where Buck and his wife were living with Grant and Julia. Ward took father and son aside and said that Marine Bank, which handled some of Grant & Ward's accounts, was suffering short-term liquidity problems. Marine needed an emergency bridge loan.

Buck knew that Grant & Ward had more than $700,000 deposited with Marine. He asked if the bank was good for that amount. Ward said it was, but if word got out that Marine was in trouble, the spillover effect could damage Grant & Ward. Neither Buck nor Grant had any reason to doubt Ward, and when Ward inquired if Grant could raise $150,000 quickly, the general was disposed to try. Ward asked if Grant knew William Vanderbilt; Grant acknowledged that he did. Could he ask the railroad magnate for a loan? Grant supposed he could. Grant drove to Vanderbilt's house and related the story Ward had told him. Vanderbilt said he cared nothing for Marine Bank and little more for Grant & Ward, but he respected and admired Grant and would give him the money as a personal loan.

Grant handed Vanderbilt's check to Ward, and briefly all seemed to be well. But Marine Bank's troubles proved to be deeper than Ward had let on, and two days later the bank was forced to close its doors. Almost immediately Grant & Ward suspended operations too, as it became known that Ward and Marine president James Fish had speculated heavily in real estate and lost. Ward disappeared and Fish refused to come out of his office. The financial community shuddered, fearing a repetition of the panic of 1873. But Jay Gould, by now the acknowledged sage of Wall Street, shrugged his shoulders and said the failed companies weren't important enough to cause wide worry. The business of the street proceeded almost as usual.

Yet the Grant name evoked interest, and the nation watched to see the response of the famous silent partner. "General Grant was informed of the difficulties of the firm early in the day," the *New York Times* reported. "He reached the firm's office about noon and remained in the private office until 2 o'clock, when he stepped into a carriage and was driven home. He was as calm as usual, but declined to talk about the trouble." Grant's supporters wanted to lend a hand. "Many offers of aid were made to the ex-President, but he said that he did not feel at liberty to accept any of them."

Explaining and resolving the firm's failure took months. As examiners and prosecutors scrutinized the books they discovered that Ward had been cheating for years. The high returns were illusory, artifacts of an unsustainable pyramid scheme. Ward was tried for grand larceny, found guilty and sentenced to ten years' hard labor at Sing Sing prison.

*T*he verdict and sentence presumably satisfied public demands for accountability in the case, but they did nothing for Grant financially. After decades of striving to achieve material security, he was worse off financially than on the day he had left home for West Point. "The Grant family is ruined," he wrote a longtime friend. He wasn't merely penniless; he was deeply in debt. The $100,000 he had invested in Grant & Ward was gone, and so too the $150,000 he had borrowed from Vanderbilt. The second amount he considered a debt of honor, to be paid whatever the sacrifice. He sold some of his and Julia's property and deeded much of the rest to Vanderbilt, to whom he also handed over the various presents and souvenirs he had brought back from his world tour, along with ceremonial swords and other mementos given him by his American admirers. Vanderbilt didn't need the money and tried to forgive the debt, but Grant wouldn't hear of it.

In his desolation in the 1850s he had lamented that "poverty, poverty" stared him in the face; he felt its icy gaze again. He tried to maintain the appearance he considered necessary for one who had been president of the United States, but he had trouble simply meeting the expenses of his household. Merchants with whom he and Julia did daily business had to wait to be paid, until they learned to insist on cash. He and she cut corners where they could and worried where they couldn't.

Editors, recognizing his straits, renewed their interest in his life story. The *Century* magazine's Robert Johnson sought an article on Shiloh, a battle that remained as controversial as when it had been fought. Johnson would pay five hundred dollars. Grant didn't relish revisiting the war, especially the battles for which he had been criticized, but he now lacked the luxury of declining good money.

To his surprise he discovered that the writing came easily. The episodes of the war had stuck in his head, and he could envision the placement and movement of forces almost as readily as he had amid the smoke and noise of the war. And there was something else. Returning in his mind to the scenes of his greatest challenges and victories distracted him from his current distress. He was young again and at the height of his powers; the cares of the present fell away before the freedom and singleness of purpose of war.

He finished the piece and gave it to Johnson, who suggested making it more personal. Grant resisted at first but, for the money, did as told. He found a rhythm, and while the Shiloh article went to press he set to work on three others: on Vicksburg, the Wilderness and Chattanooga. Meanwhile he began to think about a book. Johnson and the *Century's* publisher, Roswell Smith, offered him a contract. He thanked them for the offer but said he wanted to start writing the long-form manuscript before he made a commitment.

.

*I*n the summer of 1884 Grant felt a scratchiness at the back of his throat. This wasn't the first time his throat had bothered him; he had recurrently experienced the heavy smoker's dryness and irritation. But the scratchiness persisted, then grew painful. He noticed a swelling visible on the outside of his throat. Julia insisted that he see his doctor, who summoned a specialist. The latter prescribed gargles and ointments and said the situation should be monitored closely.

Grant suspected more than the doctors were telling him, and he decided to sign a contract for his memoir. He let Roswell Smith know he was willing and terms were discussed. He had the signing pen almost in hand when Samuel Clemens heard of the negotiations and pushed himself into the middle of them. Clemens declared that the contract Smith was offering didn't do justice to such a distinguished figure as Grant. Clemens had a second, less altruistic motive: he had just entered the publishing business with his nephew-in-law Charles Webster and wanted to publish Grant's memoir himself. Clemens knew the book business better than magazine man Smith did, and he calculated that the life story of the greatest hero of the age would be a publishing coup.

He approached Grant indirectly. "I pointed out that the contract as it stood"—the *Century* contract—"had an offensive detail in it which I had never heard of in the ten per cent contract of even the most obscure author," he recalled. "This contract not only proposed a ten per cent royalty for such a colossus as General Grant, but it also had in it a requirement that out of that ten per cent must come some trivial tax for the book's share of clerk hire, house rent, sweeping out of the offices, or some such nonsense as that." Grant should insist on much better terms. "I said he ought to have three-fourths of the profits and let the publisher pay running expenses out of his remaining fourth."

Clemens's words upset Grant, who felt an obligation to Smith but nonetheless had his and especially Julia's financial future to consider. Fred Grant happened to be present and suggested that his father sleep on the matter. Grant agreed.

Overnight Clemens developed his business plan. He would sell the Grant memoir by subscription, requiring readers to pay in advance of publication and enlisting subscription agents to drum up interest. The plan diminished the risk to the publisher, in that every book would be presold. And it perfectly suited an icon like Grant, as most purchasers would buy the book simply because they liked Grant and what he stood for. Of the millions who had served under Grant or voted for him, at least several hundred thousand ought to be willing to pay a few dollars to buy his book.

The next day he found Grant skeptical. Grant had talked to William Sherman, who said he had made twenty-five thousand dollars from his memoir. Grant doubted he could do that well. Clemens asked why. Grant said he had offered to sell his memoir for that amount to Roswell Smith and Smith had nearly fainted.

Clemens saw his opening. "Sell *me* the memoirs, General," he said. "I am a publisher. I will pay double the price. I have a checkbook in my pocket; take my check for fifty thousand dollars now and let's draw the contract."

Grant refused. He said the book might be a failure. He considered Clemens a friend and didn't want him to carry all the risk.

Clemens explained the subscription model and how it reduced the risk. He specified terms: "Seventy-five per cent of the profits on the publication go to you, I to pay all running expenses such as salaries, etc., out of my fourth."

Grant asked what Clemens thought would be left out of his fourth. "A hundred thousand dollars in six months," Clemens replied confidently.

Grant was startled by the number. He and Clemens spoke further and Clemens's confidence gradually persuaded him. But before he signed he called in George Childs, a friend who knew the publishing business. Childs queried Clemens about the capacity of his publishing firm, Webster & Co., to produce a book of the magnitude he projected for Grant's memoir. Satisfied at the answers he received, Childs told Grant: "Give the book to Clemens." And Grant did.

86

NOW HE HAD TO WRITE THE BOOK. HE BEGAN WORKING SEVERAL hours a day at his Wall Street office. The drafting went smoothly, with the pieces of his past falling into their logical and narrative places. Adam Badeau helped with the research; Fred Grant located documents and checked facts. Clemens received chapters and at first read them without comment, since he didn't presume to tell the great general how to write about war. But he heard that Grant was taking his silence amiss, as indicative of literary disapproval. Clemens had been reading Caesar's *Commentaries*, and he told Grant that his manuscript compared favorably in its directness, balance and honesty with that model of the military memoir. "I learned afterward that General Grant was pleased with this verdict," Clemens remarked. "It shows that he was just a man, just a human being, just an author. An author values a compliment even when it comes from a source of doubtful competency."

*A*merica followed his progress, and it followed the course of his illness. The papers got his medical status wrong about as often as they got it right. In February 1885 the *New York Times* scooped the *Medical Record* by quoting an article about to appear in that journal giving Grant a promising prognosis. His symptoms were diminishing and the responsible tumor was not malignant, the article said. "It is a matter for great congratulation that all fear of grave complications are for the present at an end and that our beloved ex-President is spared an affliction the bare contemplation of which would be distressing in the extreme."

At that very moment Grant's throat specialist was reaching the opposite conclusion. John Douglas discovered that the tumor was malignant and said the symptoms would get only worse. Just days after its buoyant piece, the *Times* headlined the grim truth: "Sinking into the Grave. General Grant's Friends Give Up Hope. Dying Slowly from Cancer." The article recounted the course of Grant's affliction, the consultations of his various doctors and the diagnosis of inoperable cancer. "The doctors, of course, make no predictions as to the rapidity with which the disease will work," the paper said. "But their opinion seems to be that the gallant old warrior has at the most only a few months to live, and that his death may occur in a short time."

The paper appended a progress report on Grant's writing. "Throughout his troubles General Grant has worked constantly on his literary projects. Of late his attention had been given to his own autobiography, feeling that if it was to be completed it must be done at once."

Since Vicksburg the eyes of the nation had been on Grant. For more than two decades the country had followed its hero through war and peace. Now it followed him into his final battle, the one he couldn't win. Or perhaps he could, for even as the cancer pronounced his mortality, his manuscript proclaimed his immortality—*if* he could finish it. Most of the papers, not wishing to appear impertinent, didn't play the story as a race, but that was what it seemed: Grant against death.

For a time death appeared to have the advantage. It nearly carried him off in late March when a coughing spell briefly stopped his heart. His doctor revived him with an injection of brandy and ammonia and administered digitalis thereafter. The crisis passed but the pain persisted. Swallowing was agony; he lost twenty pounds, then thirty and forty. He resorted to opiates, which rendered him too groggy to work. He had been dictating the manuscript to a stenographer, but speaking often became so difficult that he turned to writing by hand.

The effort required for him to continue made credible a story published by the *New York World* asserting that Adam Badeau had taken over the drafting. Badeau apparently inspired the story as part of an effort to negotiate better terms with Grant, from whom he demanded a larger stipend and a share of the profits of the book sale. Sam Clemens was outraged at the *World*'s story, which, if believed, would have diminished the book's credibility and therefore marketability; he urged Grant to sue the paper for libel.

Grant had neither energy nor inclination to sue. He confined himself to a simple affirmation of his authorship. "The composition is entirely my own," he wrote in a letter to his publisher, which Clemens released to the *World*. But he did fire Badeau from the project.

He meanwhile put on a convincing show for a reporter from the rival *Times*, who described a day in the life of an author in firm command of his subject. "It was a busy time at General Grant's yesterday," the paper explained. "The General resumed work on his book at an early hour. His easy chair was drawn up beside the library table, which was strewn with papers bearing on the records that he is compiling." Grant spent part of the day organizing his material and part dictating to his stenographer. "At the close of the day he expressed himself fully satisfied with what he had done, the narrative having been carried forward to events preparatory to the Appomattox campaign. . . . All that is needed now is a straight narrative to join and explain the records that close and follow actual hostilities."

*B*ut he couldn't keep it up. The approach of summer caused his doctor to recommend the slower pace and cleaner air of the country; he traveled in June to Mount McGregor, near Saratoga. The change of scenery didn't much ease his pain but did promote reflection. "Since coming to this beautiful climate and getting a complete rest for about ten hours, I have watched my pains and compared them with those of the past few weeks," he wrote in a journal he commenced on arrival. "I can feel plainly that my system is preparing for dissolution in three ways: one by hemorrhages, one by strangulation, and the third by exhaustion. The first and second are liable to come at any moment to relieve me of my earthly sufferings; the time for the arrival of the third can be computed with almost mathematical certainty. . . . I have fallen off in weight and strength very rapidly for the last two weeks. There cannot be a hope of going far beyond this time. All any physician, or any number of them, can do for me now is to make my burden of pain as light as possible." He didn't want new doctors brought in on the case, although he realized his family and his doctor might insist. He wouldn't refuse in that event. "I dread them, however, knowing that it means another desperate effort to save me, and more suffering."

He continued to work, though he could feel the cost. "I presume every strain of the mind or body is one more nail in the coffin," he recorded.

He monitored his reactions to the medicines he was given. "I do not feel the slightest desire to take morphine now. In fact when I do take it it is not from craving, but merely from a knowledge of the relief it gives. If I should go without it all night I would become restless, I know, partly from the loss of it and partly from the continuous pain I would have to endure." His doctors had experimented with injections of cocaine, a new drug, but now were cutting back the dosage. "It is a little hard giving up the use of cocaine when it gives so much relief. But I suppose that it may be used two or three times a day without injury, and possibly with benefit when the overuse of it has been counteracted." Eventually the positive effect wore off. "Cocaine is a failure in my case now. It hurts very much to apply it, and I do not feel that it does me much good." The interactions among his medicines sometimes caused a nervous agitation. "I feel very badly probably because of a cross fire between opium and laudanum. . . . The alcoholic stimulants must absolutely be given up. . . . I feel as if I cannot endure it any longer."

Yet he could recognize the humor in his situation. He knew the papers were conducting a death watch and had him hurtling toward the grave. "I see the *Times* man keeps up the character of his dispatches to the paper. They are quite as untrue as they would be if he described me as getting better from day to day." For most of one week he felt less pain than usual, thereby spoiling the story line—or so he thought until he read the accounts. "The newspapers gave that as a sure indication that I was declining rapidly." Visitors cherished whatever fragments he scribbled. "I will have to be careful about my writing. I see every person I give a piece of paper to puts it in his pocket. Some day they will be coming up against my English." Even on the worst days he could joke with himself. "I do not sleep, though I sometimes doze off a little. If up, I am talked to and, in my efforts to answer, cause pain. The fact is I think I am a verb instead of a personal pronoun. A verb is anything that signifies to be, to do, or to suffer. I signify all three."

He pondered mortality and destiny. "If it is within God's providence that I should go now I am ready to obey his call without a murmur." He was pleased to have lived as long as he had. "It has enabled me to see for myself the happy harmony which has so suddenly sprung up between those engaged but a few short years ago in deadly conflict." The silver lining of his illness was the broad sympathy it elicited from his countrymen. "It has been an inestimable blessing to me to hear the kind expressions towards me in person from all parts of the country; from people of all nationalities, of all religions, and of no religion, of Confederate and National troops alike, of soldiers' organizations, of mechanical, scientific, religious, and all other societies, embracing almost every citizen of the land. They have brought joy to my heart, if they have not effected a cure." Until far into adulthood he couldn't have imagined what life would bring him. "I never thought of acquiring rank in the profession I was educated for; yet it came with two grades higher prefixed to the rank of General officer for me. I certainly never had either ambition or taste for a political life; yet I was twice President of the United States. If anyone had suggested the idea of my becoming an author, as they frequently did, I was not sure whether they were making sport of me or not."

Some days his symptoms retreated and he sat on the porch in the summer sun. "I feel pretty well. . . . Took a half hour's nap. . . . I am as bright and well now, for a time at least, as I ever will be." He posed for a photograph with his family gathered around. But his relentless companion always returned. "The disease is still there and must be fatal in the end."

Sam Clemens came to visit; they discussed the book—Clemens speaking, Grant communicating by pencil. "He asked me with his pencil, and evidently with anxious solicitude, if there was a prospect that his book would make something for his family," Clemens wrote later. "I said that the canvass for it was progressing vigorously, that the subscriptions and the money were coming in fast, that the campaign was not more than half completed yet, but that if it should stop where it was there would be two hundred thousand dollars coming to his family. He expressed his gratification, with his pencil."

Simon Buckner arrived as Clemens was leaving. Buckner hadn't seen Grant since the Union capture of Fort Donelson, when he had surrendered the garrison's fifteen thousand troops to Grant. He laughed with Grant about the old days, reminding him and others present about the time in 1854 when he had loaned Grant fifty dollars. "I have my full share of admiration and esteem for Grant," he said. "It dates back to our cadet days. He has as many merits and virtues as any man I am acquainted with, but he has one deadly defect. He is an incurable borrower, and when he wants to borrow he knows of only one limit—he wants what you've got. When I was poor he borrowed fifty dollars of me; when I was rich he borrowed fifteen thousand men."

Other soldiers remembered Grant as fondly. Letters from comrades conveyed respect and admiration. "I am older than your Father and of

a shorter lived race than he, therefore never dreamed of outliving him,"
William Sherman wrote Fred from St. Louis. "Still, if so ordained I wish
to be present when he is entombed, and to be a willing witness to the
great qualities which made him the conspicuous figure of our eventful
epoch. Keep these facts in your memory and act on them when the time
comes, but meantime as long as there is life I have hope." The Grand
Army of the Republic made its annual encampment in Maine and sent
Grant its "profound sympathy in his continued illness." He replied with
thanks and a farewell. "Tell the boys that they probably will never look
into my face again nor hear my voice, but they are engraved on my heart
and I love them as my children. What the good Lord has spared me for is
more than I can tell, but it is perhaps to finish up my book, which I shall
leave to the boys in blue."

He bade Julia farewell also. She couldn't talk about his death without
breaking down, so he wrote her a letter. "Look after our dear children
and direct them in the paths of rectitude," he said. "It would distress
me far more to think that one of them could depart from an honorable,
upright and virtuous life than it would to know they were prostrated on a
bed of sickness from which they were never to arise alive." He told her to
make the decision as to where he should be buried. West Point would be
suitable except that she couldn't lie beside him. Galena was a possibility.
New York City, their current residence and a place where she could visit
the grave, appeared the most likely. But the decision was hers. "With
these few injunctions," he concluded, "and the knowledge I have of your
love and affections and of the dutiful affections of all our children, I bid
you a final farewell until we meet in another, and I trust better, world."

Through it all he kept working. "I must try to get some soft pencils.
I could then write plainer and more rapidly." He drafted the last chapter.
"I have been writing up my views of some of our generals, and of the
character of Lincoln and Stanton. I do not place Stanton as high as some
people do. Mr. Lincoln cannot be extolled too highly."

By the middle of July the end was in sight. "Buck has brought up the
last of the first volume in print," he wrote. "In two weeks if they work
hard they can have the second volume copied ready to go to the printer. I
will then feel that my work is done." Things went faster than he thought.
On July 16 he decided he had made all the additions and corrections
he wanted to make. "There is nothing more I should do to it now." He

added, "Therefore I am not likely to be more ready to go than at this moment."

He took his leave days later. His body was starving from lack of nourishment; his weight fell below one hundred pounds. He couldn't sleep and grew ever more exhausted. For months he had slept in a chair, the better to clear his throat; now, too weak to sit, he went to bed. He drifted in and out of consciousness; Julia and the children gathered around him. In the predawn hours of July 23 he slipped into a final reverie. His limbs began to grow cold. His breathing grew fainter until, a few minutes past eight, it stopped and didn't resume.

THE COUNTRY HAD BEEN BRACING FOR THE NEWS, BUT NO ONE expected the flood of emotion that followed. In cities and towns all across America, memorials and resolutions were read extolling the accomplishments of the great man. The South joined the North and the West in commemorating his virtues; New Orleans and Richmond matched New York and Chicago in celebrating the life well lived. Condolences came from most countries of Europe and several in Asia and Latin America; London's Westminster Abbey held a special service in his honor.

The African American community mourned particularly. "In General Grant's death the colored people of this and all other countries, and the oppressed everywhere, irrespective of complexion, have lost a preeminently true and faithful defender," a group of black veterans resolved in New York City. Hundreds of black churches prayed for the soul of their departed champion.

People recalled and related stories about Grant. A veteran of the Richmond campaign told of entering the Confederate capital and seeing graffiti scrawled in charcoal on the wall of a church: "Ulysses S. Grant: May he be hung, drawn, and quartered." Angry Union troops prepared to burn the church. But one of the soldiers discovered a statement riposting the first: "Hung with laurels of victory, drawn in the chariot of peace, and quartered in the White House at Washington." The church was spared. M. D. Leggett, who had served on Grant's military staff, remembered his leadership traits. "I heard him say once with a little impatience that he had less concern for an officer who was afraid to face the enemy than for one who hesitated in forming a judgment when he knew all the necessary facts. He said that the most cowardly officer in the command of troops was the one that was afraid of his own judgment. . . . His confidence in his own judgment seemed to be unbounded. Of all the men I ever met he was the most self-poised and the most self-reliant. It seemed impossible to confuse him or even to annoy him in great emergencies." His bravery allowed him to focus on the problem at hand. "When under fire Grant never gave an indication that he was thinking of the bullets. He went where his duty took him, regardless of personal considerations. This was just as true of him in everything else. He seemed always to drop himself out of his consciousness in his devotion to the especial work before him." Leggett acknowledged that Grant was criticized for adhering too long to friends. "It is a trait of every unselfish nature. A selfish, ambitious man will use a friend as long as he can serve his selfishness, and then will throw him aside as he would the rind of a well-squeezed lemon. A man with an honest, unselfish nature cannot be thus, but will remember the friend that stood by him when he needed friends."

A reporter caught Phil Sheridan on a train. The cavalryman was at a loss for words. "Everything has been said about General Grant that can be said," he declared. "I would willingly add to it if I could, for everybody knows how I regarded him. He was the greatest soldier in our history." Oliver Howard told of a moment just after the war when fear of a renewed insurgency gripped the capital. Grant assigned a particular officer to command the troops guarding Washington. "Why, you cannot trust that officer; he is 'coppery'!" another officer exclaimed, referring to the man's known Southern connections. Grant looked calmly at the speaker and said, "You must trust him. If you do not have confidence, soon you can trust nobody. Trust him, sir, and he will be true." The impugned officer performed magnificently. James Longstreet spoke succinctly from Georgia: "He was the truest as well as the bravest man that ever lived."

For a week the papers filled their columns with the preparations for the funeral. Julia had decided on New York as his resting place. Washington put in a late bid, with advocates of the capital contending that a national hero should be buried on national ground. Samuel Clemens rejoined: "Wherever General Grant's body lies, *that* is national ground."

*T*he final leg of his journey began with a predawn artillery salute on the slopes of Mount McGregor. A thousand people arrived for the outdoor service that sent him on his way to New York. Thousands more lined the track from Mount McGregor to Saratoga and from there to Albany. Bells in each town tolled a dirge as the funeral train, draped in furlongs of black cloth, rolled past. The casket was taken from the train at Albany and placed in the state capitol, where a constantly replenished line of mourners with bared and bowed heads filed slowly past. The casket was returned to the train the next day and continued south. The crowds grew thicker along the tracks as the train neared New York. It reached Grand Central Station in the late afternoon. "There was a burst of sunlight and a rainbow spanned the eastern sky," an onlooker observed. The casket was again removed from the train and this time carried to City Hall. During nineteen hours of public showing, 125,000 people paid their respects to the Union's savior.

The last several miles, from City Hall to Riverside Park, took half a day to traverse. A million and a half people, the largest crowd in New York's history, clogged the procession's route; their black attire, against the black that hung from doors and windows and lampposts, cast a fitting gloom over the city. A hundred thousand pedestrians streamed across the recently finished Brooklyn Bridge; the city's commuter railroads, ferries and trolleys carried more passengers than ever before. The city's hotels and restaurants broke all records for business.

Tens of thousands of people marched in the procession. Dozens of active-duty regiments from several states—infantry, cavalry, artillery—tramped, clopped and rumbled along the streets. Grizzled veterans of the Grand Army showed equal fervor if less energy. Winfield Scott Hancock, on a glistening charger, led the procession; Virginia's Fitzhugh Lee represented the Confederacy. President Grover Cleveland was accompanied by former presidents Rutherford Hayes and Chester Arthur. Cabinet secretaries, Supreme Court justices, senators and representatives likewise paid the federal government's respects. Mayor William Grace conveyed the regards of the city of New York, while police commissioner Fitz John Porter, fully rehabilitated after Grant's exoneration of him, oversaw security. Dozens of foreign diplomats bespoke the respect in which the hero was held in their home countries.

Twenty-four black horses pulled the catafalque to the tomb site. As it reached the ridge crest and came in sight of the Hudson, more than a hundred feet below, the guns of several warships in the river boomed a salute. The pallbearers, including William Sheridan, Phil Sherman, Admiral David Porter and Confederate generals Joseph Johnston and

Simon Buckner, guided the casket to the cedar box into which it was lowered, pending the construction of the permanent tomb. The drums of the U.S. Marine band rolled while the undertaker screwed on the lid. A wreath of oak leaves was placed on top. Several moments of silence ensued. Then the people of New York were permitted in. They moved quietly through the site for several hours until, at six o'clock, the police closed the doors, with instructions to the thousands still in line that they could return the next day.

They returned the next day and for days and weeks following. Only gradually did their number diminish, till Grant's resting place became a tourist site the locals mostly left alone. But a dozen years after the funeral the city and country turned out again in force. By 1897 Grant's legacy was coming into view. His stature as a military hero had never been higher. A few white Southerners still dreamed that secession could have succeeded and slavery been preserved, but most had let the Lost Cause go. Those who nursed a grudge against the bluecoats reserved their special animus for Sherman, who outlived Grant by a half decade without evincing second thoughts about the march to the sea. Students of the military arts rehearsed and analyzed Grant's campaigns and observed that for all the honor paid Lee for brilliance and daring, it was Grant who had the harder task in their epic struggle. Grant fought in enemy territory against an army that typically stood behind developed defenses; Grant had to win while Lee had merely to avoid losing. Attackers almost always suffer greater casualties than defenders, but Grant's casualties, as a portion of his army, were lower than Lee's. His mistakes were few and never decisive. And in the reckoning that overrode all others, he came out on top: he won the war.

Grant's presidency was evoking mixed reactions. In the years since he had left office, influential groups on both sides of the Mason-Dixon Line had consciously sought reconciliation, which had been Grant's goal too. But where Grant's approach to reconciliation was premised on the egalitarian ideals of the Fourteenth and Fifteenth Amendments, these new reconciliationists—white Southern Democrats and Northern capitalist-minded Republicans—preferred the path of amnesia. The Southern Democrats forgot that secession was about slavery, they recast the Civil War as a difference over states' rights, and they recalled Reconstruction as a carnival of corruption from which they had at length redeemed the

South. The Northern capitalist Republicans lost touch with the anti-slavery roots of their party, they pushed aside Lincoln in favor of J. P. Morgan and company, and if they didn't actively embrace the Southern redefinition of the war and its aftermath, they didn't bother to dispute it. They transmuted the Fourteenth Amendment from a charter of citizenship rights into a guarantor of corporate rights; the Fifteenth Amendment they and their Southern allies-in-amnesia ignored.

To both groups Grant's presidency posed a problem, for it stood against their revision of recent history. They responded by attacking his presidency and him as president. They emphasized the scandals, neglecting Grant's role in defeating the Black Friday gold corner and in bringing the whiskey culprits to justice, and conflating the transgressions that occurred under his authority with such extraneous bilkings as Crédit Mobilier and the Tweed Ring. They reiterated the tales of Grant's drinking without demonstrating a single instance where alcohol impaired his performance of duty. They threw his efforts to enforce the Constitution, especially as it pertained to civil rights in the South, back in his face as evidence of a militaristic mindset.

Yet if Grant's presidential reputation fared poorly with the elites, it resonated positively with those for whom he had fought. Southern blacks and the Northerners who revered Lincoln honored Grant for striving to uphold the vision of the Great Emancipator. They couldn't know that nearly a century would pass before the country had another president who took civil rights as seriously as Grant did. American Indians recalled Grant as the president whose peace policy offered a distinct alternative to the aggressive exploitation favored by his predecessors and most of his contemporaries. The Indians, like the African Americans, could not claim lasting success for Grant's endeavors on their behalf; his struggle for minority rights against majority hostility or indifference was a battle he couldn't win. But he waged a good and honorable fight.

One thing all Americans could agree on was Grant's central role in saving the Union. As commanding general in the Civil War he had defeated secession and destroyed slavery, secession's cause. As president during Reconstruction he had guided the South back into the Union. By the end of his public life the Union was more secure than at any previous time in the history of the nation. And no one had done more to produce that result than he.

It was Grant's role as unifier that those who gathered in New York in April 1897 came to celebrate. Many present had purchased his book,

which sold hundreds of thousands of copies and let Samuel Clemens pay
Julia Grant $400,000 while keeping a nice profit for himself. The book
impressed critics, who then and later accounted it a historical landmark
and a literary gem. Grant's clarity in depicting his campaigns enabled
his Northern admirers to relive their side's stirring victories; at the same
time, his generous tone and the respect he displayed for his Confederate foes allowed Southerners to read it with equal benefit, if perhaps less
enthusiasm.

By the time Grant's tomb was completed, he had become a symbol
of national unity around whom Northerners and Southerners both could
rally. Veterans of the war took the lead in the procession to his monument that blustery spring day. They were men who had fought beside
Grant in the Union armies of the Tennessee and Potomac; they were
men who had served with Lee in the Confederate Army of Northern
Virginia. Their general officers were nearly all gone, although John Gordon, scarred from battle and crippled by age and recent accident, rode
in a carriage. The Union veterans of the Virginia campaign lined up to
shake this former enemy's hand, with several nonetheless remarking that
in their prime they would have shot him. He cheerfully returned the sentiment, and all shared in the comradeship of battles survived. A sturdy
Confederate sallied into the Union ranks in worn but mended grays; he
boasted that he was proud of his service on behalf of his cause but had
come to honor a valiant soldier and a great man. He was met with back-
slaps and hurrahs. A company of Confederates reproduced the rebel yell;
a Union band struck up "Dixie."

ACKNOWLEDGMENTS

The author would like to thank the many people who made this book possible. The librarians and archivists at the University of Texas at Austin, the Library of Congress and the other institutions where I conducted research provided indispensable assistance. Bill Thomas, Kristine Puopolo and Stephanie Bowen at Doubleday were insightful and professional from start to finish. Roslyn Schloss did her usual brilliant job of copyediting. My colleagues and students at the University of Texas allowed me to test my thinking on them. Gregory Curtis, Stephen Harrigan and Lawrence Wright offered weekly literary consultation.

SOURCES

The principal sources for the present work are the letters, orders, memoranda, presidential messages and other writings of Ulysses S. Grant. The most comprehensive collection of these materials is *The Papers of Ulysses S. Grant*, carefully and revealingly edited by John Y. Simon and published in thirty-one volumes by Southern Illinois University Press between 1967 and 2009. The great majority of entries are from Grant's own hand, but numerous incoming letters and other supporting material are included in the extensive notes. Many of these incoming letters have not been available to previous biographers, and they afford new insight into Grant's presidency, in particular his campaign against the Ku Klux Klan. In the source references below, letters and other documents written by Grant and taken from this collection are cited by date alone. Collateral materials from this collection (which often appear out of chronological order) are cited in the form *Papers of Grant*, volume, page.

The Ulysses S. Grant Papers at the Library of Congress cover much of the same ground as the published collection, especially for the years of Grant's presidency. To an even greater degree than the published Grant papers, this collection includes incoming and collateral correspondence. References to this collection are given as "Grant Papers, Library of Congress."

Grant's *Memoirs* are another essential source. Widely considered the finest autobiographical work by any president, they merit this distinction in part by avoiding the presidency. The memoirs recount Grant's early life and especially his service in the Union army during the Civil War. The memoirs convey the authority of command and indeed echo the clear, direct prose of his wartime orders. They gain additional credibility from the unusual circumstances of their composition, during Grant's final months of life, when he knew he was dying of cancer. The edition cited in the present work is the one published by the Library of America in 1990.

Any account of the military campaigns of the Civil War must depend heavily on the mammoth collection of orders and reports published by the War Department in seventy volumes between 1880 and 1901 as *The War of the Rebellion: The Official Records of the Union and Confederate Armies*. The collection is unwieldy, as the user often has to jump between series and volumes to follow a given campaign, but it is invaluable. It is cited here as *Official Records*.

The letters and papers of Abraham Lincoln shed great light on Grant's relations with his commander in chief, as well as on the broader aspects of Lincoln's policies during the Civil War. *The Collected Works of Abraham Lincoln* is the published version; the Abraham Lincoln Papers at the Library of Congress are the unpublished counterpart.

Very many of the military officers and civilian officials active during Grant's lifetime published memoirs. Several of these are cited in the notes below; the most important and revealing by one of Grant's fellow officers is William T. Sherman's. The Library of America edition of Sherman's memoir, published in 1990, is the one cited here. Many of these same officers and officials left collections of papers; the most important repository is the Library of Congress.

The Personal Memoirs of Julia Dent Grant occupy a special category. They convey aspects of Grant family life unavailable in other sources, as well as Julia Grant's occasional comments on the politics of the army and the presidency.

Digital archives have become indispensable to historians and biographers. One devoted to Grant, the Ulysses S. Grant Homepage (granthomepage.com), includes transcripts of interviews of individuals who knew Grant, as well as clippings from nineteenth-century newspapers. The best digital archive of the American presidency is the American Presidency Project (presidency.ucsb.edu), which includes the public papers of Grant and every other president. This collection is cited as "Public Papers."

The secondary literature pertaining to Grant's life and career is much too large to summarize in even a cursory fashion. Substantially more than a hundred biographies of Grant have been published; significant studies of the Civil War number in the tens of thousands. Many of these have been cited in the notes below, but absence from the notes does not imply lack of importance. This said, special mention should be made of a small number of works: William S. McFeely, *Grant* (1981); Brooks D. Simpson, *Let Us Have Peace: Ulysses S. Grant and the Politics of War and Reconstruction, 1861–1868* (1991), and *Ulysses S. Grant: Triumph over Adversity, 1822–1865* (2000); Geoffrey Perret, *Ulysses S. Grant: Soldier and President* (1997); Jean Edward Smith, *Grant* (2001); and Charles Bracelen Flood, *Grant and Sherman: The Friendship That Won the Civil War* (2005).

NOTES

PART ONE: PROUD WALLS

CHAPTER 1

7 "I was not studious": Ulysses S. Grant, *Memoirs and Selected Letters* (Library of America, 1990), 21.

7 "He was always a steady, serious sort of boy": Hannah Simpson Grant interview, *New York Graphic*, Sept. 16, 1879, granthomepage.com.

8 "He would rather do anything else . . . the bridle reins": Jesse Root Grant interview, *Ulysses S. Grant Association Newsletter*, Oct. 1970 and Jan. 1971, granthomepage.com.

8 "Papa says . . . from the peculiarity": *Memoirs*, 22-27.

9 "Ulysses, I believe . . . had been reached": *Memoirs*, 28-31.

11 "I slept for two months": to R. McKinstry Griffith, Sept. 22, 1839.

11 "When the 28th of August came": *Memoirs*, 31.

11 "We have tremendous long . . . 'or an animal?'": to Griffith, Sept. 22, 1839.

12 "With his commanding figure": *Memoirs*, 33.

12 "There is much to dislike": to Griffith, Sept. 22, 1839.

13 "I saw in this": *Memoirs*, 32.

13 "A clean-faced, slender, blue-eyed young fellow": James Fry interview (unattributed), granthomepage.com.

14 "While I was riding . . . appreciate it so highly": *Memoirs*, 35.

CHAPTER 2

15 "an exceedingly fine looking young man": Mary Robinson interview, *St. Louis Republican*, July 24, 1885, granthomepage.com.

18 "I looked at it a moment": *Memoirs*, 38-39.

18 "Old man Dent was opposed to him": Mary Robinson interview.

19 "The country is low . . . through in streams": to Julia Dent, June 4, 1844.

20 "Our orders": to Julia Dent, July 6, 1845.

20 "I have waited so long": to Julia Dent, Aug. 31, 1844.

20 "Julia, can we hope": to Julia Dent, Jan. 12, 1845.

20 "San Antonio has the appearance": to Julia Dent, Jan. 2, 1846.

21 "Benjamin and I": *Memoirs*, 55.

21 "Our national birth . . . multiplying millions": Edward L. Widmer, *Young America* (2000), 43; Thomas R. Hietala, *Manifest Design* (2003), 255.

CHAPTER 3

24 "Everyone rejoices . . . engraved in it": to Julia Dent, March 3, 1846.

25 "The country was a rolling prairie": *Memoirs*, 61-62.

25 "A parley took place . . . intimidate our troops": to Julia Dent, March 29, 1846.

26 "We marched nearly all night": to Julia Dent, May 3, 1846.

26 "A young second-lieutenant": *Memoirs*, 65.

27 "Our wagons were immediately parked . . . sergeant down besides": to Julia Dent, May 11, 1846; *Memoirs*, 66.

27 "It was a terrible sight": to Julia Dent, May 11, 1846.

28 "an honor and responsibility . . . when in anticipation": *Memoirs*, 68-69; to Julia Dent, May 11, 1846.

CHAPTER 4

31 "After reiterated menaces": Polk message to Congress, May 11, 1846.

31 "Fortune, which has showered . . . a soldier's life": *Democracy in America*, ed. J. P. Mayer (1969), 646, 651.

32 "Matamoros contains probably": to John Lowe, June 26, 1846.

32 "Low with a flat or thatched roof": to Julia Dent, June 10, 1846.

32 "The whole country is low and flat": to Julia Dent, July 2, 1846.

33 "General Taylor never made any great show . . . or physical courage": *Memoirs*, 69-71.

34 "When we left Matamoros": to Julia Dent, Aug. 14, 1846.

35 "About one in five is sick": to Julia Dent, Sept. 6, 1846.

35 but some fifteen hundred: John S. D. Eisenhower, *So Far from God: The U.S. War with Mexico, 1846-1848* (1989), 110.

35 "I respectfully protest": to Bvt. Col. John Garland, undated (Aug. 1846).

35 "The tents and cooking utensils": *Memoirs*, 72-73.

35 "Monterrey is a beautiful city": to Julia Dent, Oct. 3, 1846.

36 "My curiosity got the better . . . 'what it was all about'": *Memoirs*, 76-82.

CHAPTER 5

39 "I have found in Lieutenant Grant": John W. Emerson, "Grant's Life in the West and His Mississippi Valley Campaigns," *Midland Monthly Magazine* (1897), 34.

39 "He died as a soldier dies": to Mrs. Thomas L. Hamer, undated (Dec. 1846).

40 "Hamer was one of the ablest men": *Memoirs*, 71.

40 "He is evidently a weak man": *The Diary of James K. Polk during His Presidency, 1845 to 1849* (1910), 2:249-50.

40 "Here we are": to unknown addressee, undated (Dec. 1846), Emerson, "Grant's Life in the West," 139-40.

41 "I was bitterly opposed": *Memoirs*, 41.

41 "I begin to think": to Julia Dent, Feb. 1, 1847.

41 "As soon as Gen. Scott": to Julia Dent, Feb. 1, 1847.

41 "A great part of the time": to Julia Dent, Feb. 25, 1847.

42 "Why, the thing looks": *Memoirs*, 86.

42 "The city is a solid, compact place": to Julia Dent, April 3, 1847.

43 "From Vera Cruz to this place": to Julia Dent, April 24, 1847.

43 "I *must* and *will* accompany my regiment": to unrecorded recipient, undated (April 1847).

44 "Lieutenant Grant is informed": from John Garland, undated (appended to Grant's request of April 1847, just above).

44 "Perhaps there was not a battle": *Memoirs*, 91.

45 "It was war pyrotechnics": to unidentified recipient, April 24, 1846.

45 "As soon as the Mexicans . . . without resistance": to John Lowe, May 3, 1846.

CHAPTER 6

46 "It surpasses St. Louis . . . resign or not": to Julia Dent, May 17, 1847.

48 "I happened to notice . . . without further loss": *Memoirs*, 103-04.

49 "When I knocked for admission": *Memoirs*, 106-09.

49 "most nobly": Walter Allen, *Ulysses S. Grant* (1901), 31.

49 "Mexico is one of the most beautiful cities": to Julia Dent, Sept. 1847.

49 "From my map . . . *ignorance* of the situation": to unknown addressee, undated (Sept. 12, 1847).

50 "The battles of Molino del Rey and Chapultepec": *Memoirs*, 104.

50 "that things are seen plainer": *Memoirs*, 113.

50 "The contrast between the two . . . pleasant to serve with": *Memoirs*, 94-95.

51 "Everything looks as if peace": to Julia Dent, Sept. 1847.

52 "If the treaty in its present form is ratified": *Diary of Polk*, Feb. 28, 1848, 3:366.

53 "not wishing to leave": *Memoirs*, 119.

53 "The day that we arrived . . . where they were": to Julia Dent, May 7, 1848; *Memoirs*, 123-28.

54 "I have no doubt": to Julia Dent, May 22, 1848.

CHAPTER 7

55 "I remember one day": *Memoirs of General W. T. Sherman* (1990 ed.), 64.

55 "At the Academy": *Memoirs of Sherman*, 16.

55 "I asked their business": *Memoirs of Sherman*, 64-65.

56 "Stories reached us": *Memoirs of Sherman*, 70, 78.

56 "The most moderate estimate": H. W. Brands, *The Age of Gold* (2002), 45-46.

57 "The accounts of the abundance": Polk annual message, Dec. 5, 1848, Public Papers.

58 "If he cannot or will not do this": *Works of Lincoln*, 1:439.

59 "No man was governed by higher or purer motives": Brands, *Age of Gold*, 304.

60 "I had had four years": *Personal Memoirs of Julia Dent Grant*, 55.

60 "How I marveled . . . I was well satisfied": Ibid., 56-57.

61 "Two years were spent": *Memoirs*, 130.

61 "A little frame house . . . a slicked bullet": James E. Pitman interview, William Conant Church Papers, Library of Congress, granthomepage.com.

62 "Sackets Harbor is as dull a little hole": to Julia Dent Grant, Aug. 31, 1851.

62 "Take good care of little Fred": to Julia Dent Grant, June 29, 1851.

62 "It distresses me, dearest": to Julia Dent Grant, undated (July 5, 1852).

62 "I was very much disappointed": to Julia Dent Grant, July 1, 1852.

62 "Mr. Clay's death": to Julia Dent Grant, July 4, 1852.

63 "The streets of the town": *Memoirs*, 131-33.

64 "My dearest": to Julia Dent Grant, Aug. 9, 1852.

CHAPTER 8

65 "I consider that city": to Julia Dent Grant, Sept. 19, 1852.

65 "Often broken places were found": *Memoirs*, 139.

66 "During my year on the Columbia River": *Memoirs*, 138.

66 "Everyone speaks well . . . within the year": to Julia Dent Grant, Sept. 19 and Oct. 7, 1852.

66 "I have been up to the Dalles": to Julia Dent Grant, Oct. 26, 1852.

66 "About pecuniary matters, dear Julia": to Julia Dent Grant, Dec. 3, 1852.

67 "The snow is now some ten inches": to Julia Dent Grant, Dec. 19, 1852.

67 "Captain Ingalls and myself": to Julia Dent Grant, Jan. 3, 1853.

67 "The climate of Oregon": to Julia Dent Grant, Jan. 29, 1853.

68 "I am farming extensively": to Julia Dent Grant, March 4 and 19, 1853.

68 "I have my health perfectly . . . bring you with me": to Julia Dent Grant, Oct. 26 and Dec. 19, 1852, and Jan. 29, 1853.

68 "The Columbia is now far over its banks . . . the commission way!": to Julia Dent Grant, June 28, 1853.

70 "I have purchased for them": to Julia Dent Grant, June 28, 1853.

70   "Besides the gambling in cards": *Memoirs*, 139-40.

71   "I cannot say much in favor of the place": to Julia Dent Grant, Jan. 18, 1854.

71   "I do nothing here . . . with his Grandpa": to Julia Dent Grant, Feb. 2, 1854.

71   "I have not been a hundred yards . . . necessities of life": to Julia Dent Grant, March 6 and 25, 1854.

72   "There is but one thing to console": to Julia Dent Grant, Feb. 6, 1854.

72   "There was not a day passed": *General George Crook: His Autobiography*, ed. Martin F. Schmitt (1986), 7.

73   "One glass would show . . . preferred against him": Charles G. Ellington, *The Trial of U. S. Grant: The Pacific Coast Years, 1852-1854* (1987), 167.

73   "Grant's friends at the time . . . on such a charge": Hamlin Garland, *Ulysses S. Grant* (1898), 127.

74   "I very respectfully tender": to Col. S. Cooper, April 11, 1854.

CHAPTER 9

75   "sink in hell": David M. Potter, *The Impending Crisis, 1848-1861* (1976), 155.

75   "It will raise a hell of a storm": Potter, *Impending Crisis*, 160.

76   "Do you suppose": *Congressional Globe*, 33:1:337-38.

76   "I adjure you": *Congressional Globe*, 33:1:342.

76   "a gross violation": Potter, *Impending Crisis*, 163.

76   "a terrible outrage . . . forever continue free": James M. McPherson, *Battle Cry of Freedom* (1988), 124.

76   "whip and spur": Potter, *Impending Crisis*, 166.

77   "I would be much gratified": Jesse Grant to Jefferson Davis, June 21, 1854, *Papers of Grant*, 1:330n.

77   "I have to inform you": Davis to Jesse Grant, June 28, 1854, *Papers of Grant*, 1:331n.

77   "Grant landed in New York in 1854": Simon Bolivar Buckner interview, Hamlin Garland Papers, Doheny Library, University of Southern California, granthomepage .com.

78   "West Point spoiled one of my boys": Hamlin Garland, *Ulysses S. Grant* (1898), 129.

78   "Mamma, is that ugly man my papa?": Garland, *Grant*, 74.

78   "How very happy": Garland, *Grant*, 75.

79   "I worked very hard": *Memoirs*, 141.

79   "I cannot imagine . . . call it Hardscrabble": *Personal Memoirs of Julia Dent Grant*, 78-79.

80   "I feel as if the *Mission*": Stephens to Robert Burch, June 15, 1854, *American Historical Review*, vol. 8 (1902-03), 92-96.

80   "I remember he impressed me": Paul M. Angle, ed., *The Lincoln Reader* (2005), 202-03.

81   "I pledge myself . . . destruction of slavery": Evan Carton, *Patriotic Treason: John Brown and the Soul of America* (2006), 82.

82 "Bleeding Kansas . . . abandon the Territory": Potter, *Impending Crisis*, 220; *New York Times*, May 30, 1856.

82 "The late civil war in Kansas": Dale E. Watts, "How Bloody Was Bleeding Kansas?" *Kansas History*, Summer 1995, 123.

83 "Crime Against Kansas . . . the harlot, slavery": George H. Haynes, *Charles Sumner* (1909), 195.

CHAPTER 10

84 "Every day I like farming better . . . advantage to me": to Jesse Grant, Dec. 28, 1856.

85 "Spring is now approaching . . . no more from you": to Jesse Grant, Feb. 7, 1857.

86 "I have seen many farmers": Mary Robinson interview, *St. Louis Republican*, July 24, 1885, granthomepage.com.

86 "My hard work is now over": to Mary Grant, Aug. 22, 1857.

87 "He was not a hand to manage Negroes": Louisa Boggs interview with Hamlin Garland, 1896, Hamlin Garland Papers, Doheny Library, University of Southern California, granthomepage.com.

87 "He was like a man thinking": Hamlin Garland, *Ulysses S. Grant* (1898), 139.

87 "I suppose I was the Jonah": Lloyd Lewis, *Sherman* (1932), 123.

88 "West Point and the Regular Army": Lewis, *Sherman*, 97.

CHAPTER 11

90 "We gave him an unfurnished back room": Louisa Boggs interview (unattributed), granthomepage.com.

90 "We are living now . . . additional commissions": to Jesse Grant, March 12, 1859.

90 "With four children": to Jesse Grant, March 12, 1859.

92 "You are the homeliest man": *Recollected Words of Abraham Lincoln*, ed. Don E. Fehrenbacher and Virginia Fehrenbacher (1996), 401-02.

93 "Liberty and Union": *Works of Lincoln*, 2:341.

93 "A house divided against itself cannot stand": *Works of Lincoln*, 2:461-62.

93 "Henry Clay once said": *Works of Lincoln*, 3:29.

94 "It was a hard situation for him": Louisa Boggs interview, Hamlin Garland Papers, Doheny Library, University of Southern California, granthomepage.com.

94 "He seemed to me to be much depressed": Louisa Boggs interview.

95 "It was evident to my mind": *Memoirs*, 143.

95 "Should your honorable body see proper": to St. Louis County Board of Commissioners, Aug. 15, 1859.

95 "He always maintained": Reynolds to Board of County Commissioners, Aug. 1, 1859, *Papers of Grant*, 1:348-49n.

95 "The question has at length been settled . . . will support me": to Jesse Grant, Sept. 23, 1859.

95   "I am still unemployed . . . when you were here": to Simpson Grant, Oct. 24, 1859.

96   "They were very poor in money": Louisa Boggs interview.

PART TWO: THE RAGE OF ACHILLES

CHAPTER 12

99   "Talk! talk! talk!": Stephen B. Oates, *To Purge This Land with Blood: A Biography of John Brown* (1970), 272.

99   "You will never get out alive": Evan Carton, *Patriotic Treason*, 288.

100   "Reached Harpers Ferry at 11 p.m.": *Recollections and Letters of General Robert E. Lee*, ed. Robert E. Lee (Jr.) (1905), 22.

100   "I see a book kissed": Oates, *To Purge This Land with Blood*, 327.

101   "The irrepressible conflict . . . at the South": Oates, *To Purge This Land with Blood*, 354-55.

101   "preposterous": Oswald Garrison Villard, *John Brown* (1910), 568.

101   "fervid Union man . . . and northern outrage": James M. McPherson, *This Mighty Scourge: Perspectives on the Civil War* (2007), 36; Joseph Carlyle Sitterson, *The Secession Movement in North Carolina* (1939), 152.

101   "I arrived here": to Julia Dent Grant, March 14, 1860.

102   emancipated the one slave he personally owned: Manumission of Slave, undated (March 29, 1859).

102   "Papa was not willing": *Personal Memoirs of Julia Dent Grant*, 82-83.

103   "In my new employment": to unrecorded addressee, undated (Dec. 1860).

103   "He was a bit shorter than Orvil": Mary Grant (Mrs. Orvil Grant) interview, *Troy Intelligencer*, April 17, 1892, granthomepage.com.

103   "I told the Captain . . . his father to arise": *Personal Memoirs of Julia Dent Grant*, 84-86.

CHAPTER 13

105   "I would as soon try the faro table": *Home Letters of General Sherman* (1909), 151-53.

105   "Avoid the subject . . . and the Northwest": *The Sherman Letters* (1894), 55; John E. Marszalek, *Sherman* (1994), 109; Lloyd Lewis, *Sherman* (1932), 119; *Home Letters*, 163.

106   "Colonel Sherman . . . not possibly be cultivated": *Memoirs of General W. T. Sherman* (1990 ed.), 167-68.

107   "When Lincoln rose to speak . . . since St. Paul": Noah Brooks, *Abraham Lincoln* (1901), 123-24.

109   "Since leaving St. Louis": to Mr. Davis, Aug. 7, 1860.

109   "My pledges would have compelled me": *Memoirs*, 144-45.

110   "Should a Black Republican President": Steven A. Channing, *Crisis of Fear: Secession in South Carolina* (1974), 161, 280-82.

110   "The union now subsisting": South Carolina ordinance of secession, Dec. 20, 1861.

CHAPTER 14

111 "How do you feel . . . all the present difficulty": to unknown addressee, undated (Dec. 1860).

111 "I declare to you this morning": David Herbert Donald, *Lincoln* (1995), 256.

112 "take from the disunionists . . . in their hands": *Works of Lincoln*, 4:134-35.

112 "Each and all of the States": *Works of Lincoln*, 4:141.

112 "This is just as I expected": *Works of Lincoln*, 4:146.

113 "The President of the United States is no emperor": *The Rebellion Record*, ed. Frank Moore (1861), 1:220.

113 "The country is certainly in great peril": John G. Nicolay and John Hay, *Abraham Lincoln* (1890), 3:271.

113 "Do the people in the South . . . is the rub": *Works of Lincoln*, 4:160.

113 "The political horizon looks dark": *Works of Lincoln*, 4:160.

113 "Let there be no compromise": *Works of Lincoln*, 4:149-50.

113 "Hold firm": *Works of Lincoln*, 4:151.

113 "They won't give up the offices": David Potter, *The Impending Crisis, 1848-1861* (1976), 432.

114 "My opinion": *Works of Lincoln*, 4:154.

114 "If the United States should merely hold": *New York Times*, Feb. 13, 1861.

115 "I have no purpose . . . of our nature": Lincoln's first inaugural address, March 4, 1861, Public Papers.

CHAPTER 15

117 "It was generally believed . . . must be the result": *Memoirs*, 145-47.

119 "We are at the end": *Works of Lincoln*, 4:317-18.

120 "A State for a fort": David Herbert Donald, *Lincoln* (1995), 290.

121 "I appeal to all loyal citizens": *Works of Lincoln*, 4:331-32.

121 "We solemnly resolve . . . the God of battles": Albert D. Richardson, *A Personal History of Ulysses S. Grant* (1868), 170-71.

122 "The sole reason": *Memoirs*, 152.

122 "In these exciting times . . . worth fighting over again": to Frederick Dent, April 19, 1861.

123 "We are now in the midst . . . with the latter": to Jesse Grant, April 21, 1861.

CHAPTER 16

124 "On account of the cars": to Julia Dent Grant, April 27, 1861.

124 "The evening I was to quit": *Memoirs*, 154.

125 "The only place I ever found": *Memoirs*, 154.

125 "I am convinced": to Mary Grant, April 29, 1861.

125 "Galena has several more companies . . . up to log-rolling": to Jesse Grant, May 2, 1861.

125 "My own opinion": to Jesse Grant, May 6, 1861.

126 "Kiss the children for me": to Julia Dent Grant, May 15, 1861.

126 "After listening to his remarks . . . has assigned me": *Recollections and Letters of General Robert E. Lee*, ed. Robert E. Lee (Jr.) (1905), 24-28.

127 "Having served for fifteen years": to Lorenzo Thomas, May 24, 1861.

127 "I felt some hesitation": *Memoirs*, 159.

127 "Your father is in the room . . . strong for the Union": to Julia Dent Grant, May 10, 1861.

128 "I went down to the arsenal": *Memoirs*, 155-56.

128 "Up to this time . . . young man subsided": *Memoirs*, 156-57.

129 "I was in hopes": *Memoirs*, 159.

130 "In accepting this command": Orders no. 7, June 18, 1861.

130 "Hereafter no passes": Orders no. 8, June 19, 1861.

130 "It is with regret": Orders no. 14, June 26, 1861.

130 "The guard house was not large enough": *Papers of Grant*, 2:46-47n1.

130 "It was in a terribly disorganized state": to Julia Dent Grant, July 7, 1861.

131 "It breathed a loyalty": *Memoirs*, 162.

CHAPTER 17

132 "These measures . . . suppress a rebellion": *Collected Works of Abraham Lincoln*, 4:426-39.

133 "Fred was delighted": to Julia Dent Grant, June 26, 1861.

133 "The soldiers and officers": to Julia Dent Grant, July 7, 1861.

133 "I thought it would be good preparation": *Memoirs*, 162.

133 "which he did in double-quick time": *Jacksonville Journal*, July 11, 1861, *Papers of Grant*, 2:59.

134 "Fred started home": to Julia Dent Grant, July 13, 1861.

134 "Do not send him home . . . his own knapsack": *Personal Memoirs of Julia Dent Grant*, 92.

134 "Last night we had an alarm": to Julia Dent Grant, July 13, 1861.

134 "My sensations as we approached . . . and ran away": *Memoirs*, 163.

135 "Tomorrow I start for Monroe": to Jesse Grant, July 13, 1861.

135 "When we got on the road . . . as I had his": *Memoirs*, 164-65.

CHAPTER 18

137 "I have never been a politician . . . as you best can": *Memoirs of Sherman*, 174, 185-86.

138 "I hold myself now . . . render most service": *Memoirs of Sherman*, 189.

138 "Their uniforms were as various": *Memoirs of Sherman*, 196.

139 "We start forth today": *The Sherman Letters* (1894), 125.

140 "For the first time . . . he would do it": *Memoirs of Sherman*, 201-08.

CHAPTER 19

143 "Colonel Grant is an old army officer": Pope to Frémont, Aug. 5, 1861, *Papers of Grant*, 2:86n.

143 "Fighting here looks to me": Edward Castle to Frémont, Aug. 8, 1861, *Papers of Grant*, 2:87n.

143 "No wandering will be permitted": General Orders No. 1, July 25, 1861.

143 "When we first come": to Julia Dent Grant, July 19, 1861.

144 "The majority in this part": to Jesse Grant, Aug. 3, 1861.

144 "I see from the papers": to Jesse Grant, Aug. 3, 1861.

144 "I certainly feel very grateful": to Julia Dent Grant, Aug. 10, 1861.

145 "I took it in a very disorganized": to Jesse Grant, Aug. 3, 1861.

145 "People here will be glad": to Julia Dent Grant, Aug. 3, 1861.

145 "I called to see Harry Boggs": to Julia Dent Grant, Aug. 10, 1861.

145 "You ask my views": to Mary Grant, Aug. 12, 1861.

146 "The last we heard of him": Ron Powers, *Mark Twain* (2005), 98.

147 "In time I came to learn": Mark Twain, "The Private History of a Campaign That Failed" (1885).

CHAPTER 20

148 "My present command": to Julia Dent Grant, Aug. 10, 1861.

148 "Many of the officers": to John Kelton (for Frémont), Aug. 9, 1861.

148 "Commanders will see that the men": General Orders No. 9, Aug. 9, 1861.

148 "Order was soon restored": *Memoirs*, 171.

149 "As I turned the first corner": *Memoirs*, 172-73.

149 "When I came to know him better": *Memoirs*, 173.

150 "There was no time for delay": *Memoirs*, 174.

150 "Found numerous secession flags": to Frémont, Sept. 6, 1861.

150 "I have come among you": Proclamation, Sept. 6, 1861.

151 "You have seen my move": to Julia Dent Grant, Sept. 8, 1861.

151 "All is quiet here now": to Julia Dent Grant, Sept. 20, 1861.

151 "I am very sorry": to Julia Dent Grant, Oct. 20, 1861.

151 "But after we started": *Memoirs*, 178.

152 "At daylight we proceeded": to Brigadier General Seth Williams, Nov. 10, 1861.

152 "We fought the rebels slowly but steadily": *The War of the Rebellion: The Official Records of the Union and Confederate Armies*, 1:3:296-97.

152 "The officers and men": *Memoirs*, 179-80.

153 "I saw at the same time . . . lodged in the floor": *Memoirs*, 180-84.

154 "All the troops behaved": to Seth Williams, Nov. 10, 1861.

154 "The two objects": *Memoirs*, 185.

CHAPTER 21

155 "By some strange operation of magic": *The Civil War Papers of George B. McClellan: Selected Correspondence, 1860-1865,* ed. Stephen W. Sears (1992), 70.

155 "serious disaster": McClellan to Lincoln, Oct. 22, 1861, Lincoln Papers, Library of Congress.

156 "a great national idea": Catherine Coffin Phillips, *Jessie Benton Frémont* (1995), 250.

156 "The late battle at Belmont . . . lauding his gallantry": *New York Times,* Nov. 11, 1861; from *Chicago Journal,* Nov. 7, 1861, in *Times,* Nov. 12, 1861.

156 "All with you have done honor": Lincoln to McClernand, Nov. 10, 1861, Lincoln Papers.

156 "An energetic, enterprising and judicious commander": McClernand to Lincoln, Nov. 22, 1861, Lincoln Papers.

156 "If a department could be established there": John Logan to McClernand, Jan. 14, 1862, *Papers of Grant,* 3:207n.

156 "The victory was most complete": to Jesse Grant, Nov. 8, 1861.

157 "You will send reports in writing": from Halleck, Nov. 21, 1861, *Papers of Grant,* 3:202n.

157 "The true line of operations": *Memoirs,* 185.

157 "I have now a larger force": to Mary Grant, Jan. 23, 1862.

157 "I was received": *Memoirs,* 190.

158 "Two ironclad gunboats": Smith to John Rawlins, Jan. 21, 1862, *Papers of Grant,* 4:91n.

158 "Fort Henry on the Tennessee . . . of this week": Foote to Halleck, Jan. 28 and 29, 1862, *Papers of Grant,* 4:99n.

158 "I would respectfully suggest": to Halleck, Jan. 29, 1862.

158 "Make your preparations": from Halleck, Jan. 30, 1862, *Papers of Grant,* 4:104n.

158 "Very little preparation": to Smith, Jan. 31, 1862.

158 "I will leave here": to Halleck, Feb. 1, 1862.

158 "No firing": General Orders No. 7, Feb. 2, 1862.

159 "On your arrival at Paducah": to McClernand, Feb. 3, 1862.

159 "I went up on the *Essex*": to Halleck, Feb. 4, 1862.

159 "All the troops will be up": to Julia Dent Grant, Feb. 4, 1862.

159 "The sight of our campfires . . . of Fort Henry": to Julia Dent Grant, Feb. 5, 1862. Grant actually wrote "4,000 troops" but doubtless meant "40,000," as the former number would not have impressed the Confederate defenders.

159 "The fire on both sides . . . as long as possible": Tilghman report, Feb. 12, 1862, *Official Records,* 1:7:140-41.

160 "Fort Henry is ours": to Halleck, Feb. 6, 1862, *Official Records,* 1:7:124.

160 "Fort Henry is ours . . . never be removed": Halleck to McClellan, Feb. 7, 1862, *Official Records,* 1:7:590.

160 "Thank Grant": McClellan to Halleck, Feb. 7, 1862, *Official Records,* 1:7:591.

CHAPTER 22

161 "I was very impatient . . . of National troops": *Memoirs*, 196-97, 206.

162 "At present we are perfectly locked": to George W. Cullum, Feb. 8, 1862.

162 "You have no conception": to Mary Grant, Feb. 9, 1862.

162 "From the first his silence was remarkable": Lew Wallace, "The Capture of Fort Donelson," *Battles and Leaders of the Civil War* (1887), 1:404-05.

163 "Last night was very severe": to Halleck, Feb. 14, 1862.

163 "The enemy was running from his batteries": Foote to Halleck, Feb. 15, 1862, *Official Records*, 1:22:584-85.

163 "The fort cannot hold out twenty minutes": Floyd to Johnston, Feb. 14, 1862, *Official Records*, 1:52(2):274.

163 "The enemy had been much demoralized": *Memoirs*, 203.

163 "The gunboats have been driven back": Floyd to Johnston, Feb. 14, 1862, *Official Records*, 1:52(2):274.

163 "If all the gunboats that can": to Foote, Feb. 15, 1862.

164 "Appearances now indicate": to Cullum, Feb. 15, 1862.

164 "Here and there the musicians": Wallace, "Capture of Fort Donelson," 415.

164 "The first charge against him was repulsed": "Capture of Fort Donelson," 417.

164 "Just then General Grant": "Capture of Fort Donelson," 421-22.

165 "There was now no doubt": *Memoirs*, 206.

165 "No terms except an unconditional and immediate surrender": to Buckner, Feb. 16, 1862.

165 "ungenerous and unchivalrous": Buckner to Grant, Feb. 16, 1862, *Official Records*, 1:7:161.

165 "He said to me": *Memoirs*, 212.

CHAPTER 23

166 "Honor to the brave!": *New York Tribune*, Feb. 18, 1862.

166 "You have Fort Donelson safe": Lincoln to Halleck, Feb. 16, 1862, Lincoln Papers.

166 "Give me command in the West": Halleck to McClellan, Feb. 17, 1862, *Official Records*, 1:7:628.

166 "Give it to me": Halleck to McClellan, Feb. 19, 1862, *Official Records*, 1:7:636.

166 "I must have command": Halleck to McClellan, Feb. 20, 1862, *Official Records*, 1:7:641.

166 "General Halleck did not approve": *Memoirs*, 197.

167 "I received no other recognition": *Memoirs*, 214.

167 "After the fall of Fort Donelson": *Memoirs*, 214.

167 "'Secesh' is now about on its last legs": to Julia Dent Grant, Feb. 24, 1862.

167 "General Halleck is clearly the same way": to Julia Dent Grant, Feb. 24, 1862.

167 "Don't be rash": G. W. Cullum (for Halleck) to Grant, Feb. 15, 1862, *Official Records*, 1:7:619.

167 "Smith, by his coolness and bravery": Halleck to McClellan, Feb. 19, 1862, *Official Records*, 1:7:637.

167 "This operator afterwards proved": *Memoirs*, 219.

168 "Why do you not obey my orders . . . at Fort Henry": from Halleck, March 4, 1862, *Official Records*, 1:10(2):3.

168 "Your going to Nashville": from Halleck, March 6, 1862, *Official Records*, 1:10(2):15.

168 "I am not aware": to Halleck, March 5, 1862.

168 "I am in a very poor humor": to Julia Dent Grant, March 5, 1862.

168 "I have done my very best": to Halleck, March 7, 1862.

169 "You are mistaken": Halleck to Grant, March 8, 1862, *Official Records*, 1:10(2):21.

169 "I renew my application": to Halleck, March 9, 1862.

169 "You cannot be relieved": Halleck to Grant, March 13, 1862, *Official Records*, 1:10(2):32.

CHAPTER 24

170 "I should like to hear from you": Sherman to Grant, Feb. 15, 1862, *Papers of Grant*, 4:215n.

170 "They are all friends . . . on reaching Washington": *Memoirs of Sherman*, 219-20.

171 "I know that others than yourself": Sherman to John Sherman, Nov. 21, 1861, *The Sherman Letters* (1894), 135.

171 "General Sherman was completely 'stampeded'": Halleck to McClellan, Dec. 2, 1861, *Official Records*, 1:52(1):198.

172 "insane": *Cincinnati Commercial*, Dec. 11, 1861, in James Ford Rhodes, *History of the United States from the Compromise of 1850* (1906), 5:5.

172 "These newspapers have us in their power": Sherman to Halleck, Dec. 12, 1861, *Official Records*, 1:8:819.

172 "The newspaper attacks are certainly shameless": Halleck to Sherman, Dec. 18, 1861, *Official Records*, 1:8:445.

172 "As evidence that I have every confidence": Halleck to Thomas Ewing, Feb. 15, 1862, *Memoirs of Sherman*, 236.

172 "one of the noblest men . . . 'none to give you'": Jefferson Davis, *The Rise and Fall of the Confederate Government* (1881), 2:38.

172 "We have suffered great anxiety": Davis to Johnston, March 12, 1862, *Official Records*, 1:7:257-58.

173 "The test of merit in my profession": Johnston to Davis, March 18, 1862, *Official Records*, 1:7:261.

173 "If we obtained possession of Corinth": *Memoirs*, 222.

173 "When all reinforcements": *Memoirs*, 223.

174 "I would fight them if they were a million": William Preston Johnston, "Albert Sidney Johnston at Shiloh," *Battles and Leaders of the Civil War* (1887), 1:555.

174 "We had just left the bleak, frozen North . . . to give up that they were whipped": Leander Stillwell, *Personal Recollections of the Battle of Shiloh* (1892), 7-17.

178 "From about the 1st of April": *Memoirs of Sherman*, 249.

178 "All is quiet along my lines": Sherman to Grant, April 5, 1862 (two messages), *Official Records*, 1:10(2):93.

178 "About 8 a.m. . . . rest of the day": Sherman to Capt. J. A. Rawlins, April 10, 1862, *Memoirs of Sherman*, 256-58.

179 "I wish I could make a visit": to Julia Dent Grant, April 3, 1862.

180 "Found all quiet": to Halleck, April 5, 1862.

180 "I was intending": *Memoirs*, 224.

180 "Heavy firing is heard up the river": to Buell, April 6, 1862.

180 "The attack on my forces": to Commanding Officer, Advance Forces near Pittsburg, April 6, 1862.

180 "It stood on the ridge": *Memoirs*, 226-31.

181 "I haven't despaired of whipping them yet": Adam Badeau, "General Grant," *Century Illustrated Monthly Magazine*, May-Oct. 1885, 156.

182 "The last time I was with him . . . the first fire": *Memoirs*, 228.

182 "Staff officers were immediately dispatched . . . have been hoped for": P. T. G. Beauregard, "The Campaign of Shiloh," *Battles and Leaders of the Civil War*, 1:590-91.

183 "I visited each division commander in person": *Memoirs*, 234.

183 "It rained hard during the night": *Memoirs of Sherman*, 259.

183 "Rain fell in torrents": *Memoirs*, 234-35.

184 "Well, Grant": Charles Bracelen Flood, *Grant and Sherman* (2005), 114.

184 "I saw Willich's regiment": *Memoirs of Sherman*, 259-60.

185 "My force was too much fatigued": to Nathaniel McClean (for Halleck), April 9, 1862.

CHAPTER 25

186 "More Glorious News . . . and irregular fighting": *New York Times*, April 9, 10 and 14, 1862.

186 "There was no more preparation": Larry J. Daniel, *Shiloh* (1997), 304.

187 "I will go on and do my duty": to Jesse Grant, April 26, 1862.

187 "The troops with me . . . by complete conquest": *Memoirs*, 238-40, 246.

188 "I did not know Grant": A. K. McClure, *Abraham Lincoln and Men of War-Times* (1892 ed.), 179-80.

188 "The soldiers of the great West": Halleck, General Orders No. 16, April 13, 1862, *Official Records*, 1:10(2):105.

189 "I have felt my position as anomalous": to Halleck, May 11, 1862.

189 "I am very much surprised, General": Halleck to Grant, May 12, 1862, *Official Records*, 1:10(2), 182-83.

189 "I have a father, mother, wife": to Washburne, May 14, 1862.

189 "I have been so shockingly abused": to Julia Dent Grant, May 11, 1862.

190 "I was silenced so quickly": *Memoirs*, 252.

190 "We found the enemy had gone": to Julia Dent Grant, May 31, 1862.

190 "I rode from my camp . . . his true place": *Memoirs of Sherman*, 275-76.

191 "I have just received your note": Sherman to Grant, June 6, 1862, *Papers of Grant*, 5:141.

192 "I have never done half justice by him": to Julia Dent Grant, June 9, 1862.

192 "In General Sherman": to Julia Dent Grant, May 4, 1862.

192 "I prefer Lee to Johnston": McClellan to Lincoln, April 20, 1862, Lincoln Papers.

192 "Your call for Parrot guns": Lincoln to McClellan, May 11, 1862, Lincoln Papers.

193 "We are quietly closing in": McClellan to Lincoln, May 26, 1862, Lincoln Papers.

193 "I have lost this battle": McClellan to Stanton, June 28, 1862, *Official Records*, 1:11(1):61.

193 "If we had a million men . . . and will bring it out": Lincoln to McClellan, July 1 and 2, 1862, Lincoln Papers.

193 "If not attacked today": McClellan to Lincoln, July 7, 1862, Lincoln Papers.

193 "Prisoners all state": McClellan to Lincoln, July 11, 1862, Lincoln Papers.

194 "I will start for Washington": Halleck to Lincoln, July 11, 1862, *Official Records*, 1:11(3):315.

CHAPTER 26

195 "The day I started": *Personal Memoirs of Julia Dent Grant*, 93.

195 "I remember one of them": *Personal Memoirs of Julia Dent Grant*, 95.

196 "As we entered the encampment": *Personal Memoirs of Julia Dent Grant*, 102-03.

196 "With my staff and small escort . . . of Dr. Smith": *Memoirs*, 259-60.

198 "His impudence was so sublime": *Memoirs*, 262.

198 "There is a great disloyalty": to Halleck, June 27, 1862.

198 "You will suspend the further publication": Hillyer to *Memphis Avalanche*, July 1, 1862, *Papers of Grant*, 5:182n.

198 "Government collections . . . receive such treatment": General Orders No. 60, July 3, 1862.

198 "The families now residing": Special Orders Nos. 14 and 15, July 10 and 12, 1862, *Papers of Grant*, 5:192n.

199 "I feel it my duty to remark": Thompson to Grant, July 14, 1862, *Papers of Grant*, 5:193n.

199 "But if it is to make him": to Washburne, July 22, 1862.

CHAPTER 27

200 "I learned with great pleasure": Washburne to Grant, July 25, 1862, *Papers of Grant*, 5:226n.

200 "I write plainly and slowly . . . for not shipping it": Sherman to Chase, Aug. 11, 1862, *Memoirs of Sherman*, 286-90.

202 "I found so many Jews and speculators here": Sherman to Rawlins (for Grant), July 30, 1862, *Official Records*, 1:17(2):140-41.

203 "Fugitive slaves may be employed": General Orders No. 72, Aug. 11, 1862, *Papers of Grant*, 5:273n.

203 "I have no hobby of my own": to Jesse Grant, Aug. 3, 1862.

203 "On the face of this wide earth": Greeley to Lincoln, Aug. 19, 1862, Lincoln Papers.

203 "I would save the Union": Lincoln to Greeley, Aug. 22, 1862, Lincoln Papers.

204 "One morning he asked me . . . the end of the war": David Homer Bates, "Lincoln in the Telegraph Office," *Century Illustrated Monthly Magazine*, May-Oct. 1907, 372-73.

204 "I said to the cabinet . . . to the government": F. B. Carpenter, *Six Months at the White House with Abraham Lincoln* (1867), 21-22.

205 "He said that nothing but foul play": William Roscoe Thayer, *The Life and Letters of John Hay* (1915), 1:128.

205 "A splendid army almost demoralized": John J. Hennessey, *Return to Bull Run* (1999), 471.

205 "The President was in deep distress": Bates note in *Collected Works of Lincoln*, 5:486n.

205 "The will of God prevails": Lincoln note, undated (Sept. 2, 1862), *Collected Works of Lincoln*, 5:404.

206 "much weakened and demoralized": Lee to Davis, Sept. 3, 1862, *Memoirs of Robert E. Lee*, ed. A. L. Long (1886), 516.

206 "To the People of Maryland": Lee proclamation, Sept. 8, 1862, in James D. McCabe Jr., *Life and Campaigns of Robert E. Lee* (1866), 239-40.

206 "When I say that they were hungry": Mary Bedinger Mitchell, "A Woman's Recollections of Antietam," *Battles and Leaders of the Civil War* (1887), 2:687.

206 "My army is ruined by straggling": McCabe, *Life and Campaigns of Robert E. Lee*, 31.

207 "Here is a paper": Stephen W. Sears, *George B. McClellan* (1999), 282.

207 "I have all the plans of the rebels": McClellan to Lincoln, Sept. 13, 1862, Lincoln Papers.

207 "God bless you": Lincoln to McClellan, Sept. 15, 1862, *Collected Works of Lincoln*, 5:426.

207 "The thought of General Lee's perilous position": John G. Walker, "Sharpsburg," *Battles and Leaders*, 2:675.

207 "The blue uniforms of the Federals": James Longstreet, "The Invasion of Maryland," *Battles and Leaders*, 2:667.

207 "Every stalk of corn": Hooker report, Nov. 8, 1862, *Official Records*, 1:19(1):218.

208 "To those who have not been witnesses": Walker, "Sharpsburg," *Battles and Leaders*, 2:675-77.

208 "The line swayed forward and back": Longstreet, "Invasion of Maryland," *Battles and Leaders*, 2:668.

208 "No tongue can tell": James M. McPherson, *Crossroads of Freedom: Antietam* (2002), 129.

208 "We awaited without apprehension": Lee report, March 6, 1863, *Reports of the Operations of the Army of Northern Virginia from June 1862 to and including the Battle at Fredericksburg, December 13, 1862* (1864), 35-36.

208 "I concluded that the success of an attack": McClellan report, Aug. 4, 1863, *Official Records*, 1:19(1):65.

208 "As we could not look for a material increase": Lee report, March 6, 1863, *Reports of the Operations*, 36.

209 "I was among the last": Walker, "Sharpsburg," *Battles and Leaders*, 2:682.

209 "The President directs": Halleck to McClellan, Oct. 6, 1862, *Official Records* 1:19(1):10.

209 "The time has come now": *The Salmon P. Chase Papers: Journals, 1829-1872*, ed. John Niven (1993), 394.

209 "Commander-in-chief of the Army and Navy": Preliminary Emancipation Proclamation, Sept. 22, 1863, *Collected Works of Lincoln*, 5:433-34.

CHAPTER 28

210 "I am concentrated and strong . . . a rapid decline": to Julia Dent Grant, Sept. 14, 1862.

210 "There is a large force": to Julia Dent Grant, Sept. 15, 1862.

211 "Besides": *Memoirs*, 275-76.

211 "You must engage the enemy": to Ord, Sept. 20, 1862.

211 "We were in a country": *Memoirs*, 278.

211 "It is now clear that Corinth is the point": to Halleck, Oct. 1, 1862.

212 "The rebels are now massing": to Halleck, Oct. 4, 1862.

212 "We should attack if they do not": to Rosecrans, Oct. 2, 1862.

212 "The combined force of the enemy": to Hurlbut, Oct. 4, 1862.

212 "Make all dispatch": to Hurlbut, Oct. 4, 1862.

212 "If the enemy fall back": to Rosecrans, Oct. 4, 1862.

212 "We move at daylight in the morning": from Rosecrans, Oct. 4, 1862, *Papers of Grant*, 6:115n.

212 "The enemy are in full retreat": to Halleck, Oct. 5, 1862.

212 "Everything looks most favorable": to Halleck, Oct. 5, 1862.

212 "Push the enemy to the wall": to Rosecrans, Oct. 5, 1862.

212 "You will avail yourself": to Rosecrans, Oct. 6, 1862.

213 "Although partial success might result": to Halleck, Oct. 8, 1862.

213 "I congratulate you": Lincoln to Grant, Oct. 8, 1862, *Works of Lincoln*, 5:453.

213 "About eight hundred rebels already buried": to Lincoln, Oct. 10, 1862.

213 "The victory was most triumphant": to John Kelton, Oct. 30, 1865.

213 "With small reinforcements at Memphis": to Halleck, Oct. 26, 1862.

CHAPTER 29

214 "It is, however, a very grave question": to Chase, July 31, 1862.

215 "The mania for sudden fortunes": Dana to Stanton, Jan. 21, 1863, in Charles A. Dana, *Recollections of the Civil War* (1899), 18-19.

215 "A greater pack of knaves never went unhung": Porter to Sherman, Oct. 29, 1863, *Official Records*, 1:25:521.

215 "Gold and silver will not be paid": General Orders No. 64, July 25, 1862, *Official Records*, 1:17(2):123.

215 "There is an evident disposition": Grant to Halleck, July 28, 1862.

215 "It is very desirable . . . into market": Halleck to Grant, Aug. 2, 1862, *Official Records*, 1:17(2):150.

216 "embarrassment . . . none of their dangers": *Memoirs*, 266-67.

216 "It will be regarded as evidence": General Orders No. 8, Nov. 19, 1862, *Official Records*, 1:52(1):302-03.

217 "My plans are all complete": to Mary Grant, Dec. 15, 1862.

217 "Examine the baggage": to Quinby, July 26, 1862.

217 "Refuse all permits to come south": to Hurlbut, Nov. 9, 1862.

217 "Give orders to all the conductors": to Webster, Nov. 10, 1862, *Official Records*, 1:17(2):337.

217 "I have long since believed": to Christopher Wolcott, Dec. 17, 1862.

218 "The Jews, as a class": General Orders No. 11, Dec. 17, 1862.

218 "The order was issued": to I. N. Morris, Sept. 14, 1868, printed in *New York Times*, Nov. 30, 1868.

219 "I would write you many particulars": to Jesse Grant, Sept. 17, 1862.

220 "It will be immediately revoked": Halleck to Grant, Jan. 4, 1863, *Official Records*, 1:17(2):530.

220 "It excluded a whole class": Kelton to Grant, Jan. 5, 1863, *Papers of Grant*, 7:54n.

220 "The President has no objection": Halleck to Grant, Jan. 21, 1863, *Papers of Grant*, 7:54n.

220 "It is a great annoyance": to Edward C. Ord, Oct. 24, 1862.

CHAPTER 30

221 "Vicksburg is the key": David D. Porter, *Incidents and Anecdotes of the Civil War* (1886), 95-96.

222 "At this stage of the campaign": *Memoirs*, 285.

223 "As soon as possible": to Sherman, Dec. 8, 1862.

223 "The surrender of Holly Springs": *Memoirs*, 290.

223 "The women came with smiling faces": Adam Badeau, *Military History of Ulysses S. Grant, from April 1861 to April 1865* (1881-85), 1:140-41.

225 "I found there was not sufficient confidence": to Halleck, Jan. 20, 1863.

225 "General McClernand was a politician": *Memoirs*, 294-95.

225 "We are now on the brink of destruction": David Herbert Donald, *Lincoln* (1995), 402-03.

225 "The draft would be resisted": *Memoirs*, 296.

226 "I propose running a canal through": to Halleck, Jan. 20, 1863.

226 "Work on the canal is progressing": to Halleck, Feb. 3, 1863.

226 "The continuous rise in the river": to Halleck, Feb. 9, 1863.

226 "There is no question": to Halleck, Feb. 4, 1863.

227 "With this we were able": *Memoirs*, 299.

227 "Hurry up": Porter, *Incidents and Anecdotes of the Civil War*, 161.

227 "I am very well but much perplexed": to Julia Dent Grant, March 27, 1863.

228 "When these gunboats once go below": Porter to Grant, March 29, 1863, *Official Records*, 1:24:518.

228 "The Mississippi at Milliken's Bend . . . of that aristocracy": Charles A. Dana, *Recollections of the Civil War* (1899), 28-29.

228 "He received me cordially": Dana, *Recollections of the Civil War*, 30.

229 "Grant's staff is a curious mixture": Dana, *Recollections of the Civil War*, 72-73.

229 "A very brilliant man": Dana, *Recollections of the Civil War*, 57, 76.

229 "Grant was an uncommon fellow": Dana, *Recollections of the Civil War*, 61-62.

230 "It was an ugly place . . . and twenty-five discharges": Dana, *Recollections of the Civil War*, 36-37.

230 "The sight was magnificent": *Memoirs*, 307-08.

231 "Our experiment of running the batteries": to Halleck, April 19, 1863.

CHAPTER 31

232 "I move my headquarters to Carthage": to Halleck, April 21, 1863.

232 "In company with Admiral Porter": to Sherman, April 24, 1863.

232 "I am now embarking troops": to Halleck, April 27, 1863.

232 "virtual possession of Vicksburg": to Julia Dent Grant, April 28, 1863.

232 "From a tug out in the stream": Grant report, July 6, 1863, *Official Records*, 1:19(1):48.

233 "The gunboats made another vigorous attack": to Halleck, May 3, 1863

233 "When this was effected": *Memoirs*, 321.

233 "The march immediately commenced . . . in our possession": to Halleck, May 3, 1863.

234 "Stop all troops": Sherman to Grant, May 9, 1863, *Official Records*, 1:24(3):285.

234 "I do not calculate": to Sherman, May 9, 1863.

234 "I shall communicate with Grand Gulf": to Halleck, May 11, 1863.

234 "The enemy would have strengthened": *Memoirs*, 328.

235 "The enemy is badly beaten": to Sherman, May 3, 1863.

235 "Every day's delay": to William Hillyer, May 5, 1863.

235 "Two days more, or Tuesday next": to Julia Dent Grant, May 9, 1863.

235 "Move your command tonight": to McPherson, May 11, 1863.

235 "The enemy was driven at all points": to McClernand, May 12, 1863.

235 "So I finally decided": *Memoirs*, 332.

235 "Move one division of your corps": to McClernand, May 13, 1863.

236 "Move directly towards Jackson": to Sherman, May 13, 1863.

236 "Send me word": to McPherson, May 14, 1863.

236 "He set about his work": Adam Badeau, *Military History of Ulysses S. Grant, from April 1861 to April 1865* (1881-85), 1:250.

236 "Just as I was leaving Jackson": Sherman, *Memoirs of Sherman*, 347-48.

237 "I am concentrating my forces": to Halleck, May 15, 1863.

237 An intercepted message: Badeau, *Military History of Grant*, 1:252n.

237 "I have just received information": to McClernand, May 16, 1863.

237 "Great celerity should be shown": to Sherman, May 16, 1863.

237 "It is one of the highest points": *Memoirs*, 342.

238 "Had I known the ground": *Memoirs*, 347.

238 "The enemy were driven": to Sherman, May 16, 1863.

238 "While a battle is raging": *Memoirs*, 348.

238 "The enemy were found": Grant report, July 6, 1863.

238 "If possible, the forces": from Halleck, May 11, 1863, *Official Records*, 1:24(3):36.

239 "I immediately mounted my horse": *Memoirs*, 350.

239 "Notwithstanding the level ground": Grant report, July 6, 1863.

239 "My men are now investing": to Porter, May 19, 1862.

239 "Until this moment": John S. C. Abbott, *The Life of General Ulysses S. Grant* (1868), 137.

CHAPTER 32

240 "If Haynes' Bluff is untenable": Johnston to Pemberton, May 17, 1863, *Official Records*, 1:24(3):888.

240 "The opinion was unanimously expressed": Pemberton to Johnston, May 18, 1863, *Official Records*, 1:24(3):889-90.

240 "Johnston was in my rear": *Memoirs*, 355.

241 "The assault was gallant": Grant report, July 6, 1863.

241 "I don't believe a word of it": *Memoirs of Sherman*, 352.

241 "This last attack only served": *Memoirs*, 356.

242 "The enemy has placed . . . but very palatable": Pemberton report, Aug. 25, 1863, *Official Records*, 1:24(1):279-81.

242 "Even the very animals . . . young innocent life": *My Cave Life in Vicksburg*, by "A Lady" (Mary Ann Webster Loughborough) (1864), 78-80.

243 "Unless the siege of Vicksburg . . . a yet indefinite period": Pemberton report, Aug. 25, 1863, *Official Records*, 1:24(1):281-83.

244 "It was a glorious sight": *Memoirs*, 375.

244 "The useless effusion of blood": to Pemberton, July 3, 1863.

244 "The conference might as well end": *Memoirs*, 376.

245 "I will march in one division": to Pemberton, July 3, 1863 (second letter).

CHAPTER 33

246 "Rawlins could argue": Jacob Dolson Cox, "How Judge Hoar Ceased to Be Attorney-General," *Atlantic Monthly*, Aug. 1895, 164.

247 "I told them Grant was sick": Charles A. Dana, *Recollections of the Civil War* (1899), 83.

247 "The great solicitude I feel": Rawlins to Grant, June 6, 1863, in James Harrison Wilson, *The Life of John A. Rawlins* (1916), 128-29.

248 "My God! My God!": David Herbert Donald, *Lincoln* (1995), 436.

248 "If successful this year": Stephen W. Sears, *Gettysburg* (2004), 15.

248 "Our resources in men": Lee to Davis, June 10, 1863, *Memoirs of Robert E. Lee*, ed. A. L. Long (1886), 620-21.

248 "Will it not promote the true interest": Hooker to Lincoln, June 10, 1863, *Official Records*, 1:27(1):34.

249 "I think Lee's army": Lincoln to Hooker, June 10, 1863, *Works of Lincoln*, 6:257.

249 "If Harrisburg comes within your means": Sears, *Gettysburg*, 103.

249 "I really think the attitude": Lincoln to Joel Parker, June 30, 1863, *Works of Lincoln*, 6:311.

249 "Yesterday morning, at 3 a.m.": Meade to Mrs. Meade, June 29, 1863, in *The Life and Letters of George Gordon Meade*, ed. George Gordon Meade (1913), 2:11-12.

250 "to find and fight the enemy": *Life and Letters of Meade*, 11.

250 "The sun of the 2nd of July . . . anywhere else": *The Reminiscences of Carl Schurz* (1908), 3:20-21.

251 "We heard a confused noise . . . the hostile wave": *Reminiscences of Carl Schurz*, 22-23.

251 "We had a great fight yesterday": Meade to Mrs. Meade, July 3, 1863, *Life and Letters of Meade*, 2.103.

251 "Great God! . . . to strike him": George E. Pickett, *The Heart of a Soldier: As Revealed in the Intimate Letters of General George E. Pickett, C.S.A.* (1913), 94.

252 "I found him like a great lion . . . 'lead my division on'": Pickett, *The Heart of a Soldier*, 98-99; James Longstreet, *From Manassas to Appomattox* (1896), 392.

252 "Every eye could see his legions": *Haskell of Gettysburg: His Life and Civil War Papers*, ed. Frank L. Byrne and Andrew T. Weaver (1970), 158.

252 "And so all across . . . ended and won": *Haskell of Gettysburg*, 160-70.

254 "All this has been my fault": "A Piece of Secret History," *Scribner's Monthly* (1875-76), 520.

CHAPTER 34

255 "How long ago is it?": Lincoln response to serenade, July 7, 1863, *Works of Lincoln*, 6:319-20.

255 "If General Meade can complete his work": Lincoln to Halleck, July 7, 1863, *Works of Lincoln*, 6:319.

256 "If I had gone up there": Hay diary entry for July 15, 1863, in William Roscoe Thayer, *The Life and Letters of John Hay* (1915), 1:194.

256 "I do not believe you appreciate": Lincoln to Meade (not sent), July 14, 1863, *Works of Lincoln*, 6:327-28.

256 "I was deeply mortified": Lincoln to Howard, July 21, 1863, *Works of Lincoln*, 6:341.

256 "The Father of Waters again goes unvexed": Lincoln to James Conkling, Aug. 26, 1863, *Works of Lincoln*, 6:409.

256 "Look at his campaign": *Chicago Tribune*, May 29, 1863, in *Recollected Words of Abraham Lincoln*, ed. Don E. Fehrenbacher and Virginia Fehrenbacher (1996), 11.

256 "I do not remember": Lincoln to Grant, July 13, 1863, *Works of Lincoln*, 6:326.

257 "On every floor": David M. Barnes, *The Draft Riots in New York, July 1863* (1863), 83-84, 87.

CHAPTER 35

259 "Not only the length of the war": Halleck to Sherman, Aug. 29, 1863, *Memoirs of Sherman*, 360.

260 "The inhabitants of the country . . . end is attained": Sherman to Halleck, Sept. 17, 1863, *Memoirs of Sherman*, 360-67.

261 "The people in the Mississippi Valley": to Chase, July 21, 1863.

262 "It is earnestly recommended": General Orders No. 50, Aug. 1, 1863.

262 "At all military posts": General Orders No. 51, Aug. 10, 1863, *Papers of Grant*, 9:135-36n.

263 "All able-bodied negro men": General Orders No. 53, Aug. 23, 1863, *Papers of Grant*, 9:136n.

263 "I believe it is a resource": Lincoln to Grant, Aug. 9, 1863, *Works of Lincoln*, 6:374.

263 "I have given the subject of arming the negro": to Lincoln, Aug. 23, 1863.

264 "I never was an abolitionist": to Washburne, Aug. 30, 1863.

CHAPTER 36

265 "My going could do no possible good": to Washburne, Aug. 30, 1863.

265 "He considers it indispensible": Stanton to Halleck, Oct. 19, 1863, *Papers of Grant*, 9:298n.

266 "By the middle of October . . . to dislodge us": Charles A. Dana, *Recollections of the Civil War* (1899), 127-30.

267 "Am still confined to my bed": to Halleck, Sept. 19, 1863.

267 "Hold Chattanooga at all hazards": to Thomas, Oct. 19, 1863.

267 "I arrived here . . . I cannot tell": to Halleck, Oct. 26, 1863.

267 "We were within easy range": *Memoirs*, 413.

267 "We held him at our mercy": Bragg report, Dec. 28, 1863, *Official Records*, 1:30(2):37.

268 "In a week the troops . . . I rode off": *Memoirs*, 418-21.

269 "If we can hold Chattanooga": Lincoln to Rosecrans, Oct. 4, 1863, *Works of Lincoln*, 6:498.

269 "There was no relief possible": *Memoirs*, 425.

269 "I do not know how to impress on you": to Burnside, Nov. 15, 1863.

269 "Drop everything east of Bear Creek": to Sherman, Oct. 24, 1863.

270 "As I sat on the porch . . . because of his looks": *Memoirs of Sherman*, 383-84.

271 "Leave directions for your command": to Sherman, Nov. 13, 1863.

271 "Sherman's advance has reached Bridgeport": to Burnside, Nov. 14, 1863.

271 "If you retreat now": Halleck to Burnside, Nov. 16, 1863, *Official Records*, 1:31(3):163.

271 "I fear he will not fight": Halleck to Grant, Nov. 16, 1863, *Official Records*, 1:31(3):163.

271 "I am pushing everything": to Halleck, Nov. 16, 1863.

271 "So far you are doing exactly": to Burnside, Nov. 17, 1863.

272 "Grant was always sanguine": Adam Badeau, *Military History of Ulysses S. Grant, from April 1861 to April 1865* (1881-85), 1:464-65.

272 "There was the greatest hopefulness": Dana, *Recollections of the Civil War*, 141.

272 "I think the rebel force": to Halleck, Nov. 2, 1863.

272 "I felt restless beyond anything": to John Kelton (for Halleck), Dec. 23, 1863.

272 "We had a magnificent view": *Memoirs of Sherman*, 387.

272 "Every arrangement is now made": to Burnside, Nov. 14, 1863.

273 "If you can communicate": to Willcox, Nov. 20, 1863.

273 "It will be impossible": to Halleck, Nov. 21, 1863.

273 "Until we opened fire". Meigs report, Nov. 26, 1863, *Official Records*, 1:31(2).77.

274 "It was marvelous . . . so quietly and so well": Dana, *Recollections of the Civil War*, 147.

274 "Hooker will attack Lookout": to Halleck, Nov. 15, 1863.

274 "A full moon made the battlefield": Dana, *Recollections of the Civil War*, 148.

274 "The fight today progressed favorably": to Halleck, Nov. 24, 1863.

274 "Well done": Lincoln to Grant, Nov. 25, 1863, *Works of Lincoln*, 7:30.

275 "I congratulate you": Halleck to Grant, Nov. 25, 1863, *Official Records*, 1:31(2):25.

275 "At daylight on the 25th": Meigs report, Nov. 26, 1863, *Official Records*, 1:31(2):78.

275 "The whole field was in full view": *Memoirs*, 443.

275 "The enemy kept firing shells at us": Dana, *Recollections of the Civil War*, 149.

276 "The rebel pickets . . . thunder upon them": Meigs report, Nov. 26, 1863, *Official Records*, 1:31(2):79.

276 "The storming of the ridge . . . whole corps went up": Dana, *Recollections of the Civil War*, 150-51.

277 "Glory to God!": Dana, *Recollections of the Civil War*, 150.

277 "Although the battle lasted": to Halleck, Nov. 25, 1863.

277 "The next thing now": to Sherman, Nov. 25, 1863.

277 "I made this change": to Halleck, Nov. 29, 1863.

277 "Do not be forced into a surrender": to Burnside, Nov. 29, 1863.

278 "Approaching from the south and west": Sherman, *Memoirs*, 393-94.

CHAPTER 37

279 The Western Victory: *New York Times*, Nov. 28, 1863.

279 "I wish to tender you": Lincoln to Grant, Dec. 8, 1863, *Works of Lincoln*, 7:53.

279 "most distinguished for courage, skill, and ability": H.R. 26, 38th Congress, 1st session, Dec. 14, 1863.

279 "Look at what this man has done": *Congressional Globe*, 38:1:430.

280 "Your successful military career": from Burns, Dec. 7, 1863, *Papers of Grant*, 9:542n.

280 "The question astonishes me": to Burns, Dec. 17, 1863.

281 "I am not a politician": to Morris, Jan. 20, 1864.

281 "It is on a subject": to Blair, Feb. 28, 1864.

281 "I am glad to say": to Mrs. Isaac Quinby, Dec. 13, 1863.

282 "Bragg was a remarkably intelligent . . . *superior military genius*": *Memoirs*, 449-50.

283 "You are Southern": *Personal Memoirs of Julia Dent Grant*, 106.

284 "captured property: *Memoirs of Sherman*, 373-75.

284 "Why should I ever": Sherman to Ellen Sherman, Oct. 10, 1863, *Home Letters of General Sherman* (1909), 276.

285 "My Dear Friend": *Memoirs,* 373-75.

CHAPTER 38

286 "I shall direct Sherman": to Halleck, Jan. 15, 1864.

286 "The expedition is one of celerity": Special Field Orders No. 11, Jan. 27, 1864, *Official Records*, 1:32(1):182.

287 "The bill reviving the grade": to Sherman, March 4, 1864.

287 "You are now Washington's legitimate successor . . . of the Atlantic": Sherman to Grant, March 10, 1864, *Memoirs of Sherman*, 428-29.

288 "I cannot make a speech": *Missouri Democrat*, Jan. 29, 1864, in *Papers of Grant*, 10:71n.

289 "I shall make a very short speech": John G. Nicolay and John Hay, *Abraham Lincoln* (1890), 8:340-41.

289 "The nation's appreciation": Lincoln speech, March 9, 1864, *Works of Lincoln*, 7:234.

289 "The general had hurriedly": Nicolay and Hay, *Lincoln*, 8:341-42.

289 "I accept the commission": Grant speech, March 9, 1864.

290 "I listened respectfully": *Memoirs*, 474.

291 "Well, I hardly know": William O. Stoddard, *Inside the White House in War Times* (1890), 220-21.

CHAPTER 39

292 "to move against Johnston's army": to Sherman, April 4, 1864.

293 "This incident gave me": *Memoirs*, 470.

293 "Grant is not a striking man": *The Life and Letters of George Gordon Meade*, vol. 2 (1913), 191.

293 "I do not know that the enemy's attack": to Julia Dent Grant, April 17, 1864.

294 "Nothing prevents my advancing now": Lee to Davis, Aug. 24, 1863, *Official Records*, 1:29(2):665.

294 "our crying necessity for food": Lee to Davis, Jan. 11, 1864, *Official Records*, 1:33:1076.

294 "I can learn of no supply": Lee to Davis, Jan. 2, 1864, *Official Records*, 1:33:1061.

294 "If it requires all the meat": Lee to J. L. Kemper, Jan. 29, 1864, *Official Records*, 1:33:1128.

294 "Today closes the gloomiest year": *Richmond Examiner*, Dec. 31, 1863, in *The Rebellion Record*, ed. Frank Moore (1865), 8:29.

294 "A cruel enemy seeks to reduce": General Orders No. 102, Nov. 26, 1863, James D. McCabe Jr., *Life and Campaigns of General Robert E. Lee* (1866), 426.

295 "He said that with the great responsibilities": Charles S. Venable, "General Lee in the Wilderness Campaign," *Battles and Leaders of the Civil War* (1887), 4:240.

295 "The reports of General Lee's scouts . . . which confronted them": John B. Gordon, *Reminiscences of the Civil War* (1904), 235-36.

295 "Each plan presents great advantages": to Meade, April 9, 1864.

296 "What I ask is that": to Butler, April 16, 1864.

296 "I will move against Lee's army": to Halleck, April 29, 1864.

297 "This is my forty-second birthday": to Julia Dent Grant, April 27, 1864.

297 "Before you receive this": to Julia Dent Grant, May 2, 1864.

297 "Not expecting to see you": Lincoln to Grant, April 30, 1864, *Works of Lincoln*, 7:324.

297 "The confidence you express": to Lincoln, May 1, 1864.

297 "The movement of this Army": to Burnside, May 2, 1864.

298 "The crossing of Rapidan effected": to Halleck, May 4, 1864.

298 "It was uneven": Alexander S. Webb, "Through the Wilderness," *Battles and Leaders of the Civil War*, 4:154.

298 "My command had cut its way": Gordon, *Reminiscences*, 239-41.

299 "By the blessing of God": Lee report, May 5, 1864, *Official Records*, 1:36(1):1028.

299 "We have engaged with the enemy": to Halleck, May 6, 1864.

299 "The enemy advanced": Lee report, May 6, 1864, *Official Records*, 1:36(1):1028.

299 "Yesterday the enemy attacked our lines": to Halleck, May 7, 1864.

300 "More desperate fighting has not been witnessed": *Memoirs*, 534.

300 "We are very much troubled": Charles A. Dana, *Recollections of the Civil War* (1899), 188, 194.

301 "He discussed the dominant characteristics": Gordon, *Reminiscences*, 267-68.

301 "General Grant is not going to retreat . . . answer — Spotsylvania": Gordon, *Reminiscences*, 268-70.

302 "Rank after rank": Horace Porter, *Campaigning with Grant* (1907), 110-11.

302 "Firing into one another's faces": Gordon, *Reminiscences*, 284.

302 "The ground around the salient": Dana, *Recollections*, 196-97.

303 "Our losses have been heavy . . . takes all summer": to Stanton, May 11, 1864.

CHAPTER 40

304 "I am satisfied the enemy are very shaky": to Halleck, May 11, 1864.

304 "The world has never seen": to Julia Dent Grant, May 13, 1864.

304 "Lee's army is really whipped": to Halleck, May 26, 1864.

304 "One of the most important results": Charles A. Dana, *Recollections of the Civil War* (1899), 204.

305 "There has been a very severe battle": to Julia Dent Grant, June 1, 1864.

305 "In passing along on foot": Horace Porter, *Campaigning with Grant* (1907), 174-75.

306 "The Second Corps assaulted the enemy's position": Hancock report, Nov. 8, 1864, *Official Records*, 1:36(1):366-67.

306 "Our loss was not severe": to Halleck, June 3, 1864.

306 "I have always regretted": *Memoirs*, 588.

307 "the very bad news from Fort Pillow": John Sherman to William Sherman, April 17, 1864, *The Sherman Letters* (1894), 233.

307 "The river was dyed": Forrest to Thomas Jack, April 15, 1864, *Official Records*, 1:32(1):610.

307 "Three hundred blacks murdered": from Sherman, April 15, 1865, *Official Records*, 1:32(3):367.

307 "We all feel that we must disband": John Sherman to William Sherman, April 17, 1864, *Sherman Letters*, 233-34.

307 "Having determined to use the negro": Lincoln speech, April 18, 1864, *Works of Lincoln*, 7:302.

307 Lincoln drafted an order: Lincoln to Stanton, May 17, 1864, *Works of Lincoln*, 7:345.

CHAPTER 41

308 "I now find . . . without this protection": to Halleck, June 5, 1864.

308 "But the move had to be made": *Memoirs*, 591.

309 "We must destroy this army": *Personal Reminiscences, Anecdotes and Letters of Gen. Robert E. Lee*, comp. J. William Jones (1875), 40.

309 "Every rail on the road": to Meade (instructions for Sheridan), June 5, 1864.

309 "The complete destruction of this road . . . destroy the canal": to Hunter, June 6, 1864.

309 "His cigar had been thrown aside": David Porter, *Campaigning with Grant* (1907), 199-200.

310 "Since Sunday we have been engaged": to Julia Dent Grant, June 15, 1864.

310 "The enemy show no signs": to Halleck, June 14, 1864.

310 "I begin to see it": Lincoln to Grant, June 15, 1864, *Works of Lincoln*, 7:393.

310 "I believed then": *Memoirs*, 599.

310 "We will rest the men": to Meade, June 18, 1864.

310 "Our work progresses here slowly": to Julia Dent Grant, June 22, 1864.

311 "You people up North": to J. Russell Jones, July 5, 1864.

311 "The immense slaughter of our brave men": Welles diary, June 2, 1864, *Diary of Gideon Welles* (1911), 2:44.

311 "I hope you are very well . . . that very stuff": Porter, *Campaigning with Grant*, 217.

312 "Like most men . . . a genuine friendship": Porter, *Campaigning with Grant*, 218-24.

CHAPTER 42

313 "immediate efforts be made": Democratic platform, Aug. 29, 1864.

314 "It was the saddest affair": to Halleck, Aug. 1, 1864.

315 "Admiral Porter has always said": Welles diary, Aug. 2, 1864, *Diary of Gideon Welles* (1911), 2:92.

315 "I write to put you in possession": Smith to Foot, July 30, 1864, *Papers of Grant*, 11:207-09n.

316 "The General was at the front today": Rawlins to Mrs. Rawlins, June 29, 1864, in James Harrison Wilson, *The Life of John A. Rawlins* (1916), 239.

316 "There never was any such happening": *Autobiography and Personal Reminiscences of Major-General Benjamin F. Butler* (1892), 698, 713.

317 "I have sometimes thought . . . are upon us": Welles diary, July 6, 8, 11, 1864, *Diary of Welles*, 2:68-72.

317 "Let us be vigilant": Lincoln to Thomas Swann et al., July 10, 1864, *Works of Lincoln*, 7:438.

317 "General Halleck says": Lincoln to Grant, July 10, 1864, ibid., 437.

317 "I have sent from here": to Lincoln, July 10, 1864.

318 "Could see the line of pickets": Welles diary, July 11, 1864, *Diary of Welles*, 2:72-73.

318 "We haven't taken Washington": *The Shenandoah Valley Campaign of 1864*, ed. Gary W. Gallagher (2006), xi.

318 "The Rebels have lost": Welles diary, July 11, 1864, *Diary of Welles*, 2:73.

318 "The sun was just sinking": Isaac N. Arnold, *The Life of Abraham Lincoln* (1885), 375.

318 "The people are wild for peace . . . hope of success": Weed to Seward, Aug. 22, 1864, in John G. Nicolay and John Hay, "Abraham Lincoln: A History," *Century* (1889), 548.

319 "No, sir . . . *badly beaten*": J. K. Herbert to Benjamin Butler, Aug. 11, 1864, *Private and Official Correspondence of General Benjamin F. Butler* (1917), 5:35.

319 "This morning, as for some days past": Lincoln memorandum, Aug. 23, 1864, *Works of Lincoln*, 7:514.

319 "I would say . . . my own conscience": John Hay diary, Nov. 11, 1864, *Inside Lincoln's White House: The Complete Civil War Diary of John Hay*, ed. Michael Burlingame and John R. Turner Ettlinger (1997), 248.

CHAPTER 43

320 "It is enough to make the whole world start": Sherman to Ellen Sherman, June 30, 1864, *Home Letters of General Sherman* (1909), 299.

320 "Dalton will be our first point": Sherman to Ellen Sherman, April 27, 1864, *Home Letters*, 289.

320 "Thomas is my centre": Sherman to Ellen Sherman, May 22, 1864, *Home Letters*, 292-93.

321 "I cannot leave the railroad": Sherman to Ellen Sherman, June 30, 1864, *Home Letters*, 299-300.

321 "All of Georgia": Sherman to John Sherman, June 9, 1864, *The Sherman Letters* (1894), 235-36.

321 "I propose to study the crossings": Sherman to Halleck, July 6, 1864, *Official Records*, 1:38(5):65-66.

321 "I immediately inquired of General Schofield": *Memoirs of Sherman*, 543-44.

322 "McPherson was then in his prime": *Memoirs of Sherman*, 550.

322 "Poor Mac": Sherman to Ellen Sherman, July 26, 1864, *Home Letters*, 303.

322 "He was not out of his place": Sherman to Ellen Sherman, no date given, *Home Letters*, 302n.

323 "I know the country swarms with thousands": Sherman to Ellen Sherman, June 26, 1864, *Home Letters*, 298.

323 "We have Atlanta close aboard": Sherman to Ellen Sherman, July 26, 1864, *Home Letters*, 302-03.

323 "Atlanta is on high ground": Sherman to Ellen Sherman, Aug. 2, 1864, *Home Letters*, 305-06.

323 "I have no faith": Sherman to Thomas Ewing, Aug. 11, 1864, *Home Letters*, 307.

323 "I sometimes think our people": Sherman to Ellen Sherman, Aug. 2, 1864, *Home Letters*, 306.

323 "It was the Gordian knot": Sherman to Thomas Ewing, Aug. 11, 1864, *Home Letters*, 307.

323 "That night I was so restless": *Memoirs of Sherman*, 581.

324 "Atlanta is ours, and fairly won": Sherman to Halleck, Sept. 3, 1864, *Official Records*, 1:38(5):777.

324 "The marches, battles, sieges": Lincoln order of thanks to Sherman et al., Sept. 3, 1864, *Works of Lincoln*, 7:533.

324 "In honor of your great victory": to Sherman, Sept. 4, 1864.

324 "As soon as your men are properly rested": to Sherman, Sept. 10, 1864.

CHAPTER 44

325 "highly spiced . . . and do it": David Porter, *Campaigning with Grant* (1907), 84.

326 "I want Sheridan put in command": to Halleck, Aug. 1, 1864.

326 "This, I think, is exactly right": Lincoln to Grant, Aug. 3, 1864, *Works of Lincoln*, 7:476.

326 "Carry off the crops . . . hang them without trial": to Sheridan, Aug. 16, 1864 (two messages).

326 "Do all the damage to railroads": to Sheridan, Aug. 26, 1864.

326 "I endorsed the program": *Personal Memoirs of P. H. Sheridan* (1888), 1:487-88.

327 "Mr. Stanton kept reminding me": *Memoirs of Sheridan*, 2:6.

327 "I have just received": to Sheridan, Sept. 20, 1864.

327 "Be ready to move": H. G. Wright to Sheridan, Oct. 16, 1864, *Memoirs of Sheridan*, 2:63.

328 "I noticed that there were many women . . . almost irresistible": *Memoirs of Sheridan*, 2:72-81.

329 "Turning what bid fair": to Stanton, Oct. 20, 1864.

CHAPTER 45

330 "All we want now": to Washburne, Aug. 16, 1864.

331 "I have no objection": to Washburne, Sept. 21, 1864.

331 "I hope it is not the intention": to Stanton, Sept. 11, 1864.

332 "The first, third, and fourth regiments": Stanton to Grant, Oct. 27, 1864, *Papers of Grant*, 12:353n.

332 "The exercise of the right of suffrage": to Stanton, Sept. 27, 1864.

332 "The Government is bound": to Lee, Oct. 3, 1864.

333 "I shall always regret": to Lee, Oct. 20, 1864.

333 "Congratulate the President for me": to Stanton, Nov. 10, 1864.

CHAPTER 46

334 "It would have gladdened my heart": Davis speech, Sept. 23, 1864, *Papers of Jefferson Davis* (2004), 11:61.

334 "Davis seemed to be perfectly upset": *Memoirs of Sherman*, 616.

334 "It once in our possession": Sherman to Grant, Sept. 20, 1864, *Official Records*, 1:39(2):411-13.

335 "It will be better to drive Forrest": to Sherman, Sept. 26, 1864.

335 "I take it for granted": Sherman to Halleck, Sept. 29, 1864, *Memoirs of Sherman*, 619.

335 "It was by such acts": *Memoirs of Sherman*, 626.

335 "It will be a physical impossibility": Sherman to Grant, Oct. 9, 1864, *Official Records* 1:39(3):162.

336 "I do not believe": to Sherman, Oct. 11, 1864.

336 "We cannot now remain on the defensive": Sherman to Grant, Oct. 11, 1864, *Official Records*, 1:39(3):202.

336 "If you are satisfied": to Sherman, Oct. 12, 1864, *Official Records*, 1:39(3):202.

336 "I am now perfecting arrangements": Sherman to Grant, Oct. 22, 1864, *Official Records*, 1:39(3):394-95.

336 "On the 1st of November": Sherman to A. Beckwith, Oct. 19, 1864, *Official Records*, 1:39(3):358-59.

337 "On mature reflection": to Stanton, Oct. 13, 1864.

337 "Great good fortune attend you": to Sherman, Nov. 7, 1864.

337 "Oh, God, the time of trial . . . ever seeing again!": Lunt diary, Nov. 17-19, 1864, in Dolly Sumner Lunt, *A Woman's Wartime Journal* (1918), 17-30.

339 "My orders are not designed": Sherman to James Calhoun et al., Sept. 12, 1864, *The Rebellion Record*, ed. Frank Moore (1868), 11:318.

339 "Stone Mountain . . . to be his freedom": *Memoirs of Sherman*, 656-67.

340 "The army will forage liberally": Special Field Orders No. 120, Nov. 9, 1864, *Official Records*, 1:39(3):713.

340 "Often I would pass these foraging parties . . . exceptional and incidental": *Memoirs of Sherman*, 659.

340 "The weather was fine": *Memoirs of Sherman*, 669.

341 "Grant says they are safe": *Memoirs*, 647.

341 "I congratulate you": to Sherman, Dec. 18, 1864.

341 "To His Excellency President Lincoln": Sherman to Lincoln, Dec. 22, 1864, Lincoln Papers.

CHAPTER 47

342 "If Hood is permitted . . . to attain this end": to Thomas, Dec. 2, 1864 (two messages).

342 "Hood should be attacked": to Thomas, Dec. 5, 1864.

342 "Attack Hood at once": to Thomas, Dec. 6, 1864.

342 "If you delay any longer": to Thomas, Dec. 11, 1864.

343 "General Thomas with the forces": John C. Van Duzer to Thomas T. Eckert, Dec. 15, 1864, *Papers of Grant*, 13:125n.

343 "I was just on my way to Nashville": to Thomas, Dec. 15, 1864.

344 "The Wilmington expedition": to Lincoln, Dec. 28, 1864.

344 "Please hold on": to Porter, Dec. 30, 1864.

344 "Here there is not the slightest suspicion": to Stanton, Jan. 3, 1865.

344 "It is exceedingly desirable": to Terry, Jan. 3, 1865.

345 "Desertion is increasing": Lee statement, undated, in James D. McCabe Jr., *Life and Campaigns of General Robert E. Lee* (1866), 572.

345 "The enemy will certainly use them": Lee to Barksdale, Feb. 18, 1865, ibid., 574.

345 "If I were he": Edward A. Pollard, *Life of Jefferson Davis* (1869), 437.

345 "Deeply impressed with the difficulties": Lee General Orders No. 1, Feb. 9, 1865, *Official Records*, 1:46(2):1226.

345 "I think General Grant will move": to Mary Lee, Feb. 22, 1865, *Recollections and Letters of General Robert E. Lee* (1905), 146.

345 "I could not see how it was possible": *Memoirs*, 688.

346 "I felt that the situation": *Memoirs*, 687-88.

346 "I know this trip is necessary": Sherman to Grant, Jan. 29, 1865, *Official Records*, 1:47(2):154-56.

347 "It is utterly impossible": Sheridan to Grant, Feb. 12, 1865, *Official Records*, 1:46(2):545.

347 "As soon as it is possible": to Sheridan, Feb. 20, 1865.

347 "We desire to pass your lines": Stephens et al. to Grant, Jan. 30, 1865, in Grant to Lincoln, Jan. 31, 1865.

348 "I found them all very agreeable . . . ever you did see?": *Memoirs*, 685-87.

349 "The peace feeling": to Sherman, Feb. 1, 1865.

349 "General Howard will cross the Saluda": Special Field Orders No. 26, Feb. 16, 1865, *Official Records*, 1:47(2):444.

349 "The northern and western sky": "The Burning of Columbia Again," *Harper's New Monthly Magazine*, Oct. 1866, 643.

349 "Oh, that long twelve hours": Diary entry for Feb. 18, 1865, in *When the World Ended: The Diary of Emma LeConte*, ed. Earl Schenck Miers (1987 ed.), 48-50.

350 "If I had made up my mind to burn Columbia": Sherman in Marion B. Lucas, *Sherman and the Burning of Columbia* (2000 ed.), 154.

350 "During the night": *Autobiography of Oliver Otis Howard* (1907), 122-23.

350 "One thing is certain": *Memoirs*, 681.

CHAPTER 48

351 "Whilst the enemy holds": to Meade, March 3, 1865.

351 "I feel no doubt": to Charles Ford, March 1, 1865.

351 "Lieutenant General Longstreet has informed me": Lee to Grant, March 2, 1865, *Official Records*, 1:46(2):824.

352 "General Ord and General Longstreet": to Lee, March 4, 1865.

352 "I can assure you": to Stanton, March 4, 1865.

352 "Please accept": Lincoln to Grant, March 7, 1865, *Works of Lincoln*, 8:339.

353 "I accept the medal": Grant speech, March 11, 1865.

353 "The officers soon selected": David Porter, *Campaigning with Grant* (1907), 393-94.

353 "Save him! Oh, save him!": Porter, *Campaigning with Grant*, 394-95.

354 "We are now having fine weather": to Jesse Grant, March 19, 1865.

354 "I have never felt any uneasiness": to Sherman, March 16, 1865.

354 "Your problem will be": to Sheridan, March 19, 1865.

354 "When this movement commences": to Sherman, March 22, 1865.

355 "A large part of the armies": to Meade, March 24, 1865.

356 "In the fight today": to Edward Ord, March 25, 1865.

356 "The President was not very cheerful . . . on the left": *Memoirs of Sheridan*, 2:130-31.

356 "After having accomplished the destruction": to Sheridan, March 28, 1865.

356 "This portion of your instructions": *Memoirs*, 696.

357 "The heavy rains and horrid roads": to Lincoln, March 31, 1865.

357 "The weather is bad for us": to Julia Dent Grant, March 30, 1865.

357 "General Sheridan will attack": Porter to Rawlins, April 1, 1865, in Grant to Lincoln, April 1, 1865.

357 "The result of this combined movement": Sheridan to Grant, April 2, 1865, *Official Records*, 1:46(1):1100-01.

357 "We are now up": to Theodore Bowers, April 2, 1865.

CHAPTER 49

359 "I see no prospect of doing more": Lee to J. C. Breckinridge, April 2, 1865, *Official Records*, 1:46(1):1264.

359 "To move tonight": Jay Winik, *April 1865* (2001), 120.

359 "It is absolutely necessary": Lee to Breckinridge, April 2, 1865, *Official Records*, 1:46(1):1265.

359 "On the morning of Sunday . . . streets of Richmond": LaSalle Corbell Pickett, *What Happened to Me* (1917), 159-62.

360 "I have got my army": Winik, *April 1865*, 120.

361 "The first object of the present movement": to Sheridan, April 3, 1865.

361 "Efforts will be made": to Ord, April 3, 1865, *Papers of Grant*, 14:335-36n.

361 "Sheridan, who was up with him": to Sherman, April 5, 1865.

361 "We have Lee's army": to Sherman, April 6, 1865.

361 "These troops were sent out": to Theodore Bowers, April 6, 1865.

361 "Nearly twenty-four hours were lost . . . the progress slow": Lee report to Davis, April 12, 1865, *Official Records*, 1:46(1):1265-66.

362 "The result of the last week": to Lee, April 7, 1865.

362 "I reciprocate your desire": Lee to Grant, April 7, 1865, *Official Records*, 1:46(1):56.

362 "There is but one condition": to Lee, April 8, 1865.

363 "I did not intend to propose": Lee to Grant, April 8, 1865, *Official Records*, 1:46(1):57.

363 "The captured trains": *Personal Memoirs of P. H. Sheridan* (1888), 2:190.

363 "The necessity of getting Ord's column . . . to General Grant": *Memoirs of Sheridan*, 2:196-98.

365 "On the 8th I had followed": *Memoirs*, 730.

365 "I received your note of this morning": Lee to Grant, April 9, 1865, *Official Records*, 1:46(1):57.

366 "When the officer reached me": *Memoirs*, 731.

366 "I am at this writing": to Lee, April 9, 1865.

366 "Is it a trick?": Adam Badeau, *Military History of Ulysses S. Grant, from April 1861 to April 1865* (1881-85), 3:601n.

366 "Lee was tall": Badeau, *Military History of Grant*, 3:603.

366 "As he was a man of much dignity": *Memoirs*, 735.

367 "In accordance with the substance": to Lee, April 9, 1865.

368 "The Confederates were now our prisoners": *Memoirs*, 741.

368 "Thanks be to Almighty God": Stanton to Grant, April 9, 1865, *Papers of Grant*, 14:375n.

PART THREE: AND GIVE THE PEACE

CHAPTER 50

372 "I had never had the courage": *Personal Memoirs of Julia Dent Grant*, 126-27.

373 ""I don't know . . . their despair, would you?": *Personal Memoirs of Julia Dent Grant*, 135, 152-53.

373 "Everyone was wild . . . You may go now": *Personal Memoirs of Julia Dent Grant*, 154-55.

375 "It would be impossible": *Memoirs*, 750-51.

375 "The joy that I had witnessed": *Memoirs*, 751.

376 "Permit me to suggest": from Dana, April 15, 1865, *Official Records*, 1:46(3):756.

376 "General Grant, thank God": *Personal Memoirs of Julia Dent Grant*, 157.

376 "Extreme rigor will have to be observed": to Ord, April 15, 1865.

376 "I want you to get your cavalry": to Sheridan, April 15, 1865.

376 "I enclose herewith a copy . . . composing said armies": from Sherman, April 18, 1865, with enclosure, *Official Records*, 1:47(3):243-44.

378 "They are of such importance": to Stanton, April 21, 1865.

378 "I thought the matter": *Memoirs of Sherman*, 852.

379 "It was an exercise": *New York Times*, April 24, 1865.

379 "I have never in my life": from Sherman, April 28, 1865, *Official Records*, 1:47(3):334-35.

CHAPTER 51

381 "Johnson was a man of the coolest": Oliver P. Temple, *Notable Men of Tennessee, from 1833 to 1875* (1912), 465-67.

382 "Although it would meet with opposition": to Halleck, May 6, 1865.

383 "By going now": to Stanton, May 18, 1865.

383 "Until a uniform policy is adopted": to John Schofield, May 18, 1865.

383 "The sight was varied and grand": *Memoirs*, 768-69.

383 "To say that I was merely angry": *Memoirs of Sherman*, 861-62, 866.

384 "Mr. Stanton never questioned his own authority": *Memoirs*, 769.

384 "In what manner has Mr. Stanton": Grant testimony, May 18, 1865.

384 "The Rio Grande should be strongly held": to Sheridan, May 17, 1865.

385 "I regard the act": to Johnson, June 19, 1865.

385 "Nonintervention in Mexican affairs": to Johnson, Sept. 8, 1865.

387 "Treason is a crime": Eric L. McKitrick, *Andrew Johnson and Reconstruction* (1960), 20.

CHAPTER 52

390 "General Grant was in the council-room": Diary entry for Dec. 15, 1865, *Diary of Gideon Welles* (1911), 2:396-97.

390 "I saw much and conversed freely . . . in whom they rely": to Johnson, Dec. 18, 1865.

391 "The aspect of affairs is more promising": Johnson special message, Dec. 18, 1865, Public Papers.

392 "They have torn their constitutional states . . . to its center": *Congressional Globe*, 39:1:72-74.

393 "In all our history": Johnson veto message, March 27, 1866, Public Papers.

393 "This is a country for white men": Eric L. McKitrick, *Andrew Johnson and Reconstruction* (1960), 184.

395 "fatal and total surrender": Eric Foner, *Reconstruction* (1988), 255.

395 "wanton betrayal of justice and humanity": Kenneth M. Stampp, *The Era of Reconstruction* (1965), 142.

395 "shilly-shally bungling thing": Stampp, *The Era of Reconstruction*, 141.

395 "In my youth": *Congressional Globe*, 39:1:3148.

CHAPTER 53

396 "I look upon it as an indication . . . Kick 'em out!": *New York Times*, Sept. 10, 1866.

397 "I am getting very tired": to Julia Dent Grant, Aug. 31, 1866.

397 "I never have been so tired": to Julia Dent Grant, Sept. 9, 1866.

398 "I am no politician . . . 'next President of the United States!'": *New York Times*, Sept. 13, 1866 (including excerpt from *St. Louis Commercial*).

398 "I regret to say": to Sheridan, Oct. 12, 1866.

399 "absolute massacre": Eric Foner, *Reconstruction* (1988), 263.

399 "thrown in like sacks of corn . . . God damned niggers": Ted Tunnell, *Crucible of Reconstruction: War, Radicalism, and Race in Louisiana, 1862-1877* (1984), 104-06.

399 "So far there seems": to Johnson, Oct. 24, 1866.

399 "There is ground to apprehend danger": Stanbery to Grant, undated (Nov. 2, 1866), Andrew Johnson Papers, Library of Congress.

400 "General Grant desires me to say": Comstock to Meade, Nov. 2, 1866, *Papers of Grant*, 16:363n.

400 "General Grant is of the opinion": *New York Times*, Nov. 3, 1866.

400 "Give my respects to the dead dog": Eric L. McKitrick, *Andrew Johnson and Reconstruction* (1960), 361.

401 "One of the most ridiculous veto measures": to Washburne, March 4, 1867.

402 "Delay may cause further demands": to Ord, Dec. 6, 1866.

402 "There is but little difference": to Sherman, Jan. 13, 1867.

402 "I am not egotistical enough": to Washburne, April 5, 1867.

CHAPTER 54

403 "I was not in favor": Grant testimony to Congress, July 18, 1867.

404 "the great danger": to Johnson, Aug. 1, 1867.

404 "In notifying you of my acceptance": to Stanton, Aug. 12, 1867.

405 "It is unmistakably the expressed wish": to Johnson, Aug. 17, 1867.

405 "I feel that your relief": to Sheridan, Sept. 8, 1867.

405 "It is truly an unenviable one": to Sherman, Sept. 18, 1867.

406 "Our place of meeting": *Memoirs of Sherman*, 910.

406 "Learning on Saturday": to Johnson, Jan. 28, 1868.

407 "According to the provisions": to Johnson, Jan. 14, 1868.

407 "though to soften": to Johnson, Jan. 28, 1868.

407 "I confess my surprise": to Johnson, Feb. 3, 1868.

408 "thoroughly ill-bred dog . . . to this house": Gene Smith, *High Crimes and Misdemeanors: The Impeachment and Trial of Andrew Johnson* (1977), 238.

408 "never in history . . . Mr. Wade has done it": Smith, *High Crimes and Misdemeanors*, 236; Michael Les Benedict, *A Compromise of Principle: Congressional Republicans and Reconstruction, 1863-1869* (1974), 300.

CHAPTER 55

411 "The Great Spirit raised both the white man": *Report of the Commissioner of Indian Affairs to the Secretary of the Interior for the Year 1871* (1872), 23.

412 "I want men": from Carrington, Dec. 21, 1866, *Papers of Grant*, 16:419-20n.

412 "All Sioux found outside": Sherman report in Grant to Stanton, Jan. 15, 1867.

412 "The protection of the Pacific railroad": to Stanton, Jan. 15, 1867.

413 "The Indian Bureau should be transferred": to Sherman, Jan. 15, 1867.

413 "If the present practice": to Stanton, Feb. 1, 1867.

413 "War exists": in letter to Sherman, May 29, 1867.

413 "This conflict of authority": from Sherman, June 12, 1867, *Papers of Grant*, 17:174n.

414 "It will be well to prepare": to Sherman, March 2, 1868.

414 "These posts are kept up": to Stanton, March 10, 1868.

414 "I did not first commence": Dee Brown, *Bury My Heart at Wounded Knee* (1970), 144.

414 "Your peace commission": to Sherman, May 19, 1868.

414 "We are on the mountains": Robert M. Utley, *The Indian Frontier, 1846-1890* (2003 ed.), 118.

415 "The Government of the United States": *Indian Affairs: Laws and Treaties* (1904), 2:998.

CHAPTER 56

416 "We profoundly deplore": Republican party platform, May 20, 1868, Public Papers.

416 "It would hardly seem": *New York Times*, May 19, 1868.

417 "The proceedings of the convention": to Joseph R. Hawley, May 29, 1868.

418 "I have seen in the papers": from Sherman, June 7, 1868, *Papers of Grant*, 18:293n.

418 "You understand my position perfectly": to Sherman, June 21, 1868.

419 "The reconstruction policy of the Radicals": *New York Times*, July 3, 1868.

419 "Alarm the people?": James D. McCabe Jr., *The Life and Public Services of Horatio Seymour* (1868), 465-66n.

419 "The country to this place": to Julia Dent Grant, July 17, 1868.

420 "I do not regret it now": to Julia Dent Grant, July 21, 1868.

420 "I fully appreciate the compliment": to Charles R. Morehead Jr., July 14, 1868.

420 "I find it so agreeable here": to Rawlins, Aug. 18, 1868.

420 "My friends": Remarks at Dubuque, Aug. 18, 1868, *Papers of Grant*, 19:23n.

421 "I have chosen this": Alphonse B. Miller, *Thaddeus Stevens* (1960), 404.

421 "If the contest was to be determined": *New York Times*, Aug. 23, 1868.

422 "Give Mr. Moses assurances": to Isaac N. Morris, Sept. 14, 1868.

422 "I know General Grant": *Boston Transcript*, Aug. 6, 1868, excerpted in *Papers of Grant*, 19:18-19n.

422 "A person would not know": to Washburne, Sept. 23, 1868.

422 "I presume military affairs": to Schofield, Sept. 25, 1868.

423 "I want to put off the evil day": to Morris, Oct. 22, 1868.

CHAPTER 57

425 "The choice has fallen upon me": Speech of Nov. 4, 1868.

425 "I am not on speaking terms": to Daniel Ammen, Nov. 23, 1868.

425 "You all know how unaccustomed": *New York Herald*, Dec. 9, 1868.

426 "The offers of the managers": to Scott, Dec. 11, 1868, *Papers of Grant*, 19:93n.

426 "The proposition was to pay me": to Sherman, Jan. 5, 1869.

426 "People looking at it": *New York Times*, March 7, 1869.

427 "The office has come to me unsought": Inaugural address, March 4, 1869, Public Papers.

CHAPTER 58

429 "I have come to the conclusion": Speech to congressional delegation, Feb. 13, 1869.

430 "I would ask": to the Senate, March 6, 1869.

430 "It is a matter for profound consideration": *New York Times*, March 11, 1869.

432 "It has been my intention": to Fish, March 10, 1869.

432 "I cannot . . . forbids it": from Fish, March 11, 1869 (telegram and letter), *Papers of Grant*, 19:150n.

433 "Not receiving your dispatch": to Fish, March 11, 1869.

433 "You have exceptional qualifications": Allan Nevins, *Hamilton Fish* (1957 ed.), 1:112.

433 "I am 'in for it'": Nevins, *Hamilton Fish*, 116.

433 "The Cabinet is a surprise . . . classed among statesmen": Editorial excerpts in *New York Times*, March 7, 1869.

434 "The Cabinet is not strong": John Bigelow, *Retrospections of an Active Life* (1913), 4:263.

434 "There was nothing": to George Stuart, Feb. 26, 1869.

434 "I scarcely get one moment": to Mary Grant Cramer, March 31, 1869.

435 "There is one subject": Special message to Congress, April 7, 1869, Public Papers.

436 "I leave here tomorrow": to Badeau, July 14, 1869.

CHAPTER 59

437 "Mr. Corbin is a very shrewd old gentleman . . . was a contractionist": *Investigation into the Causes of the Gold Panic* (1870), 152-53.

439 "I took a letter": *Investigation into the Causes of the Gold Panic*, 172.

439 "I think it had become . . . the whole question": *Investigation into the Causes of the Gold Panic*, 153.

440 "About the 4th day of September": *Investigation into the Causes of the Gold Panic*, 358.

441 "You will be met by the bulls and bears": to Boutwell, Sept. 12, 1869.

441 "The President was reported": *Investigation into the Causes of the Gold Panic*, 35.

441 "Nothing ever occurred to me": *Investigation into the Causes of the Gold Panic*, 154.

442 "We started . . . delivered all right": *Investigation into the Causes of the Gold Panic*, 231-32.

443 "Who is that man? . . . a few moments": *Investigation into the Causes of the Gold Panic*, 444.

443 "Write this": *Personal Memoirs of Julia Dent Grant*, 182. Julia Grant was reproducing the letter from memory. Delicacy or fear of a lawsuit prompted her to leave the name "Jay Gould" blank; the present author has supplied it.

443 "I was very much excited . . . 'letter gets out'": *Investigation into the Causes of the Gold Panic*, 251-56, 257.

444 "I became satisfied": *Investigation into the Causes of the Gold Panic*, 344.

444 "I went over to the President": *Investigation into the Causes of the Gold Panic*, 345-46.

445 "It was each man drag out his own corpse": *Investigation into the Causes of the Gold Panic*, 176.

445 "The President conversed": *New York Times*, Oct. 4, 1869.

445 "The committee find": *Investigation into the Causes of the Gold Panic*, 20.

CHAPTER 60

447 "What a wonderful shot . . . and earnest": Borie to Badeau, Oct. 3, 1869, *Papers of Grant*, 19:220n.

447 "Your beloved husband": to Mary Rawlins, Sept. 6, 1869.

447 "Yet his final taking off": to Washburne, Sept. 7, 1869.

447 "You and I know": Wilson to Babcock, Oct. 13, 1869, *Papers of Grant*, 19:257n.

448 "The executive department": John Sherman, *Recollections of Forty Years* (1896), 375.

449 "I think it advisable": to Fish, Aug. 14, 1869.

450 "The United States are willing": Memorandum, Aug. 31, 1869.

450 "For more than a year": Annual message, Dec. 6, 1869, Public Papers.

452 "I did not dream": to the Senate and House of Representatives, April 5, 1871, in *Report of the Commission of Inquiry to the Island of Santo Domingo* (1871), 1.

452 "He stated further": *Report of the Commission*, 1-2.

453 "Great and good friend": to Báez, July 13, 1869.

453 "He visited San Domingo": to the Senate and House of Representatives, April 5, 1871, in *Report of the Commission*, 2.

453 "What do you think!": Jacob Dolson Cox, "How Judge Hoar Ceased to Be Attorney-General," *Atlantic Monthly*, Aug. 1895, 166-67.

454 "A list was opened": Perry to Fish, June 7, 1870, in *Report of the Select Committee Appointed to Investigate the Memorial of Davis Hatch* (1870), 105.

455 "It is an island of unequaled fertility . . . in the Antilles": Grant memorandum, undated, *Papers of Grant*, 20:74-76.

CHAPTER 61

457 "When we consider . . . he didn't write it": George S. Boutwell, *Reminiscences of Sixty Years in Public Affairs* (1902), 2:214-15, 251.

457 "a colossus": Gamaliel Bradford, *Union Portraits* (1916), 236, 242.

457 "'I advise you'": Bradford, *Union Portraits*, 240-45.

458 "Mr. President": *Memoirs and Letters of Charles Sumner*, ed. Edward Lillie Pierce (1893), 4:434.

458 "I feel an unusual anxiety": Special message to the Senate, May 31, 1870, Public Papers.

459 "The condition of the insurgents": Special message to Congress, June 13, 1870, Public Papers.

460 "The moment it is known": Annual message, Dec. 5, 1870, Public Papers.

461 "Rather than carry out . . . rudely assailed": *Charles Sumner: His Complete Works*, ed. George Frisbie Hoar (1900), 18:262ff; *Congressional Globe*, 41:3:226-31.

462 "This report more than sustains": Special message to Congress, April 5, 1871, Public Papers.

462 "If Mr. Sumner": *New York Times*, March 30, 1871.

CHAPTER 62

463 "Knowing your great desire": from Angier, Jan. 20, 1870, *Papers of Grant*, 20:105-06n.

463 "Governor Bullock has assumed": from Tift, Jan. 3, 1870, *Papers of Grant*, 20:104n.

464 "These bands are having a great effect": Allen W. Trelease, *White Terror: The Ku Klux Klan Conspiracy and Southern Reconstruction* (1971), 123.

464 "Armed bands of banditti": Trelease, *White Terror*, 138.

465 "Please answer quickly": from A. Alpeora Bradley et al., Feb. 9, 1870, *Papers of Grant*, 20:107n.

465 "President has received": Porter to Bradley, Feb. 9, 1870, *Papers of Grant*, 20:108n.

465 "She ratified her constitution": Annual message, Dec. 6, 1869, Public Papers.

466 "The ratification of the Fifteenth Amendment": to Washburne, Jan. 28, 1870.

466 "The adoption of the Fifteenth Amendment": Special message, March 30, 1870, Public Papers.

467 "force, bribery, threats, intimidation": *Statutes at Large*, 16:146.

467 "There is a deplorable state": to Blaine, March 9, 1871.

467 "A condition of affairs": Special message, March 23, 1871, Public Papers.

468 "I can scarcely believe": *Congressional Globe*, 42:1:Appendix, 75.

468 "He is invited": *Congressional Globe*, 42:1:Appendix, 231-32.

468 "It is to divert": *Congressional Globe*, 42:1:355-57.

469 "Public affairs are growing": Garfield to Jacob Cox, March 23, 1871, *Papers of Grant*, 21:247n.

469 "Politics have again": Sherman to Ord, March 18, 1871, *Papers of Grant*, 21:351n.

469 "powerful and armed combinations": *Statutes at Large*, 17:14-15.

470 "extraordinary public importance": Proclamation, May 3, 1871, Public Papers.

CHAPTER 63

471 "There is a Ku Klux organization": from Flournoy, May 1 and 3, 1871, *Papers of Grant*, 21:337-38n.

471 "The Ku Klux attacked us": Flournoy and C. C. Culling to William Belknap, May 18, 1871, *Papers of Grant*, 21:338n.

471 "The first appearance": from Huggins, April 7, 1871, *Papers of Grant*, 21:342n.

472 "Give us poor people": from Boulding, May 2, 1871, *Papers of Grant*, 22:13-14n.

472 "Armed bands styling themselves": from J. Pinckney Whitehead et al., June 16, 1871, *Papers of Grant*, 22:15n.

472 "There were about twenty": *Testimony Taken by the Joint Select Committee to Inquire into the Condition of Affairs in the Late Insurrectionary States: Georgia* (1872), 1:2.

473 "The object of it is to kill out": *Testimony Taken by the Joint Select Committee: Miscellaneous and Florida*, (1872), 95.

473 "The cause of this treatment": *Testimony Taken by the Joint Select Committee: Alabama* (1872), 11:1188.

473 "When they were taking me out of the door": *Testimony Taken by the Joint Select Committee: Miscellaneous and Florida*, 43

473 "We are fast drifting": from Diver, Sept. 1, 1871, *Papers of Grant*, 22:166n.

473 "All eyes are turned": from Bryant, Sept. 8, 1871, *Papers of Grant*, 22:167-68n.

474 "The cruelties that have been inflicted": from Scott, Sept. 1, 1871, *Papers of Grant*, 22:164n.

474 "A surrender in good faith": Lou Falkner Williams, *The Great South Carolina Ku Klux Klan Trials, 1871-1872* (2004 ed.), 44.

474 "Order the troops in South Carolina": to Belknap, May 13, 1871.

475 "Unlawful combinations": Proclamation, Oct. 12, 1871, Public Papers.

475 "These combinations": from Akerman, Oct. 16, 1871, *Papers of Grant*, 22:179n.

475 "The public safety": Proclamation, Oct. 17, 1871, Public Papers.

476 "What has been": *Testimony Taken by the Joint Select Committee*, 1410-11.

476 "giving the names": *Congressional Globe*, 42:2:3.

476 "As a member": *Congressional Globe*, 42:2:14.

477 "fermentation": *The Reminiscences of Carl Schurz* (1908), 3:320.

477 "I stand in the Republican party": *Reminiscences of Carl Schurz*, 3:331-32.

477 "Akerman introduces Ku Klux": Hamilton Fish diary, Nov. 24, 1871, Library of Congress.

478 "It seems to me": Richard Zuczek, *State of Rebellion: Reconstruction in South Carolina* (1996), 100.

478 "deep criminality": Akerman to David Corbin, Nov. 10, 1871, Zuczek, *State of Rebellion*, p. 99.

478 "The feeling here . . . from the past": Akerman to J. R. Parrott, Dec. 6, 1871; to "Mr. Atkins," Dec. 12, 1871; to Benjamin Conley, Dec. 28, 1871, Zuczek, *State of Rebellion*, 58-59.

478 "At the Superior court": from Tourgée, Dec. 28, 1871, *Papers of Grant*, 22:370n.

CHAPTER 64

482 "At a moment of profound peace": *Charles Sumner: His Complete Works*, ed. George Frisbie Hoar (1900), 13:53-93.

482 "If it were not for our debt": Allan Nevins, *Hamilton Fish* (1957 ed.), 1:397.

483 "Its provisions": Annual message, Dec. 6, 1869, Public Papers.

484 "The President further expressed": Hamilton Fish diary, Oct. 21, 1870, Library of Congress.

484 "Should the time come": Annual message, Dec. 5, 1870, Public Papers.

484 "Upon a certain class": Fish diary, Jan. 8, 1871.

484 "Sumner is malicious": Nevins, *Hamilton Fish*, 2:460.

485 "Sumner is bitterly vindictive": Nevins, *Hamilton Fish*, 2:461.

485 "I never asked": to Alexander G. Cattell, March 21 (or probably 23), 1871.

CHAPTER 65

486 "I have never been": *New York Herald*, June 8, 1871.

486 "You may say for me": William Sherman to John Sherman, May 18, 1871, *The Sherman Letters* (1894), 330.

486 "General Sherman, Mr. President": *New York Herald*, June 6, 1871.

487 "Under no circumstances": to John Sherman, June 14, 1871.

487 "I told him plainly": William Sherman to John Sherman, July 8, 1871, *Sherman Letters*, 331.

489 "With what face": *Congressional Globe*, 42:1:305.

489 "The President's education": *Congressional Globe*, 42:1:Appendix, 60.

489 "Unless I greatly mistake": Schurz to Cox, April 4, 1871, *Papers of Grant*, 21:370n.

490 "Grant and his faction": Schurz to Sumner, Sept. 30, 1871, *The Reminiscences of Carl Schurz* (1908), 3:338-39.

490 "gross exaggeration": *New York Times*, Jan. 27, 1872.

490 "You know our house room": to Childs, Nov. 28, 1871.

491 "Sumner, Schurz, Dana". to Jones, Nov. 7, 1871.

491 "I simply replied": to Colfax, Nov. 14, 1871.

491 "My own convictions": to Charles Ford, May 3, 1871.

491 "It will be a happy day": to Badeau, Nov. 19, 1871.

491 "My trials here": to Washburne, May 17, 1871.

492 "We have men among us": from Wilson, Nov. 11, 1871, *Papers of Grant*, 22:233n.

492 "Whenever I have done injustice . . . execute their will": to Wilson, Nov. 15, 1871.

493 "President says": Hamilton Fish diary, Dec. 6, 1871, Library of Congress.

493 "It looks to me": to Charles Ford, Oct. 26, 1871.

493 "My prediction": to Charles Ford, April 23, 1872.

494 "He has never left": *Reminiscences of Carl Schurz*, 3:358.

494 "Carl Schurz was the most industrious": Matthew T. Downey, "Horace Greeley and the Politicians: The Liberal Republican Convention in 1872," *Journal of American History*, vol. 53 (1967), 738.

495 "I have no hesitation": *Congressional Globe*, 42:2:4110-22.

496 "The atrocious speech": from Pope, June 8, 1872, *Papers of Grant*, 23:164n.

496 "The wild enthusiasm": from Pierrepont, June 6, 1872, *Papers of Grant*, 23:162-63n.

496 "How do you like": *New York Herald*, June 14, 1872.

497 "Experience may guide me": to Thomas Settle et al., June 10, 1872.

497 "The conversation turning": *Louisville Courier-Journal*, Aug. 16, 1872, in *Papers of Grant*, 23:100n.

497 "I was not anxious": *New York Herald*, Aug. 6, 1872.

498 "The Greeleyites": to Washburne, Aug. 26, 1872.

498 "There has been no time": to Russell Jones, Sept. 5, 1872.

498 "I do not think": to Elihu Washburne, Aug. 26, 1872.

CHAPTER 66

500 "The history of the government connections": *Report of the Commissioner of Indian Affairs, Made to the Secretary of the Interior for the Year 1869* (1870), 47.

501 "I come without an invitation . . . those obligations yourself": Conversation with Red Cloud et al., May 28, 1872, *Papers of Grant*, 23:146n; Grant speech, May 28, 1872.

503 "The President inquired": *New York Herald*, Sept. 29, 1872.

504 "I hear that in a few months": *Papers of Grant*, 23:147n.

504 "If the present policy": to Stuart, Oct. 26, 1872.

CHAPTER 67

505 "The policy which was adopted . . . the highest importance": Annual message, Dec. 2, 1872, Public Papers.

506 "Under Providence . . . support and encouragement": Second inaugural address, March 4, 1873, Public Papers.

507 "Will you do me the favor": to Colfax, March 4, 1873.

509 "Good government": Maury Klein, *Union Pacific* (1987) 1:298.

509 "pitiful and shameful": *New York Times*, Feb. 27, 1873.

CHAPTER 68

510 "Much to my astonishment": to Sartoris, July 7, 1873.

511 "When Nellie came back": *Personal Memoirs of Julia Dent Grant*, 181.

512 "The President's levees": *Personal Memoirs of Julia Dent Grant*, 175.

512 "The servants I had": *Personal Memoirs of Julia Dent Grant*, 174.

512 "I was somewhat annoyed": *Personal Memoirs of Julia Dent Grant*, 174.

513 "The papers make the most": Sherman to Ellen Sherman, June 5, 1872, *Papers of Grant*, 23:82-83n.

513 "I hope Fred": from Sherman, April 24, 1872, *Papers of Grant*, 23:83n.

513 "We certainly": from Sherman, May 23, 1872, *Papers of Grant*, 23:85n.

513 "Oh, mamma!": *Personal Memoirs of Julia Dent Grant*, 179.

513 "Oh, yes": *Personal Memoirs of Julia Dent Grant*, 178.

514 "He expressed himself": to Adolph Borie, July 3, 1873.

514 "You spoke of mixing lime": to Elrod, June 23, 1871.

514 "I send you $600": to Elrod, July 8, 1871.

515 "I do not want any land": to Elrod, Nov. 16, 1871.

515 "I engaged a thoroughbred Alderney": to Elrod, Oct. 2, 1871.

515 "You had better purchase": to Elrod, March 15, 1872.

515 "Fred tells me": to Elrod, Feb. 27, 1873.

515 "I telegraphed you": to Ford, June 15, 1873.

516 "I see by the morning papers": to Ford, Feb. 22, 1873.

516 "No building": to Adolph Borie, Feb. 25, 1873.

516 "The receipts": Levi Luckey to John Long, July 3, 1873, *Papers of Grant*, 24:234n.

CHAPTER 69

517 "Results of today": from Morton, Sept. 19, 1873, Grant Papers, Library of Congress.

518 "Relief must come": from Murphy, Sept. 19, 1873, Grant Papers.

518 "All assistance of the government": to Morton, Sept. 19, 1873.

518 "The presence of President Grant": *New York Times*, Sept. 22, 1873.

519 "The Government is desirous": to Horace B. Claflin and Charles L. Anthony, Sept. 27, 1873.

519 "Panics generally occur": *New York Times*, Oct. 13, 1873. Grant's remarks were quoted indirectly, per the custom of the day. But his words are straightforward to reconstruct.

520 "Pure fright": *New York Times*, Oct. 5, 1873.

CHAPTER 70

522 "Minnesota will furnish": from Austin, Dec. 5, 1873, Grant Papers, Library of Congress.

522 "I appeal to you": from Mrs. Gebhard, Dec. 15, 1873, *Papers of Grant*, 24:245-46n.

523 "The United States are weak": Jeanie Mort Walker, *Life of Capt. Joseph Fry, the Cuban Martyr* (1875), 449.

523 "The summary infliction": to Fish, Nov. 7, 1873.

524 "This seemed to be": Message to Congress, Jan. 5, 1874, Public Papers.

524 "His family": to J. C. Bancroft Davis, May 8, 1873.

524 "A chief justice": to Roscoe Conkling, Nov. 8, 1873.

524 "My dear Senator": to Conkling, Nov. 8, 1873.

525 "My transfer now": from Conkling, Nov. 20, 1873, *Papers of Grant*, 24:253 54n.

525 "When the President": *Personal Memoirs of Julia Dent Grant*, 193-94.

526 "The Judiciary Committee": Porter to Bristow, Dec. 18, 1873, *Papers of Grant*, 24:285n.

CHAPTER 71

528 "great wrongs and frauds": from Davis, Jan. 6, 1874, *Papers of Grant*, 25:10n.

528 "This may cause": from Davis, Jan. 11, 1874, *Papers of Grant*, 25:10n.

529 "The act of the legislature": to Davis, Jan. 12, 1874.

529 "Gentlemen": *New York Daily Tribune*, March 31, 1874.

529 "silent contempt": Hamilton Fish diary, March 27, 1874, Library of Congress.

529 "The importance of doing something": from Morton, March 22, 1874, *Papers of Grant*, 25:68-69n.

530 "I know from information": from L. Montgomery Bond, April 15, 1874, *Papers of Grant*, 25:70n.

530 "Who are these men?": from Redstone, April 18, 1874, *Papers of Grant*, 25:72-73n.

531 "In my intercourse": from Martin B. Anderson, April 15, 1874, *Papers of Grant*, 25:70n.

531 "This bill is a violation": from Edward S. Jaffray, April 16, 1874, *New York Daily Tribune*, April 17, 1874.

531 "inflict a stain": *New York Times*, April 16, 1874.

532 "I deem this course": Draft message, April 22, 1874, *Papers of Grant*, 25:65-67.

532 "He had given it": Fish diary, April 21, 1874.

533 "The President thought": Fish diary, April 21, 1874.

533 "I must express": Veto message, April 22, 1874, Public Papers.

533 "God Almighty bless you": from Pierrepont, April 22, 1874, *Papers of Grant*, 25:77n.

533 "It is Vicksburg": from Manning Force, April 23, 1874, *Papers of Grant*, 25:78n.

534 "I do not forget": from Elias Derby, April 24, 1874, *Papers of Grant*, 25:79n.

534 "You have done *your* duty": from McCosh, May 4, 1874, *Papers of Grant*, 25:80n.

534 "noble stand": from Drexel, May 9, 1874, *Papers of Grant*, 25:80-81n.

534 "The president is mistaken . . . next term": *New York Times*, April 23, 1874.

CHAPTER 72

535 "I believe it to be": Memorandum, June 1, 1874.

536 "He speaks": Hamilton Fish diary, June 7, 1874, Library of Congress.

537 "A wedding at the White House": *New York Times*, May 22, 1874.

CHAPTER 73

538 "I heartily approve": to Baxter, April 22, 1874.

538 "Frauds may have been committed": from Williams, May 15, 1874, *Executive Documents Printed by Order of the Senate*, 43:2:12.

539 "all turbulent and disorderly persons": Proclamation, May 15, 1874, Public Papers.

539 "Even our opponents": from Kellogg, Aug. 19, 1874, *Executive Documents*, 43:2:9-10.

540 "We assure your excellency": from Ward, Sept. 4, 1874, *Papers of Grant*, 25:216-18n.

540 "En route they were all shot": Kellogg to George Williams, Aug. 31, 1874, *Executive Documents*, 43:2:11-12.

540 "The purpose of the riot": S. B. Packard to George Williams, Sept. 14, 1874, *Executive Documents*, 43:2:14.

541 "Under Article 4": from Kellogg, Sept. 14, 1874, *Executive Documents*, 43:2:13.

541 "Turbulent and disorderly persons": Proclamation, Sept. 15, 1874, Public Papers.

541 "The result of our election": from Blaine, Sept. 14, 1874, Grant Papers, Library of Congress.

542 "Not before the meeting": to Cameron, Nov. 3, 1873.

CHAPTER 74

543 "There is no duty": Annual message, Dec. 5, 1870, Public Papers.

544 "The rules adopted": Annual message, Dec. 7, 1874, Public Papers.

545 "I never sought the office": to White, May 29, 1875.

546 "I followed the President": *Personal Memoirs of Julia Dent Grant*, 184-85.

547 "The whole subject . . . of sectional interference": Annual message, Dec. 7, 1874, Public Papers.

CHAPTER 75

549 "I think the terrorism": Sheridan to William Belknap, Jan. 5, 1875, in *New York Times*, Jan. 6, 1875.

550 "Coming among us": Cotton Exchange statement, in *New York Times*, Jan. 6, 1875.

550 "The Administration": Statement by Illinois Democratic State Central Committee, in *New York Times*, Jan. 6, 1875.

550 "They seem to be trying . . . No trouble is apprehended": Sheridan to Belknap, Jan. 7, 1875, *Executive Documents Printed by Order of the Senate*, 43:2:25-26.

550 "I am not afraid": Sheridan to Belknap, Jan. 6, 1875, *Executive Documents Printed by Order of the Senate*, 43:2:25.

550 "The President and all of us": Belknap to Sheridan, Jan. 6, 1875, *Executive Documents Printed by Order of the Senate*, 43:2:25.

551 "You had better mend": from "Conservative," Jan. 7, 1875, *Papers of Grant*, 26:19n.

551 "If you cannot well back out": from "Deadshot," Jan. 15, 1875, *Papers of Grant*, 26:19n.

551 "There will also be": from "Charles Howard," Jan. 18, 1875, *Papers of Grant*, 26:19-20n.

551 "To say that lawlessness": Special message, Jan. 13, 1875, Public Papers.

CHAPTER 76

554 "currency of a fixed known value": Special message, Jan. 14, 1875, Public Papers.

555 "honest graft": William L. Riordon, *Plunkitt of Tammany Hall* (1905), 3-4.

556 "Let no guilty man escape": Endorsement on letter from William Barnard, July 19, 1875, forwarded to Bristow, July 29, 1875.

557 "Poor Ford is dead . . . Sylph": *Cases Determined in the United States Circuit Courts for the Eighth Circuit* (1876), 3:593, 610.

557 "To General Bristow": *Testimony Before the Select Committee Concerning the Whisky Frauds*, House of Representatives, 44th Congress, 1st Session, Misc. Doc. No. 186 (July 25, 1876), 3.

557 "The President manifested . . . in the negative": Hamilton Fish diary, Feb. 8, 1876, Library of Congress.

558 "How long have you known . . . Never": Deposition, Feb. 12, 1876.

560 "The President then": *Miscellaneous Documents of the House of Representatives*, 44:1:369.

560 "Belknap felt very much hurt": *Personal Memoirs of Julia Dent Grant*, 190.

560 "The President spoke": Fish diary, March 3, 1876.

561 "Did you ever know Orvil Grant": *Alleged Frauds in Contracts for Government Surveys in Wyoming Territory* (1876), 26.

CHAPTER 77

562 "I feel sorry for Belknap": William Sherman to John Sherman, March 4, 1876, Sherman Papers, Library of Congress.

563 "Being thoroughly of the opinion": from Ely Adams et al., March 17, 1875, *Papers of Grant*, 26:85n.

563 "I would like to start": Sheridan to Sherman, May 1, 1874, *Papers of Grant*, 26:89n.

563 "Such an expedition": from Hare, June 9, 1874, *Papers of Grant*, 26:87n.

564 "A general war": from Delano, June 9, 1874, *Papers of Grant*, 26:86.

564 "We have had great difficulty": Speech to Sioux delegation, May 26, 1875.

564 "I do not believe": Red Cloud statement, undated, *Papers of Grant*, 26:122n.

565 "We might just as well settle": Sheridan to Sherman, May 29, 1876, *Executive Documents Printed by Order of the House of Representatives*, 44:1:14:54.

565 "The President has just": Sherman to Sheridan, April 28, 1876, *Papers of Grant*, 27:71n.

565 "Please intercept him": Sherman to Sheridan, May 2, 1876, *Papers of Grant*, 27:72n.

565 "The recent reports": from Sherman, July 8, 1876, *Papers of Grant*, 27:171-72n.

565 "I regard Custer's massacre": Interview in *New York Herald*, Sept. 2, 1876.

CHAPTER 78

567 "excellent ticket": Speech, June 19, 1876.

568 "I am not aware": to Hayes, Aug. 16, 1876.

568 "It seems impossible": from Chamberlain, July 22, 1876, *Papers of Grant*, 27:200-01n.

569 "The lives of white": from Simonton, June 3, 1876, *Papers of Grant*, 27:239-40n.

569 "The scene at Hamburg": to Chamberlain, July 26, 1876.

570 "Our people are being shot": from James Major et al., Sept. 25, 1876, *Papers of Grant*, 27:332n.

570 "Guns and pistols": from "Detective," Nov. 2, 1876, *Papers of Grant*, 27:335n.

570 "Insurrection and domestic violence": from Chamberlain, Oct. 11, 1876, *Papers of Grant*, 27:330-01n.

CHAPTER 79

571 "See that the proper": to Sherman, Nov. 10, 1876.

571 "There is such apprehension": to Sheridan, Nov. 11, 1876.

572 "All they ask": from William Stage, Nov. 12, 1876, *Papers of Grant*, 28:20-21n.

572 "We have a government": from James Rusling, Nov. 14, 1876, *Papers of Grant*, 28:21n.

572 "The President must be": Hamilton Fish diary, Nov. 14, 1876, Library of Congress.

572 "The course you have pursued": from "Baltimore Secret Government," Dec. 11, 1876, *Papers of Grant*, 28:35n.

572 "Hostilities there have grown": Annual message, Dec. 5, 1876, Public Papers.

574 "again the Louisiana trouble": Fish diary, Jan. 7, 1877.

575 "To do so would be": to Kellogg, Jan. 7, 1877.

575 "These different kinds": Special message, Jan. 22, 1877, Public Papers.

576 "The bill may not be perfect": Special message, Jan. 29, 1877, Public Papers.

576 "In my daily intercourse": from Asbury Hanes, Dec. 18, 1877, *Papers of Grant*, 28:132n.

576 "There is 200,000 men": from John Adams, Dec. 18, 1877, *Papers of Grant*, 28:132n.

576 "Wherever you can": Sherman to Sheridan, Dec. 11, 1877, *Papers of Grant*, 28:37n.

576 "While he most earnestly desired": Fish diary, Jan. 17, 1877.

577 "Three weeks remain": to Pierrepont, Feb. 11, 1877.

CHAPTER 80

579 "After an unusually stormy passage": to George Childs, June 6, 1877.

579 "I have no plans": to John Long, Jan. 28, 1877.

579 "There are books enough already": *St. Louis Globe-Democrat*, April 2, 1877, in *Papers of Grant*, 28:183-84n.

580 "Through your statesmanship": to Fish, March 9, 1877.

580 "I feel overcome": *New York Times*, May 18, 1877.

580 "What was my surprise": to George Childs, June 6, 1877.

581 "Once an emperor": Pierrepont to William Evarts, June 27, 1877, *Papers of Grant*, 28:261n.

581 "He has been the recipient": Badeau to Washburne, June 8, 1877, *Papers of Grant*, 28:215n.

581 "My reception": to Fish, June 22, 1877.

582 "Yesterday and the day before": to Ulysses Grant Jr., Sept. 23, 1877.

582 "My reception has been": Speech, June 28, 1877.

582 "There is no reception": Speech, July 3, 1877.

582 "There is one subject": Speech, Oct. 17, 1877.

583 "We have now been in Paris": to Borie, Nov. 19, 1877.

583 "The weather in Paris": to Daniel Ammen, Dec. 10, 1877.

583 "All the romance": to Ulysses Grant Jr., Jan. 7, 1878.

583 "I have seen more in Egypt": to Fred Grant, Jan. 25, 1878.

583 "Our visit to Jerusalem": to Badeau, Feb. 22, 1878.

584 "The Russian army": to Fred Grant, March 22, 1878.

584 "These horses": to Edward Beale, March 6, 1878.

584 "They seem to me": to Fred Grant, March 22, 1878.

584 "My impression of peoples": to Ammen, March 25, 1878.

585 "The General saunters . . . I believe so": John Russell Young, *Around the World with General Grant* (1879), 1:409-17.

586 "I propose to stay away": Interview, Aug. 29, 1877.

587 "The United States should always": to Ammen, Aug. 26, 1877.

587 "The country, and the country's credit": to Sherman, March 21, 1878.

587 "It shows a willingness": to Drexel, March 22, 1878.

587 "It looks to me": to Abel Corbin, March 29, 1878.

588 "They have designs": to Badeau, March 22, 1878.

588 "I cannot tell you": *New York Herald*, July 24, 1878.

588 "Everything that our armies did": *New York Herald*, May 27, 1878.

589 "It is bliss": to Washburne, Oct. 7, 1878.

589 "We have seen the capitals": to Edward Beale, Dec. 6, 1878.

589 "Anchored outside the harbor . . . trade of the East": Grant journal, Jan. 23-July 26, 1879.

591 "I am ready to admit": *New York Herald*, Aug. 16, 1879.

592 "To it we owe": *New York Herald*, Aug. 13, 1879.

592 "We all know . . . solemn business sessions": *New York Herald*, Aug. 15, 1879.

593 "Nagasaki we found . . . the whole people": Grant journal, Jan. 23–July 26, 1879.

593 "What I have learned in Japan . . . their own advantage": Conversation with Meiji emperor, Aug. 10, 1879.

CHAPTER 81

595 "Some time has passed . . . of your city": *New York Times*, Sept. 21, 1879.

597 "I cannot venture": to Borie, Sept. 28, 1879.

597 "It seems like returning home": Speech, Oct. 13, 1879.

597 "It is gratifying": Speech, Oct. 14, 1879, *Papers of Grant*, 29:258n.

597 "No honors that I received": Speech, Oct. 28, 1879.

597 "When I was in Europe": Interview in *Chicago Inter Ocean*, Oct. 31, 1879, in *Papers of Grant*, 29:275n.

597 "I am very glad": *Chicago Tribune*, Nov. 5, 1879.

597 "I always like to come here": *Cincinnati Enquirer*, Nov. 12, 1879, in *Papers of Grant*, 29:285n.

598 "We think now of going": to Ellen Grant Sartoris, Nov. 8, 1879.

598 "The first time I ever saw General Grant": *The Autobiography of Mark Twain*, ed. Charles Neider (1959), 316-18.

598 "He never moved . . . his body ached": Ron Powers, *Mark Twain* (2005), 428-31.

CHAPTER 82

600 "All I want": to Washburne, Feb. 2, 1880.

601 "The election before us": H. Wayne Morgan, *From Hayes to McKinley* (1969), 91-92.

602 "Individually": to Conkling, June 10, 1880.

602 "Oh, Ulys": *Personal Memoirs of Julia Dent Grant*, 197.

602 "Do you not desire success?": *Personal Memoirs of Julia Dent Grant*, 321-22.

603 "I have nothing to say": Statement to Chicago *Advance*, July 1880, *Papers of Grant*, 29:439.

603 "I feel a very deep interest": to Garfield, Aug. 5, 1880.

603 "I have never made": Speech, Aug. 27, 1880.

603 "I am a Republican": *New York Times*, Sept. 29, 1880.

604 "He is vain": *Cincinnati Gazette*, Oct. 5, 1880, in *Papers of Grant*, 29:461-62.

604 "Hancock is a man": *Chicago Inter Ocean*, Oct. 6, 1880, in *Papers of Grant*, 29:465n.

604 "Out there": Speeches (two), *New York Times*, Oct. 22, 1880.

604 "Every Northern state": *New York Times*, Oct. 31, 1880.

605 "I heartily congratulate you": to Garfield, Nov. 11, 1880.

CHAPTER 83

606 "By years of colossal labor": *New York Herald*, Oct. 17, 1880.

607 "One thing is certain": to Badeau, Aug. 12, 1880.

607 "You know Buck is married!": to Ellen Grant Sartoris, Nov. 4, 1880.

607 "But he has something": to John Long, Nov. 12, 1880.

607 "We are boarding": to Ellen Grant Sartoris, Nov. 4, 1880.

607 "Under no circumstances": to Logan, Feb. 9, 1881.

607 "In any other great nation": Morgan et al. to Pierrepont, Nov. 9, 1880, *Papers of Grant*, 30:137n.

608 "I am sure I turned": *Personal Memoirs of Julia Dent Grant*, 323.

608 "I hope with you": to John Creswell, Nov. 14, 1880.

608 "Harmony in the Republican party": to Garfield, Jan. 26, 1881.

609 "I sincerely hope": Remarks quoted in *Methodist Quarterly Review*, Oct. 1881, 648.

CHAPTER 84

610 "Your kind letter": to Clemens, Jan. 14, 1881.

611 "They have thirteen years": *New York Times*, Nov. 12, 1880.

611 "I have long been of the opinion": Speech, April 22, 1881.

612 "I am completely disgusted": to Badeau, May 7, 1881.

612 "Garfield is a man": *Pittsburg Times*, June 17, 1881, in *Papers of Grant*, 30:237-38.

613 "dastardly attempt": to Badeau, July 27, 1881.

613 "Of course my hopes": *New York World*, July 5, 1881.

613 "During the months of August": *Chicago Inter Ocean*, Sept. 7, 1881, in *Papers of Grant*, 30:265.

614 "You will please excuse me": *New York Times*, Sept. 20, 1881.

614 "I can hardly say": to Badeau, Dec. 11, 1882.

614 "The defeat was expected": to John Russell Young, Nov. 28, 1882.

615 "The reading of the whole": to Arthur, Dec. 22, 1881.

615 "An Undeserved Stigma": *North American Review*, Dec. 1882, 539, 545.

615 "The undersigned": from Theodore Lyman et al., Nov. 27, 1882, *Papers of Grant*, 30:434.

616 "As you state": from Longstreet, Dec. 30, 1882, *Papers of Grant*, 30:435.

617 "He had lost his hat": *New York Times*, June 30, 1882.

CHAPTER 85

618 "I have washed my hands": Interview for *Louisville Courier-Journal*, June 3, 1883, in *Papers of Grant*, 31:42.

618 "There is no man": *New York Times*, July 16, 1883.

619 "I am willing that Mr. Ward": to Fish, July 6, 1882.

619 "It is my plan": Hamlin Garland, "A Romance of Wall Street: The Grant and Ward Failure," *McClure's Magazine*, April 1898, 500.

620 "We are much better off": to Ellen Grant Sartoris, Nov. 24 and Dec. 15, 1883.

620 almost a millionaire: Deposition, March 26, 1885.

621 "General Grant was informed": *New York Times*, May 7, 1884.

621 "The Grant family is ruined": to Clara Cramer, June 8, 1884.

623 "I pointed out": *The Autobiography of Mark Twain*, ed. Charles Neider (1959), 237.

623 "Sell *me* the memoirs": *Autobiography of Mark Twain*, 240-41.

CHAPTER 86

625 "I learned afterward": *The Autobiography of Mark Twain*, ed. Charles Neider (1959), 252.

625 "It is a matter for great congratulation": *New York Times*, Feb. 20, 1885.

626 "Sinking into the Grave": *New York Times*, March 1, 1885.

627 "The composition is entirely my own": to Webster & Co., May 2, 1885.

627 "It was a busy time": *New York Times*, May 2, 1885.

627 "Since coming . . . I signify all three": Notes, June 17 to July 20, 1885, *Memoirs*, 1111-20.

628 "If it is within God's providence . . . in the end": *Memoirs*, 1116-19.

629 "He asked me with his pencil": *Autobiography of Mark Twain*, 252.

629 "I have my full share": *Autobiography of Mark Twain*, 253.

629 "I am older than your Father": from Sherman, March 17, 1885, *Papers of Grant*, 31:388n.

630 "profound sympathy": Resolution of Grand Army of the Republic, June 24, 1885, in Robert B. Beath, *History of the Grand Army of the Republic* (1889), 296.

630 "Tell the boys": Message, May 14, 1885.

630 "Look after our dear children": to Julia Dent Grant, June 29, 1885.

630 "I must try": *Memoirs*, 1118, 1115.

630 "Buck has brought up": *Memoirs*, 1118.

CHAPTER 87

632 "In General Grant's death": *New York Times*, July 31, 1885.

632 "Ulysses S. Grant": *Washington Post*, Aug. 3, 1885.

632 "I heard him say once": *New York Times*, Aug. 3, 1885.

633 "Everything has been said": *New York Times*, Aug. 1, 1885.

633 "Why, you cannot trust": *New York Times*, Aug. 3, 1885.

633 "He was the truest": *New York Times*, July 24, 1885.

633 "Wherever General Grant's body lies": Ron Powers, *Mark Twain* (2005), 504.

634 "There was a burst of sunlight": *New York Times*, Aug. 6, 1885.

635 . . . Grant's casualties . . . were lower than Lee's: James M. McPherson, *The Mighty Scourge: Perspectives on the Civil War* (2007), 113; Jean Edward Smith, *Grant* (2001), 15, 629n6.

INDEX

About the Author

For nearly two decades, H. W. Brands has been writing a six-volume history of the United States in the form of a series of linked biographies. Four volumes have been published before now; these are Volume 1: *The First American* (on Benjamin Franklin, 1706–1790), Volume 2: *Andrew Jackson* (1767–1845), Volume 4: *T.R.* (Theodore Roosevelt, 1858–1919), and Volume 5: *Traitor to His Class* (Franklin Roosevelt, 1882–1945). The present work, *The Man Who Saved the Union* (Ulysses Grant, 1822–1885), becomes Volume 3.

The author continues to teach at the University of Texas at Austin, where he is the Dickson Allen Anderson Professor of History, while he works on Volume 6.

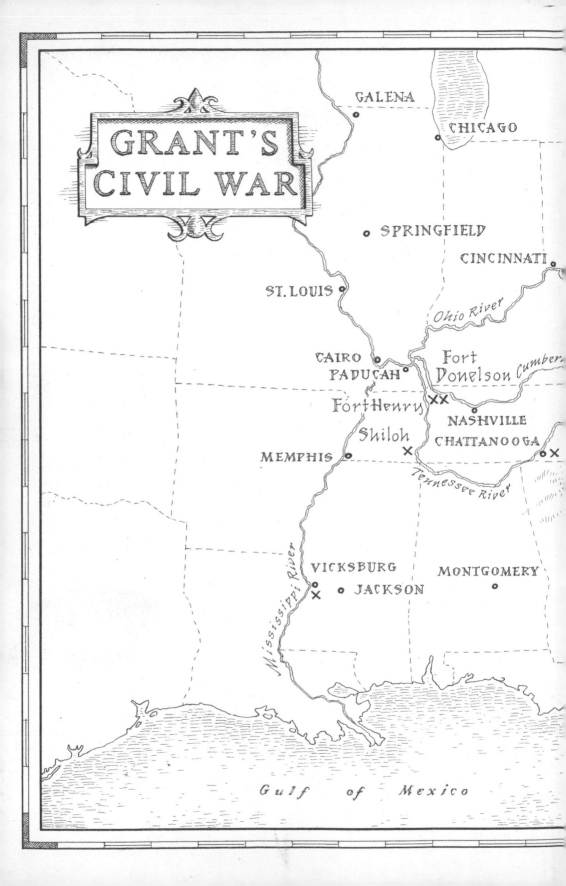